The Economics of Imperfect Labor Markets

The Economics
of Imperfect Labor Markets

SECOND EDITION

Tito Boeri *and* **Jan van Ours**

PRINCETON UNIVERSITY PRESS

Princeton and Oxford

Published by Princeton University Press, 41 William Street,
Princeton, New Jersey 08540
In the United Kingdom: Princeton University Press,
6 Oxford Street, Woodstock, Oxfordshire OX20 1TW

press.princeton.edu

ISBN 978-0-691-15893-8
Library of Congress Control Number: 2013940972

British Library Cataloging-in-Publication Data is available

This book has been composed in Minion and Whitney with ZzTEX
by Princeton Editorial Associates Inc., Scottsdale, Arizona

Printed on acid-free paper ∞

Printed in the United States of America

10 9 8 7 6 5 4

Contents

Boxes and Available Datasets

Boxes

* Available datasets.

Available Datasets

* Available datasets.

Which labor market institutions worked better in containing job losses during the Great Recession of 2008–2009? Is it good for employment to increase the progressiveness of taxation? Does it make sense to contrast "active" and "passive" labor market policies? Who actually gains and who loses from employment protection legislation? Why are minimum wages generally diversified by age? Is it better to have decentralized or centralized bargaining systems in monetary unions? Should migrants have access to welfare benefits? Should governments regulate working hours? And can equal opportunity legislation reduce discrimination against women or minority groups in the labor market?

Current labor economics textbooks neglect these relevant policy issues. In spite of significant progress in analyzing the costs and benefits of labor market institutions, these textbooks have a setup that relegates institutions to the last paragraph of chapters or to a final institutional chapter. Typically a book begins by characterizing labor supply (including human capital theory), labor demand, and the competitive equilibrium at the intersection of the two curves; it subsequently addresses such topics as wage formation and unions, compensating wage differentials, and unemployment without a proper institutional framework. There is little information concerning labor market institutions and labor market policies. Usually labor market policies are mentioned only every now and then, and labor market institutions are often not treated in a systematic way. When attention is given to these institutions, reference is generally made to the U.S. institutional landscape and to competitive labor markets in which, by definition, any type of policy measure is distortionary.

The novelty of our book is that from the start the focus is on labor market institutions operating in *imperfect* labor markets, that is, markets that depart from perfect competition. Unlike competitive markets, imperfect labor markets allow employers and employees to enjoy rents, and hence a job is a big deal. Losing a job for a worker or having to replace an employee leaving the firm is costly in such markets, while employees and employers involved in these types of events would not suffer any loss in competitive labor markets. Imperfect markets are also characterized by the presence of many labor market *institutions*, that is, systems of laws and programs that shape the behavior of individual workers and employers. Institutions result from a political process aimed at (1) increasing economic efficiency and (2) achieving some redistributive goal. Efficiency is pursued by remedying market imperfections, such as excessive monopsonistic power, informational asymmetries that give rise to moral hazard and adverse selection problems, and externalities associated with social customs or the job-matching process, as well as transaction costs and frictions that restrict the size of markets. Redistribution provides a rationale for these institutions even when there are no market imperfections. In imperfect markets redistribution sometimes can be achieved while pursuing efficiency, as in the case of institutions, such as minimum wages or employment subsidies, that counteract excessive monopsonistic power. In most cases, however, the traditional trade-off between efficiency and equity arises. Actually, the redistribution brought about by these institutions may well not promote a more egalitarian society or represent the interests of the median voter. There are frequent policy failures in the design of labor market institutions that give disproportionate representation to some pressure group pursuing very specific interests.

This book also takes into account that institutions rarely operate in isolation. Hence, from a positive standpoint, the effects of each institution on the labor market are investigated by considering not only its direct effects on employment, unemployment, and wages, but also its indirect effects, mediated by the presence of other institutions. For example, a change in the generosity of the unemployment benefit system affects unemployment directly by reducing search intensity and increasing the reservation wage of jobseekers and indirectly by increasing the bargaining power of unions and the level of the efficiency wage. Incidentally, this interaction provides a third rationale for the presence of some institutions: they are created to counteract or complement the effects of other institutions. Policy failures also may arise in this context because the institutions responsible for the distortions are rarely reformed. Often the political process creates chains of distortions and clusters of institutions, so that some institutions are used to compensate for the undesirable effects of others.

We place much attention on precisely defining institutions and measuring them along their relevant dimensions (e.g., eligibility for unemployment benefits, level of the benefits, and maximum duration for which they can be provided), because we believe that accuracy in describing the way in which the institution operates and the goals it pursues is essential for characterizing its effects on the labor market. Statistical information on the evolution over time of these institutions is also provided, whenever possible, for all member countries in the Organisation for Economic Co-operation and Development. Contrary to common wisdom, there has indeed been considerable variation over time in these institutions. We also discuss policy enforcement issues.

Position of This Book in the Literature

As mentioned earlier, available labor economics textbooks devote one or a few chapters to institutions. Ehrenberg and Smith (2006), Kaufman and Hotchkiss (2006), McConnell et al. (2008), Borjas (2009), and Laing (2011) are just a few examples.

In these chapters the key distortions associated with the presence of labor market institutions are only briefly touched on, and no attempt is made to examine how the institutions operate when labor markets are not competitive.

A few specialized books analyze labor market institutions. Because they are not conceived as textbooks, they do not provide systematic coverage of the different institutions and do not offer an integrated framework. A partial exception is Layard et al. (1991), which, however, is confined to the analysis of unemployment. Manning (2003) is another partial exception: it offers a clear overview of monopsony in all its dimensions. However, except for unions and minimum wages, it does not deal with institutions in much detail. Finally, Cahuc and Zylberberg (2004) offers wider and in-depth coverage of labor market institutions, but it does not provide a unifying framework, and the book is, in any event, intended for graduate students.

A huge literature exists on the effects of institutions on labor market performance. Current textbooks do not provide a survey of this rich empirical literature, which has been enriched in the past two decades by much wider access to micro data. We aim to fill this gap, providing in each chapter an account of the main findings of the literature on the effects on the labor market of the institution being investigated in that chapter. This does not mean that we account for *all* works that have been written on the subject. We concentrate on those findings and issues that have, in our view, more relevance in real-world labor markets.

Although we discuss why institutions exist, we do not offer full coverage of the political economy of labor market institutions, which is addressed by other specialized books, such as Saint-Paul (2000) and Persson and Tabellini (2000).

Audience

Our book targets a composite readership, including undergraduate students taking courses in labor economics (a compulsory requirement for many BAs) as well as graduate students specializing in this field. Professional economists in international organizations and government agencies are another potential target.

This book can be taught at the undergraduate level in programs that specialize in economics. It can also be used in business and political science schools where human resource–oriented courses are taught by economists. The description of the institutions and the technical annexes can also be useful references for graduate courses in labor economics, which can benefit from the datasets and applications provided on our webpage (see link at http://press.princeton.edu/titles/10142.html) and referred to in the book. Finally, scholars in the field may find the book a useful reference for their personal libraries.

Prerequisites and Technical Level

In light of the audience we have in mind, the technical level required by the book is modest. Ideally, readers should have taken an introductory course in microeconomics, a semester of calculus, and an introductory course in statistics. In practice it will be possible to read the book even when these prerequisites are partially or totally unfulfilled. The viability of the latter option rests on the various numerical examples presented in the book and on the graphical treatment of some key results. In this simpler treatment all the main arguments are presented and the main results are outlined, even though they lack the rigor and the generality that the use of calculus allows. Boxes and, above all, technical annexes provide these features.

The Second Edition

This second edition features a new chapter (chapter 4) on institutions dealing with labor market discrimination. In addition, we no longer have a separate chapter on institutional interactions, as there are so many of those that we preferred to add a separate section on institutional interactions to each chapter in this edition and offer a formal treatment of these interactions in the technical annex to chapter 13. The latter is devoted to payroll taxes, which by definition interact with other institutions, as these taxes typically finance a broad range of institutions.

We also added new material to each chapter. In particular, chapter 1 now refers to lessons from the 2008–2009 Great Recession and the links between financial and labor markets. The revised chapter 2 considers in more detail minimum wage–fixing mechanisms and the scope for subminima for young workers. Chapter 3 now contains stylized facts and theories on strike activity, and chapter 4 is a brand new chapter on antidiscrimination legislation. Chapter 5 on working time regulations now features a discussion of subsidized short-time work schemes, an institution that was revived under the Great Recession. Chapter 6 on early retirement now contains a discussion of notionally defined contribution systems. Chapter 7 on family policies in this second edition features a section on the interaction between labor market participation and fertility and considers within-household decision making. Chapter 8 on education has a new section on signaling and a richer technical annex explaining, inter alia, the rationale behind Mincer-type wage equations. Chapter 9 on migration policies has a new section on the labor market position of immigrant children. Chapter 10 on employment protection legislation discusses the rationale behind severance pay measures addressing labor market dualism, such as the single employment contract. Chapter 11 on unemployment benefits has new sections on the variation of the generosity of unemployment benefits over the cycle and the importance of the liquidity constraint. Chapter 12 on active labor market policies now considers profiling and provides a new analytical framework in its technical annex. Finally, the chapter on payroll taxes has been quite extensively restructured and is now located at the end of the text (chapter 13), allowing for a more informed discussion on interactions between taxes and the other institutions covered.

While teaching from the previous edition, we used various numerical examples that are quite useful in better understanding some of the results of the literature. These numerical examples are now included in this edition. We also added a section with exercises at the end of each chapter. The solutions of these exercises (as well as new exercises) are available on the webpage (see link at http://press .princeton.edu/titles/10142.html). Finally, the first edition of a textbook almost unavoidably contains mistakes, repetitions, and material lacking clarity. Thanks to hundreds of students and a few careful readers who worked hard in editing the translations of our book, we were able to identify most of these problems and address them.

Plan and Guidelines for Instructors

This second edition of the book consists of 13 chapters, including an overview chapter. Each chapter except the first focuses on a different institution. The overview chapter sets out the unifying line of reasoning and the structure of the book. Then the institutions are discussed separately in 12 chapters:

2. Minimum wages
3. Unions and collective bargaining
4. Antidiscrimination legislation
5. Regulation of working hours
6. Early retirement plans
7. Family policies
8. Education and training
9. Migration policies
10. Employment protection legislation
11. Unemployment benefits
12. Active labor market policies
13. Payroll taxes

Each chapter can be dealt with separately. The theoretical framework is formally presented in the technical annexes to the chapters.

This organization of the book allows the instructor to choose particular sequences of institutions. For instance, a basic course (not requiring dynamic frameworks) on *price-based institutions* could cover chapters 2, 3, 4, and 13; a basic course on *quantity-based institutions* could use chapters 5–9. More advanced courses, requiring some dynamic modeling, could focus on chapters 10–12. Shorter courses can also be organized by topics, for example, a course on *flexicurity* (chapters 10–13), a course on *wage-compressing institutions* (chapters 2 and 3), one on *human capital investment* (chapters 8 and 9), or on *gender issues* (chapters 4, 5, and 7).

In all chapters except chapter 7, where we concentrate on family labor supply decisions, the analytical unit is the individual. We also treat labor supply decisions along extensive margins (participation) in all chapters except chapter 5 (and to some extent chapters 7 and 13), where we also consider adjustment along the intensive margin (hours of work).

Each of the 12 chapters that concerns a separate institution is set up in the same way:

1. definition of the institution and the way in which it is enforced, measurement issues and stylized facts about the institution (cross-country variation and time-series evolution);
2. theories (the plural is used because for each institution several theories may apply);
3. empirical evidence (macro and micro evidence);
4. policy issues (relevant trade-offs and design features);
5. interactions with other institutions;
6. overall assessment and rationale for the presence of the institution;
7. suggestions for further reading;
8. review questions and exercises; and
9. technical annex.

Distinguishing Features

Two distinguishing features of our approach are (1) a thorough discussion of measurement issues that tries, where possible, to complement institutional indicators with information on the actual enforcement of these norms and (2) an attempt to highlight the rationale behind each institution, its efficiency and distributional properties, and to identify those who benefit and those who lose from its presence.

The nature of the empirical research very much depends on the nature of the institution. For many institutions elements of change can be exploited to establish an effect of labor market outcomes. However, some institutions, like unions, change relatively slowly over time. For antidiscrimination legislation the empirical research is not on how legislation affects behavior but on whether discrimination exists. This fundamental question needs to be addressed before the effects of legislation can be established. To establish causal effects between labor market institutions and the functioning of labor markets is not easy. In our book we favor reporting on studies that use a difference-in-differences approach and occasionally a regression discontinuity design. These studies employ a quasi-experimental setup that makes the identifying assumptions rather mild. In a difference-in-differences approach a policy change that affects some groups but not others is exploited. Such a policy change allows for a before-after comparison: the first difference. Then, there is the difference between a *treatment group* that is affected and a *control group* that is not affected: the second difference. The difference of these two differences gives the treatment effect of the policy change. A regression discontinuity methodology exploits one or more discontinuities in the relationship between a labor market institution and a variable that is exogenous for the individual, for example, age. The assumption is that individuals on either side of the discontinuity only differ slightly, except for their different exposures to an institution. The difference in behavior of individuals close to either side of the discontinuity then reveals how this difference in exposure to the institution affects behavior.

In the review of the empirical evidence, one or two studies are selected and discussed in greater detail in boxes in each chapter. On our webpage we also provide the links to the original study and the data and programs that can be used to replicate the results of the study, test their robustness, and potentially extend them in new directions. This allows students to deepen their knowledge of institutional data and its measurement and to better learn the econometric techniques that can best be used to analyze the effects of these institutions, nicely complementing their training in microeconometrics. The suggestions for further reading in each chapter complement this enrichment with a few seminal publications. Detailed references are provided at the end of this book.

Acknowledgments

While working on the second edition, we received comments and suggestions from Andrea Bassanini, Samuel Bentolila, Alison Booth, Stephane Carcillo, Magnus Carlsson, Daniela Del Boca, Christian Dustmann, Vincenzo Galasso, Dan Hamermesh, Tim Hatton, Rafael Lalive, Nicola Pavoni, Michele Pellizzari, Matteo Picchio, Dan-Olof Rooth, Konstantinos Tatsiramos, John Van Reenen, and Rudolf Winter-Ebmer.

We are particularly indebted to the colleagues who agreed to supply the datasets that are now available on the webpage and that allow students to replicate the results reviewed in the book. In particular, we warmly thank Orley Ashenfelter, Andrea Bassanini, Richard Blundell, Espen Bratberg, David Card, Romain Duval, Tor-Helge Holmås, Jennifer Hunt, Dean R. Hyslop, Juan Jimeno, Alan Krueger, Rafael Lalive, Ghazala Naz, David Neumark, Thomas Piketty, Cecilia Rouse, Øystein Thøgersen, Milan Vodopivec, and William Wascher. Roberta Marcaletti skillfully assisted us in the final editing of the book and in preparing the references. She hates us by now, but it is much easier for our students to find the references mentioned in the book. We are also grateful to Seth Ditchik, economics editor at Princeton University Press, for having supported us in our work on this second edition.

Finally, we are indebted to Giulia Tagliaferri and Ali Palali, who provided us with unflagging research assistance and picked up many mistakes (thanks also to the contributions of our students). All remaining errors are ours.

Symbols and Acronyms

Some symbols have multiple meanings, but the correct interpretation should be clear from the context. For example, β in theoretical parts represents bargaining power of the unions, while in empirical sections it could be a vector of parameters.

Latin Alphabet

A	parameter of production function, parameter of matching function
B	pension benefits, bond holdings
b	benefit level, workers' outside option in employment protection legislation
c	consumption, recruitment cost
C	total labor cost
c_c	variable childcare cost
c_d	consumption of goods and services generated domestically without monetary transaction
c_m	consumption of marketed goods
C_S	costs related to S years of schooling
D	duration of unemployment
e	employment rate, effort level, date of early retirement
F	fixed cost of working
F_c	fixed cost of childcare
$g(w^r)$	density function of reservation wages
$G(w)$	labor supply
h	hours of work
h_d	amount of time devoted to home production
h_m	hours of market work
$\overline{h}$	standard workweek
i	market interest rate
I_f	indicator of whether there is discrimination among co-workers or customers
J_e	asset value of a job to an employer
J_v	asset value of vacancy to an employer
k_t	fraction of working time devoted to training
l	leisure
l_0	maximum available leisure hours
L_f	number of female workers hired
L^d	labor demand

L^s	labor supply
m	nonlabor income, outflow from unemployment
M	number of hirings
MLC	marginal labor costs
MRS	marginal rate of substitution
$MRTS$	marginal rate of technical substitution
OV	option value
N	sample size
NPV	net present value
p	probability parameter, participation rate, penalty
r	rate of return to additional year of schooling
R	threshold value of match productivity
s	probability of being sanctioned, continuum of labor markets, search intensity, skill
S	years of schooling
t	tax on wages, wedge in disemployment bias, calendar year
t_e	payroll taxes paid by workers
t_f	payroll taxes paid by firms
T	test score
U	number of unemployed workers
u	unemployment rate
U_c	marginal utility of consumption
U_l	marginal utility of leisure
V	number of vacancies
v	vacancy rate, productivity, unobserved characteristics
V_{un}	value of unemployment for those who are not entitled to benefits
V_u	asset value of unemployment
V_e	asset value of employment
V_t	potential earnings at age t
W	social welfare
w	wage rate, marginal wage cost
$\underline{w}$	minimum wage
w_f	wages for female workers
w^e	efficiency wage
w^r	reservation wage
w^m	monopsony wage
w_t	annual earnings
w^u	monopoly union wage, wage of union member
w^n	wage of nonunion member
y	value of job, marginal value of production

Greek Alphabet

α	state of the labor market, parameter in matching function, shape parameter in baseline hazard, parameter in utility function, per worker lump-sum tax or employment subsidy, vectors of parameters in regression equations
α^h	high innate ability
α^l	low innate ability

β	bargaining power of the unions, distributional weight of labor in social welfare maximization by government
β^G	importance attached to employees by the government in welfare maximization
γ	inverse of conversion (annuitization) coefficient, fraction of vacancies not filled, search cost function
δ	imputed indexation rate, job separation rate
Δ	difference
ε	inverse elasticity of labor supply (between 0 and infinity)
η	inverse labor demand elasticity (between 0 and 1)
μ	mark-up imposed by the institution over the competitive wage
θ	labor market tightness
κ	cost of posting a vacancy
λ	job offer arrival rate
$\lambda(t)$	hazard function
$\lambda_0(t)$	baseline hazard
μ^G	post-government legislation mark-up
μ	job offer rate
ξ	change in annuitization in pensions
π	profit
π^m	monopoly profit
Π_e	net present value of profits from a filled job
Π_u	net present value of profits from a vacant job
ρ_t	return to training
ρ	replacement rate, discount rate
ρ_w	discounting of employee taxes by employees
ρ_e	valuation of employer taxes by employees relative to cash income
τ	amount of general training, contribution rate to labor earnings
$\phi(x)$	systematic part of hazard rate
ϕ	monitoring rate
ω	overtime premium; individual-specific coefficient of discrimination for employers, customers, or co-workers
Ω	coefficient of market discrimination

Acronyms

AFP	Norwegian early retirement system
ALMP	active labor market policy
DB	defined benefit
DC	defined contribution
ECHP	European Community Household Panel
ECI	employment-conditional incentives
EITC	Earned Income Tax Credit
EPL	employment protection legislation
EU	European Union
FTE	full-time equivalent
GDP	gross domestic product
IALS	International Adult Literacy Survey
ILO	International Labour Organization
ISCED	International Standard Classification of Education

ISSP	International Social Survey Program
MGI	minimum guaranteed income
NDC	notionally defined contribution
NMW	national minimum wage
OECD	Organisation for Economic Co-operation and Development
PAYG	pay as you go
PISA	Program for International Student Assessment
STW	short-time work
UB	unemployment benefit
UI	unemployment insurance
UNESCO	United Nations Educational, Scientific and Cultural Organization
VAT	value-added tax
WFTC	Working Family Tax Credit

The Economics of Imperfect Labor Markets

CHAPTER ONE **Overview**

W hat have we learned so far from the labor market response to the Great Recession of 2008–2009? Should we modify our way of teaching labor economics in light of these developments? Surprisingly enough, these questions are rarely addressed in our profession. Although many state that "this time is different" and that "nothing will be like before," there has been so far little innovation in the teaching. Everything looks very much like before.

It was, no doubt, a crisis that developed outside the labor market, and yet it heavily invested the markets where labor services are exchanged for pay. The job death toll was on the order of 30 million. Youth unemployment was still on the rise worldwide five years down the road. In the United States unemployment almost doubled from peak to trough, within one and a half years: every quarter about one million jobs had disappeared. There were, at the same time, very important cross-country differences in the responsiveness of unemployment to output falls. In Germany unemployment actually fell, in spite of a very severe recession, involving a cumulative 7 percent decline in gross domestic product (GDP), almost twice as bad as in the United States. Since the recession was global, it gave us the opportunity to evaluate differences in the way in which labor markets respond to shocks originated elsewhere. There is potentially a lot to learn from this: the differences are indeed quite striking, even when account is made of cross-country variation in output fall, as shown in figure 1.1. A GDP fall of the same magnitude is accompanied in some countries by a huge rise in unemployment, while in others unemployment hardly changed from peak to trough.

Looking at figure 1.1 through the lens of the macro-labor literature developed in between the mid-1990s and the Great Recession, one is tempted to attribute entirely to labor market institutions the huge cross-country variation in the responsiveness of unemployment to output changes. A large body of academic papers and policy reports had examined the effects of labor market institutions on economic performance before the Great Recession. This literature was summarized in the initial paragraphs of the first edition of this book, as it offers a wealth of facts and theoretical insights on the relationship between institutions and labor markets, deeply affecting our way of thinking about labor market institutions. This literature was inspired by cross-country analyses. The focus was on transatlantic comparisons of employment and unemployment performance: the most influential policy report—the Organisation for Economic Co-operation and

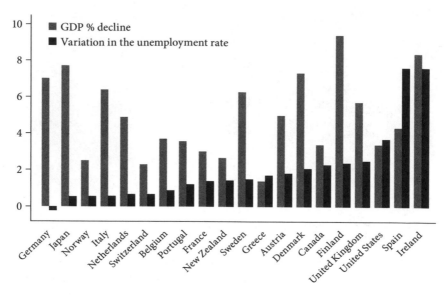

FIGURE 1.1 Changes in unemployment rates and GDP decline, 2008/2009 peak to trough

Development (OECD) (1994) report commissioned by the G7 (the intergovern-
mental group of—at the time—the seven largest economies in the world: Canada,
France, Germany, Italy, Japan, the United Kingdom, and the United States) in
the early 1990s and completed in 1994—is an attempt to explain the dismal
employment/unemployment performance of Europe vis-à-vis the U.S. "jobs miracle." The key message provided by this report, as well as by many subsequent
cross-country studies, is that there are institutional "rigidities" in Europe that prevent the labor market from creating as many jobs in the private sector as it does
in the United States. Many academic researchers followed the same route in analyzing various dimensions of the so-called *Eurosclerosis*, for example, Bean (1994),
Alogoskoufis et al. (1995), Snower and de la Dehesa (1996), Nickell (1997), Nickell and Layard (1999), Blanchard and Wolfers (2000), Nickell et al. (2005), and
Blanchard (2006).

According to this institutional perspective, it is in particular the strict employment protection legislation in Europe that is the smoking gun responsible for the
asymmetric responses to the global shock of 2008–2009 on the two sides of the
Atlantic. High costs of dismissals typically involve lower labor market volatility.
This means, during a recession, a slower growth of unemployment. However, the
countries with the strictest employment protection legislation, like Spain, this time
experienced the largest increase in unemployment. Output fall in Spain was half
as large as in Denmark, the land of flexicurity, where layoffs are fairly inexpensive for employers and there are instead generous unemployment benefits (UBs), a
mix that is supposed to give rise to relatively large unemployment inflows during
downturns. However, Denmark during the Great Recession experienced a much
lower rise in unemployment than did Spain (figure 1.1).

One should therefore go beyond the cross-country analysis of labor market
institutions to understand these asymmetric and largely unprecedented develop-

ments. To start with, it is important to acknowledge the nonuniformity of labor market institutions. National regulations allow for significant within-country variation in labor market institutions. For instance, the levels of the minimum wage differ across age groups, if not across industries or regions. Even when regulations do not allow for within-country variation, they are often not enforced uniformly. There is often a sizable informal sector, where most regulations are weakly enforced or not enforced at all. Thus, considering an institution at the country level may conceal significant within-country variation, and the coexistence of, say, "rigid" and "flexible" segments in the same labor market may involve nontrivial interactions between the two. An explanation for the strong rise in unemployment in Spain during the Great Recession is that its labor market is characterized by a dual structure, with a flexible temporary fringe alongside a rigid stock of regular contracts. This dualism could have increased labor market response to adverse business conditions precisely in those countries displaying the strictest employment protection provisions for regular contracts.

Another key factor behind the asymmetric response of labor markets to the Great Recession is likely to be in the nature of the shocks that led to the global output fall. In particular, one should look at the interactions between labor and financial markets, where the crisis originated and became global in the aftermath of the Lehman bankruptcy in the fall of 2008. Financial markets and the banking sector experienced a credit crunch well into 2009. Such a global credit crunch is likely to have played a key role in labor market adjustment during the downturn, if not the recovery. A different exposure to financial shocks may help explain the transatlantic differences in the rise in unemployment in 2008–2009, which are well characterized on the right-hand side of figure 1.2. Over a few quarters, U.S. unemployment, which previously had been virtually one-half of the average European Union (EU) unemployment, rose above European levels. One of the key differences between the two sides of the Atlantic is the degree of financial deepening. A simple empirical measure to account for this difference is the stock market capitalization as a percentage of GDP. While the size of the financial shocks, measured in terms of *changes* in stock market capitalization, appear very similar in terms of timing and size, what is striking is the fact that the *level* of financial deepening is very different. Whereas in the U.S. stock market capitalization amounts to some 100 percent of GDP, the same ratio in Europe is about 75 percent. Similar comparisons can be made by looking at the volumes of credit to the private sector on the two sides of the Atlantic.

Perhaps we did not need a Great Recession to understand the importance of the interactions between labor institutions and macroeconomic shocks. It would have been sufficient to have a bit longer memory. The focus of the institutional literature of the mid-1990s was differences in labor market performance of Europe vis-à-vis the United States over the decade. However, the institutions that were deemed to bear the brunt of blame for the poor employment performance of Europe had also been there some 30–40 years before, when the fate of labor markets was the other way around. Consider again figure 1.2 and look at it this time along the timeline from the left-hand corner. Clearly, it was only in the mid-1980s, after two oil shocks (the first two vertical lines in the figure), that unemployment in Europe

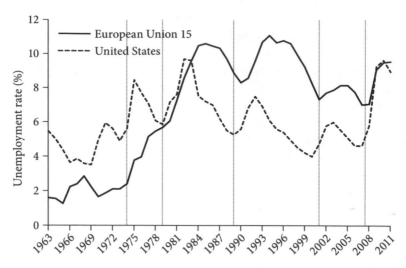

FIGURE 1.2 U.S. and European Union unemployment rates

Note: The European Union 15 (EU-15) is the group of countries belonging to the EU before the Eastern Enlargement: Austria, Belgium, Denmark, Finland, France, Germany, Greece, Ireland, Italy, Luxembourg, the Netherlands, Portugal, Spain, Sweden, and the United Kingdom.

started rising above U.S. levels, and it took another global shock at the end of the 1980s (the interest rate hike) to create a sizable gap in unemployment between the two sides of the Atlantic. The dot-com crisis (2001) reduced the gap; the Great Recession closed it. The same "rigid institutions" considered in the mid-1990s responsible for European unemployment were pointed out by the U.S. literature as one of the main factors behind the European success story. For instance, in 1964 U.S. policymaker Robert Myers (1964) wrote in a report that he was "looking enviously at our European friends to see how they do it" and invited everybody to take a look at institutions on the other side of the Atlantic: "it would be short-sighted indeed to ignore Europe's recent success in holding down unemployment." It took another 45 years and the Great Recession to have a new celebration in the United States of European institutions. This time it was Nobel Prize winner Paul Krugman writing in the widely read *New York Times* op ed (dated November 12, 2009):

> Germany's jobs miracle hasn't received much attention in this country—but it's real, it's striking. . . . Germany came into the Great Recession with strong employment protection legislation. This has been supplemented with a "short-time work scheme," which provides subsidies to employers who reduce workers' hours rather than laying them off. These measures didn't prevent a nasty recession, but Germany got through the recession with remarkably few job losses.

The Great Recession told us after all that labor market institutions are so important that they should be handled with care. It is of fundamental importance to understand how they operate. We need to know the institutional details and identify which of them are most important from an economic perspective to be able to shed light on their impact on labor market performance. It is also of paramount importance to understand how these institutions operate when the economy is under strain. Do institutions operate symmetrically over the business cycle? How do they interact with shocks coming from the product or the financial market? Who is most affected by them, and who is protected or penalized by these institutions? What type of redistributions do they involve?

A problem with much institutional literature predating the Great Recession is that it is not fair to labor market institutions. It often fails to explain why these institutions are in place to start with. Institutions are described as something that distorts the work of the market mechanism and prevents the attainment of efficient outcomes. It is assumed that if a government could remove these institutions, it should do so without further ado. It is an offense to the rationality of citizens and of their democratically elected governments that most of these institutions still exist.

This book aims at providing a comprehensive treatment of labor market institutions while introducing the key concepts and frameworks of labor economics. In this initial chapter we start by offering a few definitions that are crucial to understand what we are talking about. Next we discuss what makes the labor market taken as the reference in standard textbooks—the competitive labor market—so much different from the labor markets that we observe every day. Going beyond the competitive labor market paradigm to frame *imperfect* labor markets is essential to properly understand why labor market institutions exist. At the same time, the imperfections of labor markets together with shocks from other markets also explain pressures for change in these institutions and why institutional reforms are often asymmetric. It is better to be aware from the start that in this book we cover institutions that are changing over time. Rather than being an immanent feature of the country we live in, like the Thames River or the Alps, institutions are changing at relatively high, often unexpectedly high, frequencies. We shall see this in section 1.4, which is devoted to an analysis of institutional reforms.

1.1 A Few Key Definitions

It is useful to start with a few key definitions that will be used henceforth:

- A *labor market* is a market where a quantity of labor services L, corresponding to tasks specified in an *unfilled* assignment or job description (*vacant job*), is offered in exchange for a price or remuneration, called *wage w*. Not all labor services offered by an individual are paid. For instance, the time we devote to cleaning our own apartments is not paid. It becomes market work only if we hire a house cleaner. To be in the labor market, there must be an exchange of a labor service for a wage.

- According to internationally accepted OECD–International Labour Organization (ILO) definitions, the entire population of working age (15–64 years) can be classified in three main labor market states: employed, unemployed, or inactive:

  1. An *employed individual* is someone in the armed forces or who has worked for pay (in cash or in kind) for at least 1 hour during the reference period

(a week or a day) or has a formal attachment to a job but is temporarily not at work (e.g., because of an illness, a holiday, or maternity leave).

2. A person of working age is classified as an *unemployed individual* if that individual is willing to work at the going wage. To be classified as unemployed the following five conditions need to be fulfilled:
   (a) The person is currently not working.
   (b) The person has looked for work in the 4 weeks before the survey.
   (c) The person has looked for work actively (e.g., sending applications to employers or contacting a private placement agency or a public employment office).
   (d) The person is willing to work.
   (e) The person is immediately available for work, meaning that the person can start a job within 2 weeks following the interview.

3. *Inactive individuals* are persons who are neither employed nor unemployed according to these definitions. This residual group consists of a highly heterogeneous population, including people who are voluntarily inactive and individuals who are disabled.

Let U be the number of unemployed workers, L the number of employed workers, and O measure inactivity:

- The labor force LF is given by employment plus unemployment: $LF = L + U$.

- The working-age population adds up the three mutually exclusive categories of employed, unemployed, and inactive individuals: $N = LF + O$.

  Clearly comparing these numbers across countries with different sizes of the working-age populations is meaningless. In this book we adopt several widely used (but not always well understood) *normalization rules*. Here are the most important:

  - unemployment rate $u = \frac{U}{LF}$
  - employment rate $e = \frac{L}{N}$
  - participation rate $p = \frac{LF}{N}$

  These indicators are clearly not independent of each other, as $e = p(1 - u)$.

- If the labor force is fixed, the *steady state* (dynamic) equilibrium is defined by the equality of inflows into and outflows from unemployment. If δ is the rate at which workers lose their jobs and μ is the rate by which unemployed workers find jobs, the steady state equilibrium is defined by $\delta L = \mu U$. From this we may derive that the unemployment rate $u = \frac{\delta}{\mu + \delta}$. In other words, the steady state unemployment rate is defined by the job separation rate and the job finding rate.

- The *value of a job* y is the value of the labor product obtained when a firm and a worker engage in production. One can think of it as the revenues from the job, that is, the product of the quantity of output produced by that job and the price of this output. Both the value of a job and the price of the good produced by this job may not be fixed but may vary with the quantity of jobs and output. Thus we typically refer to the value of the *marginal* product of labor, that is, the price of the good multiplied by the increase in output made possible by hiring an additional worker.

- The *worker's surplus* or *rent* is the difference between the wage actually earned by the worker and that worker's *reservation wage* w^r, that is, the lowest wage at which the worker is willing to accept a job offer. The reservation wage is defined as the wage that makes the worker indifferent between working and not working. Any wage earned above this level represents a net gain over the option of not working, or a *surplus* from the standpoint of the worker. Formally, the worker's surplus is given by $(w - w^r)$.

- Similarly, the *surplus (or rent) of the firm* is the difference between the value of a job (the revenues from the job) and its costs, notably the wage paid to the worker engaged in that job, that is, $(y - w)$.

- The *total surplus* from a job is the sum of the firm's and the worker's surplus: $(y - w) + (w - w^r) = y - w^r$. Notice that the wage, the value of a job, and the reservation wage can all be expressed in monetary terms, for instance, in euros. Hence, given y, w, and w^r, one can readily obtain the worker's surplus, the firm's surplus, and the total surplus. Notice further that the wage cancels out in the total surplus.

Based on these definitions, we can characterize the key difference between a perfectly competitive (or "perfect" for short) and an imperfect labor market:

- A *perfect labor market* is one where there is no total surplus associated with the marginal job. Neither the worker nor the firm enjoys any rent with respect to their outside options. In other words, it is a market where $y = w$ and $w = w^r$, so that also $y = w^r$; that is, wages are ultimately immaterial at the equilibrium: they simply align the value of the job to the employer to the reservation wage of the worker. Put another way, employers and workers are indifferent between continuing or terminating any job relationship. Losing a worker for an employer or losing a job for an employee is not a big deal. Another worker or job can be found instantaneously without suffering any loss in profits or reduction in well-being. The market is transparent, workers and firms are perfectly informed about wages and labor services offered by other firms, and there are no *frictions* or costs (e.g., no time related to job search and no transportation costs when going to job interviews) involved in the matching of workers and vacancies, that is, of labor supply and demand.

- An *imperfect labor market* is one where there are rents associated with any given job, so that the total surplus is positive. Wages are, in this context, a rent-splitting device. They decide which fraction, if any, of the surplus goes to the employer, and which fraction, if any, goes to the worker. In an imperfect labor market wage setting is therefore of paramount importance. Depending on the market power of employers or workers, wages can bring either one of the two surpluses to zero while allowing the other party to enjoy a rent. The above implies that at least for one of the parties involved in the employment relationship, job destruction is a big deal—it involves loss. Imperfect labor markets are associated with frictions, informational asymmetries, or market power at least on one of the two sides of the market.

Finally, we have the definition most widely used in this book:

- A *labor market institution* is a system of laws, norms, or conventions resulting from a collective choice and providing constraints or incentives that alter individual choices over labor and pay. Single individuals and firms consider the institutions as given when making their own individual decisions. To give an example, an individual has limited choice over the number of hours of work to be supplied when working time is determined via a collective choice mechanism. As discussed in chapter 5, regulation of working hours is an institution aimed, inter alia, at coordinating the allocation of time to work, leisure, or home activities across and within households. Because of their foundations in collective choices, institutions are the by-product of a political process. Often, institutions are established by laws, but this does not need to be the case. For instance, collective bargaining institutions (chapter 3) are most frequently regulated by social norms and conventions rather than by formal legislation. What matters is that they constrain individual choice. For instance, they make the wage exogenous for the single worker or employer.

Labor market institutions operate by introducing a *wedge* between the value of the job for the firm and the reservation wage of the individual. In other words, they can create rents even in perfect labor markets. At the same time, in imperfect labor markets, they can also be a rent-reducing device. As rents are already there, they can be diminished by a proper set of institutions. Clearly, jobs can be created only if both workers and employers make some nonnegative surplus. Institutions can therefore destroy or create jobs, depending on whether they raise the reservation wage of workers above the value of a job for the employer. If $y < w^r$ in all jobs, then a labor market cannot operate.

To characterize the wedge introduced by labor market institutions, we need to derive from first principles the reservation wage of the workers and the value of a job for the employer. This is the task set out for the next section.

1.2 The Reservation Wage and the Value of a Job

Individuals participate in the labor market and supply labor services if they can get some nonnegative surplus from working. Thus, their reservation wage must be lower than or equal to the wage offered in the labor market. How is the reservation wage defined? Consider an individual whose utility function is defined over consumption c and leisure l, which are both assumed to be normal goods: $U(c, l)$, whose partial derivatives are U_c, $U_l > 0$. The individual allocates the endowment of time, say l_0, alternatively to work h hours earning at the hourly wage w, or to

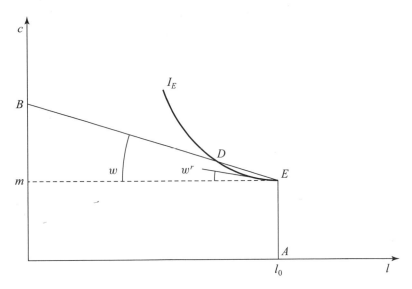

FIGURE 1.3 Reservation wage

leisure (clearly, $h = l_0 - l$). Define nonlabor income (the income when working zero hours) as m, and take the price of the consumption good as the numeraire (the price of c is 1 euro).

The *budget constraint* is given by

$$c \leq m + wh.$$

In the consumption/leisure space this constraint has a kink that corresponds to the level of nonlabor income, as depicted in figure 1.3. When $m = 0$, the budget constraint is a straight line crossing the horizontal axis at l_0, where no hours of work are supplied and hence income to buy consumption goods is zero. To the left of the kink at point E, income grows at rate w, because each additional hour of work yields an extra hourly wage.

The utility function can be graphically represented as a set of *indifference curves*. Each curve maps the combinations of consumption and leisure that yield the same level of utility to the worker. Because utility is increasing in both arguments, the indifference curves are negatively sloped: more consumption is needed to compensate the worker for the loss of an hour of leisure, and vice versa. The degree of convexity of these curves is decreasing with the degree of substitutability between labor and leisure. Because of our assumptions, indifference curves do not intersect, and utility is increasing farther away from the origin.

The reservation wage w^r is given by the slope of the indifference curve crossing the kink of the budget constraint at E, evaluated precisely at the point where the individual allocates m euros to the purchase of consumption goods and works zero hours. Any wage w lower than the reservation wage will not be accepted by the individual, because the marginal value of leisure (the reservation wage) exceeds its opportunity cost (the market wage). Conversely, when $w > w^r$, as in figure 1.3, the individual who is maximizing utility will work some hours and devote the remaining time to leisure.[1]

This definition of the reservation wage applies to conditions in which the individual can choose freely how many hours to work and how many hours to devote to leisure. In real life individuals rarely have an unconstrained choice of h. They have, at best, some leverage in deciding among a subset of possible hours of work, for example, between full-time and part-time jobs. This is because there is an institution (mandatory working-time legislation or collective bargaining agreements regulating working hours) that imposes, via a collective choice mechanism, constraints on individual decisions.

The reservation wage with restrictions on hours no longer coincides with the slope of the indifference curve at the kink of the budget constraint (see box 1.1). The reservation wage with restrictions on hours can be graphically represented as the slope of the segment going from the kink of the budget constraint (point E) to the locus where the indifference curve through the (m, l_0) pair crosses the vertical hours constraint, as depicted by point F in figure 1.4. This hours-constrained choice yields a lower level of utility than the unconstrained choice, provided that the latter, at the market wage, involves some positive number of hours of work; otherwise the hours constraint is not binding.[2]

BOX 1.1   *The Reservation Wage with and without Constraints on Hours*

When there are no constraints on the choice of hours, the reservation wage is given by the condition

$$\left(\frac{U_l}{U_c}\right)_E = w^r, \tag{1.1}$$

where U_l and U_c denote the marginal utility of leisure and consumption, respectively, and their ratio is the marginal rate of substitution between consumption and leisure. The rate is evaluated at the locus of zero hours of work (E in figure 1.3), where the individual is buying consumption goods by drawing only on nonlabor income.

An individual free to choose how many hours to work equates the marginal rate of substitution to the market wage. Hence, when $w^r = w$, the individual is indifferent between working and not working. When $w^r < w$, the optimal choice of hours h^* is greater than zero. When $w^r > w$, $h^* = 0$.

---

1. This definition of the reservation wage separates employment from nonemployment. When the reservation wage is higher than the market wage, the individual is simply not working. In the dynamic search model setting of chapters 10–13, a reservation wage separates employment from unemployment: individuals having a reservation wage higher than the wage offered to them will not accept the job offer and will search for alternative employment. In other words, according to our proposed definitions, they will be unemployed.

2. The reasons hours are regulated, although such institutions apparently reduce the well-being of an individual, are discussed in chapter 5.

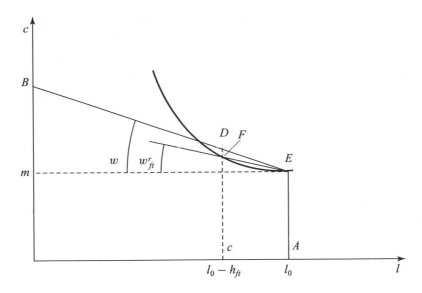

FIGURE 1.4 Reservation wage with a constraint on hours

Consider now a constrained choice. Suppose for simplicity that individuals actually have no choice over working hours and can only work h_{ft} hours, corresponding to a full-time job. The reservation wage will now be implicitly defined as the wage that would make the individual indifferent between not working at all and working exactly h_{ft} hours, that is,

$$U[m + w^r_{ft}h_{ft}, l_0 - h_{ft}] = U(m, l_0). \qquad (1.2)$$

The interpretation of this condition is that when $w = w^r_{ft}$, the constrained choice is on the same indifference curve that intersects the zero-hours locus. In other words, the individual is indifferent between working exactly h_{ft} hours and not working at all.

More important, the reservation wage of an individual who is constrained in terms of hours of work (w^r_{ft}) is higher than that of an individual free to choose hours of work (w^r). Because of the concavity of the utility function, the slope of the indifference curve increases as we move to the northwest along the same indifference curve. The labor supply decision of the individual will now obey a simple rule: supply h_{ft} hours if $w \geq w^r_{ft}$, or do not offer labor services (supply zero hours) otherwise.

If the wage increases, more individuals will be tempted to enter the labor market. Hence, in terms of the number of individuals, a wage increase will always lead to an increase in labor supply. Once an individual has entered the labor market, the effect of a wage increase is ambiguous, as there are two compensating effects:

1. Income effect: if the wage goes up with the same hours of work, income goes up. If leisure is a normal good, individuals will buy more leisure, thereby reducing their hours of work.

2. Substitution effect: if the wage goes up, the price of leisure goes up, causing consumption of leisure to go down and working hours to increase.

With leisure as a normal good, the income effect negatively affects labor supply. The substitution effect is always positive on the hours worked. The overall effect depends on the relative magnitudes of income and substitution effects. Generally, the substitution effect dominates for low-wage earners, while the income effect is most important for high-wage earners. Only if leisure is an inferior good will the income and substitution effects reinforce each other. Then, a wage increase always leads to an increase in working hours. At the participation margin, the income effect is irrelevant. Since the substitution effect is positive, an increase in the wage will always lead to an increase in the probability that an individual enters the labor market.

1.2.1 From Individual to Aggregate Labor Supply

Consider now a plurality of individuals who may well have different preferences about consumption and leisure and varying endowments of nonlabor income. The reservation wage will then vary across individuals, depending on their nonlabor income, as well as on their preferences about leisure and work. As discussed in chapter 7, time spent outside work can also be devoted to (unpaid) activities, such as household tasks generating goods and services that increase the welfare of the household. For instance, some workers may have childcare responsibilities, which increase their reservation wage.

Denote by $G(w)$ the fraction of individuals of working age with a reservation wage equal to or lower than w. By multiplying this fraction by the number of persons of working age, we obtain the *aggregate labor supply* schedule. Insofar as work involves some effort, the percentage of individuals willing to work will be increasing with the wage offered to them. Thus, we expect $G(w)$ to be monotonically increasing with w. By construction, $G(w)$ also takes values only in the interval bounded from below by 0 (nobody is willing to take the job at a wage lower than the lowest reservation wage) and above by 1 (when nobody of working age has a higher reservation wage). It is certainly possible that more than one individual has the same reservation wage, in which case aggregate labor supply will involve some flat segments. It is also plausible that some individuals, for example, a rich heiress, would not work whatever the wage offered to them.

Many surveys, such as labor force surveys, in several OECD countries ask respondents about the lowest wage at which they would be willing to take a full-time job offer. This reported reservation wage is an empirical proxy for our w^r. Longitudinal data (observations of the same individuals at different times) suggest that respondents take this question quite seriously. For instance, individuals observed to be unemployed at a given date and employed at the time of the next interview generally work at a wage that is not lower than the reservation wage stated in the first place. (Needless to say, it is possible that individuals revise downward their reservation wage when they perceive that their human capital is depreciating or they no longer have family responsibilities, but this does not seem to happen very frequently.) Thus, individuals appear to follow consistently a reservation wage policy in their labor supply decisions (they accept only jobs offering $w \geq w^r$).

1.2.2 The Value of a Job

Production takes place by combining labor with capital. In the short run, capital is fixed, so that there is no possibility to substitute labor with capital. Suppose that there is only one type of worker from the standpoint of a firm; that is, labor is homogeneous.[3] A profit-maximizing firm will hire workers up to the point where y, the value of the marginal job, equals the marginal cost of labor, that is, the wage. In a competitive market all firms will take this wage as given. Hence all firms will also have the same y at the equilibrium, and the *aggregate labor demand* will simply add up the number of jobs in each firm, yielding the same y. Put another way, y provides the *marginal willingness to pay* of firms for labor services or their *inverse labor demand* schedule $y(L)$. To obtain labor demand, we simply have to substitute y with w and solve for L. Formally, we set $y(L) = w$ and solve for L, obtaining $L^d(w)$.

Can we say anything about the slope of this labor demand function? By the law of diminishing marginal returns, the marginal product of labor is declining with the number of jobs for each individual firm. If not only the labor market but also the product market is competitive, then each firm will sell the product of labor at a given price, independently of the level of output. In this case the labor demand function will have the same slope as the (declining) marginal productivity of labor; that is, it will be decreasing with L, the quantity of labor being used. If instead firms have some monopoly power in product markets, the value of the marginal product of labor will include an additional term that captures the change in price associated with the extra output produced by the additional job, multiplied by total output.[4] Intuitively, when a firm faces a downward-sloping product demand curve,

---

3. Notice that we could as well assume that workers differ in terms of productivity but that these differences are fully offset by wage differentials, so that each employer is indifferent between hiring a high-productivity or a low-productivity worker.

4. Formally, for a competitive firm (superscript c), the value of the marginal product of labor VMP is

$$VMP^c = pf_L,$$

where p is the (given) price at which output can be sold, and f_L is the marginal product of labor. For a firm operating in a noncompetitive product market, we have instead

$$VMP = pf_L + p_L fy,$$

where p_L is the marginal effect on prices of the increase in the quantity produced by the firm associated with the use of an additional unit of labor, from which it follows that $VMP = VMP^c$ when $p_L = 0$; that is, the firm is also a price-taker in product markets. Because p_L is negative, labor demand of a monopolist will always be to the left of the demand curve of a competitive firm. Notice further that the difference between y^c and y is increasing in f, hence in the amount of labor being used. Thus, the labor demand of a monopolist will be steeper than that of a competitive firm.

increasing production lowers prices of all units being sold. The less competitive the product market is, the stronger will be the decline in prices associated with an increase in the quantity of jobs and output. By the same token, more competition in product markets involves a flatter labor demand curve.

To summarize, independently of the product market structure, labor demand L^d will be declining with wages, or the inverse labor demand, $y(L)$, will be declining with L. When product markets are noncompetitive, labor demand will be less responsive to wage changes (steeper labor demand).

1.2.3 A Perfect Labor Market Equilibrium

Figure 1.5 depicts a downward-sloping labor demand together with an upward-sloping aggregate labor supply. In a perfect labor market the equilibrium wage level w^* will lie at the intersection of the two curves. It is important to notice that there is only one wage level being determined at the equilibrium in this context. Thus, workers with a reservation wage strictly lower than w^* will realize a positive surplus from participating in the labor market. The sum of all these individual surpluses is given by the shaded area (W_s) below the equilibrium and above the labor supply curve. Firms will also realize some surplus or profits. This is depicted as the shaded area (F_s) above the equilibrium wage and below the labor demand schedule.

Workers with a reservation wage larger than w^* will instead decide not to work. In other words, $L^* = G(w^*)$ will be the *employment rate* (the fraction of the working-age population holding a job), while $1 - G(w^*)$ will be the equilibrium *nonemployment rate*. Notice that the equilibrium wage level may well be in a flat segment of the labor supply curve. In this case there will be individuals with $w^r = w^*$ who are not working, even if they are willing to work at the equilibrium wage. These individuals are, strictly speaking, *unemployed*, as denoted by the segment U in the right-hand panel of figure 1.5, although they do not suffer any welfare loss from not working ($w^r = w^*$ means that they are just indifferent between working and not working). All other nonemployed individuals are *inactive*, according to the internationally accepted definitions of labor market status reviewed in section 1.1.

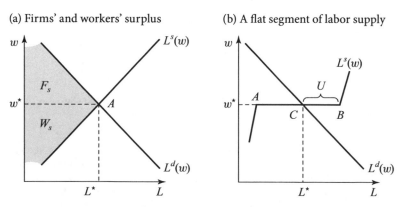

(a) Firms' and workers' surplus   (b) A flat segment of labor supply

FIGURE 1.5 Equilibrium in a competitive labor market

1.3 Labor Market Institutions

We are now ready to describe how labor market institutions operate. According to our definition, they are outcomes of collective choice mechanisms that interfere with the exchange of labor services for pay. They do so by introducing a wedge between the reservation wage of the workers and the value of a job, that is, between the labor supply and labor demand schedules. Thus, even in a perfect labor market, the marginal job may involve a rent, either for the employer or the worker.

1.3.1 Acting on Prices

Let us give a few examples of how labor market institutions operate. Formal descriptions are provided in technical annex 1.6. An institution like the *minimum wage* (see chapter 2) sets a lower bound $\underline{w}$ to the wage paid to individual workers. By doing so, it changes the slope of the labor supply schedule, preventing employer-firms from hiring workers at a lower wage than the minimum wage, even when the reservation wage of those supplying labor services is lower than $\underline{w}$. The actual labor supply faced by employers is now represented by the dotted line in the top panel of figure 1.6. The latter coincides with the reservation wage schedule only to the right of $L^s(\underline{w})$ (point C in the figure). Notice further that the segment $L^s(\underline{w}) - L^d(\underline{w})$ denotes *unemployed* individuals, that is, persons who are not working but who would be willing to work at the equilibrium wage. Insofar as their reservation wage is lower than $\underline{w}$, these individuals will not be indifferent between working and not working. In other words, unlike in a competitive and institution-free labor market, we now have strictly a welfare loss associated with unemployment. Put another way, even the marginal worker (job) enjoys a rent; her wage is higher than her reservation wage, $\underline{w} - w^r > 0$.

There are various ways to implement a minimum wage. In some countries there is a statutory minimum wage set by the government. In other countries a trade union (see chapter 3) imposes floors for wages via collective wage agreements in specific industries. Collective bargaining is itself an institution that interferes with wage setting not only by setting minima for pay but also by affecting wages above these minima, for example, by imposing egalitarian wage scales. When unions are present in the workplace, employers face a labor supply schedule that departs from the reservation wage of each individual worker. Unions thus impose on employers the payment of a *mark-up* over the reservation wage of individuals. Again we will have therefore an equilibrium involving a rent for the marginal worker-job.

Taxes on labor (chapter 13) are another institution that introduces a wedge between reservation wages and the value of labor productivity. They reduce labor demand but also labor supply, because some individuals drop out of the labor force who would be willing to work in the absence of taxes. This means lower employment and participation, but in a competitive labor market there is no unemployment unless the net wage happens to be in a flat segment of the labor supply schedule.

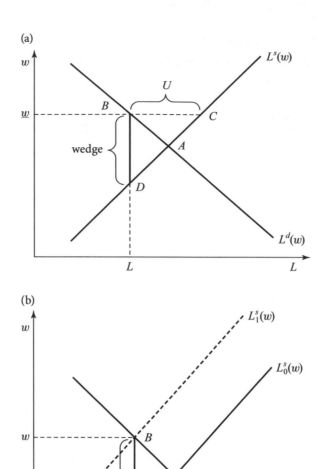

FIGURE 1.6 (a) Price-based and (b) quantity-based institutions and the wedge

The proceeds of labor taxes are generally used to finance retirement plans (chapter 6), family allowances (chapter 7), and UBs (chapter 11). All *nonemployment benefits* (subsidies provided conditional on not working) shift labor supply upward, reducing the employment rate and the size of the labor market. Part of this reduction in employment is accommodated by an increase in unemployment, and the remaining part by an increase in inactivity. The magnitude of the effects on inactivity and unemployment depends on the institutional details, notably on whether payments are contingent on nonemployment or require some job search effort (e.g., UBs may be accompanied by the activation measures outlined in chapter 12, which implement work tests, eliciting job search effort, for those receiving the benefits).

1.3.2 Acting on Quantities

Minimum wages, trade unions, taxes, and UBs operate mainly on the price of labor. They directly introduce a wedge between y and w^r by forcing employers to pay more than the reservation wage of the marginal job or workers to receive less than the labor cost paid by employers. Other institutions act on the quantity of labor being supplied or demanded and hence introduce a wedge only indirectly, because the actual or *effective labor supply* faced by employers departs from the cumulative distribution of individuals' reservation wages.

For instance, regulations on working hours (see chapter 5), restrictions to immigration (see chapter 9), or an increase in the compulsory schooling age (education policies are discussed in chapter 8) cut away a segment of the population of working age. It is plausible that most of the individuals who can no longer supply labor under these restrictions (e.g., women after maternity, first-time jobseekers, and migrants) have a relatively low reservation wage; that is, for them, $w^r < w^*$. Thus, the quantitative restrictions cut away a segment of labor supply to the left of w^*, involving a shift to the left of the entire schedule, as depicted in the bottom panel of figure 1.6. The new equilibrium will feature higher wages and less employment, just as in the case of institutions that act on prices. Once more, labor market institutions operate by introducing de facto (in this case indirectly) a wedge between the value of the marginal product of labor and the reservation wage. By reducing the segment of the population for which $w > w^r$, they reduce the size of the labor force, the employment rate, and in some cases (e.g., migration restrictions) also the working-age population. At the same time, they create rents, allowing at least one segment of the labor market—employers or workers—to enjoy at the equilibrium a surplus with respect to their outside options.

Another common quantity restriction in industrialized countries is *employment protection legislation* (EPL) (see chapter 10). This legislation makes it more costly for employers to adjust the number of workers in a firm in response to shocks. Unlike payroll taxes, EPL involves taxes and transfers to workers that are paid only in case of dismissal. Employers must pay social security contributions to employ labor, and they reduce employment in the face of higher payroll taxes if labor demand is downward sloping. But they can avoid paying firing costs by choosing a stable employment path around a level that may be slightly lower or even higher on average than what would obtain, for the same wage and contributions level, in the absence of EPL. This does not imply that firms should be happy to do so: by definition, when firms fail to equate w to y for the marginal job, they earn lower profits. In this sense it is quite reasonable to think of EPL as imposing a tax on employers. Still, EPL does not reduce profits through lower average employment levels but rather through poor synchronization of productivity and wages around roughly unchanged average levels.

1.3.3 Institutional Interactions

As just argued, EPL that imposes dismissal costs acts mainly on labor market flows. It does so by reducing the incentives for firms to shed labor. It is perhaps a little less intuitive that EPL also reduces incentives to hire: if employers anticipate that layoffs will be difficult or costly, they should try to reduce the amount of labor shedding called for by future labor demand downturns or wage upturns. This means hiring fewer people from the start. Because both firings and hirings decline, the net effect on employment and unemployment levels is ambiguous.

Yet EPL may indirectly affect employment by giving more power to trade unions in wage bargaining, and in this case the impact is likely to be unambiguous. Stronger bargaining power of workers shifts the labor supply faced by employers upward, increasing the equilibrium wage and reducing aggregate employment. In other words, EPL negatively affects employment by interacting with other institutions, such as collective bargaining institutions.

These institutional interactions can be complex, and there can be many of them, given that there are several possible combinations of institutions in place. At the end of each chapter, we discuss the interactions that appear to us most relevant. Unavoidably the list is not exhaustive. The important thing to remember at this stage is that one should never confine the analysis to the simple direct effect of one institution on the labor market. We live in labor markets in which institutions never operate in isolation.

It is customary to describe the institutional landscape of OECD countries in terms of a *cluster of institutions*. For instance, the so-called Nordic model (Denmark, Finland, the Netherlands, and Sweden) features generous nonemployment benefits combined with rather strict activation policies and the involvement of unions in the administration of UBs. Another example is the Southern model (including Greece, Italy, Portugal, and Spain), which features traditionally relatively strict EPL, early retirement provisions, and a rather strong influence of trade unions.

These different clusters of institutions involve very different labor market outcomes. As shown in figure 1.7, for both men and women there is wide variation across OECD countries in employment and unemployment rates. The cross-country variation in unemployment rates is very much the same for men and women, but the variation in employment rates is substantially larger for women than it is for men. For men (top panel of figure 1.7) there is a clear negative relationship between employment and unemployment rates. For women (bottom panel of figure 1.7) this cross-country negative relationship is less strong. Turkey is a clear outlier with a very low employment rate of prime-aged women. In addition, the lower panel of figure 1.7 shows that the same employment rate can be achieved at less than 5 percent or at unemployment rates above 20 percent. This suggests that it is important not to neglect labor force participation effects, notably among women.

(a)

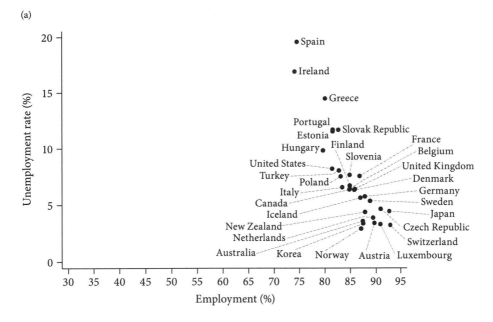

(b)

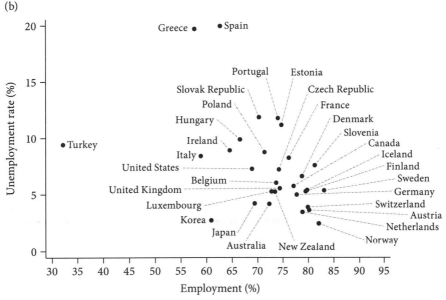

FIGURE 1.7 Employment and unemployment rates in OECD countries: (a) prime-aged men, (b) prime-aged women, 2011

1.3.4 Why Do Labor Market Institutions Exist?

Because all labor market institutions introduce a wedge between labor demand and supply, they reduce the size of labor markets. If the labor market is competitive, there will be an efficiency loss, because in principle, by increasing the size of the labor market and redistributing the surplus, it should be possible to make everybody better off. The obvious question is then why these institutions are so important in modern labor markets. They are certainly not imposed by Heaven. They are introduced by democratically elected governments. If voters did not like these institutions, they would sooner or later be removed. If these institutions reduce the size of the economic pie, then it should be possible to make everybody happier (or at least as happy) without them.

We offer three arguments for the existence of labor market institutions:

1. *Efficiency.* A first-best competitive labor market outcome is unattainable; there are second-best arguments justifying the presence of these institutions.

2. *Equity.* In the absence of nondistortionary taxes and transfers, these institutions are best suited to achieve some redistribution that is supported by voters.

3. *Policy failures.* There are failures in the political process that make it possible for minority interest groups to succeed in imposing their preferred institutions on majorities who would be better off without them.

Often these three reasons coexist, but we discuss them separately for the sake of simplicity. We confine ourselves here to a few illustrations of how these mechanisms operate. Later chapters contain a thorough discussion of the rationale for each institution.

Efficiency

Labor market institutions exist because there are *market imperfections* that prevent the institution-free equilibrium from attaining the competitive equilibrium outcome. In practice, a perfect labor market does not exist. Labor markets are far from competitive, because there are important informational asymmetries between employers and employees, as well as externalities (i.e., goods produced and consumed that are not subject to market interactions). In both cases—asymmetric information and externalities—labor markets violate the transparency and complete market properties of a perfect labor market. Well-designed labor market institutions, in this context, may remedy these failures of markets and increase the size of the pie compared with the laissez-faire outcome.

Equity

Even when institutions reduce the size of the economic pie, they may make one side of the market (those supplying labor services or those purchasing them) strictly better off than it would be without the institutions. In principle, redistribution could also be achieved by taking the laissez-faire outcome and then taxing employers or employees and transferring the proceeds to the other side of the market. In practice, however, redistribution via *lump-sum taxes and transfers* is not possible, because redistributive policies can only rely on information—on signals, which can be altered at will by individuals. Thus, any type of redistribution is unavoidably distortionary, and labor market institutions, such as distortionary labor taxes and transfers, can be the most efficient way to redistribute.

Policy Failures

Because of these redistributive properties of institutions, there are also instances in which some powerful minorities succeed in imposing a set of institutions on a majority of citizens. This happens particularly when the benefits of an institution are concentrated in a small segment of the population while the costs are spread over a very large crowd of individuals. Under these conditions, groups organized as a lobby may succeed in influencing political decisions disproportionately.

A Few Examples

In practice, labor market institutions perform several functions at once: they remedy market failures but, at the same time, affect the income distribution or meet the requests of specific interest groups. For example, in the absence of perfect capital markets, the welfare of risk-averse individuals can be increased by offering insurance against the risk of income fluctuations. Job loss is one of the occurrences against which workers could be protected. However, no private insurer will ever want to provide insurance against unemployment, because *moral hazard* and *adverse selection* stand in the way of these potential contractual arrangements. Workers would not try as hard to avoid unemployment and find new jobs if they were covered against the negative consequences of the event by purchasing insurance at a given market price (moral hazard), and workers who know that their unemployment risk is particularly high would make the scheme unprofitable for insurance providers and unattractive to workers with average risk (adverse selection). This explains why collective action (institutions) tries to remedy the inequitable or unfair labor market treatment of workers who, lacking insurance, become or remain unemployed despite their best efforts. UBs and EPL are remedies for this failure of markets. By supplying insurance, however, they involve some trade-offs. For instance, provision of insurance in the presence of asymmetric information unavoidably decreases productive efficiency. Workers have no less incentive to decrease their jobseeking effort when they are covered by social rather than private insurance, and protection from supposedly unfair developments unavoidably decreases the labor market's speed of adjustment.

While remedying a market failure, EPL and UBs transfer resources from employers to employees, creating a vertical redistribution of income. Most of the institutions analyzed in this book address distributional tensions by attributing a larger share of the economic pie to workers or to nonworking individuals and extracting surplus from employers. Minimum wages, restrictions on hours of work, collective bargaining institutions, and unions respond to distributional concerns by assigning a larger share of the pie to workers even at the cost of generating overall a smaller pie. At the same time, these institutions remedy market imperfections, such as the presence of monopsonistic power of firms and externalities in the wage-setting process and in bargaining over hours. Migration restrictions also have a well-defined distributional objective: they insulate native workers from competition from foreign workers. Their presence can also be explained in terms of market failures associated with interactions with other institutions. In the presence of minimum wages, migrants may crowd out native workers, or migrants who do not find a job may exert a negative fiscal externality on the native population by drawing nonemployment benefits without perhaps having contributed to their financing. Taxes on labor are often progressive, which suggests that they pursue vertical redistribution. At the same time, however, they can be rationalized by interactions with other institutions: someone has to pay for nonemployment benefits, active labor market policies, family policies, and formal education.

In technical annex 1.6 we provide a simple formalization of the redistributive role of labor market institutions. We model a competitive market with a government caring about income distribution or agents bargaining over wages, and we obtain the optimal size of an institution. Institutions are not always optimally sized, because specific interests prevail. Strict employment protection, for instance, involves large implicit transfers from the unemployed to employees or to some categories of employees who are de facto insulated from competition from *outsiders*. More broadly, the combination of price and quantity institutions that is present in many labor markets is successful in protecting *insiders* from negative labor market developments: not only are wages compressed and stable, but also tenure lengths of regular workers are clearly much longer in more rigid labor markets. Unsurprisingly, it is the insiders who oppose reforms of these institutions, even when they are a minority and when the optimal size of the wedge (operating the desired amount of vertical income distribution) would be lower. Often labor market institutions tend to privilege minority subsets of the market's labor force. Such policy failures can emerge over time as economies are hit by shocks (Blanchard and Wolfers 2000) or the economic environment is altered (Ljungqvist and Sargent 2003). The model in technical annex 1.6 suggests that the redistributive properties of institutions should be adjusted to the economic environment in which they operate. If product markets become more competitive, then redistribution involves higher costs in terms of forgone efficiency (Bertola and Boeri 2002). Under these conditions, it is better to pursue the same distributional objectives by imposing a smaller wedge between labor demand and labor supply. But policy failures may make this adjustment more difficult or altogether prevent it.

1.4 Reforms of Labor Market Institutions

As stressed earlier, it is always important to recognize that institutions fulfill a useful purpose from the point of view of at least some economic agents. Otherwise it would hardly be possible to see why they were introduced in the first place and why they are frequently reformed.

Labor market institutions have been subject to frequent policy changes in the past 30 years. This activism can be preliminarily characterized by looking at cardinal indicators of institutional intensity—notably some widely used indexes devised by the OECD—whose properties and shortcomings are discussed in detail in various chapters. Figures 1.8 through 1.11 display the level of these indexes in the mid-1980s or mid-1990s (horizontal axis) and for the most recent observation available (vertical axis). Countries located below the bisecting line through the origin have reduced over time the level of any given institution, whereas those located

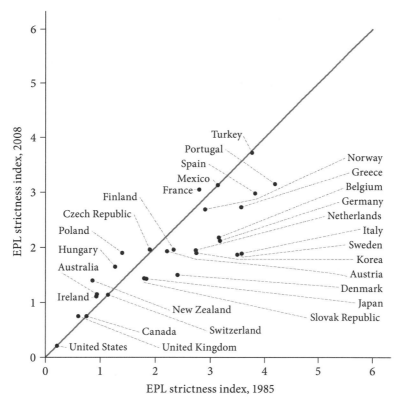

FIGURE 1.8 Evolution of the index of strictness of EPL

above the diagonal have increased it. Only countries located along the bisecting line have been keeping their institutions unchanged with respect to the initial year of observation.

We consider the following four institutional indicators: the index of strictness of EPL, the summary generosity measure of UBs, the ratio of active labor market policy (ALMP) expenditure to GDP, and the total tax wedge on low wages. The first two measures are widely used in the literature: they draw on detailed information about national regulations and are increasing in the strictness of EPL and generosity of UBs. Details on the OECD "Overall strictness of EPL" index are offered in chapter 10. The summary generosity measure is defined as a simple average of the de jure gross replacement rates over the first 2 years of an unemployment spell, still drawing on OECD data. The ALMP budget includes a variety of so-called activation programs providing job counseling, placement, and subsidized hiring typically at low durations of unemployment or among youngsters and sanctioning with benefit reductions those who did not actively seek employment (see chapter 12 for details). Finally, the total tax wedge on low pay captures a wide array of employment-conditional incentives (ECI) introduced to increase incentives to work at relatively low wages. It relies on detailed information on national tax and benefit systems collected in the OECD tax database (see chapter 13). Reference is made to a single worker earning two-thirds of the average worker pay.

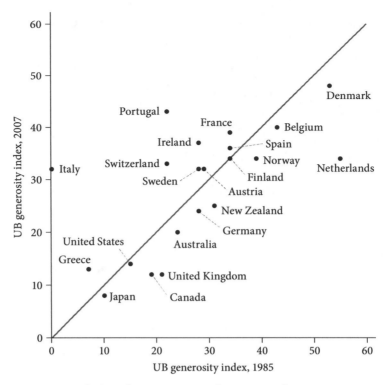

FIGURE 1.9 Evolution of summary generosity measure of UBs

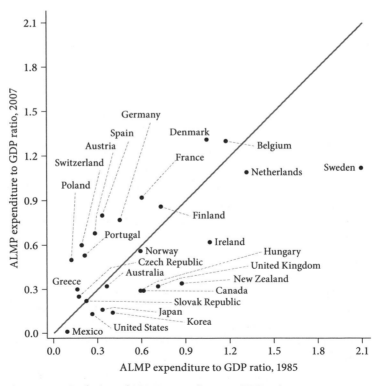

FIGURE 1.10 Evolution of ALMP expenditure to GDP ratio

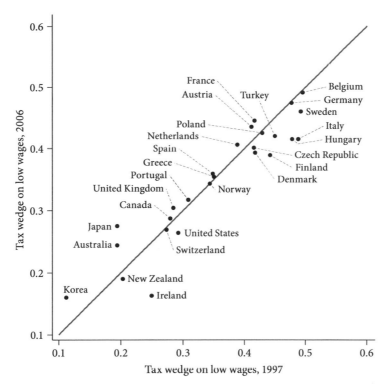

FIGURE 1.11 Evolution of the total tax wedge on low wages

The message delivered by these figures is one of much activism. There are only 3 countries (out of 28) that did not change EPL over time, only 1 country (out of 21) that did not modify UB generosity, 1 country out of 26 that did not adjust the size of ALMP programs, and 1 country out of 26 that did not adjust taxes and benefits for low-wage earners (although the available series cover only a 10-year period in this case).

Table 1.1 provides information on the number and characteristics of reforms carried out in the EU in the field of labor market and social policies during 1980–2007. It draws on the "Social Policy Reform Inventory," assembled by the Fondazione Rodolfo Debenedetti (recently in co-operation with the Institute for the Study of Labor [IZA]), which takes stock of reforms carried out in Europe in the field of EPL, UBs, activation programs, ECI, and early retirement plans. The full details on each reform are offered on the webpage of the Fondazione Rodolfo Debenedetti (www.frdb.org).

Many reforms of labor market institutions are taking place. In the observation period almost 883 reforms were counted in just 14 countries, that is, more than 2 reforms per year and country. In the areas of UB and EPL as well as in early retirement there are many reforms going in both directions, increasing and decreasing the wedge. This may be related to political opposition to reforms. There is much more consistency in activation programs and ECI reforms.

Most reforms, however, appear to reduce the wedge. This holds for each policy area. Moreover, the share of reforms reducing the wedge is increasing over time

TABLE 1.1 Number of labor market reforms by orientation and scope in Europe, 1980–2007

Reform area	Number	Effect on the wedge (%)		Scope of the reform (%)	
		Decreasing	Increasing	Two-tier	Complete
EPL	199	56	44	52	48
UB	253	55	45	46	54
AP	242	95	5	64	36
ECI	124	91	9	60	40
ER	65	58	42	75	25
Total	883	72	28	56	44

Source: Fondazione Rodolfo Debenedetti–IZA Social Policy Reforms database.
Note: AP = activation program; ER = early retirement.

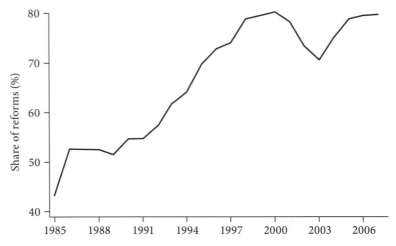

FIGURE 1.12 Share of reforms decreasing the wedge
Note: 5-year backward weighted moving average.

(figure 1.12). This trend can be explained as a reaction to pressures arising from product market competition, which, by flattening the demand for labor, increase the employment bias of labor market institutions (Bertola and Boeri 2002). At the same time, greater competition in product markets increases the political resistance to the downscaling of institutions protecting against labor market risk. Social norms or cultural factors supporting redistributive (typically, wage compressing) institutions may become more important at times of globalization (Agell 1999). This helps explain why several reforms also go opposite to the direction implied by increased product market competition. Moreover, several empirical studies (e.g., Rodrik 1998; Wacziarg and Welch 2003) found a positive correlation between exposure to product market competition—measured in terms of trade openness—and the presence of redistributive institutions, pointing to stronger demand for protection in competitive environments.

Reforms can also be categorized by considering whether they are two-tier or complete. In particular, we can look at the *target share,* that is, the share of the population potentially affected by the reform which was actually targeted by the reform. If the "treatment group" of the reform represents less than 50 percent of the potentially eligible population (i.e., it is only young people out of the entire working-age population or temporary workers out of the total dependent employment), then the reform was classified as a *two-tier reform*. As shown by table 1.1, two-tier reforms are predominant in all institutional areas except UBs. Not all two-tier reforms necessarily increase the dualism of regulatory regimes, as they may also reduce pre-existing asymmetries among the different regimes. However, four two-tier reforms out of five actually widen the asymmetries in regulatory regimes.

Whatever the reasons for the reforms of labor market institutions, many of them occur every year. This offers a great opportunity to understand their effects on the labor market. In this book we often refer to studies that use reforms as *policy experiments*, allowing researchers to better isolate the effects on the labor market of any specific institution and identify the underlying causal relationships. Often not only do institutions affect labor market outcomes, but also the underlying conditions of the labor market affect the institutions. The labor market itself gives rise to political pressures to introduce, preserve, or reform these institutions.

At the same time, it is important to be aware that most reforms are marginal and they may frequently involve the creation of two-tier regimes with the coexistence of reformed and unreformed segments of the labor market. Studying the interactions between these segments and defining a theory of two-tier reforms providing guidance to empirical work in this area is perhaps one of the most challenging areas of research in labor economics.

1.5 Review Questions and Exercises

1. What happens to the participation rate if unemployment goes up?

2. Who are the discouraged workers?

3. Why is the wage elasticity of labor supply always positive for nonparticipants?

4. What happens to labor supply if wages go up and leisure is an inferior good?

5. Why is the reservation wage higher with restrictions on hours?

6. What is the difference between a two-tier and a complete reform?

7. Provide clear examples of price-based and quantity-based labor market institutions.

8. Under what conditions can labor market institutions increase labor market efficiency?

9. Why is labor demand called derived demand?

10. Why is the labor supply curve always upward sloping?

11. Andrea's utility function is $U(C, l) = (C - 40) \times (l - 40)$, where C denotes consumption and l leisure. Andrea earns 10 euros per hour, can at most work 84 hours per week, and has no nonlabor income.

(a) Please display Andrea's budget line. Would it be different if she had some nonlabor income?

(b) What is Andrea's marginal rate of substitution when $l = 50$ and she is on her budget line?

(c) What is Andrea's reservation wage?

(d) Compute the amount of consumption and leisure, C^* and l^*, that maximize Andrea's utility.

12. Mike's preferences over consumption C and leisure l are given by $U(C, l) = Cl$. The hourly wage is 20 euros and there are 168 hours in the week.

(a) Write down Mike's budget constraint and graph it.

(b) What is Mike's optimal amount of consumption and leisure?

(c) What happens to employment and consumption if Mike receives 200 euros of nonlabor income each week?

13. (Advanced) Revenues of employers are given by

$$f(L) = \frac{A}{1 - \eta} L^{1-\eta},$$

with $0 \leq \eta < 1$, in which L is labor input and A and η are constants. Labor supply is specified as $L^s = w^{\frac{1}{\varepsilon}}$, where ε is a constant.

(a) Show that a government trying to maximize the joint surplus obtains the perfect labor market outcome.

(b) Specify the outcome of Nash bargaining over the market surplus, where β represents the bargaining power of the workers.

(c) Show under which conditions the bargaining outcome is equal to the perfect equilibrium outcome.

(d) Assume that employers have all the bargaining power, then illustrate that the magnitude of their power depends on the slope of the labor supply curve.

(e) Provide an intuition for these results.

1.6 Technical Annex: A Simple Static Framework

A simple static model originally developed by Bertola and Boeri (2002) can be valuable in characterizing equilibriums in competitive labor markets, as well as the role of labor market institutions.

1.6.1 A Competitive Labor Market

In the model below a crucial role is played by labor demand and supply elasticities, defined as the percentage change in labor demand and supply, respectively, associated with a 1 percent change in the wage. On the demand side of the market, profits are maximized when the marginal wage cost w is equal to the marginal value of production y. In the short run (when capital is fixed) there is no loss in generality in assuming that the marginal value of a job is a decreasing (at a constant elasticity) function of the employment rate L, that is, $y = AL^{-\eta}$, where A is an index of the production function, and the index of the (inverse) labor demand elasticity η takes values between 0 (flat labor demand at A) and 1. We can then write the labor demand schedule as

$$L^d = \left(\frac{A}{w}\right)^{\frac{1}{\eta}}. \tag{1.3}$$

The supply side of the labor market is given by the cumulative distribution function of the reservation wages, which is, by construction, increasing with w. We assume also that this schedule has a constant-elasticity functional form so that

$$L^s = G(w) = w^{\frac{1}{\varepsilon}}. \tag{1.4}$$

The elasticity parameter may range between 0 (in which case the labor supply is flat and normalized to unity) and plus infinity: larger values of ε denote increasingly inelastic labor supply schedules, and as ε tends to infinity, labor supply becomes perfectly vertical.

We consider first the equilibrium in a competitive and wedge-free labor market, where $y = w^r = w^*$. By equating the two schedules, solving for L, and substituting the result in the labor supply function, we obtain

$$L^* = (A)^{\frac{1}{\varepsilon+\eta}}, \qquad w^* = A^{\frac{\varepsilon}{\varepsilon+\eta}}. \tag{1.5}$$

It is easy to show that this equilibrium maximizes the total surplus from labor exchange. The profit of the employer is equal to the difference between the area under the demand curve and the labor costs:

$$\int_0^L Ax^{-\eta}dx - wL = \frac{A}{1-\eta}L^{1-\eta} - wL. \tag{1.6}$$

Similarly, the total surplus of workers is given by

$$wL - \int_0^L x^\varepsilon dx = wL - \frac{L^{\varepsilon+1}}{\varepsilon+1}. \tag{1.7}$$

Maximizing the joint surplus (the *sum* of the firm's profits and of the workers' surplus from employment),

$$\max_L \left(\left[\frac{AL^{1-\eta}}{1-\eta} - wL\right] + \left[wL - \frac{1}{\varepsilon+1}L^{\varepsilon+1}\right]\right)$$

$$= \max_L \left(\frac{AL^{1-\eta}}{1-\eta} - \frac{1}{\varepsilon+1}L^{\varepsilon+1}\right), \tag{1.8}$$

yields the wedge-free, perfect labor market wage and employment levels (1.5). Hence the competitive outcome has the desirable property of maximizing the total surplus of production over the opportunity cost of employment, or the size of the economic pie generated by the labor market. Since maximization entails equality at the margin of the value of a job for the employer and workers' reservation wages, the competitive outcome also features no welfare loss from unemployment. Yet as long as w^* lies on a flat segment of the function $G(w)$, at the equilibrium there may be individuals unemployed, meaning in this particular case that they are indifferent between working and not working.

1.6.2 Labor Market Institutions

As discussed in this chapter, the presence of labor market institutions can be rationalized in terms of market failures as well as distributional tensions, either related to general interest redistribution in favor of workers or special interests of specific categories of workers-citizens. Market failures may arise from imperfect or asymmetric information or because of an excessive concentration of power in the hands of employers (monopsony power), forcing both employment and wages to be lower than at the optimum. Distributional concerns may arise with and without market failures. In the absence of lump-sum redistribution, even equilibriums that maximize the joint surplus (the equilibrium in a competitive economy) do not necessarily address distributional tensions in the economy.

1.6.3 The Wedge

All labor market institutions operate by introducing a wedge between labor supply and demand. Their rationale can be illustrated by comparing the institution-free, laissez-faire, equilibrium with the solution of a government problem involving the choice over the size of this wedge. If the wedge is zero, the solution of the problem coincides with the laissez-faire equilibrium and there is no role for labor market institutions. The size of the wedge measures the deviation of the social optimum (or the equilibrium imposed by bargaining over the distribution of the surplus) from the laissez-faire equilibrium.

In particular, consider an institution introducing a wedge between labor supply and demand in terms of a proportional tax on labor income, t. Suppose that the government maximizes over t a Bernoulli-Nash social welfare function of the type

$$W = \max_{t} \left(\left[\frac{AL^{1-\eta}}{1-\eta} - w(1+t)L \right]^{(1-\beta)} \left[w(1+t)L - \frac{1}{\varepsilon+1}L^{\varepsilon+1} \right]^{\beta} \right), \quad (1.9)$$

where the parameter β measures the distribution weight of labor, that is, the importance given by the planner to the (functional) share of the pie going to the workers. Conversely, $(1 - \beta)$ is the distribution weight of employers.

By taking the log of (1.9) (a monotonic transformation that does not alter the first-order conditions) and imposing the condition that employers and workers are optimizing their choices over labor and leisure (employers on the labor demand

and workers on their labor supply), we can rewrite the maximization problem as

$$\max_t (1 - \beta) \log \left(\frac{AL^{1-\eta}}{1 - \eta} - (1+t)AL^{1-\eta} \right) + \beta \log \left((1+t)L^{\varepsilon+1} - \frac{L^{\varepsilon+1}}{1 + \varepsilon} \right),$$

$$(1.10)$$

where we substituted $w = AL^{-\eta}$ in the definition of the employers' surplus and $w = L^{\varepsilon}$ in the definition of the employees' surplus, or

$$\max_t (1 - \beta) \log \left(AL^{1-\eta} \left(\frac{\eta - t(1 - \eta)}{1 - \eta} \right) \right) + \beta \log \left(L^{\varepsilon+1} \left(\frac{\varepsilon + t(1 + \varepsilon)}{1 + \varepsilon} \right) \right).$$

$$(1.11)$$

The first-order condition is

$$\frac{AL^{1-\eta}(1 - \beta)}{AL^{1-\eta}(\frac{\eta}{1-\eta} - t)} = \frac{L^{\varepsilon+1}\beta}{L^{\varepsilon+1}(\frac{\varepsilon}{1+\varepsilon} + t)}.$$

Then simplifying,

$$\frac{(1 - \beta)}{\frac{\eta}{1-\eta} - t} = \frac{\beta}{\frac{\varepsilon}{1+\varepsilon} + t},$$

and then solving for the wedge, we obtain

$$t = \beta \frac{\eta}{1 - \eta} - (1 - \beta) \frac{\varepsilon}{1 + \varepsilon}, \qquad (1.12)$$

which implies that the wedge is zero if and only if

$$\frac{\beta}{1 - \beta} = \frac{\varepsilon}{(1 + \varepsilon)} \frac{(1 - \eta)}{\eta}. \qquad (1.13)$$

In other words, a laissez-faire equilibrium when governments care about the (functional) distribution of income requires that the ratio of the distribution weight of employees to that of employers equals a product of the labor demand and supply elasticities. The larger is ε, the lower the elasticity of labor supply will be, and the larger the distribution weight of employees justifying a laissez-faire equilibrium should be. Analogously, the larger is η, the lower the elasticity of labor demand will be, and the higher the distributional weight of employers justifying a laissez-faire equilibrium should be. The economic intuition behind these results is that, in line with optimal taxation theory, it is better to tax more the less elastic side of the market, as this maximizes tax revenues. Only a strong distributional concern of this less elastic side of the market could move the equilibrium away from this optimal taxation rule.

Importantly there is no reason to expect a priori that the condition (1.13) is satisfied, as β bears no systematic relationship to labor demand and supply elasticities. Put another way, it can only be by chance that (1.13) is satisfied. In the general case, when distributional concerns are relevant, it is optimal to have some wedge between labor supply and demand, even at the cost of deviating from the equilibrium, which maximizes the joint surplus. Redistribution is one of the key functions of the labor market institutions discussed in this book. The other cases for labor market institutions arise when the laissez-faire equilibrium does not maximize (1.11) and hence labor market institutions do not necessarily involve an efficiency-equity trade-off.

1.6.4 Product Market Competition and the Employment Bias of Institutions

Notice that the distribution weight compatible with the competitive, laissez-faire equilibrium is decreasing with the elasticity of demand and supply. By the same token, the *disemployment bias* of labor market institutions (the reduction in employment induced by the wedge with respect to the institution-free outcome) is larger in the presence of a larger elasticity of demand. In particular, by denoting by the superscript I the presence of some institution, the disemployment bias is given by the wedge t, where

$$1 + t = \frac{(1 - \eta) + \beta(\eta + \varepsilon)}{(1 - \eta)(1 + \varepsilon)}. \tag{1.14}$$

Let $\mu \equiv 1 + t$ denote the mark-up imposed by institutions over the competitive wage. The above result suggests that the equilibrium with institutions involves lower employment than at the laissez-faire competitive equilibrium when the mark-up is greater than 1.[5]

Suppose now that labor demand becomes more elastic (moving, say, from η_0 to η_1, where $\eta_1 < \eta_0$), for example, as a result of a globalization shock involving greater competition in product markets. Insofar as labor market institutions do not automatically adjust to the changes in the economic environment, the employment levels before and after globalization (denoted by the subscripts 0 and 1, respectively) are given by

$$L_1^I = A\mu_0^{-\frac{1}{\varepsilon + \eta_1}} < L_0^I = A\mu_0^{-\frac{1}{\varepsilon + \eta_0}}.$$

Thus, if the wedge remains at its optimal level (μ_0) before the globalization shock and does not adjust to the changes in the labor demand elasticity parameter, an increase in product market competition leads to lower employment, and by (1.8) there is a larger employment bias of labor market institutions with respect to the laissez-faire outcome. Increased product market competition may also involve improvements in production technologies (a larger A), such as ones brought

---

5. When the mark-up is strictly lower than 1, it is labor supply that is the short side of the market. Also in this case there is less employment than at the competitive equilibrium.

about by the externalities associated with having a larger market. This may increase the laissez-faire equilibrium employment level with respect to its level before the shock, shifting the labor demand schedule upward. But under greater product market competition, the employment bias of labor market institutions with respect to the laissez-faire outcome is larger. Put another way, if the rationale for labor market institutions is only in terms of (functional) income distribution, then the wedge should be downscaled after globalization, because there is a steeper efficiency-equity trade-off.

Overall, an increase in product market competition leads to pressures to reduce the wedge that labor market institutions entail with respect to the competitive outcome. At the same time, however, unreformed labor markets have worse employment outcomes than before globalization. Thus, stronger competitive pressures in product markets also increase the risk of job loss, potentially creating strong constituencies against the retrenchment of institutions that protect against unemployment risk, like nonemployment benefits, employment protection, and ALMPs, whose reform pattern is characterized in table 1.1.

CHAPTER TWO **Minimum Wages**

The minimum wage is a labor market institution that sets a wage floor, that is, a lower bound to the wage paid to individual workers. The first minimum wage was introduced in the United States in 1938 and paid 25 cents per hour. In 2010 the federal minimum wage was $7.25, in nominal terms almost 30 times larger, but, in real terms, less than twice as high as 70 years before. In the United Kingdom a national minimum wage was introduced as late as 1999.

Although most countries in the world have some form of minimum wage, the scale, eligibility, and operational details change from country to country, so providing a cross-country comparable definition and measure of the minimum wage is not an easy task. Some statistics, like the ratio of the minimum wage to the median wage, are, however, commonly used to summarize the relevance of the minimum wage in affecting the distribution of earnings in different countries. A key difference between the minimum wage and the other price-based institutions analyzed in the following chapters (e.g., unions and collective bargaining) is that the minimum wage mostly affects the low end of the wage distribution. Because the minimum wage sets a wage floor, there may be a spike in the wage distribution at the minimum wage. This spike indicates how many individuals are directly affected by the minimum wage. The fraction of the workers affected will vary to the extent that the minimum wage is binding.

A large body of theoretical and empirical research examines the effects of the minimum wage. Theory offers clear-cut predictions only in the case of a competitive labor market. Empirical results point in both directions—positive and negative effects of the minimum wage on employment—which is possible in a monopsonistic labor market where individual firms face upward-sloping labor supply curves.

In some countries the minimum wage is unilaterally set by the government, while in other countries it is the outcome of negotiations between workers and firm representatives. When it is government legislated, the minimum wage in principle applies to all workers who have a legal contract. When it is the outcome of collective bargaining, the wage floor agreed to by the parties involved in wage negotiations may also cover the workers who are not unionized. In this case it becomes a minimum wage applied to all workers covered by the collective agreements. Overall, it is convenient to classify the different types of minimum wages applied in OECD countries according to their coverage and determination on the basis of the following threefold taxonomy:

1. a national, government-legislated (perhaps after consultations with trade unions and employers' associations) minimum wage;

2. a national minimum wage that is the outcome of collective bargaining agreements and is extended to all workers;

3. an industry-level minimum wage that results from industry-level collective bargaining and is extended to all workers in that industry.

All these minima can be set on an hourly, daily, weekly, or monthly basis. Beyond the single minimum wage, there is often a reduced or subminimum rate for some specific groups of workers, for example, those without work experience and youngsters. Often, subminimum rates do not exist de jure but exist de facto, since special employment programs allow employers to pay lower wages to youth workers. In some countries premiums to the minimum wage are allowed to reward specific and time-varying workers' characteristics. For instance, the minimum wage may increase with workers' experience, workers' qualifications, and family status. Legislated minimum wages may or may not be automatically indexed to price inflation; in the latter case they may be discretionally adjusted by governments. It is also possible that the minimum wage is determined in parallel at different levels. For example, in the United States there is a federal minimum wage, but some states also have their own minimum wage. The actual minimum wage is then the highest of the two minimum wages.

2.1 Cross-Country Comparisons

Despite the various differences that we have pointed out, one can still try to compare minimum wages across countries by measuring their value relative to some central measure of the wage distribution. In particular, the ratio of the minimum wage to the median wage is often used in international comparisons.[1] In principle, using the median rather than the average wage as a denominator would be preferable, because the average wage may be affected by large values at the upper tail of the distribution, but micro data are not always available to obtain the median wage.

The minimum wage to the median wage ratio is clearly affected by how both the numerator (the minimum wage) and the denominator (the median wage) are measured. Because the minimum wage is generally exempted from income taxes, which are often progressive, it may also be preferable to use net wages (median wages after taxes) as the denominator in computing this measure. Particular attention should also be paid to using the appropriate earnings measure, which should possibly exclude any overtime and bonus payments.

The ratio of minimum to median wage ignores potential spillovers associated with the setting of minimum wages. Especially when minimum wages are embedded in collective bargaining, an increase in the minimum wage may also induce pay

---

1. The *Kaitz index* (Kaitz 1970) was developed with the idea of taking the coverage of the minimum wage into account. The index is defined as the ratio of the minimum wage to the median wage adjusted for the industry-level coverage of the legislation. Nevertheless, since the eligible population is not always well defined, the coverage part of the index is often ignored.

increases above the minimum, shifting a relevant portion of the wage distribution to the right and hence leading to a significant increase in the median wage. Under these circumstances a change of the minimum wage will hardly be perceived from looking at the ratio of the two wages, because both the numerator and the denominator move in the same direction.

Another drawback of this measure is that it does not take into account the fact that there may be subsets of the workforce, such as informal sector workers, who are not covered by the minimum wage. In most developing countries and in a number of OECD countries (including formerly planned economies of Central and Eastern Europe and southern European countries), alongside a formal (and often urban) labor market where the minimum wage is enforced, there is a large informal labor market in which the minimum wage legislation does not apply. There is no country in the world where there are enough labor inspectors to check every plant. Because of these enforcement issues, an increase in the minimum wage may paradoxically reduce the wage of the lowest-paid workers: low-productivity workers, crowded out from the covered sector by the rise in the minimum wage, could increase labor supply in the uncovered sector, driving down wages therein.

With these caveats in mind, the first three columns of table 2.1 display the ratios of minimum to median wage for several countries as compiled by the OECD. As shown in the table, there is a wide range of values of the index. In 1990 it went from a low of 17 percent in Poland to a high of 63 percent in Australia. In 2010 the index ranged from 19 percent in Mexico to 67 percent in Turkey. In 2010 minimum wages were lower in Canada, Japan, Korea, and the United States than in many European countries. The new member states of the European Union—Hungary, Czech Republic, Slovak Republic, and Estonia—are at the low end of the European distribution of minimum wages, together with Spain and United Kingdom, which introduced a national minimum wage in 1999.

Column (3) of table 2.1 shows that the evolution of the ratio of the minimum wage to the median wage between 1990 and 2010 widely differs across countries. Whereas in Australia, Mexico, Greece, and the Netherlands the ratio dropped substantially, the ratio increased significantly in Turkey and Poland. As indicated by figure 2.1, the minimum wage in the United States has been falling since the end of the 1990s relative to the median wage, to increase again at the end of the 2000s. In the Netherlands the ratio has been decreasing since the late 1970s, while in France there is an almost continuous increase over a period of 40 years.

Column (4) of table 2.1 compares the level of monthly minimum wages specified in euros. The differences are substantial. The new member states of the European Union are at the lower end of the distribution with monthly minimum wages in the range of 250–350 euros. Australia and Luxembourg are at the high end of the distribution with a range of 1,650–1,750 euros, while in the second highest group of about 1,350–1,450 euros there are France, Ireland, and the Netherlands.

A taxonomy of the minimum wage is presented in columns (5) and (6). The minimum wage can apply to the national, sectoral, regional, or provincial level. Column (6) presents the threefold taxonomy discussed at the start of this chapter. Almost all countries have a national, government-legislated minimum wage. A national minimum wage that is the outcome of collective bargaining agreements and

TABLE 2.1 Minimum wages in OECD countries

	Ratio MW to median wage (%)			Monthly MW, 2010 (euros)	Taxonomy		Percentage earning MW (2005)	Youth subminimum
	1990 (1)	2010 (2)	Difference (3)	(4)	System[a] (5)	Type[b] (6)	(7)	(8)
Australia	63	54	−9	1,670	N-S	1	—	Yes
Belgium	56	52	−4	1,388	N	2	—	Yes
Canada	38	44	6	1,187	P	1	—	Limited
Czech Republic	—	35	—	311	N	1	2.0	Yes
Denmark	—	—	—	—	S	3	—	Yes
Estonia	—	41	—	278	N	1	4.8	No
France	52	60	8	1,344	N	1	16.8	Limited
Germany	—	—	0	—	S	3	—	Some
Greece	57	49	−8	863	N	2	—	No
Hungary	44	47	3	257	N	1	8.0	No
Ireland	—	52	—	1,462	N	1	3.3	Yes
Italy	—	—	—	—	S	3	—	Some
Japan	30	37	7	1,069	R	1	—	Limited
Korea	30	41	11	605	N	1	—	Yes
Luxembourg	37	42	5	1,725	N	1	11.0	Yes
Mexico[c]	31	19	−12	—	R	1	—	No
Netherlands	56	47	−9	1,416	N	1	2.2	Yes
New Zealand	52	59	7	1,196	N	1	—	Yes
Poland	17	45	28	318	N	1	2.9	No
Portugal	53	56	3	554	N	1	4.7	No
Slovak Republic	—	46	—	308	N	1	1.7	Yes
Slovenia		58	—	734	N	1	2.8	No
Spain	47	44	−3	739	N	1	0.8	No
Sweden	—	—	—	—	S	3	—	Yes
Turkey	46	67	21	—	N	1	—	Yes
United Kingdom	—	46	—	1,169	N	1	1.8	Yes
United States	36	39	3	949	N-S	1	1.3	Limited

Sources: Dolton and Bondibene (2011); OECD Minimum Wage Database.

Note: MW = minimum wage; — = not available.

a. System: N = national; N-S = national-state; S = sectoral collective agreement; R = regional; P = provincial.

b. Type: 1 = national, government legislated; 2 = national, bargaining; 3 = industry level, bargaining (see main text).

c. The ratio of MW to median wage is for 2005 instead of 2010.

is extended to all workers is present in Belgium and Greece. Finally, an industry-level minimum wage that results from industry-level collective bargaining and is extended to all workers in that industry is present in Denmark, Germany, Italy, and Sweden.

The percentages of workers earning the minimum wage in 2005 are presented in column (7). By far the highest percentage is for France, where in 2005 almost 17 percent of all workers earned the minimum wage. At the other extreme is Spain, where less than 1 percent of the workers earned the minimum wage. Except for Hungary and Luxembourg, where respectively 8 and 11 percent of the workers

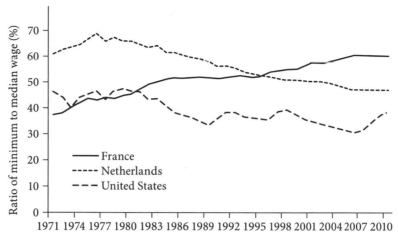

FIGURE 2.1 Ratio of minimum to median wage, 1971–2010
Source: OECD minimum wage database.

earned the minimum wage, in all other countries for which information is available the percentages are between 1 and 5.

Finally, the last column of table 2.1 indicates whether the minimum wage applies to workers of all ages or whether there is a youth subminimum wage. In section 2.4.2 we provide more detailed information on youth minimum wages.

2.2 Theory

2.2.1 A Perfect Labor Market

Economic theory offers unambiguous predictions about the effects of a minimum wage in a competitive labor market. A minimum wage set above the market-clearing level tends to reduce employment and increase the equilibrium wage level. Because the wage actually paid by employers is higher and employment is lower, some workers who were previously working at a lower wage are displaced by the introduction of the minimum wage, while other workers who were not supplying labor at the market-clearing level are now willing to work at the minimum wage. As a result of these two effects—displacement of some workers and higher participation—the introduction of a minimum wage above the market-clearing level involves some unemployment.

Figure 2.2 illustrates how the introduction of a minimum wage affects a competitive labor market. Before the introduction of the minimum wage, labor market equilibrium is at A, the intersection of the labor supply (L^s) and the labor demand (L^d) curves. The minimum wage, $\underline{w}$, changes the slope of the labor supply schedule, which is now flat at $\underline{w}$ until point C and then upward sloping along the original labor supply curve. The new labor supply schedule prevents employer-firms from hiring workers at a lower wage than $\underline{w}$ even when their reservation wage is lower than the minimum wage. Furthermore, the segment BC, that is, the difference $(L^s(\underline{w}) - L^d(\underline{w}))$, denotes the number of unemployed individuals

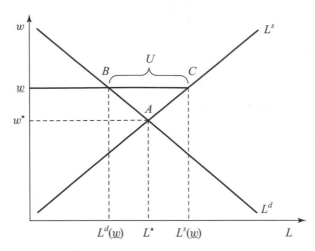

FIGURE 2.2 The minimum wage in a competitive labor market

(U), persons who are not working but would be willing to supply labor at the minimum wage. Insofar as their reservation wage is lower than $\underline{w}$, these individuals will not be indifferent between working and not working: there is strictly a welfare loss associated with unemployment in this case.

2.2.2 An Imperfect Labor Market

The effects of the introduction of a minimum wage in a labor market with distortions are much harder to predict. In some circumstances (e.g., when employers have monopsony power in wage setting, notably when there are matching frictions and externalities associated with job search), the introduction of a relatively low minimum wage may actually end up increasing employment.

When employers can unilaterally set wages, their profit-maximizing choice involves lower employment and wage levels than in a competitive labor market. As first pointed out by Stigler (1946) and Lester (1947), there is a theoretical possibility that a minimum wage set above the equilibrium wage could increase employment. The reason this happens can be readily grasped by turning upside-down the well-known case of a pure monopoly. As a pure monopolist (in the product market) faces a downward-sloping *demand* curve for its products, a pure monopsonist (in the labor market) faces an upward-sloping labor *supply* curve. Thus, the marginal cost of hiring a worker for this unique employer is higher than the reservation wage of any additional worker because the pay increase necessary to induce the individual to supply labor has to be granted not only to the marginal worker but also to the entire workforce (just as an increase in the supply of a monopolist involves a decline in the price of all goods being sold, not just of the last unit of output). The marginal labor cost (MLC) of a monopsonist is depicted in figure 2.3: it is located above the $L^s(w)$ curve and deviates more and more from the latter, as hiring an additional worker implies a wage increase to a larger and larger workforce. The profit-maximizing employment choice of a monopsonist then equals the marginal labor cost to the marginal revenues from labor, $L^d(w)$ (the price of the good mul-

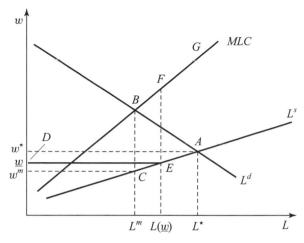

FIGURE 2.3 Monopsony and the minimum wage

tiplied by the marginal productivity of labor). Graphically, this optimal choice lies at point B, at the intersection of the marginal labor cost and labor demand curves. The monopsonist hires L^m workers, compared with L^* in a competitive economy. It also pays a lower wage (w^m) than any firm in a competitive equilibrium (w^*), because a monopsonist pays at the equilibrium less than the marginal productivity of labor. The degree of *monopsonistic power* of a firm is measured by this wedge BC between labor demand and supply, $y(L^m) - w^m$. This wedge is larger the steeper is the labor supply curve. More precisely, it is decreasing with the responsiveness of labor supply to wages, as shown analytically in box 2.1.

The Degree of Monopsonistic Power

BOX 2.1

The results in figure 2.3 clearly have an analytical counterpart. Denote, as usual, by $y(L)$ the value of the marginal product of labor and by $L^s = G(w)$ the aggregate labor supply faced by the monopsonist. Total labor costs C are equal to the product of wage and employment: wL. For marginal labor costs it holds that $\frac{dC}{dL} = w + \frac{dw}{dL}L = w(1 + \frac{dw}{w}\frac{L}{dL})$. So marginal labor costs $\frac{dC}{dL} = w(1 + \varepsilon)$, in which ε is the inverse elasticity of labor supply. At the monopsony equilibrium the value of the marginal product of labor must equal the marginal cost of labor:

$$y(L^m) = w^m(1 + \varepsilon). \tag{2.1}$$

The wedge between labor demand (the value of the marginal product of labor for the firm) and supply (the way in which labor is rewarded) expressed as a fraction of the latter measures the degree of monopsonistic power of the firm. By rearranging this equation it is easy to derive an expression for the degree of monopsonistic power,

$$\frac{y(L^m) - w^m}{w^m} = \varepsilon, \tag{2.2}$$

which tends to zero as the wage elasticity of labor supply tends to infinity. Thus, monopsonistic power is decreasing with the wage elasticity of labor supply: the less elastic the labor supply is, the larger the difference becomes between the equilibrium value of a job for the monopsonist and the wage that the monopsonist pays to workers. Conversely, when labor supply is infinitely elastic (the employer is a price-taker in the labor market), ε tends to zero, and hence monopsonistic power is zero.

In the presence of a monopsony the introduction of a minimum wage slightly above the monopsony wage generates a new marginal labor cost curve given by the segment $DEFG$ in figure 2.3 (i.e., the curve is initially horizontal until it hits the old labor supply curve and then jumps from E to F to follow the original marginal labor cost curve). The new equilibrium between marginal revenues and marginal labor costs is at point F. Clearly, a minimum wage set at an intermediate level between the monopsony and the competitive economy levels increases both wages and employment.

However, if the minimum wage happens to be above w^*, as depicted by point A in figure 2.3, then the minimum wage involves instead a lower employment level than in the competitive economy equilibrium. For even higher values of the minimum wage (i.e., above point B), employment falls below the level attained in the pure monopsony equilibrium. In the presence of a monopsony, there is therefore a nonmonotonic relationship between the minimum wage and employment: for sufficiently low levels of the minimum wage, an increase in the minimum wage is accompanied by an increase in employment, while above some threshold, the traditional negative relationship exists.

Overall, introducing a minimum wage in a monopsony model has the following effects:

1. If the minimum wage is set between the monopsony wage and the competitive equilibrium, it is the labor supply curve that determines the relationship between minimum wage and employment (i.e., an increase in the minimum wage leads to more employment).

2. If the minimum wage is set above the competitive equilibrium, it is the labor demand curve that determines the relationship between minimum wage and employment (i.e., an increase in the minimum wage reduces employment).

3. If the minimum wage is set above the marginal labor cost for the monopsonist (above point B in figure 2.3), employment is lower than at the monopsony equilibrium.

4. The introduction of a minimum wage above the monopsony wage reduces the profits of the monopsonist, but in the range BC, between the monopsonist wage and the monopsonist marginal labor costs, total surplus increases. Thus, in this range the introduction of a minimum wage increases labor market efficiency.

5. The introduction of a minimum wage above the monopsonist marginal labor costs reduces total surplus and therefore reduces labor market efficiency.

The case of a minimum wage in the presence of a pure monopsony is often neglected, because it is considered of limited practical relevance. Labor markets with only one employer are rarely observed. The standard example is the one-company towns in Russia, a legacy of central planning. Like mountain gorillas, these monopsonies are a sort of endangered species. A case like that described by figure 2.3, however, may also arise when there is more than one employer in a labor market, but these employers collude in wage setting. Collusion among employers may be favored by collective bargaining institutions, but collective bargaining means that the worker side is also organized, and hence employers cannot unilaterally set wages. There are in such cases *bilateral monopoly* conditions that reduce the power of employers in setting wages.

Even labor markets in which each individual employer is infinitesimally small relative to the market as a whole, however, may confer to employers some degree of monopsony power. This happens when there are search frictions and mobility costs, making it costly for workers to change jobs. These costs prevent the labor market from arbitraging away any difference in the way in which different employers pay for (homogeneous) labor services. Job creation and hiring costs also attribute to employers some degree of monopsony power. When it is costly to establish a new job or hiring is highly regulated, there are fewer vacancies, and hence for workers it is harder to find openings to apply for. All these modern monopsony cases are rather frequent in practice (Manning 2003) and arise even when there are many employers, but many fewer vacancies to apply for.

Can a minimum wage also increase employment in the presence of these modern monopsonies? Yes, if the minimum wage is not too large and workers' search efforts and participation decisions are sufficiently responsive to the wage that they can earn if they find a vacancy. The intuition is straightforward. In a labor market without frictions, a minimum wage, on the one hand, reduces labor demand (we move up and to the left along the L^d schedule in figure 2.2), but, on the other hand, it also increases labor supply (we move up and to the right along the L^s schedule). In a labor market with frictions and where individuals can choose whether or not to search, as well as the level of search intensity, a higher wage paid to those who succeed in finding a job induces more people to participate in the labor market and put effort into job search. At the same time, the minimum wage reduces the surplus that employers can earn over and above the marginal productivity of workers once a vacancy is filled. However, the presence of more jobseekers and the fact that each of them is seeking jobs more intensively increases the probability that a vacancy is filled. To the extent that this second, labor supply, effect dominates the negative labor demand effect associated with the reduction in the surplus of employers, there will be both more jobseekers and more vacancies at the equilibrium with the minimum wage than at the equilibrium without the minimum wage. Because the labor market is larger, equilibrium employment will also be larger, even if each individual worker now faces a lower job-finding rate per any given level of search effort. Minimum wages can also have positive effects on employment when employers

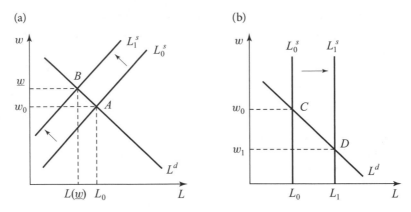

FIGURE 2.4 A dual labor market and the minimum wage: (a) formal sector;
(b) informal sector

imperfectly monitor the productivity of workers in large firms. A minimum wage, in this context of an efficiency wage model, may force firms to grow larger (Rebitzer and Taylor 1995). The intuition is that firms pay higher wages but also obtain higher productivity in return, as the penalty associated with disciplinary layoffs is larger (see technical annex 2.9.3 for a presentation of the efficiency wage model).

Minimum wages may not have negative effects on employment in *dual labor markets,* where the minimum wage does not apply to the secondary or informal labor market. Under these conditions there are important spillover effects between the two sectors. As pointed out by Mincer (1974), Gramlich (1976), and Welch (1976), after a minimum wage increase, workers displaced in the formal sector move to the uncovered sector.

This is illustrated in figure 2.4. Initially, both the formal and the informal sectors are in equilibrium at the same wage w_0, point A in the left graph and point C in the right graph. If in the formal sector a minimum wage is introduced, labor demand is reduced along the labor demand curve from point A to point B. This would create unemployment, as now labor supply is larger than labor demand. However, workers that would have become unemployed move from the formal sector to the informal sector. In the formal sector there is an upward shift of the labor supply curve from L_0^s to L_1^s, whereas in the informal sector there is a shift of the labor supply curve to the right. Therefore, wages fall in the informal sector (from w_0 to w_1). The minimum wage then reallocates jobs from the formal to the informal sector, increasing the difference between formal and informal sector wages. This adjustment mechanism prevents employment losses only insofar as there is perfect labor mobility between the two sectors.

Finally, positive effects of the minimum wage on welfare, although not necessarily on employment, can be generated when the productivity of a job depends on the investment in education and training by the employee (Cahuc and Michel 1996; Acemoglu and Pischke 1999). Under these conditions a binding minimum wage induces workers to raise their productivity by acquiring education to avoid being crowded out by the minimum wage. Hence, at the equilibrium with the minimum wage, there are more high-productivity jobs. The same type of effect may be induced on the demand side (Acemoglu 2001), because the minimum wage increases the number of vacancies for high-productivity jobs issued by employers. Nevertheless, the traditional view is that if a minimum wage is set too high, employers may find it too expensive to invest in training of low-skilled workers, as the employers cannot retrieve the training costs through a lower wage. Workers may not have an incentive to invest in their human capital, because they are entitled to the minimum wage irrespective of obtaining extra skills.

Overall, what really matters is the level rather than the presence of a minimum wage. Although the standard prediction from economic theory is that a minimum wage should reduce employment, some market imperfections may allow the introduction of a minimum wage, set at relatively low levels, to be consistent with the attainment of higher levels of employment and welfare.

2.3 Empirical Evidence

2.3.1 Studies Based on Firm-Level Data

Many studies on the effects of the minimum wage are based on firm-level data and estimate the impact of minimum wages on labor demand. The impact of the minimum wage is clearly dependent on the characteristics of the bottom end of the wage distribution and on the actual enforcement of minimum wages. Earlier studies used the Kaitz index to control for limited enforcement of the minimum wage. More recent empirical work typically measures the proportion of people earning a wage between the old and the new minimum wages (Card 1992; Card and Krueger 1995a; Brown 1999), or the *fraction affected* by the minimum wage increase. An increasingly used measure of enforcement is the *spike*, defined as the proportion of people earning exactly the minimum wage (Dolado et al. 1996). If the minimum wage is properly enforced, we generally expect the spike to increase after a minimum wage is raised as lower wages align with the new minimum.

Dolado et al. (1996) provide an overview of studies on the effects of the minimum wage on employment in several OECD countries. The minimum wage is generally found to affect employment negatively, although the magnitude of the effects varies from country to country and depends on the category affected (e.g., minimum wages for youngsters generally have stronger negative effects on employment). OECD (2006a) more recently reviewed the empirical literature on the effects of the minimum wage and found some, albeit small, negative effects on employment of the minimum wage, notably for young workers.

Although most of these studies use data on the formal sector, where minimum wage legislation is enforced, a few studies apply the same methodology to data on the informal sector. These studies mostly concentrate on developing countries (Lemos 2004 for Brazil; Gindling and Terrell 2004 for Costa Rica; Jones 1997 for Ghana), where the informal sector is larger. Notwithstanding problems in measuring informal sector employment, a few studies surprisingly found an increase in wages also in the informal sector after a minimum wage hike. The interpretation provided by this literature is that the minimum wage of the formal sector serves as a reference throughout the economy. If firms have monopsonistic power in the informal sector, and fair remuneration considerations are relevant, it is possible that changes in the minimum wage in the formal (and covered) sector lead to corresponding increases in the median wage of the informal sector. Spillover effects between the formal sector and the informal sector—increasing the wage in the latter as a result of a signal being given in the former—have been termed *lighthouse effects.*[2]

More recently, studies have been performed that use matched worker-firm data to establish whether individual firms are facing an upward sloping labor supply curve. There is evidence of market power and potential positive effects of the minimum wage. Staiger et al. (2010) find that labor supply to individual hospitals in the United States is quite inelastic, with a short-run elasticity of about 0.1. Falch (2010) finds labor supply elasticities in the range of 1.0–1.9 in the Norwegian teacher labor market, while Ransom and Sims (2010) find a labor supply elasticity of about 3.7 for public schools in Missouri.

2.3.2 Studies Based on Natural Experiments

Most of the studies just reviewed compare employment and wage outcomes of workers whose wages have to be raised (to comply with the minimum wage) with employment and wage outcomes of workers higher up the wage distribution, presumably unaffected by changes in the minimum wage. The problem with this approach is that persons receiving the minimum wage are not representative of the entire population. Thus, we may end up attributing to the minimum wage effects that are related to different characteristics of workers (e.g., lower labor market attachment) located at varying portions of the wage distribution.

The empirical methodology of a natural experiment in economics (Meyer 1995; Angrist and Krueger 1999; Blundell and Dias 2000) takes these selection problems into account and makes it possible to better identify the effects of the minimum wage. It consists of exploiting exogenous changes in the economic environment of certain agents to compare their reactions to those of other (a priori identical) agents who have not undergone these changes. In practice this means finding a counterfactual or *another difference* that makes it possible to control for the difference in the compositions of those affected by the minimum wage and those not affected by it. For this reason, the estimators obtained by applying this methodology are also called *difference-in-differences* or double-difference estimators.

Difference-in-differences estimators have been used in the United States, exploiting cross-state variation in setting minimum wages above the federal level. In particular, Card and Krueger (1994, 1995a) investigated the impact of increases in the minimum wage in New Jersey in 1992 from \$4.25 to \$5.05. They used as the control group Pennsylvania, where the minimum wage remained at \$4.25 throughout this period. New Jersey and Pennsylvania are bordering states and have similar

---

2. The literature on lighthouse effects deals mainly with Latin America; see, for example, Bell (1997). See also Boeri et al. (2011).

economic structures. Because this study has been widely debated, it is discussed in some detail in box 2.2.

Effects of Minimum Wage Hikes in the U.S. Fast-Food Industry   BOX 2.2

David Card and Alan Krueger collected data on employment in 410 fast-food restaurants in New Jersey and Pennsylvania, two bordering states in the United States with similar economic structures. The minimum wage was initially the same ($4.25 per hour) in both states and was raised in 1992, only in New Jersey, to $5.05 per hour. The data were collected in February–March 1992 (when both states had the same minimum wage) and in November–December 1992 (after the increase of the minimum wage in New Jersey). The changes in the wage distribution in the two U.S. states are totally characterized in figure 2.5: there is a visible shift of the distribution in New Jersey, with a spike corresponding to the new level of the minimum wage, while the wage distribution in Pennsylvania remains roughly unchanged. The effects of the minimum wage increase on employment were estimated by Card and Krueger by simply taking the difference between the November–December 1992 and February–March 1992 employment variations in the two states. Hence, Card and Krueger found that after the minimum wage was increased, the level of employment in fast-food establishments in New Jersey rose faster than in Pennsylvania. Their conclusion was that an increase in the minimum wage can lead to an increase in employment when this wage is sufficiently low to start with. In the case studied by Card and Krueger, the variation in the minimum wage was 80 cents, and in the table below they found an employment increase of 2.7 workers, which implies that an increase in the minimum wage by one dollar has the potential to create 3.4 (2.7/0.8) more jobs in every firm.

	Employment		Price	
	New Jersey	Pennsylvania	New Jersey	Pennsylvania
February–March 1992	20.4	23.3	3.35	3.04
November–December 1992	21.0	21.2	3.41	3.03
Difference	0.6	−2.1	0.06	−0.07
Difference-in-differences	2.7		0.07	

Note: Employment = number of full-time equivalents working in a fast-food restaurant; Price = price of a full fast-food meal in U.S. dollars.

The research by Card and Krueger generated a large and very informative debate along three dimensions. The first debate focused on the interpretation of the results and on whether consumers of fast food can be taken to be representative of the population at large, since it may well be that persons earning minimum wages represent the typical consumers of fast food. The second debate relates to the interpretation of their finding from a theoretical point of view. An increase in the minimum wage inducing an increase in employment suggests that fast-food restaurants have monopsony power. However, an increase in the minimum wage should have led to an increase in production, which could only have been achieved by a reduction of the product price. As shown in the table above, this is not in

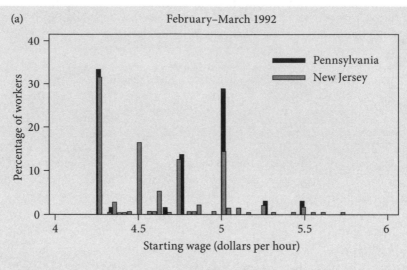

(a) February–March 1992

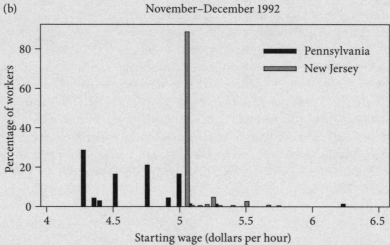

(b) November–December 1992

FIGURE 2.5 The wage distribution (a) before and (b) after an increase in the minimum wage

line with the observed increase in the price of a full fast-food meal. Nevertheless, a competitive market in which there would have been a price increase cannot explain why employment increased. The third debate concerned the quality of the data and the fact that the original Card and Krueger study was based on a survey that used telephone interviews and was not the result of administrative data. Despite the large debate between Card and Krueger (1994) and Neumark and Wascher (2000), the results of the early study seem to be confirmed.

Sources: Card and Krueger (1994); Neumark and Wascher (2000).

Difference-in-differences estimators have also been used, for instance, by Stewart (2004) to investigate the effects of the introduction of the national minimum wage in the United Kingdom in 1999 (with the adult rate set at 3.6 pounds per hour) and of the subsequent increases in 2000 (3.7) and 2001 (4.1). As documented by table 2.1, the United Kingdom has a ratio of minimum to median wage located roughly in the middle of the distribution of European countries. Stewart compared employment outcomes of individuals just above the minimum wage and higher up the wage distribution before and after the introduction of the minimum wage. He repeated this exercise for different demographic groups (males and females in different age groups) and controlled for cyclical conditions. Stewart found no adverse effect of the introduction of the minimum wage in Britain for any of the demographic groups considered.

Draca et al. (2011) also exploit the introduction of the national minimum wage in Britain in 1999 to study its economic consequences using a difference-in-differences approach. They focus on the effects of the minimum wage on profits and productivity of firms. Their study is discussed in some detail in box 2.3.

Minimum Wages and Firm Profitability   BOX 2.3

Mirko Draca, Stephen Machin, and John van Reenen study the impact of minimum wages on firm profitability, exploiting the changes induced by the introduction of a UK national minimum wage (NMW) in 1999. Using firm-level data, they are able to exploit a difference-in-differences approach. They distinguish two types of firms—low-wage and non-low-wage firms—and pre-NMW and post-NMW periods. The pre-NMW period corresponds to the three financial years from April 1, 1996, to March 31, 1999, and the post-NMW period refers to the three financial years from April 1, 1999, to March 31, 2002. Low-wage firms are defined as firms with an average wage equal to or below 12,000 pounds per year in the pre-policy financial year up to March 31, 1999. Non-low-wage firms have average wages between 12,000 and 20,000 pounds in the pre-policy financial year up to March 31, 1999. The general idea is that the introduction of the minimum wage will have an effect on low-wage firms but no effect—or a much smaller effect—on non-low-wage firms. Indeed, this is what the authors find when investigating the effects of the introduction of the NMW on average wages and profit margins (see the table below).

	Low (average wage)		Profit margin	
	Low-wage firm	Non-low-wage firm	Low-wage firm	Non-low-wage firm
Pre-NMW	2.149	2.775	0.128	0.070
Post-NMW	2.378	2.893	0.089	0.058
Difference	0.229	0.118	−0.039	−0.012
Difference-in-differences	0.111		−0.027	

Note: NMW = national minimum wage; Profit margin = ratio of profits to sales.

Draca et al. found that average wages in the non-low-wage firms were 11.8 log points higher in the post-NMW period compared to the pre-NMW period. For the low-wage firms, this was 22.9 log points. They conclude that the introduction of the NMW caused wages in low-wage firms to rise by 11.1 log points. Furthermore, the authors found that the profit margin in non-low-wage firms dropped by 1.2 percentage points, while in low-wage firms the drop was 3.9 percentage points, suggesting that the NMW caused profit margins in low-wage firms to drop by $3.9 - 1.2 = 2.7$ percentage points. Both the effects on average wages and on profit margins are statistically significant. Performing similar analyses for employment and productivity, they found no significant effects caused by the introduction of the NMW. They also found that the negative effect of the NMW on profits was much larger in industries that had some product market power, which makes sense, as there are rents to be redistributed there. The authors conclude that their findings are consistent with a "no behavioral response" model, where firms do not adjust employment and thus wage increases from minimum wages map into profit reductions.

Source: Draca et al. (2011).

2.3.3 Studies Based on Workers' Histories

Two problems with the empirical literature on the minimum wage literature are that (1) it typically focuses on specific industries in analyzing the effects of the minimum wage, while the standard predictions of the competitive model apply to the labor market as a whole and (2) it neglects potential effects of the minimum wage on hours rather than on persons employed.

These issues can be tackled by using longitudinal data on representative samples of workers, tracking labor market histories of persons whose wages are at the minimum wage or close to it. Recent studies in this category found that changes in the minimum wage have a significant impact on employment among this group of workers. Nevertheless, there is no agreement about the directions of these changes. Abowd et al. (1999) found that in France an increase of 1 percent in the minimum wage reduces the probability that men receiving the minimum wage keep their previous jobs by 1.3 percent, while for women this figure is 1 percent. In the United States a reduction by 1 percent in the minimum wage increases the probability that workers paid at this level will keep their jobs by 0.4 percent for men and by 1.6 percent for women. Portugal and Cardoso (2001) found different results using the same type of methodology. They exploited changes made in 1987 to Portuguese legislation regarding the minimum wage of young people aged 19 and under. The minimum wage was raised by 50 percent for youths aged 17 and by 33 percent for youths aged 18 and 19. They found that these minimum wage hikes reduced hiring, but also that workers had a greater tendency to keep their jobs. In other words, Portugal and Cardoso observed fewer separations, which partly offset the fall in hires. Note that this result is consistent with the predictions of the monopsony model, since it reveals greater attachment of youth to their jobs when wages improve. Neumark et al. (2004) found negative effects of minimum wage hikes in the United States on both employment and hours of workers initially earning the minimum wage or slightly more, contrary to Zavodny (2000), who found that an increase in the minimum wage reduced the probability that an affected worker remained employed, but for those who kept their jobs, there was a positive effect on hours.

Overall, this large body of empirical research shows that the minimum wage can have significant effects on both job-finding and job-loss probabilities. However, it does not invariably find a positive effect on the probability of job loss among the affected population. Furthermore, there may also be a publication selection bias in minimum wage research. Doucouliagos and Stanley (2009) claim that there is such a bias (see also Card and Krueger 1995b). They perform a meta-analysis of 1,474 estimated minimum-wage elasticities, finding strong evidence of publication selection for significantly negative employment elasticities but no evidence of a meaningful adverse employment effect when selection effects are taken into account.

2.4 Policy Issues

As discussed, recent empirical evidence fails to provide unambiguous results on the effects of the minimum wage on employment (Flinn 2007). In particular, only two-thirds of the studies reviewed by Neumark and Wascher (2007) found negative employment effects of minimum wages, and these effects were not always statistically significant. This explains why some researchers advocate an increase in the minimum wage, while others argue in favor of marked reductions of the minimum wage.

2.4.1 Should the Minimum Wage Be Reduced or Increased?

Models of the minimum wage under realistic conditions, that is, allowing for some degree of monopsony power by individual firms, suggest that the setting of the minimum wage is a matter of fine-tuning: if it is too low, it is not binding; if it is too high, it can do worse than the market failure that it was supposed to address, where "worse" here means that the total labor market surplus is lower than without the minimum wage.

The main rationale for advocating a reduction in the minimum wage is that the labor market is ill functioning, and some low-productivity workers (e.g., youngsters and the unskilled) inflate the ranks of unemployment. This argument is clearly stronger in the presence of double-digit unemployment rates for these groups, notably when these rates are not paralleled by adverse labor market conditions for other workers.

An increase in the minimum wage is often advocated on the grounds that some groups of workers have a particularly weak position at the bargaining table, and levels of earnings inequality are deemed to be too large. In this context the minimum wage is seen as an instrument to reduce the number of *working poor,* that is, individuals who hold a full-time job but nevertheless appear to live close to the poverty line. The natural supporters of this view are those who are likely to enjoy a wage increase in the presence of a wage floor. For income redistribution the minimum wage is a rather blunt instrument. The very poor are probably not employed, so they will not be affected by the minimum wage, while workers in the noncovered or informal sector may face a decrease in their wages after a minimum wage increase.

Because economic theory does not offer unambiguous results about the effects of the minimum wage on poverty, it is important to examine this issue empirically. Applied studies typically look at the distributional impact of the minimum wage by analyzing wage distributions in a neighborhood of the minimum wage level. If crowding-out effects are important, then we should observe a spike in the wage distribution close to the legally imposed minimum. If there is no spike or the spike lies to the right of the minimum, the data indicate that the minimum wage has little effective "bite." Most studies (including Card and Krueger 1994; see box 2.2 and figure 2.5) actually found a spike in the wage distribution corresponding to the minimum wage. There is also less ambiguity in the empirical literature on the employment effects of minimum wages when the focus is unskilled workers: in this case the evidence of disemployment effects is particularly strong. Concerning the effect of the minimum wage specifically on poverty, the study of Addison and Blackburn (1999) suggests that the increases in the minimum wage that occurred in the United States in the 1990s contributed to reducing the poverty rate among youth aged 24 and under and workers older than 24, but only among school dropouts. Finally, Flinn (2007) found positive effects on welfare of young Americans for the 1997 minimum wage increase (from \$4.75 to \$5.15) but no evidence of a positive effect on welfare of the minimum wage increase that occurred in 1996 (from \$4.25 to \$4.75), which seems not to have exerted significant spillovers on the wage distribution.

2.4.2 Should There Be a Youth Minimum Wage?

In many countries the minimum wage does not depend on the age of the worker, but in some countries it does. Figure 2.6 shows the relationship between the youth minimum wage and the adult minimum wage by age of the worker for eight countries. Clearly, there are big differences in the age gradient of the youth minimum wage. While in France, New Zealand, and the United States there is just one youth minimum wage; in the Czech Republic and the United Kingdom there are two youth minimum wages; and in Australia, Belgium, and the Netherlands there is a minimum wage that is different for (almost) every age. Also, the level of the youth minimum wage compared to the adult minimum wage is very different across countries. The youth minimum wage for workers aged 16 ranges between 82.5 percent in the United States and 80 percent in the Czech Republic, France, and New Zealand to 50 percent in Australia and even 34.5 percent in the Netherlands.

Unemployment rates among youth are always substantially higher than unemployment rates among prime-aged workers. Figure 2.7 confirms that this is the case. Nevertheless, the figure also shows that both unemployment rates are highly (though not perfectly) correlated. In Spain both unemployment rates are highest among the group of countries represented. In Korea and the Netherlands prime-aged workers' unemployment rates were lowest in 2010, while youth unemployment rates are among the lowest as well. Apparently, the very high

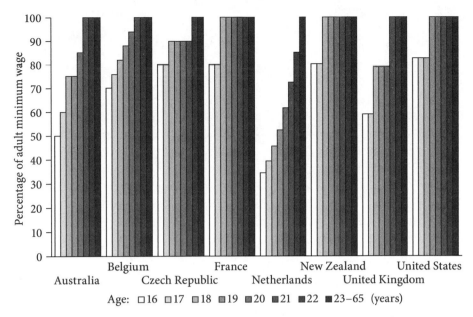

FIGURE 2.6 Youth minimum wage as a percentage of the adult minimum wage by age, 2010
Source: ILO Minimum Wage Database.

youth unemployment rates in some countries need not be the result of an age-specific policy. Countries with low adult unemployment rates apparently have a favorable mix of labor market institutions, which also keep youth unemployment rates relatively low.

When considering the question of whether there should be an age-specific minimum wage, other potential effects have to be taken into account. In particular, effects on training and schooling are likely to be important. If there is no separate youth minimum wage, young workers may be too expensive for employers (i.e., because of their lack of work experience, their productivity is insufficient to cover their wage costs). It may also be the case that in the absence of a youth minimum wage young workers are too expensive to receive general training, because firms cannot offset the training costs through a lower wage. Finally, young workers may leave school too early, because the minimum wage is too attractive to stay in education.

Recently quite a few studies have been performed to study the relationship between youth minimum wage and youth labor market position. These studies all adopt a difference-in-differences approach, exploiting changes in the age gradient of the minimum wage. In 1987 the legal minimum wage for workers aged 18 and 19 in Portugal was raised by almost 50 percent. Pereira (2003) compares the employment growth of 18- and 19-year-old workers with the employment growth of older workers. Her main findings are that the increase in the minimum wage significantly reduced employment of 18- and 19-year-olds, but it increased employment of 20- to 25-year-olds. The latter results from a substitution effect: the relative increase in the minimum wage of younger workers made slightly older workers more attractive to hire. New Zealand introduced some changes in the age gradient of the

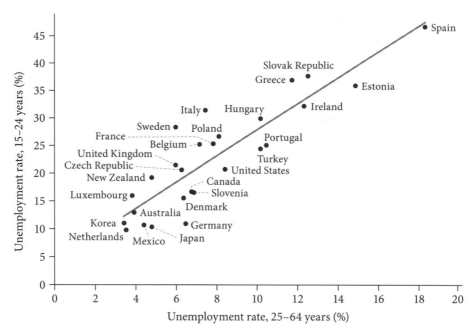

FIGURE 2.7 Unemployment rates of prime-aged workers and young workers, 2010
Source: OECD (2011b).

youth minimum wage in 2001 and 2002, making it less steep. In 2001 a change was introduced that entitled 18- and 19-year-olds to the adult minimum wage, while the minimum wage of 16- and 17-year-olds was increased from 60 to 70 percent of the adult minimum wage. For the youngest group there was a further increase to 80 percent of the adult minimum wage in 2002. Hyslop and Stillman (2007) exploit these changes in the structure of the youth minimum wage to establish its effects on employment rates and working hours. They find no significant effects on employment rates, but they do find a significant positive effect on working hours. Their study is discussed in some detail in box 2.4. Pacheco (2011) exploits the same changes in the relative youth minimum wage for New Zealand as Hyslop and Stillman but draws different conclusions. Pacheco focuses on individuals who have a higher probability of being affected by a rising minimum wage. She concludes that for these individuals a higher minimum wage has significant and negative employment effects. Between 1986 and 1998, six of the ten Canadian provinces abolished their lower minimum wage rates for 15- and 16-year-old workers. Shannon (2011) uses these province-specific changes to establish the relationship between minimum wage and employment. The findings are mixed. For some provinces a significant negative effect is found, while for others no employment effect is observed. Finally, Antón and Muñoz de Bustillo (2011) perform an analysis for Spain exploiting a similar type of policy change. From 1995 to 1998 the Spanish youth minimum wage, which was applicable to 16- and 17-year-olds, was abolished. The authors find that this relative increase in youth minimum wage depressed youth employment levels, increased unemployment among youngsters, and decreased the probability of remaining in formal education.

In 2001 and 2002 a large reform in the youth minimum wage was carried out in New Zealand. Prior to the reform in 2001 the youth minimum wage, applying to 16- to 19-year-olds, was set at 60 percent of the adult minimum wage. In March 2001 the minimum wage for 18- and 19-year-olds was set at 100 percent of the adult minimum wage, while the minimum wage for 16- and 17-year-olds was increased to 70 percent of the adult minimum wage. For the 16- and 17-year-olds there was a further increase in March 2002 to 80 percent of the adult minimum wage. Dean Hyslop and Steven Stillman investigated the consequences for employment and working hours of these changes in the youth minimum wage. They use 20- to 25-year-olds as the control group and distinguish two obvious treatment groups, the 16- and 17-year-olds and the 18- and 19-year-olds. For the adult workers during 2000–2003 the minimum wage increased by 13 percent, while the minimum wage of the 16- and 17-year-olds increased by 50 percent, and for the 18- and 19-year-olds the minimum wage increased by 87 percent, as shown in the following table.

	Minimum wage (percentage of adult wage)		
	Treatment group		Control group
	Aged 16–17	Aged 18–19	Aged 20–25
Before March 5, 2001	60	60	100
From March 5, 2001	70	100	100
From March 18, 2002	80	100	100
Increase 2000–2003 (%)	50	87	13

The authors use information from the second quarter 1998 to the third quarter 1999 as the before period, and from the second quarter 2002 to the third quarter of 2003 as the after period. Using a difference-in-differences approach, they find that the employment rates of the two treatment groups grew by 0.5 and 1.0 percentage points, respectively. Both increases were not significantly different from zero. The increase in youth minimum wage caused significant increases in the hours of work: 3.4 hours per week for the 16- to 17-year-olds and 1.8 hours per week for the 18- to 19-year-olds.

	Treatment group		Control group
Indicator	Aged 16–17	Aged 18–19	Aged 20–25
Employment rate (%)			
Before	41.3	53.8	64.0
After	43.2	56.2	65.4
Difference	1.9	2.4	1.4
Difference-in-differences	0.5	1.0	
Weekly working hours			
Before	16.4	27.4	34.8
After	19.0	28.2	33.8
Difference	2.4	0.8	−1.0
Difference-in-differences	3.4	1.8	

The authors also find a decline in educational enrollment and an increase in unemployment, inactivity, and benefit receipt rates. The authors conclude that while the minimum wage reform increased the labor supply of teenagers, this increase was not matched by an equally large increase in employment.

Source: Hyslop and Stillman (2007).

All in all, the results from the difference-in-differences studies do not all point in the same direction. Some studies find clear negative effects of a relative increase in the youth minimum wage on the employment of youngsters, sometimes accompanied by positive employment spillover effects for older age groups. However, there are also studies that do not find a significant relationship between youth minimum wage and employment rates of youngsters. The changes in the relative youth minimum wage all went in the same direction: an increase, often to the level of the adult minimum wage. Nowhere has there been a reduction of the youth minimum wage. On the basis of the available evidence, it is difficult to draw strong conclusions as to whether there should be a separate youth minimum wage, and if so, what the optimal age gradient is.

2.5 Interactions with Other Institutions

Minimum wages bear a close relationship with other institutions acting over the entire wage distribution. Minimum wages are integrated into union wage platforms when the minimum wage is set and enforced under collective agreements (see chapter 3). Boeri (2012) finds that the level of the minimum wage is affected by whether there is a government-legislated minimum wage or a wage floor set by collective agreement. In the latter case the minimum wage is usually higher (see also technical annex 2.9). Active labor market policies (see chapter 12), notably ECI, also interact with the minimum wage to reduce its potential disemployment effects.

Sometimes institutional complementarities are created as a result of policy failures. A minimum wage set too high creates unemployment among low-productivity workers. The solution to this problem is to reduce the statutory minimum wage. However, governments facing strong political resistance to reducing the minimum wage may decide instead to tighten employment protection legislation (see chapter 10), reducing the risk of job loss among those low-productivity workers who still have a job. Thus, to address a distortion induced by the bad setting of an institution, another distortion is created.

Some adverse effects of minimum wages on unemployment among low-productivity workers can be mitigated when the minimum wage is combined with in-work benefits (see chapter 13). Actually, the combination of minimum wages and in-work benefits is often advocated as a rather effective antipoverty device (Gregg 2000; OECD 2006c), providing *wage insurance* to those with low earnings. Moreover, a substantial portion of minimum wage earners may not be poor, because other family members have earnings. Thus, the minimum wage may have a low *target efficiency,* helping many workers in nonpoor families and providing only limited earnings support to the truly needy.

2.6 Why Does a Minimum Wage Exist?

Minimum wages can achieve both goals typically assigned to labor market institutions:

1. They can increase efficiency by remedying market failures, such as those deriving from excessive monopsonistic power.
2. They can reduce earnings inequality by supporting incomes of relatively low-paid workers, for example, low-skilled workers.

The setting of the minimum wage requires careful fine-tuning if either of these two goals is to be achieved. When the minimum wage is too low, it is ineffective. When it is set at a level that is too high, it reduces welfare and may have perverse effects on income inequality by completely crowding out low-skilled workers from the labor market.

The strongest arguments in favor of an increase in the minimum wage rely on equity considerations. However, economic theory also does not provide firm guidance on the impact of the minimum wage on poverty. A working poor person employed at the minimum wage may experience an increase in income if that person's job is not destroyed, reducing the poverty rate (the percentage of individuals having incomes below the poverty line), but if the minimum wage hike destroys jobs, some individuals will experience a drop in their incomes, increasing the incidence of poverty (the difference between the average incomes of those above and below the poverty line), if not the poverty rate itself (Brown 1999). In dual labor markets an increase in the minimum wage could quite paradoxically end up increasing earnings inequality.

To improve the efficiency and distributional properties of a minimum wage, governments have to adjust it over time, but it may prove politically difficult to do so. The political economy literature on the minimum wage (Sobel 1999; Saint-Paul 2000; Bacache-Beauvallet and Lehmann 2008) highlights which institutional features can increase or reduce political support for the minimum wage. The decisive (median) voter is generally an employed worker whose wage is slightly above the minimum wage. The key dimension along which to assess political support for the minimum wage is whether this pivotal group of workers experiences (1) a sufficiently high degree of substitutability with workers who are potentially crowded out by the minimum wage and (2) a positive wage spillover from the introduction of the minimum wage or a high degree of complementarity with capital. When an increase in the minimum wage, eliminating the least skilled, increases the marginal value of the semi-skilled and hence their wages, the ruling middle class will support a rather high minimum wage. Conversely, the ruling middle class will oppose a reduction in the minimum wage when it fears that firms will try to replace them with cheaper workers.

Hence the future of the minimum wage is likely to depend on these cross-skill (and capital-labor) complementarities and on the spillovers that the minimum wage can exert over the entire wage distribution. As discussed in chapter 3, these spillover effects are likely to be more pronounced in the presence of strong unions, setting wage scales from this minimum.

2.7 Suggestions for Further Reading

A good starting point is the book by David Card and Alan Krueger (1995a). Their book also summarizes their controversial study, which is described in some detail in box 2.2 and can be replicated with the data provided on the website http://press.princeton.edu.titles/10142.html. The debate over their seminal article (Card and Krueger 1994) is also particularly instructive: in particular, we recommend David Neumark and William Wascher (2000) and the reply by Card and Krueger (2000) in the same issue of the *American Economic Review*. For a survey of the new minimum wage research, see Neumark and Wascher (2007). The earlier literature, mostly focused on the United States, is surveyed by John Kennan (1995).

A bundle of papers in a 2004 issue of the *Economic Journal* was devoted to the introduction of the minimum wage in Britain (see Metcalf 2004 for an introduction). A special issue of the *Journal of Labor Economics* in 2010 was devoted to empirical studies on monopsony (see Ashenfelter et al. 2010 for an overview). The book by Alan Manning (2003) on monopsony provides a wide coverage of this type of labor market, including the relation to minimum wages. Finally, Juan Dolado et al. (1996) offer one of the few cross-country analyses of the effects of minimum wages. Although it is not very recent, the discussion of the fallacies of the common wisdom on the effects of the minimum wage is particularly instructive.

2.8 Review Questions and Exercises

1. What is the Kaitz index? What are the pros and cons of this measure of the minimum wage?

2. Why is there a spike in the wage distribution at the minimum wage?

3. How does an increase in the youth minimum wage affect the labor market position of youngsters?

4. When does a minimum wage increase employment?

5. Why would an individual firm face an upward-sloping labor supply curve?

6. How does a minimum wage affect poverty?

7. Why does an increase in the minimum wage unambiguously increase unemployment in a competitive labor market?

8. The degree of monopsonistic power depends on the slope of the labor supply curve. Explain.

9. Why did Card and Krueger study the fast-food industry?

10. Why is the main result of Card and Krueger—an increase in the minimum wage increases employment—not in line with the monopsony theory or with the theory of the fully competitive market?

11. Suppose that w is the wage and L is employment. The supply curve of low-wage workers is given by $w = 10 + 2L$. The demand curve is given by $w = 70 - 2L$.

   (a) What are the equilibrium levels of wage, employment, and unemployment?

   (b) What happens to employment and unemployment if a minimum wage of 40 euros is introduced?

   (c) What happens to employment and unemployment if a minimum wage of 60 euros is introduced?

12. A firm faces a perfectly elastic demand for its products at a price of 10 euros per unit. The firm is also confronted with an upward-sloping labor supply curve specified as $w = 10 + 2L$, where L is the number of workers hired per hour and w is the hourly wage. Each hour of labor produces 5 products. Assume that the firm uses only labor to produce its products. Also assume that the firm is profit-maximizing.

   (a) How many workers should the firm hire each hour?

   (b) What wage will the firm pay and how much profit does it make?

   (c) What happens to employment and profits if a minimum wage of 40 curos is introduced?

   (d) What happens to profits if the firm does not adjust employment in response to the minimum wage?

13. (Advanced) Consider the problem of a pure monopsonist choosing wages to maximize profits: $\pi = (p - w)G(w)$, where $p > w$ denotes the value of the marginal product (the firm operates under constant returns to scale), w is the wage, and $G(w)$ is the aggregate labor supply.

   (a) Derive the first-order condition for wages as a function of the relevant elasticities.

   (b) How does this wage equation react to changes in productivity?

   Suppose further that labor supply is given by $G(w) = (w - b)^2$, where b is the value of leisure (inclusive of any UB), and clearly $w > b$.

   (c) Derive the wage equation under this specialization of labor supply and interpret the results.

   (d) What happens if a minimum wage of b is introduced?

2.9 Technical Annex: Minimum Wage Revisited

2.9.1 Minimum Wage and Monopsony

Specify labor demand and supply as in technical annex 1.6. Suppose that labor demand is originated by just one employer facing the aggregate labor supply. This pure monopsonist (superscript m) chooses the employment level L that maximizes profits π:

$$\pi^m = \frac{AL^{1-\eta}}{1-\eta} - wL, \tag{2.3}$$

subject to being on the labor supply curve $w = L^\varepsilon$, where η is the inverse labor demand elasticity, and ε is the inverse labor supply elasticity. Therefore, $\pi^m = \frac{AL^{1-\eta}}{1-\eta} - L^{1+\varepsilon}$. Deriving the first-order condition $\frac{d\pi^m}{dL} = 0$, we find $AL^{-\eta} - (1+\varepsilon)L^\varepsilon = 0$. From this, we obtain the equilibrium employment level under a pure monopsony:

$$L^m = \left[\frac{A}{1+\varepsilon}\right]^{\frac{1}{\varepsilon+\eta}} < A^{\frac{1}{\varepsilon+\eta}} = L^*. \tag{2.4}$$

Hence employment is lower than in a competitive labor market (L^*). Substituting the monopsonist employment in the labor supply, we obtain the monopsony wage

$$w^m = \left[\frac{A}{1+\varepsilon}\right]^{\frac{\varepsilon}{\varepsilon+\eta}} < A^{\frac{\varepsilon}{\varepsilon+\eta}} = w^*; \tag{2.5}$$

hence the equilibrium with a monopsonist involves both a lower wage and lower employment than the equilibrium in a competitive labor market (w^*). The efficiency loss associated with the presence of a monopsony can be reduced by a binding minimum wage. In particular, any minimum wage that forces the monopsonist to pay at least $\underline{w}$ will increase employment, provided that the minimum wage is lower than or equal to the wage maximizing the total surplus:

$$\left[\frac{A}{1+\varepsilon}\right]^{\frac{\varepsilon}{\varepsilon+\eta}} < \underline{w} \leq A^{\frac{\varepsilon}{\varepsilon+\eta}}. \tag{2.6}$$

A minimum wage set in this range has an efficiency-enhancing role. When the minimum wage is larger than $A^{\frac{\varepsilon}{\varepsilon+\eta}}$, it is itself a source of inefficiency, potentially leading to an even lower total surplus than under a monopsony. This happens when $L(\underline{w}) < L^m$.

In other words, there is a nonmonotonic relation between the minimum wage and employment: employment is first increasing and then decreasing in the minimum wage.

2.9.2 Bargaining or Government Setting?

As indicated in the main text, there are two common ways of setting national minimum wages: through collective bargaining agreements or through government legislation. Let us first consider the bargained minimum wage. From technical annex 1.6 we know that with bargaining, the socially optimal wage will deviate by a mark-up factor $\mu = 1 + t$, where t is the wedge between labor demand and supply (which is a function of labor demand and supply elasticities, as well as of distributional weights of employers and workers):

$$\mu = \frac{(1-\eta) + \beta(\eta + \varepsilon)}{(1-\eta)(1+\varepsilon)}, \tag{2.7}$$

where β represents the bargaining power of the unions. Thus, the minimum wage will increase with the bargaining power of the unions.

If minimum wages are set through government legislation, the outcome depends on the weights the government attaches to workers and employers. Assume that the government maximizes a Bernoulli-Nash social welfare function like in (1.9); the mark-up imposed by the government over the reservation wage can be specified in a similar way:

$$\mu^G = \frac{(1-\eta) + \beta^G(\eta + \varepsilon)}{(1-\eta)(1+\varepsilon)} \tag{2.8}$$

where β^G represents the distribution weight that the government attaches to wage earners and $1 - \beta^G$ is a measure of the electoral power of employers and profit earners (see Boeri 2012). Clearly, if the electoral power of profit earners is larger than their bargaining power, a minimum wage set by the government will be lower than the minimum wage set through collective bargaining. Conversely, if workers or unions have relatively low bargaining power, they may find themselves better off with a pro-union government that would set a higher statutory minimum wage than the wage floor achieved through bargaining.

2.9.3 Efficiency Wages

In an efficiency wage model employers have market power, which allows them to set the wage. Employers are assumed to have only imperfect information about the effort of their employees. Hence they pay a wage above the market-clearing level to discourage their workers from shirking. This is the so-called *efficiency wage*. The line of reasoning is as follows. The labor input is the product of the quantity of workers L and the effort e they put into production. Effort is assumed to be a continuous variable depending on the wage w, so that $\frac{de}{dw} > 0$, and $\frac{d^2e}{dw^2} < 0$. Thus, effort increases in wages but less than proportionally. Taking the price of the final good as numeraire ($p = 1$), the profits of the firm are equal to

$$\pi = f(e(w)L) - wL,$$

where $f(\cdot)$ is the production function using labor as the only input. The firm has two degrees of freedom, wage and employment, so there are two first-order conditions:

$$\frac{\partial \pi}{\partial L} = 0 \rightarrow f'e(w) - w = 0 \rightarrow \frac{f'e(w)}{w} = 1 \tag{2.9}$$

$$\frac{\partial \pi}{\partial w} = 0 \rightarrow f'\frac{\partial e(w)}{\partial w}L - L = 0 \rightarrow f'\frac{\partial e(w)}{\partial w} = 1. \tag{2.10}$$

Combining these two first-order conditions, we find that

$$\frac{\frac{\partial e(w)}{e(w)}}{\frac{\partial w}{w}} = 1, \tag{2.11}$$

which is the so-called Solow condition: the employer chooses a wage such that the elasticity of effort with respect to the wage is equal to one. In words, wages should be increased to the level where they elicit a one-to-one increase in effort, irrespective of the employment levels. The employer pays a wage above the market clearing wage, because it is profitable to do so. This will generate unemployment, which will act as a disciplinary device (see also box 11.3). If a minimum wage is introduced above the market clearing wage, but below the efficiency wage, labor market outcomes will not be affected.

CHAPTER THREE Unions and Collective Bargaining

Labor (or trade) unions are voluntary membership organizations. Like political parties and churches, they represent the interests of their members. They do what their members want them to do.

Historically, unions emerged in the eighteenth century in the United Kingdom and the United States as craft unions, occupational organizations providing mutual insurance to their members against unemployment, death, and sometimes old age. Later, well into the nineteenth century, they gradually became industrial unions representing workers in semi-skilled positions, who are harder to replace with unemployed workers or immigrants. Increasingly at the beginning of the twentieth century they became national organizations aiming at representing all workers and having an enhanced political role. Membership in these general unions was stronger among manual workers, while skilled workers were less keen to join unions because of their egalitarian wage platforms; nowadays unions are often strongest in the public sector.

The potential membership of unions also depends on the underlying *collective bargaining* system. In some countries bargaining takes place at the national level, involving unions and employers' associations, with the government acting as mediator. In other countries there are only sectoral wage agreements or even more decentralized, plant-level agreements. Hybrid or multilevel bargaining structures with both centralized and plant-level agreements also exist, notably in Europe. Depending on the structure of the bargaining system, industrial or craft unions coordinate themselves within national federations of unions. Sometimes unions also coordinate across countries, as in the case of the European Trade Unions Confederation.

Because of the interests of their members and their ideological roots, unions tend to pursue egalitarian wage policies, reducing wage differentials by education and skill level. At the same time, what unions do affects their membership. Unions are generally not very successful in recruiting highly skilled workers and seem to be aging more rapidly than the workforce, which points to growing difficulties in involving young people in the activities of unions.

Trade unions typically bargain over all aspects of an employment contract: wages, working hours, overtime pay, fringe benefits, employment security, and health and safety standards. They negotiate with employers on a collective basis, overruling (when incompatible with the collective agreement) or complementing individual contracts. By coordinating wage claims of a plurality of workers, unions force employers to pay for labor services at a rate above the reservation wages of otherwise uncoordinated individuals. The bargaining power of unions is related to the extent of wage coordination that unions achieve and to the coverage of the collective contracts signed by the unions.

3.1 Measures and Cross-Country Comparisons

Unfortunately, not much effort has been spent to date on developing cross-country-comparable measures of the influence of trade unions. This is because unions are reluctant to provide reliable figures on their membership, and surveys may not be accurate in eliciting membership, because workers may not be keen to disclose this information. Available data suggest that the presence and influence of trade unions vary considerably across countries and have changed quite dramatically over time. The most visible change has been an increasing divergence between unions' *presence* at the workplace, as measured by the number of active members in the workforce, and unions' *influence*, proxied by the fraction of workers involved in agreements negotiated by unions. The difference between union influence and union presence, which is generally referred to as the *excess coverage* of unions, has been increasing over time.

3.1.1 Union Density

The most intuitive measure of the relevance of trade unions is given by the *union density* (or *membership*) *rate*, that is, the fraction of workers registered with some trade union. Unions often have nonworking individuals among their members. For instance, in Italy there are more pensioners than workers in the ranks of the three largest trade unions, the Italian General Confederation of Labor (CGIL), the Italian Confederation of Workers' Trade Unions (CISL), and the Italian Labor Union (UIL).

The second column of table 3.1 shows recent information about union density rates (counting only members of working age). Union density in 2010 was very low in Estonia, France, and Turkey, where the union density was below 10 percent. In Korea (10 percent) and the United States (11 percent) union density was also low. In most of the Scandinavian countries union density is high; it is about 70 percent in Denmark, Finland, and Sweden and even close to 80 percent in Iceland.

Over the past decades unions have lost a large number of members. Figure 3.1 plots union density rates in five OECD countries since 1960. In four of these countries—France, the Netherlands, the United Kingdom, and the United States—union density in 2010 was substantially below union density in 1960. Deunionization was particularly strong in the United States (where union density halved, and nowadays membership in the private sector is below 10 percent) and the United Kingdom (where after an initial increase in the 1960s and 1970s unions lost almost 4 million members in the 1979–1987 period, during the Thatcher era). In France union density dropped from about 20 percent in 1960 to 8 percent in 2010. In the Netherlands there was also a strong decline in union density, in particular from the

TABLE 3.1 Coverage, union density, excess coverage, level of bargaining, and coordination, 2010

Country	Coverage[a] (%)	Union density[b] (%)	Excess coverage (%)	Level of bargaining[c]	Coordination[d]
Australia	40	19	21	2	2
Austria	99	28	71	2	4
Belgium	96	52	44	4	4
Canada	32	30	2	1	1
Czech Republic	42	17	25	2	2
Denmark	80	69	11	2	3
Estonia	19	7	12	1	1
Finland	90	70	20	2.5	3
France	90	8	82	2	2
Germany	62	19	43	3	4
Greece	65	24	41	3	4
Hungary	34	17	17	2	2
Iceland	88	79	9	—	—
Ireland	44	37	7	1	2
Italy	80	35	45	2	4
Japan	16	18	−2	1	3
Korea	10	10	0	1	3
Luxembourg	58	37	21	2	2
Netherlands	82	19	63	2	4
New Zealand	17	21	−4	1	2
Norway	74	54	20	4	4
Poland	38	15	23	1	1
Portugal	45	19	26	2	3
Slovak Republic	40	17	23	1	2
Slovenia	92	30	62	3	3
Spain	85	16	69	3	4
Sweden	91	69	22	3	3
Switzerland	48	18	30	2	3
Turkey	25	6	19	—	—
United Kingdom	33	28	5	1	1
United States	13	11	2	1	1

Source: Visser (2011).

Note: The information refers to 2010 or the last year available (often 2008 or 2009).

a. Employees covered by wage bargaining agreements as a proportion of all wage and salary earners in employment with the right to bargain, expressed as percentage, adjusted for the possibility that some sectors or occupations are excluded from the right to bargain.

b. Union density = union members in the active, dependent, and employed labor force as a percentage of wage and salary earners in employment.

c. The dominant level(s) at which wage bargaining takes place: 5 = national or central level; 4 = national or central level, with additional sectoral/local or company bargaining; 3 = sectoral or industry level; 2 = sectoral or industry level, with additional local or company bargaining; 1 = local or company bargaining.

d. Coordination of wage bargaining: 5 = economy-wide bargaining; 4 = mixed industry and economy-wide bargaining; 3 = industry bargaining; 2 = mixed or alternating industry- and firm-level bargaining; 1 = none of the above: fragmented bargaining, mostly at company level.

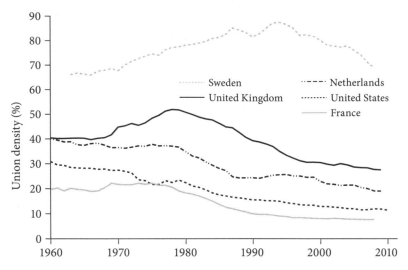

FIGURE 3.1 Union membership in five countries, 1960–2010
Source: Visser (2011).
Note: For details see table 3.1.

late 1980s (when it was about 35 percent) to 2010 (17 percent). In Sweden union density is substantially higher. From 1960 to the mid-1990s union density in Sweden increased to about 85 percent. In the years thereafter union density in Sweden declined to about 70 percent in 2008.

The decline in union membership has gone hand in hand with the aging of unions. According to the Eurobarometer survey, during 1988–2001 the median age of a union member increased by more than 2 years in the four largest nations of the continental EU (France, Germany, Italy, and Spain) while because of a significant reduction in youth unemployment, the age of a median worker was declining.

Membership, however, has not meant the same thing over time. Historically, membership in a trade union required mutual support, attendance at meetings, and involvement of time and effort in the running of the union's internal affairs. Nowadays membership may require only voting over the internet and paying a low voluntary contribution. In October 2005, for instance, the AFL-CIO enrolled members over its website (www.workingamerica.org), asking for $5 voluntary dues. The reduction in union dues should encourage membership. At the same time, unions no longer (or do not always) provide exclusive services to their members, such as higher pay or better work conditions, because contracts negotiated by the unions are extended also to nonunionized workers. This reduces the incentive to become a member of a trade union, because one can free-ride on the services provided by the organization. Another historical reason for workers to join a union is related to the organization of the unemployment insurance system. When unemployment insurance was introduced some countries opted for a compulsory system administered by government agencies, while others chose a voluntary but publicly supported scheme administered by unions or union-dominated funds (Calmfors 2001). The latter system is also called the Ghent system, after the

Belgian town where the first agreement was signed, envisaging an active role of unions in the running of unemployment benefits. The Ghent system is still operating in Denmark, Finland, Iceland, and Sweden. Needless to say, under a Ghent system workers have a bigger incentive to join a union.[1] And indeed, as shown in table 3.1, union density is by far the highest in the countries with a Ghent system of UBs.

3.1.2 Coverage and Excess Coverage

A better measure of the bargaining power of trade unions is provided by the coverage of trade unions, that is, the percentage of the eligible workforce—employees with bargaining rights—whose contract is regulated by the collective agreements signed by the unions. The first column of table 3.1 provides a cross-country overview of coverage. Clearly, there is a wide range in the coverage from as low as 10 percent in Korea and 13 percent in the United States to 90 percent or more in Austria, Belgium, Finland, France, Slovenia, and Sweden. In some countries the excess coverage (i.e., the difference between union coverage and union density) is low or even negative. In the United Kingdom, coverage is close to membership, because collective agreements are applied only if a majority of workers in a firm are members of a union.

However, it is also noticeable that in many countries coverage is much larger than union density. For instance, in France, the country of the general strike, 9 workers out of 10 have their wage negotiated by trade unions, but fewer than 1 out of 10 is a member of a trade union. This excess coverage of trade unions is a rather recent phenomenon. It is the result of (1) the decline in union density rates and (2) the presence in many countries of laws or practices that extend coverage beyond membership. These regulations may themselves contribute to increasing the gap between coverage and membership, because there are fewer incentives for workers to join a union, given that they benefit, in any event, from the wages negotiated by the unions (these extension clauses exacerbate the so-called free-rider problem of unions). Unions supporting the legal extension of the coverage of agreements are, in some sense, operating for their self-destruction.

To cope with the free-rider problem, unions in a number of countries have begun providing services exclusively to their members, for example, retirement counseling and tax advising (de facto outsourcing of government functions, as in Belgium and Italy), training and retraining (as in Denmark, France, Germany, and Italy), or even financial services (the Netherlands). In countries that have adopted the Ghent system, unions are directly involved in the administration of UBs (Calmfors 2001).[2]

---

1. In practice, under the Ghent system nonmembers also may receive UBs but at a lower replacement rate (ratio of benefits to wages) than for those who are union members.

2. Böckerman and Uusitalo (2006) document that membership in the Finnish trade unions declined by about 10 base points after the introduction of a UB system competing with the system run by the unions and not imposing membership as a requirement for receiving income support in the case of job loss.

3.1.3 Centralization and Coordination

The fourth column of table 3.1 provides information on the level of bargaining, that is, the level at which contracts are negotiated, following a fivefold classification provided by the OECD (ranging from 1, which stands for local or company bargaining, to 5, which stands for national or central level). While in some countries (e.g., the United Kingdom or the United States) negotiation occurs mainly at the level of the firm, in continental and southern Europe it is more frequently carried out at the industry level, and there have been many "social pacts" implementing income policies (imposing ceilings on wage growth) at the national level. Even decentralized bargaining can be coordinated at the industry or national level by unions. Thus, it is useful to complement information on the institutional level of bargaining with measures of the degree of coordination in collective bargaining, reported in the last column of table 3.1. It is also important to distinguish between *formal centralization,* which has to do with the actual level at which wage contracts are signed and the existence of parallel union (or employer) organizations, and overall or *implicit coordination,* which could result also from informal (tacit) coordination between independent unions and employers.[3]

Figure 3.2 shows the cross-country relationship between coordination and union density. Cross-country there is a positive but imperfect relationship between the two indicators of union power. The Ghent countries—Denmark, Finland, and Sweden—are clear outliers. The positive relationship between coordination and union density is thought to be related to the interaction between the two. In countries with high coordination employers' resistance to unions will be smaller and unions will get easier recognition as workers' representatives while, at the same time, in countries with a high union density it is easier for unions to organize bargaining in a coordinated way.

3.1.4 Strike Activity

Sometimes hours of strike or the so-called wage share (the ratio of the total wage bill to GDP) are used as measures of unions' power. However, a powerful union uses strikes only as a deterrent, and wage shares are outcome measures that do not necessarily correspond to the objectives of trade unions, maximizing wages only of their members rather than of the population at large. Nevertheless, both hours of strikes and wage shares in Europe display trends broadly similar to those of union membership. In particular, in the EU-15 the number of working days lost as a result of labor conflicts dropped from 85 million in 1979 (at the peak of union membership) to less than 7 million at the end of the 1990s (Calmfors 2001), while wage shares declined by about 10 percentage points over the same time span. Importantly, wage shares did not decline in the 1980s and 1990s in the

---

3. For alternative measures of coordination, see Elmeskov et al. (1998) and OECD (2004), as well as Nickell and Layard (1999).

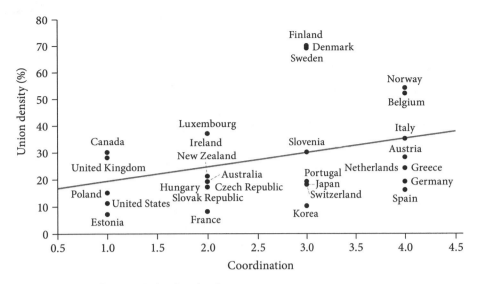

FIGURE 3.2 Coordination and union density, 2010
Source: Visser (2011).
Note: See definitions of coordination and union density in table 3.1.

United States (Blanchard and Wolfers 2000), which experienced a decline in union militancy similar to that in Europe.

Table 3.2 provides more detailed information about strike activities. Unfortunately, this information is not very recent, referring to 2000–2004. Clearly, there is a huge cross-country variation in strike activities. The overall strike rate, defined as the number of work days lost per 1,000 workers, is highest in Iceland, where about 0.6 work days per worker were lost on strikes and in Spain, where about 0.23 work days per worker were lost. In countries like Germany, Japan, Poland, and Switzerland strike rates were extremely low. The strike rate can be split up into two components, the average duration of the strike and the incidence of workers involved. Strike durations are longest in Turkey (about 38 days), while in the United States strikes lasted on average about 25 days. More often than not strike durations are very short. The incidence of strike activity is highest in Italy, where 157 out of 1,000 workers were involved in strikes, which on average did not last for more than one day. In Spain also the incidence of strike activity is relatively high, and the average duration of a strike is less than 3 days. Finally, the intensity of work stoppages defined as the number of stoppages per 100,000 workers is highest in Denmark.

Unfortunately, no cross-country-comparable information is available on the frequency of collective bargaining, notably on how long national collective agreements last and on how these periods of bargaining truce are treated by national bargaining systems. In particular, no data exist on whether there are automatic adjustments to inflation and productivity in between any two agreements. This is highly unfortunate as the frequency of bargaining is very important in understanding the behavior of wages over the business cycle (Gertler and Trigari 2009).

TABLE 3.2 Information on strikes, 2000–2004

Country	Strike rate	Average duration	Incidence of workers involved	Intensity of work stoppages
Australia	48.6	1.7	29.6	8.7
Austria	80.3	1.8	49.1	—
Belgium	76.1	—	—	—
Canada	171.4	14.8	12.6	2.4
Denmark	39.4	1.3	27.9	37.6
Finland	49.1	1.9	28.8	4.4
France	101.0	—	—	5.9
Germany	3.5	1.4	4.0	—
Iceland	597.5	16.7	22.6	3.4
Ireland	41.7	5.1	11.1	1.8
Italy	140.3	1.0	157.4	4.9
Japan	0.4	2.0	0.2	1.7
Korea	100.6	11.1	9.7	2.2
Mexico	21.6	15.7	1.7	0.2
Netherlands	10.7	2.5	5.5	0.2
New Zealand	16.6	2.6	7.8	2.2
Norway	75.9	13.3	10.9	0.6
Poland	1.6	5.1	0.2	0.2
Portugal	15.7	1.4	11.3	5.4
Spain	234.2	2.7	138.5	5.3
Sweden	34.2	3.6	4.9	0.3
Switzerland	5.6	1.1	4.8	0.2
Turkey	20.2	38.1	0.8	0.3
United Kingdom	28.7	2.7	13.4	0.6
United States	46.8	24.5	1.4	0.0

Sources: OECD database derived from ILO Laborsta, Eurostat New Cronos, and the National Statistics Offices websites. Paid civilian employee data are from the OECD Labor Force Statistics.

Note: The strike rate is defined as the number of work days lost per 1,000 workers; the average duration of work stoppages refers to average work days lost per worker involved; the incidence is the number of salaried workers involved in strikes or affected by lock-outs of workplaces per 1,000 workers; the intensity of work stoppages is defined as the number of work stoppages per 100,000 workers. — = not available.

3.2 Theory

Bargaining models offer a useful characterization of the effects of union activity on employment and wages. The implications of these models are dependent on the objectives of unions, which are themselves related to their membership when we go beyond the case of workers with identical preferences and productivity. Hence we first discuss collective bargaining models, assuming identical union members, and then models of endogenous membership.

3.2.1 Collective Bargaining

The effects of unions on wages and employment can best be characterized as outcomes of a collective bargaining process involving, on the one hand, unions and, on the other hand, organizations of employers. The outcomes of this process depend on the bargaining power of the two parties and on the scope of bargaining, notably on whether it involves only wages or both wages and employment levels.

A standard (and realistic) characterization of collective bargaining is one in which unions and employers' organizations bargain over wages, which are then taken as given by individual employers who have the *right to manage* (Nickell and Andrews 1983) their firms, choosing the employment levels that maximize the profits of the firm, given the wage agreed on at the collective bargaining table. It is assumed that the union is composed of identical workers, having the same reservation wage and being equally productive for their employers. Thus, when labor is not unionized, labor supply is flat at the level of the reservation wage. The union maximizes the utility of these identical workers, while employers maximize profits. The outcome of the process depends on the bargaining power of unions. The latter is captured by a parameter (like β in box 3.1) ranging from 0, the competitive equilibrium case, to 1, the case where the union is instead a *monopoly union* (Dunlop 1944) that unilaterally sets wages.

Bargaining over Wages (Right to Manage) — BOX 3.1

Consistent with bargaining theory (Binmore et al. 1986; Osborne and Rubinstein 1990), the outcome of a right-to-manage bargaining process is given by the maximization of the product of the surplus of workers and employers over the no-agreement outcome (the fallback or status quo option) weighted by the bargaining power of unions (Nash 1950, 1953). Assuming that union members are risk-neutral—that is, their utility only depends on the wage, so that $u(w) = w$—the surplus of each union member is given by the difference between the bargained wage and the utility while being nonemployed or the reservation wage, that is, $(w - w^r)$. For the union as a whole, this surplus will have to be multiplied by the number of active members (unemployed members obtain no surplus), determined by labor demand $L^d(w)$, given the right-to-manage structure of bargaining. When no agreement is reached, the firm does not produce, making zero profits. Hence the surplus of the employer is simply given by the profits π, that is, the difference between revenues and costs, $\pi(w) \equiv R[L^d(w)] - wL^d(w)$.

The right-to-manage agreement then obtains the wage level that maximizes the Nash product

$$[L^d(w)\,(w - w^r)]^\beta [R(w) - wL^d(w)]^{(1-\beta)}, \tag{3.1}$$

where β is the bargaining power of unions. The wage level that solves this problem is implicitly given by the first-order condition of the Nash product:

$$\frac{w - w^r}{w} = \frac{\beta}{\frac{\beta}{\eta} + (1-\beta)\varepsilon_w^\pi}, \tag{3.2}$$

where η and $\varepsilon_w^\pi = \left| \frac{\partial \pi}{\partial w} \frac{w}{\pi} \right|$ are, respectively, the inverse wage elasticity of labor demand and the elasticity of profits with respect to wages. Thus, the larger the bargaining power of unions is, the larger will be the surplus that union members enjoy with respect to being unemployed. This union wage mark-up is decreasing with the absolute value of the two elasticities of labor demand and profits, with the latter becoming more important with decreasing bargaining power of the unions. When β tends to zero, the mark-up goes to zero, indicating that workers are paid their reservation wage, as in the competitive (and the pure monopsony) equilibrium. Notice further that as β tends to unity (the union has all the bargaining power), the mark-up is simply given by the inverse of the elasticity of labor demand. Then the wage set by the unions is the monopoly union wage (denoted by the superscript u) and the wage mark-up is equal to

$$\frac{w^u - w^r}{w^u} = \eta. \tag{3.3}$$

The above clearly states that the more elastic is the labor demand (e.g., brought about by stronger competitive pressures), the lower the mark-up obtained by the union will be.

This model predicts that the stronger the bargaining power of unions is, the higher will be the wedge or *mark-up* imposed by unions over the reservation wage (see box 3.1) and the lower the resulting employment level. These predictions can be graphically represented as in figure 3.3. The right to manage implies that employers decide on employment L; hence the collective bargaining outcome must be on the downward-sloping labor demand curve L^d. There is also a restricted range of wage (and employment) levels that can possibly be achieved. Wages cannot be lower than the reservation wage; otherwise nobody would work, because the reservation wage, the utility of nonemployment, would be higher than the wage. This lower bound of wage negotiations corresponds to the competitive equilibrium level w^*, because both the labor demand and the (nonunionized) labor supply schedules apply.

The upper bound of wage negotiations is the wage level w^u that maximizes the surplus of union members, subject to being on the labor demand curve. The union has to take into account that higher wage claims, while increasing the surplus enjoyed by each worker over that worker's utility when unemployed (the reservation wage), reduce employment levels and hence the number of union members enjoying this surplus. As shown in box 3.1, the mark-up imposed by the unions over the competitive equilibrium wage is decreasing with the elasticity of labor demand and hence with the employment costs of wage hikes. In the intermediate cases (where $0 < \beta < 1$), the responsiveness of profits to wages—the costs imposed by unions on employers—will also matter in the bargaining outcome.

To summarize, under collective bargaining of the right-to-manage type, wages will increase with the strength of the bargaining power of unions, and decrease with the responsiveness of labor demand and of profits to wages. These two elas-

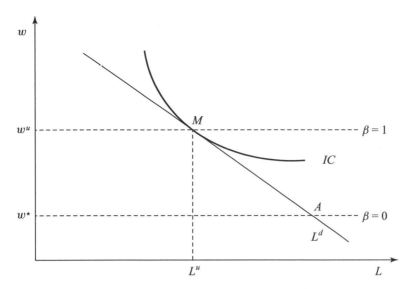

FIGURE 3.3 Right-to-manage outcomes and the bargaining power of unions

ticities are increasing with the degree of competition in product markets. Hence, consistent with the results discussed in chapter 1, stronger competition in product markets reduces the wedge between labor supply and demand introduced by labor market institutions. Technical annex 3.9 extends this result to the case where labor supply is not infinitely elastic (it is upward sloping) and where the case of zero bargaining power of workers coincides with the pure monopsony equilibrium characterized in chapter 2.

A right-to-manage structure of collective bargaining is inefficient in that employment is not involved in the bargaining process. Equilibriums must be on the demand curve of firms, and this may rule out wage and employment outcomes that improve the situation of at least one bargaining agent without reducing the welfare of the other agent. In other words, there may be Pareto-superior equilibriums that are disregarded in the right-to-manage model because of the assumption that only wages are bargained over. Graphically, the equilibriums described in figure 3.3 may well not be on the *contract curve*, the curve denoting all Pareto-optimal allocations.

Efficient contracts (McDonald and Solow 1981; Ashenfelter and Brown 1986; MaCurdy and Pencavel 1986)—that is, outcomes of collective bargaining involving both wages and employment—will typically feature, for any given bargaining power of unions, more employment and lower wages than outcomes of bargaining over wages only.[4] This is represented in figure 3.4, which displays again the right-to-manage outcomes (along the AM segment of the labor demand schedule), as well as the contract curve (the line segment AB). As shown by the figure, the monopoly union outcome at point M equates the slope of the labor demand to the

---

4. The only case where efficient bargaining involves less employment than the right-to-manage model is when workers are risk lovers, a case that is of limited empirical relevance.

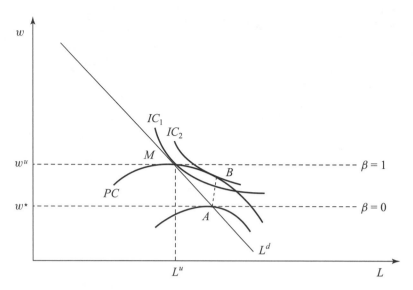

FIGURE 3.4 Efficient bargaining outcomes

slope of the indifference curve of unions, trading higher wages for less employment, but it is not tangent to any isoprofit curve (e.g., curve PC), trading wages and employment levels from the standpoint of the firm. Note that the labor demand curve is the locus of peaks of the isoprofit curves of the firm. Thus, at the union monopoly point there are "gains from trade." In figure 3.4 it is possible to move, for instance, from M to B, attaining a higher indifference curve of the union while being on the same isoprofit curve PC, generating the same profits as at M. In fact, anywhere in the area of figure 3.4 that lies between the union indifference curve IC_1 and isoprofit curve PC, the bargaining outcome of both union and firm would be superior to the outcome at point M. However, bargaining is only efficient insofar as it equates the slope of the union indifference curves to the slope of the isoprofit curves. If this condition holds, no gains from trade are possible; one party can only improve its position at the expense of the other. The locus of tangency points, the line AB in figure 3.4, is defined by this condition.

The contract curve starts at point A, which represents a perfectly competitive labor market. Here, irrespective of the level of employment, workers do not benefit from being union members. Therefore, the union indifference curve is horizontal and A is the point of tangency between an isoprofit curve and a union indifference curve. The slope of the contract curve AB is positive (i.e., except for point A both employment and wages are higher than in a perfectly competitive labor market). So, although bargaining is efficient, employment outcome is not. Therefore this situation is sometimes referred to as "weakly efficient" bargaining.[5] In an efficient bargaining system with an upward-sloping contract curve, a higher bargaining

5. This situation in which the firm hires more workers than in the competitive labor market is also referred to as "featherbedding."

power of the union no longer implies less employment. In figure 3.4 the higher β is, the closer will be the outcome to B along the AB segment; thus, higher levels of employment are attained than at any other outcome of right-to-manage bargaining. While the unions achieve higher levels of utility for their members by moving to the northeast in the figure, profits are increasing at lower wage levels. Hence the position along this contract curve depends on the relative bargaining strengths. Moreover, only the point A of the contract curve can be attained under a right-to-manage structure, because it corresponds to the competitive equilibrium outcome, which is attained when unions have no bargaining power. Finally, the length of the contract curve (i.e., length of the segment AB) depends on the extent of the rents that can be shared between employers and workers. The stronger the competition is in product markets, the shorter the contract curve will be.

A special case occurs when the contract curve AB is vertical. In that case the bargaining is strongly efficient. The bargaining is efficient because it occurs along the contract curve; at the same time, the employment outcome is the same as in a perfectly competitive labor market. A vertical contract curve originates from unions (i.e., union members) who are risk-neutral. It is also possible that the contract curve has a negative slope (see technical annex 3.9.2 for details). Note that efficient bargaining is only possible at the decentralized bargaining level. With national or centralized bargaining it is not possible to implement an arrangement where both wages and employment go up. At the central level the right-to-manage model is likely to apply.

An interesting application of efficient bargaining models is when contracts are negotiated over wages and standard workweek hours (Booth and Ravallion 1993; Contensou and Vranceanu 2000). Unions, in this context, can trade off higher hourly wages for shorter working hours. As in the models reviewed in chapter 5, the higher the value attributed to leisure relative to purchasing power by union members, the more likely it is that agreements will involve fewer hours worked. Reductions in working hours will not necessarily involve work sharing, that is, a "less hours–more workers" bargaining outcome. For work sharing to materialize, hourly labor productivity must be steeply decreasing with working hours, and unions should have a fairly low bargaining power, so they can accept reductions in hourly wages or, at least, hourly wage increases that are lower than the increase in the value of the hourly labor product.

3.2.2 Union Membership

The outcomes of collective bargaining previously discussed rest on the assumption that all union members have the same preferences and are equal also from the standpoint of firms. When workers' preferences differ, maximization of the total surplus of union members involves interpersonal comparisons of utility. For instance, simply adding up the surplus of each individual worker implies giving the same weight to all union members, independent of their income level, or choosing more egalitarian objective functions of a trade union (e.g., a maximin rule, maximizing the well-being of the least well-off worker). By arbitrarily defining the function that maps heterogeneous preferences into a scalar measure of the union's objectives, one is therefore making a number of normative assumptions.

A positive approach to modeling the objectives of trade unions requires analyzing the internal decision structure of unions. Because trade unions are voluntary membership associations, their objectives ultimately depend on their membership, notably on the preferences of those paying the union dues. If the union has a democratic decisionmaking process, its objectives will be the outcome of a majority voting process. If members vote sincerely, there is a single decision (e.g., a wage platform), and preferences of individuals around this choice variable are single-peaked. Then the objectives of the trade union will coincide with those of the median union member. Endogenous membership models are therefore also useful for characterizing the objectives of trade unions. They can be incorporated into monopoly union models by adding a membership equation that defines the identity of the marginal member who is indifferent between joining or not joining the union. It is then possible to locate the median union member and take that member's preferences as the objective function maximized by the monopoly union.

The models of endogenous membership provide an explanation of why workers join a union when there are dues to be paid, even when the results of union activity are available as a free good to all workers, independent of their membership in a trade union. This *union free-rider puzzle* is solved by pointing to the exclusive provision to union members of private goods, such as on-the-job training (Acemoglu et al. 2000), retirement and tax counseling (Booth 1995), UBs, or access to soft-landing retirement plans (Brugiavini et al. 2001). An alternative explanation of union membership under regimes where a legal extension of collective agreements is provided relies on social norms (Akerlof 1980; Naylor and Cripps 1993; Corneo 1997) that assign to union members a reputation, for example, for "good societal values."

The literature on membership also helps explain why unions typically pursue egalitarian wage policies. In addition to ideological factors, this egalitarianism can be motivated as the provision of insurance against wage fluctuations for risk-averse individuals (Agell and Lommerud 1992) or as a way to achieve savings on renegotiation costs and improve the relative position of low-skilled wage earners in the presence of strict EPL (Kramarz et al. 2008). Unions may also be involved in the enforcement of equal opportunity legislation, particularly as women become more and more important in the membership of trade unions.

Not only does membership affect the objectives of unions, but also the wage platforms of unions affect membership. This is because, unlike minimum wages, unions act over the entire wage distribution, interfering with the way in which markets reward differences in productivity across workers. To give an example, in Italy during periods of double-digit inflation, unions sponsored a wage-indexing mechanism that granted the same absolute adjustment for inflation to all workers (the so-called "punto unico di contingenza"), deeply compressing the wage distribution. Suppose that inflation is 10 percent and that the uniform adjustment to inflation is 100 euros. Those initially earning less than 1,000 euros would increase or at least keep unaltered their real wage after the price change as a result of the automatic indexing mechanism. Those earning initially more than 1,000 euros would experience a decline in their real wage.

Often unions tend to pursue egalitarian wage policies that compress earnings differentials. This may crowd out the least-skilled workers, located at the low end of the wage distribution, and reduce the skill premiums that would prevail in the absence of unions. In turn, this result may induce high-skilled workers to walk out of the union (in Italy, middle managers and high-skilled workers actually went on strike against the unions with the so-called "marcia dei 40,000"). Because the most skilled are not in the union and many of the least skilled are unemployed, membership becomes concentrated around intermediate-skill positions. A middle-skilled median union member is likely to vote for wage platforms increasing that member's pay relative to those workers with higher skills. To date, these interactions between union wages and membership have hardly been investigated in the literature.

3.2.3 Strikes

Although strikes are a rare phenomenon, they are interesting to study (see Kennan 1986 for an overview). After all, they are an indicator of a bargaining process that comes to a standstill, at least for a while. The first model of the bargaining process was developed by Hicks (1932) and is illustrated in the top panel of figure 3.5. The model assumes that firms and unions are bargaining on wages only. Unions want a higher wage than the firm offers, and so they go on strike. At the start of the strike unions want w_0, while firms offer w_e. Strikes are costly for unions because of forgone earnings and are costly for firms because of forgone production. Therefore, the duration of the strikes affects both the wage the union demands and the wage that the firm is willing to offer. During the strike the income of workers is substantially below the income they would earn while working. As the strike continues workers lower their wage demands. This process is illustrated through the union resistance curve UR_1. For firms a strike is also costly, as nothing is produced during the strike. Therefore, firms are also willing to give in. This process is illustrated by the employers' concession curve EC_1. The resistance curve and the concession curve intersect at point A in figure 3.5a. After a strike of duration t_A firms and unions agree on the wage w_A. Interestingly, if each party in the bargaining process is aware of the position and the shape of the resistance curve and the concession curve, they could both predict the equilibrium outcome and a strike would not occur. It would be rational to avoid the costs of the strike and agree on wage w_A without a strike. The irrationality of strikes in the Hicks model is known as the Hicks paradox. Nevertheless, a strike may occur in the case of asymmetric information. If the union thinks that EC_2 is the concession curve of the employers, the union will expect the equilibrium wage to be w_B. If the employer thinks that UR_2 is the resistance curve of the unions, it will expect w_C to be the equilibrium outcome. Because of the difference in expectations, there is no possibility to agree in advance and a strike will occur.

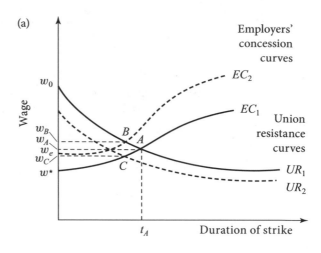

(a)

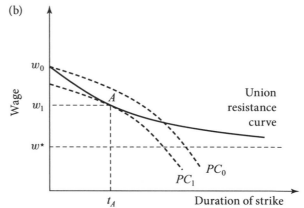

(b)

FIGURE 3.5 Union resistance curves, employer concession curves, and strikes: (a) the Hicks paradox; (b) the employer maximizing profits

Ashenfelter and Johnson (1969) argue that the asymmetry in information refers to unions having imperfect information about the financial situation of the firm. The employers are aware of the concession curve of the union and choose the point on this curve that provides maximum profits. This model is illustrated in figure 3.5b. The union resistance curve is the same as in the top panel with the addition of wage w^*, which is the reservation wage (the wage that workers can earn in a different firm or industry). Union resistance goes down as the strike continues, converging to w^* asymptotically. If the firm would pay w_0, its profits would be on isoprofit curve PC_0. This profit curve shows the combination of wages and strike duration that will generate the same profits. Profits are higher at lower isoprofit curves. Maximum profits conditional on unions' behavior are obtained at point A, where the profit curve is tangent to the union resistance curve.

The outcome in this model is determined by a simple trade-off. If the firm gives in too soon, it pays a higher wage. If the firm gives in too late, the forgone production increases. In the Ashenfelter-Johnson model strikes are necessary to reveal the financial position of the firm to the union. Note that the high initial demand of w_0 is the consequence of the asymmetry in information. If the union knew the exact situation, it could ask for a lower wage, but the firm has an incentive not to reveal its true financial situation. If unions would never strike, the firm has an incentive to claim it is in a bad financial position.

3.3 Empirical Evidence

There are two main avenues of research in the empirical literature on the effects of unions on the labor market:[6]

1. estimates of the effects of unions on wages of members vis-à-vis non-members, that is, *union wage gaps,* and on the entire wage distribution, drawing mainly on individual data; and

2. estimates of the effects of union density and bargaining coordination on employment, unemployment, and inflation, drawing mainly on macroeconomic time series.

3.3.1 Effects of Unions on Wages

In some countries it pays to be a union member, and a gap between the wages of a union member and a nonunion member occurs (see box 3.2). Booth (1995) provides a survey of the literature in which she reports estimates of the union wage gap ranging from 12 to 20 percent in the United States and from 3 to 19 percent in the United Kingdom. Estimates for other countries, which allow for legal extensions of the coverage of collective agreements, are not particularly informative, because even workers who are not members are covered by union contracts. Although this literature suggests that union membership is associated with higher wages, estimates of the union wage gap can be very imprecise. Measurement errors can significantly affect the results, because workers in the nonunionized segment may be less informed about their pay, or some union members may not want to disclose their affiliation. A large union wage gap estimated in these regressions may also reflect the fact that workers decide to be members of trade unions (technically speaking, they *self-select* themselves into unions) in industries or firms where there are more rents to be split between employers and workers, and hence wages are higher. Self-selection of workers into unions (which are voluntary associations) generates a positive correlation between wages and membership that is due to reverse causality: it is because wages are higher in these jobs or occupations that workers are unionized rather than the other way around.[7]

---

6. Union membership and strike activity have been declining over the past decades; see Hirsch (2008) on union decline in the United States and Godard (2011) on the decline in strike activity in the United Kingdom.

7. This endogeneity problem can be addressed, inter alia, by estimating (jointly with the wage equation) an endogenous membership equation, relating the decision to join a union to a number of covariates, including membership dues, industry-level labor productivity (or some measure of product market power to capture the size of the pie to be shared between workers and firms), and skill levels. This approach takes into account that egalitarian wage policies of unions are bound to attract some skill groups more than others.

BOX 3.2   *The Union Wage Gap*

Economic theory suggests that unions increase wages above the reservation wages of individuals, extracting rents, if any are available, from employers. This prediction inspired an extensive empirical literature estimating the so-called union wage premiums, drawing on micro data. To bring the theory to the data, one has to acknowledge that all workers and jobs may not be equally productive and find appropriate controls for sources of heterogeneity in pay that are independent of unions' presence.

The union wage gap is therefore estimated via cross-sectional regressions of wage equations of the type (where we omit error terms and a constant for simplicity)

$$\log w_i = \beta_m D_i + X_i' \gamma, \tag{3.4}$$

where D_i is a dummy variable denoting membership in a trade union (it takes the value 1 when individual i is a member of a trade union and 0 otherwise); X is a vector of personal characteristics affecting wages, such as age, educational attainment, and tenure on the job; and γ is a vector of parameters. If we denote by w^u and w^n mean wages of union and nonunion members, respectively, the estimated union wage gap is given by the parameter β_m:

$$\frac{w^u - w^n}{w^n} \approx \log w^u - \log w^n = \beta_m. \tag{3.5}$$

Some authors also make D_i interact with personal characteristics, so that unions are allowed to affect not only the average wage but also the way in which age, gender, and seniority are rewarded by employers. The union wage gap indeed reflects both differences in the way in which personal characteristics are rewarded in the two segments and differences in the characteristics of union versus nonunion members.

In countries where the coverage of collective bargaining extends far beyond membership, it is difficult to assess the effects of unions on wages, because there is no counterfactual wage distribution (no indication as to what wages would be without the unions). Di Nardo et al. (1996) developed an ingenious method to identify the effects of unions on the entire wage distribution and found that unions mainly affect wages of middle-skilled workers. Blau and Kahn (1996), Kahn (1998, 2000), and Card (2001) also provided estimates of the effects of unionization (or deunionization) on the entire wage distribution. Even in countries where union membership and coverage of collective bargaining are closely associated, the presence of trade unions may exert spillovers on the entire wage distribution. This happens for a number of reasons. Unions may increase the bargaining position of nonunionized workers, alter the skill composition of the workforce and hence also the substitutability of labor with capital, or affect the sectoral composition of labor demand. If these spillover effects are important, the effects of union activity on wages can be evaluated only by considering the entire wage distribution. Similar problems arise also in the (much smaller) literature evaluating the effects of unions on productivity, hours of work, and employment. The empirical literature evaluating the effects of unions on the entire wage distribution typically finds that unions reduce wage dispersion, notably in countries with higher centralization/coordination of bargaining.

3.3.2 Bargaining Coordination, Union Density, and Unemployment

Some studies have addressed the relationship between, on the one hand, union density and bargaining structure and, on the other hand, real wages and unemployment.[8] This literature draws on the highly imperfect measures of bargaining structure discussed in section 3.1.3. These measures also exhibit a limited time-series variation. This is a serious problem, because estimates draw on panel data seeking to explain variations both across countries and over time.

With these caveats in mind, a consistent finding in the macro empirical literature is that when broader coordination measures are used, a monotonic negative relationship between the degree of coordination and unemployment is observed, with higher coordination leading to lower unemployment. When centralization measures are instead used, a hump-shaped relationship is obtained (Calmfors and Driffil 1988), with low unemployment at low and high degrees of centralization and high unemployment with hybrid, intermediate bargaining regimes. However, Di Tella and MacCulloch (2005) found more recently that greater bargaining centralization is associated with higher unemployment, a result that helps us better understand the trend toward greater bargaining decentralization in the OECD area (see also section 3.4.2).

It is interesting to compare the results on bargaining coordination with those using union density and coverage of collective agreements as right-hand-side variables. In general, these latter variables have lower explanatory power than bargaining coordination. Most studies suggest that the difference between high and low density/coverage accounts for a smaller difference in unemployment than the difference between high and low coordination. A possible interpretation of these results is that changes in bargaining coordination are more important for macroeconomic outcomes than are changes in union membership and coverage of union contracts. But it is not clear that one can treat density/coverage and bargaining coordination as independent of each other. It may be easier to achieve high coordination in the union sector when union density and coverage are higher, because the benefits of coordination become larger when more employees are encompassed (Holden and Raaum 1991).

Overall, the (fragile) estimates from this macroeconomic literature suggest that the employment performance of an economy with both high bargaining coordination and high unionization is, ceteris paribus, superior to that of an economy

---

8. See OECD (2006a), chapter 3, for a survey of econometric evidence on the influence of coverage, density, centralization, and coordination on equilibrium unemployment.

with low coordination and unionization. At the same time, when coordination is lacking, better macroeconomic outcomes are observed under either centralized or decentralized regimes, with intermediate regimes offering the worst performance.

3.4 Policy Issues

3.4.1 Do Unions Increase Efficiency?

At least since the seminal works by Hirschman (1970) and Freeman and Medoff (1984), economists have usually characterized unions as organizations with two faces, having both a good (efficiency-enhancing) face and a bad (rent-seeking) face. The good face of unions is associated with their function as a collective voice of atomistic agents. Without such a voice, workers asking in vain for higher pay when productivity increases would have only the option of quitting the job and searching for another job with better pay (the *exit* option). Unions provide workers the option to continue to stay on the job and agitate for better pay, being at least as effective as when they exert the exit option, which is more costly because of the disruption of production associated with this mobility. By transmitting complaints, grievances, and demands, unions can also improve and correct the work relationship, making it possible to improve productivity in the firm. For instance, unions can force employers to provide more on-the-job training. Moreover, unions may help achieve higher efficiency by reducing transaction costs involved in individual bargaining.

In imperfect markets there are several second-best arguments for an efficiency-enhancing role of unions. For instance, unions can play the same role as a minimum wage in the presence of a monopsony (Robinson 1989). Indeed, historically, unions were created as a reaction to excessive monopsonistic power, and, as argued in chapter 2 and formally derived in technical annex 3.9.1, there can be efficiency gains in counteracting, at least up to some level, excessive bargaining power of employers. Unions may also provide protection through ex post redistribution against uninsurable labor market risk (Jones and McKenna 1994; Agell 2000), both by reducing wage differentials (hence earnings of workers in firms hit by adverse shocks) and by providing income in case of job loss, notably when unions are involved in the running of UBs, as in countries with a Ghent system. Clearly, it is not granted a priori that unions are more efficient than the state in providing unemployment insurance. Finally, unions, by compressing wage structures, may improve economic efficiency.

The bad face of unions is their rent-seeking behavior. Table 3.3 gives an overview of coverage, union density, and hence excess coverage by industry in the United States. Within industries, there is not much difference between coverage and union density, so the excess coverage is small. However, there are substantial differences in union density across industries. Union density is low in manufacturing (which faces international competition), and it is low in wholesale and retail trade (in which many small businesses operate). Union density is relatively high in education, public administration, utilities, and transport (i.e., industries that hardly face any international competition). Table 3.3 suggests that unions are typ-

TABLE 3.3 Coverage, union density, and excess coverage in different industries in the United States, 2011

Industry	Coverage (%)	Union density (%)	Employment share (%)
Utilities	28.7	27.5	1.0
Manufacturing	11.3	10.6	10.9
Construction	16.1	15.2	5.3
Transportation	30.5	28.8	4.3
Wholesale and retail trade	5.4	4.8	14.5
Education	37.0	33.3	10.1
Health care and social assistance	10.7	9.5	14.0
Public administration	36.3	32.7	5.4
Other industries	3.9	3.3	34.5
Total	13.0	11.8	100.0

Source: Dataset constructed by Barry Hirsch and David Macpherson; see Hirsch and Macpherson (2003).

Note: Employment = wage and salary employment; union density = percentage of employed workers who are union members; covered = percentage of employed workers who are covered by a collective bargaining agreement.

ically stronger in industries where there is less competition and hence there are more rents to be split between workers and firms. According to the Eurobarometer Survey, in all EU countries unions are stronger in the public than in the private sector. In markets where competition erodes profits, unions cannot extract wages above the marginal product without forcing firms to exit or to shed labor. Put another way, when competition is stronger, the segment AB in figure 3.4 becomes shorter. In Britain, one of the few countries with a long time-series of micro data on union membership and firms' characteristics, the decline in union membership was stronger in industries and years when product market competition increased the most (Pencavel 2003). Blanchflower (2007) also reported that deunionization in Canada, the United Kingdom, and the United States was concentrated in the private sector, the union density rate among public-sector employees being five times larger than among private-sector workers.

The same mobility costs that confer monopsony power on firms (see chapter 2) may also confer bargaining power on workers and allow them to extract rents from their employers. This typically happens when employers have to make irreversible investments, for example, they need to train their workforce to make it productive. This irreversible investment creates a substantial asymmetry between the incumbent workers (those for whom the investment has already been carried out) and outsiders, who need to be trained before becoming at least as productive as the incumbents. This asymmetry can then be exploited by incumbents to extract some surplus from their employers. In other words, after the investment in training is made, workers can renegotiate their wage and obtain higher pay. This *hold-up* problem (Williamson 1975; Grout 1984) can be particularly serious in innovative sectors requiring substantial investment in human capital at start-up. Unless unions can credibly commit to a wage schedule negotiated ex ante, the threat of ex post wage renegotiation can discourage start-ups of innovative firms and job creation.

Although redistribution in favor of low-skilled workers may be desirable from an equity standpoint, unions, by pursuing the interests of their members, often end up reducing employment opportunities for those who are not represented (because they do not have a job). In particular, egalitarian wage scales may crowd out the least-skilled workers from the labor market. Unions also generally support EPL (see chapter 10), which makes entry and reentry into the labor market harder. Thus, unions reduce the size of the labor market, leaving out new entrants and low-skilled workers.

Finally, the bad face of unions can materialize in their opposition to restructuring plans or to reforms aimed at increasing economic efficiency via reductions of rents in services less exposed to foreign competition. Coalitions of employers and workers' organizations often oppose regulatory reforms aimed at increasing competition in these sectors.

3.4.2 Should Collective Bargaining Be Decentralized?

These empirical results are consistent with the view that unions encompassing a very large set of workers can better take into account the macroeconomic effects of bargaining. In particular, centralized wage agreements can take into account the effects on inflation associated with excessive wage claims (Calmfors and Driffil 1988) and internalize aggregate demand externalities associated with consumer price inflation (Alesina and Perotti 1997; Soskice and Iversen 2000), as well as fiscal externalities (Flanagan 1999) related to the payment of UBs. However, bargaining systems in the OECD area have recently been evolving toward greater decentralization (OECD 2006c), and this trend is generally not imposed by governments but is chosen by unions and employers' associations (with the noteworthy exception of Australia, where the government actively encouraged decentralization). How can we reconcile this trend toward greater decentralization with the theoretical predictions and empirical findings previously reviewed on the advantages of centralized wage bargaining?

Figure 3.6 shows possible relationships between coordination of bargaining and bargaining outcomes (i.e., real wages or unemployment). Coordination in bargaining increases from left to right. This has two effects. First, if there is more coordination, negative externalities of bargaining are internalized, which tends to reduce wage pressure (curve I). Second, if there is more coordination, bargaining power increases, which tends to increase wage pressure. Initially the effect of increased bargaining power dominates, while later on internalizing externalities becomes more important. This creates a hump-shaped relationship between the degree of coordination and the real wage and thus unemployment (curve II). Therefore, at intermediate levels of bargaining, unemployment is highest (Calmfors and Driffil 1988). The power of unions is limited by product market competition. Therefore in more competitive markets there is a flatter relationship between bargaining coordination and bargaining outcomes (curve III).

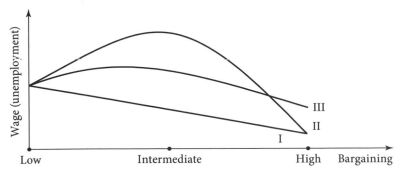

FIGURE 3.6 Relationship between bargaining coordination and bargaining outcomes

Note: I = the effect of internalization of negative externalities; II = hump-shaped relationship in the case of limited competition; III = hump-shaped relationship in more competitive markets.

The presence of a hump-shaped relationship between bargaining centralization and unemployment suggests that countries with an intermediate degree of centralization (industry-level bargaining) can achieve a better employment (and inflation) performance by pursuing greater decentralization in wage setting. A strong theoretical argument in favor of decentralization can be made in the presence of large productivity differentials across industries and regions. Centralized wage agreements make wages unresponsive to these differences in productivity, increasing unemployment in the low-productivity industry or region. Another explanation for the superior macroeconomic outcomes of decentralized versus hybrid bargaining structures is that the former can better accommodate incentives to achieve higher levels of efficiency, for example, by productivity-related pay.

Centralized or industry-level wage agreements can only replicate right-to-manage outcomes when unions agree with employers' associations on aggregate (or industry-level) wage levels, letting employment be determined by the individual employers, who are represented by their associations at the national or industry-level bargaining table. The right-to-manage model provides a more realistic description of how collective bargaining takes place under centralized or industry-level bargaining. This is because it is, in any event, difficult for employers' associations to commit their associates to the employment levels specified in the contract. In addition, a choice of the efficient employment level would require local knowledge of the technology of firms and would prescribe contingent contracts when the environment is uncertain. Thus, efficient bargaining outcomes, where both wages and employment are agreed on simultaneously, can only be replicated at the plant level. Hence by decentralizing bargaining, it is possible to achieve more efficient outcomes, potentially involving higher employment *and* wages, than in the right-to-manage model, as suggested by figure 3.4.

The decision on the bargaining regime does not truly belong to governments, because it is agreed on by unions and employers' associations. At most, governments can act as mediators in wage negotiations. However, governments may or may not allow the legal extension of collective agreements to nonunion members, and this indirectly affects the degree of centralization of bargaining. Some (rather weak) arguments in favor of this extension can be made on the grounds that it can reduce wage negotiation costs and, potentially, labor disputes. Employers sometimes favor legal extension of egalitarian union-sponsored wage scales as a device to level the playing field and to reduce wage costs of skilled workers. However, extension enables voluntary associations representing the interests of a subset of workers to affect the entire workforce, while union leaders are accountable only to the members of the trade union. Legal extension of collective agreements is not suitable when productivity levels are heterogeneous across firms.

3.5 Interactions with Other Institutions

National labor unions bargain with governments over the minimum wage (chapter 2); labor laws, like EPL (chapter 10); the age of retirement (chapter 6); family policies (chapter 7), UBs (chapter 11); and payroll taxes (chapter 13). Historically, unions played a role in some countries when unemployment insurance was introduced. In these countries UBs were introduced as a voluntary but publicly supported scheme administered by unions. Currently, this Ghent system operates in only a few countries. To the extent that unions compress earnings differentials, they reduce the returns to education, making investments in education less profitable (chapter 8).

3.6 Why Do Unions Exist?

Unions have a bad face and a good face. On the one hand, unions can increase the efficiency of the labor market. If employers have too much power, they not only reduce wage income but overall economic efficiency. Unions can act as a countervailing force reducing the monopsony power of employers and thereby increase economic efficiency. On the other hand, unions are rent-seekers: in their search for higher wages, they may increase unemployment.

In spite of falling densities, unions continue to exert significant influence over wage bargaining (and, more broadly, redistributive policies) in many countries, notably in Europe, because the coverage of collective bargaining did not decline together with membership. This widening excess coverage of unions suggests that simple measures of unions' strengths, which are typically based on membership or union presence in the workplace, can be quite misleading. In other words, unions' influence can be significantly larger than their presence.

Like any voluntary organization, unions exist because they are popular among some socioeconomic groups. In this chapter we have shown who gains from the presence of unions. Those who gain are not necessarily low-skilled workers, who may actually be displaced by the relatively high minimum wages imposed by the unions. Support of the egalitarian wage policies promoted by unions may come mainly from individuals with middle skill levels who can reduce their wage gap vis-à-vis highly skilled workers. Employers of skilled workers can also favor an extension of the coverage of union wages beyond the presence of unions at the workplace, notably when the presence of unions reduces negotiation costs (i.e., when unions have not only a redistributive but also an efficiency-enhancing function). In any event, more theoretical work on the reasons for the large excess coverage rates observed in some EU countries is warranted.

Although trade unions are not keen to release information on the age distribution of their members, household surveys suggest that the median age of a union member is increasing faster than that of the median worker. The fast aging of the median union member in some countries suggests that unions may be caught in a vicious circle of aging membership and reduced attractiveness among the young and active population. The share of retirees among union members is increasing everywhere; in Italy they are already a majority. Thus, unions increasingly favor older people in intergenerational conflicts, for example, in the design of public pensions. Unless unions solve this intergenerational problem, they may be headed for the grave.

3.7 Suggestions for Further Reading

A thorough survey of the earlier theoretical and empirical literature on unions is provided by Alison Booth's book on the economics of trade unions, which was published in 1995. The first part of the Oxford University Press book *The Role of Unions in the Twenty-First Century*, edited by Lars Calmfors, Agar Brugiavini, and Tito Boeri in 2001 (Calmfors 2001), offers a more recent review of the literature on deunionization. An overview of the activities of unions around the world is offered by Richard Freeman's "What Do Unions Do?" in a symposium issue of the *Journal of Labor Research* published in 2005 and in chapter 3 of the *2004 OECD Employment Outlook* (OECD 2004). Alan Manning's chapter of the *Handbook of Labor Economics* (Manning 2011) offers a nice survey of models of wage determination and estimates of rent splitting.

3.8 Review Questions and Exercises

1. What are the pros and cons of the various measures of the strength of labor unions provided in the literature?

2. What is the Hicks paradox?

3. Why are unions stronger in industries where there is less competition in product markets?

4. What happens in a right-to-manage model when the bargaining power of workers increases?

5. Why is a right-to-manage bargaining system inefficient?

6. Why do unions pursue egalitarian wage policies?

7. How does competition affect efficient bargaining?

8. Why, in your view, does excess coverage exist?

9. Why is it sometimes profitable for firms to have a strike before reaching an agreement on wages?

10. Wages in Kumbekistan are set via national agreements, in spite of large within-country disparities in economic and labor market performance. In Eastern Kumbekistan labor demand is given by $L_e^d = 1,000,000 - 20w$, where w is the annual wage, while in Western Kumbekistan it is given by $L_w^d = 800,000 - 20w$. Labor supply is the same in each region, and there is no interregional mobility of the workforce: $L^s = 700,000 + 10w$. Suppose that collective bargaining, involving mainly Eastern workers and employers, imposes the wage that clears the market in Eastern Kumbekistan.

    (a) What would be the employment and unemployment level in the two regions?

    (b) Suppose that there is a labor supply shock, e.g., brought about by migration to the richest region, and hence labor supply in the East is now $L_e^s = 790,000 + 10w$ and national wage contracts are revised accordingly. What happens to employment and unemployment levels in the two regions?

    (c) Finally, suppose that wage setting is decentralized and workers and firms in the West are allowed to set wages clearing the regional labor market. What would be the wage differential between the two regions? And how large should be the West–East flow of workers that brings this wage differential to zero?

11. Assume that the firm's labor demand curve is given by $w = 120 - 0.02L$, where w is the hourly wage, and L is the level of employment. Assume further that the union's objective function is given by $U = wL$.

    (a) What wage would a monopoly union impose?

    (b) How many workers would be employed under the union contract?

    Consider now a different objective function for the union. Suppose that the union's utility function is given by $U = (w - w^*)L$, where w^* is the competitive wage equal to 50 euros per hour.

    (c) What wage would a monopoly union demand?

    (d) How many workers will be employed under the union contract?

    (e) Is your answer different than with the previous specialization of the objective function of the union? Why?

12. Strikes reduce the profits of a firm π according to the function $\pi = (60 - 2s)(20 - w)$, where s denotes strike duration and w wages. The resistance of unions, hence strike duration, is a decreasing function of the wage: $s = 40 - w$. Supposing that the employer knows exactly the resistance of unions, which wage should she offer?

13. (Advanced) Consider a firm that faces a constant per unit price of 1,500 euros for its output. The firm hires L workers from a union at a daily wage of w, to produce output q, where the production function is $q = \sqrt{L}$, so the marginal product of labor implied by this production function is $1/\sqrt{L}$. There are 324 workers in the union. Any union worker who does not work for the firm can

find a nonunion job paying 50 euros per day. The union wants to maximize total earnings for its members.

(a) What is the firm's labor demand function?

(b) If the firm is allowed to specify w and the union is then allowed to provide as many workers as it wants (up to 324) at the daily wage of w, what wage will the firm set? How many workers will the union provide? Calculate the output, the profit of the firm, and the total income of the 324 union workers.

(c) If the union is allowed to specify w and the firm is then allowed to hire as many workers as it wants (up to 324) at the daily wage of w, what wage will the union set to maximize the total income of all 324 workers? How many workers will the firm hire? Calculate the output, the profit of the firm, and the total income of the 324 union workers. Compare this with the result of part (c).

3.9 Technical Annex: Unions Revisited

3.9.1 How Strong Should Unions Be to Be Efficient?

Specify labor demand and supply as in technical annex 1.6. Collective bargaining in a right-to-manage environment involves the maximization of the product (rather than the sum, as in the case of a perfect labor market) of the surplus of employers and workers, that is, the Nash-bargaining rule

$$w = \arg \max \left(\left[\frac{AL^{1-\eta}}{1-\eta} - wL \right]^{1-\beta} \left[wL - \frac{1}{\varepsilon+1} L^{\varepsilon+1} \right]^{\beta} \right), \qquad (3.6)$$

where the first term is the surplus of employers (profits) and the second the surplus of workers (the difference between the wage bill and reservation wages). Consistent with the framework developed in technical annex 1.6, the fallback option of employers is zero (no production, hence no profits), and the fallback option of workers is the reservation wage represented by the constant-elasticity labor supply ($w = L^{\varepsilon}$).

The two surpluses are weighted by the parameter β measuring the relative bargaining power of unions. Another interpretation of (3.6) is in terms of a benevolent government that cares about the (functional) income distribution and assigns weights β and $(1 - \beta)$ to the welfare of workers and employers, respectively. More generally, equation (3.6) offers a qualitatively appropriate characterization of any situation where the contractual and institutional structure of the labor market addresses distributional concerns across two groups of agents (employers and employees), using nonmarket instruments (e.g., unions and employers' associations, which provide a voice to their members) to redistribute purchasing power within each group.

As discussed in this chapter, a realistic (albeit inefficient) bargaining regime is one in which employers and workers bargain only over wages and then employers read from labor demand the employment level associated with this contracted wage (the right-to-manage model). Assume then that employment is on the labor demand schedule. Then maximizing (3.6) with respect to w under the constraint that $L = (w/A)^{-\frac{1}{\eta}}$, we obtain

$$w^b = (\mu)^{\frac{\varepsilon}{\varepsilon+\eta}} (A)^{\frac{\varepsilon}{\varepsilon+\eta}} = (\mu)^{\frac{\varepsilon}{\varepsilon+\eta}} w^*, \tag{3.7}$$

where $\mu \equiv \left(\frac{1-\eta}{1+\varepsilon} + \beta \frac{\eta+\varepsilon}{1+\varepsilon} \right) \frac{1}{1-\eta}$ is the optimal mark-up imposed by collective bargaining over the opportunity cost of working, the superscript b denotes equilibriums with collective bargaining institutions, and w^* is the wage prevailing at the equilibrium without unions. This solution encompasses the case of a *monopoly union* (setting wages) faced by a right-to-manage (setting employment) employer: when $\beta = 1$, all weight is on worker welfare, and

$$w^b = w^u = \left(\frac{1}{1-\eta} \right)^{\frac{\varepsilon}{\varepsilon+\eta}} (A)^{\frac{\varepsilon}{\varepsilon+\eta}} = \left(\frac{1}{1-\eta} \right)^{\frac{\varepsilon}{\varepsilon+\eta}} w^*. \tag{3.8}$$

Notice that the monopoly union wage w^u converges to the competitive equilibrium wage only when the aggregate labor demand is infinitely elastic (because η tends to 0). If labor supply is infinitely elastic ($\varepsilon = 0$), the monopoly union wage would be

$$w^u = \left(\frac{1}{1-\eta} \right) w^*. \tag{3.9}$$

To put it another way, unions introduce a wedge between labor demand and supply that is decreasing with the wage elasticity of labor demand. In the cases where market power is on both sides (employers and workers), the elasticity of labor supply also matters. This helps explain why unions typically represent workers (e.g., prime-aged males) with inelastic labor supply.

When instead all bargaining power is on the side of employers ($\beta = 0$) and labor demand is infinitely elastic ($\eta=0$), we have that

$$w^b = w^m = \left(\frac{1}{1+\varepsilon} \right) w^*, \tag{3.10}$$

that is, we go back to the pure monopsony case (hence the superscript m) characterized by (2.5) in technical annex 2.9. Like the monopoly union case, the pure monopsony equilibrium can replicate the competitive equilibrium wage only when labor demand is infinitely elastic (e.g., the firm has no monopoly power in product markets, and technologies are of the constant returns to scale type).

In all the more interesting cases where both labor demand and supply are inelastic, the competitive equilibrium outcome can only be replicated by an intermediate value of the bargaining-power parameter β. In particular, the equilibrium under Nash bargaining coincides with the competitive equilibrium when

$$\beta = \frac{\varepsilon}{\varepsilon + \eta} (1 - \eta), \quad 1 - \beta = \frac{\eta}{\varepsilon + \eta} (1 + \varepsilon), \tag{3.11}$$

because in this case $\mu = 1$ and the labor market generates the competitive equilibrium wage. In fact, the equilibrium in a perfect economy is supported by any combination of weights such that the ratio of the profit share to the labor share is

$$\frac{1-\beta}{\beta} = \frac{\eta}{1-\eta}\frac{1+\varepsilon}{\varepsilon}. \qquad (3.12)$$

This condition is similar to the Hosios (1990) condition for efficiency when individual workers and jobs meet randomly, according to a given matching technology, under constant returns.[9] There is no reason to expect a priori that this condition is fulfilled when there is uncoordinated individual bargaining. In the latter case β can be simply interpreted as a subjective discount factor that reflects the relative impatience (hence weakness) of the two parties at the bargaining table. However, insofar as β is a reduced-form representation of an allocation mechanism different from perfect competition, it may be expected to react to changes in the relevant elasticities ε and η. For instance, β can be interpreted as requiring that unions are not too strong when the labor demand elasticity is large to keep from reducing too much the size of the labor market and hence the pie to be shared between workers and firms.

To the extent that β is a (reduced-form) representation of politically supported equilibriums, this parameter may react to shocks (e.g., the competitive pressures arising from globalization that have been characterized in chapter 1) that increase the employment costs of redistributive institutions. For instance, collective bargaining institutions encompassing a rather broad range of interest groups may adjust wage claims to the new environment. Unions engaged in nationwide wage bargaining internalize the fact that unemployment will increase unless pay concessions are made. Small, decentralized unions may instead resist changes in their members' take-home pay. If every union follows the same policy, the outcome will be excessively high wages at the macroeconomic level, implying a bigger employment cost than with a nationwide union. This result is consistent with the arguments originally developed by Calmfors and Driffil (1988) on the labor market effects of macroeconomic shocks under different bargaining structures. The adjustment of wage claims under collective agreements to environmental changes may take some time to materialize, depending on the frequency of contracts, but eventually it will take place.

3.9.2 Deriving the Contract Curve

As indicated in the main text, the contract curve consists of the locus of the tangency points between iso-utility curves of unions and isoprofit curves of firms. Here we derive the conditions under which the contract curve is vertical, upward sloping, or downward sloping (see Booth 1995; Cahuc and Zylberberg 2004).

---

9. See chapter 12 for the description of matching technologies. It should be stressed that in a matching framework unemployment is present at the equilibrium, but if the Hosios condition is satisfied, unemployment efficiently coordinates the search decisions of workers and firms in a frictional labor market.

Unions are interested in employment and the difference between the utility derived from the wage ($u(w)$) and the utility derived from the reservation wage $w^r(u(w^r))$. The utility function of unions can be specified as

$$U^U = L^d(w)\left[u(w) - u(w^r)\right].$$

(3.13)

Profits of firms are equal to the difference between revenues and costs

$$\pi = R(L^d(w)) - wL^d(w).$$

(3.14)

The tangency between indifference curves and isoprofit curves can be obtained by equating the marginal rate of substitutions MRS for both curves. For the utility function of unions, the MRS is equal to the ratio of two marginal utilities

$$MRS^U = -\frac{MU_L}{MU_w} = -\frac{\partial U/\partial L}{\partial U/\partial w} = -\frac{u(w) - u(w^r)}{L^d(w)u'(w)}.$$

(3.15)

For the profit function of the employers, the marginal rate of technical substitution $MRTS$ is equal to the ratio of two marginal products

$$MRTS^\pi = -\frac{MP_L}{MP_w} = -\frac{\partial \pi/\partial L}{\partial \pi/\partial w} = \frac{R'\left(L^d(w)\right) - w}{L^d(w)}.$$

(3.16)

The tangency is given by

$$MRS^U = MRTS^\pi \Rightarrow -\frac{u(w) - u(w^r)}{L^d(w)u'(w)} = \frac{R'\left(L^d(w)\right) - w}{L^d(w)}.$$

(3.17)

Simplifying (3.17) yields the following equation for the tangency points:

$$u(w) - u\left(w^r\right) = u'(w)\left[w - R'\left(L^d\right)\right].$$

(3.18)

Since 3.18 does not yield a clear functional form for w in terms of L, we can use the implicit function theorem or total differentiation to obtain the slope of the contract curve. Specifying $G: u(w) - u\left(w^r\right) - u'(w)\left[w - R'\left(L^d\right)\right]$, it follows that

$$\frac{\partial w}{\partial L} = -\frac{\partial G/\partial L}{\partial G/\partial w} = -\frac{u'(w)R''\left(L^d\right)}{-u''(w)\left[w - R'\left(L^d\right)\right]} = \frac{u'(w)R''\left(L^d\right)}{u''(w)\left[w - R'\left(L^d\right)\right]}.$$

(3.19)

Since it is likely that revenues increase with L, we have $R'\left(L^d\right) \geq 0$, and since the revenues are likely to increase less than proportionally, we have $R''\left(L^d\right) < 0$. The slope of the contract curve specified in (3.19) depends on the nature of the utility function:

1. Unions are risk-neutral: $u(\cdot) = w$, therefore $u'(\cdot) = 1$, and $u''(\cdot) = 0$. Then the contract curve is vertical.

2. Unions are risk-averse: $u'(\cdot) > 0$, and $u''(\cdot) < 0$. Then the slope of the contract curve is positive.

3. Unions are risk lovers: $u'(\cdot) > 0$, and $u''(\cdot) > 0$. Then the slope of the contract curve is negative.

If unions are risk-neutral, employment does not influence their preferences, and they are only interested in the difference between wage and reservation wage. Employment will be at the efficient outcome of the competitive labor market. Since both bargaining and employment outcomes are efficient, this is called "strongly efficient" bargaining. If unions are risk-averse, they want to equalize marginal utilities over time. Thus, they are interested in both employment and wages. Unions want to protect their members against unemployment and at the same time increase their wage above their reservation wage. If unions are risk-averse, employment will be above the competitive level. Bargaining is efficient, since it occurs along the contract curve. However, the level of employment is not efficient. Hence the expression "weakly efficient" bargaining. If unions are risk lovers, they do not mind giving up employment in exchange for higher wages. Then the bargaining curve has a negative slope, albeit the curve is still above the labor demand curve.

CHAPTER FOUR Antidiscrimination Legislation

The labor market position of individuals may depend on their personal characteristics, such as education, training, and work experience. Some individuals will be more likely to have a job, and if they have a job, they will have higher wages. To the extent that these differences are related to productive characteristics, there is no economic inefficiency involved. However, sometimes the differences in labor market position are related to irrelevant characteristics (i.e., characteristics that do not affect the productivity of the worker). Then there is discrimination. Discrimination is defined as "the valuation in the market place of personal characteristics of the worker that are unrelated to worker productivity" (Arrow 1973). Discrimination may occur according to gender, race, ethnicity, sexual orientation, age, beauty, or the like.

Rational workers and profit-maximizing employers do not deviate from the optimal rule that marginal wage costs should equal the value of the marginal product. Discrimination may originate from differential market power, prejudice, lack of information, and employment barriers. Employers may have different market power over different groups of workers. Exploiting this market power, they will create differences between groups of workers. Prejudiced employers may be willing to pay men more than women or white workers more than black workers. Lack of information may occur if employers observe a noisy signal of individual productivity and therefore use group characteristics as an indicator of individual productivity. Some occupations may have barriers at entry for certain groups of workers. Thus, the labor supply for these occupations is restricted, inducing the affected group to seek employment in other occupations and driving down the wages in these occupations.

This chapter deals with labor market discrimination and (anti)discrimination legislation (i.e., legislation developed to prevent discrimination). While we are aware that discrimination may occur before individuals enter the labor market— for example, in the educational system—we focus on discrimination in the labor market.[1] In most of the chapter we focus on gender discrimination. However, the theories presented can also be applied to discrimination by race, ethnicity, and so

---

1. We are aware that premarket discrimination and market discrimination are intertwined. For example, individuals who expect to be discriminated against may invest less in human capital, which is rational, insofar as the expected returns to investment are lower.

forth. Also, although we are aware that there are many types of discrimination (e.g., discrimination in hiring and firing, promotions, and working conditions), we focus on two manifestations of labor market discrimination: in employment and earnings.

4.1 Measures and Cross-Country Comparisons

All OECD countries have a legal and institutional framework to fight labor market discrimination on gender and ethnic grounds. The labeling of laws varies across countries and types of discrimination. For instance, there is a sex discrimination act, a racial discrimination act, an equal treatment act, and an equal pay act. The bottom line of all laws is that there should not be discrimination against workers on the basis of characteristics not related to productivity. Whether the legal discrimination framework is effective depends on how difficult it is for workers to take action and how severe violations of employers are punished. Table 4.1 provides an overview of some of the cross-country differences in worker incentives to bring a case to court and employer incentives to comply with antidiscrimination policy. For the worker incentives we distinguish between elements of proof to be provided by the plaintiff and protection against victimization of the plaintiff. For the employer incentives we distinguish three types of sanctions in case of noncompliance: publicity, fines, and prison sentences.[2]

The first column of table 4.1 shows which elements of proof have to be provided by the plaintiff who wants to charge an employer with discrimination. Presumption of discrimination refers to a situation where the employee has to introduce his/her claim before the court by presenting facts establishing disparate treatment and from which a presumption of discrimination can be inferred. In most countries presumption or strong presumption has to be provided, but in others, such as Australia, Canada, Japan, and the United States, proof of discrimination has to be provided.

The second column of table 4.1 shows the protection of the plaintiff against retaliatory victimization. Limited protection against victimization refers to cases where the claimant employee (or any employee providing evidence in a proceeding against discrimination) is protected against wrongful discharge (dismissal) only. Clearly, protection against victimization varies considerably. Many countries have plaintiff protection, but there are also many where this protection is limited. In some countries, such as Finland, Italy, and Korea, the protection depends on the kind of discrimination: gender discrimination or ethnic discrimination.

The third to fifth columns of table 4.1 provide information about incentives of employers to comply with antidiscrimination legislation. The third column shows whether publicity is used as a sanction—that is, courts (or other relevant bodies)

---

2. In OECD (2008) more incentives for workers and employers are mentioned. With respect to worker incentives, OECD (2008) mentions institutional support provided to the plaintiff (legal guidance and counseling, investigation, legal representation), redress with back pay, additional compensation, and protection against victimization of witnesses. With respect to employer incentives OECD (2008) mentions other civil or administrative sanctions and affirmative and positive action.

TABLE 4.1 Worker incentives to bring a case before the courts and employer incentives to comply with antidiscrimination legislation

	Worker incentives		Employer incentives to comply		
	Burden of proof	Protection	Publicity	Fines	Prison
Australia	Proof	Yes	Yes	Penal	Yes
Austria	Strong presumption	Yes	No	Penal, rare, low	No
Belgium	Presumption	Yes	Yes	Gender: none Ethnicity: penal, low	Gender: no Ethnicity: yes
Canada	Proof	Limited	No	None	No
Czech Republic	Strong presumption	Limited	No	Administrative	No
Denmark	Gender: presumption Ethnicity: strong presumption	Limited	No	Penal	No
Finland	Presumption	Gender: yes Ethnicity: limited	No	Penal	Yes
France	Presumption	Limited	Yes	Penal	Yes
Germany	Presumption	Yes	Yes	Administrative and penal, low	No
Greece	Presumption	Yes	Gender: yes Ethnicity: no	Administrative	Yes
Italy	Gender: strong presumption Ethnicity: proof	Gender: no Ethnicity: limited	Yes	None	No
Japan	Proof	Yes	Yes	Penal	Yes
Korea	Gender: presumption Ethnicity: proof	Gender: yes Ethnicity: limited	Yes	Penal	Yes
Mexico	Strong presumption	Limited	Yes	Labor law	Yes
Netherlands	Presumption	Limited	Yes	Penal	Yes
Norway	Presumption	Yes	No	Administrative	Gender: no Ethnicity: yes
Poland	Presumption	Limited	No	None	Yes
Portugal	Presumption	Yes	Yes	Some	No
Spain	Strong presumption	Yes	Yes	Some	Yes
Sweden	Presumption	Yes	No	None	No
Switzerland	Presumption	Limited	Yes	Some	No
United Kingdom	Strong presumption	Yes	Yes	None	No
United States	Proof	Yes	Yes	Some	No

Source: OECD (2008).

Note: Worker incentives = incentives to bring a case before courts; proof = elements of proof to be provided by the plaintiff; protection = protection of the plaintiff against victimization; publicity = publicity as sanctions in case of noncompliance; fines = administrative, civil, or penal fines in case of noncompliance; prison = prison sentences in case of noncompliance.

can order the nominative publication of a discrimination case, or issue a notice outside the firm in question. As shown in the table, in the majority of the countries publicity can be used as a sanction. The fourth column indicates whether administrative, civil, or penal fines can be used as a sanction in case of noncompliance with antidiscrimination legislation. Such fines are used in many but not all countries. Finally, the fifth column of table 4.1 shows whether a prison sentence can be used as a sanction in case of noncompliance with the discrimination law. In about half the countries there is a possibility for using a prison sentence as a sanction.

4.2 Theory

Discrimination refers to valuation of personal characteristics that are unrelated to productivity in contrast to those that are related. A gender wage gap may occur if men and women differ in productive characteristics, such as education or working experience. Psychosocial research points to the possibility that men and women also differ in psychological traits and preferences. These differences may make some types of jobs more attractive to women and other jobs more attractive to men. The most commonly used personality traits are the "big five": extroversion, agreeableness, conscientiousness, neuroticism, and openness to experience. Laboratory-based research has documented gender differences in these five personality traits, but as yet the empirical relevance in real-life data is unclear (Bertrand 2010).[3]

Leaving aside potential psychosocial differences between men and women, there are several theories that analyze the phenomenon of discrimination (i.e., valuation of personal characteristics that are unrelated to individual productivity). We distinguish them by whether they are based in the context of a competitive or a noncompetitive labor market. In the setting of a competitive labor market the main theory is the taste-based discrimination model. In the setting of a noncompetitive labor market there are three discrimination theories: monopsony-based discrimination, statistical discrimination, and discrimination due to occupational crowding. Each of these theories will be presented and discussed in detail.

4.2.1 A Perfect Labor Market

Becker (1971) provides a framework that allows economists to analyze the nature and consequences of discrimination based on prejudice (i.e., taste-based discrimination). For ease of argument we assume that labor is homogeneous and that labor markets are competitive (i.e., all workers are equally productive and both firms and workers are wage-takers). We assume that discrimination, if any, is against women and in favor of men. Discrimination may lead female workers to have a wage w_f

---

3. Mueller and Plug (2006) present an early analysis of the effects of personality traits on earnings by gender. Using U.S. data, they find that only 3–4 percent of the gender gap in earnings is explained by gender differences in mean personality traits and gender differences in the returns to those personality traits.

that is below the wage w_m of male workers. Both wages are determined at the market level.

Employer Prejudice

Prejudiced employers have a preference for male workers. The utility U employers derive from employing workers depends on the profits, Π, that they make and the wage costs that they pay to women:

$$U = \Pi - \omega w_f L_f, \tag{4.1}$$

where L_f is the number of female workers hired, and ω is the *employer-specific coefficient of discrimination*. This coefficient varies across employers and is distributed over the interval $0 \leq \omega \leq \omega^{\max}$. For unprejudiced employers $\omega = 0$, while for the employer with maximum prejudice $\omega = \omega^{\max}$. The wage costs for male workers are equal to $w_m L_m$, and the (perceived) wage costs for female workers are $(1 + \omega)w_f L_f$. Because men and women are perfect substitutes in production, firms hire either men or women. Utility-maximizing prejudiced employers will hire only men if $w_m \leq w_f(1 + \omega)$, and they will hire only women if $w_m > w_f(1 + \omega)$. Hence, the workforce will be segregated. Conditional on the female wage, the higher the coefficient of discrimination is, the lower will be the number of females hired. Because of the existence of prejudiced employers, in equilibrium the wages of women can be lower than those of men. The *coefficient of market discrimination* Ω depends on the proportionate wage gap between male wage and female wage:

$$\Omega = \frac{w_m - w_f}{w_f}. \tag{4.2}$$

Note that the coefficient of market discrimination is the outcome of a market process, while the coefficient of discrimination is a subjective parameter of each individual employer. Obviously, the two are related. Figure 4.1 shows the equilibrium situation in the labor market. The relative wage w_f/w_m is plotted on the vertical axis and female employment is on the horizontal axis. L_0^d denotes labor demand of unprejudiced firms. The curve BCA shows the labor demand curve for women. If male and female workers have the same wage, only L_0^d jobs are available for women. Female employment can only increase if the relative wage falls. Point A represents an employer who is sufficiently prejudiced to hire no female workers even at a zero wage. The diagram also shows the female labor supply curve L_f^s, which is assumed to be perfectly inelastic. Equilibrium is at E, the intersection of the demand and supply curves, where $w_f^* < w_m^*$.

This simple model generates the following predictions:

1. All firms that employ women—even those with unprejudiced employers—pay the same low wage $w_f^* < w_m^*$. Wages are the outcome of a market process and are not influenced by individual employers.

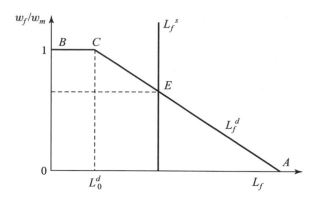

FIGURE 4.1 Employer discrimination and the gender wage gap equilibrium

2. The equilibrium level of wage discrimination is determined by the marginal employer and not by the average employer. Even if many employers are prejudiced, an increase in the number of unprejudiced firms (point C moves to the right, the slope of CA increases, shifting the relative wage upward) will reduce the gender wage gap. If $L_0^d > L_f^s$, there is no wage effect of discrimination despite the presence of many prejudiced employers. Note also that an increase in female labor supply will reduce women's wages relative to men's wages and thus increase the equilibrium level of labor market discrimination.

3. The profits of firms that hire at least some female workers will be higher than those of firms that only hire male workers. The relationship between profits and the coefficient of discrimination is illustrated in figure 4.2. A firm will hire only women if its coefficient of discrimination ω is smaller than the coefficient of market discrimination Ω, and it will hire only men if its coefficient of discrimination is larger than the coefficient of market discrimination.[4] Profit is at its maximum Π_1 at point A, where the employers are not prejudiced. The unprejudiced firms hire only female workers to maximize their profits. With a positive coefficient of discrimination, profits go down. The employer still only hires female workers, but the number of women hired goes down, because decisions are based on (dis)utility and not just profits. At $\omega = \Omega$ profits drop from B to C, as from then on the firm only hires male workers. A further increase in prejudice does not lower profits, as the number of male workers hired is not affected.

4. Prejudiced firms have lower profits than unprejudiced firms. This is a short-run phenomenon. In a competitive market, prejudiced firms cannot survive in the long run. They will be forced to leave the market either through

---

4. A firm hires only women if $w_m > w_f(1 + \omega)$, hence $\omega < \Omega$. Similarly, a firm will hire only men if $\omega \geq \Omega$.

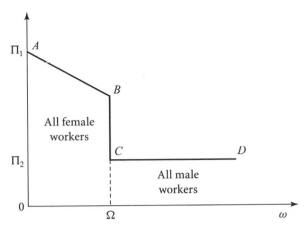

FIGURE 4.2 Profits and coefficient of discrimination

takeovers by unprejudiced firms or through competition from unprejudiced firms entering the market.

Co-worker Prejudice

There may also be discrimination against women because male workers prefer not to work with female co-workers. The utility U_m that a male prejudiced worker derives from his wage depends on whether he has female co-workers:

$$U_m = w_m(1 - \omega I_f),$$ (4.3)

where ω now is the coefficient of co-worker discrimination, and I_f is an indicator of whether this worker has at least one female co-worker. Prejudiced male workers will want to be compensated for the disutility of having female co-workers. Alternatively, for a given wage they will prefer to work in a male-only firm.

This model has the following predictions:

1. In firms in which women and men cooperate the male worker has to earn more to overcome his dislike of female co-workers. Therefore, firms hire either men or women, and the workforce will be segregated.

2. If employers are not prejudiced, there will be no gender wage gap, even if all men are prejudiced. This is the case even in the short run.

Customer Prejudice

If customers do not like to be served by women, the perceived price of a product or service may differ from the actual price. Discrimination occurs if the perceived price p_w for a particular product depends on the presence of female workers in the production process or when the transaction takes place:

$$p_w = p(1 + \omega I_f),$$ (4.4)

where p is the actual price, and here ω is the coefficient of customer discrimination. Conditional on the price, prejudiced consumers will only buy from firms that have no female workers. Alternatively, prejudiced consumers will only buy from firms with female workers if the price is sufficiently low.

This model has the following predictions:

1. Since firms pay workers according to their marginal product, in an environment with customer discrimination women will have a lower wage.

2. Firms will be segregated. For an all-woman firm the product price is low; hence this firm cannot afford to hire a male worker. For an all-man firm the product price is high, but this price would fall once a female worker is hired.

Comparing Types of Taste-Based Discrimination

In the short-run equilibrium, the workforce will be segregated irrespective of whether the taste-based discrimination is related to employers, co-workers, or customers. In a labor market with employer discrimination market forces will eventually remove discrimination through competition, but no such market force exists in a labor market with customer discrimination. Co-worker discrimination does not cause a gender wage gap. With customer and co-worker discrimination, workforce segregation may persist.

Taste-based discrimination is a bundle of theories that are founded in the context of a competitive labor market. Of course taste-based discrimination may also occur in an imperfect labor market. In an imperfect labor market taste-based discrimination by employers can survive. In a market with search frictions and employer discrimination it is more difficult for women to find a job, since an application at a prejudiced employer may not be successful. If women need to apply more often to generate a job offer than men do, job search for women is more expensive and the bargaining power of women is weaker. Unprejudiced employers may exploit this by offering women a lower wage (Black 1995). Note that in this case the equilibrium level of discrimination depends on the subjective coefficient of discrimination of the average employer rather than of the marginal employer.

4.2.2 An Imperfect Labor Market

Employers may have market power over some groups of workers and exploit this by paying them lower wages than they would in a competitive labor market. An early explanation of the gender wage gap is based on monopsony power of employers in the female labor market and is discussed in more detail in the next subsection. Other types of discrimination in a noncompetitive labor market are statistical discrimination and discrimination related to occupational crowding.

Monopsony and the Gender Wage Gap

Joan Robinson's (1933) theory of monopsony provides an explanation of the gender wage gap. Employers may have more monopsony power over women than they have over men. To illustrate the general idea we assume that the labor market for men is fully competitive, whereas the labor market for women is character-

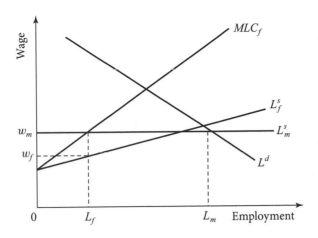

FIGURE 4.3 The gender wage gap in a monopsony model

ized by monopsony power, for example, because women have high mobility costs, and hence their labor supply curve slopes upward. Figure 4.3 illustrates the line of reasoning.

The employment of women L_f is determined by the intersection of their upward-sloping marginal labor cost curve MLC_f and the horizontal labor supply curve of men. Here the marginal hiring costs for men and women are equal. However, to hire L_f women, the employer has to pay a wage $w_f < w_m$ (see also technical annex 4.9.2). Total employment is determined by the intersection of the male labor supply curve L_m^s and the labor demand curve L^d. Thus, the number of employed men is $L_m - L_f$. The gender wage gap originates from the labor supply of women being inelastic.

Empirical studies usually find that the labor supply of women is more elastic than that of men. Does this invalidate the monopsony explanation of the gender wage gap? Not necessarily. It may be that at the market level the labor supply of women is more elastic than at the level of individual firms (see Manning 2003, 2011). For example, Hirsch et al. (2010) find that women's labor supply to German firms is less elastic than men's labor supply. Using the estimated value of the labor supply elasticities, they conclude that at least one-third of the gender wage gap may be due to wage discrimination of profit-maximizing monopsonistic employers.

Statistical Discrimination

The theory of statistical discrimination is based on the assumption that employers have imperfect information—that is, they observe a noisy signal of the true productivity of individual workers (Aigner and Cain 1977). To assess individual productivity, employers will use individual "test scores." These test scores may be actual scores from a test but may also be scores based on past experience with similar workers, interpretation of an application letter, or an assessment of a CV. Because the test scores are imperfect, they are combined with information about the group the applicant belongs to. The perceived productivity of an individual worker is the weighted average of the individual test score and the perceived group productivity (i.e., the average test score of the group the individual belongs to):

$$q_{ji} = \alpha_j T_j + (1 - \alpha_j) T_i,$$ (4.5)

where q_{ji} is the perceived productivity of individual i from group j, T is the test score, and α is weight attached to information about group productivity.[5] There are two types of statistical discrimination. The first type arises when employers have a different perception of group productivity, but there is no difference in the weight attached to individual test scores ($\alpha_j = \alpha$). Then, individuals belonging to different groups may be treated differently, even if they share identical observable characteristics in every other aspect:

$$q_{ji} = \alpha T_j + (1 - \alpha) T_i.$$ (4.6)

This type of statistical discrimination is illustrated in figure 4.4a. Lines 1 and 2 are parallel, indicating that the test score has the same accuracy for both groups. However, the mean productivities T_1 and T_2 are different. At test score T_2 an individual of group 2 has a perceived productivity of q_2, while an individual from group 1 with the same test score has a perceived productivity of q_1, and thus is not hired or, if hired, is paid a lower wage. This type of statistical discrimination could be based on stereotyping, where the perceived productivity differences between groups are based on prejudice or lack of information. To the extent that the perceived group differences are real, on average there will be no discrimination between groups as, on average, perceived productivity coincides with actual productivity.

The second type of statistical discrimination occurs if employers value the individual test score of one group more than that of another group, even though the average productivity of the two groups is perceived to be the same ($T_j = T$):

$$q_{ji} = \alpha_j T + (1 - \alpha_j) T_i.$$ (4.7)

This type of statistical discrimination is illustrated in figure 4.4b. Now the mean perceived productivities are the same for both groups, but outside the mean, for the same test score expected individual productivity differs, because the accuracy of the test scores differs. If the test score is T_a, individuals from group 1 are perceived to have productivity q_{a1}, while individuals from group 2 are perceived to have productivity q_{a2}. Again, for the same test score individuals from group 1 are more likely to be hired or to receive a higher wage, and again on average there is no discrimination between groups.

Occupational Crowding

The theory of occupational crowding explains how wage differences between occupations may occur because some groups of workers are restricted in their en-

---

5. Note that, on average, the test score is equal to the perceived productivity: $\sum_i q_{ji} = q_j = \alpha_j T_j + (1 - \alpha_j) \sum_i T_i = T_j$.

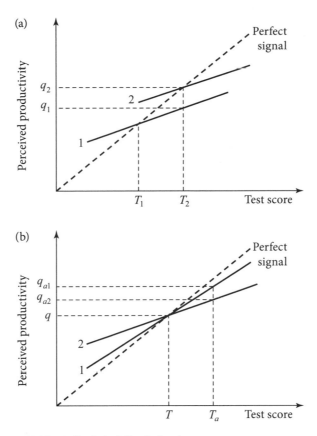

FIGURE 4.4 Statistical discrimination

trance to certain occupations. Wage discrimination is not within occupations or industries but across occupations and industries. The theory focuses on male-female earnings differences. If women are not allowed (or are not supposed) to enter a particular occupation, they will enter other occupations, pushing wages in these occupations down. The barriers for women to enter specific occupations may come from unions, through custom, or because of self-selection. Historically, some occupations—mainly teaching and clerical jobs—had "marriage bars," which prohibited employment of married women. Employed single women would have to give up their jobs as soon as they got married. If they wanted to remain employed after marriage, they had to look for a job outside the marriage-bar occupations. The marriage bars caused highly skilled women to work in low-wage jobs. In the United States marriage bars were in place from the late 1800s until the 1950s (Goldin 1988). In the Netherlands a law that prohibited married women in government service was introduced in 1937, at a time when unemployment was high. This law was abolished in 1957. Although they were not legally obliged to do so, some big companies followed the example of the government and also fired women as soon as they got married or became pregnant (Portegijs et al. 2008).

Figure 4.5 shows how occupational barriers affect the labor market. Without occupational crowding, the labor markets are in equilibrium at wage w_0 and the

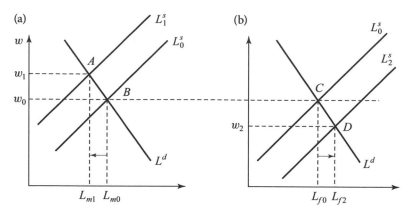

FIGURE 4.5 Occupational crowding: (a) male jobs; (b) female jobs

label "male jobs" and "female jobs" is not relevant. The distinction between male and female jobs is artificial in the sense that women can work in male jobs and men can work in female jobs. If barriers are introduced for women to enter male jobs, this situation changes. The supply curve for male jobs shifts to the left, reducing employment and increasing wages in male jobs to w_1 (figure 4.5a). Assuming that the women who are banned from male jobs still want to work, they have to work in female jobs. Thus, the labor supply curve for female jobs shifts to the right and wages go down to w_2 (figure 4.5b). Note that the wage is determined by the type of job and not by the gender of the worker. This generates earnings differences which are occupation-specific (i.e., men working in female occupations will earn less than men in male occupations). Thus, on average women earn less than men, but within industries there is no earning differential between men and women.

A key assumption of the occupational crowding model is that men working in female jobs do not respond to the wage differential by moving to male jobs. This may be because of preferences or mobility costs.

Discrimination and Economic Efficiency

Discrimination is inefficient from an economic point of view. For occupational crowding this can be illustrated using figure 4.5. Because of occupational crowding, the market surplus in male jobs goes down with the area $ABL_{m0}L_{m1}$, while the market surplus in the female jobs goes up with $CDL_{f2}L_{f0}$. Clearly, the loss of market surplus in male jobs is bigger than the gain of market surplus in female jobs. Male jobs are more productive at the equilibrium than are female jobs. Hence, too little is produced in male jobs and too much is produced in female jobs. This outcome is not specific to the occupational crowding explanation of wage discrimination but holds more generally. For example, as discussed before, prejudiced employers may hire fewer women than is optimal from the point of view of profit maximization.

4.3 Empirical Evidence

We begin the overview of empirical evidence with a presentation of unconditional differences in employment and earnings for male and female workers. Then we discuss studies on wage discrimination. This type of study is usually based on the estimation of wage equations. These estimates are then used to disentangle the part of the wage differences between groups of workers that can be attributed to differences in human capital, while residual wage differentials are considered to be evidence for the existence of wage discrimination. Therefore, discrimination is often equivalent to a "measure of ignorance." Finally, we discuss empirical studies on employment gaps. Here it is possible to use a quasi-experimental approach by randomizing information about job applicants.

4.3.1 Unconditional Gender Employment and Earnings Gaps

Estimated unconditional employment and earnings gaps can sometimes provide suggestive evidence of potential discrimination. The statistical information about both gaps can be readily obtained for men and women. The gender employment gap is defined as the percentage difference between the employment-population ratios of men and women. The gender earnings gap is calculated as the difference between earnings of men and women relative to earnings of men, usually at the median or mean of the earnings distribution. Of course these unconditional gaps as such do not provide evidence of gender discrimination, because men and women may differ in relevant labor market characteristics. Conditional gaps, that is, gap measures for specific categories of workers (e.g., depending on educational attainment), can also be misleading, as the difference in characteristics may be due to pre-labor market discrimination. When pre-market wage discrimination is important, unconditional wage differentials may be more informative than conditional differences.

Table 4.2 gives an overview of cross-country differences for both gaps. The first column shows the 2010 gender employment gap for prime-aged workers (aged 25–54). The employment gap is very large in Turkey (50 percentage points) and Mexico (38 percentage points) and relatively small in Nordic countries. In Finland and Norway the 2010 employment gap is 5 percentage points.

The second to fourth columns of table 4.2 provide information about the 2009 gender earnings gap for full-time wage and salaried workers evaluated at the median (second column) and at the 20th and 80th percentiles (third and fourth columns, respectively) of the earnings distribution. At the median the earnings gap is particularly large in Korea (39 percent) and Japan (28 percent) and relatively small in Hungary (4 percent). In Belgium, New Zealand, and Norway the gender earnings gap at the median of the distribution is below 10%. The third and fourth columns of table 4.2 show that in some countries the gender earnings gap does not vary significantly over the earnings distribution, while in other countries there are substantial differences. In countries such as Canada, Czech Republic, Denmark, and the Netherlands, the difference in the earnings gap at the 20th and 80th

TABLE 4.2 Gender employment gap and gender earnings gap

| | Employment gap, 2010 (%) | Earnings gap, 2009 (%) | | | Change in gap (%) | |
| | | Median | Percentile | | Employment, 1994–2010 | Median wage, 1980–2008 |
			20th	80th		
Australia	15	16	7	20	−6	−7
Austria	9	19	26	22	−12	—
Belgium	11	9	12	10	−15	—
Canada	7	20	21	20	−7	—
Czech Republic	17	18	24	23	48	—
Denmark	5	12	14	15	−5	—
Finland	5	20	16	25	2	−5
France	10	13	9	17	−9	−8
Germany	10	22	25	22	−11	—
Greece	24	10	9	5	−18	—
Hungary	11	4	2	13	−2	—
Iceland	6	14	11	20	−4	—
Ireland	8	10	12	16	−25	—
Italy	25	12	7	−4	−14	—
Japan	23	28	26	36	−9	−11
Korea	26	39	29	41	−12	—
Luxembourg	19	—	—	—	−20	—
Mexico	38	—	—	—	−15	—
Netherlands	11	17	18	19	−17	—
New Zealand	15	8	7	14	−4	—
Norway	5	9	5	16	−5	—
Poland	11	10	8	3	−2	—
Portugal	9	16	14	9	−11	—
Slovak Republic	11	—	—	—	−2	—
Spain	12	12	13	5	−26	—
Sweden	6	15	—	—	4	1
Switzerland	13	15	20	22	−11	—
Turkey	50	—	—	—	−6	—
United Kingdom	11	20	17	21	−4	−14
United States	12	20	14	24	−4	−16

Sources: OECD various statistics; OECD (2008); OECD earning database.

Notes: The gender employment gap is the difference in employment-population ratios of prime-aged men and women. Estimates of earnings used in the calculations refer to gross earnings of full-time wage and salaried workers. — = not available.

percentile is less than 1 percent. In countries where there is a difference across the distribution the earnings gap is most often much bigger at high incomes. For example, in Korea the earnings gap at the 20th percentile is 29 percent, while it is 41 percent at the 80th percentile. Portugal and Spain are exceptions: in these countries the gender earnings gap is much bigger at the 20th percentile than at the 80th percentile.

Figure 4.6 shows the cross-country variation in gender employment and gender earnings gap. There is a positive association between the two gaps, although this is predominantly driven by most countries having similar gaps of 10–20 percent and

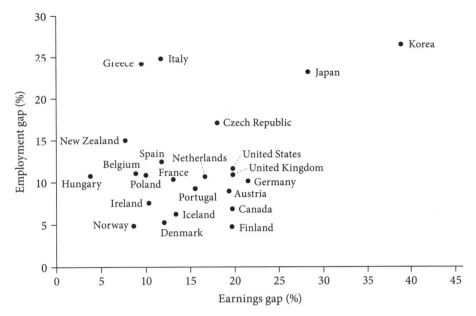

FIGURE 4.6 Gender earnings gap and gender employment gap
Source: Data are from the first two columns of table 4.2.

Japan and Korea having both large employment and earnings gaps. Greece and Italy are outliers in this positive association, because they combine a relatively high employment gap with a relatively low earnings gap.

The last two columns of table 4.2 show changes in the employment gap and earnings gap over time. In all countries except the Czech Republic, Finland, and Sweden there has been a decline in the gender employment gap, which was particularly large (approximately 25 percent) during 1994–2010 in Ireland and Spain. Information about the change in earnings gap is available only for a few countries. Except for Sweden, where there was a mild increase in the earnings gap during 1980–2008, there were substantial reductions in the median earnings gap during this period.

4.3.2 Empirical Evidence on Discrimination in the Labor Market

Using regression analysis differences in, for example, male and female wages, can be explained through differences in observed characteristics between men and women and through differences in returns to these observed characteristics. This last type of differences is considered to be evidence of discrimination (for a more detailed discussion, see boxes 4.1 and 4.2). However, this approach may understate as well as overstate the extent of wage discrimination (Altonji and Blank 1999). Some of the observed characteristics may be influenced by the existence of discrimination. Women may invest less in education in anticipation of wage discrimination that reduces the return to education. Then the true effect of discrimination is understated. However, it may also be that the regression analysis suffers from omitted variables which are related to human capital variables and personal tastes (see also section 4.2). Then, the extent of discrimination may be overstated.

BOX 4.1   *Blinder-Oaxaca Decomposition*

A popular way to establish the extent of wage discrimination between any two groups of workers (e.g., men and women) is based on estimates of wage equations. This is done separately for men and women:

$$\log w_j = \alpha_j + x_j \beta_j, \quad \text{with } j = m, f,$$

where w represents hourly wages, x is a vector of personal and job characteristics, and α and β are vectors of parameters. We ignore for simplicity the statistical error term. Taking the differences of the two equations, the wage gap between male and female workers can be attributed to differences in characteristics and differences in rewards for given characteristics:

$$\log w_m - \log w_f = \alpha_m - \alpha_f + (x_m - x_f)\beta_m + x_f(\beta_m - \beta_f). \tag{4.8}$$

The part related directly to discrimination is $(\beta_m - \beta_f)$, as this represents a different reward for the same characteristics. However, $(x_m - x_f)$ may also be due to discrimination, for example, if women invest less in their human capital because of the expectation that they will be discriminated against. And $(\alpha_m - \alpha_f)$ may also be related to discrimination, as there is no reason women with the same characteristics and the same reward for observed characteristics should receive a lower pay. Whether the wage gap is measured correctly this way depends on whether all relevant personal and job characteristics are included. If there are omitted characteristics, such as motivation and commitment to career, the decomposition would overstate the gender wage gap. For example, if few very low-paid women choose to work, those with the lowest wage offers are not observed, and the wage gap would be understated. Note also that (4.8) can also be split up in a different way, evaluating the extent of discrimination based on the male characteristics:

$$\log w_m - \log w_f = \alpha_m - \alpha_f + (x_m - x_f)\beta_f + x_m(\beta_m - \beta_f). \tag{4.9}$$

This alternative split up will lead to a different estimate of the extent of discrimination.

Source: Blinder (1973), Oaxaca (1973).

BOX 4.2   *Sensitivity of the Blinder-Oaxaca Decomposition*

The sensitivity of the Blinder-Oaxaca decomposition is shown by Joseph Altonji and Rebecca Blank in their overview chapter on race and gender in the *Handbook of Labor Economics*:

Groups compared	Wage difference, 1979 (%)		Wage difference, 1995 (%)	
	Model 1	Model 2	Model 1	Model 2
Male-Female				
Characteristic	2.6	12.6	0.8	7.6
Coefficient	43.8	33.5	27.9	21.1
White-Black				
Characteristic	6.3	10.8	8.2	11.4
Coefficient	10.2	6.1	13.4	9.8

Note: The numbers indicate the percentage wage difference of males-females and whites-blacks; model 1 includes education, potential experience, and region; model 2 includes in addition occupation, industry, and job characteristics.

Using data from the Current Population Survey, they show that when only education, potential experience, and regional variables are included (model 1), in 1979 2.6 percentage points of the gender wage gap was due to differences in characteristics, while 43.8 percentage points was due to differences in coefficients (i.e., differences in rewards to characteristics). However, it is incorrect to attribute the latter differences to discrimination. Model 2, in addition to the variables in model 1, also includes occupation, industry, and job characteristics. Then the contribution of differences in characteristics goes up to 12.6 percentage points, while the contribution of the difference in coefficients goes down to 33.5 percentage points. In 1995 the gender wage gap was smaller, and both components of the gap became less important. For the wage gap between black and white workers, introducing additional explanatory variables also reduces the contribution of the coefficients (i.e., the part of the wage attributed to discrimination).

Source: Altonji and Blank (1999).

It is difficult to establish the extent of discrimination using information from natural experiments because they are hardly available. A rare example of a natural experiment that was performed in auditions for American orchestras is presented in box 4.3.

Gender Discrimination in Hiring

BOX 4.3

Claudia Goldin and Cecilia Rouse studied gender bias in hiring by analyzing data from auditions at American orchestras. These orchestras introduced blind rounds in their audition procedures such that the applicants would perform behind a screen. The applicants could play their instrument concealing their identity from the recruitment committee. Because different orchestras adopted the blind selection procedure at different times, the authors could compare the effect of the blind procedure on the gender composition of the new hires as if these were the result of a natural experiment. The authors collected a sample of auditions for eight major orchestras from the late 1950s through 1995. Using a subsample of musicians who auditioned through both blind and not-blind selection procedures, they find the following hiring probabilities:

Group	Selection procedure	
	Blind	Not blind
Female	2.7	1.7
Male	2.6	2.7
Difference	0.1	−1.0
Difference-in-differences	1.1	

As shown for women, the probability of being hired with a blind audition was 2.7 percent, while in a non-blind audition it was only 1.7 percent. For male musicians it hardly matters which hiring procedure was used. Because the use of the screen can be interpreted as a natural experiment, a difference-in-differences approach can be used to establish the effect of the change in hiring procedure. It is clear that the increase in the hiring probability of women was 1.1 percentage points, a growth of 65 percent. Over the sample period the female share of new hires increased substantially. This was partly due to the increased pool of female candidates. But according to Goldin and Rouse, about one-third of the increase in the proportion of women among new hires can be attributed to the introduction of the blind hiring procedures.

Source: Goldin and Rouse (2000).

The extent of discrimination is also investigated using field experiments in so-called audit and correspondence studies. In audit studies "live" job applicants—actors—are used, who are identical except for the characteristic that may lead to discrimination. Audit studies have been criticized, because it is virtually impossible to have live applicants from different groups appearing identical to employers. Live applicants know that the application is fake, and they know the reason they are applying—to establish whether employers are discriminating. Thus, they may behave differently than they would in a real application procedure. Correspondence studies use fictitious application letters. On paper (or through the internet) it is easy to make personal characteristics and CVs identical across groups. Comparing callback rates of individuals from different groups with otherwise identical characteristics should be informative about the extent of discrimination between these groups. Nevertheless, correspondence studies have also been criticized for their limitations (Heckman 1998). If the callback rate is influenced by unobserved characteristics that are distributed differently across groups, even correspondence studies can generate spurious evidence of discrimination or absence of discrimination (see technical annex 4.9.3 for an example). Furthermore, random applications may overstate the extent of discrimination, if applicants are aware of discriminatory behavior and avoid discriminating employers. Riach and Rich (2002) provide an overview of early correspondence studies, and Neumark (2012) discusses the criticism of audit and correspondence studies in more detail. Table 4.3 provides an overview of some recent correspondence studies investigating potential discrimi-

TABLE 4.3 In search for discrimination: correspondence studies

Study	Group	Callback (%)	Country	Sample size
Booth and Leigh (2010)	Male	32	Australia	3,365
	Female	25		
Bertrand and Mullainathan (2004)	White	10	United States	2,435
	African-American	6		
Carlsson and Rooth (2007)	Swedish	29	Sweden	1,552
	Middle Eastern	20		
Ahmed et al. (2011)	Male heterosexual	30	Sweden	1,978
	Male homosexual	26		
	Female heterosexual	32		2,018
	Female homosexual	26		
Ruffle and Shtudiner (2010)	Male plain	9	Israel	2,656
	Male attractive	20		
	Female plain	14		2,656
	Female attractive	13		

Note: Correspondence studies are faked job applications submitted by mail or over the internet.

nation along dimensions of gender, race, immigrant status, sexual orientation, and beauty:

- *Gender.* In 2007 Booth and Leigh (2010) sent application letters to employers with job vacancies in the three largest cities of Australia—Brisbane, Melbourne, and Sydney. They selected four female-dominated types of jobs: wait staff, data entry, customer service, and sales. For each job category four fake CVs were created, tailored to the particular job. Male and female names were randomly assigned to CV types. The typical female applicant received a callback 32 percent of the time, while the typical male candidate received a callback 25 percent of the time. Men looking for work in these types of jobs would have to apply 28 percent more frequently to receive the same number of callbacks as women received. Apparently, it is not easy for men to enter female-dominated jobs, as is probably the case for women to enter male-dominated jobs.

- *Race.* Between July 2001 and January 2002 in Boston and between July 2001 and May 2002 in Chicago, Bertrand and Mullainathan (2004) surveyed all employment advertisements in the Sunday editions of *The Boston Globe* and *The Chicago Tribune* in the sales, administrative support, and clerical and customer services sections. They sent four resumes in response to each ad: two higher quality and two lower quality ones. They randomly assigned African-American–sounding names and white names to the resumes. The authors find that resumes with white names have a 10 percent chance of receiving a callback. Equivalent resumes with African-American names have a 6 percent chance of being called back. So, a white applicant can expect one callback for every 10 applications, while an African-American applicant would need to apply to about 15 ads to achieve the same result.

- *Immigrant status.* Carlsson and Rooth (2007) investigate the presence of discrimination between natives and immigrants in hiring in Sweden. They sent applications to vacancies in 12 occupations and two cities, Gothenburg and Stockholm. Applications with identical skills were randomly assigned Swedish or Middle Eastern names. They find that, on average, 29 percent of the applicants with Swedish names got a callback for an interview, while only 20 percent of the applicants with Middle Eastern names got such a callback. The authors were able to relate the callback rates to employers and recruiters. For example, they found that female recruiters are less likely to discriminate, while in small firms and in occupations with many immigrants discrimination is more likely to occur.

- *Sexual orientation.* Ahmed et al. (2011) investigated whether homosexuals experienced discrimination in the hiring process in Sweden. In the fake application letters they indirectly labeled applicants as gay, lesbian, or heterosexual by showing the gender of the applicants' partner and adding information about doing voluntary work in a homosexual organization or a neutral help organization. On average gay men received 4 percent fewer callbacks than did heterosexual men, while lesbian women received 6 percent fewer callbacks than did heterosexual women. They also find that this type of discrimination varied across occupations and appeared only in the private sector. The gay applicant was discriminated against in male-dominated occupations, while the lesbian applicant was discriminated against in female-dominated occupations.

- *Beauty.*[6] Ruffle and Shtudiner (2010) sent out application letters to employers in Israel in pairs: one was without a picture, while the second—otherwise almost identical—letter contained a picture of either an attractive or a plain man/woman. They find that attractive men are much more likely to receive callbacks than are plain men, while for women the difference in callback rates between attractive and plain applicants was small.

4.4 Policy Issues

Historically, women have typically experienced some sort of discrimination in the workplace. Some of these early measures originated from being protective toward women. In the early 1900s there was legislation limiting how many hours per day a woman could work, as it was believed to be bad for her reproductive health if she overexerted herself (Hoffman and Averett 2010). Since the 1960s legislation shifted from protection to equal opportunity, and laws were introduced to prevent discrimination according to gender, race, age, sexual preferences, and possibly other dimensions. We discuss typical ingredients of antidiscrimination legislation in more detail: equal pay legislation and affirmative action. In a perfectly competitive labor market neither equal pay legislation nor affirmative action are needed,

---

6. For an early study on beauty, see Biddle and Hamermesh (1994). For a recent overview, see Hamermesh (2011).

as competition among discriminatory employers will remove discrimination. In an imperfect labor market equal pay legislation may not be the answer to the problem of discrimination, while affirmative action may be useful.

4.4.1 Equal Pay Legislation

Equal pay legislation implies that men and women in the same jobs should be paid the same wage. Both from a theoretical and a practical point of view such legislation is thought to be ineffective. Although equal pay is a step toward elimination of wage differentials, it also suppresses a market mechanism that helps women obtain greater access to jobs. If their wages are lower, women are more attractive for employers, and discriminatory employers will suffer in terms of loss of profits. Equal pay removes this competitive advantage. From a practical point of view equal pay for equal work is difficult to implement, since "equal work" is difficult to measure. Employers who want to discriminate between men and women will not suffer significantly from equal pay legislation. To eliminate labor market discrimination, legislation must require both equal pay and equal opportunities in hiring and promotions for people with comparable productivity.[7]

This is what happened in the United States where the Equal Pay Act of 1963 made it illegal for a firm to have separate pay scales for women and men doing the same job. It applied only to wage discrimination for the same job in the same firm and did not address discrimination in hiring, promotion, training programs, and so on. In 1964 Title VII of the Civil Rights Act was passed. This law explicitly prohibited discrimination by employers, employment agencies, or trade unions in the spheres of employment, wage practices, training, and union membership.

The goal of equal pay for equal jobs is sometimes implemented by adopting a comparable worth approach. Comparable worth policies rely, for example, on job-rating schemes to determine or justify pay differentials associated with various job titles or promotion steps. The process by which points are awarded to each job is obviously critical. The principle of comparable worth implies that women should be paid according to the intrinsic value of their jobs.[8] The main criticism of the comparable worth approach is that it ignores the situation in the labor market (i.e., supply and demand for particular workers). Sometimes wages in particular markets are low because of low demand and high supply and not because of discrimination.

4.4.2 Affirmative Action

Affirmative action policy regulates the allocation of scarce positions in education, employment, or business contracting so as to increase the representation in those

---

7. Women are often supposed to be confronted with a "glass ceiling," which is the name given to the set of subtle barriers believed by many to inhibit women and minorities from reaching the upper echelons of firms, governments, and academia.

8. One procedure to estimate the size of the adjustment to female wages that would be required to implement comparable worth is to augment the traditional earnings equation to include a variable measuring the percentage of an occupation that is female.

positions of persons belonging to certain groups (Fryer and Loury 2005). Affirmative action can be distinguished from other antidiscrimination policies by its requirement of proactive steps (Holzer and Neumark 2000). In an affirmative action plan the extent of the underutilization of women and minorities is analyzed, and a plan is made to remedy any such underutilization. This could go as far as reverse discrimination—or "positive" discrimination—for example, by hiring a less-qualified female or minority worker in place of a more-qualified white male. Reverse discrimination is motivated by arguing that it is necessary to correct for a history of past discrimination.

Affirmative action in the form of employment quotas may be problematic. If a firm wants or has to increase its share of workers from minority groups in general or for specific jobs, such as managers, this may not be easy. If turnover is low, it will take a long time to reach the goals. Also, the use of quotas is illegal in some countries, since discrimination is considered to be illegal, irrespective of whether it is positive discrimination. Aiming for quotas may lead to (un)intended discrimination against nonquota groups.

Affirmative action may not only affect discriminatory firms but also nondiscriminatory ones. An example is given in figure 4.7, in which male and female workers are assumed to be imperfect substitutes in the production process. The curve $\overline{y}$ represents the isoquantity curve, which shows all combinations of male and female labor that produce quantity $\overline{y}$. For a nondiscriminatory firm the minimum costs of producing $\overline{y}$ are given by point A, where the slope of the isocost curve BC is tangent to the isoquant. The slope of the isocost curve is equal to the ratio of male to female wages $\frac{w_m}{w_f}$. If the female wage goes down, more women will be employed. Affirmative action would force the firm to hire a predetermined share of women in the workforce, for example, represented by the line OG. Then the minimum production costs are at point D on the new isocost curve EF. Clearly, affirmative action forces this nondiscriminatory firm to produce the same output at higher costs.

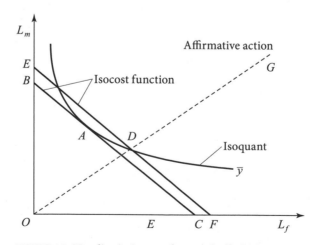

FIGURE 4.7 Nondiscriminatory firms and affirmative action

4.5 Interactions with Other Institutions

Antidiscrimination legislation is an institution that interacts with several other institutions, such as education and training, family policies, working hours legislation, EPL, and unions. To the extent that there is pre-market discrimination, a role exists for intervention perhaps at a young age. This may be more of an issue for ethnic discrimination when ethnic minorities are already disadvantaged at a young age. Individuals may underinvest in education in expectation of discrimination in the future. Smaller expected benefits will imply less investment. With respect to family policies, it could be that the gender wage gap discourages women from entering the labor market. Antidiscrimination policies might reinforce family policies that aim at increasing female labor force participation. Furthermore, there may be an interaction between antidiscrimination legislation and working hours legislation through part-time labor. Legislation that hinders individuals to work part-time may especially affect the labor participation of women and hence have a discriminatory impact. Finally, there is an interaction between antidiscrimination policy and EPL. A worker can be reinstated if a layoff appears to be discriminatory. The costs of layoffs may increase if there is a risk that a worker will start legal action against the employer for discriminatory action irrespective of whether this is actually the case. Unions may fight discrimination, but they may also represent some groups of workers more than others. For example, unions may oppose part-time work, and this opposition may go against the interest of women, who on average are more likely to work part-time.

4.6 Why Does Antidiscrimination Legislation Exist?

There are two main reasons for antidiscrimination legislation: equity and efficiency. According to Article 23 sub (2) of the Universal Declaration of Human Rights, everyone, without any discrimination, has the right to equal pay for equal work. From an economic point of view antidiscrimination legislation improves labor market efficiency through better allocation of workers to jobs and more generally, a better use of scarce resources. To assess the importance of antidiscrimination legislation, it is necessary to make a distinction between competitive labor markets and imperfect labor markets. In competitive labor markets discriminatory employers will be punished. This is different in imperfect labor markets, as some market power may be used to sustain discrimination against women or minority groups. The competitive nature of the labor market also determines the severity of discrimination by employers. In competitive labor markets it is the marginal employer who determines the relevance of discrimination. According to Heckman (1998) "there may be evil lurking in the hearts of firms that is never manifest in consummated market transactions." However, in imperfect labor markets it is the average employer that determines the severity of discrimination.

Blau et al. (2010) conclude that the direct effects of labor market discrimination may explain 40 percent or more of the pay differential between men and women. However, it is difficult to establish the magnitude of the effects originating from discrimination, if only because of the existence of feedback effects. Direct discrimination has to do with differences in economic outcomes, such as wage, employment position, and promotion, which are unrelated to productivity differences. To the extent that individuals are aware of the existence of discrimination against their group, they may react to it by investing less in human capital. Such feedback effects imply that estimates of direct effects of discrimination will be no more than a lower bound on the overall effect.

4.7 Suggestions for Further Reading

Chapter 3 in OECD (2008), "The Price of Prejudice: Labor Market Discrimination on the Grounds of Gender and Ethnicity," is informative about antidiscrimination legislation. The *Handbook of Labor Economics* contains various chapters on labor market discrimination. In particular, Joseph Altonji and Rebecca Blank (1999) provide an overview of theoretical work and empirical studies on race and gender in the labor market. Marianne Bertrand (2010) has a chapter about new perspectives on gender issues and discusses recent studies on differences in psychological traits between men and women. Roland Fryer (2010) has a chapter on racial inequality that discusses the declining significance of discrimination between black and white workers in the United States. Another recent survey of theoretical and empirical work on racial discrimination is offered by Kevin Lang and Jee-Yeon Lehmann (2012).

4.8 Review Questions and Exercises

1. Consider discrimination based on occupational crowding: what is the most important empirical prediction for the gender wage gap?

2. In a competitive labor market, what is the main difference between the short-run and long-run effects of taste-based discrimination?

3. What is statistical discrimination? What is the impact of statistical discrimination on the wages of affected workers? What happens if a test is a better predictor of productivity for white workers than for black workers?

4. Women may earn less than men because of wage discrimination. Sometimes this difference is related to the type of job. Men who work in "female jobs" may earn less than men who work in "male jobs." Explain why.

5. Explain Becker's taste theory of discrimination. Explain also why in this theory discrimination can be economically inefficient for firms.

6. Use a production function in which black labor and white labor are imperfect substitutes. Explain graphically how affirmative action can increase the production costs of a color-blind firm.

7. In Becker's discrimination theory, firms, workers, or customers may be prejudiced against women. Discuss the main differences between these three possibilities in terms of the effects on the gender wage gap.

8. Explain the difference between the coefficient of discrimination and the coefficient of market discrimination, and explain what happens if the two are different in size.

9. What is the main mechanism driving the gender pay gap in the monopsony model of wage discrimination?

10. A firm can use either white or black workers to produce output. The firm faces the following production function: $q = 10L_w + 10L_b$, where q is output, L_w is the number of white workers, and L_b is the number of black workers.

    (a) If the market wage for white workers is $W_w = 40$, market wage of black workers is $W_b = 35$, and the output produced by these workers sells for a price of 6, how many workers of each type will the firm hire if it expects to produce 100 units of output and is a cost minimizer?

    (b) If the firm is discriminatory and has a discrimination coefficient equal to 0.2, how many workers of each type would it hire?

    (c) What is the cost of the firm's discriminatory behavior in dollars?

11. The production function of a firm is specified as $q = 10\sqrt{L_m + L_f}$, where L_m and L_f are the number of male workers and female workers employed by the firm. Suppose that the market wage for female workers is 4, the market wage for male workers is 5, and the price unit of output is 8. The firm needs only labor to produce.

    (a) How many female workers and male workers would a nondiscriminatory firm hire? How much profit does this firm earn?

    (b) A firm discriminates against female workers with a discrimination coefficient of 0.2; how many female workers and male workers will this firm hire?

    (c) At what discrimination coefficient would a firm be indifferent between female workers and male workers?

    (d) A firm discriminates against female workers with a discrimination coefficient of 0.5; how many female workers and male workers will this firm hire?

12. Wages for males (w_m) and females (w_f) depend on years of schooling s and years of experience e:

    $$w_m = 200 + 10s + 5e$$
    $$w_f = 200 + 5s + 3e$$

    Men have on average 10 years of schooling and 14 years of experience. Women have on average 9 years of schooling and 10 years of experience.

    (a) How big is the gender wage gap?

    (b) Use the Blinder-Oaxaca decomposition to calculate what share of the gender wage gap is due to discrimination.

    (c) What share of the gender wage gap would be due to discrimination if we ignore experience?

13. (Advanced) Suppose that an employer has monopsony power over women but not over men. The labor supply curve of women is given by $L_f = w_f^{1/\eta}$. The labor supply curve of men is flat at w^*. In labor demand

$$\left(L_d = \left(\frac{A}{w}\right)^{1/\eta}\right),$$

men and women are perfect substitutes.

(a) Determine the equilibrium level of employment and wages for men and women.

(b) Show that both employment and wage for women go up if the wage for men goes up.

(c) What happens to employment and wages for women if the monopsony power over women goes up?

4.9 Technical Annex: Discrimination

4.9.1 Prejudice in a Competitive Labor Market

If employers prefer to hire male workers because they are prejudiced against female workers, they maximize their utility instead of their profits. As presented in the main text, the utility U an employer derives from employing female workers depends on the profit Π it makes and the wage costs it pays to women:

$$U = \Pi - \omega w_f L_f, \tag{4.10}$$

where L_f is the number of female workers hired, and ω is the *employer-specific coefficient of discrimination*, with $0 \leq \omega \leq \omega^{\max}$. If female and male workers are perfect substitutes, a discriminatory employer will hire either only male workers or only female workers. Female workers are hired if $w_m > (1 + \omega)w_f$. If this is the case, a utility-maximizing employer determines the optimal number of female workers to be hired through

$$\frac{\partial U}{\partial L_f} = \frac{\partial \Pi}{\partial L_f} - \omega w_f = 0. \tag{4.11}$$

Clearly, the larger the coefficient of discrimination ω is, the larger the difference between utility maximization and profit maximization will be. Therefore, the larger ω is, the lower the utility will be. If $w_m < (1 + \omega)w_f$, a discriminatory employer will only hire male workers and in this case,

$$\frac{\partial U}{\partial L_m} = \frac{\partial \Pi}{\partial L_m} = 0. \tag{4.12}$$

In this case, utility maximization and profit maximization are identical, and the magnitude of the coefficient of discrimination does not affect profits.

A discriminatory employer is indifferent between hiring a particular number of male workers or the same number of female workers if $w_m = (1 + \omega)w_f$. The employer is indifferent, since its utility does not depend on the gender composition of the workforce. However, the gender composition of the workforce has an impact on profits. Clearly, if the number of workers is the same, the profits from hiring female workers are substantially higher than the profits from hiring male workers.

4.9.2 Monopsony and Gender Discrimination

In a monopsony model the employer maximizes profits if the marginal hiring costs of male and female workers are equal to the value of the marginal product. If the labor supply curves of female workers are given by $w^f = L_f^{\varepsilon_f}$, the hiring costs of female workers are equal to $L_f^{\varepsilon_f + 1}$. Therefore, the marginal hiring costs of a female worker are equal to $(\varepsilon_f + 1)L_f^{\varepsilon_f}$. Similarly, the marginal hiring costs of a male worker are equal to $(\varepsilon_m + 1)L_m^{\varepsilon_m}$. Therefore,

$$(\varepsilon_f + 1)w_f = (\varepsilon_m + 1)w_m, \tag{4.13}$$

and

$$w_f = \frac{1 + \varepsilon_m}{1 + \varepsilon_f} w_m. \tag{4.14}$$

If the labor supply of women is less elastic, $\varepsilon_f > \varepsilon_m$, and therefore, $w_f < w_m$.

4.9.3 Unobserved Heterogeneity in a Correspondence Study

Heckman (1998) criticizes audit and correspondence studies, because they may generate spurious evidence of discrimination or lack of discrimination. Correspondence studies are able to make all observed characteristics between individuals of two groups identical and focus on the potentially discriminatory characteristic. However, correspondence studies do not take into account that the distribution of unobserved characteristics may differ between groups. Heckman provides the intuition of his criticism by presenting an example of black and white high jumpers. They both use the same equipment and have the bar set at the same level. The assumption is that the chance of a jumper clearing the bar depends on the observed person's height and the unobserved jumping technique. Black and white jumpers can be paired so that they have identical heights, but their techniques are not observed directly. Even if the mean jumping technique is equal for the two groups, the outcome may still be race dependent if the distribution of the jumping techniques is race specific. Assume for the sake of the argument that the variance in jumping techniques is larger among black jumpers. If the bar is set at a low level, most jumpers of a given height are likely to clear the bar, with the white jumpers being more likely to clear it. If the bar is set at a high level, then the black jumpers, who have a higher variance in jumping technique, will be more likely to clear the bar.

This line of reasoning can easily be demonstrated using a numerical example. Assume two groups A and B which have an unobserved ability that is distributed uniformly but with a different variance. The distribution of group A ranges from 1.5 to 2.5 with a mean of 2.0. The distribution of group B ranges from 1 to 3 with a mean of 2.0. The assumption is that callback depends on the distribution of unobserved ability and on the threshold for callbacks. We distinguish three situations:

1. *No discrimination* (same low threshold for A and B of 1.5). All individuals from group A will receive a callback, while only 75 percent of group B will receive a callback. No discrimination occurs, while the correspondence study would suggest that group B is discriminated against.

2. *No discrimination* (same high threshold for A and B of 2.5). None of the individuals from group A will receive a callback, while 25 percent of group B will receive a callback. No discrimination occurs, while the correspondence study would suggest that group A is discriminated against.

3. *Discrimination* (different thresholds for A and B). Group B is discriminated against, because for individuals from group B the threshold is 2.5, while it is 2.25 for individuals from group A. Nevertheless, the probability of receiving a callback is 25 percent for each individual, irrespective of whether they are from group A or B. Discrimination occurs, while the correspondence study would suggest no discrimination.

CHAPTER FIVE **Regulation of Working Hours**

Working hours have been a topic of heated debate between unions and employers for a long time. May 1, 1886, was a day of strikes and bloody riots in the United States for the introduction of an eight-hour working day. To commemorate the working-hours struggle between unions and employers, May 1 was declared Labor Day, which is still a holiday in many countries.

The discussion of the optimal length of the working day concerns wages, leisure, and productivity. Past decades have seen several clear trends in hours of work. Working hours per week have been declining slowly in the four decades from 1950 to 1990 but have remained constant in many countries more recently. Average working hours go down not only through a reduction of standard working hours but also through part-time work. Part-time work has been increasing in most countries, especially for women.

The regulation of working hours has three key dimensions. The first is the regulation of standard working hours. There are generally restrictions as to the maximum number of hours that can be worked within a week and the number of normal hours, so that any additional hour of work involves higher (overtime) pay. The second dimension concerns the barriers workers and employers face when choosing part-time work instead of a full-time job. There can be restrictions (e.g., imposed by collective bargaining) to the share of workers in a firm who are in part-time jobs, or fiscal disincentives to offering part-time jobs may exist. The third dimension relates to short-time work, that is, the schemes encouraging employers to reduce hours rather than the number of employees when experiencing a negative shock. These rules and regulations originated from government interference in private contractual arrangements or through collective agreements between unions and employers.

There are large cross-country differences in working hours: for instance, an average U.S. employee works about 15 percent more hours than a typical European worker. These wide differences in the allocation of time are not only a byproduct of the regulations discussed in this chapter. They also have to do with preferences and social customs. Indications as to the importance of these non-institutional factors come from in-depth analyses of the allocation of time not devoted to market work, drawing on time-diary or *time-use surveys*. Burda et al. (2008) document that Americans work more than Europeans also when account is made of nonmarket, home work, and such activities as gardening, care, and babysitting. We deal with *home production,* time allotted neither to work nor to leisure, in chapter 7.

5.1 Measures and Cross-Country Comparisons

The usual measure of the intensive margin of labor supply is the average number of working hours per week. This can be averaged over all workers or can be specified separately for full-time and part-time workers. Often the number of weekly working hours of part-time workers is roughly half the number for full-time workers. The choice concerning weekly hours of work is determined by workers' preferences, but the menu to choose from is determined by legislation and collective agreements. As discussed in more detail later, annual working hours are also strongly affected by the number of working weeks per year, since in some countries workers have many more holidays than in others.

Table 5.1 presents an overview of legal restrictions on weekly working hours. In many countries the legal maximum of a *normal* working week is 40 hours; in Denmark the maximum is as low as 37 hours. The maximum number of weekly *overtime* hours varies widely, from 2 in Spain to 16 in Switzerland, while several countries have no legal restrictions on the amount of overtime hours. There is also wide variation in the maximum number of total (normal + overtime) weekly hours. In some countries this legal maximum is not the sum of legal normal hours and legal overtime hours, because for a short period of time the maximum weekly overtime hours may sometimes be higher.[1] During overtime hours employers have to pay premiums that are usually in the range of 25 to 50 percent but in some countries may go up to 100 percent or even higher in case of night weekend work. Because of the overtime premiums, employers have an incentive to stick to normal working hours, but overtime hours allow employers to deal with temporary fluctuations in economic activity. The fourth column of table 5.1 shows that the normal weekly hours set by collective agreements are often substantially lower than the legal maxima of normal weekly hours.

Average working hours per employee are affected by changes in the *incidence of part-time,* that is, the fraction of dependent employment on part-time jobs. Cross-country differences in part-time work are determined by the characteristics of part-time jobs, for example, wages and prospects for promotion or on-the-job training. This induces more or fewer people to apply for part-time jobs. Labor demand is also important in determining the incidence of part-time: some sectors, notably services, may better accommodate than others the spread of part-time employment. Furthermore, taxes and social security contributions may affect the choices of employers as to the number of part-time positions in their firms. In countries like Italy social security contributions involved fixed costs for several years, making part-time jobs more costly than full-time jobs on a hourly basis. This regulation discouraged the spread of part-time employment and was supported by

---

1. For example, in Austria the usual legal maximum of weekly overtime hours is 5, but for 12 weeks per year it is 10.

TABLE 5.1 Legislative limits on normal weekly hours of work and overtime work

Country	Legal maximum on working hours			Bargained normal hours	Wage premium on overtime hours (%)
	Normal	Overtime	Maximum		
Australia	38–40	None	None	35–40	50
Austria	40	5	50	36–40	50
Belgium	40	10	50	38	50
Canada	40–48	None	None	35–40	50
Czech Republic	40.5	8	51	—	25
Denmark	37	None	48	37	50
Finland	40	5	45	37.5–40	50
France	39	9	48	39	25
Germany	48	12	60	35–39	25
Greece	40	8	48	40	25
Hungary	40	12	52	—	50
Ireland	48	12	60	38–40	25
Italy	48	12	60	36–40	10
Japan	40	None	None	40–44	25
Korea	44	12	56	—	50
Luxembourg	40	8	48	40	25–50[a]
Mexico	48	9	57	—	100
Netherlands	45	15	60	36–40	[b]
New Zealand	40	None	None	40	[b]
Norway	40	10	50	37.5	40
Portugal	40	12	54	35–44	50
Spain	40	2	47	38–40	[b]
Sweden	40	12	52	40	[b]
Switzerland	45 or 50	16	61 or 66	40–42	25
Turkey	45	—	—	—	50
United Kingdom	None	None	None	34–40	[c]
United States	40	None	None	35–40	50

Source: OECD (1998).

Notes: Bargained normal hours refer to normal weekly hours set by collective agreements; legislative wage premiums for overtime hours concern the first overtime hours worked during the week. — = not available.

a. Luxembourg has a 25 percent rate for blue-collar workers and a 50 percent rate for white-collar workers.

b. Has no legislation on overtime hours wage premiums.

c. Has a collectively bargained wage premium.

male-dominated unions opposing part-time jobs, considered to be inferior to full-time work. In most countries social security arrangements are nowadays neutral with respect to the choice between part-time and full-time jobs.

Most countries during the 2008–2009 Great Recession activated *short-time work* (STW) schemes, which had been in place before on a relatively large scale only in Germany, Italy, and Japan. STW encourages adjustment along the intensive margin in case of negative shocks by subsidizing hourly wages, so that employees do not suffer a reduction in their earnings as large as the reduction in working hours. STW differs from country to country in terms of the strictness of eligibility criteria, that is, the categorical or procedural conditions required to activate an STW scheme at the workplace: to reduce deadweight losses, in fact, firms must prove that they are facing negative demand shocks.

These cross-country differences are summarized in table 5.2. Most countries require an explicit agreement between the social partners or at least a consultation with workers; in some countries (e.g., Germany) worker councils can initiate STW. While some countries offer short-time work to all workers irrespective of their employment status (Denmark, Finland, Ireland, Spain, and the United Kingdom), workers qualify for STW only if they have a minimum contribution record in most countries. This prevents many workers with fixed-term contracts or part-time workers with few working hours to be eligible for STW. In the course of the Great Recession, these eligibility criteria were relaxed for workers with atypical contracts in many countries.

Beyond these eligibility criteria many countries impose entitlement conditions on users of STW, which set behavioral requirements on firms and workers participating in STW schemes. Some countries require that workers receiving STW benefits are obliged to participate in compulsory training measures (the Czech Republic, Hungary, the Netherlands, Portugal), while others provide subsidies for the participation in training programs (Germany). Moreover, most countries that finance STW by social security contributions require that workers participate in job search under the same rules designed for workers receiving UBs (Denmark, Finland, Germany, Ireland, Norway, and Spain). A few countries request that firms participating in STW schemes do not dismiss workers during the period they receive STW (Austria, France, Hungary, the Netherlands, and Poland), while other countries expect a business plan from participating firms (Belgium, Italy, Luxembourg, Poland, and Spain).

Some countries require that the use of STW is supported by a collective agreement or is at least approved by the unions when white-collar workers are involved. In some countries (e.g., Germany) worker councils can initiate STW. Other countries require that only workers otherwise eligible for unemployment insurance are involved and only if they have a minimum contribution record. This prevents many workers with fixed-term contracts or part-time workers with few working hours to be eligible for STW. Other eligibility conditions relate to the requirement that the scheme be applied to at least a significant portion of the total workforce (it should be a work-sharing device) and that the reduction exceeds a minimum fraction of the standard working hours. The rationale behind these minimum requirements is to allow only firms facing serious falls in demand to have access to STW. Ten out of the twenty countries having STW feature minimum hour requirements. Formal "justification of economic need" is also often required: firms must prove that they are facing negative demand shocks (e.g., by documenting some reduction in production or sales). It is a condition aimed at reducing abuse and associated deadweight losses. STW differs across countries also in terms of the strictness of entitlement criteria, that is, the conditions that have to be fulfilled by the firm or worker to *continue* to be eligible for STW. These provisions may include the obligation for the employer to provide training to short-time workers (as in the

TABLE 5.2 STW eligibility and entitlement conditions for STW schemes

Country	Eligibility conditions		Entitlement conditions			
	Justification of economic need	Social partner agreement	Compulsory training	No dismissal	Job search requirement for employee	Recovery plan
Austria	Yes	Yes	No	Yes	No	No
Belgium	Yes	BC: No WC: Yes (or business plan)	No	No	No	BC: No WC: Yes
Canada	Yes	Yes	No	No	No	No
Czech Republic	Yes	Yes	Yes	No	No	No
Denmark	No	Yes	No	No	Yes	No
Finland	Yes	Consultation	No	No	Yes	No
France	Yes	Yes	No	Yes	No	No
Germany	Yes	Yes	No	No	Yes	No
Hungary	Yes	No	Yes	Yes	No	No
Ireland	No	No	No	No	Yes	No
Italy	Yes	CIGO: No CIGS: Consultation	No	No	No	Yes
Japan	Yes	Yes	No	No	No	No
Luxembourg	Yes	Yes	No	No	No	Yes
Netherlands	No	Yes	Yes	Yes	No	No
Norway	Yes	No	No	No	Yes	No
Poland	Yes	Yes	No	Yes	No	Yes
Portugal	—	—	Yes	No	—	No
Slovak Republic	Yes	Yes	No	No	No	No
Spain	Yes	No	No	No	Yes	Yes
Switzerland	Yes	Individual Agreement	No	No	No	No
United States	Yes	Yes	No	No	No	No

Source: Hijzen and Venn (2011).

Notes: Justification of economic need = firms must provide a proof, such as a minimum reduction in production and/or business activity; Social partner agreement = an explicit agreement between the social partners is required; Compulsory training = workers have to participate in special training programs; No dismissal = prohibition of dismissal during participation in STW schemes; Job search requirement = workers are required to search for a job while participating in STW schemes; Recovery plan = firms must develop recovery plan. BC = blue collar; WC = white collar; CIGO = Cassa Integrazione Guadagni Ordinaria; CIGS = Cassa Integrazione Guadagni Straordinaria; — = not available.

Czech Republic, Hungary, Netherlands, and Portugal), the definition of a restructuring plan (Belgium, Italy, Luxembourg, Poland, and Spain), and the absence of dismissals throughout the period in which the firm is using STW (as in Austria, France, Hungary, Netherlands, New Zealand, and Poland). Some conditions may also apply to the employees: for instance, Denmark, Finland, Germany, Norway and Spain include job search requirements for the workers involved similar to those involving workers receiving UBs, although these workers are still formally on the payroll of the firm. Needless to say, some of these conditions are rather poorly enforced: job search requirements are, for instance, rarely enacted, notably during downturns. A third key feature of STW is the cost to the employers of activating this institution. In some countries, STW schemes are mainly funded by general tax revenues, while in others they are financed by social security contributions. Firms participate in the costs of STW benefits either by paying a part of the working costs for the hours not worked (e.g., France, Germany, Hungary, Japan, the Netherlands, Poland, Portugal, and the Slovak Republic) or by paying full wages for an initial period (e.g., Norway and Sweden). In some of these cases firms are obliged to pay the full amount or a part of the social security contributions for the hours not worked (e.g., Germany), which discourages abuse of STW. In other countries (e.g., Italy and the United States) bonus-malus arrangements are also envisaged, whereby employers making use of the scheme have to pay higher contributions (this method of partly internalizing the fiscal externalities associated with STW is also termed "experience-rating"). In most countries the replacement rate for the hours not worked (the percentage of the wages not paid when under STW that are replaced by the subsidy) equals the replacement rate of the UBs (see chapter 11). Since the average reduction of working hours is usually well below 100 percent, workers who participate in STW schemes are usually better off than their unemployed counterparts, in addition to still being formally attached to the firm. In some countries, hours reductions can be as high as 100 percent, putting the worker in a condition similar to a leave or a temporary layoff, although the worker is still on the firm's payroll.

5.2 Theory

5.2.1 A Perfect Labor Market

As usual, we start by characterizing a perfect labor market with competitive workers and firms. We shall see why employers must pay sometimes an overtime premium to elicit more work from their employees. This can be shown by considering again the labor/leisure choice analyzed in chapter 1 and the constraints imposed on this choice. Next we look at what drives decisions of employers to offer jobs with a fixed number of hours of work, that is, the choice on how to share the labor input between hours and workers.

5.2.2 Labor Supply: Overtime Pay and Availability of Part-Time Work

As discussed in chapter 1, individuals choose the number of hours they want to work on the basis of the hourly wage rate and their preferences for leisure, income,

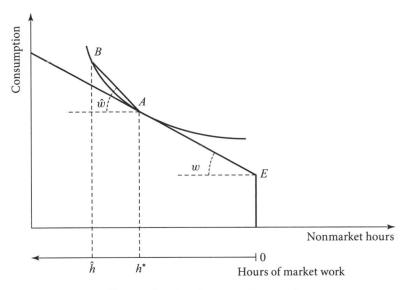

FIGURE 5.1 Choice of hours of work and the overtime premium

and home production. The preferred number of hours may relate to working hours per day, working days per week, workweeks per year, and working years over the lifetime. Individuals supply labor to obtain an optimal combination of income, nonmarketed goods and services produced at home, and leisure. Pool together the time spent either carrying out home production or enjoying leisure as non-market time. Individuals will supply working hours until the marginal value of nonmarket hours (relative to the marginal value of income) equals the wage rate. This is depicted in figure 5.1 where the horizontal axis from left to right gives the nonmarket hours, and from right to left the hours of work. The vertical axis indicates the total income, which partly consists of labor income and partly of income from other sources. The optimal choice of hours h^* is where the indifference curve is tangent to the budget constraint. Suppose that an employer wishes to induce the worker to supply more hours of work, say up to $\hat{h}$. To do so, she should pay the worker more, increasing the amount of goods that the worker can buy with an additional hour of market work. This is shown by the segment AB in figure 5.1, which is clearly steeper than the budget constraint. This higher wage rate $\hat{w}$, which has to be paid to the left of point A, allows the worker to remain on the same indifference curve as at the initial optimal choice, even after being requested to work more hours. The ratio of $\hat{w}$ to w (the slope of the segment AB relative to the slope of the budget constraint) is the overtime premium that has to be paid by the employer to convince the worker to supply more hours of work.

In reality the choice of working hours is often restricted to a limited set, most commonly full-time work, part-time work, and not working for pay. Under these conditions, workers can no longer maximize their utility as in the unconstrained choice depicted in figure 5.1. They will work for pay only if, by doing so, they can get to a higher indifference curve than the curve crossing the zero labor earnings locus (the kink of the budget constraint).

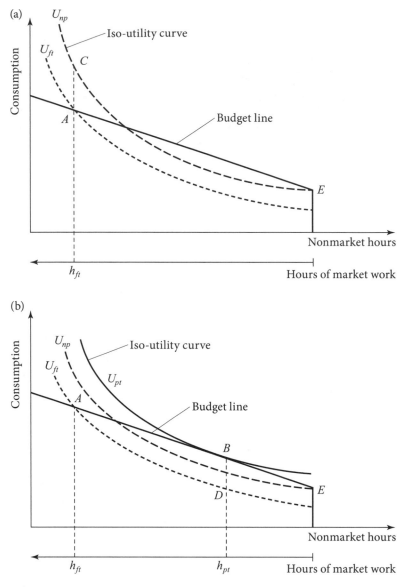

FIGURE 5.2 Choice of hours of work: (a) only full-time jobs available, choice is nonparticipation; (b) introducing part-time work, choice is participation

If a worker can choose only between a full-time job or no job, it may be that the reservation wage is too high for the worker to enter the labor market. This is shown in figure 5.2a. A worker who works for pay zero hours—a nonparticipant—is at point E, the endowment point where utility equals U_{np}. This worker could also work full-time and reach point A on the budget line EA—whose slope represents the wage—where utility equals U_{ft}. If the labor market offers only full-time jobs, the worker will prefer not to work, since $U_{ft} < U_{np}$. For this individual to work full-time, the wage would have to increase until the slope of the budget line would be at least equal to EC. However, if a worker can choose between a full-time job, a part-time job, or no job, it may be that the wage is sufficiently high to induce the worker to enter the labor market. This is the case in figure 5.2b, since at point B the worker derives a higher utility from the combination of part-time work and labor income than at points E and A. This worker will decide to enter the labor market as soon as it is possible to work part-time. In this case, the worker is looking specifically for a part-time job, and the segment BD measures the extent of the hourly wage reduction that the worker is willing to accept to get a part-time job instead of being forced to choose between working full-time or not working at all.

The above explains why the availability of part-time work is generally associated with higher participation rates: it allows persons with a higher reservation wage to obtain a relatively convenient combination of work and nonwork time. The womenization of employment was in many countries associated with the spread of part-time employment, as in all countries women are more involved than men in nonmarket activities related to home production.

For workers having a relatively low reservation wage—as for many prime-aged men who are the primary breadwinners in their families—part-time may be an involuntary choice. In figure 5.3 for instance, the worker can only choose to work part-time or not work for pay at all. By working instead full-time, the worker would attain a higher indifference curve than not working for pay (at the kink, point E, of the budget constraint) or working part-time (point A, at the intersection between the budget constraint and the part-time constraint). Notice that the worker would accept moving to a full-time job even at a discount in this case. Indeed, even at the lower hourly wage $\hat{w}$ (the slope of the AB segment), the individual would still be willing to move from a part-time to a full-time job. This condition is often referred to as *underemployment* or *involuntary part-time work*, and the difference between the market wage, w, and $\hat{w}$ provides a measure of the welfare loss of the part-time worker in this case.

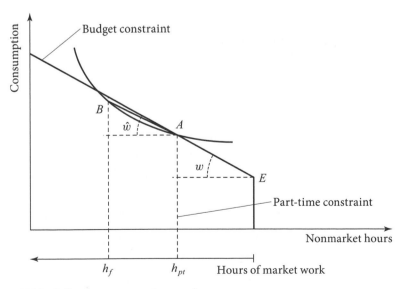

FIGURE 5.3 Involuntary part-time work

The number of hours of work is typically specified by the contract offered by the employer. Thus, we turn our attention to the labor demand side.

5.2.3 Labor Demand and the Choice between Hours and Workers

Profit maximization requires that employers use labor until the marginal value of an additional hour of work equals the wage costs, but they can achieve this targeted level of labor either by increasing the number of workers in the firm or by increasing the number of hours per worker. Hence it is important to characterize the choice of employers between hours and workers, extending the simple labor demand framework developed in chapter 1.

Suppose that firms produce output y, using only labor that requires some combination of workers L and hours of work h. In particular, assume that the production function is multiplicatively separable, that is, given by

$$y = Lh^{\alpha},$$

where $0 < \alpha < 1$. This functional form takes into account that production would be zero if either the number of hours or the number of workers is zero, and it allows for decreasing marginal returns to hours (i.e., working longer hours reduces productivity at the margin). The curve displaying the same level of effective labor input, the so-called *isolabor curve*, is depicted in figure 5.4. A special case is when reductions in hours worked per employee are equivalent to reductions in the number of employees from the standpoint of production technologies. This happens when $\alpha = 1$. In this case the isolabor curve is a hyperbola, and the elasticity of the labor input to hours and workers is always one.

While the isolabor curve displays all combinations of hours and workers enabling the employer to attain any targeted level of production, the *isocost of labor* curve displays all combinations of hours and workers that are equally costly for the employer. Labor costs C typically feature not only variable costs (the hourly wages, w times the number of hours h worked) but also fixed costs per worker, F (e.g., related to medical programs or fringe benefits provided independently of actual hours worked):

$$C = L(F + wh).$$

The optimal choice of the firm will combine hours and workers in such a way as to attain its targeted level of output at the lowest cost, that is, it will position itself where the isocost of labor curve is tangent to the isolabor curve corresponding to this targeted level of output.

As shown in technical annex 5.9, the optimal choice of hours of the firm is generally independent of the targeted scale of production, say $\overline{y}$, while this is not the case for the choice of workers. In other words, changes in the scale of production affect the number of workers but not the hours of work per employee. This is consistent with the observation in several industries (where firms possibly adopt the same type of technologies) of broadly the same number of hours worked per em-

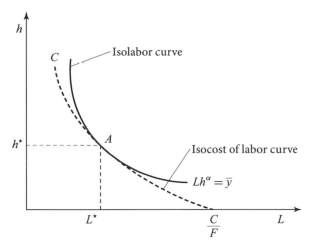

FIGURE 5.4 Isolabor curve (continuous curve) and isocost of labor curve (dashed curve)

ployee, independently of the size of the firms. By the same token, a reduction in costs required to match a decline in the targeted output level associated with an adverse shock will be accommodated by reducing the number of workers rather than by reducing the hours of work. This result, also formally proved in technical annex 5.9, stems from the production technologies allowing for substitutability between hours and workers as well as the presence of fixed costs per worker. As we will scc, this property of labor adjustment, together with labor market imperfections, provides a rationale for STW schemes and for the restrictions to working-time flexibility imposed in OECD countries.

5.2.4 An Imperfect Labor Market

In a perfect labor market, depending on sector-specific or firm-specific technologies, different employers would offer different combinations of hours and number of posts, and perfectly informed workers would choose according to their preferences among this choice set. If an employer offers a level of hours of work that is considered suboptimal by the worker, the latter can costlessly move to another firm with job characteristics better matching her preferences. In other words, even if the hours requirement of a job is determined unilaterally by the employer, the worker always has the option to exit. In this sense labor supply and the preferences of individuals matter at the equilibrium even with respect to the hours of work.

Real world labor markets, however, feature costs of mobility of workers across jobs. This gives some monopsonistic power to employers in the setting of hours of work, and it reduces the size of the labor market, forcing many potential workers to stay out of the labor market. Organized labor may react to monopsonistic power by imposing—through its monopolistic power—some combination of hours and workers that optimizes the preferences of the union workers, perhaps at the costs of leaving out of the market those workers with different preferences. Moreover, in an imperfect labor market there can be unemployment, and this unemployment is a source of welfare losses for the individuals involved and—in cases where UBs are offered to job losers (see chapter 11)—also for the taxpayers who have to pay for these transfers.

Under these imperfections, labor adjustment concentrated entirely on the number of workers rather than on hours may be socially, if not economically, very costly. STW and constraints on the maximum number of working hours are institutions for coping with these problems.

5.2.5 Short-Time Work

STW encourages reductions in working time by making adjustment along the intensive margin less costly for employers and workers. This is done by essentially subsidizing workers accepting a reduction in the amount of hours they work in such a way that their weekly or monthly wage is not affected "too much" by the reduction in hours. In other words, STW allows the effective hourly wage to increase for workers experiencing reductions in working time without, at the same time, preventing the firm from attaining substantial cost savings through the reduction in hours. As depicted in figure 5.5, an increase in the hourly wage from w to w_{st} could in principle compensate even a worker who is optimizing the hours-leisure choice before the reduction in working time. It is clearly a policy tool for dealing with temporary negative shocks hitting individual firms or aggregate shocks, such as a recession.

As discussed above, under fairly general characterizations of production technologies and costs of firms, employers tend to react to negative shocks by laying off workers rather than by reducing the number of hours of work for the average employee. This concentration of employment adjustment at the extensive margin leads to "excessive" job losses (Hall and Lazear 1984; Farber 1993; Hall 1995) during recessions or to shocks that temporarily reduce the demand for specific industries and firms. It would instead be both "more equitable and efficient" (Reid 1985) to reduce hours of work for everybody. The inefficiency of the adjustment along the extensive margin of the number of employees is related to the different degree of risk aversion of workers and firms. Workers are risk averse and would be better off by working fewer hours (and earning less) but avoiding job losses during downturns. Employers having access to capital markets are instead risk neutral and could in principle "sell" a form of insurance to their workers, which avoids job losses in exchange for lower wages throughout the employment relationship.

An additional source of inefficiency in labor adjustment, carried out along the extensive margin, rather than the intensive margin, of hours of work is related to the fiscal costs of dismissals (Burdett and Wright 1989; van Audendrode 1994): in the presence of UB systems, employers laying off their workers exert a negative fiscal externality by imposing a higher expenditure for UBs.[2]

---

2. The negative externality is reduced when UBs are experience-rated, as in the United States or Denmark. See chapter 11.

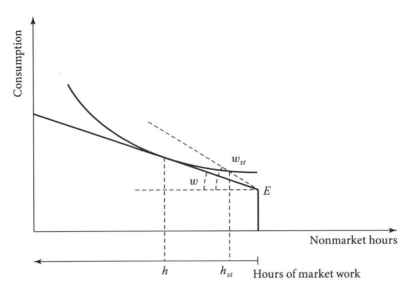

FIGURE 5.5 STW: compensating the worker for the reduction in working time

5.2.6 Regulating Weekly Working Hours

Governments often regulate working hours by imposing constraints on the decisions of firms. As discussed in section 5.1, generally these constraints are in terms of the maximum number of weekly hours of work. Regulations often also specify the number of *normal hours,* above which overtime premiums apply. Sometimes these regulations simply give a legal status (and hence stronger enforcement) to decisions already made within collective bargaining institutions. Workers' organizations trade higher wages for more leisure time; under some circumstances, a reduction in working hours increases the marginal product of labor (Marimon and Zilibotti 2000), giving more bargaining power to workers, so that they can also increase their wages. Of course, individual workers would like to deviate from the agreement and work longer hours at the higher wage, just as producers have an incentive to deviate from a cartel agreement. There are a number of cases where it is directly up to the government to set statutory maximum and normal hours of work. For instance, the EU Working Time Directive imposes a 48-hour weekly limit to hours of work, inclusive of overtime, and this regulation is also supposed to apply in countries where there are no limits established by collective bargaining over a relatively large set of occupations.

As the regulation imposes ceilings on working time, it bites only insofar as it forces employers to reduce the number of hours of work that they would have otherwise asked their employees to perform. These reductions are generally legitimized as measures reducing the monopsony power of employers and their overexploitation of workers. Under these conditions, shorter working hours may increase the standard of living of workers in line with their preferences. As shown by Manning (2004), in the presence of a monopsony not only is the wage rate less than the value of the marginal product, but also the firm can induce employees to work more than would be optimal given the monopsony wage. In the same way that a minimum wage can enhance welfare in the case of a monopsony, reductions in working hours can improve welfare in this context.

At the same time, reductions in working time force firms to produce without optimizing on workers' choice of hours. This, in turn, may induce employment losses even if the intention of the policymaker is the opposite: reductions in working time are generally introduced with the aim of forcing employers to substitute reduction of workers' hours for laying off workers.

The problem with the idea that reducing working time stimulates higher employment is that there is no such thing as a *lump of labor*, a fixed number of total hours of work demanded by firms, independently of government regulations and of the labor supply response to these changes (see box 5.1).

BOX 5.1

The Lump of Labor Fallacy

The *lump of labor theory* can be traced back to Mayhew's (1851) *London Labour and the London Poor*, in which he argued that reducing the number of working hours (per job) would create more jobs and reduce unemployment. This argument does not receive support from economic theory, and it is commonly considered a fallacy by economists (the so-called *lump of labor fallacy*). To illustrate this problem, consider the case where hours and workers are equally productive, and there are no fixed costs per worker. Under these conditions, both the isolabor curve and the isocost of labor curve would be hyperbolas and would coincide, as depicted in the box figure, part a. In this case, the combination of workers and hours per worker does not matter for the employer: only the product of the two matters. Indeed, there can be an infinite combination of hours and workers minimizing the costs of the employer. By the same token, the employer can move from one combination of hours per worker and number of workers to another combination without incurring any additional costs and without suffering any production loss. Suppose that initially all employees work h_1 hours, hence the firm needs L_1 workers to attain the targeted level of output. If the number of working hours per worker is reduced by government regulation to h_2, the firm will need L_2 workers: the working-time reduction has created new jobs for workers. This is the essence of the lump of labor argument.

Unfortunately, there are several factors that stand in the way of this simple characterization of the adjustment of firms to statutory reductions in the number of hours of work. Calmfors and Hoel (1989) listed five channels preventing firms from remaining on the same isolabor curve when forced to reduce working time by government regulations. First, hourly wages may increase, because workers want to protect their real income. As discussed while characterizing STW, employees typically require some compensation, in terms of an increase in hourly wages, to accept reductions of their working time. Second, even if hourly wages do not change, labor costs per unit of time may increase because of the presence of fixed costs per worker. To give an example, fringe benefits like company cars or mobile phones are independent of the number of hours worked.

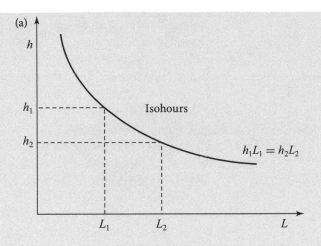

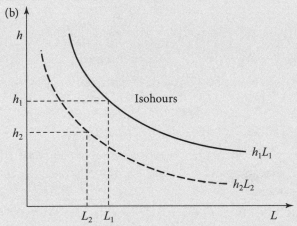

Changing standard working hours ($h_1 \rightarrow h_2$): (a) lump of labor; (b) No free lunch

Third, labor productivity may actually fall if nonproductive time—start-up and finishing work—remains constant. Thus, hours and workers are never perfectly substitutable from the technological standpoint. Fourth, the relative costs of adjusting along the intensive and extensive margins may change as a result of the aggregate, economywide, effects of the regulation. In particular, the costs of hiring new workers may rise relative to the costs of increasing working time when standard hours are cut. Finally, capital utilization may decrease if operating time is reduced parallel to working time. This will be typically the case if capital and labor are complements.

Thus, the statutory reduction in the number of hours per worker will almost unavoidably involve a reduction in the total number of hours, causing an inward shift to a lower isohours curve. This situation is depicted in the figure, part b, in box 5.1. Again the number of hours per worker is reduced from h_1 to h_2, but

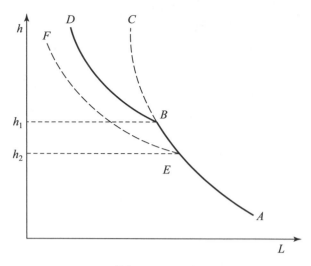

FIGURE 5.6 Isocost of labor curve with overtime premium

because the total number of hours worked falls from $h_1 L_1$ to $h_2 L_2$, employment falls from L_1 to L_2.

The Effects of Reductions in Standard Working Hours

So far, we have ignored the fact that overtime hours often pay a higher wage. In the presence of overtime, the isocost of labor curve will have a kink corresponding to the standard hours. Above that level, any extra hours of work will have to be paid for at a higher rate by the employer and hence will result in a stronger reduction in the number of employees to keep the costs of labor constant (figure 5.6). Without overtime premiums, the isocost of the labor curve is ABC. Supposing that h_1 is the standard number of working hours and there are overtime payments, there will be a kink in the isocost of labor curve at point B, and the new isocost of labor curve will be ABD. A reduction in normal (or standard) working hours enforced by government regulation would shift the kink from B to E, and the isocost of labor curve would become AEF.

As discussed in technical annex 5.9, in the presence of overtime premiums, mandatory reductions of standard working hours will have different effects on firms, depending on their initial location along the isocost of labor curve. There are three cases to be considered:

1. If hours of work are initially to the right of point E in figure 5.6, then the policy change has no effect on the decisions of the firm. Indeed, there is no modification in the portion of the isocost that is relevant for the firm.
2. If employees initially work overtime, that is, to the left of point B, then the reduction in standard hours causes the number of workers to fall, because employment of each individual worker becomes more expensive, while the price of marginal hours does not change. Therefore, firms will reduce their production levels.

3. If all employees initially are working exactly the standard hours (i.e., we are at the kink *B* of the initial isocost of labor curve), then, when the regulation takes effect, the firm finds itself in the overtime portion of the isocost curve. As the wage for the last hour goes up, the firm may reduce employment, hours, or both, depending on the slope of the isolabor curve (i.e., on the marginal productivity of hours and workers). The firm may increase or reduce employment levels, depending on whether it moves organization of work to the new kink or decides to pay the overtime premium. In other words, the effects are indeterminate. As theory has no clear predictions in this case, it is particularly important to look at the empirical evidence on the effects of mandatory reductions in standard working hours.

5.3 Empirical Evidence

5.3.1 Working Hours

Table 5.3 presents a long-term perspective on the annual number of hours worked by employees. For all countries listed, there was a substantial decline in the annual hours of work between 1950 and 2010. In 1950 workers in Ireland had the most annual working hours (2,762), while Swedish workers had the fewest (1,871). In 2010 Korean workers still worked 2,204 hours per year, whereas Dutch workers on average worked only 1,381 hours per year. Over the 60-year period the decline in annual working hours was strongest in Luxembourg; on average each year workers worked 16.5 fewer hours than the year before. The decline in annual working hours was smallest in Mexico, where, on average, each year workers worked 2.3 fewer hours than the year before.

Annual hours of work are influenced by the number of working hours per week and the number of workweeks per year. Table 5.3 also presents the anatomy of a typical workweek for employees in 2010. There is a wide range in weekly hours, from 31 in the Netherlands to 49 in Turkey. The low number of weekly hours in the Netherlands has to do with the high share of part-time employment (discussed later). Similarly, there is also a wide range in the number of workweeks per year, from a low of 36 weeks in Norway to a high of 48 weeks in Australia.

In some countries the reduction of standard working hours was mandatory. Through collective agreements in Germany the standard workweek was reduced from 40 to 36 hours between 1984 and 1994 (see Hunt 1999). In 1985 (West) German unions began to reduce standard hours on an industry-by-industry basis, stating that this was done in an attempt to reduce unemployment. In the late 1970s and early 1980s unions went on strike for shorter working hours. In 1984 the unions were successful, and the standard working week in the metalworking sector was reduced from 40 to 38.5 hours in 1985. In exchange for shorter working hours, the unions agreed to greater flexibility in the use of standard hours, which could vary daily within a week, from week to week, or across employees. The restriction was that, averaged over a period of time and across workers, the working week would consist of 38.5 hours. In her analysis to establish the extent to which work-sharing affected employment, Hunt (1999) used individual-level data from

TABLE 5.3 Average annual hours actually worked per worker (1950–2010) and the anatomy of a typical working year for employees (2010)

Country	Average annual hours		Average annual change (hours)	Anatomy of annual hours, 2010	
	1950	2010		Hours per week	Weeks per year
Australia	2,023	1,693	−5.5	36	48
Austria	2,405	1,663	−12.4	38	41
Belgium	2,337	1,546	−13.2	37	41
Canada	2,063	1,713	−5.8	—	44
Czech Republic	—	1,795	—	41	42
Denmark	2,145	1,536	−10.1	34	38
Finland	2,035	1,690	−5.8	37	39
France	2,098	1,439	−11.0	38	39
Germany	2,387	1,408	−16.3	36	41
Greece	2,712	2,017	−11.6	42	45
Hungary	—	1,947	—	40	43
Iceland	2,483	1,698	−13.1	39	40
Ireland	2,762	1,804	−16.0	35	43
Italy	2,469	1,778	−11.5	38	41
Japan	2,076	1,735	−5.7	—	—
Korea	2,358	2,204	−2.6	46	—
Luxembourg	2,492	1,504	−16.5	37	41
Mexico	2,217	2,077	−2.3	43	—
Netherlands	2,299	1,381	−15.3	31	42
New Zealand	2,045	1,700	−5.8	37	—
Norway	2,136	1,424	−11.9	34	36
Poland	—	2,050	—	41	43
Portugal	2,290	1,942	−5.8	39	42
Slovak Republic	—	1,749	—	41	44
Spain	1,960	1,674	−4.8	39	41
Sweden	1,871	1,624	−4.1	36	37
Switzerland	2,225	1,628	−10.0	—	43
Turkey	2,712	1,877	−13.9	49	—
United Kingdom	2,201	1,650	−9.2	36	41
United States	1,909	1,695	−3.6	—	46

Sources: Average annual hours: Groningen Growth and Development Center and the Conference Board, Total Economy Database, 2012 (www.ggdc.net); anatomy of annual hours: OECD (2010, p. 35).
Notes: The estimates for average annual working hours are intended to include paid overtime and to exclude paid hours that are not worked because of sickness, vacation, and holidays. Annual weeks worked equals 52 minus holidays and vacation weeks, absences due to nonholiday reasons, and absences due to sickness and maternity. — = not available.

the German Socioeconomic Panel and industry-level samples roughly covering 1984–1994. The main results concerning the effects of a reduction of the standard working week by 1 hour are the following. Actual working time declined by 0.9 hour, hourly wages increased by 2.2 percent, employment of women increased by 0.2 percent, and employment of men decreased by 1.2 percent. Therefore, actual working hours follow standard hours quite closely. Monthly wages were hardly affected by the reduction in working hours; workers bargained sufficient increases in their hourly wages to compensate for the reduction in working hours. Finally, the results suggest that reductions in standard hours caused employment losses among men.

In France the standard (mandatory) workweek was reduced from 40 to 39 hours in 1982 (see Crépon and Kramarz 2002 and box 5.2). Studies show that the reduction in the standard workweek also reduced the average number of hours worked weekly and increased the average wage rate, but total employment declined. In other words, work sharing held weekly incomes relatively constant but increased unemployment. In 1998 a Socialist French government introduced new mandatory restrictions on working hours with the deliberate goal of reducing unemployment. This attempt was also unsuccessful, although this time the employment costs were partly mitigated by large state transfers to firms reducing working time (see Estevão and Sá 2008 and box 5.3). While France had government-imposed reductions in working hours, Germany faced weekly working-hour reductions imposed as the outcome of negotiations between unions and firms. More recently these negotiations have opened up the possibility of longer working hours (see Kramarz et al. 2008). Andrews et al. (2005) analyze the German labor market using establishment data to investigate the effects of working-time reductions. They find no evidence of work sharing, that is, reductions in the length of the working week leading to more jobs. This finding is irrespective of whether firms operate with workers on standard hours, on overtime hours, or with a combination of the two. Kapteyn et al. (2004) analyze cross-country differences in level and developments—reductions—in actual working hours that they interpret as work sharing, assuming that the reductions in actual working hours are driven by changes in standard hours.[3] They find that work sharing has a significant positive long-run effect on the wage rate and a positive but insignificant long-run effect on employment. Kawaguki et al. (2012) analyzed reductions in standard working hours in Korea, finding that they did not increase time devoted to home production.

Mandatory Reduction of Working Hours in France

At the beginning of 1982 the workweek in France was reduced from 40 to 39 hours. Bruno Crépon and Francis Kramarz use labor force survey data to study the effects of this working-time reduction. One way to establish the effects of working-time reduction is to compare the employment losses of two groups of workers. The first group consists of workers who worked 40 hours per week, the second group of workers who worked 39 hours. The first group was affected by the mandatory

---

3. Indeed, there is ample empirical evidence that actual hours follow standard hours. The analysis of Kapteyn et al. (2004) is based on data from 16 OECD countries during 1960–2001.

reduction of working hours; the second group was not. The employment losses cumulated over two years were as follows:

Length of workweek	Employment loss (%) 1982–1984	1985–1987	Difference (%)
40 hours	16.5	11.9	4.6
39 hours	12.6	12.1	0.5
Difference (%)	3.9	−0.2	4.1

Whereas shortly after the introduction of the 39-hour workweek the first group experienced an employment loss of 16.5 percent, the second group faced an employment loss of 12.6 percent, a difference of 3.9 percentage points. A couple of years later, in 1985, the difference in employment loss between the two groups was only 0.2 percentage points. Under a difference-in-differences approach, this result suggests that the mandatory reduction of working hours caused an employment loss of 4.1 percent for the workers working 40 hours per week. All in all, Crépon and Kramarz (2002) find an impact of annual employment losses between 2 and 4 percentage points. A special feature of the French situation was that hourly minimum wages were increased shortly before the workweek reduction. For minimum wage workers already employed, the nominal weekly wage was fixed, while for newly hired minimum wage workers, the weekly wage was based on the new working week of 39 hours, causing them to be 2.5 percent cheaper than workers already employed. Minimum wage workers were obviously most affected by the reduction of the workweek. Crépon and Kramarz conclude that for low-wage workers the annual probability of losing their jobs increased by 8.4 percentage points.

Source: Crépon and Kramarz (2002).

BOX 5.3   *Effects of the 35-hour Working Week*

Estevão and Sá (2008) investigated the effects of the policy of mandating 35 hours per week pursued by the French government in 1998. The policy actively promoted by the Labor Minister Martine Aubry used a mixture of sanctions and incentives to induce firms to reduce working hours to 35 hours per week with the deliberate goal of reducing unemployment. The policy allowed for a gradual increase in the new norms. In particular, the so-called Aubry I law of June 1998 set the length of the workweek to 35 hours, effective February 2000 for firms employing more than 20 people and January 2002 for smaller firms. A second law—Aubry II—of January 2000 reduced the overtime premium for small firms and increased their annual limit to overtime work compared with large firms. This way, small firms could continue operating on a 39-hour basis, paying the difference with a reduced overtime premium. Social security contributions were also reduced to contain the effects of these provisions on labor costs. Estevão and Sá (2008) used the gradual enforcement of the restrictions (firms with more than 20 employees were supposed to comply by February 2000, while those with fewer employees were given two additional years to adjust to the 35-hour week) to analyze the effects of this policy.

Unlike previous studies (e.g., Crépon et al. 2005), they could look at several effects of the policy changes going beyond the simple employment effects. In particular, they also considered the effects on dual-job holdings, wages, and transitions from large to small firms. They used data from the French labor force survey (Enquête Emploi) from 1993 to 2000. Firms with 20 or fewer employees were used as the control group, while the medium-sized firms (those with more than 20 but fewer than 49 workers) were used as the treatment group. The following table illustrates the fraction of employees working less than 35 hours, in firms with 20 or fewer and more than 20 employees, respectively.

Year	Small firms (%)	Medium-sized firms (%)	Difference (%)
1997	25.5	24.6	−0.9
1998	26.3	25.9	−0.4
1999	27.1	27.6	0.5
2000	31.4	43.6	11.2
2001	34.3	52.1	17.8
2002	57.3	64.4	7.1

As expected, the increase occurs in large firms in 2000, while in small firms there is a jump in the proportion of employees working 35 hours in 2002. This indicates that the choice of the treatment and control groups is accurate. Estevão and Sá (2008) investigated the effects of the policy on wages (either hourly or monthly), employment (level, inflow, and outflow), multiple job holdings, and self-reported job satisfaction. Their results, displayed below as differences with respect to 1997 levels, show that the law increased the proportion of employees with more than one job and increased transitions from large to small firms. As Estevão and Sá put it, their results "cast serious doubts on whether the reduction in hours benefited French employees."

Year	From employment to unemployment		Share of workers with multiple jobs (%)		Hourly wage (%)		Monthly wage (%)	
	Men	Women	Men	Women	Men	Women	Men	Women
1998	0.8	0.1	0.1	−1.1	0.9	−0.4	0.2	−0.4
1999	3.9	−0.5	−0.1	0	2.1	−1.7	0.6	0.2
2000	2.7	0.6	0.7	−0.03	3.4	1.3	0.5	−0.4
2001	1.0	2.1	−0.1	−0.2	3.7	2.0	1.1	−0.8
2002	1.4	−1.2	0.04	−0.03	3.0	0.0	0.3	0.1

Note: All values expressed as differences with respect to 1997 levels.

Source: Estevão and Sá (2008).

5.3.2 Part-Time Work

An overview of part-time employment is given in table 5.4. In 2011 part-time work among men was most common in the Netherlands, where more than 17 percent of male employees worked part-time. Also in Denmark, Ireland, and Australia many men worked part-time. In the Czech Republic, Slovak Republic, Hungary, and

TABLE 5.4 Part-time employment (%)

Country	PT employment		Involuntary part-time		Part-timers preferring FT		Full-timers preferring PT	
	Men	Women	Men	Women	Men	Women	Men	Women
Australia	12.6	37.4	37.9	26.8	—	—	—	—
Austria	5.9	32.8	11.9	7.3	—	—	—	—
Belgium	7.1	33.6	16.0	9.7	31	25	9	36
Canada	11.9	25.6	29.4	26.1	—	—	—	—
Czech Republic	1.6	6.1	12.4	17.6	—	—	—	—
Denmark	14.3	25.4	10.4	12.8	69	8	7	21
Finland	8.2	15.2	19.5	30.5	—	—	—	—
France	5.7	22.4	26.6	28.4	69	35	11	25
Germany	8.1	38.3	20.8	12.9	52	12	5	10
Greece	6.8	15.1	41.7	34.9	33	25	8	9
Hungary	3.4	6.3	35.1	31.5	—	—	—	—
Ireland	12.8	39.2	38.0	22.7	78	30	8	12
Italy	6.2	32.6	44.8	39.6	83	42	22	32
Japan	—	—	22.0	19.2	—	—	—	—
Korea	—	—	—	—	—	—	—	—
Luxembourg	4.3	29.6	8.1	8.1	—	—	—	—
Netherlands	17.1	61.6	6.7	5.0	25	7	13	23
New Zealand	10.6	32.6	27.2	18.7	—	—	—	—
Norway	10.9	30.1	6.1	5.9	—	—	—	—
Poland	3.6	11.1	15.6	14.6	—	—	—	—
Portugal	3.1	9.9	22.0	39.8	100	40	7	2
Slovak Republic	3.2	6.0	68.7	53.4	—	—	—	—
Spain	5.6	22.6	67.5	54.9	36	37	8	14
Sweden	8.6	17.8	21.0	21.9	—	—	—	—
Switzerland	8.3	44.1	—	—	—	—	—	—
Turkey	2.7	8.0	—	—	—	—	—	—
United Kingdom	10.5	38.1	27.0	12.2	72	22	3	9
United States	8.4	17.1	13.7	10.3	—	—	—	—

Source: Online OECD database.

Notes: Part-time employment is measured counting the persons who usually work less than 30 hours per week in their main job. It is measured as a percentage of dependent employment (2011); involuntary part-time employment is the percentage of part-time workers who state that they are working part-time because they could not find a full-time job (2011); part-timers who prefer to work full-time and full-timers who prefer to work part-time (1994). FT = full-time; PT = part-time; — = not available.

Luxembourg hardly any men worked part-time. Among women the variation in part-time work is much larger. Whereas in the Czech Republic, Slovak Republic, and Hungary fewer than 10 percent of female employees had a part-time job, in the Netherlands more than 60 percent of female employees worked part-time.

In theory, part-time employment is negotiated between workers and employees. In the same way that nonstandard working hours provide flexibility to both sides of the labor market, part-time employment enables employers to meet staffing and production requirements and enables employees to match working hours with family life. For employers, part-time jobs may be attractive because they also are often temporary jobs, creating much flexibility to adjust the workforce. According to Jaumotte (2003), there are at least three reasons for firms to offer part-time jobs. The first reason concerns optimal staffing. Part-time jobs make it easier for firms to match workers to a changing workload because of demand peaks during the day or during the week. The second reason is to have cheap and flexible workers: part-time workers typically have lower hourly wages and less employment protection. The third reason is related to vacancies. Some vacancies cannot be filled or some workers cannot be retained if no part-time jobs are offered. However, this is not the case in every country. In some countries part-time jobs have all the ingredients of full-time jobs except the weekly working hours. Nevertheless, a choice for part-time work is not always voluntary for workers. Some employees work part-time involuntarily when they would prefer to have a full-time job. Table 5.4 gives an overview of the share of involuntary part-time work among part-time workers. Both for men and women, the Netherlands has a low proportion of involuntary part-timers, while Spain and the Slovak Republic are at the other extreme. The United States has a relatively low share of involuntary part-time, perhaps because full-time employees work longer than in most countries. Table 5.4 also indicates to what extent full-time and part-time work are in line with personal preferences. To the extent that individuals working part-time would prefer to work full-time, there is underemployment; to the extent that individuals working full-time prefer to work part-time, there is overemployment. Here too the cross-country differences are quite large. In Portugal all men working part-time would prefer to work full-time, while in the Netherlands only 7 percent of the women working part-time prefer to work full-time. There are also large gender differences in the share of individuals working full-time who prefer to work part-time.

There is a clear negative relationship between the incidence of part-time work for women and the share of women who work part-time involuntarily. This is shown in figure 5.7. In Finland, in 2011, where only about 15 percent of women worked part-time, 30 percent of them worked part-time involuntarily. In the Netherlands, where 61 percent worked part-time, only about 5 percent worked part-time involuntarily. Apparently, in a situation where there are many part-time workers, part-time work is more attractive. This may have to do with unions being more interested in representing part-time workers once their number is large enough. Or it may be that part-time work can only grow if it is sufficiently attractive for workers.

Another reason for the fact that involuntary part-time is lower when the incidence of part-time is higher is that part-time increases labor supply per any given labor demand, lowering the equilibrium wage rate. Under these conditions persons who were before working full-time may decide to move to part-time jobs. Nevertheless, there is concern that part-time jobs marginalize women in the labor market when part-time jobs are characterized by poor wages and benefits, low job tenure, and absence of training, reducing women's prospects of promotion and putting them at higher risk of dropping out of the labor force.

On the basis of an international overview of part-time work, OECD (2001) concludes that hourly earnings in part-time jobs are lower than in full-time jobs, and employer-provided training is less frequent in part-time jobs than in full-time

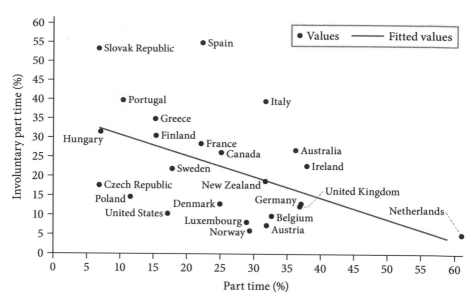

FIGURE 5.7   Part-time and involuntary part-time work of women

jobs. Nevertheless, many part-time workers, especially women, have no desire to work full-time. Similarly, many full-time workers prefer to work part-time but have no opportunity to do so.

Garibaldi and Mauro (2002) investigate employment growth in 21 OECD countries. They find that the increase in part-time work in many countries is not associated with net gains in total hours of work. The exception is the Netherlands, where the strong employment growth is largely accounted for by a net increase in part-time jobs in the service sector taken by women aged 25–49. The result for the Netherlands is confirmed by van Lomwel and van Ours (2005). They investigate the relationship between the growth of part-time work and growth of total employment in the Netherlands and find that the two developments are strongly related: the growth of part-time labor is at least partly responsible for the "Dutch employment miracle."

Manning and Petrongolo (2005) perform a cross-EU-country analysis of the pay penalty related to part-time jobs. They find evidence of this penalty, with the United Kingdom having the highest part-time pay penalty, making it difficult for women to move between full-time and part-time work without occupational demotions. At the same time, they also find that part-time work in the United Kingdom carries a higher job satisfaction premium than in most other countries. Apparently, women experience part-time jobs as having compensating wage differentials. Perhaps part-time jobs allow women to combine work and care, and therefore the lower wages attached to part-time jobs do not cause job dissatisfaction. This is consistent with the framework proposed in figure 5.1: just as workers require compensation to work more, they can also accept a reduction in their hourly wages to better conciliate work and nonwork time (home production and leisure).

Buddelmeyer et al. (2005) study recent developments in part-time work in EU countries. They find that part-time employment is significantly affected by institutions and policy. Both the legal framework affecting part-time positions and the creation of financial incentives (subsidies and improvement of social protection) to take a part-time job are important.

In a sequence of studies Booth and van Ours investigate preferences of partnered women for part-time work. Part-time jobs are common among partnered women in many countries. There are two opposing views on the efficiency implications of so many women working part-time. The negative view is that part-time jobs imply wastage of resources and underutilization of investments in human capital, since many part-time working women are highly educated. The positive view is that, without the existence of part-time jobs, female labor force participation would be substantially lower, since women confronted with the choice between a full-time job and zero working hours would opt for the latter.

Booth and van Ours (2008) investigate the relationship between part-time work and hours-of-work satisfaction, job satisfaction, and life satisfaction in Britain. It turns out that men have the highest hours-of-work satisfaction if they work full-time without overtime hours, but neither their job satisfaction nor their life satisfaction are affected by how many hours they work. Women present a puzzle. Hours satisfaction and job satisfaction indicate that women prefer part-time jobs irrespective of whether these are routine or challenging, but their life satisfaction is virtually unaffected by hours of work. Booth and van Ours (2009) investigate the relationship between part-time work and family well-being in Australia. They find that part-time women are more satisfied with working hours than full-time women are and that women's life satisfaction is increased if their partners work full-time. Male partners' life satisfaction is unaffected by their partners' market hours but is increased if they themselves are working full-time. Booth and van Ours (2013) investigate whether in the Netherlands, where the majority of partnered working women have a part-time job, part-time work is likely to be a transitional phase that will culminate in many women working full-time. Their results indicate that partnered women in part-time work have high levels of job satisfaction, a low desire to change their working hours, and live in partnerships in which household production is highly gendered. Taken together, these results suggest that part-time jobs are what most Dutch women want.

5.4 Policy Issues

5.4.1 Should Governments Regulate Working Hours?

Regulation of working hours may originate from a bargaining agreement between unions and employers or through government intervention.[4] If regulation

---

4. Here we only discuss regulation of the number of working hours, not the timing of working hours over days or weeks. This timing is an issue, for example, for shop opening hours and concerns coordination of leisure activities across individuals (within the same family). Governmental regulations face a trade-off between economic efficiency and welfare attached to the collective enjoyment of free time (see Burda and Weil 2008).

is through a bargaining agreement, governments usually do not have any reason to intervene, as unions would coordinate heterogeneous preferences of members and internalize externalities associated with different working-time regimes. If such a bargaining agreement does not exist, there may be an efficiency reason for governments to intervene and impose working-hours regulations. This may be the case if employers have monopsony power. Just as a small increase in the minimum wage may have positive employment effects, but a large increase may reduce employment, there may be a small range of working-time reductions that can lead to an increase in employment, whereas a large reduction will be at the expense of employment. The explanation of this phenomenon is in the noncompetitiveness of the labor market. Because of monopsony or bargaining power, labor market imperfections arise that can only be balanced through government intervention (as in the case of a minimum wage; see chapter 2).

However, some governments want to influence working hours on the basis of the idea that reducing working hours will increase demand for workers and thus lower unemployment. To the extent that this is the driving force, there is no urgent need for governments to interfere. One of the few issues on which economists agree is that employment is not a lump of labor that can be redistributed without costs. On the contrary, mandatory reductions of working hours are often imposed at the expense of employment.

A century ago there may have been good reasons for the government to counter the monopsony position of employers by introducing mandatory reductions in working hours, increasing overall welfare. Nowadays it is difficult to find strong arguments for government intervention. Mandatory reductions of working hours are still advocated as an instrument to reduce unemployment, possibly because this policy seems to come as a free lunch. If the lump-of-labor story held, governments could reduce unemployment without much effort. Because this is not the case, there does not seem to be an important reason for governments to interfere in the labor market and regulate working hours.

5.4.2 Should Governments Subsidize STW?

During the Great Recession, many countries introduced STW schemes and others expanded the scope of existing programs. Table 5.5 provides some information on the scale of STW before and during the Great Recession in the countries for which this information is available and meaningful cross-country comparisons can be carried out. In particular, three measures of the scale of these programs are provided. The first measure is the number of participants as a percentage of all employees. Some short-time workers may reduce hours of work by a very small amount, and yet they would be counted by this measure just like workers involved in a 100 percent reduction in hours. The second measure involves some adjustment for the actual hours of reduction: it is based on an estimate of the number of full-time equivalent (FTE) jobs involved in these schemes, normalized by the population of full-time employees. The estimate of the FTEs draws on information collected by Hijzen and Venn (2011) on the average reduction of

TABLE 5.5 The scale of STW programs

| Country | Average quarterly take-up rates (%) | | | | | |
| | Stock of participants over total (dependent) employment | | FTE over full-time employees | | STW hours over total hours worked | |
	2007	2009	2007	2009	2007	2009
Austria	0.0	0.7	0.0	0.2	0.0	0.2
Belgium	3.2	5.6	1.8	3.0	1.4	2.4
Canada	0.0	0.3	0.0	0.1	0.0	0.1
Finland	0.4	1.7	0.4	2.0	0.4	1.5
France	0.4	0.9	0.1	0.2	0.1	0.2
Germany	0.1	3.2	0.2	1.8	0.0	1.1
Italy	0.7	3.3	0.7	3.2	0.4	2.0
Japan[a]	0.0	2.7	0.0	1.1	0.0	0.7
Norway	0.1	0.6	0.1	0.2	0.1	0.7
Switzerland	0.0	1.1	0.0	0.5	0.0	0.4

Sources: Data on short-time workers drawn from Hijzen and Venn (2011); data on total hours worked and employment from OECD.

Notes: FTE take-up rate = (stock of participants into STW × average hours reduction)/ (full-time employees + STW full-time equivalents). STW hours over total hours calculated as follows: total STW hours/(previous five-year average of total hours worked in the economy + total STW hours), where total STW hours = (STW FTEs × average number of hours worked by a full-time worker in a year). FTE = full-time equivalent.

a. Japan 2007 refers to 2008:Q2.

hours in different STW schemes. Finally, the third measure takes hours of STW over total hours worked in the previous five years (a proxy for standard hours at the aggregate level).

As shown in the table, in many countries these schemes were rather insignificant in 2007, while they had climbed to relatively high levels by 2009. In Belgium, Germany, Italy, and Japan between 2.5 and 6 percent of the workforce participated in STW schemes at the trough of the recession. Finland and Switzerland also enrolled in these schemes more than 1 percent of the labor force and up to 2 percent of the total hours worked under normal business conditions. Were these schemes successful in reducing job losses during the recession? Focusing in particular on the German and Italian experiences, Boeri and Bruecker (2011) investigated the employment effects of STW during the Great Recession. Their results suggest that for severe recessions, STW contributes to saving jobs. Similar results were obtained by Cahuc and Carcillo (2011). However, the number of jobs saved is generally smaller than the number of persons involved in the schemes, and deadweight costs are likely to rise substantially for milder recessions. Thus, it is very important that STW is made responsive to changes in macroeconomic conditions. Experience rating and cofinancing by the employers of a significant share of the costs of the instrument are crucial in this respect. At the same time, high costs for employers reduce take-up rates and may end up increasing the tax burden on firms at just the time when they need to be encouraged to hire more. One possible way out of this problem is to let average contribution rates increase during upturns, allowing accumulation of a surplus, which could then be used to finance a reduction in contribution rates during downturns. Moral hazard problems are also likely to be less important during a recession, when most firms have to reduce the labor input. The specific design features of STW also matter in setting the scale of these programs. Thus, the relevant policy issue is not whether to have an STW in place, but which type of STW, if any, should be adopted. After all, most OECD countries already have some form of STW scheme by now.

5.5 Interactions with Other Institutions

The regulation of working-hours institution has clear relationships with collective bargaining institutions (see chapter 3), because unions typically bargain about working hours and wages, trading pay increases with adjustments of working hours. Unions representing mainly prime-aged men, for instance, may oppose the development of part-time work, as this would increase labor supply, reducing hourly wages, and does not match preferences of the members of the unions. The level of bargaining may also affect regulations on working time. In countries with decentralized bargaining structures, collective bargaining covers hours, employment, and wages (as in the efficiency bargaining models), unlike national agreements, which can be meaningfully negotiated only over pay. This may reduce the scope for government regulations of working time when collective bargaining is decentralized.

Working-hours regulations also bear a strong relationship with family policies (see chapter 7), because the presence of part-time work allows the combination of work and family responsibilities.

There is also a clear relationship between working-time regulations and EPL (see chapter 10), because strong EPL induces firms to adjust employment through the intensive margin rather than through the extensive margin. Boeri and Bruecker (2011) find that take-up rates of short-time work are larger in countries with high costs of dismissals, as employers find it more convenient to reduce working hours than to lay off workers in this context.

Boeri and Bruecker also find that STW is negatively associated with the generosity of UBs (see chapter 11), as the latter reduce costs of employers to use the extensive margin of labor adjustment. At the same time STW may work as an extended period of UB and hence be partly a substitute for the latter.

It should be finally stressed that working time is affected by many other regulations besides those setting maximum hours, overtime pay, and STW. For instance, according to Prescott (2004), Ohanian et al. (2006), as well as Rogerson (2009), transatlantic differences in hours of work can be largely explained by differences in tax rates. Although these interpretations of the fact that Americans work longer hours than Europeans neglect adjustments along the extensive margins (e.g., higher youth unemployment in Europe) and would imply implausibly large wage elasticities of labor supply (Blundell et al. 2011), there is little doubt that payroll taxes (chapter 13), together with culture and social customs (Blanchard 2004) do affect significantly choices along the intensive margin.

5.6 Why Does Regulation of Working Hours Exist?

The determination of hours of work is rarely the outcome of a market process. Market failures occur for several reasons, in particular, because preferences of workers and employers are conflicting or because of institutional restrictions. Workers' preferences with respect to weekly working hours, for example, may vary greatly, and providing individualized contracts may be too costly for employers. Employers may prefer that working hours vary considerably over a week because of peak hours in the production process, and accommodation may be too costly for workers (if only for social reasons). There may be institutional restrictions on hours of work because unions and employers have bargained a specific number of working hours per week, have agreed on an annual number of holidays, or have provided opportunities for workers to retire early. Negotiations about working hours cannot always be left to unions if these represent the interests of their members only. Sometimes governments influence hours of work for social reasons (family life) or because they want to influence the level or composition of unemployment (early retirement schemes).

5.7 Suggestions for Further Reading

Pietro Garibaldi and Paolo Mauro (2002) provide a general analysis of employment growth that investigates the importance of part-time work. Alan Manning and Barbara Petrongolo (2005) compare job satisfaction and part-time wages across OECD countries. One of their surprising findings is that in Britain women who work part-time have higher job satisfaction despite their lower wages. The book *Working Hours and Job Sharing in the EU and USA: Are Europeans Lazy? Or Americans Crazy?* edited by Boeri et al. (2008) provides interesting information about labor-leisure choices, working hours, part-time work, and the functioning of labor markets. Chapter 4 of the 2010 *Employment Outlook* of the OECD (2010) is devoted to part-time employment. Finally, Vera Brusentsev and Wayne Vroman (2012) offer an overview of STW schemes in OECD countries.

5.8 Review Questions and Exercises

1. Under what conditions does work sharing lead to an increase in employment, and how plausible are these conditions?

2. Why do firms employ part-time instead of full-time workers?

3. How do fixed hiring costs affect the trade-off between hours and workers?

4. How does overtime work affect the trade-off between hours and workers?

5. What happens if the standard working week is reduced in a situation where workers work overtime? And if the workers were working just normal hours?

6. Why are hourly earnings for part-time jobs often lower than for full-time jobs?

7. Why do overtime premiums exist?

8. How does STW affect employment adjustment during recessions?

9. Give an explanation for the cross-country negative correlation between the share of involuntary part-time work and the share of part-time jobs in total employment.

10. Illustrate the hours-workers trade-off.

    (a) What happens when there is an overtime premium?

    Suppose now that there is no choice in terms of hours.

    (b) Show graphically what happens to the reservation wage of a single individual in this case.

    (c) How does this reservation wage change when part-time jobs are introduced?

    (d) Can this explain why unions oppose the introduction of part-time jobs?

11. Suppose that hours and workers in a firm are combined in such a way that the isolabor function is $y = L\sqrt{h}$, where L denotes the number of workers, and h is the number of hours.

    (a) Display the isolabor curve and compute the elasticities of labor with respect to L and h.

    Suppose further that labor costs are given by $C = L(F + wh)$, where w is the hourly wage, and F denotes fixed costs per worker.

    (b) Obtain the cost-minimizing choice of hours and workers for a given level of output, say, $\bar{y}$.

    (c) Interpret the results, notably, the relationship that the two factor demand functions have with the scale of production.

12. (Advanced) Let the isolabor curve be $y = g(L, h) = Lh^{\alpha}$, where L denotes workers, h is hours, and y is an arbitrary constant. There is an overtime premium ω, so that the cost of production is given by

$$C = \begin{cases} (F + wh)L & \text{if } h \leq \bar{h} \\ [F + \omega(h - \bar{h})]L & \text{if } h < \bar{h}, \end{cases}$$

where $\bar{h}$ denotes normal hours.

    (a) Derive the optimal levels of h and L if there is no overtime premium.

    (b) Derive the optimal levels of h and L when $\omega > 0$.

    (c) Display graphically the cases $h^* < \bar{h}$, $h^* = \bar{h}$, and $h^* > \bar{h}$.

5.9 Technical Annex: Intensive and Extensive Margins

To analyze the effects of a reduction in standard hours, two components of the cost of labor are important. First, for every worker there are fixed costs $F > 0$ that are independent of working hours. These are mainly the costs of medical insurance, holiday pay, social security contributions with a binding ceiling, or, in a dynamic setting, hiring and firing, as well as training costs. Second, every overtime hour worked above the standard is compensated at a higher rate. The total labor costs of a firm are therefore

$$C = (wh + \omega w(h - \overline{h})d + F)L, \tag{5.1}$$

where C is the total labor costs of the firm, w is the hourly wage, h is the actual weekly working hours, ω is the hourly overtime premium, $\overline{h}$ is the standard work-week, d is a binary variable that has a value of 1 if $h \geq \overline{h}$ and a value of 0 otherwise, and L is the number of workers in the firm.

For simplicity we assume that wages are constant, workers are identical, and production y depends only on hours and workers,

$$y = Lh^{\alpha}, \tag{5.2}$$

where $\alpha \leq 1$. We are interested in interior solutions, so that h^*, the optimal number of hours, exceeds standard hours $\overline{h}$. For any given level of production $\bar{y}$, the firm minimizes labor costs Λ, solving

$$\min_{L,h} \Lambda = (wh + \omega w(h - \overline{h})d + F)L + \lambda(\bar{y} - Lh^{\alpha}), \tag{5.3}$$

where λ is the Lagrange multiplier. From the first-order condition $\frac{\partial \Lambda}{\partial L} = 0$, we find that

$$wh + \omega w(h - \overline{h})d + F = \lambda h^{\alpha}, \tag{5.4}$$

and from $\frac{\partial \Lambda}{\partial h} = 0$, we find that

$$w(1 + \omega d)L = \lambda \alpha L h^{\alpha-1}. \tag{5.5}$$

Taking the ratio of both equations yields

$$\frac{\alpha}{h} = \frac{w(1 + \omega d)}{wh(1 + \omega d) - \omega w \overline{h} d + F}. \tag{5.6}$$

After some rewriting, we find the optimal number of hours,[5]

$$h^* = \frac{\alpha(F - \omega w \overline{h} d)}{(1 - \alpha)w(1 + \omega d)}, \tag{5.7}$$

5. Notice that this condition holds when fixed costs are sufficiently large, that is, $F > \omega w \overline{h} d$.

and the optimal number of workers,

$$L^* = \bar{y} \left(\frac{\alpha(F - \omega w \bar{h} d)}{(1 - \alpha)w(1 + \omega d)} \right)^{-\alpha}.$$ (5.8)

From these two optimal conditions we can derive the following results:

Effects of changes of	on hours (h^*)	on employees (L^*)
$\bar{y}$	0	+
F	+	−
$\bar{h}$	−	+

In words:

1. If the scale of production increases, working hours are unaffected and employment increases.

2. If the fixed costs of employment increase, the hours per worker increase and the number of workers declines.

3. If the standard number of working hours goes down, the hours per worker increase and employment goes down.

Result 1 is very important in understanding the rationale for STW schemes. Without STW, cost-minimizing employers facing a reduction of the scale of production (e.g., during a recession) will tend to reduce the number of workers rather than the hours of work. Result 2 is fairly intuitive, insofar as F is the only cost component independent of hours. Result 3 is somewhat counterintuitive. It indicates that reducing standard working hours reduces employment and that in a firm with overtime hours, reductions of standard hours increase hours of work. This happens as initially $h^* > \bar{h}$.

If a firm is initially operating below standard working hours ($h < \bar{h}$), then a reduction in standard hours, say $\bar{h}_1 < \bar{h}$, does not affect the choice of the firm, provided that $h^* < \bar{h}_1$. If $\bar{h}_1 < h \le \bar{h}$, the firm will reduce working hours, and it may be that employment increases.[6] If the working-hours reduction affects productivity, wages, and levels of production, the employment effects depend on the magnitude of the changes in wage costs and production. If only wages increase—without productivity increase or, worse, with a productivity decline—in addition to demand for labor going down, the incentives to substitute workers by hours will increase even further. Finally, if initially $h^* = \bar{h}$, then the effect on both hours and workers is ambiguous.

---

6. Note that without overtime hours, $\frac{\partial C}{\partial h} = wL$, while with overtime hours, $\frac{\partial C}{\partial h} = (1 + \omega)wL$. If standard hours of work are reduced to a level below actual working hours, the marginal cost of an additional hour of work increases. This induces firms to reduce hours of work.

CHAPTER SIX Early Retirement Plans

E arly retirement occurs when the retiring individual is still of working age. Unlike other flows from employment to inactivity, retirement decisions tend to be irreversible, inducing permanent declines of the labor force in any given cohort of individuals. From a historical perspective, large-scale retirement of workers is a rather recent phenomenon. Until the beginning of the twentieth century, not many workers retired. They worked as long as they could, and if they stopped working, retirement often involved a few years of dependence on children at the end of life. In the course of the twentieth century retirement programs were introduced in all industrialized countries. Today, retirement is typically an extended period of self-financed independence and leisure, and in many countries workers are even forced to retire because of a mandatory retirement age. The presence of early retirement programs in many countries makes it possible for workers to retire even long before the mandatory retirement age, so there is a gap between the statutory and the effective retirement age. This gap arises for a variety of reasons: the existence of early retirement programs, professions in which the official retirement age is lower than the standard age (e.g., civil servants, teachers, police, the armed forces, and firemen), and the use of unemployment insurance and disability programs by those who may not be incapable of work (Pestieau 2003).

Many studies indicate that older workers strongly respond to incentives to retire early. Gruber and Wise (1997) conclude, on the basis of an analysis of 11 industrialized countries, that there is a strong correspondence between the age at which retirement benefits are available and departure from the labor force. Retirement decisions are a typical example of individuals optimizing on the basis of constraints provided by the institutional structure.

In many countries the labor market attachment of older workers is low. Early retirement is an important exit route for older workers to leave work, but it is not the only one. Older workers may become disabled or sick, or they may become unemployed. Sometimes UBs (Finland and Spain), disability benefits (Australia, Austria, Ireland, the Netherlands, Norway, and the United Kingdom), and long-term sickness benefits (Czech Republic, Norway, and Sweden) are used as pathways to early retirement (OECD 2006c). In some countries older unemployed workers face less demanding search requirements or are even exempted from looking for work.

6.1 Measures and Cross-Country Comparisons

Early retirement is generally financed through a *pay-as-you-go* (PAYG) system, where current workers are taxed to pay for current retirees. There is, in other words, an intergenerational transfer—from the current workers to the current pensioners—involved in these schemes. The PAYG systems are not well adapted to future demographics, because in many countries the population is aging. Unlike funded systems (individual financial accounts, where individuals put their own savings for old age), PAYG systems are put under strain not only when longevity increases (hence pensions have to be paid for a longer period of time) but also when fertility declines. Pension programs are either *defined benefit* (DB) or *defined contribution* (DC). DB systems typically define the final pension as a function of the length of employment attachment and final earnings. Other than the risk of becoming unemployed, which reduces the length of employment attachment, there is no risk for the worker concerning the replacement of earnings provided by pension benefits; this replacement level is guaranteed. In DC systems the contributions to a pension fund are defined, but the level of retirement benefits depends on lifetime contributions. DC systems typically require that the entitlements acquired at retirement be transformed into annual payments. This *annuitization* also involves some risk, because it is related to the current level of interest rates. Another factor affecting annuitization is the year of retirement: later retirement leads to higher annuity rates. For this reason DC systems tend to induce higher retirement ages than DB systems do (see also box 6.1).

BOX 6.1   *DC and DB Systems and the Retirement Decision*

Pension wealth is the present value of the stream of expected pension benefits. Supposing that pension benefits are constant at level B for the entire period in which the individual draws benefits (from the date of retirement to death) and denoting by a the date of the (early) retirement, we can define the pension wealth PW as

$$PW(a) = \sum_{t=a}^{T} \frac{B(a)}{(1+i)^{t-a}} = B(a) + \sum_{t=a+1}^{T} \frac{B(a)}{(1+i)^{t-a+1}}, \tag{6.1}$$

where i is the rate at which future pension benefits are discounted.

If she instead decides to work an additional year, until the age $a+1$, her pension wealth would be

$$PW(a+1) = \sum_{t=a+1}^{T} \frac{B(a+1)}{(1+i)^{t-a+1}}. \tag{6.2}$$

Thus, the benefit accrual BA is given by

$$BA(a+1) = PW(a+1) - PW(a) = -B(a) + \sum_{t=a+1}^{T} \frac{B(a+1) - B(a)}{(1+i)^{t-a}}. \tag{6.3}$$

Now, suppose that we are in a DB system where the pension benefit is established as a fixed proportion of the final earnings and the individual is in a flat wage-tenure profile. It follows that in this case

$$B(a + 1) = B(a) = B; \qquad (6.4)$$

hence

$$BA(a + 1) = -B. \qquad (6.5)$$

In other words, the worker suffers a loss in her pension wealth by postponing retirement. Consider now a DC system where

$$B(a + 1) = B(a)(1 + \xi), \qquad (6.6)$$

where ξ is the change in the annuitization (in the yearly pension amount) brought about by an additional year of work. For large T, $BA(a + 1) \simeq -B + \frac{\xi B}{i}$. Thus, a sufficient condition for $BA(a + 1)$ to be positive is that $\xi > i$, that is, the benefit accrual associated with an extra year of work is higher than the market interest rate.

In recent years *notionally defined contribution* (NDC) systems were introduced in several countries (Italy, Latvia, Sweden, and Poland). At the time of writing, plans to move in this direction are being made in Norway, while Germany has adopted some of its features (see Börsch-Supan and Jürges 2006), and even in France there is a discussion about the pros and cons of adopting an NDC system (see Holzmann and Palmer 2006; Legros 2006). NDC systems are the new conventional wisdom on retirement plans and are now recommended by international organizations as a blueprint for other countries to follow (Holzmann and Palmer 2012 and Whitehouse 2011). The idea behind an NDC retirement scheme is to bring a PAYG system to mimic a financial account scheme in which workers contribute during their working lives and draw (defined) benefits after retiring. Unlike financial account schemes, however, contributions to an NDC system are not invested in financial assets, and hence the returns on these contributions do not depend on stock market or bond returns. The system is notional in that contributions flow to the national social security administration, which uses them to cover current pension benefits: it is still a PAYG scheme. The returns on these defined contributions are determined in such a way as to guarantee solvency of the scheme; in particular, such returns are generally approximated by the growth rate of GDP or wages (the tax base of NDC, as social security contributions funding current pensions are paid as a proportion of gross wages). Once a worker retires, the total capitalized value of his/her lifetime contributions is transformed into a real annuity: the pension benefit. This annuity depends, among other things, on the life expectancy at retirement and hence on the retirement age. The specific features of an NDC system and its relation with the labor market are described in more detail in box 6.2.

BOX 6.2

Notionally Defined Contribution and the Labor Market

An NDC system is a PAYG pension scheme, in which contributions made during the working years are treated as if they were accumulated into a pension fund invested in assets. Contributions are typically proportional to labor earnings (floors and ceilings on contributions may apply), but they do not go to an actual fund or individual account, and thus do not receive a market return. They are only notionally accounted as if they were deposited in a fund, and the returns on these contributions are determined by law, using proxies to establish system solvency that are often linked to the growth rate of the economy or contribution base. Upon retirement, individuals who contributed to the system acquire pension rights on the pension wealth accumulated over their working years. This pension wealth is then converted into an annuity—the pension benefit—according to a benefit formula. The following two equations provide a basic representation of how pension benefits are calculated in an NDC pension system:

$$B = \tau \sum_{t=t_0}^{a-t_0} w_t \prod_{j=t_0+1}^{a-t_0-1} (1+r_j^w)\frac{1}{\gamma} \tag{6.7}$$

$$\gamma = \sum_{t=a}^{T}(1+\delta)^{a-t}, \tag{6.8}$$

where B is the pension benefit, τ is the contribution rate on the labor earnings w_t, $a - t_0$ is the number of years of contributions (the age of retirement a minus the age at which the individual starts working, t_0), r^w is the rate of return on the contributions, γ is the inverse of the conversion (annuitization) coefficient, δ is an imputed indexation rate, and T is the expected length of life.

Equation (6.7) shows that pension benefits depend on the accumulated pension wealth and the conversion coefficient. The pension wealth is obtained by accumulating every year pension contributions τw_t, according to a rate of return on contributions r^w. At retirement, these accumulated contributions are converted into a stream of incomes (the pension benefits) through the (inverse of the) conversion coefficient γ. As shown by (6.8), this coefficient depends on the average expected longevity at retirement and on an indexation rate δ that regulates the returns on the pension entitlements. Finally, notice that the age of retirement affects both equations by modifying the number of working years a as well as the length of the retirement period T.

The *pension wealth* of a worker is the present value of the stream of expected pension benefits. The difference between the pension wealth at retirement age, a, and at retirement age, $a + 1$, is the *benefit accrual*. The ratio of the accrual to the net wage earnings is an implicit *tax* on earnings (if the accrual is negative) or an implicit *subsidy* to earnings (if the accrual is positive). A negative accrual stimulates retirement, while a positive accrual stimulates continuation of work.

TABLE 6.1 Standard age and earliest age of entitlement to public old-age pensions; pension replacement rate

Country	Earliest (Men) 1969	Earliest (Men) 2001	Earliest (Men) 2011	Standard (Men) 1969	Standard (Men) 2011	Standard (Women) 1969	Standard (Women) 2011	Pension replacement rates (%) Men	Pension replacement rates (%) Women
Australia	65	55	60	65	67	60	67	65.9	63.2
Austria	65	65	62	65	65	60	65	89.9	89.9
Belgium	60	60	60	65	65	60	65	66.0	66.0
Canada	66	60	60	66	65	66	65	61.5	61.5
Czech Republic	—	58.3	60	—	65	—	62/65	72.5	72.5
Denmark	67	65	n.a.	67	67	67	67	94.5	94.5
Finland	65	62	62	65	65	65	65	64.8	64.8
France	60	60	56	65	60	65	60	60.8	60.8
Germany	65	63	63	65	67	65	67	58.4	58.4
Greece	60	60	60	60	65	55	65	110.3	110.3
Hungary	—	62	63	—	65	—	65	99.5	99.5
Iceland	67	65	62	67	67	—	67	111.7	111.7
Ireland	70	65	n.a.	67	66	70	66	40.8	40.8
Italy	55	57	61	60	65	55	60	76.2	63.0
Japan	60	60	60	65	65	65	65	41.4	41.4
Korea	—	55	60	—	65	—	65	51.8	51.8
Luxembourg	62	60	57	65	65	62	65	96.2	96.2
Mexico	—	65	60	—	65	—	65	46.9	46.9
Netherlands	65	60	n.a.	65	65	65	65	103.3	103.3
New Zealand	60	65	n.a.	65	65	65	65	49.6	49.6
Norway	70	67	62	70	67	70	67	62.3	62.3
Poland	—	65	n.a.	—	65	—	60	68.2	50.7
Portugal	65	55	55	65	65	65	65	65.5	65.5
Slovak Republic	—	60	60	—	62	—	62	72.9	72.9
Spain	65	60	61	65	65	55	65	84.5	84.5
Sweden	63	61	61	67	65	67	65	53.3	53.3
Switzerland	65	63	63	65	65	62	64	66.4	65.5
Turkey	60	60	n.a.	65	65	55	65	98.0	98.0
United Kingdom	65	65	n.a.	65	68	60	68	48.0	48.0
United States	62	62	62	65	67	65	67	53.4	53.4

Sources: Duval (2003); OECD (2011a).
Notes: Pension replacement rates concern *net* replacement rates for mandatory retirement programs of full-career workers with average earnings. n.a. = early retirement is not allowed in any part of the pension system; — = not available.

Table 6.1 shows that until 2001 the earliest age of entitlement to public old-age pensions (first three columns) went down or remained unchanged in most countries. In the last decade, however, several countries have increased the earliest age of retirement in an attempt to contain public pension outlays. The tightening is more visible in terms of standard age of retirement (next four columns). The

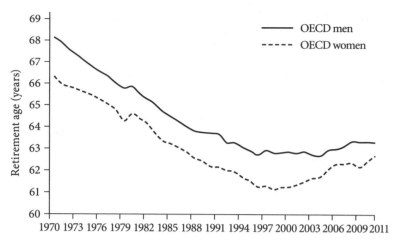

FIGURE 6.1 Average effective retirement age in OECD countries

Source: OECD online statistics; estimates based on national labor force surveys; and, for earlier years in some countries, national censuses.

Note: Included countries: Austria, Belgium, Canada, Denmark, Finland, France, Germany, Greece, Iceland, Ireland, Italy, Japan, Luxembourg, the Netherlands, Norway, Portugal, Spain, Sweden, Switzerland, Turkey, the United Kingdom, and the United States.

most common standard age of entitlement to public old-age pensions is still 65. For men there is less variation than for women. By 2011 the standard retirement age was highest in the United Kingdom (68) and lowest in France and Poland (60). The incentives to retire vary greatly across countries. The net replacement rate for public old-age pensions (mandatory retirement programs) for full-career workers on average earnings is more than 100 percent in Greece, Iceland, and the Netherlands, but about 40 percent in Ireland, Japan, and Mexico.

The evolution over time of the effective average retirement age in OECD countries is displayed in figure 6.1. This shows that actual retirement decisions of individuals have been closely following the evolution of early retirement rules. In particular, the reduction of earliest retirement age in the 1970s and 1980s provoked a drastic decline in the actual retirement age in the OECD countries, which dropped by about five years, from 68 to 63 years old for men, and from 66 to 61 years old for women. The subsequent increase in the legal retirement age since the mid-1990s in many countries induced an increase also in the effective retirement age, above all for women.

6.2 Theory

In the theoretical literature on optimal retirement, the concept of *option value* is frequently used. Pension plans often provide a large bonus if the individual works until a certain age, typically the early retirement age. If the worker retires before that age, the option of a later bonus is lost. Continuing to work preserves the option, hence the terminology "the option value of work." The main characteristic of the option value model is that a person will continue to work at any age if the expected present value of continuing work is greater than the expected present value of immediate retirement (Stock and Wise 1990). A person will postpone retirement if the option value of work is positive and will retire as soon as this option value becomes negative. In other words, a worker will retire when the value of continuing work falls below the value of retiring. The option value of working will decrease as the age of the individual comes closer to the optimal retirement age. The decline in option value does not have to be smooth. For instance, if an individual becomes eligible for an early retirement option at a particular age, there is a negative shift in the option value of working at that age. In making a retirement decision, a person takes future income from work and retirement into account (see technical annex 6.9 for details on the option value model).

The determinants of the decision to retire are a mix of push and pull factors (OECD 2006c). The *push* factors restrict the available set of attractive job opportunities open to older workers and consist of the true or perceived imbalance between wage and productivity for older workers, problems that firms face in adjusting their labor force due to EPL, lack of incentives to invest in human capital to avoid skills obsolescence, bad health, and constraints on changing working hours. The *pull* factors primarily consist of financial incentives that make it attractive for workers to retire. These financial incentives concern both old-age pensions and early retirement programs.

Retirement decisions are the outcome of individual optimization in the context of an institutional framework. The effect of the type of pension on retirement age is rather straightforward. In a DB system an individual who continues to work adds to the level of pension benefits in two ways. First, the length of labor market attachment increases. Second, if the wage increases with labor market tenure, the end salary increases. The increase in future pension benefits induces individuals to stay in the labor market. As soon as an individual reaches the standard or early retirement age, there is often no longer an increase in the expected pension benefits, while if an individual keeps on working, the number of pension years is reduced. This provides strong incentives to retire.[1] In DC systems continuation of work also leads to higher benefits, because there is an additional contribution to the pension fund and the annuity rate increases. The incentives to retire in both DB and DC systems will depend on specific design features, as the devil is very much in the details (Banks and Smith 2006). However, in presence of a flat (or even declining) wage-tenure profile (i.e., wages not increasing as the worker enters the ages where she could possibly retire) a DC system tends to encourage a higher retirement age than a DB system. This difference is explained analytically in box 6.1. Figure 6.2 drawn from Boeri and Brugiavini (2008) displays the pension wealth of a woman with median earning and career profiles in Italy before and after the 1996 pension reform that involved a switch from a DB to a DC system. As shown by the figure, pension wealth under the pre-reform regime was

---

1. Note that as long as the level of pension benefits depends on the final salary, workers have little incentive to reduce their number of weekly working hours shortly before retirement.

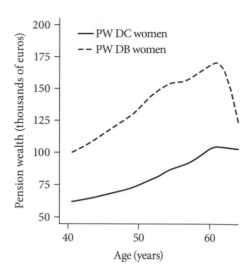

FIGURE 6.2 Pension wealth under the pre-reform (DB, dotted line) and post-reform (NDC, continuous line) rules by age for working women in Italy
Source: Boeri and Brugiavini (2008).

higher at all ages than under the new regime. At the same time, the DB system encouraged retirement before reaching the age of 60, as after that age pension wealth falls dramatically, while the DC system is relatively flat after the age of 60, meaning that it becomes rather neutral with respect to the decision about the retirement age.

6.3 Empirical Evidence

6.3.1 Age and Employment

Table 6.2 shows the effects of the introduction over past decades of early retirement programs; the average age of transition to inactivity went down considerably. Between 1967 and 2002 this age went down by as much as 14.8 years for Turkish men, but also in countries like Hungary and Poland the decline in retirement age for men was substantial. For women the largest decline occurred in Hungary and Poland. Only in Korea and, for women, in Italy was there an increase in the average age of transition to inactivity, but starting from low levels. Notice that all this happened just while longevity was increasing roughly at 2.5 years per decade. In other words, working lives were getting shorter and shorter as lives were getting longer and longer.

Figure 6.3 shows 2010 employment rates for prime-aged (aged 25–54) and older (aged 55–64) women and men. Concerning prime-aged workers, two stylized facts arise from these diagrams. First, the range in employment rates is much smaller for men than for women. Second, in every country employment rates are higher for men than for women. The differences are smallest for the Scandinavian countries, which have high rates for women, and largest for southern European countries, where female employment rates are relatively low. For men, there does not seem to be a strong correlation between the employment rates of prime-aged and older workers. Apparently early retirement policies differ consid-

TABLE 6.2 Average age of transition to inactivity

	Men (years)			Women (years)		
	1967	2002	Change	1967	2002	Change
Australia	67.3	63.2	4.1	67.7	60.6	7.1
Austria	—	62.6	—	—	59.4	—
Belgium	64.2	61.2	3	63.5	61.9	1.6
Canada	66	63.1	2.9	61.4	61.4	0
Denmark	—	63.2	—	—	61.4	—
Finland	69.3	62.3	7	62.2	61.1	1.1
France	67.3	60.3	7	66.8	59.8	7
Germany	—	62.6	—	—	61.9	—
Greece	68.1	61.3	6.8	64.5	61.6	2.9
Hungary	70.5	60.1	10.4	69.5	58.7	10.8
Iceland	—	69.5	—	—	67.8	—
Ireland	—	63.5	—	—	64.7	—
Italy	64.3	60.8	3.5	59.6	59.8	−0.2
Japan	72.2	69.6	2.6	68.9	65.7	3.2
Korea	67.1	68	−0.9	65.5	66.7	−1.2
Luxembourg	66.1	58.1	8	66.1	57	9.1
Netherlands	—	63.9	—	—	63.1	—
New Zealand	—	64.2	—	—	62.2	—
Norway	68	63.0	5	69.2	63.3	5.9
Poland	73.4	61.4	12	72.4	57.5	14.9
Portugal	—	62.9	—	—	62.3	—
Spain	—	61.2	—	—	63.4	—
Sweden	69.3	64.7	4.6	67	64.0	3
Switzerland	72.5	64.8	7.7	73	62.2	10.8
Turkey	77.3	62.5	14.8	63.1	61.8	1.3
United Kingdom	—	64.1	—	—	62.0	—
United States	69.9	65	4.9	68.6	62.9	5.7

Sources: OECD estimates derived from the European and National Labor Force Surveys. Austria, Belgium, Poland, Portugal, and Italy (women), 2007; Ireland, 2006; Luxembourg, 2003; Australia, Canada, Iceland, Japan, Korea, New Zealand, Turkey, United States, 2002.

Notes: The average effective age of retirement is derived from observed changes in participation rates over a five-year period for successive cohorts of workers (by five-year age groups) aged 40 and older. — = not available.

erably from country to country. Indeed, the cross-country range in employment rates for older men is substantial, from a low of 40 percent in Hungary to a high of 85 percent in Iceland. For women, there is also variation in early retirement regimes, but a clear positive correlation also exists between the employment rates of prime-aged and older workers, as highlighted by the upward-sloping regression line.

Older workers who want to stop working have a variety of ways to do so; they may became disabled, sick, or unemployed as a way to leave employment before early retirement. An example of the importance of the various exit routes from

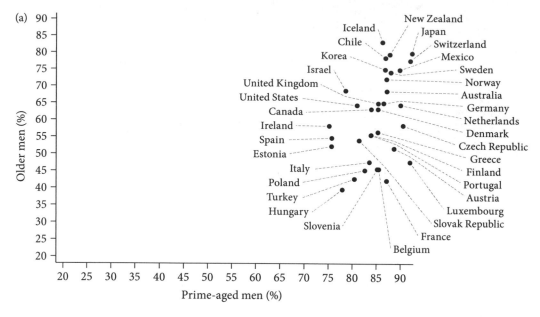

(a)

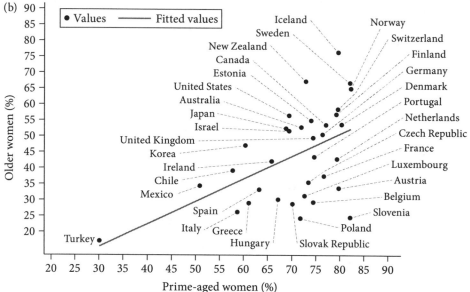

(b)

FIGURE 6.3 Employment rates of (a) men and (b) women, 2010
Source: OECD Labor Force Statistics.
Note: Prime age = 25–54; older = 55–64.

work is given by Bratberg et al. (2004), who study the effects of a change in early retirement programs in Norway (see box 6.3 for details). When a fairly generous early retirement program was introduced, many Norwegian workers who were entitled actually used it to retire early. To a large extent the early retirement system reduced the employment of older workers, and it also reduced outflows from work to other destinations, such as disability, unemployment, or sickness.

In Norway the standard retirement age is 67. In 1989 a fairly generous early retirement system called AFP was introduced. At the outset the entitlement age was set at 66, but this age was gradually lowered to 65 in 1990, 64 in 1993, 63 in 1997, and finally to 62 since 1998. In the private sector AFP is not available to everybody, because only firms that participate in the central tariff agreements can offer early retirement to their employees. In these firms early retirement is possible if workers meet some rather weak conditions in terms of past work experience and past wages. The AFP system is financially attractive for many workers. At the age of 67 the worker will receive an ordinary public pension that is calculated as if that worker had continued working until age 67. Before the introduction of AFP, a significant number of older workers retired early through such unofficial routes as disability benefits, prolonged unemployment benefits, or sickness benefits.

An argument put forward in favor of the AFP reform was that some workers would not stay in the labor force until 67 anyway, and the main effect of the new program was to offer them a more "dignified" exit from the workforce. Some of the changes in the system have the character of a natural experiment. In October 1993 the AFP age limit was reduced from 65 to 64. The first group of affected workers reached 64 years in the period from January 1 to March 1, 1993. Espen Bratberg, Tor Helge Holmås, and Øystein Thøgerson show the labor market position of these workers three months after their birthdays:

Worker status	64 years old January–February 1993 (%)			64 years old January–February 1994 (%)			Difference-in-differences
	AFP firms	Non-AFP firms	Difference	AFP firms	Non-AFP firms	Difference	
Still at work	82.6	83.8	1.2	64.7	86.0	21.3	−20.1
AFP	—	—	—	26.0	—	−26.0	26.0
Other	17.4	16.2	−1.2	9.3	14.0	4.7	−5.9
Total	100.0	100.0	0.0	100.0	100.0	0.0	0.0

About 83 percent were still at work, while about 17 percent had a different labor market position, that is, disabled, long-term sick, or other. There was a small difference between workers in AFP firms and those in non-AFP firms. The second group of workers reached the age of 64 years in the period from January 1 to March 1, 1994. Some of these workers became eligible for the AFP system on their birthdays. As shown by the table, three months after their birthdays 26 percent were in an AFP system, while about 9 percent had a different labor market position. For the workers who were not eligible for an AFP system, 86 percent were still at work three months after their birthday. Comparing both groups makes it clear that the AFP system reduced the employment rate of older workers significantly (26 percent), while it reduced other exits from work only slightly (about 6 percent).

Source: Bratberg et al. (2004).

The low participation rates of older workers have not always been considered a problem and in fact sometimes have resulted from deliberate government policy to tackle youth unemployment or as a service to older workers. As the OECD (2006a) puts it: "the claim that fewer jobs for older workers result in more jobs for younger workers, though unfounded, is proving especially stubborn." Another observation is that "older workers are just 'too tired' to carry on working." Early retirement policies were supported by governments to reduce labor supply, employers used them as a subsidized means to rejuvenate or reduce their workforce, and unions supported them because many of their older members were keen to leave the labor force. The decline in labor force participation among older workers is a long-term phenomenon partly stimulated by the high unemployment rates that emerged in the 1980s in many European countries. To reduce unemployment and make room for young workers, older workers often got attractive offers to retire early, "offers they could not refuse."

Once older workers become unemployed, it takes a long time for them to find another job. Long-term unemployment among older workers is higher than among prime-aged and young workers. In the literature there is not much attention to unemployment among older workers, except to the extent that unemployment is used as an alternative exit route to early retirement. Losing a job is a one-way street out of the labor force for many older workers (see Gielen and van Ours 2006 for an analysis of Dutch data). It is easier to extend ongoing firm-worker relationships than to stimulate employers to hire older workers. Nevertheless, older workers face difficulties in keeping their jobs partly because of employers' negative perceptions about their capacities to adapt to technological and organizational changes and partly because their wage costs may rise more steeply than their productivity. Ill health and difficult working conditions, including long working hours, may also play a role. Perhaps even more important, older workers who lose their jobs find it extremely difficult to acquire a new job and may face large potential wage losses. On average across the OECD, the hiring rate of those older than 50 is less than half the hiring rate for workers aged 25 to 49. This may have to do with employer reluctance to hire older workers but also with weak search incentives and limited support by public employment services (OECD 2006c).

Chan and Stevens (1999) study the economic consequences of late-career job loss in the United States and find large and lasting effects on wages, assets, employment expectations, and actual employment. Chan and Stevens (2001) conclude that two years after a job loss at age 55, only 60 percent of men and 55 percent of women are employed, compared with employment rates of more than 80 percent among nondisplaced men and women who were working at the age of 55. They also find that even four years after job loss there is still a gap of about 20 percent in employment rates of displaced and nondisplaced workers. The reasons for this difference are twofold. Displaced workers return to a new job slowly, and exit rates from postdisplacement jobs are higher than from other jobs.

Daniel and Heywood (2007), referring to Hutchens (1986), argue that there are two possible explanations for the widely observed phenomenon that many firms employ older workers, but few firms hire them. The first explanation is related to training issues. Older workers have more experience, firm-specific skills, and knowledge and are important in training functions within firms. If they get separated from their firms, they lose this advantage and become relatively expensive as new hires. The second explanation concerns the relationship between productivity and wages. If back-loading of the compensation profile is used to motivate greater lifetime effort, this only holds if the worker stays in the firm. Newly hired older workers do not have an incentive to put in a lot of effort in their jobs, which makes them also relatively expensive. Daniel and Heywood (2007) use British data to investigate both potential explanations for the low hiring of older workers. They find that firms that use deferred compensation and internal labor markets are unlikely to hire older workers. They also conclude that modest financial incentives may be insufficient to change the hiring practices of many employers, especially employers that use back-loading and require specific human capital. Nevertheless, Behaghel et al. (2004) find evidence that financial incentives influence the hiring behavior of French firms. When a firing tax was abolished for workers hired after the age of 50, the hiring of older workers increased.

Duval (2003) presents an analysis of participation rates of older individuals that investigates the effects of a variety of incentives. He uses an unbalanced panel dataset of 22 OECD countries over the period 1967–1999 containing information for three age groups, 55–59, 60–64, and 65 years or older. The focus is on the effect of the implicit tax rates embedded in old-age pensions and early retirement programs. Changes in implicit tax rates and standard retirement ages appear to explain a major part of the trend of decline in labor force participation by older men.

Dorn and Sousa-Poza (2005) perform a cross-country analysis to study voluntary and involuntary early retirement. They conclude that generous early retirement provisions not only make it more attractive for workers to retire early but also provide an incentive to firms to encourage more workers to retire early. In particular, firms are persuaded to use early retirement programs to lay off workers during recessions and circumvent EPL.

Studies of the effects of abolishing mandatory retirement ages may be helpful to get an idea about the effects of age-related policies on aggregate labor market performance. In the United States, to abolish age discrimination, mandatory retirement before age 65 was prohibited in 1967 and before age 70 in 1978, and it was abolished altogether in 1986. Adams (2004) finds that the prohibition of mandatory retirement did not influence the probability of older workers being hired, but it did reduce retirement and thus increased the length of the worker-firm relationship. Neumark and Stock (1999) show that wage profiles were steeper rather than flatter after the abolition of mandatory retirement, suggesting that long-term worker-firm relationships were strengthened. They also find that the abolition of mandatory retirement raised employment rates of older workers substantially, by as much as 7 percentage points. Von Wachter (2002) analyzes the labor market effects of the abolition of mandatory retirement in the United States. He finds that workers who were covered by mandatory retirement had a very high incidence of retirement at age 65, while those who were not covered had a much smaller incidence at age 65. The difference between the two groups gradually disappeared after the end of mandatory retirement. He estimates that the labor force of workers aged 65 or older increased by 10–20 percent because of the abolition of mandatory retirement.

Ashenfelter and Card (2002) find that the elimination of mandatory retirement rules for college and university professors in the United States substantially increased their labor market attachment at higher ages (see box 6.4 for details). Banks and Smith (2006), however, conclude that for the United Kingdom the employment effects of abolishing mandatory retirement are likely to be small. The main reason is that early retirement programs are more important determinants of employment rates than mandatory retirement age. They estimate that only around 1.5 percent of retirements in the United Kingdom are attributable to mandatory retirement below the age of 65.

BOX 6.4   *Elimination of the Mandatory Retirement Age in the United States*

College and university professors were among the few occupations to be exempted from the general elimination of mandatory retirement in the United States in 1986. Postsecondary institutions were granted a temporary exemption to enforce mandatory retirement at the age of 70. On January 1, 1994, this exemption expired. Orley Ashenfelter and David Card use a dataset of regular faculty who were aged 50 or older in the mid-1980s and who were followed for the next 10–11 years to study how the elimination of mandatory retirement affected faculty retirement. The dataset concerns faculty at colleges and universities that offered DC pensions. On the basis of their analysis, the following probabilities were estimated:

| | Mandatory retirement | | |
Indicator	Yes	No	Difference
Probability to stay to age 70 (%)			
From age 60	26.1	25.4	0.7
From age 65	39.2	38.6	0.6
Employment outcomes if at work at age 70 (%)			
Leave at 70	76.6	29.6	47.0
Still employed at 71	23.4	70.4	−47.0
Still employed at 72	8.4	51.6	−43.2
Still employed at 73	6.3	39.4	−33.1

It appears that the elimination of mandatory retirement had no effect on retirement rates of faculty younger than 70. However, the fraction of faculty who continued working into their 70s increased substantially. When mandatory retirement was present, less than 10 percent of the 70-year-old faculty were working at age 72. After the elimination of mandatory retirement, close to 50 percent of the 70-year-olds were still working at age 72. Ashenfelter and Card also find that faculty with higher salaries or lower pension wealth were less likely to retire at any given age.

Source: Ashenfelter and Card (2002).

6.3.2 Age and Productivity

Aging may affect productivity levels for various reasons. On the one hand, older workers are thought to be more reliable and to have better skills than average workers. On the other hand, older workers have higher health care costs and lower flexibility in accepting new assignments, and they may be less suitable for training (Barth et al. 1993). It is difficult to establish how age itself affects labor productivity not only because productivity is highly individual and sector specific but also because of the interaction of age, cohort, and selection effects. Age alone is found to be a poor predictor of individual performance. There are wide variations among jobs and workers, but older workers are generally considered to be more consistent, cautious, slow, and conscientious. Furthermore, older workers have fewer accidents and are less likely to quit, thus reducing hiring costs.

The age/productivity profile is not exogenous to labor market institutions. In the past, labor market institutions have been adjusted to facilitate early departure from the labor force. Individual productivity deteriorates if no investments are made to keep human capital up-to-date. Therefore, declining productivity for older workers may be a self-fulfilling prophecy. If a worker anticipates early retirement, that worker will be less eager to invest in training to prevent deteriorating productivity. If an employer expects a worker to retire early, that employer will also have no incentive to invest in maintaining productivity. Current generations of older workers may have anticipated that they could retire early, reducing their willingness to invest in human capital. If so, the concave relationship between age and productivity may be caused by the existence of mandatory retirement and not the other way around.

According to Johnson (1993), most employers (and probably many employees) seem to believe in a rule of thumb that average labor productivity declines after some age between 40 and 50. This assumption is so common that few attempts have been made to gather supporting evidence; why bother to prove the obvious? Nevertheless, the variance in performance is commonly greater within age groups than between age groups. Most research is based on cross-sectional comparisons and not on longitudinal analysis. Warr (1998) presents an extended overview of a variety of studies on the relationship between age and productivity. Warr's overview includes studies on a range of job behaviors in conjunction with financial indicators to determine the overall outcome of employing older staff and laboratory experiments comparing the behavior of people at different ages. According to Warr, there is no reason to think that older workers are less good at their jobs than younger workers are: across jobs as a whole there is no significant difference between the job performance of older and younger workers.

Some evidence on the relationship between productivity and age is based on general data from either workers or firms. Avolio et al. (1990) find, on the basis of a U.S. database containing individual information on personal characteristics, ability, jobs, and work performance, that the length of job experience is a better predictor of work performance than age, especially in jobs with high complexity. Hellerstein et al. (1999) use a U.S. matched worker-firm dataset to analyze the relationship among wages, productivity, and worker characteristics. They find that for prime-aged workers and older workers, productivity and earnings increase at the same rate over the life cycle, and they conclude that their evidence is most consistent with models in which wages rise in accordance with productivity, such as the general human capital model. Crépon et al. (2003), using French matched worker-firm data and a setup of the analysis similar to that of Hellerstein et al. (1999), find opposite results: older workers are relatively overpaid. The age profile of wages has a concave pattern, while the age profile of productivity stops rising and even decreases after some experience level. Crépon and colleagues conclude that for workers older than 35, increases in wages are not a reflection of human capital accumulation.[2] Ilmakunnas and Maliranta (2005) use Finnish firm data with matched average worker characteristics to investigate the relationship between wages and productivity. They find that the wage-productivity gap increases with age, which they attribute to strong seniority effects in wage setting. Dygalo and Abowd (2005) use French matched worker-firm data to compare experience/earnings and experience/productivity profiles over employment spells. They too find that earnings increase over employment spells even when productivity declines and attribute this to preferences of workers for rising earnings profiles and firms matching these preferences. However, Aubert (2003), who also uses French matched worker-firm data, does not find strong evidence of older workers being less productive than younger ones. Productivity is increasing and concave with age. In manufacturing, construction, and trade the increase slows after age 40 and is close to zero after 50, but it does not decline. In services there is also a slowdown of productivity after age 40, but even beyond this age productivity increases with age. Dostie (2006) concludes, on the basis of an analysis of Canadian linked worker-firm data, that both wage and productivity profiles are concave, but productivity diminishes faster than wages for workers aged 55 or older.[3]

The objective relationship between age and productivity may be difficult to establish, but employers may still have strong opinions about the productivity of older workers. Remery et al. (2003) report employers' opinions about aging issues in the Netherlands. They find that employers are less favorable—higher wage costs, lower productivity—about older workers the higher the share of older workers in the firm. About 40 percent of the employers indicated that they would not consider recruitment of older workers even if they suffered staff shortages.

6.4 Policy Issues

6.4.1 Should the Mandatory Retirement Age Be Increased?

A theoretical motivation for the existence of a mandatory retirement age is provided by Lazear (1979). According to Lazear, age/earnings profiles are upward slop-

2. Note that the authors conclude from this that the early retirement policy in France is consistent with this evidence and that a policy of raising the mandatory retirement age may be problematic because of the poor performance of older workers in the labor market. They do not consider the possibility that the age/productivity profile may change if the attachment between workers and firms lasts longer.

3. Dostie indicates that it is only possible to distinguish workers by age, gender, and education. An important missing variable is occupation, so it is not possible to distinguish workers in managerial positions from those in production.

ing, because this will discourage workers from shirking. Workers and firms engage in long-term relationships in which a worker is initially underpaid but later on in life is overpaid. Such delayed-compensation contracts will discourage the worker from shirking to preserve the job and enjoy the wage returns of a longer tenure. But at the same time, these contracts require mandatory retirement to avoid firms paying more than the value of the marginal product averaged over the working life (i.e., over the duration of the contract between the worker and the firm). Lazear's theory requires that workers and firms want to be engaged in long-term relationships. As wages increase with tenure, and productivity declines (or is flat) after reaching a certain age, rising earnings may coexist with declining or constant productivity.

The above suggests that using wages as a proxy for productivity, notably for older workers, can be misleading. Another complicating factor when using the age/wage profile as an indication of how age affects productivity is that the current relationship between productivity and age is at least partly determined by selective attrition from employment. The least-productive workers are most likely to be the first to retire. If not accounted for, this selection effect will lead to a downward bias in the estimated productivity decline attributed to aging. Von Wachter (2002) finds that neither job tenure nor wage profiles of older workers were affected by the change in the mandatory retirement legislation in the United States. From this finding he concludes that mandatory retirement is not a unique instrument to end long-term relationships between firms and workers. All in all, there does not seem to be a reason not to increase or even abolish the mandatory retirement age. But it should also be noted that increasing the mandatory retirement age may be neither necessary nor sufficient to increase labor force participation among older workers. It may not be necessary, because there are other barriers that hinder older workers from keeping their attachment to the labor market. It may not be sufficient, because workers use exit routes other than official retirement to leave the labor force.

6.4.2 Should Early Retirement Programs Be Phased Out?

There are basically three pension-oriented policies to reduce early retirement (OECD 2006c): reducing the generosity of early retirement benefits, improving the reward for delaying retirement, and delaying the minimum age of retirement. Most, if not all, OECD countries have reformed their pension systems using one or more of these possibilities. Studies evaluating the effects of these reforms suggest that individuals do react to incentives. Hence an increase in retirement age can be achieved not only by increasing the legal early retirement age but also by reducing pension benefits for those retiring earlier. For instance, Hanel (2010) finds that the 1997 German pension reform, reducing benefits by 0.3 percentage points for every month that claims on benefits take place prior to eligibility for the full pension, significantly postponed retirement age. In addition, there may be nonpension incentives to retire early, for example, through alternative exit routes like long-term sickness, disability, or unemployment. These schemes offer a pathway to retirement or a soft-landing scheme, which is widely used to cushion the social costs of redundancies. To give an example, in Belgium workers in the age window of 55–59 years old can exit the labor force through unemployment insurance in three ways: first, they can receive rather low unemployment benefits; second, they can exit through an early retirement scheme that offers both the unemployment benefit and extra compensation from the former employer with the consent of the government; third, they can be persuaded by their employers to take unemployment and receive a side-payment making up for some of the difference between their salary and the unemployment benefit (Pestieau 2003). Here, too, OECD countries have implemented or are implementing various policies to reduce these incentives, for example, through intensive screening of applicants for disability benefits. Finally, some countries stimulate flexible pathways to retirement through part-time pensions. Although older workers may partly determine their retirement date, the opportunities to stay in the labor force, especially after job loss, are mainly determined by employers. OECD countries use a wide variety of policies to influence employers' behavior, including large-scale information campaigns. Furthermore, many countries, following the U.S. example, have introduced new legislation to ban age discrimination. To the extent that this legislation acts as a form of EPL, the effects are unclear. If the costs of firing older workers are raised, fewer older workers will be fired, but also fewer will be hired, making the net effect unpredictable. Policies increasing costs of dismissals for older workers seem to work better if accompanied by an increase in the early retirement age (see box 6.5). Another avenue of government policy to stimulate employment of older workers is the matching of costs to productivity. Many countries have introduced wage subsidy systems to hire or retain older workers. Important problems related to some of these systems are deadweight losses and substitution or displacement effects (see chapter 12). Wage subsidies that are targeted on age alone risk being blunt instruments and may lead to small net effects at considerable costs. These age-related wage subsidies may also lead to further stigmatization of older workers.

BOX 6.5   *Effects of Costs of Dismissals on the Employment of Older Workers*

Early retirement decisions are associated not only with labor supply decisions but also labor demand contractions affecting older workers. Mario Schnalzenberger and Rudolf Winter-Ebmer investigated the effects of a tax introduced in Austria in 1996 and then tightened up in 2000, which made it more costly for firms to lay off workers aged older than 50. The purpose of the tax was to reduce the unemployment rate among older workers and the associated large inflows into costly soft-landing schemes for early retirement. In particular, the tax introduced in 1996 was proportional to wages and increasing in tenure and the number of months until the earliest possible retirement, up to a maximum of 170 percent of monthly income. Since the law in 2000 increased the early retirement age by some 18 months, the amount of the tax was increased sharply: the maximum tax rate increased by approximately one-third for men, while it doubled for women.

Drawing on social security records, Schnalzenberger and Winter-Ebmer analyzed the effects of the tax on layoff rates. They took as the treatment group workers aged 50–52.5 and as the control group those aged 47.5–50, thus choosing those just above and just below the age threshold relevant for the regulation. The table below provides evidence on layoff rates in 1996 and 2000 for the treatment and the control groups as well as a rough difference-in-differences exercise:

| | Layoff rates (%) | | | |
| | Men | | Women | |
Age range	2000	1996	2000	1996
50–52.5	0.86	0.83	1.59	1.34
47.5–50	0.85	1.27	1.27	1.14
Difference	0.02	−0.44	0.32	0.20
Difference-in-differences	−0.46		−0.12	

This suggests that the 2000 reform may have significantly reduced layoff rates among older workers. However, as stressed by Schnalzenberger and Winter-Ebmer, due to the long time span between the two observations, it is preferable to look at layoff rates four quarters before and four quarters after each of the two policy changes intervened in 1996 and 2000. By doing so, Schnalzenberger and Winter-Ebmer found that the 1996 reform did not have a significant effect on layoff rates, while the 2000 reform, increasing the early retirement age and consequently also the tax, reduced layoff rates among older workers. They report no evidence of mobbing or bribing to pressure older workers voluntarily to leave the firm. However, there seems to have been some substitution of older workers with short-tenured and untaxed younger workers, whose layoff rates increased after the 2000 reform.

Source: Schnalzenberger and Winter-Ebmer (2009).

In many countries early retirement policies were introduced as a short-term policy measure: governments wished to combat unemployment through a reduction of labor supply. When economic circumstances changed, these policies looked increasingly anachronistic (Walker 1998). Rather than reducing unemployment, early retirement increases joblessness notably among those workers who are approaching retirement age. Hairault et al. (2010) find that early retirement reduces employment rates of near-to-retirement people by negatively affecting their search intensity. Even worse, early retirement programs may have affected employers' perceptions about the potential productivity of older workers. As long as many older workers leave the labor force well before the standard retirement age, those remaining in the labor force may be perceived as too old as well. Thus, older workers are trapped in a vicious circle of perceptions that lack a solid empirical basis. All in all, there is little reason not to abolish early retirement programs.

6.5 Interactions with Other Institutions

As discussed above, early retirement programs have a clear relationship with EPL (see chapter 10). Early retirement makes it less costly for firms to lay off workers with relatively long tenures, externalizing these costs on the taxpayer. Thus, employers generally favor early retirement plans in countries with strict EPL.

UBs (see chapter 11) are also complementary to early retirement, as older workers sometimes use UBs as a pre–early retirement system. At the same time, if older workers lose their jobs and become unemployed, it is difficult for them to find new jobs.

Early retirement plans also have a close relationship with education policies (see chapter 8). A longer working life makes the investment in human capital more rewarding, as it will pay off over a longer period. At the same time, while early retirement is a scheme paid by the relatively young workers to the older ones, free public education is a transfer from the old to the young generations. Thus, there are strictly economic and political economic reasons to expect early retirement to be negatively correlated with public expenditure on education. We analyze this interaction in more detail in chapter 8.

6.6 Why Do Early Retirement Programs Exist?

An important argument against the abolition of mandatory retirement is that this will create unemployment among young people. In past decades early retirement programs were introduced in several countries to reduce youth unemployment. In both cases the argument is based on the erroneous assumption that there is a lump of labor that may be redistributed from old workers to young ones without costs. Boldrin et al. (1999) show that there is no positive relationship between youth unemployment and the retirement age; that is, early retirement of older workers does not induce lower youth unemployment. Similarly, figure 6.4 shows that on a

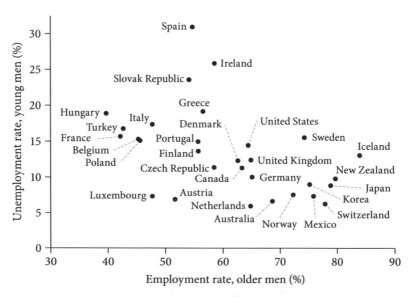

FIGURE 6.4 Employment rates of older men (aged 55–64) and unemployment rates of young men (aged 20–29), 2010
Source: OECD Labor Force Statistics.

cross-country basis there is even a negative relationship between the employment rates of older workers (aged 55–64) and the unemployment rates of young workers (aged 20–29). Another argument made in favor of early retirement programs is that older workers face health problems that prevent them from staying active in the labor market. This too seems to be erroneous. Not only has life expectancy increased substantially over past decades, but also the health of older individuals has improved greatly. Employers may support early retirement because it makes it easier for them to get rid of older, high-paid workers. Employers would support early retirement, notably in the presence of strict EPL. Unions may support early retirement because it is a benefit originally won through negotiation. Who pays for this policy failure is the young worker, who finances the pensions of individuals retiring earlier and earlier in spite of the increase in longevity, and the general taxpayer, who has to fill the funding gaps of social security.

6.7 Suggestions for Further Reading

There is a huge literature on retirement plans and their effects on labor supply. An overview of international differences in incentives to retire is given by Gruber and Wise (1999). Institutional features related to aging populations are reviewed in an OECD study on aging and employment policies titled *Live Longer, Work Longer* (OECD 2006c). The main policy issue discussed is how to increase labor force attachment among older workers. Much less is known about labor demand for older workers. The book *Ageing, Health and Productivity: The Economics of Increased Life Expectancy*, edited by Garibaldi et al. (2008), and the 2011 special issues of *De Economist* on "Ageing Workforces" provide interesting information about the relationship between age, health, and productivity. Finally, a recent National Bureau of Economic Research book by Gruber and Wise (2010) also documents the negative effects of early retirement on youth employment.

6.8 Review Questions and Exercises

1. What is the difference between a DB and a DC pension system?
2. Why do people generally retire more gradually under a DC system than under a DB system?
3. Which are the key characteristics of an NDC system?
4. To what extent do pension contributions differ from taxes?
5. Why is early retirement not a good instrument to reduce youth unemployment?
6. Why do wages increase with tenure, and how does that affect retirement programs?
7. How would an increase in the standard retirement age affect the behavior of employers and workers?
8. Sometimes the relationship between age and productivity is studied through the evolution of wages over the life cycle. Why is this a dangerous strategy?

9. Explain why many firms employ older workers, but few firms hire older workers.

10. What are the essential ingredients of the option value theory of work?

11. Joe has worked until reaching the age of 60. He now has two options. The first is to work for another 5 years, earning 40,000 euros per year, retire at age 65, and collect a pension of 10,000 euros per year for the following 15 years. The second option is to retire immediately and collect a yearly pension of X euros for the next 20 years. Suppose that a euro received today is worth 1.05 euros received next year.

    (a) What value of X gives the worker the same total income (earnings and retirement benefits) in net present value terms in the two options?

    (b) What value of X gives the worker the same pension wealth in the two options?

    (c) Consider a state-provided medical insurance which is provided free to persons as long as they continue to work up to the age of 65. Those under 65 years of age who are not working can purchase this health insurance for 5,000 euros per year. If Joe values retiring at age 60 over retiring at age 65 at 200,000 euros, for what value of X would he retire at age 60?

12. Consider a worker who is currently 65 years old and expects to live until the age of 85. Her current and future wage is 25,000 euros per year. She has the option to retire immediately or postpone retirement up to the age of 70. If she does retire immediately, she gets a yearly pension of 10,000 euros. If she postpones retirement until the age of 66, she can obtain a higher pension, say 12,000 euros per year. Retiring at the age of 67, she receives 14,000 euros, at 68 16,000 euros, at 69 18,000 euros, and at 70 (when she is in any event compelled to retire) she can get 20,000 euros per year. Assume that after retirement, the pension is the only source of income and that the utility function of the individual is given by $U = R^\alpha Y^{1-\alpha}$, where R denotes the total number of years of retirement, Y is the net present value of her (remaining) lifetime income, and $0 < \alpha < 1$. Assume for simplicity that the market (and subjective) discount factor is one.

    (a) Tabulate the net present value of income and the pension wealth for this individual at different levels of R.

    (b) Display the leisure (retirement) income trade-off for this individual, putting the retirement age on the horizontal axis.

    (c) At which levels of α does the individual decide to retire at the age of 65? At which levels of α will she retire at 70?

    (d) Supposing that $\alpha = .9$, which accrual rate of pension (increase in the amount of yearly pension if the individual postpones retirement by one year) would be required to induce the worker to postpone retirement until the age of 70?

13. (Advanced) In 1996 Italy and Sweden both introduced a NDC pension system. There are important design differences between the two regimes, however. The so-called transformation coefficients are higher in Sweden than in Italy. Moreover, Italian pensions are kept constant in real terms, independently of wage growth, whereas in Sweden they are not fully indexed to inflation when wage growth falls below a certain level (right now it is 1.6 percent).

(a) In your view what is the rationale behind such differences in the design of pension systems?

(b) What are their implications for the induced age of retirement?

(c) How do they affect the pension expenditure to GDP ratio over the business cycle?

6.9 Technical Annex: Optimal Retirement Age

The pension wealth accrual model outlined in box 6.1 assumes that there is no uncertainty as to the age of death and that individuals compare the pension wealth across any two consecutive years rather than between, say, today and some date in the future. This may overlook large spikes in wealth at a particular age (e.g., associated with different early retirement schemes). A more general framework to analyze retirement decisions is provided by the option value of retirement model Stock and Wise (1990).

Assume that retirement is irreversible and that there is a constant discount rate i. The value of retirement at a particular age a, evaluated at the contribution year t, consists of two components related to two subsequent periods. First, in the years from t_0 (age at which the individual starts working) to a, the person will have annual earnings w_t, of which the net present value NPV can be expressed as

$$NPV_{1,t}(a) = \sum_{t=t_0}^{a-1} \left(\frac{1}{1+i}\right)^{t-t_0} U(w_t), \tag{6.9}$$

where t is an indicator of age, U is a function indicating the (indirect) utility that the person derives from the wage earnings w_t, and $\frac{1}{1+i}$ is the discount factor. Second, from age a until death at a given age T the person receives pension benefits $B_t(a)$, of which the net present value NPV_2 in year t can be expressed as

$$NPV_{2,t}(a) = \sum_{t=a}^{T} \left(\frac{1}{1+i}\right)^{t-t_0} U[B_t(a)]. \tag{6.10}$$

Thus, the total net present value of retirement at age a can be expressed as

$$NPV_t(a) = \sum_{t=t_0}^{a-1} \left(\frac{1}{1+i}\right)^{t-t_0} U(w_t) + \sum_{t=a}^{T} \left(\frac{1}{1+i}\right)^{t-t_0} U[B_t(a)]. \tag{6.11}$$

Postponing retirement increases the length of the first period and reduces the length of the second one. Since earnings go up with age and pension benefits usually increase with years of service and with the wage in the last year before retirement, postponing retirement increases total income over the remaining life period. Ceteris paribus, this has a positive effect on the value of retirement. However, if a person postpones retirement, she or he will have fewer years of receipt of the pension. This second effect will decrease the value of retirement. Of the two effects, the first is initially more important, but eventually the second effect dominates. Thus, there must be some age a^* where there is a maximum value of retirement, as shown in figure 6.2.

The option value OV of retirement compares the expected lifetime utility of retiring today and the expected lifetime utility of postponing the decision until the optimal retirement age a^*, that is,

$$OV_t(a^*) = E_t[NPV(a^*)] - NPV_t(a). \qquad (6.12)$$

A worker is expected to retire if the utility of retiring at a^* is smaller than the utility of retiring today, that is, if the option value is negative.

CHAPTER SEVEN Family Policies

To cope with aging populations, many countries face the short-run challenge of raising rates of female labor force participation and the long-run challenge of raising fertility. Family policies aim at reconciling work of both parents with childcare responsibilities. There are two main types of family policies: parental leave and subsidized childcare.

Parental leave arrangements not only provide a period for the working mother to recover from giving birth and to bond with her newborn, but also make it easier for mothers to stay attached to the labor market when raising children. Indeed the leave period grants parents the right to take job-protected time off for caregiving, especially when children are younger than school age. In most countries, some or all wages during parents' time off are also replaced.

Subsidized childcare affects mothers' choices with respect to the allocation of time between childrearing and work, potentially also affecting labor supply decisions of other members of the household. Social policies that reduce the costs to raise children—increasing the availability and quality and reducing the costs of childcare—affect not only labor supply but also the decision to have a child. These choices are affected both by the availability of formal childcare and by the availability of informal childcare, including family support.

Family policies differ considerably across countries. In some cases governments strongly support parents' caregiving by subsidizing parental leaves. In other cases (e.g., in the United States), governments rely mainly on market-based solutions: there is a short mandatory parental leave that is job-protected but not subsidized, while employers voluntarily provide options for reduced hours of work, and childcare services are provided through market arrangements (Gornick and Meyers 2003). Family leave policies also vary across countries on at least two additional dimensions: the generosity of the leave available to new mothers and the degree to which policy designs encourage men's engagement in caregiving. In addition, early childhood education and care can further strengthen maternal employment by providing alternatives to full-time maternal caregiving, and high-quality early education and care can also enhance child well-being. Reconciliation of work and family responsibilities is also pursued via working-time regulations (see also chapter 5) that can free up parents' caring time for both mothers and fathers by limiting normal hours to fewer than 40 per week, by guaranteeing a minimum number of days for annual vacations, and by encouraging the development of part-time employment.

This chapter presents a taxonomy of policies reconciling work and family life, focusing on subsidized childcare facilities and parental leave. It also provides a framework highlighting the interactions among labor supply, leisure, and childcare decisions of parents and how these decisions are affected not only by preferences and labor market conditions—wages and job opportunities—but also by family policies.

7.1 Measures and Cross-Country Comparisons

Cross-country information about childcare facilities and parental leave is presented in table 7.1. There are large cross-country differences in spending for childcare: Nordic countries spend roughly 1 percent of GDP, if not more, on childcare, while Austria, Canada, Poland, and Switzerland spend less than one-third of that amount. Differences are also substantial in the coverage of formal childcare arrangements for children younger than 3. In countries such as the Czech Republic and the Slovak Republic fewer than 5 percent of young children have formal childcare arrangements, while in Denmark, Iceland, the Netherlands, and Norway more than 50 percent of these children do. These cross-country differences in coverage do not necessarily capture differences in the supply of childcare, that is, in the costs and availability of childcare facilities. Opening hours may differ substantially across countries, preventing mothers from reconciling full-time jobs with family responsibilities. For instance, childcare facilities for infants are open 5 hours per day in Spain compared with 10.5 hours in Denmark (De Henau et al. 2007). Differences in coverage may also capture differences in the demand for childcare. In some countries childcare is indeed arranged informally through grandmothers and relatives. In Italy, for example, the availability of informal care (and social stigma against mothers putting children aged 0–2 in kindergartens) is the main reason for the low use of formal childcare (Boeri et al. 2005), notably when this involves more than 30 hours per week. In countries such as the Netherlands, the availability of quality part-time opportunities makes it easier for women to reconcile work and motherhood, reducing the demand for childcare. For children aged from 3 to mandatory school age, the use of formal childcare arrangements is substantially higher. In many European countries childcare use is close to 100 percent in this age group, and the country with the lowest use, Greece, is still close to 50 percent. Only Turkey has a substantially lower use of formal childcare.

Table 7.1 also shows that there are large cross-country differences in parental leave, both in the maximum duration and in the level of benefits paid during the base (mandatory) period. Some countries, such as Spain, Portugal, and several eastern European countries have total (mandatory plus optional) parental leave lasting about three years, while other countries, such as the United States, do not have a paid maternity leave, but only 12 weeks of job-protected leave. Employers in the EU are bound by a 1992 EU directive to provide at least 14 weeks of maternity leave to their employees, that is, more than in the United States. As made clear

TABLE 7.1 Summary indicators of formal childcare coverage and maternity leave

Country	Childcare spending (percentage of GDP)	Young children having formal childcare (%) Age < 3	Age ≥ 3	Duration of base maternity leave (weeks)	Base maternity benefits (percentage of average wage)	Total duration of leave (base + optional) (weeks)
Australia	0.39	29	55	6	0	52
Austria	0.30	12	78	16	100	112
Belgium	0.80	48	99	15	77	15
Bulgaria	0.76	15	71	63	90	63
Canada	0.16	24	57	17	49	35
Czech Republic	0.44	2	80	28	60	164
Denmark	1.32	66	92	18	50	46
Estonia	0.26	18	89	20	100	172
Finland	0.90	29	74	18	66	157
France	1.01	42	100	16	100	159
Germany	0.39	18	93	14	100	162
Greece	0.12	16	47	43	59	43
Hungary	0.63	9	87	24	70	136
Iceland	0.85	55	96	13	80	26
Ireland	0.26	31	56	42	16	42
Israel	0.74	23	87	26	54	—
Italy	0.62	29	97	20	80	26
Japan	0.33	28	90	14	60	58
Korea	0.34	38	80	13	100	46
Latvia	0.63	16	81	19	100	52
Lithuania	0.60	14	65	21	100	104
Luxembourg	0.36	39	86	16	100	26
Malta	0.60	7	94	13	46	13
Mexico	0.60	6	83	12	100	12
Netherlands	0.72	56	67	16	100	26
New Zealand	0.75	38	94	14	71	38
Norway	0.96	51	94	9	80	91
Poland	0.28	8	47	18	100	156
Portugal	0.36	47	79	17	100	17
Romania	0.76	14	73	21	75	21
Slovak Republic	0.38	3	74	28	55	156
Slovenia	0.47	34	78	15	100	37
Spain	0.45	37	99	16	100	162
Sweden	1.09	47	91	9	80	51
Switzerland	0.23	—	47	14	80	14
Turkey	—	—	24	16	70	26
United Kingdom	1.09	41	93	52	25	52
United States	0.38	31	56	12	0	12

Source: OECD Family Database, 2011.
Notes: The information about childcare coverage (first three columns) concerns the years 2007–2008; the information on maternity leave (last three columns) refers to 2008. — = not available.

by the example of the United States (and Australia until very recently), maternity leave does not necessarily involve public transfers replacing the forgone earnings during the leave period. In the countries where maternity leave is paid, maternity benefits range from 16 to 25 percent of the wage in Ireland and the United Kingdom to 100 percent in many other countries. In all cases, however, the job position is protected during the entire leave period, whether this is paid or unpaid, mandatory or optional. Moreover, women may have the option to postpone taking the leave until the child is older instead of immediately after childbirth. In addition to the schemes reported in table 7.1, employers may voluntarily offer paid or unpaid maternity leave to preserve good employee matches and job-specific human capital.

Gender equality is sometimes also pursued via parental leave policies. Countries like Sweden, for instance, reserve up to one-third of total two-parent parental leave for the exclusive use of fathers. In Finland total paid parental leave can be extended up to two months if the father is to take it. A 2010 EU directive imposes on employers a minimum of four months of parental leave on the birth or adoption of a child to be granted to all workers, men and women alike. All this is done to promote a more egalitarian sharing of family responsibilities within the couple, reducing gender asymmetries in the cost of labor in the perception of employers and avoiding the association of motherhood with skill deterioration and lost opportunities for promotion and training.

Overall, all countries provide some sort of support for childcare through paid leave enabling parental childcare and through subsidies supporting nonparental childcare, but countries differ in the way they combine these two types of support as well as in the specific design features of childcare and parental leave schemes. Some countries, such as Germany, encourage mothers to take care of their children themselves by putting an emphasis on paid parental leave and providing little support for nonparental childcare (see Gregg and Waldfogel 2005). The United States aims at encouraging mothers to combine work and care for young children by providing little support for parental leave and more support for childcare. Other (Scandinavian) countries leave the choice concerning childcare to parents by supporting both parental and nonparental childcare.

7.2 Theory

7.2.1 Subsidized Childcare

The effects of the availability of subsidized childcare on labor supply of women can be analyzed using a simple static framework in which a mother maximizes utility. The mother derives utility from consumption and from being with her children. In other words, if the mother takes care of the children, this is assumed to be increasing her utility like a leisure activity, a normal good. There are fixed costs associated with childcare (e.g., because one has to pay a flat entry fee to preschools independently of the actual use of them). This income effect has asymmetric effects on hours of work and participation. Depending on the costs and on nonlabor income, some mothers will continue to work and increase hours to compensate for the income loss, while others will decide to leave employment, thus avoiding the entry fee. Subsidized childcare reducing these fixed costs will clearly operate in the opposite direction, inducing more women to keep on working, but at reduced hours. There can also be variable costs of childcare, so that every hour of work of the mother comes at the expense of one hour of child rearing, and for every hour of work, formal childcare has to be provided.[1] This reduces the net wages of women, exerting a negative substitution effect on the labor supply of women also along the intensive margin of hours of work. Subsidized childcare in this case may also increase hours of work.

These effects are illustrated geometrically in figure 7.1 and formally in technical annex 7.9.1.

Figure 7.1 illustrates how the presence of children and of subsidized childcare facilities affects individual labor supply behavior of women. Consider initially a woman without children who allocates her time between market and nonmarket hours (assumed to be a normal good), maximizing her utility. As in the labor-leisure choice framework proposed in chapter 1, the woman will choose a time allocation maximizing her utility (e.g., point A) working h_A hours. Suppose that now the mother has a child, and this involves only some fixed costs $F_{c_{low}}$, incurred independently of the number of working hours supplied by the mother. This will clearly reduce the set of consumption levels achievable by working. Geometrically, the budget line shifts downward and has a spike at the zero-hours-of-work locus, as childcare costs are not paid when the mother does not work. We have two cases here. If the fixed costs are not too large, the mother will be still working after childbirth, choosing a new combination of market work and consumption (e.g., point B in figure 7.1a). Notice that this involves a greater number of hours of work than before childbirth, as the mother has to make up for the income loss associated with the payment of childcare costs. However, if childcare costs are too large, say $F_{c_{high}}$ in figure 7.1b, then the mother will prefer not to work at all: the highest indifference curve in the feasible set will be the one crossing the zero-hours-of-work locus, E. Thus, subsidized childcare in the presence of fixed costs of childcare is likely to have a positive effect on women's participation but a negative effect on the hours of work of working mothers.

In practice, however, childcare involves not only fixed but also variable costs, as every hour of the mother's work typically comes at the cost of purchasing childcare services in the market. For simplicity, suppose that there are only these variable costs c_c associated with childcare (i.e., no fixed costs). Figure 7.1c represents this situation. Variable childcare costs reduce the net wage of the mother, so that the budget line rotates toward the origin. The new optimum is at B, and therefore working hours are reduced from h_A to h_B. In other words, because of the costs of childcare, the net wage decreases (the opportunity cost of market work increases),

---

1. Informal childcare (e.g., by other family members) is ruled out for simplicity.

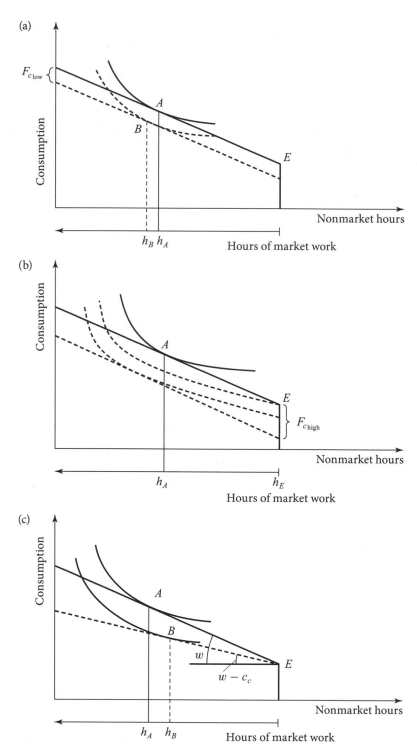

FIGURE 7.1 Labor supply of women and (a,b) fixed costs of children and (c) variable costs of children

inducing women to supply less labor in the market.[2] Thus, subsidized childcare for working mothers operating on variable rather than on fixed costs of childcare will increase not only the number of mothers working but also hours of work as long as the substitution effect is larger than the income effect.

Notice that the above considers childcare subsidies offered only to working women. A child benefit provided unconditionally, that is, independently of whether the mother is working (like the child allowances offered in some countries), would only involve a positive income effect, shifting up the entire budget constraint (including E) and reducing unambiguously the labor supply of mothers.

7.2.2 Mandated Parental Leave

Parental leave generally operates as an extension of mandated maternity leave, which is granted by employers to allow mothers to recover from childbirth and is offered for a limited time around this event. Parental leave arrangements permit both mothers and fathers additional time off to care for infants and young children. Basically, parental leave is a form of subsidized childcare in which the subsidy is not provided to external services but to the parents who are providing childcare themselves. Like childcare subsidies conditional on employment, mandatory parental leave will have a positive effect on headcount labor supply of mothers, but it may reduce hours of work.

The way in which parental leave operates can be described by considering a small extension of the standard labor/leisure framework. So far we have assumed that the preferences of parents for labor versus leisure (or market versus non-market activities) are unaffected by the birth of a child. Suppose, however, that childbirth changes preferences of mothers, increasing for them, at least temporarily, the opportunity cost of market work. This will result in an increase in the reservation wage of women, as depicted in figure 7.2. In the initial weeks after childbirth, this reservation wage w^r may then be higher than the wage offered by the job held by the mother, say, w_0. As the child ages, however, the reservation wage is bound to decline, since the time spent by the mother with the child is more valuable when children are younger.[3] Thus, at some date or age of the child, say, a_1, the mother will be willing to go back to work in her initial position, as her reservation wage falls below the market wage. If the parental leave is long enough, then the mother will take the leave up to a_1 and then go back to her original job. If instead the parental leave is not sufficiently long or is not offered at all, then the mother will quit her old job. New jobs obtained immediately after maternity

---

2. As in the case of a wage decline, which is analyzed in chapter 1, there will be also in this case income and substitution effects operating in opposite directions. In the case depicted in figure 7.1c, the substitution effect (decreasing hours of work) dominates the income effect (increasing labor supply).

3. Lalive et al. (2011) provide direct evidence that the value of home production decreases as the child ages.

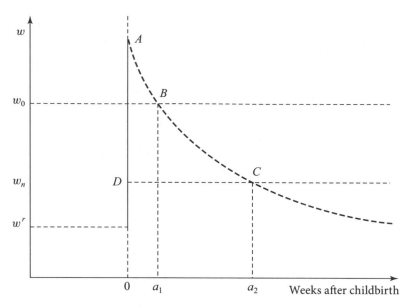

FIGURE 7.2 Parental leave and return to work after childbirth

periods are typically paid less than the old jobs. Suppose that a new job could only pay $w_n < w_0$ as in figure 7.2. Then the mother will resume working later, if there is no mandatory parental leave. Thus, quite paradoxically, mothers may spend more time not working without parental leave than with it. This longer period outside work may also hamper career advancement of women and induce a deterioration of the skills of mothers before they return to work (Rønsen and Sundström 2002). This explains why employers typically offer parental leave even when they are not legally compelled to do so. Yet the leave offered by employers is likely to be too short for those mothers who have stronger preferences for staying with their children. Government intervention can prolong the leave, preventing losses of human capital for these women. Indeed governments face a different trade-off than individual employers do. Private benefits of parental leave are generally lower than social benefits. For governments, the loss of human capital associated with inadequate parental leave is more important than for the firms involved.

The above assumes that every morning mothers compare market wages with their reservation wages, as in spot markets (Blau and Ehrenberg 1997). It is, however, plausible that at some stage women consider the option to take parental leave well before actually having a child. This creates an additional labor supply–enhancing mechanism: mandatory parental leave increases the value of a job for women, as when accepting a job offer, she anticipates that there will be higher utility gains after childbirth. Hence, the labor supply of women, at least measured in terms of headcounts rather than hours per worker, is enhanced by mandatory parental leave.

The above framework can also be used to understand why family policies encouraging formal versus informal childcare can be rather ineffective in increasing the labor supply of women. Parents often trust their relatives (e.g., their own parents) more than outside childcare givers, especially when the child is very young. If not only formal but also informal childcare is subsidized, then a lower transfer would be sufficient to convince women to resume working soon after childbirth. The increase in the market value of work under subsidized childcare is likely to be partly offset by the increase in the reservation wage of women if the type of childcare that is offered at a lower price is not that most preferred by the parents.

Parental leave can be taken by men as well as women. However, female workers are much more likely to seek time off under this policy than their male counterparts. As mandatory parental leave is costly for employers, it is likely to have negative effects on the demand for women (Ruhm 1998). It is precisely to avoid the negative effects of mandatory parental leave on employment and wages of women that more and more countries are introducing mandated or incentivized *paternity* leave. The purpose of these schemes is to reduce asymmetries between men and women in terms of labor costs in the perceptions of employers, avoiding preferential treatment for men in hiring policies.

7.2.3 Effects on Fertility

So far we have considered the effects of family policies on the labor supply of mothers, taking the number of children as given. However, maternity policies may also affect fertility plans, hence the number of children in a family. Indeed, these policies are often introduced with an explicit pro-natalist goal, particularly so after the worldwide fertility decline of the past decades. Although the effects of labor market institutions on fertility rates go beyond the scope of this book, it is nevertheless important to characterize how family policies may affect fertility plans, since fertility itself has important effects on labor supply.

Fertility is likely to be affected by family income and the price of children. Ceteris paribus, the number of children increases with family income. This relationship represents the pessimistic view of Thomas Malthus and led to economics being labeled the "dismal science."[4] However, income effects are only part of the story. The desired number of children also depends on their cost. An increase in the wage rate of the parent most responsible for childcare will make a child more expensive; thus, there is a negative relationship between female employment and fertility.

---

4. It is often stated that Thomas Carlyle gave economics the nickname "dismal science" as a response to the writings of Malthus, who predicted that starvation would result as projected population growth exceeded the rate of increase in the food supply. However, others claim that the phrase "dismal science" first occurs in Carlyle's 1849 tract titled "Occasional Discourse on the Negro Question," in which he was arguing for the reintroduction of slavery as a means to regulate the labor market in the West Indies. Carlyle argued that slavery was actually morally superior to the market forces of supply and demand promoted by economists, since, in his view, the freeing up of the labor market by the liberation of slaves had actually led to a moral and economic decline in the lives of the former slaves themselves.

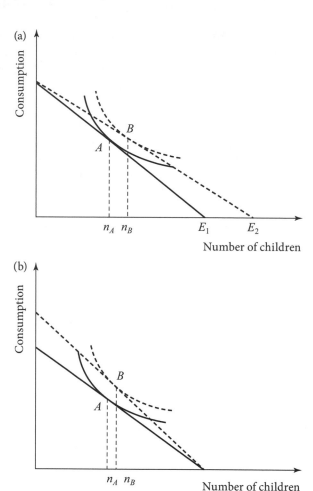

FIGURE 7.3 Fertility and family policies: (a) effect on fertility
of parental leave and subsidized childcare; (b) effect on
fertility of greater earning capacity of women

The above effects of income and net earnings of women, hence family policies,
on fertility decisions can be graphically illustrated by drawing on a simple model
in which the choice of a couple as to the number of children they have, n, is
defined in terms of a consumption fertility trade-off, as in figure 7.3. Parents
derive utility from having children. However, children reduce per capita income
in the family by being a source of direct costs or by indirectly forcing parents to
work less. Hence, a larger number of children reduces consumption possibilities of
each member of the household, as indicated by the linear budget constraint in the
figure. Depending on preferences for children and consumption (depending on the
slope of the indifference curve) and on the steepness of the trade-off, parents may
decide to have more or fewer children. They may also decide to have no children
at all. Insofar as family policies allow reconciliation of childrearing and earnings
from work, they are likely to improve the consumption-fertility trade-off, making

it flatter (i.e., allowing parents to have a larger number of children with unchanged consumption possibilities). This is bound to increase fertility, moving the decision of parents from *A* to *B* in the figure. There is no ambiguity as to the effects of policies in this case, as both the income (shifting out the budget constraint) and the substitution effect (reducing the slope of the budget constraint) operate in the same direction. An increased earning capacity of women would instead involve a positive income effect and a negative substitution effect on fertility, as depicted in figure 7.3b. This effect is important in assessing the empirical evidence, presented in the next section, on the cross-country correlation between fertility and employment of women.

The effects of family policies on fertility will clearly depend on specific design features of these schemes and on the credibility of the commitment of governments to maintain these schemes in place in the future (i.e., when the fertility plans result in an actual increase in the number of children). The decision to have children is indeed like an investment decision, as the benefits of this decision materialize only over time. Sometimes policies aim at anticipating fertility decisions by extending parental leave and hence allowing the mother to stay away from work, in case a new child is conceived within a limited period since the birth of the previous child.

7.3 Empirical Evidence

If there is a stylized fact characterizing postwar OECD labor markets, it is the womenization of the labor force. The gender employment gap—the difference in employment rates between men and women—has not yet been eliminated anywhere, although some (notably the Nordic) countries, are very close to a one-to-one female-to-male employment rate. In other countries female employment rates continue to be much below those of males. These differences have to do with preferences for work and family care, but they are also influenced by family policies or labor market discrimination (see chapter 4).

Some indications as to the role played by family policies in reconciling employment of women and family responsibilities come from analyzing the cross-country correlation between, on the one hand, fertility, and, on the other hand, employment rates of women. A remarkable phenomenon in past decades is the change in the cross-country correlation between female participation rates and fertility rates (Boeri et al. 2005). Up to the early 1980s this correlation was negative, suggesting a trade-off in time between paid work and childcare. From the late 1980s onward a positive cross-country correlation is observed: countries with higher participation rates also have higher fertility rates. This change in correlation is thought to be related to more generous parental leave, greater availability of childcare, and greater opportunities for flexible hours and part-time employment.

Indeed, as shown in figure 7.4, there is a positive cross-country correlation between the total fertility rate and the employment rate of prime-aged women. In the Nordic countries with generous provision of childcare facilities and maternity leave, high fertility rates coincide with high female employment rates. In

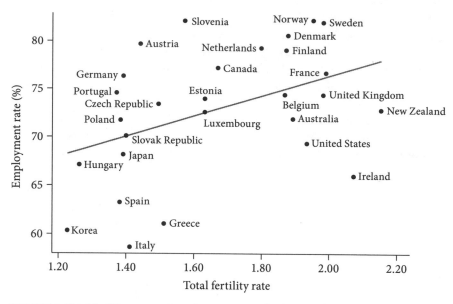

FIGURE 7.4 Total fertility rate and employment rate of prime-aged women, 2010
Source: OECD (2012b).

Note: Total fertility rate is the average number of children that would be born to a woman if she were to live to the end of her childbearing years and bear children in accordance with current age-specific fertility rates.

southern European countries, where these arrangements are less generous, low fertility rates coincide with low female employment rates. To some extent, the positive correlation is driven by Italy, Greece, Korea, and Spain, which combine a low employment rate of prime-aged women with a low fertility rate. Nevertheless, even if these countries are ignored, there is still a slight positive correlation between fertility and female employment rates.

It is also possible that countries with higher employment of women, hence a larger tax base for social policies, can afford to pay more generous family policies. Another interpretation for the coexistence of higher female employment and fertility in countries with sizable subsidized childcare and parental leave policies is that both policies and labor market outcomes are affected by social customs more or less supportive of mothers at work. To make causal inferences as to the effects of family policies, it is important to go beyond cross-country correlations.

Table 7.2 provides information on employment of women by country, depending on the presence and number of children. In particular, the table shows the difference in employment rates between women without children and those with one, two, or more children. The employment rate is affected strongly by the presence of children in some, but not all, countries. In many countries there is hardly any difference in employment rates between women without children and women with one child. Only in the case of two or more children does the employment rate drop substantially.

TABLE 7.2 Women's employment and presence of children

| Country | Female employment rate, part- and full-time (%) | | | | | | | Female employment rate, part-time (%) | | | | |
| | Number of children | | | | | Status of mothers | | Number of children | | | | |
	0	1	2	3+	Total	Single	With partner	0	1	2	3+	Total
Australia	68.4	55.3	—	43.2[a]	66.8	63.0	60	40.8	54.1	—	63.1[a]	41.8
Austria	82.8	81.8	76.3	59.9	79.7	80.2	76.2	30.3	54.7	65.8	66.6	45.4
Belgium	74.1	76.1	78.6	62.1	74.4	63.7	78.4	32.9	40.2	49.5	54.1	41.3
Bulgaria	75.5	76.1	70.1	34.8	73.6	—	—	1.6	—	—	—	1.6
Canada	76.5	74.9	—	68.2[a]	74.0	73.2	64.9	17.0	22.9	—	30.7[a]	21.4
Denmark	79.8	85.2	84.3	88.1	83.0	—	—	24.4	23.0	24.7	26.6	24.3
Finland	82.2	79.2	81.0	67.5	79.6	73.7	77.1	10.3	11.5	11.9	18.1	11.7
France	80.0	78.5	78.4	58.2	76.7	73.2	76.1	20.9	26.7	36.9	47.5	29.0
Germany	82.9	74.7	69.1	50.1	76.3	68.6	69.3	31.8	59.5	74.3	78.3	47.6
Greece	63.0	59.8	60.9	52.1	61.1	71.5	59.8	8.6	9.1	10.1	13.3	9.3
Hungary	75.3	66.0	65.5	39.4	67.1	71.1	59.7	5.0	6.5	6.9	15.3	6.4
Iceland	89.1	89.3	—	80.8[a]	87.4	—	—	—	—	—	—	28.4
Ireland	77.5	66.7	60.4	47.6	65.7	48.9	61.3	15.5	34.5	43.2	51.4	30.5
Italy	63.2	58.8	54.3	40.4	58.7	74.1	56.5	22.6	32.7	37.1	40.2	29.4
Japan	—	—	—	—	62.7	—	85	—	—	—	—	8.7
Luxembourg	77.5	74.5	70.5	57.9	72.4	88.7	68.0	18.2	37.2	54.1	57.8	36.1
Netherlands	81.4	78.4	81.6	69.7	79.5	69.3	79.7	55.3	82.4	89.2	91.1	74.0
New Zealand	80.7	66.9	—	58.9[a]	70.6	—		20.6	37.6	—	50.8[a]	32.4
Poland	74.3	73.2	70.4	62.4	71.7	71.6	71.2	6.8	7.7	8.9	14.0	8.3
Portugal	74.4	76.2	74.7	62.5	74.6	77.5	76.6	11.6	8.6	7.6	11.3	9.6
Slovak Republic	76.4	68.8	68.5	51.1	70.1	77.0	65.8	4.5	3.9	4.0	7.9	4.4
Spain	67.6	63.3	60.1	47.8	63.2	72.1	60.4	17.1	24.2	29.7	30.2	22.9
Sweden	81.2	80.9	86.8	74.5	82.0	—	—	25.4	35.6	40.5	45.0	33.7
Switzerland	84.3	75.5	—	65.5[a]	76.8	—	—	34.2	58.0	—	66.5[a]	47.1
Turkey	37.0	32.5	26.9	22.9	30.1	33.4	25.2	16.3	17.7	26.6	40.0	23.0
United Kingdom	81.7	75.4	71.1	49.2	74.3	58.8	72.2	21.5	45.4	60.1	65.6	39.0
United States	78.6	75.6	—	64.7[a]	74.1	73.0	72	10.1	15.8	—	23.6[a]	14.6

Sources: OECD (2002); Eurostat (2010).

Notes: Women aged 25–54 years. Columns 1–5 and 8–12: data for 2010, except for Australia, Canada, Iceland, Japan, New Zealand, and the United States (2000), and Switzerland (2001). Columns 6 and 7: data for 2008, except for Canada, Denmark, Japan, Sweden, and Switzerland (2005); Australia and New Zealand (2006); and Japan (2007). — = not available.

a. Estimates for women with two or more children.

Table 7.2 also provides information about childcare responsibilities. The table presents the employment rates of mothers with at least one child aged younger than 6, distinguishing between mothers in couples and lone mothers. In many countries lone mothers have a higher employment rate than mothers who are part of a couple. In other countries lone mothers have a substantially lower employment rate. The differences between the labor market position of lone mothers and married or cohabiting mothers are due to the trade-off between the need to make a living and the possibility of sharing some of the childcare responsibilities with a partner. Finally, table 7.2 shows that in most countries the share of part-time work among female employees increases with the number of children, at least up to the second child.

There is a rich microeconometric literature on the effects of family policies on employment and fertility decisions. It generally can better identify the effects of parental leave and subsidized childcare on labor supply decisions, taking into account that family policies are shaped by social and cultural customs.

An example of a natural experiment studying the effects of childcare on labor market behavior is presented by Piketty (1998). He finds that the introduction of a childcare allowance in France reduced the employment rate of mothers substantially (see box 7.1 for more details). Naz (2004) describes a similar type of natural experiment in Norway. Here the government introduced cash benefits for parents with young children who did not use state-subsidized childcare facilities. This policy change made childcare facilities relatively more expensive to use and decreased the labor supply of mothers with young children (see box 7.2 for more details).

BOX 7.1   *Mothers with Young Children in France*

In France in 1986 the Allocation Parentale d'Éducation (APE) was introduced to help parents (predominantly mothers) raise their children. The allowance of about 40 percent of the median wage (60 percent of the net minimum wage) was paid to a mother of at least three children, one of whom was younger than 3. In 1994 the allowance was extended to families with two children, one of whom was younger than 3. Mothers were entitled to the benefit from the birth of their second child, provided that it was born on July 1, 1994, or later. Because of this requirement, more and more mothers with two children, one of whom was younger than 3, became entitled to the APE benefit as time went by. By 1997 everyone in this group was entitled to the benefit. Thomas Piketty studies the effects of the introduction of the parental education allowance as a natural experiment using families with two children as treatment group and families never or always (i.e., either before and after the policy change) entitled to APE as control groups. The development of the employment rates within the different groups of mothers—living in a couple and aged younger than 55—with young children in the period 1994–1997 was as follows:

Number of children	One child younger than 3	Entitled to APE Before 1994	Entitled to APE After 1994	March 1994	March 1997	Difference	Difference-in-differences
Two	yes	no	yes	59	47	−12	
One	yes	no	no	62	64	+2	−14
Three	yes	yes	yes	31	34	+3	−15
Two	no	no	no	68	69	+1	−13

The table data indicate that the employment rate of mothers who became entitled to the APE dropped from 59 percent to 47 percent. Such a drop in the employment rate did not occur for mothers who were not entitled to APE, that is, mothers with one child aged younger than 3 and mothers with two children but no child below

---

the age of 3. Also, for mothers with three children of whom at least one was aged younger than 3—who were already entitled to the APE before 1994—a drop in the employment rate did not occur. The employment rate among these mothers was only 31 percent in 1994, but by 1997 it had increased to 34 percent. If we use a difference-in-differences approach, it is possible to draw the conclusion that the expansion of the APE to mothers with two children caused the employment rate of this group to drop 13–15 percentage points.

Source: Piketty (1998).

Childcare and Hours of Work in Norway

BOX 7.2

The rates of female labor force participation in Scandinavia are high compared with most other European countries. In Norway the labor force participation rate of married and cohabiting mothers was 75 percent if the youngest child was younger than 3 years old and 83 percent if the child was from 3 to 6 years old. One reason for the high labor force participation rate of women with preschool children is high-quality public childcare. The costs of public and private daycare centers are shared by the state, municipalities, and parents. Parental payments for daycare vary according to local rules and may be means tested, that is, conditional on having income and assets below a given threshold. In 1998 the Norwegian government introduced cash benefits to those parents with 1- to 3-year-old children who did not use state-subsidized daycare facilities. The amount provided was roughly equivalent to the state subsidy per child given to daycare centers. Parents who used daycare facilities only for a limited number of hours were entitled to receive a proportionally lower cash benefit. The main reason for introducing the cash-benefit reform was to offer an alternative to subsidized daycare to parents by giving them freedom of choice in childrearing. The presence of young children increases the value of women's time at home, which reduces their labor market activity. The cash-benefit reform increases the value of mothers' time at home, thus increasing the relative costs of childcare centers for parents and making market work less attractive. To investigate the effects on hours of work of mothers and fathers, Ghazala Naz compared the labor supply of parents with children aged from 1 to 3 (the treatment group) and the labor supply of parents with children in the age group 3–6 (the control group). Before the reform neither group of parents was entitled to the cash benefits; after the reform the first group of parents was entitled while the second was not. The table indicates what happened to the average number of hours worked (per week):

Working hours	Children age 1–3			Children age 3–6			Difference-in-differences
	Before	After	Difference	Before	After	Difference	
Mother	24.4	23.7	−0.7	24.5	26.5	2.0	−2.7
Father	40.9	41.3	+0.4	40.8	40.8	0.0	+0.4
Total	65.3	65.0	−0.3	65.3	67.3	2.0	−2.3

Hence the mother's working hours decreased by 0.7 hours per week if she had children aged 1–3, while it increased by 2.0 hours per week if she had children 3–6 years old, leaving an effect of the cash benefit of 2.7 hours. The labor supply of fathers hardly changed.

Source: Naz (2004).

Ruhm (1998) presents an empirical analysis of the economic consequences of rights to paid parental leave in nine European countries in the 1970s through the early 1990s. He argues that parental leave mandates will shift the labor supply curve of women to the right while moving the demand curve to the left. If leave benefits are primarily state funded, the effect on the demand curve will be small. This should have a positive effect on the employment of women and a negative effect on their wages. Ruhm's empirical analysis exploits changes in paid parental leave policies in the countries investigated. He finds that rights to short periods of paid parental leave increase the employment rates of women by 3–4 percent while having little effect on wages. He also finds that extended parental leave periods raise the female employment rate by the same amount, but they also decrease hourly earnings by about 3 percent.

Tanaka (2005) presents a cross-country time-series analysis investigating the relationship between parental leave (paid and unpaid) and child health. The main result of the study is that job-protected paid parental leave decreases infant mortality, whereas unpaid leave and paid leave that is not job-protective do not. Dustmann and Schönberg (2011) evaluate long-term outcomes of children whose mothers benefited from extended maternity leave. They find very little support for the hypothesis that the expansion in leave coverage improved children's outcomes. The effects on educational attainments and wages are small, and in the case of schools preparing children for attending universities, mildly negative.

Baker and Milligan (2010) concentrate on labor market behavior of mothers in the months immediately after childbirth, exploiting the wide differences in maternity leave policies in Canada to identify the effects of family policies. The methodology and the results of this study are described in some detail in box 7.3.

BOX 7.3   *Duration of Maternity Leave and Job Tenure in Canada*

A key problem faced by studies evaluating the effects of parental leave on labor supply is that mothers decide whether or not to take parental leave, and this decision will be affected by characteristics of the mothers, of their families, jobs, and so forth, which cannot always be measured and controlled for in the context of natural experiments. In other words, the exposure to maternity leave cannot be considered as an exogenous treatment to which some representative mothers are exposed while others are not, even after conditioning on observable characteristics of the two groups.

Michael Baker and Kevin Milligan have been investigating the effects on the period mothers are away from work postbirth and the likelihood they return to their prebirth employer in Canada. An advantage of working on Canadian data is that, due to differences across Canadian provinces in the extent of mandated parental leave and reforms of these regulations, mothers' leave eligibility varies over time and space rather than by their choices to work with particular employers, and their choices are therefore less likely to be correlated with their unobserved characteristics. Baker and Milligan considered two policy changes. The first was the introduction of relatively short mandatory leave (lasting at most 17–18 weeks) in several provinces. The second was the extension of these leaves to much longer periods, ranging from 29 to 70 weeks. Baker and Milligan compared the time spent by mothers at home with their infants in provinces with and without these regulations and before and after these policy changes. They also looked at whether the mothers returning to work were changing employers and losing their job-specific human capital. Figure 7.5 motivates their approach: it compares the fraction of married mothers employed and on leave one month before the childbirth in Ontario and Quebec, two states with similar economic structures, before and after (the vertical line marks the date of the reform) the introduction of a mandatory maternity leave of 18 weeks in Quebec (treatment) in 1978. During the observation period maternity leave regulations in Ontario were left unchanged. The focus is on the month before childbirth, as few private sector arrangements covered the month before birth. In contrast, the new maternity leave entitlement did allow leave in the month before birth. So, looking at the month before birth is less likely to show "crowding out" of existing private arrangements. The figure points to a widening gap between the two provinces after the reform, suggesting that the introduction of maternity leave did increase the proportion of women taking the leave. Baker and Milligan find that the extension of maternity leave succeeds in increasing the time spent by mothers at home with their infants. This effect is stronger after the

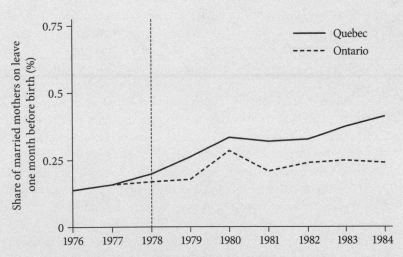

FIGURE 7.5 Married mothers employed and on leave before birth, Ontario versus Quebec

Source: Panel-based sample from the Labour Force Survey.

Notes: Sample includes married mothers aged 20–39 in the month before their children were born. Only the provinces of Ontario and Quebec are included.

introduction of European-type parental leave periods (lasting from 29 to 79 weeks). Importantly, they find that mandatory maternity leave at all lengths increases the probability that women returning to work keep their pre-birth employers. This is in line with the implication of the model of parental leave outlined in section 7.2.2.

Source: Baker and Milligan (2010).

Lalive and Zweimüller (2009) investigated the effects of maternity leave on fertility decisions, finding a positive and significant effect of these policies on the proportion of women giving birth to at least one additional child after the introduction of the possibility of having a single long leave across two or more relatively close childbirths. The approach and the results of their study are summarized in box 7.4.

BOX 7.4   *Effects of Parental Leave on Fertility in Austria*

Rafael Lalive and Josef Zweimüller investigated the effects of the duration of parental leave on the decision to have a second child shortly after having given birth to the first child. This is important in assessing the effectiveness of family policies in raising fertility rates to the replacement level of 2.1 children per woman. To identify the effects of policies, the authors use as a natural experiment a 1990 reform that increased to 27.5 months (from 15.5) the period since the birth of the first child in which a new baby should be conceived to benefit from an extended spell of maternity leave, without needing to go back to the former employer between births. They draw on data from the Austrian social security records. They use as the treatment group mothers having given birth to the first child just after the policy change, in July 1990, and as control group women not entitled to the new regulation (because they gave birth in June 1990). A key finding of their study is summarized in figure 7.6a. The vertical axis measures the percentage of women who gave birth to a second child within 36 months following the June or July 1990 birth. The figure suggests that less than one-third of women in the control group gave birth to an additional child within the 36 months since the first birth date, compared to almost 36.7 percent in the treatment group. Thus, the effect is rather sizable: almost 5 percent of women tend to give birth to an additional child in the treated cohort than in the control group. Lalive and Zweimüller also find that the effect on fertility is persistent: among women eligible for the more generous parental leave rules, 3 percent of women gave birth to an additional child within 10 years after the birth of the first child who would not have done so with a short leave. The authors also investigated the effects of this policy on the probability of returning to work in the short and in the long run. They found strikingly similar employment and earning levels for women benefiting from the extended leave and mothers in the control group nine months after the birth of the child onward. However, the fraction of women returning to work in the treatment within the

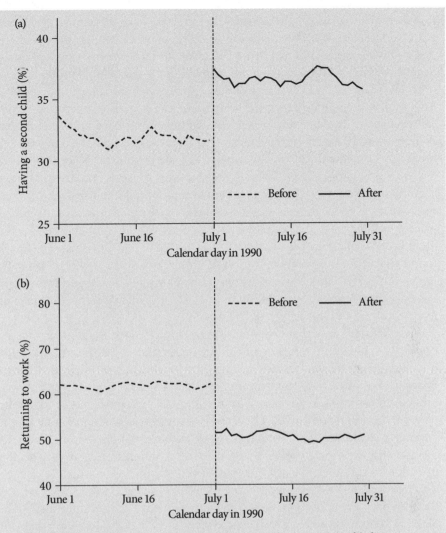

FIGURE 7.6 Extended parental leave: (a) percentage of women giving birth to a second child within three years; (b) percentage returning to work within three years

15.5 months since birth is lower, as women eligible for parental leave exploit the renewal option (figure 7.6b). This choice, however, does not seem to have lasting effects on employment and earnings.

Source: Lalive and Zweimüller (2009).

7.4 Policy Issues

7.4.1 Should Public Policies Encourage Mothers to Work?

The key argument in favor of family policies is that they increase female labor force participation, improving the position of women at the workplace. If properly designed, they can also improve the bargaining position of women in the household (see section 7.4.2). A larger proportion of women working is likely to yield a double dividend: according to the so-called *marketization hypothesis* (Freeman and Schettkat 2005), working women create demand for market substitutes for household production and thus create demand for labor producing these substitutes. This increases employment, value added, and the tax base, generating more fiscal revenues to finance childcare services. However, it is debatable whether public policies should increase employment per se. This may occur at the cost of reducing the welfare of individuals, notably when there is a surplus from home production (see technical annex 7.9.2). Encouraging mothers to work, in particular, may be harmful to children's well-being and human capital: children may be healthier and improve their noncognitive skills if they get more parental attention. While some studies find that maternal employment has positive effects on children's achievement because of increasing household incomes (Blau and Grossberg 1992), others found that it leads to a deterioration of children's cognitive skills (Baum 2003; James-Burdumy 2005). Thus, the proper balancing of work and family life requires not only considering the promotion of female employment rates but also the quality of childcare and the welfare of children.

Blau (2001) argues that childcare quality in the United States is low—not because of a failure on the supply side of the market, but because many parents are unwilling to pay for quality care. The majority of childcare subsidies in the United States do not place restrictions on the quality of the care and do not provide incentives to use high-quality care, but the subsidies are available only to employed parents. According to Blau, the childcare subsidies encourage employment of both parents in two-parent families and of the single parent in one-parent families, but it is not clear why society should wish to provide this encouragement. The system of childcare subsidies increases the well-being of families in which both parents are employed, but it does not provide benefits to families in which one parent stays home to take care of children. Indeed, as shown in box 7.2 on childcare subsidies in Norway, if subsidies are provided irrespective of whether childcare is actually used, many parents, mainly women, opt for providing childcare themselves. If childcare subsidies are provided conditional on parental employment, the demand for greater quantity but not necessarily higher quality of childcare will increase.

Blau (2001) argues that there is no compelling economic or moral reason to encourage employment of both parents in a two-parent middle-class family. For single-parent families there may be a reason for childcare subsidies, but this is at best an indirect approach and at worst an ineffective policy instrument to accomplish this goal. If governments subsidize the costs of raising children, they could do this without favoring market costs for childcare over the forgone-earnings cost of a parent who stays home to care for a child.

Policies should also take into account cultural and social customs. In some countries the use of external childcare facilities may be small because of a social stigma related to sending children to these facilities. In economic terms this implies that there are fixed—mainly psychological—costs related to the use of childcare facilities. Under these circumstances, policies to promote female employment may not be in line with social norms.

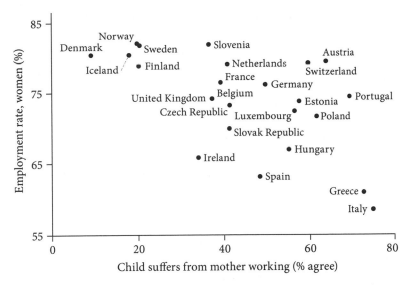

FIGURE 7.7 Cross-country relationship between norms about women working and the employment rate of prime-aged women, 1990
Sources: World Values Survey (www.worldvaluessurvey.org); OECD (2001).

Figure 7.7 shows that there is a negative cross-country relationship between opinions about mothers working and the employment of prime-aged women. In countries where many people agree with the statement that preschool children suffer when their mothers work, employment rates of prime-aged women are lower. In Denmark, for example, where many disagree with this statement, female employment rates are quite high. In Italy many agree, and the female employment rates are rather low. Nevertheless, there are also clear outliers. In Austria many think that a preschool child suffers when the mother works, but still the female employment rates are high; in Ireland and Spain many individuals do not worry, but the female employment rate is not very high. Clearly there is not a one-to-one relationship between social and cultural norms and female employment. Nevertheless, if low female employment rates in some countries represent social and cultural preferences, it may not be optimal from a welfare standpoint to promote female employment.[5] Still, it is also possible that the cultural norms merely support the existing situation. In that case an increasing female employment rate could change opinions about participation of mothers in the labor force.[6] The wives of men whose mothers worked were found by Fernandez (2004) to be significantly more likely to work. Geographical proximity to women working with children is also important in shaping preferences as to the conciliation of motherhood with

5. See Algan and Cahuc (2005) for more details.
6. For example, in the Netherlands in 1965, 84 percent of the respondents aged 17–70 years indicated that they find it objectionable for married women who have school-aged children to work. In 1970 this number was 44 percent, in 1980 36 percent, in 1991 20 percent, and in 1997 18 percent. This change in opinions coincides with a strong increase in female labor force participation (Sociaal en Cultureel Planbureau 1998).

employment (Fogli 2011). In addition to changing preferences, more mothers at work may involve an increased bargaining power of women within the household, and women are generally less negative than men about the possibility of reconciling employment of mothers and the well-being of children.

Fertility rates are below replacement level in all OECD countries, and in some countries they are barely half that level (OECD 2001). In almost all OECD countries there are similar trends in female employment rates and fertility rates. Over past decades successive cohorts of young women have had higher employment rates but lower fertility rates. Furthermore, it seems that larger increases in employment have been associated with larger decreases in fertility. In coming decades the working-age population is likely to decline in many OECD countries. Increasing rates of female labor force participation may balance this decline in the working-age population. However, if increasing female labor force participation causes lower fertility rates, the future working-age population will be reduced. At the same time, high levels of female employment are not incompatible with relatively high fertility rates. Indeed, as shown in figure 7.4, now there is even a positive cross-country correlation between fertility and employment rates of prime-aged women. Thus, with regard to the size of the future working-age population, there does not seem to be a trade-off between female employment rates and fertility rates.

All in all, the main argument for subsidizing childcare facilities to encourage mothers to enter the labor market is based on the idea that labor force participation should go up to deal with an aging society and a shrinking tax base. From the perspective of what is best for children, providing childcare subsidies is not sufficient to guarantee high-quality childcare arrangements.

7.4.2 Who in the Family Should Receive the Subsidy?

Governments may support external childcare by subsidizing providers or consumers.[7] Since only childcare providers who meet certain requirements are eligible for subsidies, only formal providers, such as daycare centers and preschools, benefit from a policy of subsidizing providers. This induces a bias in state support toward formal childcare, crowding out informal childcare arrangements that can be sometimes preferable from the standpoint of children's welfare.

More and more countries are therefore providing consumer subsidies via childcare tax credits and deductions, which are not limited to specific types of childcare providers (Blau and Grossberg 1992). An alternative, which is neutral with respect to the choice between formal and informal childcare providers, is to provide vouchers to families with children that can be used to support either type of care.

A key issue arising in this context is who in the family should receive the subsidy. The simple theoretical models presented in this chapter are not particularly insightful in this context, as they consider the family as a monolith: everybody in

---

7. Apart from subsidies, governments may also influence childcare facilities through regulations concerning child-staff ratios and the qualifications of the provider.

the family has the same preferences, and choices are made as if a single decision-maker acts for the good of everybody. Income is pooled across all household members, rather than being allocated based on some sharing rule. In this context, the so-called *unitary model of household behavior*, it is immaterial who in the family receives the subsidy. What matters is the amount and the characteristics of the transfer, not the identity of the individual within the household who is the target of the public program. A problem with this approach is that it cannot explain differences in the allocation of income and labor/leisure time in the household. It treats such differences as a willing act on the part of all household members.

The *collective models of household behavior* (Chiappori and Bourguignon 1992) allow for heterogeneity of preferences in the household and hence for intra-household bargaining to establish the allocation of incomes, consumption, and tasks. These collective decisions must be efficient in the Pareto sense—that is, it should not be possible to improve the position of one member of the household without making someone else in the same household worse off (see technical annex 7.9.3). There are many possible allocations of time and consumption that are Pareto efficient. All those along the *contract curve* satisfy this property. The equilibrium solution will depend on the sharing of nonlabor income across the members of the household. As indicated by Browning et al. (1994), this sharing rule is strongly related to the initial allocation of wealth and nonlabor income in the family.

An advantage of this approach is that it is possible to understand why policy-makers care about the allocation of transfers within the household. For instance, the decision by the UK government in the mid-1970s to make child benefits payable only to the mother was expected to be popular with women and unpopular with men (Lundberg et al. 1997). Many empirical studies, notably in developing countries, document that transfers being provided to mothers have the potential to induce behavior that is more beneficial for their children.[8] Moreover, empirical tests of the implications of the unitary versus collective household model generally speak in favor of the latter (Fortin and Lacroix 1997) except in particular circumstances and particular categories of individuals (including parents with preschool children). Thus, it is always safer when designing policies to consider that labor supply decisions within the household are interdependent, and an individual's fluctuation in income will have an impact not only on the individual's own supply of labor, but also on that of the spouse or other members of the household. Neglecting these interdependencies in the design of policies can be fairly misleading, as discussed more extensively in chapter 13.

7.5 Interactions with Other Institutions

Equal opportunity legislation (see chapter 4) is important for reducing the risk that family policies increasing gender asymmetries in labor costs induce employers to hire men preferentially over women. The family policies institution also has

---

8. See Alderman et al. (1994) for a survey.

clear relationships with hours of work (see chapter 5), because working-time regulations, notably the development of part-time employment, also enable parents to combine work and care. Indeed, across countries there is a negative correlation between the share of women involved in part-time employment and the coverage of subsidized childcare for infants (figure 7.8).

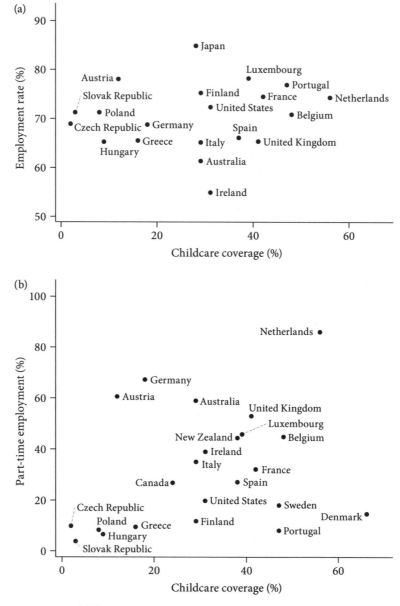

FIGURE 7.8 Childcare coverage of children younger than 3 and employment of women with at least one child, 2010 (a) and part-time employment as percentage of total employment of women with at least one child (b)
Sources: OECD Family Database, 2011; Eurostat.

Family policies interact with ALMPs, notably those targeted to women going back to work after maternity (see chapter 12). Finally, the payroll taxes institution (see chapter 13) also concerns elements of family policies, in particular, income transfers to households and the interdependencies among labor supply decisions. A discussion of interactions of family policies with other institutions in the EU is provided by Del Boca and Wetzels (2008).

7.6 Why Do Family Policies Exist?

Governments introduce mandatory parental leave because the social net benefits of parental care are generally higher than the private net benefits. If both parents have jobs, an important question is who will take care of the children and who will pay for that care. Many European countries provide heavily subsidized public childcare. In a few countries there is a market for childcare. Only the United States has a childcare policy that is mainly private. Blau (2001) distinguishes two dimensions along which childcare programs may be organized. The first dimension is the employment requirement of the program, with no requirements at the one extreme and full-time parental employment at the other. The second dimension is the quality of the childcare required to be eligible for a subsidy. According to Blau, in 1999 in the United States only one-third of the programs had a major focus on quality, while the other two-thirds had little emphasis on quality but strong emphasis on parental employment. In European countries childcare is often publicly provided with relatively generous funding and coverage, with a strong emphasis on quality. Childcare subsidies may be provided because of the existence of imperfections in the market for childcare: parents have imperfect information about its quality. This may lead to moral hazard and adverse selection. Moral hazard may occur because parents know less about the quality than the provider, and monitoring quality is costly. Adverse selection of providers may occur in the informal care sector. Because family daycare is a low-wage occupation, women with high wage offers in other occupations are less likely to choose the daycare sector. Subsidies targeted at high-quality childcare may induce parents to opt for higher quality care. Although this does not solve the information problem, it may induce parents to choose a level of childcare that is not suboptimal from a social point of view. This externality argument is related to one line of reasoning for education subsidies (see chapter 8). High-quality childcare increases the probability that children will attend higher education, which reduces costs to society related to low education: low wages, unstable employment, long-term unemployment, dependency on social transfers, and so on. Because parents may not be fully aware of these benefits, there is a difference between private and social discount rates.

7.7 Suggestions for Further Reading

The chapter "Balancing Work and Family Life: Helping Parents into Paid Employment" in OECD (2001) is very informative about cross-country differences in family policies. Francine Blau and Adam Grossberg (1992) and David Blau (2000) discuss childcare subsidy programs, focusing on the United States.

7.8 Review Questions and Exercises

1. Why do lone-parent households face above-average poverty risk?

2. Why do some countries provide family allowances only to those who are not working?

3. Why have some countries introduced mandated paternity leave?

4. Why might it improve welfare if governments subsidize childcare facilities?

5. Why did the OECD cross-country correlation between female participation and fertility rates change from negative to positive?

6. How does childcare affect the reservation wage of women?

7. How does parental leave affect employment and wages?

8. For a long time economics was called the "dismal science" because of Malthus's ideas. What is wrong with his ideas?

9. How can governments influence the market for childcare? What are the pros and cons of these policies?

10. To what extent is the targeting of policies within the household important in the design of family policies?

11. Show graphically how the cost of childcare facilities affects individual labor supply for women distinguishing between fixed and variable costs. What type of policies are likely to increase the labor force participation of women?

12. Consider a couple ranking purchased goods and services C and home-produced goods and services D as follows:

$$U = CD, \tag{7.1}$$

where D is produced via a decreasing returns-to-scale technology $f(h_d) = \sqrt{h_d}$, using as input time h_d devoted to home production as opposed to market work h. Suppose further that the individual can allocate 100 hours per week to either market work or home production.

   (a) What is the optimal allocation of time between market and home production when the wage is 10 euros per hour?

   (b) Suppose that now the couple has a child and, given the extra value of the time spent with the child, the joint utility becomes

$$U = CD^2. \tag{7.2}$$

   At the same time, any hour spent away from the child involves a cost of 5 euros to be paid to a babysitter. How does this affect the allocation of time of the family?

   (c) Would your answer differ if home production technologies improve (e.g., as a result of the introduction of disposable diapers and microwave ovens), so that household production becomes $f(h_D) = h_D^{.8}$?

13. (Advanced) Consider a household where the husband can earn a market wage of 25 euros per hour or produce at home the equivalent of 10 euros. The wife can instead earn 20 euros per hour or produce domestically the equivalent of 15 euros. Both members of the household have a total allocation of time to either market work or home production of 50 hours per week.

   (a) Does it make sense for both members of the couple to work for pay?

   (b) Would an increase of the wife's wage affect her decision? Would it affect the decision of the husband?

   Suppose now that the productivity of the husband and the wife are dependent on the amount of time spent in home production by the other partner. How does this affect their allocation of time if:

   (a) The husband and wife are substitutes in home production?

   (b) The husband and wife are complements in home production?

   (c) Their decision is based on bargaining within the household?

7.9 Technical Annex: Family Policies

7.9.1 Childcare Facilities

We assume that the mother derives utility U from consumption c and leisure l: $U = U(c, l)$. As indicated in the main text, if the mother takes care of the children, this is assumed to be a leisure activity, a normal good. Every hour of work is at the expense of one hour of leisure, and for every hour of work, formal childcare has to be provided. Informal childcare is ruled out.

First, we consider the fixed-costs case. This is the case if the childcare facilities are provided for an entrance fee, a subscription to facilities that is unrelated to the amount of use. If w is net hourly wage, h is the (weekly) hours of work, m is nonlabor income, and F_c is the fixed cost of childcare, the mother can choose between two weekly budget constraints:

$$c_1 = m \tag{7.3}$$

if the mother decides not to work and

$$c_2 = m - F_c + wh \tag{7.4}$$

if the mother enters the labor market and works h hours, where $h = l_0 - l$, and l_0 is the total time allocation. The mother will decide to enter the labor market and work h hours if $U(c_1, l_0) < U(c_2, l_0 - h)$. Even if the earnings exceed the fixed costs of childcare, the mother may not enter the labor market because of the reduction in leisure. If a childcare subsidy is provided, it raises the potential income from working, increasing the likelihood of work. At the same time, the subsidy would reduce the hours of work of the working mother because of the (negative) income effect associated with the transfer.

The second case is the one where childcare costs are variable; that is, every hour of childcare costs c_c. Now the budget constraint is

$$c_3 = m + (w - c_c)h; \tag{7.5}$$

in other words the budget constraint rotates, because the actual wage net of the childcare costs decreases. Insofar as the substitution effect dominates over the income effect, there is a reduction in hours of work, which may even lead mothers to exit the labor force. Symmetrically, a childcare subsidy will increase the net wage, having an ambiguous effect on hours of work. There is indeed a positive substitution effect and a negative income effect of the subsidy, if we assume that leisure is a normal good.

Formally, denoting by h^* the optimal choice of hours of work, the comparative statics of an increase in variable childcare costs is given by

$$\frac{\partial h^*}{\partial c_c} = \frac{\partial l}{\partial w} + \frac{\partial l}{\partial m} l_0, \tag{7.6}$$

where the first term on the right-hand side (the substitution effect) is negative and the second (the income effect) is positive. Notice that an increase in the childcare subsidy is equivalent to a reduction in c_c.

7.9.2 The Surplus from Home Production

Define by c total consumption and by c_d the consumption of goods and services generated domestically without monetary transaction. Suppose further that home production uses the technology $c_d = f(h_d)$, where h_d is the amount of time devoted to home production. The total time allocation constraint is therefore

$$l_0 = l + h_m + h_d, \tag{7.7}$$

where h_m denotes hours of market work, and the budget constraint reads

$$c_m \leq wh_m + m, \tag{7.8}$$

where $c_m = c - c_d$ is the consumption in the marketed good. Substituting (7.7) into (7.8) and using the definition of home production, we have

$$c + wl \leq m + wl_0 + [f(h_d) - wh_d]. \tag{7.9}$$

The last term on the right-hand side denotes the surplus from home production.

7.9.3 The Unitary and Collective Models of the Household

Consider a family composed of two individuals, indexed by 1 and 2. The unitary model of labor supply assumes that decisions about the labor-leisure trade-off are made maximizing a joint utility function of the type

$$U(c, l_1, l_2)$$

(7.10)

$$\text{subject to} \quad c + w_1 l_1 + w_2 l_2 \leq m_1 + m_2 + (w_1 + w_2) l_0.$$

This form implies that the distribution of nonlabor income within the household is immaterial. What matters is uniquely the sum $m_1 + m_2$, as there is *income pooling* within the household. This description of family decisionmaking implies that policymakers should not care about the targeting of family policies within the household.

The collective model of the household instead assumes that decisions maximize the utility of a single household member, say, member 1, subject to the constraint that the utility of the other household member is greater than a given level of utility, supposedly related to the nonlabor income and wage of the individual. Formally, the model solves the following problem:

$$\max U(c_1, l_1)$$

(7.11)

$$\text{subject to} \quad U(c_2, l_2) \geq \bar{U}_2$$

$$c_1 + c_2 + w_1 l_1 + w_2 l_2 \leq m_1 + m_2 + (w_1 + w_2) l_0,$$

where $\bar{U}_2$ is a given utility level.

The utility level of the two household members will depend on some sharing of family endowments in the household. Under these conditions, the targeting of policies to specific household members is likely to affect the initial allocation of resources in the family, providing a stronger representation of the preferences of the member of the household receiving the transfer. To illustrate the relation with the sharing rule, the above problem can also be specified as

$$\max U(c_1, l_1)$$

(7.12)

$$\text{subject to} \quad c_1 + w_1 l_1 \leq \phi_1 + w_1 l_0,$$

where ϕ_1 is a sharing rule such that $\phi_1 + \phi_2 = m_1 + m_2$.

CHAPTER EIGHT **Education and Training**

Governments devote a significant, and often increasing, amount of resources to education. In 1880, for example, the United States spent 1 percent of its GDP on primary and secondary public education. By 1920 this figure had doubled, and by 1980 it had reached 4.1 percent. From 1870 to 1970, the days attended during the school year doubled, and the fraction of those 10–19 years old enrolled in school increased from about 40 to 90 percent (Rangazas 2002).

Governments spend on education as an investment in their endowment of *human capital,* a notion that dates back to the *Wealth of Nations.*[1] The educational attainment of the workforce is a strong predictor of the degree of economic development of a country. In cross-country regressions, nations with, on average, 12 years of education per person of working age display income per capita levels that are up to eight times higher than those of countries with only 6 years of education. However, according to Bils and Klenow (2000), no more than one-third of these cross-country correlations can be attributed to a causal effect of education on growth. Moreover, the quality of education, as measured by test scores, matters more than the quantity (i.e., the average number of years of schooling). Based on growth regressions, Hanushek and Woessmann (2011) estimated that raising students in all OECD countries to the same average level of proficiency of the top country in international school achievement tests could increase aggregate GDP in the area in the long run by almost 14 percent.

Educational attainments are also a very strong predictor of labor market performance at the micro level. Individuals with higher levels of education typically earn more and have a higher probability of being employed than do poorly educated individuals. Thus, there is a visible monetary return to the efforts and the *real expenses* (in the words of Adam Smith) made in acquiring competences, both at the individual level and at the level of a country as a whole.

1. The acquisition of such talents, by the maintenance of the acquired during his education, study, or apprenticeship, always costs a real expense, which is a capital fixed and realized, as it were, in his person. Those talents, as they make a part of his fortune, so do they likewise of that of the society to which he belongs. The improved dexterity of a workman may be considered in the same light as a machine or instrument of trade which facilitates and abridges labor, and which, though it costs a certain expense, repays that expense with a profit. [Adam Smith, 1776]

However, when Gary Becker (1964) developed his theory of human capital investment, his ideas were considered debasing and were received with skepticism even by many of his colleagues. "You want to measure everything and reduce something that is immaterial to a pecuniary calculation!" was the kindest reaction of many sociologists and political scientists, let alone several rather old-fashioned economists. Others were calling his theory "human cattle": "you consider investment in human beings like investment in cows; you feed them not because you want to get better cows, but because you can make money getting better or more milk." But when deciding which U.S. college to send their children to, the very same colleagues who questioned Becker's approach were anxiously looking for information on the earnings of students graduating from these institutions and comparing them with tuition fees. In private, they were doing just the type of calculations envisaged by the human capital investment theory, although, in public, they were denying its relevance.

Schooling and training are investments by individuals and firms whose costs are paid in exchange for expected future profits. The human capital of individuals is influenced by their innate ability, their investment in schooling, and their investment in on-the-job training. The main difference between human capital and physical capital concerns property rights. Whereas physical capital can be sold, human capital is embodied in persons. Therefore, for firms to use human capital, workers and firms have to agree on the terms of use.

Going to school is a productive investment, since additional years of schooling lead to higher wages and better employment prospects. On-the-job training is also a productive investment, because it increases general or firm-specific productive skills of workers. Formal schooling most often takes place before an individual enters the labor market. Subject to their ability, individuals choose the educational level they wish to obtain by balancing costs and expected benefits, such as a higher wage and a higher employment rate that stem from the productivity increases from educational attainment.

Training most often takes place after entrance into the labor market. Schooling and training are often complements: training on-the-job is needed as technology changes and knowledge needs to be updated. Sometimes training is general; that is, it is useful in many firms. At other times training is firm specific: it only has a positive effect on productivity within the firm and cannot be used in other firms. The literature on schooling focuses on the decisions of individuals concerning their choice of educational attainment; the literature on training focuses on the question of who pays for the training—the worker or the employer. Standard human capital theory predicts that the costs of general on-the-job training have to be paid by workers, while the costs of firm-specific training have to be paid by firms. An important element in the discussion is the influence of the nature of the labor market, that is, whether it is competitive.

The main market failures concerning education and training are fourfold. First, individuals are confronted with incomplete capital markets, so they are restricted in their optimal decisionmaking, and their investment decision may be suboptimal. Second, it may be that the private rate of return to education and training differs from the social rate of return. Third, there is a long time lag between an educational decision and the outcome of that decision. Fourth, there is a *holdup problem:* once an investment in training is made by the employer, the worker can leave the firm and negotiate a higher wage somewhere else. Alternatively, once a worker has invested in human capital, he may be fired and thus be unable to benefit from the investment. Because of these market failures, governments influence education and training, often by making it cheaper for individuals to invest in their human capital and thus increase their productivity.

8.1 Measures and Cross-Country Comparisons

The way formal education is organized is highly country specific. Individuals may choose the type and amount of education they wish to acquire on the basis of costs and benefits. Acquiring formal education is an investment decision, with rates of return connected to that decision. Provision of in-company training also differs significantly across countries.

Table 8.1 provides a cross-country overview of expenditures on educational institutions as a percentage of GDP for all levels of education. There are substantial differences in spending levels, ranging from lows of 3.8–4.1 percent in Turkey, the Slovak Republic, and Greece to greater than 7 percent for Denmark, the United States, Norway, Korea, and Iceland. Table 8.1 also provides an overview of educational attainments in terms of the average number of years spent in formal education. There are differences between men and women, but the within-country differences are much smaller than the between-country differences. Portugal has the lowest educational attainments, with men reaching 8.3 years and women 8.7 years of formal education. Educational levels are highest in Norway, where adult men and women, on average, have 13.9 years of formal education. There is a positive relationship between educational expenditures and educational attainment, but the relationship is imperfect, with a mild slope. Portugal and Mexico are clear outliers with relatively high expenditures and low educational attainments.[2]

Teaching curricula and the quality of education differ substantially across countries. Thus, to establish some form of equivalence across different education systems, one must go beyond years of schooling (Freeman 1999). The International Standard Classification of Education (ISCED) was introduced in 1997 by the United Nations Educational, Scientific and Cultural Organization (UNESCO) to improve cross-country comparability of education statistics. It provides six categories defined on the basis of the level and field of education. Table 8.1 provides the fraction of the population having at least level 3 (upper secondary) or level 5 (first stage of tertiary) education. Finally, table 8.1 also provides some information on the quality of education, that is, on literacy levels. In particular, it provides an overview of mathematics scores, as measured through

---

2. Of course, the comparison of expenditures and educational attainment is far from perfect, since the expenditures concern a particular year, 2011, while educational attainment concerns persons aged 25–64 years, most of whom have been to school decades ago. Nevertheless, even among younger cohorts Portuguese men and women have relatively low educational attainment.

TABLE 8.1 Educational expenditures and attainments

Country	Educational expenditure (% GDP)	Years of formal education		Educational attainment		PISA math score
		Men	Women	ISCED 3	ISCED 5	
Australia	5.2	12.8	12.5	30	37	514
Austria	5.4	12.3	11.7	54	19	496
Belgium	6.6	11.4	11.4	34	33	515
Canada	6.0	13.2	13.3	26	49	527
Czech Republic	4.5	12.6	12.4	76	16	493
Denmark	7.1	13.5	13.3	42	33	503
Finland	5.9	10.9	11.4	44	38	—
France	6.0	11.7	11.4	31	30	497
Germany	4.8	13.7	13.2	52	26	513
Greece	4.1	11.0	10.7	33	24	466
Hungary	4.8	11.8	11.6	59	19	490
Iceland	7.9	9.7	11.4	30	33	507
Ireland	5.6	12.9	13.1	23	36	487
Italy	4.8	10.2	10.0	40	14	483
Japan	4.9	12.6	12.1	56	44	529
Korea	7.6	12.5	11.4	41	39	—
Luxembourg	—	13.6	13.0	45	35	489
Mexico	5.8	9.1	8.6	19	16	419
Netherlands	5.6	11.4	11.1	37	33	526
New Zealand	6.6	12.6	12.6	28	40	519
Norway	7.3	13.9	13.9	41	37	498
Poland	5.7	11.6	11.9	63	21	495
Portugal	5.2	8.3	8.7	15	14	487
Slovak Republic	4.0	12.5	12.4	75	16	497
Spain	5.1	10.6	10.6	22	31	483
Sweden	6.3	12.4	12.8	46	33	494
Switzerland	5.7	13.5	12.5	50	35	534
Turkey	3.8	9.9	9.2	18	13	445
United Kingdom	5.7	12.7	12.4	52	37	492
United States	7.2	13.2	13.4	47	41	487

Sources: OECD online statistics, 2011; OECD (2012a).

Notes: Expenditures on educational institutions are given as a percentage of GDP for all levels of education, 2011; Greece and Turkey, 2005. The average number of years in formal education are for individuals 25–64 years old, 2011. Educational attainment is given as a percentage of the adult population, 2011. The PISA normalized score is for 15-year-olds in mathematics, 2009. PISA = Program for International Student Assessment; — = not available.

the Program for International Student Assessment (PISA) survey.[3] Here too there are large cross-country variations, with Switzerland reporting the highest score and Mexico having the lowest score. Again, there is a positive but mildly sloping relationship between educational expenditures and math scores. Switzerland has the highest math score, but far from the highest educational expenditures, while

3. PISA is a three-year survey of the knowledge and skills of 15-year-olds in the principal industrialized countries. The survey assesses how far students have acquired some of the cognitive skills that are essential for full participation in society. In particular, it tests reading as well as knowledge of math and science.

TABLE 8.2 Cross-country variation in employer-sponsored continuous vocational training courses

Country	IALS data		ECVTS data	
	Participation rate (%)	Annual volume (hours/worker)	Participation rate (%)	Annual volume (hours/worker)
Australia	24	15	—	—
Austria	—	—	31	9
Belgium	13	10	41	13
Canada	28	17	—	—
Czech Republic	16	13	42	10
Denmark	45	36	53	22
Finland	42	23	50	18
France	—	—	46	17
Germany	—	—	31	9
Greece	—	—	15	6
Hungary	14	13	12	5
Ireland	10	9	41	17
Italy	14	8	26	8
Luxembourg	—	—	36	14
Netherlands	24	21	41	15
New Zealand	34	23	—	—
Norway	45	35	—	16
Poland	11	8	16	4
Portugal	—	—	17	7
Spain	—	—	25	11
Sweden	—	—	61	18
Switzerland	14	9	—	—
United Kingdom	44	22	49	13
United States	33	18	—	—

Source: OECD (2003).

Notes: Data in columns 1 and 2 are from the International Adult Literacy Survey (IALS) and refer to job-related education and training that employers provided to (or partially paid for) their workers aged 26–65 in 1994 for Canada, Ireland, the Netherlands, Poland, Switzerland (German- and French-speaking regions), and the United States; in 1996 for Australia, Belgium (Flanders only), New Zealand, and the United Kingdom; and in 1998 for the Czech Republic, Denmark, Finland, Hungary, Italy, Norway, and the Italian-speaking regions of Switzerland; data in columns 3 and 4 are from the European Continuing Vocational Training Survey (ECVTS) for 1999 and refer to firms with at least 10 employees. Participation rate is the ratio of employed persons in training to total employment. Annual volume is hours per employed person. — = not available.

the United States has one of the highest educational expenditures but is among the lowest in math scores of its 15-year-olds.[4] PISA test scores provide measures of schooling outputs. In the countries where PISA tests have not been carried out, measures of educational quality are potentially available by looking at schooling inputs, such as the pupil-teacher ratio, the ratio of average salaries of teachers to per capita GDP, or the length of the school year.

Table 8.2 gives an overview of the cross-country variation in employer-sponsored training programs. For many countries this type of information is

4. Note that this may also be due to large expenditures in tertiary education, which most 15-year-old individuals have not yet started.

missing. Furthermore, there are differences in the numbers depending on whether the information comes from workers (columns 1 and 2) or from firms with at least 10 employees (columns 3 and 4).[5] In Belgium, for example, the participation rate in employer-sponsored training programs is 13 percent according to workers and 41 percent according to firms. This difference is either due to perception or because very small firms are excluded from the firm survey.[6] In countries for which information is available, there is wide variation. According to information from workers, in Ireland the participation rate in employer-provided training is only 10 percent, while it is 45 percent in Norway. Also, the number of hours spent in employer-based training shows wide cross-country variation, from 8 hours per year in Italy and Poland to 36 hours per year in Denmark. According to information from firms, the variation in participation ranges from a low of 12 percent in Hungary to a high of 61 percent in Sweden. The average annual hours per worker range from 4 in Poland to 22 in Denmark.

8.2 Theory

8.2.1 A Perfect Labor Market

In a perfect labor market employers are informed about the productivity of each worker, and wages can freely adjust to reflect these differences in productivity. Individuals invest in the accumulation of competences, that is, their *human capital*, throughout their lives. This investment is costly: it involves not only enrollment costs for formal education, traveling, lodging, purchase of books and other learning material and so forth (the direct costs of education) but also opportunity costs insofar as the time devoted to schooling is not allocated to a remunerated activity. Training on the job is also costly in terms of effort, although it does not involve a trade-off between getting educated and getting paid. The investment in human capital pays off in terms of higher productivity and earnings in the future. Thus, the decision of each individual worker as to how much to invest in human capital compares the costs and benefits of education.

Three basic assumptions of the human capital model of education (Becker 1964) are therefore satisfied in a perfect labor market:

1. More education leads to higher productivity.
2. Higher productivity leads to a higher wage.
3. Individuals choose their level of education based on financial considerations.

The Schooling Investment

According to this model, the optimal level of schooling depends on the expected benefits and the costs of schooling. The expected benefits are determined by the

5. In addition to these differences, firm-specific training may be underestimated, because the surveys do not account for apprenticeships, for example, in Germany, where this is a very important part of firm-specific training.

6. There is a positive relationship between firm size and participation of workers in employer-sponsored training programs. In Belgium participation is 20 percent in firms with 10–50 workers, while it is 66 percent in firms with more than 1,000 employees.

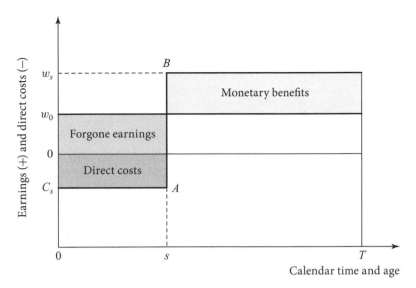

FIGURE 8.1 Benefits and costs of education

higher wages and higher employment probability associated with higher educational attainment and also by the expected length of time over which the returns to education materialize (the period between the educational attainment and the date of retirement).

Figure 8.1 represents the choice of the individual. The initial situation, which may represent high school or primary education, is normalized to zero. The individual has to compare two options. The first option is to start working immediately and have annual earnings w_0, which we consider to be constant for the remaining labor market years until retirement at age T.[7] The second option is to attend s years of schooling, during which direct educational costs have to be paid and after which the wage will be $w_s > w_0$. The total costs of s years of schooling are the direct costs C_s and the forgone earnings from 0 to s; the monetary benefits are the higher earnings over the period s to T. The individual will undertake the extra years of schooling if the present value of doing so is larger than the present value of not doing so (see technical annex 8.9.1 for details).

Attending a particular level of schooling is more attractive the longer the expected payout period is. Therefore, typically young people go to school. By comparing the net present value of the future stream of earnings with and without attending a specific number of years of schooling, individuals may find out how large their rate of return to schooling is. If the market rate of return to investment (the *external* rate) is higher than the rate of return to schooling (the *internal* rate), the individual should reduce the number of years of schooling; if the market rate of return to investment is lower, the years of schooling should be expanded.

Individuals may have different levels of human capital before acquiring education. In other words, they may have different endowments of *innate ability*, the

7. Note that we also ignore periods of unemployment.

productivity of the worker without any investment. The costs of funding study may also vary across individuals as well as the psychological costs of acquiring education, motivation, the drive to succeed, and the like. Thus, different workers will have different rates of return to schooling and will choose different levels of schooling accordingly. Accounting for this heterogeneity is one of the most challenging issues for empirical research.

General and Firm-Specific Training

After completing formal education, individuals may accumulate human capital and increase their productivity through on-the-job training (see Leuven 2005 for an overview). Before addressing the choice as to the amount of investment in human capital accumulation, it is necessarily to establish who pays for it. Either the employer or the employee could pay for on-the-job training. Becker (1964) distinguishes between *general training* and *firm-specific training*. General training in a firm increases productivity, but it can also be used by other firms, posing a problem of property rights to the employer. Because workers are free to leave, firms may never recoup their investment in general training. Therefore, workers have to pay for this, for example, by accepting wages lower than their productivity during training.

The problem of the choice of the optimal amount of general training is graphically illustrated in figure 8.2. The amount of general training τ increases the productivity and thus the output of the worker, $v(\tau)$, which is therefore upward sloping (see the top part of the diagram). However, there are diminishing returns to this investment. To reward the worker for the increased productivity, wages also increase with the amount of general training, so the wage, $w(\tau)$, is also upward sloping with diminishing returns. Training costs c will also increase with the amount of training, but increasingly so.

In perfect markets firms compete for the labor services of workers, and therefore $w(\tau) = v(\tau)$; hence the firm does not benefit from the general training. This being the case, it is obvious that the firm will not pay for the training, and the worker has

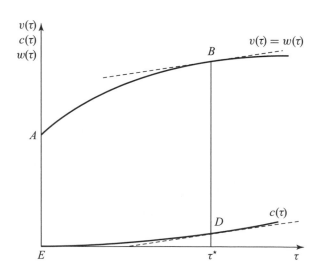

FIGURE 8.2 Training: perfect labor market—choice of workers

to bear the costs. The choice of the worker is depicted in figure 8.2. An optimizing worker will choose the level of training such that the difference between revenues and costs is at its maximum, that is, where marginal costs equal marginal benefits from training. This occurs when $\tau = \tau^*$, where the slopes of the cost and benefit functions are the same. In this situation the worker benefits from the training, and therefore it is optimal for the worker to pay for it. However, the worker's choice may be constrained. A requirement for the worker to make the investment is that the resources to invest in training are accessible. If workers are not credit constrained, in a perfect labor market, they will invest up to maximizing the private (and social) net benefits from training. In other words, there is no market failure in training (Acemoglu and Pischke 1999).

But this may not be the case. In the presence of credit market restrictions, the worker may not be able to make the investment. Since the employer cannot make the investment either, there is a market failure. In this case, even if the labor market is competitive, the government may want to intervene and provide subsidies for general training. The issue is that this type of market failure arises in the financial market rather than in the labor market. Rigid wages, however, make the problem more serious, as they prevent at least part of the costs of training being paid by workers accepting lower wages.

In the case of firm-specific training, there is no longer a property rights issue. Hence, firms appropriate the net benefits from this investment and, consequently, are willing to pay for it. Credit constraints are generally less serious for firms than for individual workers. Hence, a perfect labor market is generally also synonymous with an optimal level of investment in firm-specific training from a social standpoint. In this context the holdup problem discussed in the introduction to this chapter does not arise.

8.2.2 An Imperfect Labor Market

Schooling as a Signaling Device

In labor markets with informational asymmetries, potential employers may not be in a condition to observe the ability of workers at hiring and their productive efficiency in their future professional lives. Under these conditions, the investment made in education by each individual worker can be used by the employer to make inferences as to the productivity of the workers that she plans to hire. In other words, education is used as a *signal* (Spence 1973) of a worker's ability. This generates a positive correlation between educational attainments of workers and their wages, even when the investment in human capital per se does not increase productivity.

To gauge the importance of signaling in human capital investment, consider a case where the first of the three basic assumptions underlying the human capital model is violated. Suppose, to start with, that education does not affect the productivity of workers. Production efficiency depends only on the innate ability of individual workers, which is not observable by potential employers, while it is known to the workers applying for jobs. Suppose further that those with a higher level of innate ability find it less expensive to acquire any particular level of education than those with lower endowments of innate ability. Under these conditions, educational achievements may be used by the most productive workers as a *signaling* device, that is, as a way to inform employers about their abilities. For this to happen, there must be a *separating equilibrium* in which the most productive workers invest more in education than the less productive ones (see box 8.1 and technical annex 8.9.2). As employers use education to screen workers, it will still be worthwhile for high-ability individuals to attain a high educational level, because the signal attached to it pays off. Thus, the private returns to schooling are still there, just as in a perfect labor market. However, the social rates of return to education are much lower in this context. If education does not increase productivity, there is a waste of resources involved in educational systems. The only benefit associated with these investments is that they help employers find the employees they are looking for, improving the allocation of resources in the economy. However, this social benefit of education may be relatively small compared to the costs of education. Thus, under asymmetric information as to workers' abilities, there can be overinvestment in education from a social standpoint, and a case can be made for cross-subsidies from high-educated to low-educated individuals limiting the investment in schooling.

BOX 8.1 *The Separating Equilibrium*

The intuition behind the signaling model can be grasped with a simple numerical example, adjusted from Spence (1973). Suppose that there are just two productively distinct groups in a population facing a single employer. Individuals in the first group have a lifetime productivity of 100 euros, while those in the second group have a lifetime productivity of 240 euros. The productivity of each individual worker is private information. It is known by the individual workers but not by the employer, who knows only about the two productivity levels and the population shares of the two groups. Suppose that the first group is a proportion q of the population, and the second group is a proportion $(1 - q)$. The employer is aware that the low-productivity workers will always lie about their true productivity, and it takes a long time before the employer can find out about their true productivity. Hence the employer can only offer a weighted average of the two productivities, where weights are given by the proportions of the two groups in the population:

$$\bar{w} = 100q + 240(1 - q) = 240 - 140q.$$

Clearly this wage will underpay the high-productivity workers by a factor proportional to the share of low-productivity workers, q, in the population. However, high-productivity workers can signal their productivity to the employer by investing in schooling. Schooling can be a signal for true productivity when the costs of schooling for the high-productivity group are sufficiently lower than the costs of acquiring education for the low-productivity group (e.g., workers in this group need to spend additional money to pay for tutors). Under these conditions there is indeed a separating equilibrium induced by the investment in education. Consider, for instance, that the first group faces a cost of 25 euros per year of schooling, while the second group has a cost of 20 euros. Under these conditions, the employer can post vacancies requiring a minimum educational attainment, say $\bar{s}$, to be paid 240 euros, and vacancies not requiring this level of education pay 100 euros. Doing so separates the high-productivity workers from the low-productivity ones. Why is this threshold level of education separating the two groups? Consider first the high-productivity workers. If they do not invest in schooling, they are paid 100 euros, while if they invest $\bar{s}$ they would obtain 240 euros minus the costs of acquiring education, that is, $20\bar{s}$. Solving, we obtain the maximum level of schooling they are willing to acquire to signal their ability:

$$100 = 240 - 20\bar{s}.$$

Thus, the high-productivity workers would be willing to invest up to 7 years in school. For this to be a separating equilibrium, it must be that the low-productivity workers are not willing to invest $\bar{s}$ years in schooling. Consider then the problem of the low-productivity workers. The maximum level of schooling that they are willing to acquire is given by solving

$$100 = 240 - 25\bar{s},$$

from which it follows that $\bar{s} = 5.6$.

In other words, jobs requiring no less than 6 and no more than 7 years of education will provide the right incentives for the high-productivity workers to acquire education and apply for the highly paid jobs and for the low-productivity workers not to invest at all in schooling and apply to the lower paid jobs.

The minimum and maximum level of education required to separate the high-productivity from the low-productivity workers is displayed in the box figure. Graphically, the relevant comparison is between the segments AB (the pay in the lowest paid job) and CD (the pay in the highest paid job net of the costs of acquiring education)

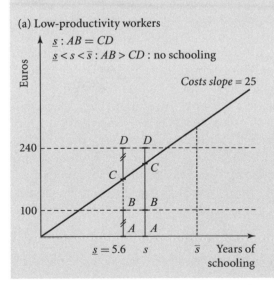

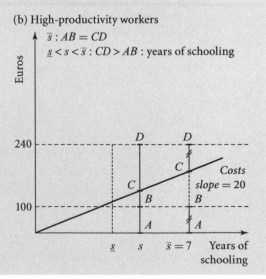

If we allow for competition among employers, the equilibrium will be at $\bar{s} = 6$, that is, at the lowest threshold level of education compatible with a separating equilibrium to exist, as high-productivity workers will always prefer to apply for the vacancies requiring less cost of acquiring education.

Source: Spence (1973).

Overeducation is an outcome of models with asymmetric information only when it is assumed that employers cannot hire workers before they complete their curricula. If hiring can be made on the same day the students enroll in long and difficult courses of study, then education can no longer be used as a signaling device (Weiss and Ching-to 1993; Swinkels 1999). Another problem with signaling theory and its predictions is that it considers only one dimension of productive efficiency, innate ability, that is revealed by the investment in education. However, a growing body of research at the borders between economics and psychology suggests that there are not only cognitive but also *noncognitive skills* (Borghans et al. 2009) affecting productivity and wages at any level of education. Such noncognitive skills may well not be revealed by educational attainments, which typically reward performance in tests of cognitive abilities. Among the noncognitive skills, motivation, perseverance, and self-esteem are particularly important in creating ability gaps between individuals at relatively early ages, that is, before entry into the labor market. Family and social environments, more than schooling (notably the upper education considered by signaling theory), are particularly important in shaping these noncognitive skills.

The Holdup Problem and Underinvestment in Specific Training

As discussed above, the case for overeducation is fairly limited. In general market imperfections lead to underinvestment (rather than overinvestment) in human capital. This is because it may be difficult for those undertaking the investment in human capital to obtain the full returns from this investment. Consider the case of an employer willing to invest in firm-specific training. This is precisely the type of investment a firm would pay for in a perfect labor market according to Becker's theory, as discussed in section 8.2.1. As we are in an imperfect labor market, there will be rents to be split between the employer and the workers according to a given wage contract. Suppose that this contract is incomplete in that it does not prevent wages from being renegotiated ex post (i.e., after the investment in training has been made). Under these circumstances, once this has been made, the workers will have all the incentives to increase their wages, appropriating a large part of the surplus from the investment. This is because the costs already paid by the firm protect the workers already in the firm—the so-called *insiders*—from the competition of *outsiders*, such as unemployed workers willing to supply labor at a lower wage. Indeed, the employer hiring outsiders would have to undertake another costly investment to make their work at least as productive as the work of insiders. In other words, the costly and irreversible investment creates a wedge between insiders and outsiders (Lindbeck and Snower 1988). All this reduces the incentives of the employer to invest in specific training, reducing if not altogether preventing the investment in human capital. A similar problem arises when it is the worker who invests in training. She will have no incentive to invest, knowing that the employer will ex post appropriate the surplus from this investment that cannot be used elsewhere.

As these examples indicate, there is a holdup problem (Williamson 1975; Grout 1984; Malcomson 1999) arising because the returns on the investment are reduced by the bargaining power of the party that does *not* invest. The stronger this bargaining power is, the larger will be the inefficiencies of imperfect labor markets in terms of underinvestment in human capital.

Why Do Employers Invest in General Training?

Another key prediction of Becker's human capital theory is that employers will only pay for training that is firm specific, as they cannot appropriate the rents from general training. This prediction is at odds with the empirical observation that few skills are firm specific, and most skills may be industry specific.[8] Furthermore, there is evidence that although many training programs are general, firms pay a major part of the costs of these programs. Acemoglu (1997) argues that because of labor market imperfections, employers have some monopsony power (see chapter 2), through which they can reap some of the benefits of general training, causing a compressed wage structure. The line of reasoning runs as follows (Acemoglu and Pischke 1998; see also technical annex 8.9.4).

As in Becker (1964), consider that the general training τ increases the productivity and thus the output of the worker, $v(\tau)$, which is therefore upward sloping, while there are diminishing returns to training. Rather than allowing increased wages to pay for any increase in productivity associated with the investment in general training, consider a monopsonistic market. In such a market the firm is able to pay the worker below productivity, and there is a gap: $\Delta(\tau) = v(\tau) - w(\tau)$. In particular, assume that the gap between the value of labor productivity and the wage is increasing with the level of training. Thus, the returns to training for a worker are less than those prevailing in a competitive market; the wage structure is compressed. This situation is depicted in figure 8.3. Now the firm has an incentive to invest. The gap between productivity and wages increases with the level of training, as does the cost of training. An optimizing firm will choose the level of training that equals marginal costs or marginal benefits, which now occurs when $\tau = \tau^f$. Thus, in an imperfect labor market a firm is willing to pay for general training of its workers, because it is profitable to do so. In a noncompetitive market workers are not paid for their full marginal product, even though their skills are general; that is, general skills are rewarded as if they were specific skills.

As also discussed in chapter 2, a firm may have monopsony power for various reasons. It may be that there are transaction costs in the labor market due to matching and search frictions. This may make it difficult for workers to leave their existing jobs and find new employers to take full benefit of their general training. It

8. Loewenstein and Spletzer (1999) report that according to NLSY data about 63 percent of the employees who received firm-provided training state that all or almost all of the skills they learned during the course are also useful in different firms.

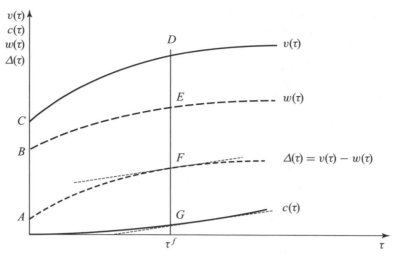

FIGURE 8.3 Training: imperfect labor markets—choice of the firm

may also be that there is asymmetric information between the current employer of the worker and other firms. The current employer knows the exact content of the training, while the other firms have incomplete information. Therefore, they are not willing to pay the worker according to that worker's marginal productivity. A similar reasoning may explain why temporary work agencies often pay for general education of their employees (Autor 2001). This would imply that in figure 8.3, the upward-sloping $w(\tau)$ only refers to wages at the current employer, whereas in the labor market $w(\tau)$ would be a horizontal line. All in all, the monopsony power of the firm makes investment in general training profitable.

8.3 Empirical Evidence

8.3.1 Returns to Schooling

Table 8.3 shows that there is a strong relationship between educational attainment and labor market status. Employment rates are substantially higher for workers with tertiary education.

Across countries there is a wide variation in employment rates among less educated workers. Employment rates among less educated women range from a low of 19.1 percent in Turkey to a high of 72.9 percent in Iceland, while for less educated men the extremes are 42 percent in the Slovak Republic and 89.9 percent in Mexico. For highly educated individuals, the cross-country range in employment rates is substantially smaller. Among highly educated men the extremes are 80.5 percent in the United States and 93.8 percent in Switzerland. Among women the range is from 60.7 percent in Korea to 93.9 percent in Norway.

Table 8.3 also shows that not only are employment rates higher among highly educated individuals, but also their earnings are substantially higher. Among men the largest range between the levels of education is in the United States. Here men with less than upper secondary education earn 33 percent less than men

TABLE 8.3 Employment rates and relative gross earnings by educational attainment, men and women aged 25–64

Country	Employment rate (%) Men			Women			Relative earnings (%) Men			Women		
	1	2	3	1	2	3	1	2	3	1	2	3
Australia	80.6	89.6	88.1	62.5	72.3	77.1	81	100	134	84	100	147
Austria	64.1	80.7	86.6	50.0	70.9	84.5	48	100	106	54	100	134
Belgium	66.4	79.4	87.3	46.4	63.7	81.4	91	100	133	76	100	126
Canada	67.3	—	84.1	50.1	—	79.0	72	100	132	75	100	151
Chile	83.2	88.4	86.5	36.6	57.6	67.9	—	—	—	—	—	—
Czech Republic	55.4	81.5	—	39.6	60.9	—	—	—	—	—	—	—
Denmark	70.7	82.7	87.1	58.8	76.9	82.6	94	100	155	96	100	148
Estonia	55.1	65.8	82.1	42.8	55.9	77.0	—	—	—	—	—	—
Finland	71.6	76.3	82.2	61.2	72.4	82.6	92	100	163	98	100	146
France	73.8	83.4	89.5	57.7	69.0	81.8	88	100	159	81	100	146
Germany	67.9	80.7	88.3	51.5	70.1	82.2	79	100	130	63	100	128
Greece	83.3	86.8	83.9	46.7	59.7	75.1	71	100	140	42	100	109
Hungary	47.7	70.5	85.2	34.0	54.9	76.1	59	100	193	59	100	161
Iceland	80.7	87.5	84.9	72.9	81.7	88.6	—	—	—	—	—	—
Ireland	68.2	—	83.8	44.2	—	75.1	79	100	154	81	100	180
Israel	64.0	80.1	85.7	41.9	63.2	72.8	61	100	115	63	100	141
Italy	75.0	82.5	81.1	40.9	60.2	65.2	74	100	162	78	100	147
Japan	—	—	92.0	—	72.4	64.9	—	—	—	—	—	—
Korea	79.6	85.8	89.2	58.0	55.7	60.7	70	—	127	—	100	176
Luxembourg	77.2	78.9	89.8	49.2	57.1	75.8	77	100	179	35	100	93
Mexico	89.9	—	—	46.2	—	—	—	—	—	—	—	—
Netherlands	81.3	82.7	85.9	55.8	71.9	76.1	72	100	131	63	100	137
New Zealand	74.4	86.0	88.9	57.3	72.2	77.6	82	100	126	89	100	136
Norway	70.6	86.0	88.1	62.3	79.8	93.9	65	100	109	66	100	113
Poland	53.4	78.1	—	31.0	59.1	—	75	100	168	62	100	139
Portugal	83.2	83.8	—	71.8	76.8	—	76	100	200	59	100	163
Slovak Republic	42.0	84.5	88.7	27.1	67.8	67.0	—	—	—	—	—	—
Slovenia	66.8	80.1	86.2	48.8	73.1	82.8	—	—	—	—	—	—
Spain	72.0	76.3	83.1	49.3	65.3	72.5	68	100	115	62	100	145
Sweden	77.7	83.9	85.4	63.0	77.9	83.4	74	100	119	76	100	123
Switzerland	78.8	84.6	93.8	61.3	73.0	87.2	74	100	131	58	100	119
Turkey	74.2	76.1	—	19.1	26.0	—	—	—	—	—	—	—
United Kingdom	56.2	83.9	86.3	34.2	71.2	78.7	73	100	151	70	100	180
United States	59.6	72.9	80.5	42.8	64.8	75.2	67	100	189	70	100	177

Sources: Educational attainment and relative earnings: OECD (2011a).

Notes: Educational attainment is the highest completed level of education, defined according to the International Standard Classification of Education (ISCED); 1 = less than upper secondary education; 2 = upper secondary education; 3 = tertiary education; data for 2011. Relative earnings are defined as mean annual earnings from employment of individuals with a certain level of educational attainment divided by the mean annual earnings from employment of individuals whose highest level of education is the upper secondary level; information year is 2009; 2005 for Finland, France, Greece, Italy, the United Kingdom, and the United States; 2003 for Korea. — = not available.

with upper secondary education. In Hungary men with tertiary education earn 93 percent more than men with upper secondary education. In other countries these differences are smaller. In Denmark men with less education earn only 6 percent less than men with average education. In Austria men with tertiary education earn only 6 percent more than men with average education. Among women there are also clear differences in earnings by educational attainment, but as for men, the magnitude of these differences depends very much on the country they live in.

Earning and employment differentials between highly educated and less educated individuals rose just when educational attainments of the workforce were increasing due to the extensive scholarization of the postwar period. Apparently the increase in labor supply of highly educated workers was not sufficient to match the increase in labor demand for this type of workers. The increase in the demand for educated workers has been generally attributed to *skill-biased technological change*, replacing routinized jobs with machines and increasing the demand for abstract tasks requiring a higher level of education (Krueger 1993). More recent analyses carried out by drawing on data on the skill content of occupations (rather than on educational attainments per se) provide support for the view that indeed, the demand for routinized jobs has fallen (Autor et al. 2006). At the same time, in a number of countries *job polarization* is observed, with more employment at the two extremes of the skill distribution, induced by an increase in high-skill jobs, a strong decline of medium-skill positions, and a milder decline of low-skill jobs (Goos et al. 2009).

8.3.2 Estimating the Returns to Schooling

The positive correlation between, on the one hand, educational attainments and, on the other hand, earnings and employment, which was documented in table 8.3, cannot be given a causal interpretation. Perhaps education indeed increases productivity, and hence wages and employment. Or it could also be the other way around: a substitution of labor with capital in some jobs requiring low levels of education might induce a better labor market performance of relatively highly skilled workers. It could also be that a third factor, such as innate ability, drives up both educational attainments and earnings.

To establish a causal relationship between education and productivity, one has to go beyond macro data and analyze individual data on earnings and educational attainments. Traditionally, empirical evidence of the rate of return to human capital investments is derived by performing wage regressions with the amount of schooling and training as explanatory variables. A huge literature has developed over the past 30 years estimating returns to schooling based on Mincer-type earning functions, in which wages are regressed against educational attainments and work experience of workers. In particular, the standard Mincerian wage equation is

$$\log(w) = \alpha + \beta s + \gamma_0 x + \gamma_1 x^2 + \epsilon, \tag{8.1}$$

where s denotes years of education, and x is years of work experience, while ϵ is an error term. This equation can be obtained from an accounting identity in which

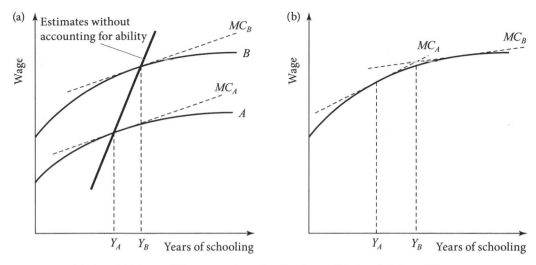

FIGURE 8.4 (a) A and B face a different earning-schooling locus; (b) A and B face different costs of acquiring education

observed earnings are given by potential earnings less the costs of human capital investment in school and on-the-job training (see technical annex 8.9.3). The key parameter is β, which measures the returns to schooling.

A problem with this approach is that individuals are far from identical before investing in human capital, and higher levels of education are generally associated to higher levels of innate ability. This correlation between ability and education is consistent not only with signaling theory (see section 8.2.2) but also with the model of human capital investment in perfect labor markets (section 8.2.1).

Consider, for instance, two individuals with different levels of innate ability, so that the person with higher innate ability enjoys higher wages than the other individual at any given level of education. Graphically, the returns to education of the two individuals will be as depicted in figure 8.4a: the education earning profile of individual A is below that of individual B. Notice that neither individual has a linear wage-education profile.

We know from the theory of human capital investment that the two individuals will choose the amount of schooling that equates the marginal return of an extra year of schooling to its marginal cost. If the marginal costs of acquiring education are independent of the years of education and are the same for the two workers (as given by the straight line MC), individual A will opt for Y_A years of schooling, while individual B will invest in education Y_B years of forgone earnings. It follows that the wage differential $w_a - w_b$ cannot be entirely attributed to the effects of education but also has to do with the fact that the more able individual has chosen a higher level of education than the other individual has. Estimating this relationship without taking into account these differences in abilities would result in fitting a regression line like the bold line in figure 8.4a. Differences in abilities may also affect the costs of acquiring education. Suppose, for instance, that individual A faces a higher marginal cost than individual B (e.g., if education for the first individual requires a lower level of effort, it would also result in different choices as to the investment in education), as depicted in figure 8.4b. When ability bias involves both differences in returns and differences in costs of acquiring education, then the component of earning differentials related to differences in innate ability would be even higher and would bias upward the estimates of the returns to schooling. This *ability bias* stems from the fact that a more able person gets more from an additional year of education and "pays" less for it in terms of effort, and hence invests more in schooling, rather than being the difference in educational attainment inducing the observed difference in pay.

To estimate properly the returns to education, this potential *selectivity*—the fact that individuals with different (unobservable) characteristics, potentially affecting wages, have different levels of education—has to be accounted for. A method often used to identify the effects of education on earnings is to use (exogenous) variations in the level of schooling of individuals, which cannot be related to their individual choices. Any variation in the amount of schooling associated with factors outside the choice set of individuals is a good candidate for this identification strategy. In particular, natural experiments are generally exploited, in which there is an exogenous change in the year of schooling, such as an increase in compulsory schooling age or draft lotteries compelling some people to leave education to join the military. Alternatively, differences in the distance to school (creating differences in the costs of acquiring education, independently of the ability of individuals) have been used.

Another approach to identifying the returns to education is to try to capture the unobserved heterogeneity in ability levels across individuals before the investment in schooling is carried out. Studies based on twins have been used to account for differences in innate ability across individuals. Identical twins have the same family and social background, which might affect choices and performance, and are assumed to have the same innate ability. Hence wage differences between two members of a twin pair can be fully attributed to differences in educational attainments. This tradition was initiated by Ashenfelter and Rouse (1998), who studied wage differences between U.S. twins. They found the ability bias to be very small; cross-sectional estimates that ignore ability differences are, according to their results, only marginally upward biased (see box 8.2 for details). This result is similar to the findings of Isacsson (1999), who compares individual characteristics of Swedish identical twins and returns to years of schooling. In his comparison he uses two physiological dimensions (weight and height) and two psychological dimensions (degrees of introversion and emotionality). He finds that the within-pair returns to schooling are 4.6 percent, which is almost identical to the average of 4.5 percent estimated using a sample of the Swedish population at large. Apparently, in Sweden the effect of selectivity in schooling choice is also not very important.

| BOX 8.2 | *Returns to Schooling: Using Data on Identical Twins* |

To establish the rate of return to schooling, one has to account for potential selectivity in the years of schooling. It could be that high-ability individuals have more education than low-ability individuals. If that is the case, the schooling effects measured in simple wage regressions represent a combination of schooling and ability. To correct for this bias, some studies use information about identical twins. The assumption is that identical twins have the same innate ability. Differences in earnings between twins may be related to differences in schooling but not to differences in ability. Wage regressions on the basis of identical twins can be used to estimate the true returns to schooling. Orley Ashenfelter and Cecilia Rouse do this on the basis of a U.S. sample of 340 twins. If they ignore the fact that the individuals in the sample are twins, they estimate a rate of return of 10.2 percent. If they base their estimates on a comparison of the twins, they find that the average return to schooling is 8.8 percent per year attained, so the ability bias is only 1.4 percentage points. Apparently, cross-sectional estimates that ignore ability differences are only marginally upward biased. A potential problem with twin studies is that the fundamental assumption of identical twins having identical abilities may not be fulfilled. Ashenfelter and Rouse find no evidence of this. They conclude that schooling investments of genetically equivalent individuals are the same, apart from random deviations that can be used to estimate the returns to schooling.

Source: Ashenfelter and Rouse (1998).

Angrist (1990) uses the U.S. government lottery during the Vietnam War, which established draft priorities among potential draftees. Men with low lottery numbers were the first to be drafted, whereas those with higher numbers completely escaped the draft. Men with low lottery numbers who did not want to go to Vietnam had going to college as an alternative. The two groups were determined by a lottery and therefore on average had the same ability. Therefore, comparing men with low lottery numbers and high education levels to those with high lottery numbers and lower education reveals the true rate of return to schooling. Angrist and Krueger (1991) use compulsory school laws that sometimes forced individuals to remain in school until they reached some predetermined age. Individuals under different regimes will have different years of schooling but are observationally equivalent in terms of ability. Comparing these individuals will generate an unbiased estimate of the rate of return to schooling. Card (1995) uses the distance to school to correct for selectivity in the schooling decision. The basic assumption is that parents decide where to live with their family without taking into account the distance to school. Differences in distance to school are therefore unrelated to the ability of their children. Nevertheless, children who live closer to school will be more inclined to stay in school. Thus, comparing individuals with different distances to school generates an unbiased estimate of the rate of return to schooling.

The estimates of the rate of return to schooling, β, provided by the literature vary considerably over time and across countries. They typically are in the range 0.05–0.15, that is, an additional year of education yields an increase in the wage of 5–15 percent. This compares with generally lower rates of return on financial investments.

Importantly, the estimates of the return to schooling that do *not* control for ability bias are often lower than those obtained by accounting for selectivity. For instance, Angrist (1991) obtained an estimate of β in the range 5–7 percent without controlling for ability bias and 6–10 percent controlling for it. Similarly, Card and Krueger (1995a) found a 7 percent return without controlling for ability bias and 13 percent when using distance from school to identify the effects of education on earnings. If ability induces persons to spend more time in school, then we should expect the estimates controlling for ability bias to be lower than those not controlling for it. Several studies find instead the opposite, that is, a higher effect when properly identifying the effects of education on earnings. This may be because the correction does not produce average effects of education, but only the effects for those individuals affected by the natural experiments (which are typically relatively poorly educated individuals forced to continue schooling), whose returns to schooling are decreasing with years of education (as also depicted in figure 8.4). Another interpretation is that there is some negative selection: the most talented individuals (typical examples are Bill Gates dropping out from Harvard after selling his first software package and Mick Jagger leaving the London School of Economics when the Rolling Stones were formed) have too high a cost of continuing school beyond a certain age because of the very high forgone earnings that this choice involves. A perhaps more plausible explanation is that there is a fair amount of measurement error in data on years of education, which may bias downward estimates that do not exploit exogenous variations in years of schooling. Some indication as to the importance of these different explanations for the difference between estimates of returns to education controlling or not controlling for ability bias come from a recent study by Oreopoulos (2006), which is summarized in box 8.3. An advantage of this study with respect to the previous literature is that Oreopoulos used an instrument affecting the behavior of a large portion of the population. Hence, unlike previous studies, the estimates of the returns to schooling controlling for ability bias do not concern a relatively small fraction of the population.

BOX 8.3   *Estimating Returns to Schooling in the United Kingdom*

In the United Kingdom an Education Act was passed in 1944 that raised the minimum school-leaving age from 14 to 15 in England, Scotland, and Wales from 1947 onward. This reform, combined with an expansion in the supply of teachers, buildings and furniture, redirected almost half the population of 14-year-olds in the 1950s to stay an additional year in school. Philip Oreopoulos exploited this natural experiment to provide estimates of the return to schooling controlling for ability bias. An advantage of his study over previous literature is that a very large fraction of the population reacted to the reform. Previous literature had obtained estimates of the returns to schooling controlling for ability bias typically by drawing on exogenous sources of variation in schooling that involved a relatively modest fraction of the population. Oreopoulos used as the control group Northern Ireland, where there was no change in compulsory schooling age until 1957. The analysis was

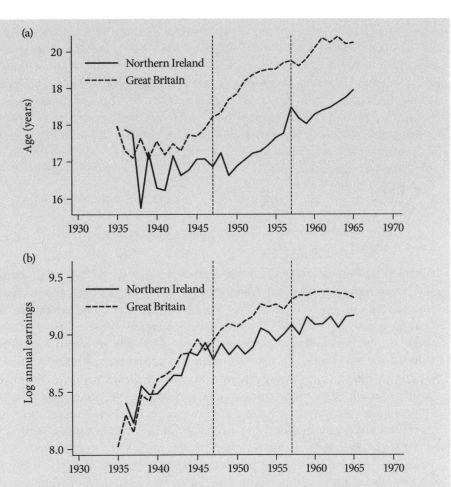

FIGURE 8.5 (a) Average age of leaving full-time education; (b) average log annual earnings by year aged 14 in Great Britain and Northern Ireland

Sources: General Household Surveys, 1983–1998.

Notes: Data are for adults aged 32–64. The vertical lines mark the years of educational reform in Great Britain (1947) and Northern Ireland (1957).

carried out drawing on data from several waves of the General Household Survey in the United Kingdom and Northern Ireland. Figure 8.5 displays educational attainments by cohort in Britain and in Northern Ireland before and after the change in school laws (described by a vertical line). In particular, the average age of leaving full-time education (vertical axis) is plotted by school cohort or generation (horizontal axis). There is a clear difference in attainment before and after the 1947 policy change. The difference in educational attainments is reduced after the same policy change was introduced in Northern Ireland in 1957. This result legitimizes the identification strategy followed by the author. Figure 8.5b presents the key results obtained by Oreopoulos. In particular, the mean log yearly earnings during 1983–1988 are plotted for Northern Ireland and the United Kingdom by the age in which each cohort turned 14. The diagram points to a significant increase in earnings, on average, associated with raising compulsory schooling to age 15.

It was, on average, on the order of 5.5–7.0 percent. The author also compared the UK estimates with those in the United States and Canada (where the increase in compulsory schooling age affected a much smaller fraction of the population) to assess whether the size of the population affected by the instrument (the policy change) does indeed matter in the estimates of returns to schooling. Encouragingly enough, he finds that "the benefits from compulsory schooling are very large whether these laws have an impact on a majority or minority of those exposed." This conclusion is important for interpreting earlier results in the literature on returns to schooling.

Source: Oreopoulos (2006).

8.3.3 On-the-Job Training

In line with the prediction from human capital theory, a worker's wage is positively related to past investments in training. However, employers almost always pay the costs of training, even though most of the training received is general training (Loewenstein and Spletzer 1998). Other than empirical analyses of the returns to schooling, there are only a few studies that estimate rates of return to training. Frazis and Loewenstein (2005) derive estimates of the rate of return to formal training using U.S. data. They find that 60 hours of formal training, the median positive amount of training, increases wages by 34 percent. Thus, rates of return at the median positive training of 60 hours are in the 150–175 percent range; after correcting for promotions, direct costs of training, and heterogeneity in wage growth and wage levels, rates of return are significantly lower, on the order of 30–40 percent.

There also appears to be much heterogeneity across jobs, with managers and professionals having higher rates of return than blue-collar workers. Booth and Bryan (2005) investigate the effects of training on wages in the United Kingdom and find that only employer-financed training has a positive effect on wages, and this holds also when the worker moves to another firm that has not invested in training. In particular, employer-financed training increases wages by nearly 10 percent. Note that the important effect of training by previous employers indicates that this training must have been general training. They also find that training self-financed by the worker has no effects on wages.

Studies by Acemoglu and Pischke (1998, 1999) on training indicate that the existence of imperfect labor markets (notably, the presence of institutions such as unions compressing wage structures) may explain why firms pay for general training (see also box 8.4 and technical annex 8.9.4). Using worker and firm data from Dutch manufacturing, Picchio and van Ours (2011) investigate how product market competition and labor market imperfections affect firm-sponsored training. They find that product market competition does not affect the firms' training expenditures. Instead, labor market imperfections influence firm-sponsored training. An increase in labor market flexibility significantly reduces the incentives of firms to invest in training. The magnitude of this effect is nevertheless small.

Picchio and van Ours (2013) investigate whether on-the-job training has an effect on the employability of workers. Using data from the Netherlands, they find that firm-provided training significantly increases future employment prospects. This also holds for older workers, suggesting that firm-provided training may be an important instrument to retain older individuals at work.

On-the-Job Training in Germany

BOX 8.4

In Germany firms voluntarily offer apprenticeships to workers entering the labor market. Firms that train apprentices have to follow a prescribed curriculum, and apprentices take a rigorous outside exam in their trade at the end of the apprenticeship. Firms are not allowed to train apprentices without permission of the industry or crafts chambers. The training is monitored by worker councils in the firm. All in all, firms have limited influence on the training content. Therefore, most skills learned during the apprenticeships constitute general training. Nevertheless, contrary to the standard prediction of human capital theory, much of the financial burden of the apprenticeships is borne by the firm. Daron Acemoglu and Steve Pischke explain this phenomenon by the existence of labor market imperfections: mobility of workers is restricted, and therefore employers earn rents on trained workers. Given that firms are able to obtain part of the marginal product of workers, they have an interest in increasing this by investing in the human capital of their workers. Because of the monopsony power of the firm, workers are not willing to pay for general training themselves, because they realize that a large fraction of the returns on the training will be appropriated by the firm. Acemoglu and Pischke compare wages of about 5,000 German apprentices who stay in their firms with those who quit for an exogenous reason, that is, to join the army. Their model predicts that military quitters should have higher wages than stayers, because the exogenous reason of their separation frees them from the monopsony power of the firm. Since the military conducts a physical exam but no other tests to determine draft eligibility, there is no selection bias. Furthermore, military service does not increase human capital of the draftees to an extent that is valued in the civilian labor market. Acemoglu and Pischke compare the gross monthly wages of the two groups with those of voluntary quitters from their firm and find for stayers a wage increase of 1.2 percent and for (military) quitters 4.5 percent. The model of Acemoglu and Pischke allows for multiple equilibria. One equilibrium is where workers who quit receive low wages. Therefore, firms will have considerable monopsony power and will support a high level of training. Another equilibrium is where workers who quit receive high wages. This limits the monopsony power of firms, and the investment in training will be small. Paradoxically, a better allocation of workers to jobs—the equilibrium with high quitting rates—may be less efficient, because the level of training is lower.

Source: Acemoglu and Pischke (1998).

8.4 Policy Issues

8.4.1 Should There Be a Compulsory Schooling Age?

All OECD countries have a compulsory schooling age that forces individuals to stay in school up to some minimum age. The question is whether such a compulsory schooling age is welfare improving. After all, if individuals drop out of school early, they may have good reasons to do so, that is, because they face negative net returns to additional schooling. Nevertheless, a compulsory schooling age may be welfare improving if individuals are shortsighted and do not take into account all future revenues of additional schooling. They may have a discount rate that is too large, for example, because they ignore the negative correlation between educational attainment and lifetime unemployment rates. A compulsory schooling age may prevent individuals from dropping out. It may also be the case that students face restrictions on the funding of their studies and therefore drop out. Here too it may be that the social returns to schooling are higher than the private returns. Having a more highly educated population has positive externalities. For instance, there is evidence that education has a positive effect on political participation, civic attitudes, and more broadly social capital, trade, crime rates, and the like (see Lochner 2004). In that case having a compulsory schooling age makes sense. The duration of compulsory education is also affected by changes in the school entry age. Although the empirical literature assessing the consequences of postponing formal education is far from conclusive, several countries are increasing the school entry age. Under these circumstances an increase in the age of compulsory education does not necessarily involve an increase in the years spent in schools, but it may significantly affect the quality of schooling.

As discussed in section 8.1, there is substantial variation in school quality, both across and within countries. Thus, increasing educational attainment can have much different implications on the human capital endowment of a country, depending on how students are distributed across schools. In principle, school choice should reward the best schools. However, the choice of parents as to the school where their children should be enrolled is seriously constrained by administrative rules (allocating students to public schools based on their district of residence) as well as by informational and financing constraints. Moreover, school tracking constrains school choice. Some educational systems force students to specialize relatively early in a given education curriculum, which may possibly segregate students in specific school tracks.

School vouchers[9] should, in principle, enhance school choices of parents and increase competition across schools, creating stronger incentives for improvements in school quality. A large literature has developed in assessing whether competition, proxied by the number of schools in any given city, affects the quality of schools. The "battle over streams" (box 8.5) illustrates the methodological and measurement issues arising when evaluating the effects of competition on school quality.

---

9. School vouchers are certificates issued by the government, which parents can apply toward tuition at a private school (or, by extension, to reimburse home schooling expenses) rather than at the state school to which their child is assigned.

The empirical literature on the relation between competition and school quality has been using the number of school districts in any given urban area as a measure of competition. When there are more districts, parents have a richer menu of choices as to where to live and enroll their children. And there is a relatively large variation in the number of school districts in U.S. cities. For instance, some metropolitan areas, like Boston, have dozens of school districts, while others, such as Las Vegas, are dominated by just one. A problem with this measure of school competition is that the number of school districts in a city is itself endogenous and may well depend on the quality of schooling. As districts with low school quality cannot be readily merged with other districts, quality affects the number of schools.

A way out of this problem was found by Caroline Hoxby (2000), who used the number of (water) streams in any given urban area in the United States—a geographical characteristic creating natural borders around which districts are created—as an instrument for the number of districts. She indeed found that cities with lots of streams had more school districts than those with few streams. At the same time, the number of streams should not directly affect school quality. Instrumenting the number of districts with the number of streams, she claimed to have found a way to recover a causal relationship between competition and school quality. Her results point to a positive effect of the number of school districts on school quality, measured in terms of the performance of students on standardized tests.

This result was challenged by Rothstein (2007), who questioned both the choice of the instrument as well as its measurement. According to Rothstein, streams not only affect the number of districts but also local economic development and hence school quality. Large, navigable streams are likely to affect commerce and wealth in an area and the kind of population it attracts. As the count of small streams would not suffer from this problem, Hoxby then divided her streams into larger and smaller ones and entered them into her equations separately to make the distinction clear. Studying detailed maps published by the U.S. Geological Survey, she measured dimensions of water bodies in hundreds of metropolitan areas with methods which were also challenged by Rothstein. The academic debate on the relationship between competition and school quality therefore turned into—quite unusually for economists—a geological dispute on criteria to disentangle small from large streams. As noted by a political scientist, the debate turned into a "battle over streams," with conflicting ideas as to the best way to count streams and measure their widths. This dispute provides an illustration of the assumptions required to test hypotheses in economics. Although there are not many scholars like Rothstein, and few academic journals are willing to host disputes of this type, it is always important to submit to a very close scrutiny the identification assumptions required to make causal inferences.

Sources: Hoxby (2000); Rothstein (2007).

8.4.2 Should Governments Subsidize In-Company Training?

Governments may stimulate training in firms through direct subsidies or tax credits. This will make it cheaper for firms to provide training. The main question is whether such support is optimal from a welfare point of view. If many firms would provide training anyway, the deadweight loss is large, and the social returns to the investment are low. The answer to the question will depend on the market power of firms. In labor markets with imperfect competition, firms may have sufficient market power to provide training themselves without governmental support. In a more competitive market, employers may be reluctant to invest in training, because other firms in the same industry may reap some or all of the benefits of the investment. If the in-company training increases productivity, there are social returns to training. Thus, if the social returns are larger than the private returns, governments may step in and subsidize training.

8.5 Interactions with Other Institutions

Schooling and training laws defining the compulsory schooling age, the entry school age, the scope of public provision of education, caps to tuition fees, and subsidies (if any) to training have relevant interactions with other institutions in the labor market. The most obvious interaction is with payroll taxes (see chapter 13) as public provision of education must be at least partly funded by tax revenues. Furthermore, educational and training decisions are influenced by the potential gains of those decisions net of taxes, and progressive taxation may reduce incentives to acquire higher education.

There is also an interaction with unions (see chapter 3), because union-induced wage compression makes investment in education and training less profitable, as also suggested by the evidence collected by Acemoglu and Pischke (1998).

EPL (see chapter 10) may stimulate on-the-job training investments, because employers want to use internal labor markets to reallocate workers across jobs rather than laying them off. In the absence of employment protection, workers may also be reluctant to contribute to such investments, especially when they involve firm-specific skills, as they expect their jobs to be short lived.

Another relevant interaction is with retirement programs. A longer working life increases the lifelong returns from education by enabling individuals to enjoy education premiums for a longer time span. This prediction of human capital theory is supported by empirical evidence (see box 8.6). At the same time, on-the-job training may reduce the productivity losses that are typically associated with aging (see chapter 6), increasing the demand for older workers.

BOX 8.6   *Pensions and Training*

In 2006, the Dutch public sector was subjected to a major pension reform that treated two highly similar groups of employees differently. The reform phased out pre-pension plans for everyone born after December 31, 1949. If employees were born before 1950 and had been working in the public sector continuously since

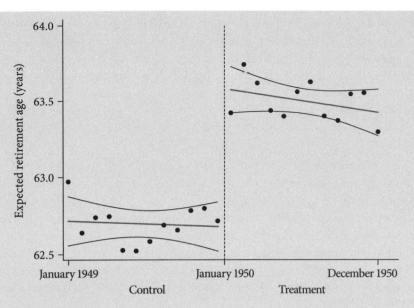

FIGURE 8.6 Expected retirement age over time, the Netherlands
Source: Montizaan et al. (2010).

Notes: This figure presents the mean of the expected retirement age for each birth month from January 1949 to December 1950. The sample consists of two birth-year cohorts; employees born in 1949 are entitled to the old pension rules and employees born in 1950 are subject to the new pension rules. The vertical line marks the threshold that divides the control group from the treatment group.

April 1, 1997, they could still retire at the age of 62 years and 3 months with a pension offering a replacement rate of 70 percent. Employees born after 1950 were instead subject to the new, less generous, pension system, which substantially lowered pension benefits, allowing workers to obtain the same replacement rate as the previous cohort more than one year later (at the age of 63 years and 4 months). The reform induced a postponement by one year, on average, of the age of retirement (see figure 8.6). Raymond Montizaan, Frank Cörvers, and Andries De Grip matched employer (surveys) and employee (administrative information from the pension fund) data for male employees in the public sector. Data were gathered one year after the introduction of the new pension system and incorporate detailed information on older employees' individual pension rights, expected sources of income after retirement, and training participation. The table below compares the training participation of employees born just after the treatment threshold (i.e., born in 1949) and those in the control group under the old system.

The results of the difference-in-differences estimation are shown as follows:

Training participation	Born in 1949 (control)	Born in 1950 (treatment)	Difference (%)
2006	0.54	0.57	3
2005	0.50	0.50	0

The table points to a positive effect (on the order of 3 percent, not conditioning on workers and firm characteristics) of the postponed retirement on training participation. This effect is confirmed in multivariate analyses. According to the authors, "workers in the treatment group participate approximately 7.3 percent more in long training courses than workers in the control group."

Source: Montizaan et al. (2010).

Correlations between education and retirement policies can also be found based on political economic arguments. Both institutions operate intergenerational redistributions, albeit typically in opposite directions. Education policies, increasing the quality and availability of education, are bound to improve the welfare of younger generations, generally by taxing current workers. Through the public financing of education, the young borrow from the middle-aged to invest in human capital. Generous PAYG retirement plans instead tend to improve the well-being of older workers at the expense of the younger generations who have to pay for their elders' pensions.

In general, aging societies experience a shift in the policy mix in favor of more generous retirement institutions (Galasso 2006) and against large-scale public education programs. Figure 8.7 displays on the vertical axis the share of public education expenditure in GDP and, on the horizontal axis, the effective retirement age in several OECD countries. There is a positive correlation between the two institutions. Nordic countries typically display relatively long working lives and high expenditures on education, while southern European countries feature short

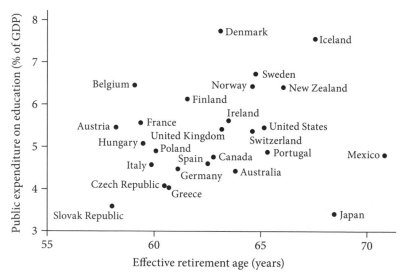

FIGURE 8.7 Public education and early retirement
Sources: OECD online statistics, 2011; World Bank (2011).

Note: The vertical axis displays expenditure on public education as a fraction of GDP (2009); the horizontal axis measures the effective age of retirement as discussed in chapter 6 (2011).

working lives and low expenditures on education. However, there are also countries like Japan, with relatively long working lives but low spending on education.

8.6 Why Do Governments Subsidize Education and Training?

Education and training increase labor productivity. There are private returns to schooling, because individuals who invest in their education increase their productivity and will receive higher lifetime earnings than do individuals who do not invest. Because productivity goes up, education also has a social return. Through the investment in schooling, national income goes up. Having a well-educated and well-trained workforce is an important competitive asset. The main reasons for governments to intervene in education and training are the presence of market imperfections and the positive externalities related to a more highly educated workforce in terms of stronger civic attitudes; greater political participation; lower crime rates; and greater trust and hence lower transaction costs, implying more gains from trade. Individuals who want to pursue their studies will not always find it easy to finance them. Capital market imperfections may make it impossible or expensive to borrow money. This may lead to a suboptimal investment in human capital. When individuals are credit constrained, there is a strong case for governments to subsidize formal education systems. Without subsidies there would be an underinvestment in schooling.

Positive externalities also provide a reason for governments to support training. Firms may be reluctant to invest in training if this training has productive effects outside the firm as well. A firm will only invest in training if it has sufficient market power to reap at least part of the benefits.

8.7 Suggestions for Further Reading

The OECD series *Education at a Glance* (OECD 2005a) provides an interesting overview of cross-country differences in educational systems. Card (1999) surveys literature on the causal relationship between education and earnings. The *Handbook of the Economics of Education* (Hanushek et al. 2011) offers a wealth of surveys and insights on the relationship between education and labor market outcomes by top scholars of the field. Brunello et al. (2007) provide a theoretical and empirical analysis of education and training in Europe. Finally, Daron Acemoglu and David Autor's chapter in the *4th Handbook of Labor Economics* offers a discussion of trends in real wage levels by skill groups against the background of the education race (Acemoglu and Autor 2011).

8.8 Review Questions and Exercises

1. Why do firms pay for general training even though trained workers are valuable to other firms as well?

2. Why do governments provide scholarships to students even though education is an investment from which students themselves will benefit later in life?

3. Why should there be a compulsory schooling age?

4. Under which conditions might there be overeducation from a society-wide standpoint?

5. Why is it difficult to measure returns to schooling?

6. How are compulsory school laws or distance from schools used to derive unbiased estimates of returns to schooling?

7. Why should not all students try to achieve an academic degree?

8. Does it matter for the schooling decisions of the individual to what degree schooling is a signal of innate productivity?

9. Should the state subsidize on-the-job training?

10. Suppose that Andrea's wage-schooling locus is given by:

Years of schooling	Earnings (euros)
6	12,000
7	15,360
8	19,200
9	22,200
10	24,420
11	26,400
12	27,720
13	28,680
14	28,800

(a) Derive the marginal rate of return schedule. When will Andrea quit school if her discount rate is 5 percent? What if it is 15 percent?

(b) Suppose now the government imposes an income tax of 25 percent on both labor earnings and interest income. What is the effect of this income tax on Andrea's educational attainment?

11. Tom, a 18-year-old boy, has to decide how many more years to study. He knows that, if he stops studying now, he will get a wage $w_0 = 1,200$ euros; if, instead, he decides to invest s more years in education, his wage will be $w^n = w_0 + 600 \log(1 + s)$. However, if Tom decides to study, he knows he will have to pay a yearly school fee of 120 euros.

(a) Given the above data, how many more years will Tom stay in school? Given this choice, what is his expected wage?

Suppose that a reform of the education system is implemented in Tom's country: school fees are fixed to a lower level of 75 per year, but education becomes lower quality, so that the expected wage after n years of school is now $w^n = w_0 + 300 \log(1 + s)$.

(b) How will the reform affect Tom's decision on his optimal investment in years of education?

(c) How many more years will he spend in school?

(d) What is his expected wage now?

12. Suppose that there are two types of workers in the economy: low-productivity workers (75 percent of the population) and high-productivity workers (25 percent). Low-productivity individuals have a lifetime productivity of 300 euros, while highly productive workers have a lifetime productivity of 500 euros. The employer knows the two proportions and the relative productivity, but, at hiring, cannot distinguish a high-productivity from a low-productivity worker.

   (a) Which wage would a competitive employer pay in this context?

   Now consider schooling. For low-productivity workers, a year of education costs 25 euros, while for a highly productive individual, it costs only 16 euros. Education has no effect on productivity.

   (b) What is the minimum educational attainment (in terms of years of schooling) that an employer can impose to ensure that only high-productivity workers would apply for these jobs?

   (c) Suppose that jobs not requiring any educational attainment are also offered. Who loses and who gains from this policy of the employer?

13. (Advanced) John is a 16-year-old student and has to decide whether to leave school and start working or to study for another year. If he leaves school, he will earn 45,000 euros per year for the rest of his working life. If he increases his level of education with one additional year of studies, he would earn 50,000 euros per year for the rest of his working life. Attending school for one more year will cost him 30,000 euros. John plans to work until reaching the age of 70. Assume that John uses a discount rate of 5 percent per year.

   (a) Show that it is profitable for John to acquire an extra year of education.

   (b) Suppose that further years of education would increase John's annual earnings by 5,000 euros per year of education. However, the costs of additional years of education are also increasing according to $15,000s^2$, where s denotes the additional years of education. How many additional years of education should John acquire?

8.9 Technical Annex: Education and Training

8.9.1 Optimal Years of Schooling

In figure 8.1 an individual chooses between an initial number of years of schooling (which might be primary schooling but is normalized to zero) and a particular number of years of schooling s. Alternatively, we may consider the decision whether an individual who has s years of schooling should opt for another year of schooling. If the individual does not attend this additional year, the annual earnings over the remaining labor market years until age T will be w_s. If the individual attends $s + 1$ years of schooling, the annual earnings from age $s + 1$ to age T are equal to w_{s+1}. The annual costs involved at school are equal to c_s. The individual makes a decision on the basis of a comparison of present values of both flows of earnings and costs. If i is the market interest rate, the net present value NPV with s years of schooling is

$$NPV_s = \sum_{t=0}^{T} \left(\frac{1}{1+i}\right)^t w_s = w_s + \sum_{t=1}^{T} \left(\frac{1}{1+i}\right)^t w_s.$$ (8.2)

The present value for $s + 1$ years of schooling is

$$NPV_{s+1} = -c_s + \sum_{t=1}^{T} \left(\frac{1}{1+i}\right)^t w_{s+1}.$$ (8.3)

Just like the optimal retirement plan characterized in technical annex 6.9, the individual will attend another year of schooling if the present value of doing so is larger than the present value of abstaining, that is, $NPV_{s+1} > NPV_s$. After some rewriting, this leads to

$$\sum_{t=1}^{T} \left(\frac{1}{1+i}\right)^t (w_{s+1} - w_s) > w_s + c_s.$$ (8.4)

If the costs of schooling are small, $c_s \approx 0$, and again after some rewriting it follows that[10]

$$w_{s+1} - w_s = w_s\, i,$$ (8.5)

from which it follows that $w_{s+1} > w_s(1 + i)$. So

$$\ln(w_{s+1}) > \ln(w_s) + \ln(1 + i) \approx \ln(w_s) + i,$$ (8.6)

and therefore

$$\ln(w_{s+1}) - \ln(w_s) > i.$$ (8.7)

Condition (8.7) is easy to interpret, since the left-hand side represents the rate of return to an additional year of schooling: $\ln(w_{s+1}) - \ln(w_s) = r$. In other words, the individual will opt for the additional year of schooling if $r > i$ (i.e., if the rate of return to schooling at educational level s is larger than the market interest rate). In other words, the individual will invest in schooling if it is more profitable than an investment in the capital market. It may be that the rate of return to schooling decreases with the level of schooling. Since the market interest rate is independent of the level of schooling, the individual will have to make a choice concerning the optimal number of years of schooling, s^*. Optimizing behavior implies that the individual will choose s^* such that $i = r$. The individual will keep investing until the marginal rate of return to schooling equals the market interest rate.

10. Using the geometric series approximation $\sum_{t=1}^{T} \left(\frac{1}{1+i}\right)^t \approx \frac{1}{i}$ when T is large.

8.9.2 Signaling

Suppose we have two types of individuals, with either low or high innate ability/productivity levels, say α^l and α^h, with $0 < \alpha^l < \alpha^h$. Workers can achieve a level of education $s \geq 0$ at cost $\frac{s}{\alpha}$, so that a higher innate ability reduces the cost of acquiring education. However, education does not affect productivity.

Consider for simplicity a utility function W for the individual that is linear in income, net of the costs of acquiring education:

$$U(w, s, \alpha) = w - \frac{s}{\alpha}.$$

In this setup, labor market imperfections (in the form of asymmetric information) represent the only incentive to acquire education. Suppose, in fact, that ability is observable by employers and that product markets are also perfectly competitive, so that there is free entry of firms. The zero-profits condition implies that wages equal the productivity of workers. Hence, employers would pay α^h to high-ability types and α^l to low-ability ones independently of s. Hence, for any α, $s = 0$ is $\arg\max_s U(w, s, \alpha)$.

Consider instead that ability is not observed by the employer, while it is known to the worker. Workers choose how much education to acquire knowing that employers observe only s. In this context workers of type α^h will choose a level of s, say s^*, that is too costly for workers of type α^l to acquire. As a low-ability worker in this case cannot improve on the signal given by the high-ability types, she has no incentive to acquire education. It follows that s^* is implicitly given by the condition $U(w^h, s^*, \alpha^l) < U(w^l, 0, \alpha^l)$, or

$$\alpha^h - \frac{s^*}{\alpha^l} < \alpha^l,$$

which implies

$$s^* > \alpha^l(\alpha^h - \alpha^l).$$

For this to be an equilibrium, we must also check that this level of education is optimal for the high-ability types. This means that

$$U(w^h, s^*, \alpha^h) > U(w^l, 0, \alpha^h),$$

that is, high-ability types are better off in the separating equilibrium than in the pooling case, in which employers pay the same wage to all workers and nobody invests in education. Assuming that 50 percent of workers have high ability, and the remaining 50 percent have low ability, the pooling equilibrium wage is given by $w = 1/2(\alpha^h + \alpha^l)$. For s^* to maximize the utility of the high-ability types, it must require the lowest possible level of education allowing a separating equilibrium to exist, that is, $s^* = \alpha^l (\alpha^h - \alpha^l)$. Substituting w and s^* into the above condition, we obtain

$$\alpha^h > 2\alpha^l.$$

In other words, the ability difference should be sufficiently large for a separating equilibrium to exist.

8.9.3 Derivation of the Mincer Equation

The Mincer (1974) equation can be obtained from the Ben-Porath (1967) life-cycle human capital investment model. Individuals invest both at school and on the job via training. Let us start with the second type of investment, training on the job. Denote potential earnings at age t by V_t and the fraction of working time devoted to training by k_t. It follows that training costs are given by the forgone earnings $k_t V_t$. Individuals become more productive by investing in training. Denote the returns from training by ρ_t. It follows that potential earnings can be written as a function of earnings at the beginning of the working life, V_0:

$$V_t = V_{t-1}(1 + k_{t-1}\rho_{t-1}) = \prod_{j=0}^{t-1}(1 + k_j\rho_j)V_0. \tag{8.8}$$

Let us now consider the schooling investment. When involved in formal schooling, the individual is investing full-time, that is, $k = 1$. Assume that the returns to schooling investment is constant at ρ, and denote by s the years of schooling. Potential earnings at the end of the schooling period (at labor market entry) can therefore be written as

$$V_{s+1} = V_0(1 + \rho)^s. \tag{8.9}$$

Consider now the lifetime investment decision (involving both schooling and training). Taking logs and also assuming that ρ_t is constant over time, we have

$$\log V_t = \log V_0 + s\log(1 + \rho) + \sum_{j=s}^{t-1}\log(1 + k_j\rho)$$

$$\approx \log V_0 + \rho s + \sum_{j=s}^{t-1}k_j. \tag{8.10}$$

If the rate of post-school investment declines linearly over time, then

$$k_{T+x_t} = k\left(1 - \frac{x_t}{T}\right), \tag{8.11}$$

where x is the amount of work experience at time t, and T the length of the working life. The first order (Taylor) approximation of (8.10) then gives

$$\log V_t \approx \log V_0 + \rho s + \left(\rho k + \frac{\rho k}{2T}\right)x - \frac{\rho k}{2T}x_t^2. \tag{8.12}$$

Empirically, this can be estimated cross-sectionally by a Mincer-type equation with a constant capturing the term $\log V_0 - k$, a linear term for years of schooling, and linear and quadratic terms for work experience:

$$\log(w_i) = \alpha + \beta s_i + \gamma_0 x_i + \gamma_1 x_i^2 + \epsilon_i. \tag{8.13}$$

8.9.4 Who Pays for General Training?

The answer to the question of who pays for general training depends on whether the labor market is competitive. Assume that the productivity of a worker depends on the amount of general training τ:

$$v(\tau) = \overline{v} + v_0(\tau), \tag{8.14}$$

where $\overline{v}$ is the productivity without general training, and $\frac{\partial v}{\partial \tau} > 0$, $\frac{\partial^2 v}{\partial \tau^2} < 0$. The wage is also assumed to depend on the amount of general training:

$$w(\tau) = \overline{w} + w_0(\tau), \tag{8.15}$$

where $\overline{w}$ is the wage without general training, and $\frac{\partial w}{\partial \tau} > 0$, $\frac{\partial^2 w}{\partial \tau^2} < 0$. Thus, the wage gap Δ for an individual worker depends on the amount of general training:

$$\Delta(\tau) = v(\tau) - w(\tau) = \overline{v} - \overline{w} + v_0(\tau) - w_0(\tau), \tag{8.16}$$

and the effect of the amount of training on the profits of the firm is given by

$$\frac{\partial \Delta}{\partial \tau} = \Delta'(\tau) = v'(\tau) - w'(\tau). \tag{8.17}$$

Now in a situation where there is no general training ($\tau = 0$), two possibilities can be distinguished:

1. The labor market is competitive, so that $\Delta'(0) = 0$ and the firm does not benefit from general training, but the worker has an incentive to invest in training, because the wage increases with the amount of general training. The worker chooses the optimal amount of investment τ^* by maximizing the difference between the wage and the costs of general training, $c(\tau)$, with $\frac{\partial c}{\partial \tau} > 0$ and $\frac{\partial^2 c}{\partial \tau^2} > 0$. This leads to $w'(\tau^*) = c'(\tau^*)$, a situation that is depicted in figure 8.2.

2. The labor market is imperfect and there is wage compression, so that $\Delta'(0) > 0$, then the productivity increases faster than the wage. Now the firm has an incentive to invest in general training, because this increases the firm's profits. The firm chooses the optimal amount of investment τ^f by maximizing the difference between profits and costs of general training, which leads to $\Delta'(\tau^f) = c'(\tau^f)$, a situation depicted in figure 8.3.

CHAPTER NINE **Migration Policies**

International migration is the great absentee in the era of globalization. While the barriers to international trade and capital mobility have already been largely removed, cross-border worker flows are tightly restricted. Until a few decades ago many European countries were mass out-migration countries. According to historians, about 60 million Europeans moved away from the Old Continent in the period 1820–1940. Two-thirds of them went to the United States (one can find their names on the website http://www.ellisislandrecords.org). Currently Europe is attracting more migrants in proportion to its population than the United States. Countries like Italy that were sending 100,000–200,000 people to the United States every year at the beginning of the twentieth century are now receiving annual inflows of migrants on the order of 350,000. In Europe migration policies are getting stricter and stricter. At the same time, poor enforcement of these restrictions is giving rise to very large inflows of illegal migrants. According to some estimates, up to 40 percent of migration to Europe is illegal.

Migration policies introduce a complex set of restrictions on the movement of persons across jurisdictions. Migration restrictions take the direct form of *quotas* that establish a maximum number of work and residence permits to be issued to foreigners in a given year or the indirect form of admission criteria that limit access. Quotas are often allocated on a first-come, first-served basis, but an increasing number of countries are adopting a *points system*, whereby each application is attributed a score based on explicit criteria that typically reward educational attainment, experience, and language abilities. Bonus points can also be given for employment in occupations and regions where there is a shortage of workers. Migration is also deterred by increasing the administrative burdens placed on migrants and their employers. The number of bureaucracies involved in *admission procedures* is therefore another indicator of the stance of migration policies. An important feature of migration legislation relates to the *length of stay*, that is, the maximum duration of the residence or work permit. Policies related to the assimilation of migrants are also relevant in defining the more or less restrictive stance of migration policies. A good indicator in this context is the minimum number of years required to apply for *citizenship*. Finally, there are ad hoc rules for *asylum seekers*. Although asylum policies are largely inspired by noneconomic considerations, in practice most asylum seekers respond to economic incentives, just like other migrants. Hence it is important to include asylum policies when analyzing the more or less restrictive stance of any given country on international migration.

Economic theory suggests that migration increases efficiency by arbitraging away cross-country (and even cross-regional, when natives are immobile) differences in productivity and unemployment. The scope for this efficiency-enhancing arbitrage is large: in international markets for commodities and financial assets, price differentials rarely exceed a ratio of 2/1, while wages of similarly qualified individuals in advanced and low-income countries differ by a factor of 10 or more. This suggests that gains from liberalizing labor movements across countries are enormous and are much larger than the likely benefits from further liberalization in the traditional areas of goods and capital. Why then is migration so severely restricted? The answer is that migration policies are essentially redistributive tools, aiming at reducing negative effects of migration on wages and unemployment among natives. Moreover, migration tends to occur in waves. By imposing some gradualism on migration flows, migration restrictions mitigate supply shocks that may negatively affect incomes or jobs of some specific groups.

BOX 9.1   *Coming to America*

The book *Coming to America* by Roger Daniels (2002) documents the nature of the migration to the United States and the way both the volume and the composition were affected by immigration policy. According to Daniels the period between 1820 and 1920 is the "century of immigration." The U.S. Census of 1820 recorded fewer than 10 million inhabitants. In the century thereafter 36 million immigrants entered the United States, with more than 30 million coming from Europe; predominantly from Germany (5 million), Ireland (4.5), Italy (4.5), Poland (2.5), England (2.5), and Scandinavia (2). During most of the century of immigration, immigration remained largely unfettered by government regulation, but there were anti-immigrant activities. Daniels distinguishes three phases: anti-Catholic, anti-Asian, and anti-all immigrants. The second phase led to the Chinese Exclusion Act of 1882, which suspended entry by most Chinese immigrants. The third phase led first to a quota system in 1921 in which each nationality's quota was based on the number of its members residing in the United States in 1910, and then to the Immigration Act of 1924, in which quotas for Italy and Eastern Europe were reduced and those from Britain, Germany, and Ireland increased. The 1924 Act reduced immigration substantially and was used until 1965, when the amendments to the Immigration and Nationality Act abolished the national origins quota. Instead a total of 170,000 immigrant visas for the Eastern Hemisphere and 120,000 for the Western Hemisphere were allocated annually. The majority of the entry visas were assigned to those who had family members already in the United States. Some visas were also earmarked for immigrants who possessed a desirable set of skills. The 1978 amendment abolished separate quotas for the Eastern and Western Hemispheres and established an annual quota of 290,000 immigrants with a maximum of 20,000 from any one country. The Immigration Act of 1990 increased the annual immigration quota ceiling to about 675,000 persons per year. Figure 9.1 illustrates the magnitude of the immigration to the United States in which the changes in policy are clearly shown in terms of levels and fluctuations.

Sources: Daniels (2002); Clark et al. (2007). Laing (2011) provides a nice overview of U.S. immigration policy.

In addition to aiming at controlling the magnitude of migration flows, migration policies can also affect their composition, for example, by encouraging more or less skilled migration. For this reason, in most countries migration policy is a highly controversial topic. There are, on the one hand, those who are keen to host more migrants, who need them desperately to fill vacant positions or to find someone who can pay for their pensions, and, on the other hand, those who fear that migrants will ultimately steal their jobs, increase crime rates, and abuse social transfers paid out of their pockets. The same individual may at the same time support and oppose migration, and vigorously do so. Employers wish to have migrants from 7 AM to 5 PM—just during working hours—and then, when it is time to shift to their private lives, prefer not to see them any longer. As in the famous aphorism by Max Frisch on migration to Switzerland, "We wished arms, and we received persons."

9.1 Measures and Cross-Country Comparisons

It may be useful to put the numbers in a historical context. Figure 9.1 shows the evolution of immigration to the United States during 1820–2010, both in absolute terms as well as in relative terms (see also box 9.1). In the first decade of the twentieth century, 8.8 million immigrants went to the United States. In the first decade of the twenty-first century this number was 10.5 million. However, contrary to common wisdom, migration flows have not been increasing in the era of globalization. The United States is currently experiencing much lower inflows of migrants, in proportion to the native population, than at the beginning of the twentieth century. The population of the United States in 1900 was about 75 million; in 2010 it was about 310 million. In terms of percentage of the population the United States received immigrants at the rate of about 1 percent per year in the first decade of the twentieth century while this was about 0.4 percent per year in the first decade of the twenty-first century.

Europe experienced larger migration flows after the massive political disruptions of World War II and decolonization than in the past two decades. The number of people displaced by World War II is estimated to be about 30 million, not counting 13 million Germans displaced from Czechoslovakia, Poland, and the

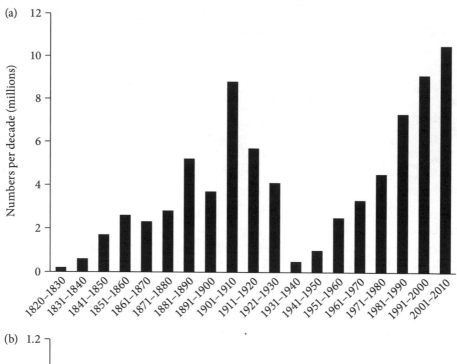

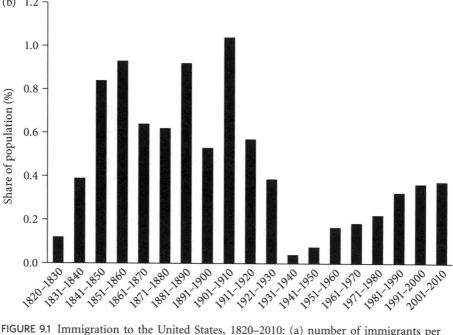

FIGURE 9.1 Immigration to the United States, 1820–2010: (a) number of immigrants per decade; (b) share of population (percent per year)
Source: US Office of Immigration Statistics (2011).

Soviet Union. In the United Kingdom there was increasing immigration from the New Commonwealth after the war, beginning with the Caribbean countries and, later, the Indian subcontinent. In France more than 1 million Algerians of French origin were repatriated after Algerian independence. Similar processes occurred in Belgium, the Netherlands, and, later, in Portugal after the dissolution of their colonies.

Migration was not only tolerated but even encouraged in Europe in the 1950s. After full employment had been achieved, labor shortages induced some countries to open their labor markets or even to recruit foreign labor. The main source countries were in southern Europe (Italy, Greece, Portugal, Spain, Turkey, and Yugoslavia) and North Africa (Morocco and Tunisia), while the main countries of destination were France, Germany, the United Kingdom, Switzerland, Belgium, and the Netherlands. The total number of foreign-born persons increased in Europe from about 4 million to 10 million from 1950 to 1970, while about 5 million workers migrated from southern Europe to these countries (Zimmermann 2005).

This liberal stance toward migration was abandoned at the beginning of the 1970s, when European unemployment was increasing. Since then, and even more in the past 20 years, migration policies have been getting stricter and stricter, not only in northern European countries but also in southern Europe.

Table 9.1 provides an overview of cross-country differences in migration integration policies specified in terms of an index that ranges from 0 (very unfavorable) to 100 (very favorable). The table distinguishes among four types of policy: labor mobility, family reunion, long-term residence, and access to citizenship. Clearly, there are substantial differences across countries. The most favorable labor market policy for migrants is in Sweden, Portugal, the Netherlands, Spain, and Canada. Labor market policy is also favorable toward migrants in other Scandinavian countries. Relatively unfavorable policies are present in former eastern European countries and in Ireland. Family reunion for migrants is easiest in Portugal and most difficult in Ireland, while long-term residence is easiest in Belgium and the most difficult in the United Kingdom. Access to citizenship is easiest for migrants in Portugal and the most difficult in Estonia.

Figure 9.2 shows, for EU countries with the largest immigration, some information on the policies affecting entrance (i.e., migration policies, strictly speaking). Regulations vary considerably from country to country. The countries having a large number of admission requirements are generally also those that prolong the period to get permanent residence. A few countries adopt an explicit quota system. These are mainly the southern European countries that are facing immigration from North Africa. The strictness of the migration policy index is developed by normalizing countries' scores in each migration policy area to be in the range 0–6 and then taking the simple average of these subindicators. Denmark and Spain have the most strict migration policies while France has the least strict. Figure 9.2 tracks the evolution over time of this summary indicator of migration policies, showing that most countries are above the bisecting line through the origin, which points to a tightening of migration restrictions over time.

TABLE 9.1 Migrant integration policy index (MIPEX) 2010

Country	Labor mobility[a]	Family reunion[b]	Long-term residence[c]	Access to citizenship[d]
Australia	58	81	61	77
Austria	56	41	58	22
Belgium	53	68	79	69
Canada	81	89	63	74
Czech Republic	55	66	65	33
Denmark	73	37	66	33
Estonia	51	65	67	16
Finland	71	70	58	57
France	49	52	46	59
Germany	77	60	50	59
Greece	50	49	56	57
Hungary	41	61	60	31
Ireland	39	34	43	58
Italy	69	74	66	63
Japan	62	51	58	33
Luxembourg	48	67	56	66
Netherlands	85	58	68	66
Norway	73	68	61	41
Poland	48	67	65	35
Portugal	94	91	69	82
Slovak Republic	21	53	50	27
Slovenia	44	75	69	33
Spain	84	85	78	39
Sweden	100	84	78	79
Switzerland	53	40	41	36
United Kingdom	55	54	31	59
United States	68	67	50	61

Source: MIPEX: www.mipex.eu.

Notes: All MIPEX scores are based on an average of four dimensions: eligibility, acquisition conditions, security of status, and rights associated. Scores: unfavorable: 0–20; slightly unfavorable: 21–40; halfway to best practice: 41–59; slightly favorable: 60–79; favorable: 80–100.

a. Are migrants excluded from taking some jobs? What is the state doing to help migrants adjust to the demands of the labor market? Can migrants easily lose their work permits? What rights do migrants have as workers?

b. Which migrants can sponsor relatives? Which relative can they sponsor? Is a migrant's right to live in a family not made conditional on requirements, tests, or courses? Does the state protect a migrant's right to settle with his or her family? Do family members have the same rights as their sponsors?

c. How long do migrants have to wait to qualify for long-term residence? Are eligible migrants not compelled to meet restrictive requirements? How easily can long-term residents lose their permits? Do long-term residents have equal access as nationals to many areas of life?

d. How long do migrants have to wait to become citizens? Are their children and grandchildren nationals at birth? Are eligible migrants not compelled to meet restrictive requirements? How easily can naturalized migrants lose their citizenship? Who is exempt from withdrawal? Can naturalizing citizens or children born in the country to migrants have dual citizenship?

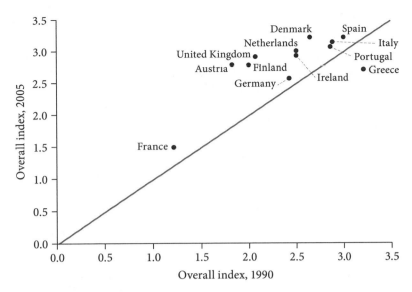

FIGURE 9.2 Evolution of the index of strictness of migration policies in the EU-15
Source: www.frdb.org.

Note: Points on the line indicate no change in policy for 1990 and 2005.

9.2 Theory

In competitive labor markets migration should negatively affect wages of natives. This effect comes from the presence of a downward-sloping demand curve. When labor supply is not rigid, migration also reduces employment among natives. The magnitudes of these effects and the extent to which migration is accommodated by reductions in wages or employment depend on the elasticity of labor supply in the relevant range. Labor market institutions that interfere with employment and wage adjustment are also important in this context. We begin, as usual, by characterizing the case of a competitive labor market where there are no other institutions (other than migration restrictions) interfering with labor market adjustment and then move to more realistic institutional configurations.

9.2.1 A Perfect Labor Market

Figure 9.3 depicts the effects of migration on a competitive labor market when labor supply is vertical (figure 9.3a) or positively sloped (figure 9.3b). For the time being, we assume that natives and migrants are perfect substitutes; that is, they are interchangeable. Later we consider skill differences and hence also complementarities between migrant and native labor that potentially shift the labor demand schedule. We also focus on the short-run effects of migration, neglecting changes in the capital stock associated with the decline in wages in the receiving country.

Migration in this context is a shock to labor supply that shifts the aggregate supply curve to the right from L_0, where labor supply involves only native workers, to L_1, where there are both natives and migrants. When labor supply is rigid, there is no reduction of employment among natives, and the adjustment is accommodated

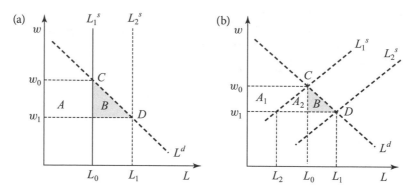

FIGURE 9.3 A competitive labor market: (a) inelastic labor supply; (b) elastic labor supply

entirely by reductions in wages. When instead labor supply is positively sloped, some reduction of employment among natives is also involved. Importantly, the reduction of employment among natives comes entirely from the withdrawal from the labor market of natives who were willing to work only at the wage levels prevailing before the migration-supply shock. No unemployment is involved in the adjustment.

Notice that in both cases workers suffer a loss in welfare (in figure 9.3a their loss is given by the area A; in figure 9.3b, by A_1), while employers' gains ($A + B$ in the first case, and $A_1 + A_2 + B$ in the second) exceed labor losses. Thus, there is an aggregate welfare increase in both cases. There is also an increase in national income accruing to natives, that is, an *immigration surplus* (Borjas 2003) given in both cases by the triangle B. As shown by figure 9.3, this *immigration surplus* can be estimated as the product $\frac{1}{2}(w_0 - w_1)(L_1 - L_0)$, which suggests that it is increasing with the changes induced by migration to native wages and with the size of migration flows. At the same time, there is a conflict of interest between native workers and native employers over migration policy. Insofar as migrants do not carry out any capital with them, labor productivity and labor income per capita decline in the recipient country. Furthermore, with an inelastic labor supply the employment of native workers is unaffected by the immigration, but in case of an elastic labor supply employment of native workers goes down (from L_0 to L_2 in figure 9.3b). Nevertheless, this is a pure labor supply effect. The reduction in wages makes it less attractive for native workers to supply labor; all native workers who want a job at the going wage have a job. With an elastic labor supply, employment of immigrant workers is equal to $L_1 - L_2$.

9.2.2 An Economy with Wage Rigidities

Migration often occurs in countries that exhibit in one way or another some form of wage rigidity. The case of an economy where downward wage adjustment is constrained by wage-setting institutions is characterized in the next figure. Figure 9.4a

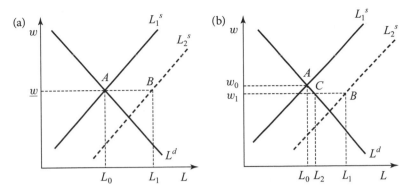

FIGURE 9.4 An economy with wage rigidities: (a) minimum wage; (b) collective bargaining with wage rigidity

depicts an economy with a minimum wage set at the market-clearing level. Thus, initially there is no unemployment. The supply shock associated with migration in this case needs to be accommodated entirely by job losses. The extent of native worker losses will depend on the market penetration of migrant workers. With a binding minimum wage, there is indeed a fixed number of jobs in the economy, and after immigration unemployment of $L_1 - L_0$ is experienced. In this case it is not clear which part of unemployment is made up of native workers and which part of immigrant workers. The more migrants who come in and find a job, the higher the unemployment among natives will be. If there are no externalities associated with unemployment (e.g., fiscal externalities related to the payment of UBs), then employers realize the same surplus with and without migration, but native workers lose out. As a result, total incomes of natives in the immigration country decline, and unemployment appears among native workers.

A more realistic scenario of partial wage rigidity (wages adjust, but not enough to allow for market clearing after migration takes place) is depicted in figure 9.4b. In this case there is no longer a one-to-one relationship between migration and unemployment, and native employers do gain something from the inflow of migrants. Initially, the labor market is in equilibrium at wage w_0 with employment L_0. After immigration the wage drops to w_1, which is insufficient to clear the market. Employment increases to L_2, while total labor supply equals L_1, leaving an unemployment gap between labor demand and labor supply of $L_1 - L_2$. Thus, it is possible that in this case the immigration country realizes a net gain from immigration, because the accrued surplus of employers hiring the migrants exceeds the welfare loss of native workers earning lower wages. Yet the net gain will be lower than in the competitive labor market case.

9.2.3 What Drives Migration Decisions?

Migration is not a random process. It is a rational choice that involves two decisions. The first decision relates to whether to migrate. The second decision is on where to relocate. The two decisions are clearly interdependent, but they can conveniently be characterized as sequential choices.

Let us consider first the decision on whether to move to another country. This choice is based on a cost-benefit analysis that weighs the pros and cons of migration. Typically the costs of migration are front loaded; they are all paid at the time of changing residence. These migration costs are very large, because they include not only transportation and relocation costs but also the huge psychological costs related to abandoning the network of relatives. The stream of benefits associated with migration comes from the earnings differentials between the destination country and the country of origin. Migration occurs if the present value of the earnings differences exceeds the front-loaded migration costs (see technical annex 9.9 for a formal exposition). Thus, migration is more likely to occur

1. the larger the earnings differential between the destination country and the home country (i.e., the larger the lifetime benefits from migration);

2. the lower the migration costs;

3. the longer the expected length of the working life (i.e., the longer the period over which the individual benefits from the earnings differential); and

4. the lower the discount rate (i.e., the more value the individual attaches to the future when the benefits from migration materialize).

Conditions 3 and 4 imply that younger individuals are more likely to migrate, because they have a longer time horizon in which the initial investment can provide returns in terms of earning differentials; youngsters also typically have a lower discount rate than older people.

The second decision relates to where to relocate. If we suppose for simplicity that the initial mobility costs are independent of the final destination (e.g., the individual is choosing among different states in the United States or in the EU), the choice of where to move will depend entirely on the potential earnings in the different destinations. Suppose that the migrant can choose between two alternative destinations, say, country 1 or 2, and that the only relevant dimension affecting the potential earnings of migrants is skill, as in the Roy (1951) model. The choice faced by the migrant is illustrated in figure 9.5, which displays on the horizontal axis the skill level of a given individual and on the vertical axis that individual's earnings, net of migration costs. As shown by figure 9.5a, the most-skilled workers (those with skills higher than s^*) will go to country 1, where their skills are better rewarded, while the least-skilled will go to country 2, because they are paid more there.

Suppose now that country 1 introduces a welfare system in the form of a floor for incomes (e.g., a guaranteed minimum income scheme), preventing natives and migrants from falling below a given poverty threshold, say, b (see figure 9.5b).[1]

---

1. Notice that a minimum wage would not necessarily prevent incomes of migrants from falling below b, as it would create unemployment among migrants and natives.

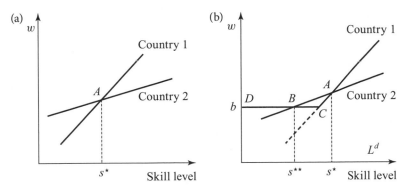

FIGURE 9.5 The choice of where to migrate: (a) skilled migrants go to country 1, and unskilled migrants go to country 2; (b) safety net in country 1, and the least skilled also go to country 1

Now some of the unskilled (those with skills lower than s^{**}) will also migrate to country 1. Therefore, the presence of a welfare state affects the skill composition of migration and may induce some workers not to go where their skills are most productive.

9.2.4 Effects on Income Distribution of Skill-Biased Migration

The introduction of a safety net in a country may alter the skill composition of its migrants, increasing the proportion of unskilled migrants moving there. Changes in the skill composition of its migrants may have not only important fiscal but also income distribution effects in the receiving country.

To illustrate this, we assume that there are just two types of labor, skilled and unskilled, and that migrants and native workers are perfectly substitutable only within each skill group. Suppose further that only one good is produced, combining both skilled and unskilled labor in a fixed proportion. Thus, skilled and unskilled labor are complements.

If migration perfectly replicates the skill composition of the native population (migrants have exactly the same proportion of skilled and unskilled workers as the native population), then we should expect no effects of migration on relative wages and hence on income distribution in the recipient country. Suppose instead that all immigrants are unskilled workers, whereas in the destination country there are some skilled workers. The effects on wages of native unskilled workers will be just as described before: unskilled wages will decline, and, depending on the type and extent of wage rigidities, unemployment among unskilled workers may increase. At the same time, because of the higher number of unskilled workers in the economy, labor demand for skilled workers will shift out, and hence wages of skilled natives will increase. Thus, wage differentials between skilled and unskilled workers in the receiving country will increase as a result of immigration of unskilled workers. The opposite clearly happens when immigration involves only skilled labor: in this case earnings inequality in the receiving country is reduced by migration.

This result is fairly robust. Relative wages will change in the direction outlined here even when some (imperfect) substitutability is allowed between skilled and unskilled labor (Dustmann and Glitz 2005). If we allow for two goods, both internationally traded and both using skilled and unskilled labor in different proportions, cross-skill substitutability reduces the effects of skill-biased migration on income distribution in the long run. This trend occurs because the country increasing its endowment of, say, unskilled workers gradually expands its production in the unskilled-labor-intensive industry (Leamer and Levinsohn 1995). But the key effect is still there, at least in the short run: unskilled migration increases income inequality, while skilled migration reduces income inequality in the recipient country. The type of labor that becomes relatively scarcer gains from migration, while the other loses. According to Card et al. (2012) immigration changes the composition of the local population, which is why people worry about immigration. Concerns about skill-biased migration may be more important than those about taxes and wages.

9.3 Empirical Evidence

9.3.1 Labor Market Effects of Immigration

Most studies estimating the effects of migration on employment and wages of natives are based on U.S. data. This literature is reviewed in Borjas (2003). The empirical literature on European migration (reviewed in McCormick 2002) is more recent, because there is still a paucity of data on migration, notably illegal migration, to the EU. More empirical work outside the United States is warranted to better characterize the effects of migration under different institutional configurations.

Table 9.2 compares employment and unemployment rates of foreign- and native-born men and women across the OECD countries. The table also shows that there are huge cross-country differences in the share of the labor force that is foreign-born. In Luxembourg almost half of the labor force is foreign-born, while in Australia, Canada, New Zealand, and Switzerland more than 20 percent of the labor force is foreign-born. At the other end of the distribution, the share of foreign-born labor force participants is very low; less than 10 percent in eastern European countries and most Scandinavian countries (except for Sweden).

Figures 9.6 and 9.7 illustrate some of the cross-country relationships between foreign-born workers and labor market performance. Figure 9.6 shows that there is a negative cross-country correlation between the share of foreign-born workers in the labor force and the unemployment rates of native-born men. However, this negative relationship is largely driven by Luxembourg, which has both a very high share of foreign-born workers and a very low unemployment rate for native-born men. Ignoring Luxembourg, there does not seem to be any correlation between the two variables. For example, Spain and Ireland have a very high unemployment rate of native-born men, but Canada—with about the same share of foreign-born in the labor force—has a substantially lower unemployment rate of native-born men. Figure 9.7 shows the cross-country relationship

TABLE 9.2 Employment and unemployment rates of native- and foreign-born residents and share of foreign-born labor force, 2010 and 2009

Country	Employment rate (%)				Unemployment rate (%)				Labor force, foreign born (%)
	Men		Women		Men		Women		
	Native born	Foreign born	Native born	Foreign born	Native born	Foreign born	Native born	Foreign born	
Australia	79.2	77.0	68.5	60.3	5.3	5.1	5.2	6.1	26.9
Austria	77.9	73.5	67.9	59.8	3.8	8.8	3.6	7.6	16.3
Belgium	68.4	60.8	58.4	44.6	6.7	17.5	7.3	17.7	13.8
Canada	74.3	74.5	70.5	63.3	8.6	10.0	6.6	9.9	21.2
Czech Republic	73.2	78.7	56.1	55.5	6.7	5.7	8.6	9.9	—
Denmark	76.6	67.6	72.6	60.0	7.7	15.1	6.0	12.1	6.9
Estonia	60.2	57.5	60.8	57.9	21.1	26.5	13.8	23.3	13.8
Finland	69.6	66.7	67.6	55.6	9.2	18.9	7.6	16.3	4.6
France	68.5	66.4	61.5	49.7	8.4	13.6	8.7	15.8	11.6
Germany	76.4	72.7	68.0	55.8	7.0	12.6	6.0	10.7	—
Greece	70.8	77.2	48.0	51.7	8.8	14.7	15.6	16.9	11.8
Hungary	60.1	68.8	50.3	63.6	11.9	19.2	10.9	7.9	2.3
Ireland	63.9	65.4	56.5	54.4	16.5	19.2	8.8	12.6	19.0
Italy	66.7	76.3	45.6	49.8	7.3	9.7	9.1	13.2	11.3
Luxembourg	68.6	78.5	53.2	62.0	2.4	5.3	3.0	6.8	48.6
Netherlands	81.9	72.0	72.6	58.8	3.8	8.5	3.8	7.7	11.5
New Zealand	79.1	75.8	68.6	61.1	6.2	7.2	6.8	7.7	23.8
Norway	77.8	72.7	74.3	64.8	3.5	9.8	2.5	7.0	9.5
Poland	65.4	59.0	53.1	42.8	9.6	—	10.1	—	0.3
Portugal	69.7	74.3	60.8	64.5	10.2	12.7	12.0	17.2	9.4
Slovak Republic	65.0	74.7	52.2	38.7	14.4	—	14.8	—	—
Slovenia	69.7	70.5	63.0	60.4	7.3	9.3	6.7	9.5	8.7
Spain	65.6	60.0	52.0	53.8	17.3	31.1	19.1	26.7	18.5
Sweden	76.6	67.3	73.5	56.0	7.4	15.9	6.8	16.7	11.2
Switzerland	84.5	84.1	75.0	66.5	3.0	6.2	3.7	9.1	26.3
Turkey	79.0	75.4	68.5	45.2	2.8	7.9	4.0	14.7	—
United Kingdom	74.4	74.4	65.7	58.0	8.8	9.2	6.6	9.0	12.9
United States	68.2	77.4	62.2	57.4	10.9	10.0	8.7	9.5	16.2

Source: OECD (2011a).

Notes: Numbers are for workers 15–64 years old. Employment and unemployment rates are for 2010. The share of foreign-born labor force is given for 2000 for Switzerland; 2006 for Canada, New Zealand, and Sweden; 2008 for Finland; and 2009 for all other countries. — = not available.

between unemployment rates of native- and foreign-born men. In the United States and Australia these unemployment rates for the two groups are about the same. In most European countries—with the exception of the Czech Republic, which has a very small foreign-born labor force—the unemployment rates of foreign-born workers are higher than those of native-born workers. At the same time, there is a strong positive cross-country correlation between the two. This trend suggests that macroeconomic conditions and labor market institutions matter for all workers, irrespective of their nationality. These conditions,

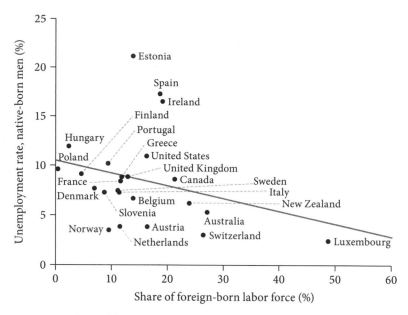

FIGURE 9.6 Share of foreign-born in the labor force and unemployment rates of native-born men
Source: OECD (2011a).

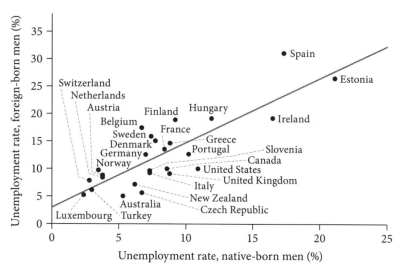

FIGURE 9.7 Unemployment rates of native- and foreign-born men
Source: OECD (2011a).

faced by all workers, have larger effects on the unemployment of foreign-born men. Presumably foreign-born men on average have more unfavorable labor market characteristics, such as lower educational attainments, than do native-born men.

Okkerse (2008) provides a recent overview of the labor market effects of immigration, from which she draws two main conclusions. First, immigration negatively affects the wages of less-skilled workers and earlier immigrants. Second, the probability that immigrants increase unemployment is low in the short run and zero in the long run. These conclusions are confirmed in recent studies. For example, Bauer et al. (2011) conclude that immigration into Germany has had very small or no effect on labor market outcomes for German natives. D'Amuri et al. (2010) conclude that immigration into Germany has had very few adverse effects on native wages and employment levels, but it had sizable adverse employment effects on previous immigrants as well as a small adverse effect on their wages.

There are differences in focus between American and European studies. The American literature mainly deals with the effect of immigration on wages, while European studies predominantly analyze the effect on employment (Kerr and Kerr 2011). Nevertheless, cross-Atlantic comparisons can be quite revealing about the consequences of immigration on the labor market. The typical framework used in these studies correlates wages or unemployment among natives with some measure of immigrant penetration in a given area, often by skill category. This area-analysis framework is justified by evidence that immigrants concentrate in some gateway regions, where the labor market adjustment to migration can be better observed.

As discussed earlier, economic theory suggests that we should observe a negative correlation between immigration and native wages or employment. However, the empirical literature until recently found very modest, if any, effects of migration on the labor market of natives. Typical estimates are that a 10 percent increase in the fraction of immigrants in a region lowers native wages by less than 1 percent (often an amount not statistically different from zero). These findings are well summarized in influential surveys concluding that "the effect of immigration on the labor market outcomes of natives is small" (Friedberg and Hunt 1995) or that "the weight of the empirical evidence suggests that the impact of immigration on the wages of competing native workers is small" (Smith and Edmonston 1997). The empirical evidence from EU countries also points to a negligible impact of migration on wages and employment opportunities of natives. Dustmann et al. (2013) find that immigration has an effect on the distribution of native wages. Immigration to the United Kingdom depresses wages below the twentieth percentile of the wage distribution. Nevertheless, they find an overall slightly positive effect of immigration on native wages. Migrants often take jobs for which they are overqualified. Insofar as natives and migrants are paid the same wage, and (more highly educated) migrants are more productive than (less educated) natives, a surplus is generated. This surplus may lead to an increase in employment. Ottaviano and Peri (2012) find that immigration to the United States had a small effect on the wages of native workers but a substantial negative effect on those of previous immigrants. Manacorda et al. (2012) draw similar conclusions on the labor market effects of immigration to the United Kingdom. Card (2012) concludes that the overall impacts of immigration to the United States on native wages are small—far smaller than the effects of other factors, such as new technology, institutional changes, and recessionary macro conditions.

These empirical results can be at least partly reconciled with economic theory when account is taken of three factors:

1. self-selection of immigrants into high-wage regions,
2. relocation of native workers, and
3. changes in the regional output mix.

The first factor stems from the non-random distribution of immigrants across labor markets. As discussed earlier, they decide to locate to a given area in light of earnings and employment opportunities offered in that area. Thus, regions with higher wages or lower unemployment are likely to attract more migrants, generating a *positive* correlation between migration and native wages. Causality in this context goes the other way around: wages of natives affect the levels and composition of migration rather than vice versa. Thus, appropriate econometric methods should be found to deal with this *endogeneity* (of migration) problem.

The second factor relates to the responses of native workers. As more migrants arrive in a given area, natives may respond by moving their labor or capital to other regions or cities. This effect is likely to be important in the United States, where interregional labor mobility is relatively large (Topel 1986; Blanchard and Katz 1992) and strongly responsive to economic incentives. In contrast, European interregional labor mobility appears to be much lower (McCormick 2002), and, if anything, foreign migrants compensate for the lack of mobility of residents. Figure 9.8 documents this fact: in Italy mobility from high-unemployment to low-unemployment regions is almost entirely accommodated by net migration of foreign workers as opposed to native workers. Nevertheless, Hatton and Tani (2005) find some evidence of native outflows in response to immigrant inflows.

Finally, the third factor explaining the modest effects of migration on the wages of natives comes from the ability of open economies to adjust to migration by changing the composition of the output mix or production technologies (Lewis 2005; González and Ortega 2011) in such a way as to reap the benefits from the increased labor supply, rather than by adjusting wages or employment to an increasing supply of labor. This adjustment in product specialization takes time and hence may play some role in explaining the small effects of migration on wages and employment of natives in low-frequency data.

For these three reasons, the effects of migration on labor market outcomes of natives can be better identified at the national level (Borjas 2003) and by correlating wages (or unemployment) of natives to the share of migrants by skill group. Results from the United States, Canada, and Mexico adopting this empirical framework (Borjas 2009) seem to indicate that migration has had a significant and negative effect on the wages of natives, in line with the predictions of the competitive model of the labor market when capital is held constant. However, some of these national labor market studies focus on the total population rather than on the relative sizes of the different skill groups, and they use low-frequency data from the census (typically carried out at 10-year intervals). Card (2005), working on higher frequency data on wages of school dropouts (people with less than a high

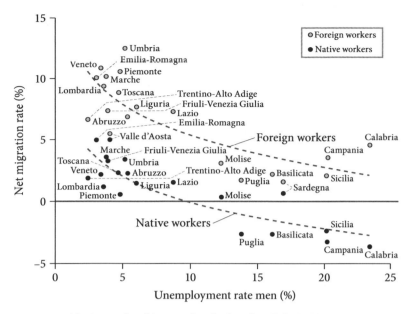

FIGURE 9.8 Net internal and international migration, Italy, 2003

school diploma) in the United States, found that their wage gap with respect to other educational groups in the workforce had remained fairly constant, in spite of substantial inflows of unskilled migrants.

Regrettably, only a few studies have used difference-in-differences techniques to isolate the effects of migration on wages and employment of natives. Among these few exceptions, Card (1990) analyzed Cuban migration to Florida following the opening of borders, Hunt (1992) studied migration to France after Algerian independence, and Carrington and de Lima (1996) investigated the effects of the inflows to Portugal of about 600,000 *retornados* after the loss of the African colonies of Angola and Mozambique. In particular, Card documented that although the 1980 Mariel boatlift to the Miami-area labor market unexpectedly increased the local labor supply by 7 percent in a four-month period, this shock had no discernible effect on native wages or unemployment in the area (see box 9.2). Bodvarsson et al. (2008) show that Card's finding of no wage effect may be due to the new Cuban immigrants inducing a strong increase in the local demand for labor. Apparently this effect was sufficiently strong to compensate for the downward pressure induced by the increased labor supply.

The Mariel Boatlift

BOX 9.2

On April 20, 1980, Fidel Castro announced that Cuban nationals wishing to move to the United States could leave freely from the port of Mariel. By September 1980 about 125,000 mostly unskilled Cubans left—mainly to Miami. Almost overnight Miami's labor force had grown by 7 percent. Between April and July 1980 the unemployment rate in Miami rose from 5.0 percent to 7.1 percent. To investigate whether this increase was related to inflows of the "Mariels" (Mariel immigrants) David Card (1990) compared the labor market of Miami with those of four other cities: Atlanta, Los Angeles, Houston, and Tampa–St. Petersburg. These four cities were selected both because they had relatively large populations of blacks and because they exhibited a pattern of economic growth similar to that in Miami over the late 1970s and early 1980s. By comparing the unemployment rates in 1979 (before Mariel) and 1981 (after) in Miami and the comparison cities, Card was able to perform a difference-in-differences analysis. For black workers, while the unemployment rate went up in Miami by 1.3 percentage points, it went up in comparison cities by 2.3 percentage points. Following the difference-in-differences approach, this suggests that the Mariel boatlift had a *negative* effect on the unemployment rate of black workers:

| | Unemployment rate | | | |
| | Blacks | | Whites | |
Group	Before	After	Before	After
Miami	8.3	9.6	5.1	3.9
Comparison cities	10.3	12.6	4.4	4.3
Difference	−2.0	−3.0	+0.7	−0.4
Difference-in-differences	−1.0		−1.1	

Following the same approach, the unemployment rate of white workers went down by 1.1 percentage points. Card also finds that wages of less-skilled non-Cuban workers were not affected. According to Card there are several explanations as to why the Miami labor market was able to absorb a 7 percent increase in the labor force with no adverse effects. It could be that the Mariels displaced other immigrants and natives who would have moved to Miami in the early 1980s had the Mariel boatlift not occurred. It could also be that the growth of industries that use relatively unskilled labor absorbed many of the Mariels.

Source: Card (1990).

De Silva et al. (2010) analyze the wage effects of the migration from New Orleans to Houston caused by Hurricane Katrina at the end of 2005. Katrina caused a 3 percent increase of the population of the Houston metropolitan area. The evacuees who remained in Houston were younger and less educated than existing residents, causing a relative increase in labor supply for low-skill jobs. Using a difference-in-differences approach, the authors consider the Houston labor market as the treatment group and the labor market in Dallas as a control group. It turns out that in the Houston area wages for low-skill jobs went down relative to wages for high-skill jobs, while no such effect occurred in Dallas.

The applications of the difference-in-differences techniques in migration research raise a number of issues, because it is not obvious how treatment and control groups should be defined in the case of immigration (see box 9.3).

In the summer of 1994, tens of thousands of Cubans boarded boats with Miami as their destination in an attempt to emigrate to the United States in a second Mariel boatlift that promised to be almost as large as the one that occurred in 1980. The U.S. government ordered the navy to divert the would-be immigrants to a base in Guantanamo Bay. Only a small fraction of the Cubans ever reached Miami. Joshua Angrist and Alan Krueger (1999) call this event "The Mariel Boatlift That Did Not Happen." They use the same research design as David Card (see box 9.2) to explore the effects of this "nonevent." Now 1993 represents the before situation and 1995 the after situation. The labor market in Miami is the treatment group, and that in the four comparison cities—Atlanta, Los Angeles, Houston, and Tampa–St. Petersburg—make up the control group. In Miami the unemployment rate of black workers in 1993 was 1.4 percentage points lower in Miami than it was in the comparison cities. In 1995 the Miami unemployment rate of black workers was 4.9 percentage points higher than in the comparison cities. Thus, the treatment effect of the nonevent on the unemployment rate of black workers was +6.3 percentage points:

| | Unemployment rate | | | |
| | Blacks | | Whites | |
Group	Before	After	Before	After
Miami	10.1	13.7	4.9	3.9
Comparison cities	11.5	8.8	5.4	4.1
Difference	−1.4	+4.9	−0.5	−0.2
Difference-in-differences	+6.3		+0.3	

For white workers the treatment effect on their unemployment rate was equal to 0.3 percentage points. The analysis of Angrist and Krueger does not necessarily invalidate the findings by Card, but it does stress that one has to be careful in proving causality by associations in nonexperimental data.

Source: Angrist and Krueger (1999).

9.3.2 Fiscal Effects of Immigration

Some studies have recently tried to evaluate the net contribution of immigrants to fiscal balances in the country of destination. This literature is relevant for evaluating the effects of migration on the labor market that come via labor taxes.

This literature is largely confined to the United States. Whether immigration increases or decreases fiscal costs for native taxpayers was analyzed by a report of the National Academy of Sciences for the U.S. Congress. The results of this study are summarized by Smith and Edmonston (1997), taking as reference cases New Jersey and California. Notwithstanding a number of conceptual and data problems, they offer a rather comprehensive overview of the transfers between natives and immigrants. In 1996 the net annual fiscal burden of immigration, considering all transfers at the local and national levels, was estimated to be between $166 and $226 per native household. The main reasons for these sizable transfers from natives to immigrants are differences in family structures and income levels: immigrant families have more dependent children who use publicly funded schools, and immigrant households are poor and hence receive more transfers and pay less in taxes. Smith and Edmonston (1997) also document large differences in transfers across U.S. states, which can be explained in terms of differences in demographic structures and welfare schemes across states. The age structure and the ethnic composition of immigrants are also very important in the fiscal impact of immigration. An average immigrant household in California receives net benefits of $4,977 if its members are from Latin America, but it contributes $1,308 if its members are from Europe or Canada.

Less information is available for Europe. Boeri (2010) and Zimmermann (2005) documented that migrants in some countries are overrepresented in the population of recipients of social assistance, housing benefits, and UBs, while they are less represented than natives among pensioners and recipients of sickness benefits. This overrepresentation can be largely explained by the personal characteristics of migrants that make them more likely to be eligible for social transfers than natives are. Indeed, regressions (run over European Community Household Panel [ECHP] data covering 1994–2001) rarely detect the presence of "residual dependency from social transfers" by non-EU citizens (Boeri 2010). In other words, being a migrant is not relevant to determining receipt of benefits once account is taken of the personal characteristics of the individual (e.g., the number of dependent children).

9.3.3 Labor Market Performance of Migrants

Table 9.2 shows employment and unemployment rates of foreign-born men and women across OECD countries. In most but not all countries the employment rate of native-born men is higher than that of foreign-born men. Notable exceptions are Greece, Italy, Luxembourg, Portugal, some eastern European countries, and the United States. For women only, a few countries have an employment rate that is higher for foreign-born than it is for native-born. Whereas in terms of employment rates the labor market position of foreign-born compared to native-born is sometimes better and sometimes worse, in terms of unemployment rates the situation is more clear. Except for men in Australia, the Czech Republic, and the United States and for women in Hungary, unemployment rates for foreign-born are always higher than those for native-born.

Some studies have analyzed the labor market performance of migrants, notably their convergence to the wages of natives (Borjas 1999). This literature is also relevant for assessing the contribution of migration to the national economy. Although most of this literature is based on cross-sections, it would be preferable to use longitudinal data that follow the same individuals over time in assessing convergence. The general finding, in any event, is that income convergence is largely determined by the human capital characteristics of migrants. While relatively high skill levels translate into a relatively favorable labor market outcome of migrants, the labor market performance of low-skilled migrants lags persistently behind that of natives. Unfortunately, this literature is mainly confined to the United States, because European countries rarely have long series of longitudinal data on migrants.

The U.S. literature also provides support for the nonrandom allocation of migrants to different areas in the country of destination. As pointed out by Borjas (2001), migrants grease the wheels of the labor market: they migrate to the most productive areas, arbitraging away differences in labor productivity. Hunt (2006), in her study of east-west migration in the context of German unification, also documents a nonrandom allocation of migrants by age and skill, very much in line with the predictions of the Roy model reviewed earlier. In particular, she found that decisions of young people to migrate strongly react to wage differentials between the sending and the receiving country, while older workers are more responsive to unemployment differentials.

Recent research shows that the location of immigrants matters. Edin et al. (2003) analyze the labor market position of refugee immigrants in Sweden. These immigrants were not allowed to freely choose their location but were allocated on the basis of the availability of housing. Thus, the usual problems related to the endogenous sorting of immigrants are not present here. The authors find that living in enclaves improves labor market outcomes of less-skilled immigrants compared to immigrants living outside enclaves.[2] Damm (2009) finds that in Denmark, refugees with unfavorable unobserved characteristics self-select into immigrant enclaves. She also finds that living in an enclave is beneficial to immigrant wages.

9.3.4 Labor Market Performance of Immigrant Children

Table 9.3 provides a cross-country overview of the labor market position of the children of immigrants by comparing unemployment and employment rates of the children of natives and native-born children of immigrants, aged 20–29. As the first four columns show, there is a wide variation in unemployment rates across countries. However, in terms of differences between children of natives and native-born children, there are two types of countries. In countries such as Belgium, France, Germany, and the United Kingdom there are substantial differences in unemployment rates with immigrant children sometimes having an unemployment rate that is twice as high as that among native-born children. In other countries, including Australia, Canada, Norway, and the United States, the differences in unemployment rates are small or even absent. The same distinction can be made in terms of average employment rates. In countries such as the United States, Switzerland, and Australia there are hardly any differences, while in other countries the differences are substantial. The right-hand side of table 9.3 shows that the differences in employment rates are mainly present among individuals with low levels of education. For example, for poorly educated men, only in New Zealand, Norway, and Spain are the differences in employment rates between native-born children and the children of immigrants small. For highly educated men, only for Belgium, Germany, Norway, and Sweden are there substantial differences; for other countries, they are small or absent.

---

2. An *enclave* is defined for each immigrant group as an area where the share of these immigrants was at least twice as large as the share over the entire population.

TABLE 9.3 Unemployment and employment rates for children of natives and native-born children of immigrants, around 2007

	Unemployment rate				Employment rate				Employment rate by education level												
	Men		Women		Men		Women		Men						Women						
									Low		Medium		High		Low		Medium		High		
Country	(1)	(2)	(1)	(2)	(1)	(2)	(1)	(2)	(1)	(2)	(1)	(2)	(1)	(2)	(1)	(2)	(1)	(2)	(1)	(2)		
Australia	6	8	5	5	88	86	76	79	71	65	91	88	96	98	43	42	77	77	92	92		
Austria	6	—	5	—	90	81	79	66	87	71	92	90	96	—	56	—	80	74	88	—		
Belgium	11	28	12	27	81	61	77	54	68	47	82	69	88	79	49	32	71	57	89	82		
Canada	8	7	7	8	85	85	78	83	70	67	86	84	92	90	50	56	76	75	88	88		
Denmark	2	6	3	8	85	75	81	72	76	69	88	79	88	86	63	61	85	76	89	84		
France	12	21	13	21	83	72	75	62	68	55	86	78	88	85	46	43	73	60	87	80		
Germany	18	27	13	20	79	69	73	62	58	54	82	76	90	81	44	43	77	73	86	64		
Luxembourg	6	11	11	22	92	86	83	75	90	85	92	—	96	—	70	67	87	—	92	—		
Netherlands	5	—	4	—	91	70	87	67	81	53	94	80	96	93	66	48	90	75	94	—		
New Zealand	5	—	7	10	92	89	78	80	88	85	95	90	97	94	65	65	83	80	94	93		
Norway	3	4	3	3	86	77	82	72	75	72	91	86	92	86	67	62	86	80	92	83		
Spain	13	—	13	—	80	76	75	57	76	73	83	92	88	—	62	60	78	—	84	85		
Sweden	—	—	—	—	85	73	82	71	63	53	88	79	92	87	53	45	83	75	92	87		
Switzerland	4	—	4	—	90	89	90	91	69	—	90	91	94	96	65	—	90	93	94	92		
United Kingdom	9	15	7	10	82	79	75	66	71	61	89	80	92	90	44	28	77	66	92	86		
United States	9	9	7	—	81	80	73	74	60	57	80	80	91	89	43	—	68	70	87	86		

Source: OECD (2009).

Notes: Population aged 20–29 and not in school or training. (1) = children of natives; (2) = native-born children of immigrants; — = not available.

9.4 Policy Issues

The preceding discussion suggests that migration, notably unskilled migration, has the potential to increase wage and income inequality among natives and to be a source of fiscal costs for an immobile native workforce. These externalities can reduce the economic gains of migration and create political opposition to it. Often governments react to these concerns by tightening migration restrictions, as documented in section 9.1. However, migration restrictions are rarely effective in preventing migration altogether. Often they end up simply increasing illegal migration, which involves mainly unskilled workers, and preventing these workers from having a regular job and hence paying social security contributions. There is a high risk in this context of a vicious circle being set in motion, where unrealistic restrictions on migration induce more illegal and unskilled migration, which strengthens public opinion against migrants and pushes governments to adopt even stricter (and unenforceable) restrictions. Two strategies attempt to address this potential vicious circle:

1. closing the welfare door to migrants, and
2. introducing a points system that rewards skilled migration.

9.4.1 Closing the Welfare Door?

There is growing concern in Europe about immigration. Citizens fear that migrants exert negative fiscal and benefit externalities on the native population. A strategy decoupling migration from fiscal pressures on welfare systems that is increasingly being used is to restrict access of immigrants to welfare (Boeri 2010). Closing the welfare door would reduce the proportion of unskilled workers in migration inflows, thus increasing the proportion (not the absolute number) of skilled workers in migration inflows. Closing the welfare door, however, would postpone the assimilation of migrants who are already in the country or who would come in any event. Thus, it might paradoxically increase negative externalities on natives of immigration to rigid labor markets by pushing many migrants into illegal activities.

Another rather subtle argument often made for closing the welfare door uses political economy considerations. A policy explicitly preventing abuse of welfare by migrants is deemed to buy popular support for more realistic migration policies in individual EU countries. Research on opinion surveys (Boeri and Bruecker 2005; Dustmann and Glitz 2005) shows that many citizens are indeed concerned about welfare abuse by migrants. Yet this does not imply that voters would support more liberal policies when migrants are banned from some citizenship rights (e.g., access to social welfare) in the country of destination.

Closing the welfare door may not be a credible policy in countries with large numbers of immigrants. The U.S. experience is revealing in this respect. In 1996 the welfare system was partly decentralized to the states, and limitations were introduced to access to welfare benefits for legal immigrants. For instance, legal nonasylum immigrants who arrived in the country after August 1996 were barred from receiving food stamps or using Medicaid for five years. The proponents of this reform were hoping that a more decentralized system would make states more cautious in providing expensive welfare benefits to immigrants. The reform failed (McCormick 2002). Since 1996 the provision excluding immigrants from some welfare services has been challenged in the courts. In 1997 the U.S. Congress started repealing the tougher provisions. Finally, the states felt political pressure to maintain benefits at previous levels under the federal system. This pressure is particularly evident in high-migration states like California, where immigrants account for more than 15 percent of the electorate. Thus, a decentralized system that strongly discriminates against immigrants can face political resistance, can easily be challenged in court, and is likely to ultimately revert to the previous system.

9.4.2 Adopting a Points System?

As discussed in the introduction to this chapter, a points system is a method to rank applications for residence and work permits. It has been adopted by Australia, Canada, New Zealand, and Switzerland, and is being introduced in the United Kingdom and other European countries. Each application is allocated a score based on explicit criteria, which typically reward educational attainment, experience, and language abilities. Bonus points can also be given for employment in occupations and regions where there is a shortage of workers. A well-designed points system could encompass and simplify the entire range of migration regulations, for example, removing the need for ad hoc policies for highly skilled migrants and possibly also integrating asylum policies into a broader framework. Hatton (2004), for instance, suggested introducing humanitarian points.

Points systems seem to be quite effective in selecting migrants. This can be seen by comparing the distribution of 2004 International Adult Literacy Survey (IALS) scores of migrants versus natives in a country without a points system (Germany) and one with a points system in place, like Canada (figure 9.9). The difference is quite striking both in absolute skill levels (the average IALS score for migrants was roughly 300 in Canada compared with 250 in Germany) and relative to the skills of natives. In Germany the skill distribution of migrants is visibly displaced to the left, while in Canada it almost perfectly overlaps the distribution among natives. Difference-in-differences analysis of changes in the skill composition of migration in Canada after the introduction of the points system and comparison with trends in the United States also confirm the effectiveness of the points system. In Canada the fraction of migrants with tertiary education increased by 5 percentage points from 1987 to 2002, while it decreased in the United States. However, the points system may also discriminate against certain countries of origin rather than simply being based on skill levels (Antecol et al. 2003).

As discussed earlier, immigration of skilled workers may reduce income inequalities in the recipient country and help contain fiscal pressures associated with access to the welfare system. Thus, it can reconcile efficiency and equity goals of

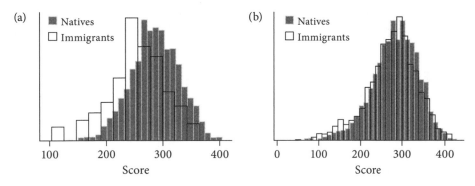

FIGURE 9.9 Distribution of IALS test scores among natives and immigrants in Germany (left) and Canada (right), 2001

migration policy. Moreover, there is evidence of skill complementarity; hence inflows of skilled migrants may even increase job opportunities for unskilled natives.

There is, however, an important drawback to a points system: its negative effect on growth in the sending country by means of the *brain-drain* effect. The brain drain, as its name suggests, is the assertion that migration tends to strip the sending nation of all its best workers. Evidence on the brain-drain effect of migration is, however, far from conclusive (Docquier and Rapoport 2012). Selective immigration policies increase individual incentives to invest in human capital in the sending countries, so the impact of migration on human capital formation in the country of origin is ambiguous. Moreover, since migration is often temporary, human capital acquired in the country of destination could subsequently be transferred to the country of origin and could promote growth in the sending region. Finally, access to higher rewards for their skills enables migrants to send generous remittances back home, supporting growth there.

9.5 Interactions with Other Institutions

Both in terms of magnitude and skill composition, migration flows are affected by wage compression and income floors. If there is little wage compression in a country, high-skilled immigrants may be tempted to enter that country. With significant wage compression, this is not likely to occur. Income floors may trigger more immigrants, especially low-skilled immigrants, to enter a country. Therefore, institutions that affect wage compression and income floors are likely to interact with migration policies. In particular, immigrant flows may be affected by minimum wage legislation (chapter 2), unions (chapter 3), family policies (chapter 7) and UBs (chapter 11). Therefore, immigration policies may be more or less necessary, depending on the other labor market institutions. Other labor market institutions may affect the size and skill composition of immigrants, but immigration policy will not affect the consequences of the other labor market institutions. A rare exception concerns the discussion about closing the welfare door (section

9.4.1), in which there is the suggestion that migrants should be banned from some citizenship rights, in particular the access to social welfare.

9.6 Why Do Migration Policies Exist?

Migration policies are essentially redistributives. They typically prevent income inequality from rising at the bottom of the income distribution by sheltering unskilled native workers from competition with foreign workers. Hence these policies are typically supported by workers at the low end of the skill distribution. Immobile taxpayers can also benefit from tight migration policies, because they are vulnerable to fiscal spillovers associated with inflows of migrants who draw benefits from social welfare systems. Aging increases the political power of these groups, while an increase in the educational attainments of the domestic workforce may weaken the antimigration constituency. The latter is becoming increasingly important in affecting policy outcomes. As documented in this chapter, the trend seems to be toward a tightening of migration restrictions.

Restricting migration, however, may not be very effective in addressing the concerns of these groups, because these restrictions may paradoxically end up selecting just that type of migrants whose assimilation and integration into the fiscal system are more problematic. In any serious policy evaluation there cannot be a zero-immigration scenario. Migration policies can, at best, induce some gradualism in migration flows that would otherwise occur in large waves, as predicted by the option value theory of migration reviewed in technical annex 9.9. Migration policies, in any event, cannot altogether prevent migration.

Pressures on welfare systems that exert negative fiscal spillovers on the domestic population can be reduced by either restricting access to welfare by migrants or by adopting a points system. We have weighed pros and cons of these two types of measures in section 9.4.

9.7 Suggestions for Further Reading

A nice history of migration is provided by Tim Hatton and Jeffrey Williamson (1998). The book edited by Tito Boeri, Gordon Hanson, and Barry McCormick (2002) offers surveys of the literature on the effects of migration on the U.S. and European labor markets. George Borjas (2001) provides an explanation of the small effects of immigration on wages and employment found by this literature in terms of self-selection of immigrants, as well as estimates of the so-called greasing-the-wheels effects. Michael Burda and Jennifer Hunt (2001) offer an assessment of the German reunification episode that sheds light on the determinants of migration flows in integrated labor markets. Christian Dustmann and Albrecht Gitz (2005) nicely review evidence from survey data on attitudes of residents about immigration. Tito Boeri and Herbert Bruecker (2005) draw lessons from the eastern enlargement of migration to the European labor market. David Card (2005) offers an up-to-date assessment of the consequences of migration to the United States for the wages of low-skilled natives. Finally, Frédéric Docquier and Hillel Rapoport (2012) discuss potential brain-drain effects of migration.

9.8 Review Questions and Exercises

1. Why do employers generally support migration, while unions do not?

2. What are the effects of migration on income distribution in the sending country?

3. What is the relation between internal and international migration?

4. Why does empirical work often not find strong effects of migration on native wages in spite of the predictions of economic theory?

5. What does the Roy model predict about the skill composition of migration?

6. How do the elasticities of labor demand and labor supply affect the economic impact of migration?

7. What is the immigration surplus and under which conditions does it occur?

8. What are the pros and cons of a points system?

9. What are the pros and cons of a policy that closes the welfare door to migrants?

10. What is the bottom line of the analysis based on the Mariel boatlift? And what are the implications of the research titled "The Mariel Boatlift That Did Not Happen"?

11. A family—husband, wife, and two young children—reside in southern Italy: the husband currently earns 30,000 euros per year, whereas the wife does not work. The couple is considering moving to northern Italy, where the husband could find a new job paying him 35,000 euros per year, and the wife could start working at 15,000 euros per year. Nonetheless, the family likes the south much better: living there has a monetary utility in present value terms of 35,000 euros. Moreover, should the wife start to work, the family would have to pay childcare costs equal to 10,000 euros per year.

    (a) If the family is supposed to live in northern Italy for the current and the next 3 years and has a discount rate of 12 percent, is it convenient for the family to (immediately) migrate to the north?

    (b) Would your answer be different if childcare was cheaper (e.g., equal to 9,000 euros per year)?

    (c) At which discount rate will the family change opinion about moving to northern Italy?

12. Suppose that a worker with an annual discount rate of 10 percent resides in the Netherlands and is considering whether to stay there or to move to Italy. There are three work periods left in his working life, and pensions are independent of earnings. If the worker remains in the Netherlands, he will earn 40,000 euros per year in each of the three periods. If he moves to Italy, he will earn 44,000 in each of the three periods. What is the highest cost of migration that the worker is willing to incur and still migrate?

13. (Advanced) John is a young worker who faces a decision on whether to migrate from the Netherlands to Italy. If he stays in the Netherlands, he

will earn 45,000 euros per year for the rest of his life. If he moves to Italy, he will earn 50,000 euros per year for the rest of his life. Moving from the Netherlands to Italy will cost him 50,000 euros.

(a) If John uses a discount rate of 5 percent per year, show that it is profitable for him to move to Italy.

(b) At what discount rate would John be indifferent between staying and moving?

(c) At what level of moving costs would John be indifferent between staying in the Netherlands or moving to Italy?

(d) Suppose that in the Netherlands (in Italy) there is a 4 percent (2 percent) probability of losing a job per year and that those losing their jobs earn for the rest of their lives a social assistance of 10,000 euros per year (5,000 euros per year). Would John migrate under these conditions?

(e) Under these conditions, at which probability of losing a job in Italy would John be indifferent between moving or remaining in the Netherlands?

9.9 Technical Annex: Net Gains from Migration

The decision to migrate can be modeled just like a human capital investment decision (see chapter 8). Suppose that an individual at the beginning of a career ($t = 0$) has to choose between staying in a given country, say, home (H), or migrating to a foreign country (F). If the individual stays at home, the annual earnings over the remaining labor market years—from $t = 1$ until age T—will be $w_H(t)$. If the individual moves from H to F, from year 1 onward the individual will earn a stream of income $w_F(t)$. The costs of moving are all incurred at the time of moving and are equal to C_0. The individual makes a decision on the basis of a comparison of present values of both flows of earnings and costs. If i is the market interest rate, the net present value of migrating NPV_M is given by

$$NPV_M = \sum_{t=1}^{T} \frac{w_F(t) - w_H(t)}{(1+i)^t} - C_0. \tag{9.1}$$

From this it follows that the lower the costs of mobility are, the younger the individual (the longer the time horizon T^e, in which the initial investment can provide returns in terms of earning differentials) will be. In addition, the larger the difference in wages between destination and origin countries is, the higher will be the probability that the individual migrates.

Suppose that wages are constant over the lifetime in both H and F. Then for large T, the net present value of migrating can be approximated by

$$NPV_M \approx \frac{w_F - w_H}{i} - C_0, \tag{9.2}$$

where we have used the properties of geometric series.

This suggests that even if the costs of migration are very large relative to the wage in H, say, six times as large as a yearly wage, and the discount rate is 5 percent, then for migration to be convenient, it is sufficient that wages in the destination country are just 30 percent larger in F than in H. To put it another way, migration costs must be very large; otherwise, we would observe large migration flows even in the presence of relatively modest wage differentials.[3] Another interpretation is that there is uncertainty associated with the stream of incomes in the country of destination, and this uncertainty implies that there is an option value for waiting. The latter explanation is consistent with the observation of large waves of migration.

When there is no uncertainty as to future earnings in the country of destination, it is always better to migrate at the beginning of the working life to capitalize on the wage differential. Suppose now that there is some uncertainty associated with the future stream of earnings in the country of destination, and allow the individual to be able to decide the date, if any, at which to migrate. As explained in technical annex 6.9 with reference to retirement decisions, there may be now an option value of postponing migration (Burda 1995). Postponing migration implies that the individual will have less time to capitalize on earning differentials. However, the individual may gather more information that allows a better choice of destination country. Suppose that this additional information comes at some date $0 < \tau < T^e$. For instance, it may be that co-nationals will come back home with information on the labor market in the country of destination.

The option value OV of waiting to migrate until time τ is given by

$$OV(\tau) = NPV_M(\tau) - E_0 NPV_M(0), \tag{9.3}$$

where E_0 indicates expectation. A person will postpone retirement if the option value of waiting to migrate is positive and will migrate as soon as this option value becomes negative. This effect induces large waves in migration when the option value becomes negative for a large group of migrants, for example, migrants coming from the same country.

---

3. Gibson and McKenzie (2011) find that even for high-skilled workers, the expected income gain from migration plays a minor role in the decision to migrate. McIntosh (2008) finds that some immigrants tend to underestimate the benefits from migration.

CHAPTER TEN Employment Protection Legislation

Employment protection legislation consists of the set of norms and procedures to be followed in case of dismissals of redundant workers. EPL imposes legal restrictions on dismissals and sets compensations to workers to be paid by their former employers in case of early termination of a permanent employment contract (i.e., an open-ended contract). EPL also imposes restrictions on the hiring of workers under temporary contracts (i.e., fixed-term contracts). Procedures are also envisaged under EPL that have to be followed in case of both individual and collective layoffs. The final decision on the legitimacy of a layoff may depend on a court ruling. From the point of view of economic analysis, it is very important to note that the firing decision is not only up to the worker and the employer but also can involve a court—a third party, which can be requested to assess the legal validity of the layoff.

EPL is a multidimensional institution, although from the standpoint of economic theory it can be reduced to two key components: a transfer and a tax. The *transfer component* is a monetary transfer from the employer to the worker, similar in nature to the wage. The *tax component*, instead, corresponds to a payment to a third party, external to the worker-employer relationship. Conceptually, the transfer component of EPL consists of *severance payments* and the mandatory *advance notice period*, while the tax component consists of *trial costs* (the payments for lawyers and the like) and all the other costs related to *administrative procedures*. *Severance payments* refer to a monetary transfer from the firm to the worker to be paid in the case of firm-initiated separation. *Advance notice* refers to a specific period of time to be given to the worker before a firing can actually be implemented. Both the severance payment and advance notice that are part of EPL refer to the *legal minima,* that is, statutory payments and mandatory rules that apply to all employment relationships, regardless of what is established by specific labor contracts. Beyond mandatory payments, collective agreements may specify larger severance payments for firm-initiated separations. Administrative procedures have to be followed before the layoff can actually take place. In most countries the employer is often required to discuss layoff decisions with workers' representatives. Furthermore, legislative provisions often differ depending on business characteristics, such as firm (or plant) size and type of industry.

In most countries legislation distinguishes between *individual* and *collective* dismissals. Individual dismissals should be further distinguished between *economic* and *disciplinary* dismissals, with most EPL clauses applying only to the former case. Disciplinary dismissals (i.e., worker's fault dismissals) typically do not involve monetary transfers. The procedure for collective dismissals applies to large-scale firm restructuring and requires the dismissal of at least a specific proportion of the workforce. When a collective dismissal is authorized by the relevant authority, the firm can then implement large-scale dismissals with lower transfers than would be required by applying the individual layoff provisions to all workers. Yet this procedure requires a much tighter administrative burden and procedural costs, in the form of prolonged consultation with workers' representatives.

10.1 Measures and Cross-Country Comparisons

From a cross-country perspective, it would be interesting to compare EPL by evaluating the average cost of a layoff under different employment protection regimes. Unfortunately, homogeneous measures of these costs relative to the average wage hardly exist. To carry out international comparisons of employment protection regimes, economists developed synthetic measures of the strictness of EPL, ranging from 0 to 6, where higher numbers denote more rigid regimes. The OECD uses the following three main indicators:

1. Strictness of the firing regulations for individual workers under *permanent contract* include notification procedures, delays involved before notice can be given, length of the notice period, severance pay, definition of justified or unfair dismissal, length of trial period, compensation following unfair dismissal, possibility of reinstatement following unfair dismissal, and the maximum time to make a claim of unfair dismissal.

2. Strictness of *collective dismissals* refers to the definition of collective dismissal, additional notification requirements, additional delays involved before notice can be given, and other additional costs for employers carrying out collective—as opposed to individual—dismissals.

3. Regulations to hire workers under *temporary contracts* include valid cases for use of fixed-term contracts, maximum number of successive fixed-term contracts, maximum cumulative duration of successive fixed-term contracts, types of work for which temporary work agency employment is legal, restrictions on number of renewals, maximum cumulative duration of agency contracts, whether the set-up of a temporary work agency requires authorization or reporting obligations, and whether regulations ensure equal treatment of regular and agency workers at the user firm.

To obtain the overall indicator of the rigidity of a country, it is necessary to consider simultaneously the strictness of permanent contracts, regulations on temporary contracts, and the strictness of collective dismissals. The weighted average of these three measures provides the overall EPL indicator used by the OECD. Several caveats apply to the interpretation of the OECD EPL index:

1. The OECD overall index averages several subindicators covering regular employment contracts, temporary contracts, and collective dismissals. The overall index can therefore change, because of variations in one or more subindicators.

2. Changes in the EPL subindicators are not independent of one another. For instance, the increasing share of employment under fixed-term contracts may also be a consequence of strict employment protection for regular workers (because more investment may be directed to activities exempted from these provisions) rather than an indication of greater labor market flexibility per se (Bertola et al. 2000). In other words, the coverage of EPL for regular workers is endogenous. As documented later, the share of employment exempted from these regulations (e.g., the share of employment with temporary contracts, the size of the informal sector, the fraction of workers in small units) is larger in countries with particularly strict EPL regimes for permanent contracts. This suggests that it is always better to weight the OECD index for regular workers by the share of workers subject to these regulations.

3. Ideally, one should obtain indicators of the two crucial components of EPL from the standpoint of economic analysis: the transfer and the tax components. However, disentangling the tax from the transfer component is not an easy task, because it is particularly difficult to measure the legal costs of dismissals, whose amount depends on the probability that the worker files the case in a court and on the probability that the court invalidates the firm's firing. To give an example, in the Italian case, if the firing decision is overruled by a judge, the firm can be forced to reinstate the employee on the payroll. Garibaldi and Violante (2005) estimated that an Italian employer with more than 15 employees who fires a worker and whose decision is overruled by a court a year after the layoff may have to bear a cost of 15 monthly wages. This amounts to roughly 20 percent of the total costs of the layoff.

With these caveats in mind, the first four columns of table 10.1 display the overall EPL index and its three subcomponents in 2008, the most recent year for which data are available. Two facts are noteworthy. First, there are marked differences across countries in the strictness of EPL. Second, these differences vary between the main components of the EPL index. The employment protection of permanent workers against individual dismissals is very low in the United States, with a value of 0.6, and by far the highest in Portugal, with a value of 4.0. Regulation of temporary forms of employment is the least strict in Canada, the United Kingdom, and the United States but is also not very strict in Ireland and Sweden. The regulation of temporary employment is by far the most strict in Turkey but is also very strict in France, Luxembourg, and Mexico. Specific requirements for collective dismissals are by far the least strict in New Zealand, with a value for this indicator of 0.4. These requirements are very strict in Italy and Belgium; even in the United Kingdom and the United States, where the employment protection of permanent workers and temporary forms of employment is rather low, the requirements for collective dismissals are relatively strict, with a value of 2.9.

TABLE 10.1 Strictness of employment protection, 2008,
and share of temporary workers, 2012

Country	OECD employment protection index				Share of temporary workers (%)	
	Regular	Temporary	Collective	Overall	Men	Women
Australia	1.4	0.8	2.9	1.4	—	—
Austria	2.2	2.3	3.3	2.4	9.3	9.7
Belgium	1.9	2.7	4.1	2.6	6.6	9.7
Canada	1.2	0.2	2.6	1.0	—	—
Czech Republic	3.0	1.7	2.1	2.3	6.0	9.0
Denmark	1.5	1.8	3.1	1.9	7.8	9.7
Estonia	2.3	2.2	3.3	2.4	3.3	2.8
Finland	2.4	2.2	2.4	2.3	10.3	16.3
France	2.6	3.8	2.1	3.0	13.8	15.2
Germany	2.9	2.0	3.8	2.6	13.8	13.9
Greece	2.3	3.5	3.3	3.0	8.5	11.1
Hungary	1.8	2.1	2.9	2.1	8.7	7.3
Iceland	2.1	1.5	3.5	2.1	9.0	9.9
Ireland	1.7	0.7	2.4	1.4	9.5	10.7
Italy	1.7	2.5	4.9	2.6	12.8	14.2
Japan	2.1	1.5	1.5	1.7	—	—
Korea	2.3	2.1	1.9	2.1	—	—
Luxembourg	2.7	3.9	3.9	3.4	5.9	6.6
Mexico	2.3	4.0	3.8	3.2	—	—
Netherlands	2.7	1.4	3.0	2.2	17.5	20.2
New Zealand	1.5	1.1	0.4	1.2	—	—
Norway	2.2	3.0	2.9	2.7	5.9	9.8
Poland	2.0	2.3	3.6	2.4	27.1	26.0
Portugal	4.0	2.5	1.9	3.2	19.9	20.2
Slovak Republic	2.5	1.2	3.8	2.1	6.5	7.2
Slovenia	3.0	2.5	2.9	2.8	16.4	19.5
Spain	2.4	3.8	3.1	3.1	22.3	25.4
Sweden	2.7	0.7	3.8	2.1	12.1	16.3
Switzerland	1.2	1.5	3.9	1.8	12.9	13.0
Turkey	2.5	4.9	2.4	3.5	8.9	8.2
United Kingdom	1.2	0.3	2.9	1.1	5.4	6.4
United States	0.6	0.3	2.9	0.9	—	—

Sources: EPL: OECD; share of temporary workers: Eurostat.

Notes: The OECD index values range from 0 to 6. To find out more about the methodology used to calculate the OECD employment protection indicators—version 3, see www.oecd.org/employment/protection. Regular = protection of permanent workers against (individual) dismissal; temporary = regulation of temporary forms of employment; collective = specific requirements for collective dismissal; overall = (5/12) × regular + (5/12) × temporary + (2/12) × collective; — = not available. The share of temporary workers is their percentage of the total number of employees aged 15 to 64 years for the first quarter of 2012.

Figure 10.1 provides a visual characterization of how the EPL index and its components changed between 1998 and 2008.[1] EPL for regular workers (workers with permanent contracts) hardly changed at all in OECD countries over the period covered by the data. In contrast, the regulation of temporary contracts was eased in most European countries. In particular, the scope of fixed-term contracts was significantly expanded, and the temporary work agency was introduced, allowing firms to face temporary peaks in demand without having to hire new workers permanently. This corresponds to a *dual-track* reform strategy, involving reforms only at the margin, on a flow basis, for new hires, while the employment security entitlements of the incumbent workers remain unchanged. Although there seems to have been some easing of collective EPL, the requirements for collective dismissals did not change much over the 10-year period. All in all, there is not a lot of change in the overall EPL-index between 1998 and 2008.

Columns five and six of table 10.1 show the share of temporary workers in the first quarter of 2012 in European countries. Whereas in Estonia only about 3 percent of the workers are in temporary jobs, in Spain and Poland about 25 percent of all jobs are temporary. Other countries with a relatively high share of temporary workers are the Netherlands, Portugal, and Slovenia.

Figure 10.2 shows cross-country variations in the share of workers in temporary jobs between 1998 and 2008. Most countries during this period increased their share of workers on temporary contracts, for men as well as women. In Poland the increase was enormous, from about 5 percent to more than 25 percent. Spain is the only country with a substantial drop in the share of workers on temporary contracts, but this occurred from a relatively high level: it declined for men from about 30 to 25 percent and for women from about 35 to 25 percent. Presumably the changes in Spain have been caused by the substantial drop in employment for workers in temporary jobs in the course of the Great Recession. Reforms reducing the protection of EPL for permanent contracts in Spain could also have played a role in this reduction.

In addition to temporary contracts, there are many other exemptions from the application of EPL rules on permanent contracts. For instance, small units are usually exempt from the reinstatement obligations and other procedural requirements, because these obligations are a source of fixed costs and hence particularly affect small units. The relatively small size of plants and the large informal sector in southern Europe might also be a by-product of the presence in these countries of rigid regimes for regular contracts.

Finally, figure 10.3 shows a cross-country scatter plot for the EPL index for regular jobs and the share of workers in temporary jobs as well as a scatter plot for the EPL index for temporary work and the share of workers in temporary jobs. There seems to be a strong positive relationship between restrictions on layoffs from permanent jobs and the share of temporary workers, but there is a much less strong relationship between the EPL indicator for temporary layoffs and the share

---

1. Note that in chapter 1 we present information about changes in the overall EPL index between 1985 and 2008; see figure 1.8.

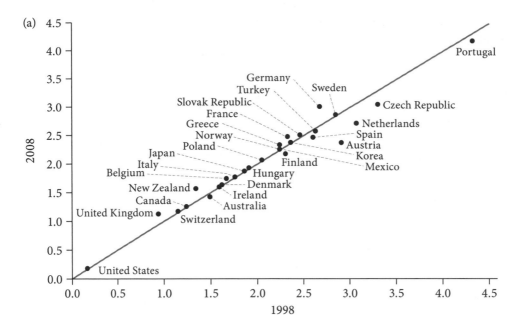

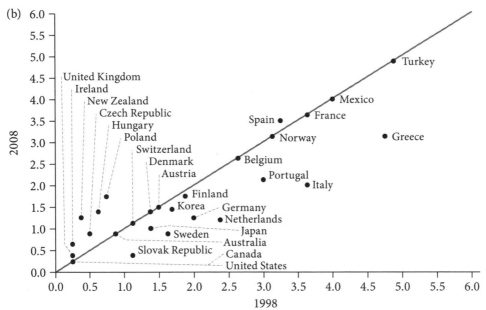

FIGURE 10.1 Change in EPL components, 1998–2008: (a) regular; (b) temporary

Source: OECD EPL database.

Note: See table 10.1 for definitions of the index components.

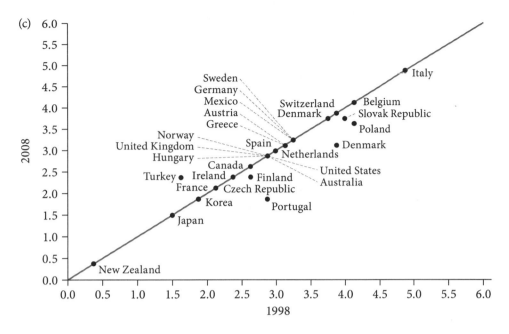

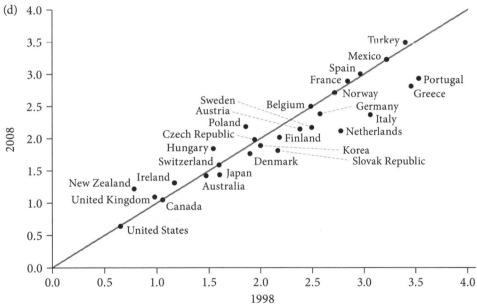

FIGURE 10.1 *(continued)* Change in EPL components, 1998–2008: (c) collective dismissals; (d) overall

Source: OECD EPL database.

Note: See table 10.1 for definitions of the index components.

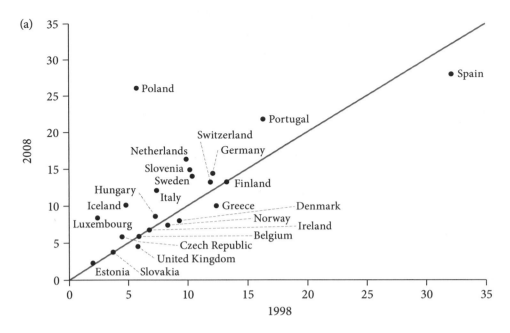

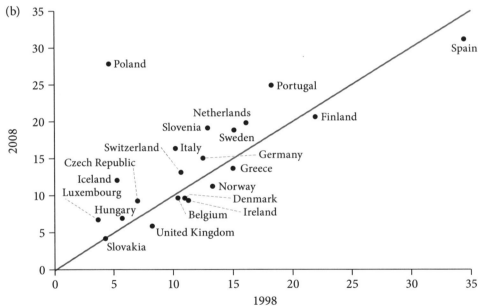

FIGURE 10.2 Change in the percentage of temporary workers, 1998–2008: (a) men; (b) women
Source: Eurostat.

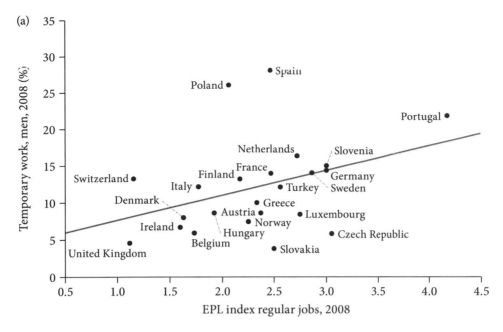

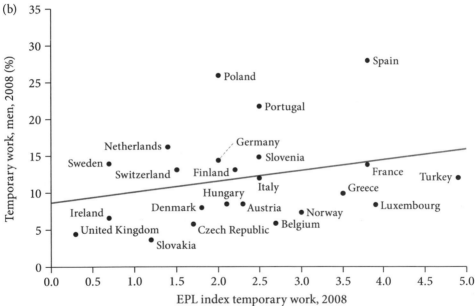

FIGURE 10.3 EPL index components and male temporary employment, 2008 (%): (a) regular;
(b) temporary

Source: Eurostat and OECD EPL database.

Note: See table 10.1 for definitions of the index components.

of temporary workers. The strictness of employment protection for permanent contracts seems to be the driving force behind the development of temporary employment.

10.2 Theory

EPL imposes costs on firms for adjustments of the levels of the workforce. Put another way, employers can avoid paying severance payments and procedural costs by deciding not to change employment levels in response to shocks. Lack of response to shocks could reduce profits of firms, but this loss could possibly be compensated by a decline in wages if employers succeed in shifting to workers the EPL transfer as a sort of voluntary insurance scheme.

10.2.1 A Neutrality Result

Under some rather extreme circumstances EPL has no effects on employment, welfare of workers, and profits. This neutrality case was first highlighted by Lazear (1990) and occurs when three conditions are met (see also box 10.1):

1. Workers are risk-neutral.
2. Wages are flexible; that is, there is no wage floor (minimum wage or collective agreement) preventing downward wage adjustment.
3. EPL consists only of the transfer component, a severance payment to be paid by the employer to the worker involved in the redundancy; the tax component is zero.

BOX 10.1   *Example of a Contract Undoing EPL*

Ed Lazear presents a model to investigate how EPL affects employment, welfare of workers, and profits of firms. Suppose that we have initially a two-period contract offering wages w in both periods. Furthermore, workers are risk-neutral, so that their utility function reads $u(w) = w$, and there are no wage floors. Now introduce employment protection as a severance scheme, paying TR to the worker at the termination of the two-period contract. To keep labor costs unchanged with respect to the situation without EPL, the employer proposes to the worker a contract offering a lower wage in the first period, $(w - B)$, where B is the *bond* entitling the worker to TR in the second period. For the worker, there is no loss in welfare as long as

$$w - B + \frac{w + TR}{1 + i} = w + \frac{w}{1 + i},$$
(10.1)

where i is the interest rate. This condition implies that $B = \frac{TR}{1+i}$, that is, the worker is lending to the firm the transfer that will be delivered at the end of the contract. Under these assumptions, EPL does not affect employment, welfare of workers, or profits of firms.

The risk-neutrality assumption is crucial in this context. Suppose in fact that the utility function $u(w)$ is concave, denoting a risk-averse worker. It follows that

$$u(w) > \frac{1}{2}[u(w-B) + u(w+B)]. \tag{10.2}$$

Hence

$$u(w) + \frac{u(w)}{1+i} > u\left(w - \frac{TR}{1+i}\right) + \frac{u(w+TR)}{1+i}. \tag{10.3}$$

Thus, a bonding arrangement will cause a welfare loss to the employees when they are risk-averse.

Source: Lazear (1990).

The neutrality occurs under these circumstances because EPL affects only the intertemporal structure of wages, leaving the net discounted value of a job for a worker and the employer unchanged. The essence of this result is that the presence of a severance payment is taken into account in the wage contract, which internalizes the future redundancy payment. Employers, in other words, initially pay a lower wage, forcing their employees to buy from them a sort of *bond* or insurance that will give the employees the right to receive a deferred compensation—the severance payment—at the time of separation.

The key to the neutrality result is that the worker receives the same payment in discounted value terms from offering labor with or without EPL. A risk-neutral worker is interested only in the discounted value of the job, not in the time profile of the wage, and the employer, when deciding whether to create a job and open a vacancy, will be indifferent to the presence of EPL, because the net discounted cost of the job is unchanged with respect to the situation without EPL. The contract has succeeded in undoing the effects of EPL.

Boeri and Jimeno (2005) show that employment protection negatively affects both economic (exogenous) layoff and disciplinary layoff probabilities. This happens via the costs of judicial procedures required to implement the dismissals. EPL usually establishes that either economic or disciplinary reasons have to be provided for dismissal by the employer, who has the burden of proof. Layoffs are considered unfair in most countries when there are neither subjective (misconduct) nor objective (economic) grounds for the interruption of the relationship. Penalties applied to employers implementing unfair dismissals do not discriminate among the two types of justifications (disciplinary and economic), and an employer who finds it hard to prove misconduct can always try to justify the dismissal on economic grounds. Thus, the costs of disciplinary layoffs are unavoidably interrelated with those of economic dismissals. Insofar as EPL negatively affects disciplinary layoffs, it increases the efficiency wage (see box 10.2). When EPL instead acts mainly on economic layoffs, it reduces the efficiency wage. Thus, the impact of EPL will vary, depending on the monitoring technology of the firm. The better this technology is, the stronger will be the effects of EPL on disciplinary versus economic layoffs. As small firms can better monitor the productivity of their workers than large firms can, this provides an argument for the exemption of small units from the strictest EPL provisions.

Efficiency Wages and Employment Protection

The efficiency wage model (see technical annex 2.9.3 for a static version) is useful for characterizing the effects of EPL on wages. Employers are assumed to have only imperfect information about the effort of their employees. Hence they pay *efficiency wages* above the market-clearing level to discourage their workers from shirking.

The workers face a trade-off. Either they put in effort, which provides a disutility to them, or they shirk and face some positive probability of being detected and fired. We can use a dynamic framework to illustrate the efficiency wage model in more detail. The flow value of a job to a person who does not shirk is

$$\rho V_e^N = w - e + \delta(V_u - V_e^N), \tag{10.4}$$

where w is the wage, e is the effort, δ is the exogenous job separation rate (independent of the behavior of the employee), and V_u is the asset value of being unemployed. For shirkers, the flow value of a job is

$$\rho V_e^S = w + (\delta + \phi)(V_u - V_e^S), \tag{10.5}$$

where ϕ is the rate at which shirkers are detected and fired, that is, the probability of a disciplinary layoff. The no-shirking condition implies that the asset value of shirking is lower than or equal to the asset value of not shirking, that is, $V_e^S \leq V_e^N$. Using this condition together with (10.4) and (10.5), we can then derive the efficiency wage:

$$w^e \geq \rho V_u + e\left(\frac{\phi + \rho + \delta}{\phi}\right). \tag{10.6}$$

The efficiency wage is increasing with the effort required in the job, with the discount rate, and with the exogenous job separation rate, while it is decreasing with the probability of a disciplinary layoff. These effects are intuitively clear. A higher effort, a higher discount rate, and a higher exogenous job separation rate all reduce the value of the job, which means that the penalty associated with being caught shirking (and so being laid off by the employer) is lower. Hence there is a need to pay higher wages to prevent shirking. A higher probability of disciplinary layoffs reduces the value of the shirking option compared with the value of nonshirking, making it less necessary for employers to pay higher wages to deter opportunistic behavior.

Unemployment is generated in efficiency wage models because employers find it optimal to pay a wage above the market clearing level and to use involuntary unemployment as a disciplining device to induce their workers to put more effort into the job. Stricter EPL causes layoffs to be more expensive and thus reduces the probability of disciplinary layoffs (ϕ). Hence, stricter EPL increases efficiency wages and through that, it increases unemployment. However, to the extent that EPL reduces not only disciplinary but also economic layoffs (δ), the effect on wages and unemployment of EPL can be mitigated.

Source: Shapiro and Stiglitz (1984).

10.2.2 Removing Risk Neutrality

It is sufficient to relax any of the three assumptions above (risk neutrality, wage flexibility, and EPL as a pure transfer) to have EPL affect labor allocation. Take first the case in which workers are risk-averse. They will then suffer a welfare loss from experiencing fluctuations in their earnings, even if the net discounted value of the job is unchanged with respect to the situation without EPL (see box 10.1).

Workers may then ask for higher wages to be compensated for the fluctuations in earnings associated with the bonding arrangement. As the labor supply curve shifts upward, the bonding scheme cannot be neutral for the employers either: the introduction of EPL is bound to affect the labor market equilibrium.

10.2.3 EPL with Rigid Wages

Suppose now that condition 2 is relaxed, so that wages are rigid and therefore do not adjust after the introduction of EPL. Because the introduction of the severance payment cannot be accompanied by a reduction of the wage, labor supply will be unaffected, and we can concentrate on labor demand, as in box 10.3. Generalizing from the results in box 10.3, we conclude that EPL with fixed wages

1. has no effects on average employment or unemployment,
2. lowers the volatility of employment over the business cycle, and
3. reduces profits.

Flexiland and Rigidland   BOX 10.3

To highlight the effects of EPL under rigid wages, it is instructive to consider an economy where only two states of the world are possible—a good and a bad state, for example, a boom and a recession. In particular, let us take a simple logarithmic production function (labor is the only factor of production) and hence write the firm's profits in the *flexible regime* (denoted with superscript F) as follows:

$$\pi^F = A^i \log L - wL, \tag{10.7}$$

where L is employment, and A^i is the price of the good being sold by the firm, which varies depending on the state of the world: A^i assumes value A^h under the good state and A^l under the bad state, where $A^h > A^l$. In every period there is

---

a probability p that the price is equal to A^h and a probability $(1-p)$ that the price is equal to A^l. The wage is fixed and equal to w independently of the cyclical conditions.

The employer has to decide how many workers to hire. Without EPL, hiring and firing can take place at no cost, and the firm can freely choose the profit-maximizing employment level (equating the value of the marginal product of labor to its marginal costs or wage rate) under any state of the world. Optimal employment in this case equates the value of the marginal product, $\frac{A^i}{L}$, to the wage, so that, solving for employment,

$$L^F = \begin{cases} \frac{A^h}{w} & \text{with probability } p \\ \frac{A^l}{w} & \text{with probability } 1-p \end{cases}$$

Because the economy experiences, on average, a fraction p of booms and a fraction $(1-p)$ of recessions, the average employment in the long run will be

$$\bar{L}^F = \frac{(1-p)A^l + pA^h}{w}. \tag{10.8}$$

Consider now the behavior of the firm when EPL is present. Assuming that with EPL, laying off workers during recessions is too expensive, the firm can only choose the employment level that maximizes the *expected* value of the profits π, holding the employment level constant over time. Then the employer in the *rigid regime R* will solve the expected profit-maximization problem

$$\pi^R = \max_L \{[(1-p)A^l + pA^h]\log L - wL\}. \tag{10.9}$$

The first-order condition of this problem provides the level of employment in the rigid regime as

$$L^R = \frac{(1-p)A^l + pA^h}{w}. \tag{10.10}$$

This optimal employment level in the rigid regime, L^R, is therefore a weighted average of the levels of employment that, without EPL, would prevail during the expansions and recessions, respectively, where weights are given by the probabilities of the two events. Note that L^R coincides with $\bar{L}^F$, the long-run employment level in Flexiland. Thus, employment in the long run is the same in the two regimes. However, during the cycle, employment in the rigid regime will never be as in Flexiland: it will be lower under upturns and higher during downturns. Finally, note that $\pi^R < \pi^F$ even in the long run, because the rigid-regime firm realizes lower profits (using suboptimal employment levels) in both booms and recessions.

The first two implications are intuitive in the light of the preceding discussion. The third follows because the employment level chosen without EPL is the only level that maximizes profits in each period. Consequently, in each period profits are higher without EPL than with it. With the same level of employment on average, the firm without EPL is able to make higher profits. In other words, the firm operating without EPL is more efficient.

10.2.4 EPL as a Tax

Finally, condition 3 of the neutrality model (see section 10.2.1) can be relaxed so that EPL no longer is a transfer but a tax—notably, a payment to a third party, say, a lawyer. Now, even when wages are flexible and workers are risk-neutral, EPL can no longer be undone by a new labor contract compensating the employer for the tax.

The effects of employment protection on employment and wages when EPL is a tax can be characterized only by using a dynamic framework. Dynamics are needed because the EPL tax is a particular type of tax on the firm, namely, one that the firm can avoid paying if it does not reduce employment levels over time. Thus, the presence of the EPL tax is taken into account by the employer also when issuing a vacancy and hiring an employee, because this hiring carries with it a higher risk of having to pay the EPL tax in the future. Put another way, the EPL tax displays its effects by acting mainly on labor market flows (i.e., on hiring and firing).

An EPL tax reduces job creation, because employers are more reluctant to open a vacancy: the net discounted value of a job is lower with EPL than without it. However, job destruction is also lower in the presence of EPL, because it is more costly for firms to lay off workers. The effects of EPL on employment and un-employment are therefore ambiguous: they can increase or decrease, depending on the relative strength of the effects on job creation and job destruction margins. An unambiguous theoretical prediction, however, is that labor market flows decline with employment protection: a world with an EPL tax is one with less job creation, job destruction, and unemployment inflows, as well as unemployment outflows, and hence it experiences longer unemployment duration (Bentolila and Bertola 1990).

As long as wages are flexible, they will also react to the introduction of EPL. As argued earlier, an EPL tax cannot be undone by contractual arrangements between the employer and the worker. Yet wages are nevertheless bound to be affected by EPL. Suppose, for instance, that wages are set as a result of a bargaining process be-tween the employer and the worker, as in the models discussed in chapter 3. These models predict that wages are increasing with the bargaining power of workers and with their fallback option, that is, the net discounted value of being unemployed. EPL has two effects on wage setting in this context. On the one hand, it increases the bargaining power of those who have a job, the *insiders*, who now are more pro-tected from wage underbidding by unemployed jobseekers, or *outsiders*. This effect increases the equilibrium wage in comparison with the situation without EPL. On the other hand, EPL reduces the fallback option of workers, because unemployed jobseekers face lower re-employment probabilities under strict EPL. This second effect reduces wages under the EPL tax regime. Because of these two offsetting effects, the relationship between EPL and wages is likely to be hump shaped: for low values of EPL, wages are bound to increase as a result of increased bargaining power of insiders, but for high values of EPL, wages may well decline, because the welfare loss associated with unemployment becomes very large.

Even when EPL does not increase wages, insiders are better off with the EPL tax, because the risk of job loss is lower. With regard to income distribution, EPL involves lower profits for firms and lower welfare for unemployed individuals, who now experience longer unemployment duration, but higher welfare for those who have jobs, notably when individuals care much about their future (have a low discount factor).

10.2.5 Two-Tier Regimes

The preceding theoretical results on the effects of EPL are relevant to predicting labor market adjustment in environments with different degrees of strictness of EPL involving all workers. However, as documented earlier, many EPL reforms are asymmetric in that they change regulations only for a subset of the eligible population. This design of reforms, reducing EPL only at the margin for new hires, seems to be a viable political economy strategy when there are strong political obstacles to reforms (Saint-Paul 1997).

As suggested by Boeri and Garibaldi (2006), two-tier reforms involve important transitory job creation (*honeymoon*) effects and a decline in productivity. The intuition is illustrated in figure 10.4 and runs as follows. In a rigid environment employers do not adjust employment to cyclical conditions (like Rigidland in box 10.3), and employment is fixed at levels between employment in bad times (L_b) and employment in good times (L_g). From time T_0 onward the firm is allowed to enjoy *flexibility at the margin;* that is, it can hire and fire workers on a temporary basis, but at the same time, it cannot reduce at will the existing stock of permanent contracts. Thus, in good times the firm hires temporary workers up to the optimal employment level in the frictionless environment L_g and employment increases from A to B. Because of natural attrition (retirement and resignations) the stock of permanent workers decreases, and so in bad times employment is decreased from B to C. In the next cycle employment is increased from C to D and goes down from D to E. All this means that during upturns there will be more employees than before the two-tier reforms, while during downturns employment will be higher than in an actually flexible labor market. This goes on until the stock of permanent workers reaches the level L_b. It follows that dual-track reforms temporarily increase average employment.

The transient honeymoon effects fade away as the stock of permanent workers is gradually replaced with flexible contracts. Hence, the firms can build up a buffer stock of workers with flexible contracts (Bentolila and Dolado 1994), allowing them from time T_1 onward to adjust employment to business conditions. When all workers are replaced, the economy is under a fully flexible regime in which the previous theoretical results apply.

Throughout the honeymoon firms enjoy higher profits and lower labor productivity, because total output is the same as in the rigid environment, but em-

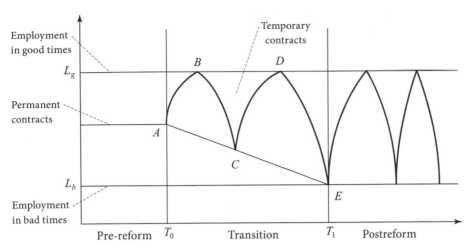

FIGURE 10.4 The honeymoon effect
Source: Boeri and Garibaldi (2006).

ployment is higher. Profits increase throughout the transition until they reach the same levels as in the flexible regime. The positive effects on employment and the negative effects on labor productivity of two-tier regimes are transitory: they fade away when the honeymoon is over.

10.3 Empirical Evidence

10.3.1 Cross-Country Analyses

Most studies of the effects of EPL take a cross-country approach; that is, they compare employment dynamics in countries that, according to some measure of the strictness of EPL, display different degrees of employment protection. A few studies have found significant effects of employment protection (generally measured using the OECD cross-country ranking) on employment and unemployment *stocks*. This finding is consistent with economic theory: as a tax on labor adjustment (or on the capitalized value of the firm), EPL should affect hirings and separations, and hence unemployment inflows and outflows, but it should not be correlated with employment and unemployment stocks. Consistent with economic theory, a robust finding of this literature is that EPL negatively affects unemployment inflows and outflows: countries with the most strict EPL have more stagnant unemployment pools. EPL also seems to affect the composition of employment and unemployment (OECD 2004): countries with stricter EPL display higher youth unemployment rates and lower unemployment among prime-aged groups. This finding is also consistent with economic theory, because prime-aged groups are typically insiders (they already have a job and are sheltered by EPL from labor market adjustment), while youngsters are typically outsiders (they are first-time jobseekers and hence are hit by longer durations of unemployment).

Some studies only investigate how EPL affects stocks of employment and unemployment. Lazear (1990) and Di Tella and MacCulloch (2005) find that EPL has a negative effect on employment and a positive effect on unemployment. Grubb and Wells (1997) find a negative effect of EPL on employment. However, Belot and van Ours (2001, 2004) find that the unemployment stock is negatively affected by EPL, while Addison and Grosso (1996) and Nickell et al. (2005) find ambiguous effects on both unemployment and employment. Other studies that investigate the effects of EPL on both stocks and flows all find negative effects on unemployment flows but ambiguous effects on stocks of employment and unemployment (Bertola 1990; Jackman et al. 1996; Garibaldi et al. 1997; Gregg and Manning 1997; Emerson 1998; Boeri 1999). Jackman et al. (1996) and Emerson (1998) find a negative effect of EPL on the flows to and from employment, while Boeri (1999) and Kugler and Saint-Paul (2000) find a positive effect on these flows.

No unambiguous result is obtained concerning the impact of EPL on *labor turnover* (the sum of hirings and separations) and *job turnover* (the sum of job creation and destruction), although economic theory unambiguously predicts a negative effect of the strictness of employment protection on labor market flows. Explanations of this discrepancy between theory and facts—for example, Boeri (1996) and Bertola and Rogerson (1997)—typically call into play the interaction of EPL with other labor market institutions. For instance, it is argued that institutions that compress wage structures tend to counteract the negative effects of EPL on labor market flows, because they reduce the scope of price-driven adjustment mechanisms. If employers cannot adjust wages when they face changes in the demand for their product, they are forced to adjust employment.

10.3.2 Studies Based on Firm and Worker Data

There are more and more empirical studies using within-country variation in enforcement of EPL and policy change. Work carried out in the United States has been drawing on cross-state differences in the adoption of wrongful-discharge protections over and above the doctrine of employment at will. Work carried out in Europe has been exploiting another dimension of within-country variation, the exemption of small units from the strictest EPL provisions. By combining these exemptions with dual-track reform strategies, it is possible to carry out difference-in-differences policy evaluation studies. For instance, Boeri and Jimeno (2005) exploit variation in enforcement of EPL in Italy, where the most restrictive legislation is not enforced in small firms (see also box 10.4). They also exploit a 1990 reform that made severance pay mandatory for firms with fewer than 15 employees in case of unfair dismissals. Before that date, small firms were not obliged to follow this rule. The authors use a difference-in-differences approach in which firms with fewer than 15 employees are the treatment group and firms with between 15 and 30 employees are the control group. Furthermore, 1986–1990 represents the before period and 1991–1995 the after period. Boeri and Jimeno find that EPL increased persistence (i.e., the probability that a firm does not change the number of workers from one year to the next).

Tito Boeri and Juan Jimeno analyzed dismissal rates for temporary and permanent employees in establishments of different sizes by drawing on data from the Italian Labor Force Survey for 1993–1995. In Italy the most restrictive EPL provisions concern permanent workers in firms with more than 15 employees. The table below gives an indication of the effects of EPL by drawing on two differences: the difference between workers in firms of fewer than and more than 15 employees, and the difference between permanent and temporary workers:

Firm size	Probability of being dismissed (%)	
	Permanent workers	Temporary workers
Fewer than 15 employees	1.7	0.8
More than 15 employees	0.9	2.2
Difference	0.8	−1.4
Difference-in-differences	2.2	

Because temporary workers are not covered by EPL provisions on termination of their contracts, their dismissal rates are expected to be higher than those of permanent employees when the strictest EPL provisions for permanent workers hold. This is confirmed by the data in the table: while below the 15-employee threshold the dismissal rate of permanent workers is higher than that of temporary workers, above this threshold it is the other way around. These difference-in-differences effects of EPL hold also in different partitions of the sample, for example, by industry, region, gender, age, and skills, and when all these personal characteristics are simultaneously taken into account. Boeri and Jimeno also carried out another difference-in-differences estimation by comparing growth rates of establishments below and above the 15-employee threshold, before and after a reform that in 1990 increased the costs of dismissals for units with fewer than 15 employees. They found that firm size became more persistent after the reform only in units with fewer than 15 employees, an indication of the role played by EPL in reducing the adjustment of employment levels in firms.

Source: Boeri and Jimeno (2005).

Some studies focus on age-specific EPL. For example, when older workers are better protected than younger ones, the age-specific discontinuity in EPL can be exploited to learn about the labor market effects of EPL. Behaghel et al. (2008) study the effects of the so-called Delalande tax, which compelled French firms laying off workers aged 50 and older to pay a tax to the unemployment insurance system. Box 10.5 provides some details on their analysis of the Delalande tax's adverse hiring effects, which they find are substantial. The authors also investigated the effect of the tax on the layoff rates for older workers, which they find hard to detect. Schnalzenberger and Winter-Ebmer (2009) study the effects of a layoff tax for older workers introduced in Austria in 1996 (see also box 6.5). Employers had to pay a tax of up to 170 percent of the gross monthly income when they fired workers aged 50 or older. Using workers aged nearly 50, they find that the firing tax reduced layoffs of older workers significantly. Boockmann et al. (2012) investigate the effect of hiring subsidies for older workers in Germany. For the identification of the effects, they exploit two policy changes in eligibility criteria. The first policy change was in 2002 when program participation for workers above the age of 50 was extended from workers who were long-term unemployed to all workers. The second policy change in 2004 trended in the opposite direction. The specific treatment of older workers above the age of 50 was ended, and younger and older workers were made equally eligible for the hiring subsidies. The authors conclude that firms' hiring behavior is hardly influenced by the hiring subsidies, which—except for women in eastern Germany—mainly led to deadweight effects.

BOX 10.5   *Layoff Taxes for Older Workers*

French firms laying off workers aged 50 and older have to pay a tax to the unemployment insurance system, known as the Delalande tax. This tax is intended to internalize the costs of laying off older workers, which are likely to be high, because older unemployed workers stay unemployed for a long time. However, because of the increase in firing costs for these older workers, firms refrained from hiring these workers as well. Since the tax had to be paid to the unemployment insurance fund, it could not be undone by a private transfer, that is, a reduction of wages for these workers. In July 1992 firms were exempted from the tax for workers who were hired after age 50. Using a difference-in-differences approach, Luc Behaghel, Bruno Crépon, and Béatrice Sédillot analyze how the 1992 policy change affected the age-specific outflow from unemployment to employment. If the Delalande tax had adverse effects on hiring, this should become apparent after the July 1992 policy change, which removed the hiring disincentive. The authors compare the monthly transition rate from unemployment to employment under indefinite-duration contracts for workers aged 49 and aged 50 before July 1992 and after July 1992 (in percentages):

Monthly transition from unemployment to employment				
	Men (%)		Women (%)	
Age of worker	50	49	50	49
Before July 1992	1.21	1.43	0.88	1.13
After July 1992	1.25	0.93	0.99	0.93
Difference	0.04	−0.50	0.11	−0.20
Difference-in-differences	+0.54		+0.31	

They find that while for 49-year-old men the outflow declined by 0.50 percentage points, for 50-year-old men, it increased by 0.04 percentage points. So the treatment effect of the change in law was 0.54 percentage points, a small absolute increase but a substantial relative increase in the outflow from unemployment to employment of about 45 percent. For women the treatment effect was 0.31 percentage points, an increase of about 35 percent. All in all, this is evidence that adverse hiring effects were indeed present before the 1992 policy change.

Source: Behaghel et al. (2008).

Employment protection may affect the behavior of workers who benefit from this protection. These workers may be inclined to put less effort in their work, thus reducing their productivity (see box 10.2). There are no empirical studies that investigate the direct relationship between EPL and individual labor productivity, if only because it is virtually impossible to measure individual labor productivity. However, there are studies that use absenteeism as an indicator of opportunistic behavior. Although no one-to-one relationship exists between absenteeism and productivity, it is clear that reduced absenteeism will lead to increased labor productivity. Ichino and Riphahn (2005) exploit a discontinuity in employment protection in Italian firms that exists because workers begin to be protected against firing after 12 weeks of probation. Firing a worker after 12 weeks is very expensive for firms. If the firing is not sustained by a just cause, the firm is forced to take back the worker and to pay the full wage lost during litigation. In addition, the firm must pay a fine up to 200 percent of the original amount due. In the first 12 weeks, during the probationary period, workers can be fired at will. The authors find that absenteeism increases significantly once employment protection is granted at the end of probation. Olsson (2009) studied the relationship between EPL and absenteeism by investigating a reform that made Swedish seniority rules less stringent for small firms. Olsson found that the policy change reduced worker absenteeism in small firms (box 10.6 discusses this study in some detail). Von Below and Thoursie (2010) use the same policy change to study its effect on employment and turnover. They find that both hires and separations increased in small firms relative to large firms by 5 percent. This implies a negative relationship between EPL and turnover, but it also implies that employment was not affected.

EPL and Sickness Absence   BOX 10.6

In January 2001 an exemption in the seniority rule in the Swedish Employment Security Act was implemented. The exemption made it possible for employers with a maximum of ten employees to exempt two workers from the seniority rule at times of redundancies. Thus, workers who were previously protected by seniority were put at risk of dismissal should the firm decide to lay off workers. The weaker employment protection resulted in an increasing risk of redundancy, especially for workers with high amounts of sickness absence. This in turn might cause workers not to report in sick for fear of being laid off. Martin Olsson used the change in policy to investigate the relationship between EPL and absenteeism through a difference-in-differences approach, finding indeed that the reduced EPL caused a decline in absence rates:

Firm size	Probability of being absent (%)	
	Firm size	
	Treatment group (2–9 employees)	Control group (12–50 employees)
2000	2.8	3.6
2001	2.4	3.6
Difference	−0.4	0.0
Difference-in-differences	−0.4	

Olsson compared the probability to be absent on a given Wednesday in 2000, before the policy change, and in 2001 once the policy change was implemented. He compared firms with 2–9 workers (to whom the new policy applied) with firms with 12–50 workers (whose employment protection was unaffected by the policy change). In the control firms there was no change in absenteeism, while in the treatment firms the probability of absenteeism dropped by 0.4 percentage points, a substantial drop of almost 15 percent. Olsson notes that the effect of EPL on sickness absence suggests that EPL lowers labor productivity. Since no one-to-one relationship exists between absence and productivity, the magnitude of the effect of EPL on productivity remains unclear. Whether reduced absenteeism increased productivity also depends on the nature of the absenteeism. If workers who are very ill report to work and possibly infect their co-workers, who then become ill, there may even be adverse effects on productivity. However, Olsson also concludes that the drop in absenteeism occurred especially for shorter spells for those who held permanent contracts, suggesting that the effect of EPL on absenteeism should not be underestimated.

Source: Olsson (2009).

Kugler and Pica (2008) study the effects of EPL on worker and job flows, exploiting the same Italian reform of 1990 as did Boeri and Jimeno (2005). They find that this reform decreased accessions and separations for workers in small relative to large firms, especially in sectors with higher employment volatility, where the increased firing costs affect potential separations the most. The authors find a negligible impact on net employment. Finally, Schivardi and Torrini (2008) study the effect of the 15-worker discontinuity in EPL on firms' growth and employment policies. They find the effect on firms' growth to be modest, because if firms pass the threshold of 15 workers, they adjust their employment policies, hiring more workers on temporary contracts.

Van der Wiel (2010) exploits a change in the term of notice that resulted from the introduction of a new law in 1999 in the Netherlands. Under the old law the terms of notice depended on the tenure of the workers, who could be dismissed with a maximum of three months' notice. For workers aged 45 or older, the maximum was six months' notice. Under the new law, age dependency disappeared, and the maximum term of notice was four months. Van der Wiel finds that longer terms of notice caused wages to be higher.

Within-country studies generally found some negative effects of EPL on dismissal rates (Miles 2000; Boeri and Jimeno 2005; Autor et al. 2006). Garibaldi et al. (2003) also found that the presence of thresholds on firm size (e.g., 15 employees, as in Italy), below which EPL does not hold, increases firms' persistence. That is, the probability increases that a firm does not change the number of employees from one year to the next, holding the number to just below the threshold. These effects are generally small but qualitatively consistent with the predictions of economic theory.

10.3.3 Endogeneity of EPL

An important issue in the empirical assessment of the effects of EPL is whether the role played by courts in the enforcement of EPL makes these regulations dependent on underlying labor market conditions. Judges may feel that under severe labor market slack in a region or during a cyclical downturn, workers should be more heavily protected against dismissals than in a buoyant labor market.

Available information on the enforcement of EPL, discussed in Bertola et al. (1999), suggests that the nature and stringency of EPL enforcement do indeed vary across countries and over time and are quite strongly influenced by underlying labor market conditions. In particular, long-term unemployment is positively correlated with the number of cases brought before courts (as a fraction of the population of working age) across the OECD countries for which data on EPL enforcement were available. Another dimension of jurisprudence that seems to be linked to labor market conditions, both across countries and over time, is the percentage of cases favorable to workers: the countries where tribunals are most frequently involved in labor disputes on the termination of a contract are those with the highest percentage of cases favorable to workers. In Spain almost 72 percent of cases in 1995 were won by workers, compared with less than 50 percent in North American countries and a low of 16 percent in Ireland, all countries where tribunals seem to intervene rather infrequently in labor disputes concerning contract termination. The high incidence of judicial procedures in France may also be partly explained by a large share (74 percent) of cases favorable to workers. The likelihood that court rulings are favorable to employees tends to play an important role in inducing workers to bring their cases to the courts, although it may, conversely, encourage employers to reach extrajudicial agreements.

With regard to time-series variation in EPL enforcement, Bertola et al. (1999) found a marked covariation of the incidence of jurisprudence (cases brought to court as a percentage of the labor force) and unemployment in Germany. Co-movements of indicators of jurisprudence and unemployment are also observed in Spain, especially when the focus is on cases ending with judgments favorable to employees, and in Italy, where evidence on case law points to a strong link between law enforcement and regional labor market conditions.

10.4 Policy Issues

10.4.1 How Much Protection Should EPL Provide?

Workers are generally risk-averse and have limited, if any, access to capital markets. Their (indirect) utility function is concave in wages. Thus, when comparing two jobs that offer, on average, the same wage, they will always opt for the one that has less variability in earnings. Employers are instead generally risk-neutral: firms have better access than workers to capital markets. Thus, firms can insure against negative shocks to their business by investing in capital markets and diversifying risk.

Under these conditions it is always optimal to have employers providing some insurance to their workers, allowing them to smooth out income fluctuations. As argued in this chapter, EPL is the most common way for employers to provide such an insurance. UBs, discussed in the next chapter, offer an alternative. But if we suppose that there is no UB system, how much insurance should be provided? Can it be made less distortional?

Blanchard and Tirole (2003) consider a simple case where wages are unaffected by employment protection, there is no asymmetric information (hence workers' effort can be fully monitored by the employer), and EPL consists only of transfers: it is a pure severance scheme. They show that under these conditions the optimal insurance offered by EPL may be a *complete insurance*, preventing any fluctuation in the income of the workers, provided that productivity exceeds the reservation wage of individuals.

However, wages do react to the provision of this insurance. EPL has two offsetting effects on wages. On the one hand, EPL strengthens the bargaining power of insiders, exerting an upward pressure on wages. On the other hand, EPL reduces the fallback option of workers, exerting a moderating effect on wages. When workers are fully insured against the risk of job loss (e.g., the severance payment offered by employers compensates them throughout their entire unemployment spell), there is no longer this second, moderating effect on wages related to the outside option of workers. Thus, wages are bound to increase unambiguously as a result of EPL, and hence firms providing full insurance to their workers will not be able to partly recover the costs of this insurance through lower wages paid to their workers. If employers are forced by regulations to provide this full insurance, employment will be reduced.

The presence of moral hazard also prevents the provision of full insurance. Workers require incentives—a penalty associated with the possibility of being fired because of misconduct—to abstain from shirking, as highlighted by the efficiency wage models summarized in box 10.2. If EPL makes disciplinary layoffs more difficult, then opportunistic behavior is encouraged.

Thus, under general circumstances there will be some optimal level of employment protection that provides less than full insurance. How much insurance should be provided depends on a number of factors, including the degree of risk aversion of employees, the depth of capital markets, and the underlying wage-setting mechanism. Interactions with other institutions, notably UBs (see chapter 11), are also important in this context.

Other important design features of EPL concern—more than the level of protection—its unpredictability and the involvement of third parties. EPL consisting of a tax is always more distortional than EPL designed as a pure transfer. However, some payments to third parties are unavoidable, because judges need to be involved in assessing the nature (economic, disciplinary, fair, or unfair) of a dismissal. Because the involvement of the judicial system is unavoidable, the costs of layoffs for employers and workers are highly uncertain. One way to reduce uncertainty about court rulings is to put some limits on the arbitrariness and the duration, and hence the costs, of judicial involvement. For instance, the Dutch dual system allows workers involved in layoffs to benefit from a quicker, more predictable, and higher severance payment. An increasing proportion of employers (from less than 10 percent in the late 1980s to more than 50 percent more recently) indeed prefer to opt for a quicker, but more costly, dismissal procedure than to wait for the authorization of a designated public authority (the Center for Work and Income), which does not require any severance payment in case of a fair dismissal.

A question of the International Social Survey Program (ISSP), a household survey carried out in the EU-15 since 1994, is particularly valuable in highlighting the coverage and extent of the protection offered by EPL. Employees with a permanent contract were asked how satisfied they were with their present jobs or businesses in terms of job security. As pointed out by Postel-Vinay and Clark (2006), the survey collected information on the respondent's perception of at least two different components of job security: (1) the probability of job loss and (2) the cost of job loss. Comparisons of the ages and occupational profiles of the respondents suggest that the first factor dominates: it is indeed the persons less protected against the risk of job loss (e.g., workers in small firms or youngsters) who report lower degrees of satisfaction with their present jobs. With this caveat in mind, figure 10.5a measures, on the vertical axis, the fraction of employees in the 2005 ISSP stating that their job is secure in the various countries and, on the horizontal axis, the OECD index of strictness of EPL. Surprisingly enough, countries with the strictest EPL provisions (at least according to the OECD index, unadjusted by coverage), notably the southern European countries, have the largest fraction of workers who are deeply concerned about their job security. A possible interpretation of this result is that EPL is highly selective in offering protection against the risk of job loss: this protection can only be offered to a limited segment of the workforce, concentrating the risk on those who are not covered. In other words, the high perceived risk may be a by-product of the fact that EPL protects only workers with permanent contracts and concentrates all risks on the others as a result of the dual-track reform strategies characterized in this chapter. It could be that the share of workers covered by EPL is important. However, even when the EPL measure adjusted for coverage is used, the correlation between perceived security and EPL is negative (see figure 10.5b). Another interpretation is that although individuals perceive a lower probability of job loss, they are aware that a job loss is more costly under strict EPL regimes because it involves longer unemployment spells. Yet another interpretation recently put forward by Wasmer (2006) is that under strict EPL employers use mobbing as a strategy to force their employees to leave the firm "voluntarily."

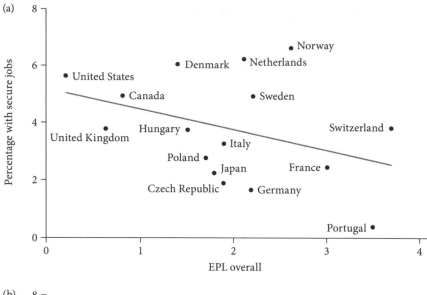

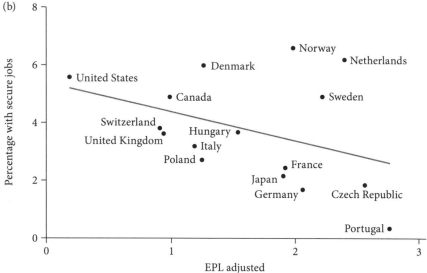

FIGURE 10.5 Perceptions of job security and strictness of EPL: (a) overall index; (b) index adjusted for coverage

Source: ISSPC (2005).

Note: The vertical axis measures the percentage of workers who responded on the ISSP survey that their jobs are secure.

10.4.2 Should There Be a Single Employment Contract?

In all countries permanent contracts and temporary contracts coexist. Thus, dual labor markets exist in which some workers are highly protected from unemployment, while other workers are hardly protected at all. To the extent that there is a substantial flow from temporary jobs to permanent jobs, the dual labor market does not have long-lasting consequences for individual workers in temporary contracts. However, it is also possible that duality coincides with segmentation. This is the case when there is a small probability to flow from a temporary job to a permanent one. Workers who are in temporary jobs mainly flow from unemployment to temporary jobs and vice versa. During the Great Recession unemployment in countries with a large difference between temporary contracts and permanent ones may have increased more than in other countries. Bentolila et al. (2012) relate the increase in unemployment over the Great Recession in Spain and France to the employment protection in the two countries. The much larger difference in firing costs between permanent and temporary contracts in Spain is responsible for the large flow from temporary employment to unemployment.

To reduce the segmentation in the labor markets, single contracts have been advocated in which employment protection gradually increases with tenure (Kramarz et al. 2008; Bentolila et al. 2012; Boeri et al. 2013). In some countries an element of employment protection increases with tenure, as severance pay generally depends on tenure (see technical annex 10.9). However, this is only the case for permanent contracts. For temporary contracts no or limited severance pay is available once the contract comes to an end. The idea of a single employment contract is that the distinction between temporary jobs and permanent jobs disappears. All jobs are open-ended, with employment protection gradually and steadily increasing with tenure without any large discontinuity. Obviously, then, workers who would have been previously protected by their permanent contracts are more likely to lose their jobs if their tenure is short. However, workers who would have previously worked under a temporary contract are now increasingly protected as their job tenure increases. García Pérez and Osuna (2012) calibrate a search-matching model of the Spanish economy to simulate the potential effects of the introduction of a single employment contract in Spain. Their simulations suggest that these contracts would be greatly beneficial for a majority of workers.[2]

10.5 Interactions with Other Institutions

EPL bears a close relationship to UB systems (see chapter 11) in providing insurance against unemployment risk. EPL protects only those who already have a job, while UBs are typically funded by a payroll tax and also protect the unemployed (at least those with previous work experience). Insofar as EPL involves payments by the employers implementing the layoffs, it internalizes the fiscal externality associated with redundancies (i.e., workers receive unemployment benefits that are paid by all workers and employers, rather than only by those responsible for the redundancies).

The term flexicurity is increasingly being used to denote countries, such as Denmark, with low employment protection and generous UBs. Algan and Cahuc (2009) argue that when it comes to institutions providing insurance against labor market risks, civic attitudes influence the trade-off between employment protection and unemployment insurance. In countries displaying low social sanctions for

---

2. Note that the honeymoon effect arising from the introduction of flexible contracts in an economy with strict employment protection is absent, as the dichotomy between permanent and temporary contracts disappears.

cheating on government benefits, providing unemployment insurance increases moral hazard. Then, it may be less costly to provide employment protection rather than UBs, even if this choice might be harmful for the efficiency of the labor market. Boeri et al. (2012) address the political economy of flexicurity, distinguishing between two conflicts of interest. The first conflict is between insiders and outsiders and arises in the transition between unemployment and employment, which is influenced by the strictness of employment protection. The second conflict is between high-skilled and low-skilled workers and occurs because both employment protection and UBs involve some redistribution across skills. Boeri et al. (2012) argue that the trade-off between employment protection and UBs also depends on the distribution of skills in the labor force. In countries with a large fraction of skilled workers, flexicurity arrangements with low employment protection and high UBs are more likely to occur.

There is also an interaction between EPL and unions (see chapter 3). Unions extract rents from employers by imposing a mark-up on the reservation wage of workers. They also tend to compress wage structures, because they typically pursue egalitarian wage policies. Thus, a stronger influence of unions on wage setting is likely to reduce both downward wage adjustment and wage differentials across workers in the same firm, industry, or country. As pointed out by Bertola and Rogerson (1997), limiting the freedom offered to employers in setting wages induces them to react to shocks by adjusting employment levels. Under compressed wage structures we would expect to observe more turnover in the labor market. By the same token, employment protection would hardly be binding if wages were completely unrestrained over time for a given individual. In response to the labor demand shocks from which EPL is meant to protect workers, wages could fall so as to make stable employment profitable or to induce voluntary quits. Thus, there are political economic reasons to believe that EPL and unions should be complementary institutions.

Finally, EPL interacts with retirement programs (see chapter 6). In many countries EPL is age specific. Older workers have a strong labor market position in the sense that they are not very likely to lose their jobs. Nevertheless, if older workers do lose their jobs, their labor market position is weak, because it is often difficult for them to find a new job and they stay unemployed for a long time. Early retirement programs exist to help older workers avoid becoming unemployed for long terms. Also, to prevent older workers from becoming long-term unemployed, it is often more difficult for employers to lay off these workers. However, this in turn makes employers reluctant to hire older workers, as documented in box 10.5, and in a sense the solution of more employment protection to avoid long-term unemployment just exacerbates the problem. Making employment protection increase gradually with tenure is a better option to protect older workers.

10.6 Why Does EPL Exist?

EPL is an institution that protects a segment of the workforce against unemployment risk. Because of the selectivity of the coverage offered by EPL, it is always better to complement measures of the strictness of regulations with information on the actual coverage of these norms. In some countries very strict EPL for regular contracts goes hand in hand with a large share of employment in the informal sector, in plants exempted from these norms, or in self-employment, while many workers are hired under temporary contracts.

For all these reasons, EPL is a strongly redistributive institution. It protects those who already have a job (notably, those with permanent contracts in the formal sector). Unemployed individuals and workers with temporary contracts generally suffer in the presence of strict EPL rules for permanent contracts. The former tend to experience longer unemployment spells in the presence of strict EPL, while the latter may be caught in a sort of parallel secondary labor market of temporary contracts with limited access to the primary labor market of permanent contracts. Employers also suffer a loss in profits in the presence of employment protection, especially when they do not succeed in making workers pay (through lower wages) for the costs of providing this insurance.

From a political economy perspective, then, depending on the relative number or political power of (1) employees with permanent contracts, (2) the unemployed, (3) workers with temporary contracts, and (4) employers, we should see more or less stringent EPL. Another important factor affecting political support for EPL is the presence of other institutions, such as UBs, that can substitute for EPL in providing insurance against unemployment risk. Under stronger competition in product markets, a case can be made for protections against job loss that are more mobility friendly. UBs are one of these. Thus, we should expect EPL to become less important over time as countries improve the coverage of their UB systems.

10.7 Suggestions for Further Reading

The chapters on EPL in OECD (1999, 2013) provide a good overview of the problems related to the measurement of this institution. Venn (2009) gives an overview of the way the recent OECD indicator of EPL is constructed. Enforcement (and policy endogeneity) issues are discussed in some detail in Bertola et al. (2000). Boeri and Garibaldi (2006) analyze the honeymoon effect and offer a survey of the main findings of the literature on dual labor market regimes. Finally, Saint-Paul (1993) is a good reference on the political economy of employment security.

10.8 Review Questions and Exercises

1. What are the main drawbacks of available measures of the strictness of EPL?

2. Why is there a nonmonotonic relationship between EPL and unemployment?

3. Why do many two-tier reforms of EPL initially increase employment?

4. What are the efficiency arguments in favor of employment protection?

5. When is EPL neutral with respect to labor market outcomes?

6. From an economic standpoint, why is it important to disentangle the transfer from the tax component of EPL?

7. Why has empirical work failed to observe the negative relationship between EPL and job and labor turnover predicted by economic theory?

8. Why do workers in countries with strict EPL feel less secure than workers in flexible labor markets?

9. Why are third parties (e.g., judges) always involved in the enforcement of EPL?

10. Why is it easier to implement changes in EPL for temporary work than for permanent contracts?

11. Consider a country in which firms produce output (assumed to be the numeraire good) using labor L as the only production factor, with the technology $Y = f(A^i, L)$, where A^i is a parameter that fluctuates with the economy. It can take the value $A^b = 100$ in bad times, which occur with probability 2/3, and the value $A^g = 300$ in good times, which occur with probability 1/3. In the labor market wages are rigid and fixed to be $w = 10$. Assume no type of employment protection is in place in the country, so that firms can adjust their stock of labor at any time by hiring and firing workers at will. Compute the equilibrium levels of employment, wages, and profits in good and bad times, and their averages, for each of the following specifications for the production function:

    (a) $Y = A^i \log L$

    Assume that employment protection is introduced: it is now unboundedly costly, for firms, to adjust the stock of labor.

    (b) How do employment and wages change?

    (c) Which of the two scenarios (no EPL versus EPL) is more profitable for firms?

    (d) And by how much?

    (e) Interpret these results.

12. (Advanced) Consider a firm operating in an imperfect labor market, where any job generates a surplus $\sigma = y - w^r$, so that a risk-neutral employee can be paid more than her reservation wage (w^r) and the firm can realize some profits ($y - w$), where y is the value of the marginal product, even when the product market is competitive. Wages are set with a rent-sharing scheme, assigning a share β of the surplus to the worker.

    (a) Express the equilibrium wage as a weighted average of the outside options of the employer and the worker.

    Suppose now that a mandatory severance pay S is introduced that is paid to the worker by the employer if the job is discontinued.

    (b) Write out the two outside options under these circumstances.

    (c) Would the equilibrium wage w be affected by the severance scheme? And what about the wage net of the severance?

(d) What happens if instead of a severance scheme, a firing tax is introduced that is paid by the employer to a third party, say, a lawyer? Would the equilibrium wage w be affected by the firing tax? And what about the wage net of the firing tax?

Interpret these results.

13. (Advanced) Consider an employed worker who has a two-period job. The worker discounts the future at a rate $\delta < 1$. In the first period the wage is given by $w_1 = w(1 - \gamma)$, while in the second period it is given by $w_2 = w(1 + \gamma)$, $0 < \gamma < 1$. In other words, γ is a parameter that encodes the wage tenure profile of the job. At the end of the first period the worker faces an involuntary separation with probability λ. If a λ shock hits the worker, he loses the second-period wage. Conditional on a λ shock, the worker faces a probability α of instantaneously finding another job. Obviously, if he finds a new job, he will obtain the first-period wage of $w(1 - \gamma)$. The outside option in the second period is the unemployment benefit b.

(a) Write down the present discounted value of a job.

(b) Which restrictions are needed for the labor market to operate?

Assume that the worker faces an increase in mobility, which can be recorded either by an increase in λ or an increase in α.

(c) What happens to the value of the job when job destruction increases?

(d) And when does α increase?

(e) How do the previous two answers change when the increase in mobility is also associated with an increase in the premium to tenure γ?

10.9 Technical Annex: When Is EPL Efficient?

Boeri et al. (2013) offer a simple illustration of the efficiency properties of a properly designed EPL in the presence of wage deferrals. EPL in this context is nonneutral even if it consists only of a transfer from the employer to the worker and workers are risk-neutral.

Consider a two-period model of junior and senior workers, in which for some reason (e.g., incentives for the worker to invest in job-specific productivity) wages are deferred over time and there is uncertainty as to the productivity of senior workers. For simplicity assume that the workers' outside option is constant at b (the value of leisure or an unemployment benefit) in both periods and ignore discounting.

Let $w_1 < b$ and $w_2 > b$ be wages in the two periods, and y_1 and y_2 denote the value of the job in each period. As stated above, productivity in the second period is stochastic. There are two possible realizations of productivity for senior workers:

- y_2^h with probability p, and
- y_2^l with probability $1 - p$, where $y_2^h > y_2^l$.

Assume further that productivity in the second period cannot be lower than the outside option of the worker, but it can be lower than the (fixed) second-period wage:

$$y_2^h > w_2 > y_2^l > b. \tag{10.11}$$

Since $y_2^l > b$, the joint surplus is always positive in the second period, and hence it is efficient that production takes place. However, in the second period, a profit-maximizing employer will always fire a worker in case of the realization of a low productivity level because

$$y_2^l - w_2 < 0. \tag{10.12}$$

EPL in the form of a mandatory payment from the employer to the firm can prevent this inefficient layoff. Indeed, consider a severance payment $TR \geq 0$ that should be made by the employer to the worker in case of dismissal. Under these conditions, firms' profits are given by

$$\pi = y_1 - w_1 + p[y_2^h - w_2] + (1 - p) \max[y_2^l - w_2, -TR]. \tag{10.13}$$

Clearly, if $TR = 0$, firms always fire conditional on a negative productivity realization. There will also be excessive layoffs insofar as

$$y_2^l - w_2 > -TR. \tag{10.14}$$

However, a severance payment $TR^* \geq w_2 - y_2^l$ would prevent inefficient separations for senior workers.

CHAPTER ELEVEN Unemployment Benefits

U nemployment benefits (UBs) protect individuals against uninsurable labor market risk. Unlike EPL (covered in chapter 10) that protects jobholders by making it more difficult for employers to dismiss them, UBs offer replacement income to workers experiencing unemployment spells after having lost their jobs.

The first UB system was introduced in the United Kingdom in 1911. Many people did not like the idea that persons not working could receive a state transfer, and beneficiaries were ironically named people "on the dole," which is derived from the "doling out" of charitable gifts of food or money. Nowadays, all OECD countries, most middle-income countries, and some developing nations have UB systems in place.

UBs are often treated as a one-dimensional institution. However, there are several key dimensions that identify these systems: *eligibility* (the norms determining access to the benefit) and *entitlement* (the rules concerning the duration of the payment) conditions and level of payments. Typically, job losers with short unemployment durations can have access to an income replacement system that mimics an insurance scheme: they draw benefits that are proportional (at least above a benefit floor and below a given threshold) to their past contributions. These contributions are generally channeled to an extra-budgetary *unemployment insurance fund* that collects compulsory payroll taxes earmarked for UBs. This *unemployment insurance* (UI) component of UBs provides transfers that are proportional to the last wage earned (hence to past contributions) and whose duration increases with the length of the contribution record. The close link between benefits and past contributions, entitlements, and insurance premiums paid during the working life reduces incentives to elude or evade payments to the social insurance fund.

Transfers to jobseekers with longer unemployment durations are generally independent of past contributions and are offered in combination with other cash transfers to individuals who are not working, notably, social assistance of the last resort. Eligibility to this second, *unemployment assistance,* component of UBs can be independent of payments made during previous work experience. Unemployment assistance is typically offered at a flat rate (independent of the previous wage) and for a maximum duration that is not conditional on the length of the contribution period. Unemployment assistance can also be integrated with general social assistance, in which case it is offered for unlimited duration but is subject to means testing; that is, it is provided only to unemployed individuals who have incomes and family assets lower than a given (poverty) threshold. Linking the transfer to household assets involves tying together individual and family labor supply decisions. For this reason, we discuss the effects of means testing on family labor supply elsewhere (chapter 13).

11.1 Measures and Cross-Country Comparisons

UBs differ in many dimensions. Table 11.1 provides a cross-country summary of the main characteristics. The numbers in the table refer to a 40-year-old worker who becomes unemployed after a long and uninterrupted employment record. Later we discuss how the level of previous earnings, family characteristics, and the duration of unemployment affect the UBs.

Sometimes there is a waiting period (i.e., a period between the day the job was lost and the first day the unemployed worker is entitled to benefits). This waiting period is motivated as a disincentive for workers to apply for benefits for unemployment spells that may be brief and as a cost-saving device. For such spells, the administration costs are relatively high. The first column of table 11.1 shows that some countries have a waiting period, while other countries do not. The longest waiting period, of 14 days, is in Canada. The maximum duration of unemployment benefits differs widely between countries, as shown in the second column. In Belgium UBs are of indefinite duration, while in Sweden, Iceland, and the Netherlands the maximum is about 3 years. Countries such as the Czech Republic, the Slovak Republic, and the United Kingdom have relatively short maximum benefit durations of about half a year.

The level of UBs in terms of the replacement rate (i.e., the ratio of the UB to previous earnings) also differs significantly between countries. As shown in the third column of table 11.1, this percentage is low in countries where the relation to previous earnings is absent. If the UB is paid as a flat rate or as a fixed amount, the replacement rate could be as low as 10 percent (United Kingdom) or 17 percent (Finland). However, there are also countries where benefits as a share of the previous earnings base are as high as 90 percent (Denmark) or 80 percent (Luxembourg, and Sweden in the initial phase of unemployment). Finally, in some countries like Belgium, the Czech Republic, Estonia, Italy, the Netherlands, Poland, Slovenia, Spain, and Sweden the replacement rate drops over the duration of unemployment such that at the end of the entitlement period benefits are sometimes 10 percentage points lower than in the beginning.

Table 11.1 shows the complexity of the UBs for a particular group of workers, 40-year-olds with long and uninterrupted employment records. For other groups of workers, the generosity of the benefit system may be different. Table 11.2 tabulates the *net replacement rate* (i.e., the ratio of the UB to previous earnings at different earning levels, both measured after taxes). Replacement rates net of taxes tend to be higher than gross replacement rates, because income taxes are progressive and UBs in some countries are tax exempt. Table 11.2 shows the effects of the level of previous earnings, family situation, duration of employment, and social assistance "top-ups" or cash housing benefits. The first column shows the net

TABLE 11.1 Unemployment insurance benefits, 2010

Country	Waiting period (days)	Maximum duration (months)	Replacement rate (%)		Note
			Initial	End	
Austria	0	9	55	55	
Belgium	0	Unlimited	60	53.8	
Canada[a]	14	11	55	55	
Czech Republic	—	5	65	50–45	
Denmark	0	24	90	90	
Estonia	7	12	50	40	
Finland[b]	7	23	17	17	Bb
France	7	24	57–75	57–75	
Germany	0	12	60	60	
Greece	6	12	27	27	Fr
Hungary	0	9	60	60	MW
Iceland[c]	0	36	34	34	Fr
Ireland[d]	3	12	32	32	FA
Italy	7	8	60	50	
Japan	7	9	50–80	50–80	
Korea	7	7	50	50	
Luxembourg	0	12	80	80	
Netherlands	0	38	75	70	
Norway	—	24	62	62	
Poland	7	12	30	23	FA
Portugal	0	24	65	65	
Slovak Republic	0	6	50	50	
Slovenia	—	9	70	60	
Spain	0	24	70	60	
Sweden	7	35	80	70	
Switzerland	5	18	70	70	
Turkey	0	10	40	40	
United Kingdom	3	6	10	10	FA
United States[e]	0	23	53	53	

Source: www.oecd.org/els/social/workincentives.

Notes: UI benefits are for a 40-year-old (where benefits are conditional on work history, the table assumes a long and uninterrupted employment record). The replacement rate refers to gross earnings except for Austria, the Czech Republic, and Germany, where it refers to net earnings. End = end-of-benefit period; AW = average worker, defined as an adult full-time worker in the private sector whose wage earnings are equal to the average wage earnings of such workers (OECD Glossary of Statistical Terms); Bb = basic benefit in percentage of AW; Fr = flat rate in percentage of AW; FA = fixed amount in percentage of AW; MW = percentage of mandatory minimum wage; — = not available.

a. The duration of unemployment insurance payments depends on the unemployment rate in the relevant insurance region. The 47-week duration shown relates to an unemployment rate of 9 percent in Ontario.

b. Basic benefit of 17 percent of AW plus 45 percent of earnings exceeding basic benefit to 81 percent of AW, then 20 percent.

c. Flat rate 34 percent of AW for 10 days, then 70 percent of previous earnings for 65 days, then back to the fixed rate.

d. If weekly earnings while in employment were below certain amounts, reduced rates of payment are made. If a dependent adult is employed, supplement is reduced or suppressed, depending on income level.

e. The information reflects the situation of the Michigan unemployment benefit scheme, for which payment duration has been extended due to high unemployment rates. Emergency unemployment compensation and extended benefits are paid after exhaustion of regular UI (26 weeks) and at lower rates.

replacement rates at the start of the unemployment spell for the baseline family, a single-earner married couple with average earnings, two children, and eligibility for social assistance and housing benefits. This baseline family has a net replacement rate of less than 50 percent in Korea (43 percent) and Turkey (45 percent) and greater than 90 percent in Luxembourg (93 percent) and Denmark (94 percent). The other columns of table 11.2 show how net replacement rates differ when one of the characteristics of the baseline family changes, holding the other characteristics constant.

The second and third columns provide information about the effect of previous earnings. Because UBs often have lower and upper bounds, average replacement rates go down with previous earnings. The extent to which this happens varies widely across countries. For example, in Estonia, France, Germany, Portugal, and Switzerland the differences are small, but there are substantial differences in net replacement rates related to earnings in Norway and Finland. In Norway an unemployed worker who earned two-thirds of the average wage has a net replacement rate of 98 percent, while a worker who earned 50 percent of the average wage has a net replacement rate of 53 percent, a difference of 45 percentage points. In Finland the difference between the two types is 36 percentage points.

The fourth and fifth columns show what happens to the net replacement rates if the family type changes. The fourth column presents the numbers if there is a single parent instead of a married couple; the fifth column shows the numbers for a two-earner instead of a single-earner married couple. For some countries the family type is not very important. For others it is. For example, in Denmark the baseline family is entitled to benefits with a net replacement rate of 94 percent, whereas a single parent is entitled to a net replacement rate of 75 percent. And in the United States the baseline family has a net replacement rate of 52 percent, whereas a two-earner couple would be entitled to 72 percent. Conditional on the earnings, some countries have a higher net replacement rate for two-earner families, while other countries have a lower net replacement rate.

The absence of children decreases the net replacement rate of UBs in almost every country presented in table 11.2. Exceptions are Korea, the Slovak Republic, and Turkey, but here the differences are very small (column 6). The duration of unemployment sometimes affects the net replacement rate, but there are also many countries where the net replacement rate does not vary over the duration of unemployment (column 7). Extreme drops in benefits are present in Italy and Turkey, where after five years unemployed workers are no longer entitled to benefits.

Column 8 of table 11.2 shows that in some countries social assistance "top-ups" or cash housing benefits are an important part of the UBs. In Denmark, for example, these benefits account for 30 percentage points of the overall benefit, and for 27 percentage points in the United Kingdom. Nevertheless, for other countries these benefits play a marginal role or no role at all.

Mapping all the various features of UBs into a one-dimensional measure is not an easy task. As table 11.2 suggests, it is difficult to make cross-country comparisons of replacement rates, because these vary considerably across earning levels and for different unemployment durations. What replacement rate should be taken as the reference in international comparisons of UB generosity? The OECD

TABLE 11.2 Net replacement rates for various earnings levels, family types, durations of unemployment, and eligibility for housing benefits, 2010

Country	(1)	(2)	(3)	(4)	(5)	(6)	(7)	(8)
Australia	58	69	47	51	61	45	58	56
Austria	69	82	54	68	81	56	65	69
Belgium	60	77	47	69	75	57	58	60
Canada	83	77	63	81	80	64	60	82
Czech Republic	70	79	51	73	88	69	57	69
Denmark	94	95	76	75	77	75	64	64
Estonia	59	57	57	60	74	56	41	59
Finland	74	93	57	74	77	61	74	61
France	70	73	67	71	81	67	52	67
Germany	75	77	70	72	88	61	62	72
Greece	61	75	44	58	71	50	4	43
Hungary	64	81	51	66	76	57	34	64
Iceland	75	81	59	74	82	69	67	72
Ireland	85	94	67	80	71	78	85	70
Italy	68	73	53	70	77	62	0	69
Japan	81	90	57	79	76	61	81	56
Korea	43	55	30	45	67	44	50	43
Luxembourg	93	100	70	91	92	82	72	88
Netherlands	85	84	62	76	80	76	72	80
New Zealand	58	74	47	54	55	53	58	52
Norway	71	98	53	86	81	66	71	69
Poland	57	72	41	74	67	53	45	44
Portugal	76	77	75	77	92	75	50	76
Slovak Republic	57	59	61	92	82	58	42	57
Slovenia	89	84	71	89	86	74	72	77
Spain	75	75	53	74	84	60	33	75
Sweden	63	86	48	64	70	53	63	52
Switzerland	90	85	82	88	89	74	68	90
Turkey	45	52	32	46	71	46	0	45
United Kingdom	71	78	51	64	58	45	71	44
United States	52	61	38	50	72	48	37	45

Source: www.oecd.org/els/social/workincentives.

Notes: Column (1) baseline family: Earnings 100 percent of average wage, two children, single-earner married couple, initial phase of unemployment but following any waiting period, eligible for social assistance "top-ups" and cash housing assistance. Any income taxes payable on UBs are determined in relation to annualized benefit values (i.e., monthly values multiplied by 12) even if the maximum benefit duration is shorter than 12 months. The percentage of average wage relates to the previous earnings of the unemployed spouse only; the second spouse is assumed to be inactive with no earnings and no recent employment history. Where receipt of social assistance or other minimum-income benefits is subject to activity tests (e.g., active job search or being available for work), these requirements are assumed to be met. Children are aged four and six, and neither childcare benefits nor childcare costs are considered. After tax and including unemployment benefits and family benefits. Columns (2) to (8) differ from the baseline family in one dimension only:

(2)–(3): Earnings 67 percent and 150 percent of average wage
(4)–(5): Single parent and two-earner married couple
(6): No children
(7): After 5 years of unemployment
(8): No social assistance "top-ups" or cash housing benefits are available in either the in-work or out-of-work situation

TABLE 11.3 Net replacement rates: OECD summary measure
of benefit entitlements, 2010

	OECD summary measure (1)	Coverage of UBs (2)	Adjusted summary measure $(3) = (1) \times (2)$
Australia	41.2	0.56	23.3
Austria	51.9	0.86	44.8
Czech Republic	20.5	0.25	5.2
Denmark	40.1	1.00	40.1
Finland	44.1	1.00	44.1
Germany	43.9	0.74	32.7
Greece	23.1	0.10	2.4
Hungary	21.8	1.00	21.8
Ireland	56.0	0.67	37.4
Italy	23.4	0.25	5.8
Luxembourg	29.4	0.35	10.2
Norway	38.4	1.00	38.4
Poland	21.9	0.13	2.8
Portugal	52.0	0.30	15.3
Slovak Republic	21.1	1.00	21.1
Spain	42.9	0.35	14.9
United Kingdom	29.3	1.00	29.3

Source: www.oecd.org/els/social/workincentives; EU Statistics on Income and Living Conditions data.
Notes: The net replacement rate summary measure is defined as the average of the net UB (excluding social assistance and cash housing assistance) replacement rates for two earnings levels, three family situations, and 60 months of unemployment. Coverage is the fraction of the labor force unemployed declaring that they were receiving UBs.

tabulates a *summary measure of benefit generosity,* which is defined as the average of the replacement rates in the first five years of unemployment for an average worker (table 11.3). The cutoff of 60 months is arbitrary. It takes into account that the average length of an unemployment spell is shorter than two years in most OECD countries and that after four years jobless people lose their attachment to the world of work. This summary measure clearly attaches the same importance to replacement rates offered at different unemployment durations and ignores the time profile of replacement rates. To give an example, a system offering 50 percent of the previous wage throughout the entire unemployment spell would be considered as generous as one offering 65 percent in the first year, 55 percent in the second, 45 percent in the third, and 35 percent in the fourth year of unemployment.

A more serious problem with the OECD summary measure is that it neglects *eligibility* (the norms determining access to the benefit) and *entitlement* (the rules concerning the duration of the payment) conditions. Because of strict eligibility conditions and short entitlement relative to the typical duration of unemployment spells, the coverage of UBs (the fraction of unemployed workers receiving the benefits) can sometimes be very low. Unfortunately, it is difficult to obtain cross-country-comparable measures of coverage. For the EU countries, UB coverage can be computed by drawing on the EU Statistics on Income and Living Conditions data.

Table 11.3 presents the OECD summary measure of generosity (based on legal norms on replacement rates) in the first column; the second column displays the fraction of individuals who are unemployed according to OECD-ILO definitions and who declared that they were beneficiaries of UBs in the 2010 EU Statistics on Income and Living Conditions. An adjusted summary measure is then displayed in the third column that corrects the OECD measure by coverage. This adjusted measure is obtained by multiplying the OECD summary generosity measure by the coverage ratio. Table 11.3 suggests that countries like Italy, Portugal, and Spain offer a much less generous UB system when account is taken not only of replacement rates but also of eligibility and entitlement conditions.

The preceding discussion suggests that UB generosity measures unadjusted for coverage can be fairly misleading. At the same time, one should keep in mind that legal replacement rates and coverage rates of UBs are not independent of one another. Coverage is endogenous to replacement rates via take-up incentives (the more generous the UB system is, the higher the benefit take-up will be) and fiscal constraints (the more generous the statutory replacement rate is, the stronger the incentive of governments to tighten eligibility criteria will be, reducing the coverage of UBs). The trouble is that the first type of correlation is positive (more generous benefits encourage more people to apply for UBs), while the second source of correlation—combining fiscal and political economy constraints—induces a negative correlation between replacement rates and benefit coverage. Governments may pursue a policy of low coverage with very generous soft-landing schemes offered to a few job losers, leaving many other displaced workers, typically those less politically represented, with low (if any) income support. This combination seems to prevail in many middle-income countries where UBs offer relatively high nominal replacement rates (e.g., 60 percent of the best earnings in the last year in Argentina) but then are offered for a short time and only to a small fraction of the workforce (workers in small businesses and in rural areas are not covered, as in China). These asymmetries in replacement rates and duration of benefits are somewhat less evident, but still present, in OECD countries. In Spain and Portugal, for instance, UBs are relatively generous in terms of replacement rates, but they cover a very small fraction of the unemployed, as documented by table 11.3. Conversely, in the United Kingdom and even more so in the United States, low replacement rates go hand in hand with almost universal coverage of job losers and are generally offered—when integrated with means-tested social assistance—with unlimited duration.

The preceding discussion offers strong arguments against the standard practice of mapping UBs into a simple scalar generosity measure. It is always better to use a variety of measures to characterize UBs. Since they are multidimensional institutions, UBs can be reformed along various dimensions. The devil is in the details, and neglecting any of these dimensions can offer a misleading picture of the relative generosity (and evolution over time) of these UB systems.

11.2 Theory

11.2.1 A Perfect Labor Market

Often the effects of UBs are only discussed in the context of perfect labor market cases. As is argued here, this discussion is not particularly instructive, because unemployment (and hence a UB system) does not arise as an equilibrium phenomenon in this context. Yet it may be useful to start from the competitive market, insofar as it helps in understanding some design features of UBs that can mitigate its adverse effects on labor supply in more realistic environments.

In competitive labor markets, UBs affect labor market outcomes along two main channels:

1. They increase the (static) reservation wage of individuals, inducing more people not to supply labor at any given market wage (the *participation effect*).

2. They affect labor market outcomes through the increased taxation (generally payroll taxes) required to finance UBs (the *taxation effect*).

The second transmission mechanism is not discussed in this chapter, because it is investigated in detail in chapter 13. Yet it is important to keep in mind that any increase in the generosity of UBs needs to be financed, and that UBs are generally funded by statutory payroll contributions. Thus, more generous UBs generally involve an increase in *proportional* taxation of earnings. When UBs are funded by taxation of general incomes, UB systems are more progressive.

To characterize the participation effect, we need to refer to the notion of the *reservation wage*, which was introduced in chapter 1. Each individual has a utility function defined over consumption c and leisure l, which are both assumed to be normal goods. The utility function is concave in c, which means that individuals are risk-averse. Thus, their welfare can be increased by giving them the opportunity to purchase some (actuarially) fair insurance scheme that reduces their uncertainty about the income/leisure pairs to which they have access. This is indeed the insurance (or income-smoothing) role attributed to UBs.

To keep things simple, however, we shall consider an environment in which there is no uncertainty as to potential incomes and labor/leisure levels. The individual then allocates the endowment of time, say, l_0, alternatively to work—earning the hourly wage w times the number of hours of work, h—or to leisure (clearly, $h = l_0 - l$). Define the individual's nonlabor income (the income when working zero hours) as m. As long as m is strictly positive, there will be a kink in the budget constraint of the individual: at zero hours of work (when $l = l_0$), the individual gets m. Income increases to the left of l_0 (for any positive amount of work) at the rate w, as depicted in figure 11.1a. The individual maximizes welfare by choosing the highest possible indifference curve that is in the budget constraint, that is, the locus A where the indifference curve $U(c, l) = k_1$ is tangent to the budget constraint. The (static) reservation wage, w^r, is given by the slope of the indifference curve $U(c, l) = k_2$ crossing the kink of the budget constraint at point E, where the individual allocates nonlabor income m to the purchase of consumption goods and works zero hours, as formally characterized in box 11.1.

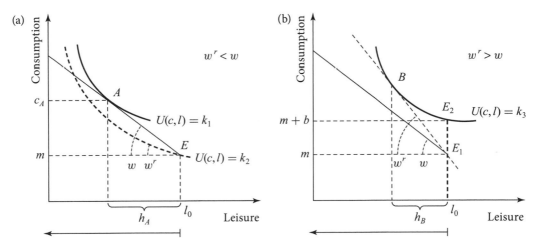

FIGURE 11.1 Reservation wage: (a) without UBs; (b) with UBs

As also discussed in chapter 1, the *reservation wage* is formally defined as the marginal rate of substitution between leisure and consumption at the kink of the budget constraint, or

$$\frac{U_l(m, l_0)}{U_c(m, l_0)} = w^r .$$ (11.1)

Notice that, in general, the slope of the indifference curve at the kink will differ from the slope of the budget constraint, which is given by the market wage w. Now, for any $w > w^r$, that is, any market wage exceeding the reservation wage, the individual will supply some positive hours of work. This is the scenario depicted in figure 11.1a, where the individual maximizes welfare at A, where $h_A > 0$ hours of work are supplied. If instead $w < w^r$, then the worker will not supply any positive hours of work, because that worker can be better off devoting time entirely to leisure and consuming m.

Suppose now that a UB b is introduced. Nonlabor income will now be $m + b$. Notice that the benefit is conditional on not working. Thus, in the presence of UBs, the reservation wage is implicitly given by

$$U(m + b, l_0) = U(m + w^r h_B, l_0 - h_B).$$ (11.2)

Since utility is strictly increasing in both arguments, the reservation wage will be increasing with the level of unemployment benefits: the larger b is, the stronger will be the increase of w^r after the introduction of the UB system. This is depicted in figure 11.1b. Note that at point B it again holds that the marginal rate of substitution between leisure and consumption equals the reservation wage. The negative participation effect can be partly fmitigated by allowing the individual to combine the UB with work income, at least partly, making the benefit also conditional on employment at low wages, as discussed in chapter 13.

Suppose now that a UB is introduced, providing some positive income b to those who are not working in addition to m, and that this additional income is provided conditional on not working. The new budget constraint will now look as in figure 11.1b: it will have a spike at the zero hours locus, because the transfer b is provided only to those working zero hours. Provided that the transfer is sufficiently large, the individual may now be better off not working at all. Indeed, in figure 11.1b at point E_2, the individual can now attain a higher indifference curve $(k_3 > k_1)$ than at the equilibrium without UBs. When UBs are present, the reservation wage is no longer represented by the slope of the indifference curve at the kink at point E_2. It will now be given instead by the lowest market wage that can allow the individual to reach at least the indifference curve $U(c, l) = k_3$ by supplying some positive hours of work. Because now $w < w^r$, the marginal value of leisure exceeds its opportunity cost (the market wage), and hence the individual is better off not working. For the individual to supply labor, hourly wages should therefore increase.

All in all, the prediction of a simple static model of labor supply is that the introduction of a UB system increases the reservation wage of individuals and thus the value of the nonparticipation option. When leisure is a normal good, the larger the UB is, the greater will be the increase in the reservation wage with respect to the case where no UB is present, and hence the more likely that the recipient will decide not to work.

What does the increase in the reservation wage imply for aggregate labor market outcomes? As long as workers have different preferences for the labor/leisure choice, there will be different reservation wages in this economy. Thus, labor supply will be increasing with the market wage, L_0^s, as in figure 11.2. The higher the market wage is, the larger will be the fraction of the population of working age willing to supply labor.

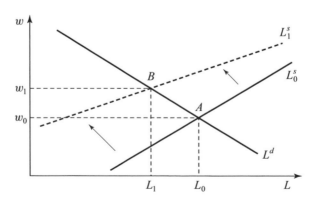

FIGURE 11.2 Aggregate labor supply with (dashed line) and without (solid line) UBs

Suppose now that a UB is introduced. We know from the preceding discussion that this will increase all reservation wages, shifting labor supply upward to L_1^s, as in the dashed line in figure 11.2. It is likely that the effect is stronger for individuals with a lower reservation wage; hence the distance between the labor supply with and without UBs will be larger the closer we are to the origin. It follows that the labor market equilibrium with UBs involves a higher wage ($w_1 > w_0$) and lower employment ($L_1 < L_0$) than the (wedge-free) equilibrium without UBs.

Notice that in this simple framework UBs reduce the size of the labor market, but they do not give rise to unemployment. In other words, UBs act like an increase in compulsory schooling, reducing labor supply. That unemployment does not arise at the equilibrium makes the competitive model not particularly interesting in analyzing the effects of UBs. If unemployment is simply not there, then why should a UB system exist?

11.2.2 An Imperfect Labor Market

In labor markets with some imperfections, such as frictions in the job creation process, wage bargaining, or imperfect information, UBs affect labor market outcomes through three main channels:

1. They increase the (dynamic) reservation wage of UB recipients, because they make workers more choosy when deciding on available job offers. So workers reduce their search intensity and hence increase the duration of their unemployment spells and in the process find a better job (the *job search effect*). Hence, longer search durations may lead to a higher quality of post-unemployment jobs.

2. They improve the fall-back option of workers, putting a higher floor in wage setting and increasing wage claims at the bargaining table, or in any event the wages required to deter shirking (the *wage effect*).

3. They induce more people to participate in the labor market, insofar as they increase the value of employment and unemployment over the value of in-activity (the *entitlement effect*), at least for those not receiving the UB.

In addition to these effects there will be the *taxation effect* that is also present in competitive labor markets. These effects can be characterized in a dynamic framework as the model formally described in technical annex 11.9. We confine ourselves here to providing the intuition behind the operation of these three transmission mechanisms.

The Job Search Effect
The static model of labor supply, where an individual optimally chooses hours of work and leisure subject to a budget constraint, is ill suited for an analysis of the effects of UBs on unemployment duration, because it does not allow unemployment to arise as an equilibrium phenomenon. To fully characterize the effects of UBs, we need a more realistic, but also somewhat more complex, model. *Job search theory*

(pioneered by Lippman and McCall 1979) provides such a framework. It pays attention to the time and costs involved in looking for jobs. This process is modeled like the search for an apartment: one surveys the market and does not necessarily accept the first offer, but keeps on searching until one finds something that corresponds to one's expectations. Bringing the theory closer to the labor market, these models also allow individuals to decide on the amount of effort to put into job search, for example, in terms of hours of leisure sacrificed to the search for a good job. A person who decides not to search at all is inactive. Those actively seeking a job are unemployed. It is also possible to build a measure of *effective labor supply* that goes beyond simple headcounts of jobseekers and considers the intensity of job search of different individuals.

While searching for jobs, individuals earn a UB that is proportional to the wage, as in earnings-related UB systems. In this framework an increase in the generosity of UBs increases the (dynamic) reservation wage and reduces search intensity (see box 11.2 and technical annex 11.9). This happens because the opportunity cost of having a job increases. As a result of the increase in reservation wages and the decline in search intensity, the job-finding probability declines as well, increasing the duration of unemployment. However, the increase in the reservation wage also implies that unemployed workers will earn higher wages once they accept a job. So, the longer the duration of search, the better the quality of the post-unemployment job will be.

BOX 11.2   *Dynamic Reservation Wages and UBs*

In addition to the static reservation wage, which determines whether an individual should enter the labor market and accept a job, there is the dynamic reservation wage, which determines whether a jobseeker should accept a wage offer from a certain wage distribution. Under some standard assumptions (jobseekers form expectations about the wage offers that they are likely to receive, because they know the distribution of wages from which job offers are randomly drawn; each job pays a constant wage; and there is no on-the-job search, so that one cannot accept a job and continue to search), it turns out that the optimal search strategy involves a *stopping rule*, that is, defining a threshold wage level such that only the jobs that offer a wage superior to this level are accepted. This threshold wage level is the (dynamic) *reservation wage* of the individual and equals the value of unemployment, because it makes the individual indifferent between working at that wage and continuing the job search. A graphical representation is as follows:

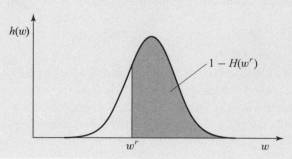

Conditional on the wage distribution $H(w)$, the reservation wage determines the probability that a random wage offer will be accepted: $1 - H(w^r)$ (the shaded area). If the reservation wage increases, the shaded area becomes smaller. Hence, the probability that a random wage offer is accepted is reduced and thus the duration of unemployment increases.

The concept of a dynamic reservation wage is clearly different from the static reservation wage characterized in box 11.1. The static reservation wage discriminates between employment and nonparticipation, while in job search theory one continues to participate in the labor market even if the wage offer is lower than the reservation wage. One just keeps on searching. Thus, the dynamic reservation wage of job search theory discriminates between employment and unemployment.

UBs influence the dynamic reservation wage, because they make job search less expensive. Higher UBs lead to higher reservation wages, thus lowering the probability that a random wage offer will be accepted. Therefore, it takes more time to find an acceptable wage offer, and the duration of unemployment will increase (see also technical annex 11.9.1). Empirical studies typically find a positive elasticity of the reservation wage with respect to the level of UBs. For instance, Lynch (1983) reports elasticities of 0.08–0.11 for young people in the United Kingdom, Holzer (1986) finds elasticities of 0.02–0.05 in the United States, and van den Berg (1990b) of 0.04–0.09 in the Netherlands.

Not only workers but also firms are searching. Employers post vacancies that will be gradually filled or matched with jobseekers. Employers' searches are also costly. Moreover, jobs do not last forever but are destroyed at some given rate. The model generates labor market flows across employment and unemployment when a jobseeker is matched to a vacancy or a job is destroyed. Equilibrium involves some positive level of unemployment. Actually, some unemployment is efficient, because it makes it easier for employers to fill their vacancies. There are *externalities* involved in the matching of vacancies and jobseekers. The more vacancies around, the easier it is to find a job. Similarly, the more unemployed workers seeking a job, the easier it is to fill a vacancy.

The Wage Effect

Because there are costs involved in job search and in posting vacancies, and the matching of jobseekers and vacancies is time consuming, even if product markets are competitive (and hence the expected profits from posting a vacancy are zero at the equilibrium), filled vacancies generate some positive rents for the employer and the worker involved. These rents are split between the employer and the worker. In particular, wages (establishing the fraction of the surplus going to the worker) are set according to a Nash bargaining rule similar to that considered in chapter 3. Also in this case wages will be increasing with the fall back option of workers and hence with the unemployment income and the job-finding probability for any given level of search intensity.

Thus, in addition to reducing search intensity, UBs increase the equilibrium market wage by means of the Nash bargaining rule. This effect will be larger the stronger the effect is of UBs on the fallback option of workers (i.e., the value of unemployment). As we have seen, the value of unemployment increases with the generosity of UBs because jobseekers get a higher income for any given level of search effort. However, more generous UBs reduce the vacancy rate, because it is more difficult to fill vacancies when people search less intensively. The increase in wages itself reduces the job-finding probability for any given level of search intensity.

The wage effects of unemployment benefits are magnified by the taxes required to finance the benefits. Because benefits are funded by payroll taxes, the contributions clearing the budget of the fund running UBs should equal the UB multiplied by the total number of unemployed individuals and divided by the total wage bill: $t = \frac{bU}{wL}$.

Wage bargaining is not the only channel through which UBs might affect wages. UBs may increase the equilibrium market wage also because they force employers to pay their employees more to deter them from shirking, as in the efficiency wage literature. The relationship between UBs and efficiency wages is discussed in box 11.3.

BOX 11.3   *Efficiency Wages and UBs*

Efficiency wage models generate involuntary unemployment as an equilibrium phenomenon. As discussed in box 10.2, the efficiency wage makes the value of shirking lower than or equal to the value of not shirking. Therefore, the efficiency wage w^e satisfies

$$w^e \geq \rho V_u + e \left(\frac{\phi + \rho + \delta}{\phi} \right),$$

(11.3)

where ρ is the discount rate, e is the effort, ϕ is the rate at which shirkers are detected and fired, δ is the exogenous job separation rate (independent of the behavior of the employee), and V_u is the asset value of being unemployed. From this relationship it follows that the efficiency wage is higher when the flow value of unemployment is higher and hence it hurts less to lose a job. If the job-finding rate μ is constant and V_e is the asset of being employed, the flow value of unemployment is given by

$$\rho V_u = b + \mu (V_e - V_u),$$

(11.4)

which is increasing with b, the level of UBs. In equilibrium, inflows into unemployment are equal to outflows from unemployment; that is, $\mu U = \delta L$, where U represents the number of unemployed workers and L the number of employed workers. From this equation it follows that $\mu + \delta = \delta \frac{(U+L)}{U}$, or $\mu + \delta = \frac{\delta}{u}$, where u is the unemployment rate. Furthermore, at the margin, the costs of effort are equal to the expected costs of shirking:

$$e = \phi(V_e - V_u). \tag{11.5}$$

Using these conditions, we can rewrite the efficiency wage as

$$w^e \geq b + e\left(\frac{\rho + \delta/u + \phi}{\phi}\right). \tag{11.6}$$

Thus, the efficiency wage increases with the level of UBs and decreases with the unemployment rate. If the unemployment rate is higher, a lower efficiency wage is needed. This is the sense in which unemployment is a worker-discipline device. A higher unemployment rate makes losing a job more costly and therefore encourages workers not to shirk. UBs have the opposite effect: they reduce the penalty associated with being detected shirking and getting fired.

Source: Shapiro and Stiglitz (1984).

The Entitlement Effect

Labor supply can also vary as a result of a change in UB generosity. Instead of being employed or unemployed, individuals may decide not to participate at all in the labor market. This choice also has a reservation property: the individual decides to be inactive if the market wage is below the reservation wage.

When UBs are paid only to active jobseekers (i.e., inactive people do not receive the benefit), an increase in the generosity of benefits increases the reservation wage while leaving the value of inactivity unchanged. Then, some individuals will move from inactivity to unemployment, increasing labor force participation in the aggregate. The intuition is that the entitlement to higher income while seeking jobs induces more people to be engaged in active job search. Thus, UBs may actually increase participation, contrary to the predictions of the perfect labor market model. This does not necessarily mean that the effective labor supply also increases, because jobseekers receiving the benefit put less effort into job search when UBs are higher.

When UBs are offered only to individuals with previous work experience, there may also be an entitlement effect among the population of jobseekers, that is, not only among inactive persons. When eligibility for benefits requires previous work experience, there are two categories of unemployed: first-time jobseekers, who do not receive the benefit, and jobseekers with previous work experience, who are eligible for UBs. The former group will actually increase their search intensity after the introduction of UBs, because the value of holding a job increases (as it also involves eligibility for benefits in case of job loss), while the second category will experience the usual negative effect on job search.

11.3 Empirical Evidence

11.3.1 Effects of UBs on Unemployment Duration

Several empirical studies drawing on aggregate data have looked at the relationship between the generosity of UBs and the level of unemployment. Using cross-sectional data on 20 OECD countries, Layard et al. (1991) found that countries with higher UB replacement rates and longer benefit durations tend to experience higher unemployment rates. In particular, they estimated that a 10 percent increase in the replacement rate involves roughly a 1.7 percent increase in the unemployment rate. More recent studies of the same group of industrialized countries offer comparable results: Scarpetta (1996) estimated an elasticity of unemployment to UBs on the order of 0.13, Nickell (1997) of 0.11, and Bassanini (2006) of 0.12.

The empirical literature using microeconomic data to establish how UI affects the exit rate from unemployment is extensive. Reviews of the early literature are provided by Atkinson and Micklewright (1991) and Pedersen and Westergård Nielsen (1993). The early literature focused mostly on the effect of the level of benefits using cross-sectional variation at the individual level. Benefit levels are generally found to have significant effects in U.S. and UK studies, while most continental European studies find insignificant or weak effects. In most U.S. studies the elasticity of unemployment duration with respect to benefit level is in the range 0.3–0.9 (Holmlund 1998). The disincentive effect of benefit levels on the exit rate from unemployment depends also on the duration of unemployment, with higher effects for short-term unemployed (Nickell 1979; Fallick 1991). The research on the effect of benefit duration on the exit rate from unemployment is extensive both in the United States and in Europe.[1] One common finding of most studies is a sharp increase in the exit rate close to benefit expiration (see also box 11.4).

BOX 11.4   *End-of-Benefit Spikes*

A stylized empirical finding is the increase in job-finding rates shortly before UBs expire. There is some debate about whether the end-of-benefit spike is a real phenomenon or a statistical artifact. In a recent study that focuses exclusively on the end-of-benefit spike phenomenon, Card et al. (2007b) find that the unemployment exit rate increases much more than the re-employment hazard rate does. Their main conclusion is that the spike in exit rates from unemployment is to a large extent due to measurement error: researchers mistakenly considered cancellations from the unemployment register as job finding.

Usually, end-of-benefit spikes are found as a by-product of an analysis focusing on the relationship between the UI potential benefit duration (PBD) and exit rates from unemployment. Katz and Meyer (1990) show that for UI recipients in the week of benefit expiration, the job-finding rate is about 80 percent higher than

---

1. Older studies for the United States and Canada include Ham and Rea (1987), Meyer (1990), and Katz and Meyer (1990). Early studies for Europe are Hunt (1995), Carling et al. (1996), and Winter-Ebmer (1998).

before, while such spikes are not present for UI nonrecipients. Using administrative data that should not be biased by statistical artifacts, Røed and Zhang (2003) for Norway, Lalive et al. (2006) for Austria, van Ours and Vodopivec (2006) for Slovenia, and Caliendo et al. (2013) for Germany also find evidence for the presence of end-of-benefit spikes.

End-of-benefit spikes can be explained both in static labor supply models and in dynamic job search models. In the static labor supply theory it is assumed that a new job can be found at any time (Moffitt and Nicholson 1982; Meyer 1990). At the time a worker loses his job he decides on consumption and the duration of unemployment subject to a budget constraint. At the expiration date T the budget constraint is kinked, and hence many indifference curves are tangent at the kink. This is illustrated in figure 11.3a. Without benefits, the fall in income over the duration of unemployment would be given by line AB, which has slope w. With benefits, but without a maximum benefit duration, the fall in income over the duration of unemployment would be given by line AC, and an individual would find maximum utility at point D. With end-of-benefits at T, this individual would receive maximum utility at the kink of the budget constraint E. Many individuals who used to have a maximum utility on the segment EC now have maximum utility at E. Therefore, many individuals choose to leave unemployment at benefit expiration T, which explains the spike in the outflow rate at T.

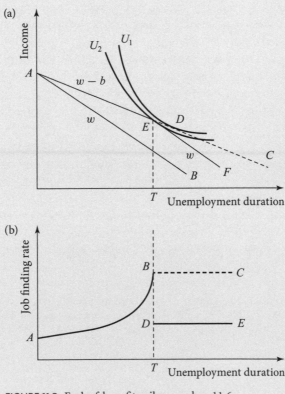

FIGURE 11.3 End-of-benefit spike—see box 11.6

Mortensen (1977) and van den Berg (1990a) developed models accounting for nonstationarity in job search. They both show that if the UI benefit drops (to zero), the value of unemployment becomes so low that almost any job becomes acceptable. This reduces the reservation wage and hence increases the job acceptance rate. As shown in figure 11.3b, nonstationary job search explains curve AB, the increase in job-finding rate over the duration of unemployment as well as the constant high level BC, but not the drop after benefit expiration (BD).

Boone and van Ours (2012) suggest that end-of-benefit spikes in job-finding rates are related to optimizing behavior of unemployed workers, who rationally assume that employers will accept delays in the starting date of a new job, especially if these jobs are permanent. This gives some workers an incentive to not immediately start working after finding a job. Instead they wait until their benefits expire.

More recently, some U.S. and European studies have exploited policy-driven changes in benefit levels. These studies examine how UI recipients react to incentives using a quasi-experimental identification of the treatment effect that allows the researchers to adopt a difference-in-differences approach. The policy change allows for a before-after comparison: the first difference. Then, there is usually a treatment group that is affected and a control group that is not affected: the second difference. The difference-in-differences gives the treatment effect of the policy change. Other recent studies use a regression discontinuity methodology exploiting one or more discontinuities in the relationship between benefit level or benefit duration and, for example, age at inflow or pre-unemployment work experience. The assumption is that individuals on either side of the discontinuity only differ slightly, except for the exposure to a different UI benefit level or benefit duration. The difference in behavior of individuals close to either side of the discontinuity then reveals how the difference in UI affects behavior. An overview of recent studies on the effects of UI on unemployment outflow is provided in the top part of table 11.4.[2] The studies are characterized in terms of country, calendar period, sample size, treated population, the identification strategy, and the effect of UI on duration and two indicators for the dose-response effects to enable a comparison between the studies.

Card and Levine (2000) study an extension of UI benefits in the state of New Jersey in 1996. For political reasons unrelated to the state of the labor market, UI benefits were temporarily—for 25 weeks—extended by 13 weeks.[3] The authors

2. This table and the related discussion draw on Tatsiramos and van Ours (2013).
3. In the United States, UI benefit durations at the state level are automatically extended once the unemployment rate is higher than a particular threshold. This may cause difficulties in estimating the effect of benefit duration on unemployment. Due to this *policy endogeneity* or *reverse causality,* higher unemployment induces governments to adopt more generous benefit systems rather than the other way around (Holmlund 1998). The study by Card and Levine (2000) does not suffer from this bias.

compare the unemployment exit rates before, during, and after the benefit extension was introduced. They find a decrease of the exit rates by about 15 percent. From simulations of the long-term effect of the benefit extension, they conclude that the 13 weeks of extra benefits would raise the average duration of regular UI claims by about 1 week.

Carling et al. (2001) study the effects of a cut in Swedish replacement rates in January 1996 from a maximum of 80 to 75 percent. Because of a ceiling on the benefit level, actual replacement rates can be lower than the maximum rates, while for high-wage earners the UI replacement rate is not affected at all. The authors compare the job-finding rates of unemployed workers who were affected by the cut in the replacement rates with the rates of workers who were not affected. They distinguish two treatment groups, one group with exactly 80 percent replacement before the change and 75 percent after the change and the other group with a replacement rate between 75 and 80 percent before the change and 75 percent after the change. There is one control group with individuals for whom the cut in benefits did not apply, because their earnings were above the threshold. The sample consists of UI recipients younger than 55 years. The authors find that the cut in UI benefits substantially increased the outflow from unemployment with an implied elasticity of the hazard rate with respect to benefits of about 1.6.

Røed and Zhang (2003) present an analysis of unemployment durations of Norwegian workers who were younger than 60 years old, became unemployed during the 1990s, and were eligible for UBs. They exploit two particular features of the Norwegian benefit system. First, UBs depend on the entry month into unemployment, because they are calculated on the basis of earnings during the previous calendar year. Second, benefits are indexed depending on the entry month. Furthermore, because of the ceiling in earnings, the replacement rate goes down with earnings for workers who earned more than the ceiling. These are sources of independent variation in replacement rates that the authors use to estimate benefit elasticities, which they find range from 0.95 for men to 0.35 for women. This implies that a 10 percent reduction in benefits may cut a ten-month duration by approximately one month for men and by one to two weeks for women.

Van Ours and Vodopivec (2006) (see box 11.5) exploit a policy change in Slovenia that involved substantial reductions in the potential duration of UBs for four groups of workers while not changing in benefits for another group, which served as a natural control. The distinction between the four groups is based on pre-unemployment work experience. Depending on this experience, the PBD could be reduced from 6 to 3, 9 to 6, 12 to 6, or 18 to 9 months. The effect of the reduction in maximum benefit duration depends on the size of the reduction but also on the age and gender of the worker. Based on their parameter estimates, they present simulation results from which it appears that for a 30-year-old male worker in good health for whom the PBD was reduced from 12 to 6 months, the median unemployment duration declined by 1.1 months; for a female worker with the same characteristics, the drop in median unemployment was 3.5 months.

TABLE 11.4 Overview of recent empirical studies of the effects of UI on unemployment duration and post-unemployment outcomes

Reference	Country	Period	Sample size	Treated population	Unemployment duration Treatment	Effect on PBD[a]	Benefit elasticity[b] (%)
Card and Krueger (2000)	United States	1995–1997	56,262	New Jersey	13 weeks PBD ↑ Calendar time variation	0.08	
Carling et al. (2001)	Sweden	1994–1996	18,429	Age < 55	Income-dependent cut in RR from 80 to 75 percent		1.6
Roed and Zhang (2003)	Norway	1990s	100,499	Age < 55	Exogenous variation in RR		Men: 0.95 Women: 0.35
Van Ours and Vodopivec (2006)	Slovenia	1997–1999	20,049	Age 19–43	Experience-related 3–9 months of PBD ↓	Men: 0.18[c] Women: 0.58[c]	
Lalive et al. (2006)	Austria	1987–1991	225,821	Age 35–54	Age-related extension of PBD 9 (22) weeks ↑ and RR ↑	0.04–0.10	0.2
Card et al. (2007a)	Austria	1981–2001	650,922	Age 20–50	Experience-related extension of PBD 20–30 weeks	0.10–0.18[d]	
Lalive (2008)	Austria	1986–1998	27,555	Age 46–53	Age-related extension of PBD from 30 to 209 weeks	Men: 0.08 Women: 0.42	
Uusitalo and Verho (2010)	Finland	2002–2004	17,783	Age < 55	Experience-related increase of RR by 15 percent[e]	0.08	0.8
Schmieder et al. (2012a)	Germany	1987–1999	329,680	Age 40–49	Age-related extension of PBD, various durations	0.10–0.13	

Post-unemployment outcomes

Reference	Country	Period	Sample size	Treated population	Basis for extension of PBD	Effect of PBD extension on	
						Earnings	Job stability
Card et al. (2007a)	Austria	1981–2001	650,922	Age 20–50	Experience: 20–30 months	No	No
Centeno and Novo (2007)	Portugal	1998–2004	9,675	Age 30–39	Age: 15–18 months	Small	—
Van Ours and Vodopivec (2008)	Slovenia	1997–1999	17,701[f]	Age 19–43	Experience: various	No	No
Caliendo et al. (2013)	Germany	2001–2006	7,216	Men 44–46 Women 43.5–46.5	Age: 12–18 months	No[g]	No[g]

Note: PBD = potential benefit duration; RR = replacement rate; — = not available.

a. Marginal effect: change in actual unemployment duration/change in PBD.

b. Benefit elasticity = percentage increase in unemployment duration in response to a 1 percentage point increase in benefit replacement rate (absolute values).

c. Based on simulations for a 30-year-old median worker in good health, with vocational school education, 10–15 years of work experience, and no dependent family members who was confronted with a drop in PBD from 12 to 6 months.

d. First 20 weeks; calculated on the basis of the reported increase in job-finding rate of 5–9 percent as a consequence of an increase in PBD of 50 percent.

e. The experience-related increase in the RR was over the first 150 days of unemployment in compensation for severance pay being abolished.

f. For the wage estimates 8,393 observations were used.

g. Unemployed who obtain jobs close to or after the time when benefits are exhausted are significantly more likely to exit subsequent employment and receive lower wages compared to their counterparts with extended benefit duration.

BOX 11.5

Shortening the Duration of Benefits

Faced with increasing unemployment, Slovenia in October 1998 drastically reduced the UI potential benefit duration (PBD). The changes depended on work experience:

Group	Experience (years)	PBD (months) Before	After	Difference (months)
1	1–2.5	3	3	0
2	2.5–5	6	3	−3
3	5–10	9	6	−3
4	10–15	12	6	−6
5	15–20	18	9	−9

Before the reform, for example, workers with 10 to 15 years of experience were eligible for up to 12 months of benefits (group 4). After the change this group of workers was eligible for up to 6 months of benefits. As shown in the next table, for the male workers of this group median unemployment duration dropped by 2.1 months. Since the unemployment duration of the reference group (1) dropped by 0.3 months, the "treatment" effect of the 6 months PBD reduction was 1.8 months reduction of median unemployment duration.

Jan van Ours and Milan Vodopivec analyzed the effects of shortening the PBD. They identify a significant increase in the job-finding rate and thus a drop in unemployment duration at various durations of unemployment spells. They also identify a clear spike in the job-finding rate in the month unemployment benefits expire. As shown below, the benefit spikes in the job-finding rates (left panel) and the survival rates in unemployment (right panel) indeed follow the change in PBD.

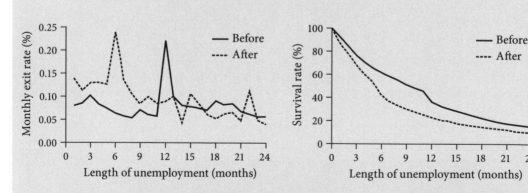

Whereas the probability of finding a job greatly increased for most groups of recipients whose benefit entitlement period was shortened, it stayed virtually unchanged for recipients whose entitlement period did not change. This suggests that the job-finding rate improved mainly because of more intense job search efforts by unemployed workers. In a follow-up study van Ours and Vodopivec (2008) investigate the effect of the reduction in PBD on the quality of the post-unemployment jobs. The average effects for each group of men are presented next:

Group	Duration (months)				Job loss within a year (%)				Wage change (%)			
	B	A	Δ	ΔΔ	B	A	Δ	ΔΔ	B	A	Δ	ΔΔ
1	3.8	3.5	0.3		51.2	48.8	−2.4		12.5	9.0	−3.5	
2	4.2	3.7	−0.5	−0.2	47.2	46.1	−1.1	1.3	17.2	11.4	−5.8	−2.3
3	5.8	4.2	−1.6	−1.3	43.2	44.4	1.2	3.6	16.3	12.8	−3.5	0.0
4	7.0	4.9	−2.1	−1.8	46.6	43.0	−3.6	−1.2	16.1	12.7	−3.4	0.1
5	9.2	5.6	−3.6	−3.3	42.1	43.0	0.9	3.3	16.6	13.6	−3.0	0.5
2–5	6.0	4.5	−1.5	−1.2	44.8	44.1	−0.7	1.7	16.5	12.6	−3.9	−0.4

Note: B = before the policy change; A = after the policy change; Δ = difference; ΔΔ = difference-in-differences.

Two indicators of the quality of post-unemployment jobs are used: the percentage of job loss within a year and the change in wage from the pre-unemployment job to the post-unemployment job. They find that the faster job finding did not occur at the cost of quality of post-unemployment jobs; that is, workers found jobs faster without accepting lower quality jobs in terms of employment stability and wages. Together, these findings imply that longer PBDs contributed to longer durations of unemployment spells of benefit recipients without improving the quality of post-unemployment jobs. These findings suggest that additional job search had a zero marginal productivity—or that recipients behaved opportunistically and did not spend additional time on job searches at all, perhaps in collusion with their prospective employers.

Sources: Van Ours and Vodopivec (2006, 2008).

Lalive et al. (2006) (see box 11.6) study a policy change in the structure of the UI benefits in Austria which affected various unemployed workers differently. The first group experienced an increase in the replacement rate, the second group experienced an extension of the PBD, the third group experienced both a higher replacement rate and a longer PBD, and the fourth group experienced no change in the policy parameters. The authors estimate hazard rate models and, on the basis of their parameter estimates, they present simulation results. An increase in PBD from 30 to 39 weeks leads to an increase of 0.4 weeks of unemployment, while an increase in PBD from 30 to 52 weeks increases the unemployment duration by 2.3 weeks. The increase in the replacement rate of 4.6 percentage points from about 41 percent leads to an increase in the unemployment duration of 0.4 weeks from about 18 weeks. So, an increase in the replacement rate of 11.2 percent ($100 \times 4.6/41$) generates an increase in unemployment of 2.2 percent ($100 \times 0.4/18$), implying a benefit elasticity of approximately 0.2.

Replacement Rates and Maximum Benefit Duration in Austria   BOX 11.6

In 1989 Austria reformed its UB system in a way that affected various unemployed workers differently: one group experienced an increase in the replacement rate, a second group experienced an extension of the maximum duration of benefits, a third group experienced both a higher replacement rate and a longer duration of benefits, and a fourth group experienced no change in the policy parameters:

	Younger than 40 years Work experience		40 years and older Work experience	
Monthly income	Low	High	Low	High
Low	RR↑	RR↑	RR↑	PBD+RR↑
High	Control	Control	Control	PBD↑

Note: RR = replacement rate.

The increase in the maximum duration of benefits depended on age and experience: for workers younger than 40 and those with little previous work experience, the duration remained unchanged; for workers with long previous work experience, the duration increased, from 30 to 39 weeks for the age group 40–49 and from 30 to 52 weeks for workers aged 50 and older. Rafael Lalive, Jan van Ours, and Josef Zweimüller used this natural experiment to derive lessons about the effects on unemployment duration of changes of UB systems along these different dimensions.

The data analyzed concerned workers' unemployment histories from two years before the policy change to two years after the change. The authors estimated the conditional probability of leaving unemployment at different durations of unemployment and for workers entitled to different durations of UBs and replacement rates. The table below summarizes the results of a simple difference-in-differences analysis, comparing the duration of unemployment (measured in weeks) in the first 104 weeks of the unemployment spell for groups involved by the various regulatory changes (the treatment groups) and groups not involved (the control group):

	Weeks of unemployment			
	Before	After	Difference	Difference-in-differences
PBD	16.3	18.7	2.4	1.1
RR	17.8	20.0	2.2	0.9
PBD and RR	19.0	23.5	4.6	3.3
Control group	15.2	16.5	1.3	

Note: Before = before August 1989; after = after August 1989; RR = replacement rate.

Both the increase in replacement rates and the extension of benefit duration significantly increase the duration of unemployment. The effect is stronger when it is the maximum duration to be increased rather than the replacement rate or when replacement rates and benefit durations are simultaneously increased. Figure 11.4 provides more detailed information about the policy effects. Figure 11.4a shows the unemployment exit rates, while figure 11.4b displays the unemployment survival rates.

Source: Lalive et al. (2006).

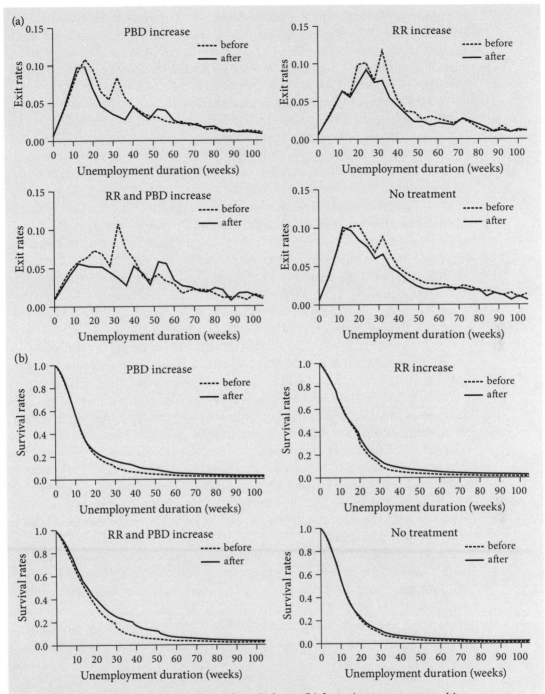

FIGURE 11.4 Unemployment exit rates (a) and survival rates (b) for various treatment combinations of changes in replacement rates and PBDs

Note: See box 11.6.

Card et al. (2007a) exploit a discontinuity in the relationship between work experience and UI entitlement for Austrian workers. Individuals with fewer than 36 months of employment in the past five years received 20 weeks of benefits, while those who worked for 36 months or more received 30 weeks of benefits. Using a sample of workers aged 20–50, the authors find that UI recipients who are eligible for 30 weeks of benefits exhibit job-finding rates during the first 20 weeks that are 5–9 percent lower than those who are eligible for only 20 weeks of benefits.

Lalive (2008) exploits an age-specific change in the maximum benefit duration in Austria in June 1988; for workers aged 50 or older the PBD was extended from 30 weeks to 209 weeks in some regions but not in others. He uses this age discontinuity in UI entitlement to establish the effect of the PBD extension on the unemployment duration. The data refer to workers aged 46–53. From the estimates it appears that the duration of job search is prolonged by about 14.8 weeks for men, while for women the increase is 74.8 weeks. This gender difference is attributed to difference in age requirements for early retirement. The early retirement age for women is 54, while for men it is 59. Apparently, for older Austrian women UI provided a quantitatively important pathway into early retirement.

On January 1, 2003, unemployment benefits in Finland were increased for workers with long employment histories. The average benefit increase was 15 percent for the first 150 days of the unemployment spell. At the same time, the severance pay system was abolished. The increase in benefits was calculated so that in the absence of behavioral effects on expectation, the costs for the UB funds would not change. Uusitalo and Verho (2010) use this policy change to analyze the effect of the UI replacement rate on unemployment duration and find that the re-employment exit rates were reduced on average by 17 percent. The effect is largest at the beginning of the unemployment spell and disappears after the eligibility for the increased benefits expires. Based on their estimates, Uusitalo and Verho conclude that the benefit increase extended the time to re-employment by 33 days or 11.9 percent. Given that the benefit increase was 15 percent this result implies that the elasticity of time until re-employment with respect to the replacement rate would be about 0.8.

Finally, Schmieder et al. (2012a) implement a regression discontinuity design using data on German workers aged 40–49 who entered unemployment between July 1987 and March 1999 when the UI system was stable. During this time there were three sharp age thresholds in the PBD: age 42 (12–18 months), age 44 (18–22 months), and age 49 (22–26 months). The authors find that for each additional month of UI duration, the unemployment duration increases on average by 0.10–0.13 months.[4]

The main conclusion that can be drawn on the basis of the overview of studies presented in table 11.4 is that there are substantial effects on unemployment duration if the replacement rate or the PBD changes. The magnitude of the effects varies across countries and type of policy change, but the variation is not so

---

4. In Schmieder et al. (2012b), the authors replicate their results using only the threshold at age 42, finding a marginal effect of 0.20, which goes down to 0.15 if nonemployment over 5 years—after the start of the initial spell—is taken into account.

big. An extension of the PBD leads to an increase in actual unemployment duration of about 20 percent of the extension of the PBD. One of the exceptions is for Slovenian women, the other is for Austrian women. The first may have to do with their attachment to the labor market, the second with the proximity to early retirement benefits. The benefit elasticity seems to range between 0.4 and 1.0, with the Swedish findings of Carling et al. (2001) being an exception. Although the ages of the workers being investigated differ, there is no evidence of age-specific treatment effects, with the exception of older Austrian women. Incentives clearly matter. The job-finding behavior of unemployed workers is influenced both by the level and the duration of UI benefits.

An important dimension in the optimal design of UI is to understand whether either of the two main components of the benefit system—benefit level and benefit duration—matter more by affecting differently the behavior of unemployed workers. The existing evidence suggests that both types of increase in the generosity of the UI system lead to longer unemployment duration. Consistent with the theory, most of the effect of the increase in benefit levels takes place early in the unemployment spell; for the extension of benefit duration, most of the effect arises near the expiration date. Lalive et al. (2006) perform an exercise in which they compare the disincentive effects of PBD and replacement rate by investigating the effects of increases in PBD and replacement rate on total increases in benefit payments. An increase in replacement rate will raise benefit payments even if individuals do not change their behavior, simply because higher benefits have to be paid for the same number of days that the individuals are unemployed. Furthermore, the replacement rate increase will induce individuals to stay unemployed longer, raising benefit payments even further. An intuitive way to compare PBD and replacement rate is to split up the total increase in benefit costs into the fraction of direct costs (without behavioral changes) and the fraction of indirect costs resulting from changes in behavior. The authors find that an increase in PBD induces a substantially higher share of behavioral costs than an increase in replacement rate. In other words, individuals react relatively strongly to increases in benefit duration, and these behavioral changes are the main factor driving the costs or benefits of the policy change. Changes in replacement rates have a relatively smaller influence on changes in behavior, because they affect every unemployed worker and not just those who are close to benefit expiration.

The finding that changes in the duration of benefits lead to stronger effects compared to changes in the level of benefits means that benefit duration is a more effective tool for influencing incentives. One concern is that the quality of post-unemployment jobs is affected too. The higher exit rate from unemployment might be associated with jobs of lower quality and with higher probability of re-entering unemployment. We discuss the empirical findings of the relationship between PBD and the quality of post-unemployment jobs in the next section.

11.3.2 Effect of UBs on Post-unemployment Outcomes

The evidence of the effect of UBs on post-unemployment outcomes (wage and stability of jobs) is mixed. In older studies the effect of UB on wages is weakly positive. There is, however, variation in the evidence, with some studies finding no effect while others find positive effects.[5]

The most recent century studies include Addison and Blackburn (2000), who find that more generous UI (in terms of either the benefit level or entitlement period) hardly increases re-employment wages. The evidence of the effect of the UI system on employment duration is rather mixed. Evidence from Canada (Belzil 2001) and the United States (Centeno 2004) suggests that jobs accepted close to benefit termination have a higher dissolution rate, while higher benefit levels increase the quality of job matching measured by the duration of the employment spell.[6] An overview of recent studies on the effects of UI on post-unemployment outcomes using a difference-in-differences or regression discontinuity approach is provided in the bottom part of table 11.4.

Card et al. (2007a)—whose results were discussed before—show that extended benefits do not affect the match quality of subsequent jobs, as measured by mean wages or the duration of subsequent jobs. Centeno and Novo (2007) exploit an age-specific change in entitlement introduced in Portugal in July 1999. For the age group 30–34, the maximum benefit duration was increased from 15 to 18 months, while for the age group 35–39, it remained at 18 months. The new law appears to have had a small positive impact on re-employment wages; the 3-month benefit extension increased wages by 2.8 percent. The increase was somewhat stronger at the bottom of the re-employment distribution. van Ours and Vodopivec (2008) use the policy change in Slovenia, which substantially reduced the PBD for many groups of workers, to investigate the quality of post-unemployment jobs (see also box 11.5). They find that the reduction in the PBD did not affect the likelihood of a worker taking a temporary rather than a permanent job, had hardly any effect on job separation rates, and did not affect post-unemployment wages.

Finally, Caliendo et al. (2013) focus on a discontinuity in the German UI system, where at the age of 45 the maximum benefit duration increases by 6 months from 12 to 18 months. They investigate a German sample of flow into unemployment from 2001 to 2003, with men ranging in age from 44 to 46 and women between ages 43.5 and 46.5. The authors find that the exit rate from unemployment decreases because of the extended benefit period (by 14 percent). The overall effect of the extended benefit duration on the exit rate from subsequent employment is negative but small and is not significantly different from zero. However, the treatment effect is heterogeneous. The same applies to post-unemployment wages. Unemployed workers who obtain jobs close to and just after the time when ben-

<hr />

5. See Burgess and Kingston (1976), Ehrenberg and Oaxaca (1976), Hoelen (1977), and Blau and Robins (1986). Classen (1977) finds no relationship between the level of UI benefits and re-employment wages.

6. Tatsiramos (2009) uses ECHP data to investigate the effect of UI on unemployment duration and subsequent employment stability for eight European countries. He finds that benefit recipients experience longer unemployment spells, but UI also has a positive effect on subsequent employment stability. The effect of UI on employment stability is more pronounced in countries with relatively more generous UI systems, such as Denmark, Germany, France, and Spain, when compared with countries, such as Greece and Italy, in which the UI system is underdeveloped.

efits were exhausted are significantly more likely to exit subsequent employment and receive lower wages compared to their counterparts with extended benefit durations.

Whereas in every study there is evidence of replacement rates and PBD affecting the job-finding rate, the results of studies on post-unemployment effects are much more heterogeneous. Many studies find no effects on the quality of the post-unemployment job, while only a few studies find some effects.

11.4 Policy Issues

11.4.1 Should the Generosity of UBs Vary over the Business Cycle?

The disincentive effect of UI may be sensitive to the business cycle, becoming lower during recessions (because of higher search costs and weaker labor demand) and higher during booms (because of lower search costs and stronger labor demand). The occurrence of longer unemployment duration during recessions may call for more generous benefits, since the trade-off between consumption smoothing and moral hazard is different than in a booming labor market with low unemployment.

This is how the U.S. system of extended benefits is organized during cyclical downturns. The regular program provides benefits up to 26 weeks. However, the Federal-State Extended Benefits Program provides up to 13 additional weeks of benefits in states where unemployment rates are relatively high. Furthermore, in the past during several recessions there have been further "emergency" extensions (Kiley 2003). As a response to the Great Recession of 2008–2009, maximum UI durations in the United States were extended to as long as 99 weeks.[7] The U.S. system of cyclical variation in UI benefit generosity is relatively unusual for other OECD countries.

There is some recent empirical evidence in support of cyclical variations in UI benefit generosity. Kroft and Notowidigdo (2010) show for the U.S. that the elasticity of unemployment duration with respect to the UI benefit level varies with the unemployment rate. Theoretically, this elasticity depends on the relative importance of search effort and reservation wage. Through the reservation wage, there is a positive correlation between the duration elasticity and the unemployment rate, while in terms of the search effort there may be a negative correlation. Empirically, a negative correlation exists between the elasticity and the unemployment rate. Thus, moral hazard is lower when unemployment is high. Schmieder et al. (2012a) find similar results for Germany. These findings suggest that extensions of UI duration during recessions can enhance welfare.

From a theoretical point of view, there are few recent studies on the optimal UI over the business cycle. Andersen and Svarer (2010) and Landais et al. (2010) find countercyclical optimal benefits. In Andersen and Svarer (2010) the

---

7. Rothstein (2011) concludes on the basis of an analysis of data from the Current Population Survey that the effects on unemployment exits of the benefit extensions has been rather limited. He attributes 0.1–0.5 percentage points of the unemployment rate to the extended duration of maximum benefits.

government uses UI to smooth consumption over the business cycle facing an intertemporal budget constraint. Landais et al. (2010) distinguish between two sources of unemployment—that stemming from matching frictions (in booms) and that from job rationing (in recessions). In recessions the moral hazard problem is smaller than in booms because of the limited number of jobs available, while the value of consumption smoothing remains constant over the cycle. Due to job rationing, the individual effort to find a job creates a negative externality for other jobseekers. In this setting, the optimal UI rule implies more generous benefits in recessions than in expansions, which correct the negative externality by reducing job search effort. Mitman and Rabinovich (2011) also study the optimal provision of UI over the business cycle by using a general equilibrium search model, in which they allow for aggregate productivity shocks. They also consider the optimal design of both the level and duration of benefits. They find that the optimal path of benefits is procyclical. The main difference with the previous studies is that they allow for wage bargaining, which implies that UI benefit changes do affect wages, instead of assuming rigid wages.

The main argument in favor of cyclically adjusted UBs is that moral hazard is less of an issue in recessions than in boom periods. Therefore, making benefits more generous during recessions—in particular by increasing the PBD—should not harm the functioning of the labor market. The main argument against cyclically dependent UBs is that workers will be more likely to enter unemployment in recessions due to the more generous UBs.

11.4.2 Is Moral Hazard All That Matters?

Workers remain unemployed longer when they receive more generous benefits. This may be due to a moral hazard effect. An alternative explanation is that it is due to liquidity constraints. To the extent that UBs induce moral hazard, there is a welfare argument for making UBs less generous, since they drive a wedge between the private and social costs of unemployment. However, if unemployment durations increase because of a liquidity constraint, this is less of an issue, as the longer benefit duration does not distort incentives but actually remedies other market imperfections. The liquidity constraint arises when imperfect credit and insurance markets prevent individuals from smoothing consumption. In this case, UBs help correct a market imperfection.

To establish the importance of the liquidity constraint, studies exploit the fact that some workers are entitled to severance payments, paid as a lump sum at separations.[8] Chetty (2008) uses variation in severance pay policies across firms in the United States to identify the effect of liquidity constraints. A severance payment is a lump-sum payment made when a separation occurs (see chapter 10) that does not influence the leisure-work trade-off and therefore should not have an effect on behavior unless through a liquidity constraint. Chetty's analysis is based on 2,441 individuals, of whom 471 (18 percent) report receiving a severance payment. There

---

8. An obvious criticism of this type of study is that the availability of severance payments is selective.

is no information about the size of these payments. From his analysis Chetty concludes that 60 percent of the increase in unemployment durations caused by UI benefits is due to a liquidity effect rather than to distortions in marginal incentives to search—the moral hazard effect. Chetty finds two pieces of evidence. First, increases in benefits have much larger effects on durations for liquidity-constrained households than for unconstrained households. Second, lump-sum severance payments increase durations substantially among constrained households.

The change in the Finnish UI system exploited by Uusitalo and Verho (2010) to investigate the effect of replacement rate on unemployment duration was not one-on-one. The eligibility criteria for the severance pay in the old system were slightly different than the eligibility criteria of higher daily allowance in the new system, and there were small groups of unemployed workers who lost the right to the severance pay without becoming eligible for the higher daily allowance (1,420 individuals) or who gained higher allowance even though they were not eligible for the severance pay before the reform (681 individuals). These small groups were used to disentangle the effect of the removal of severance pay and the effect of the higher replacement rate in the early period of unemployment. The authors find that the effect of the lost severance pay is insignificantly different from zero.

Both Chetty (2008) and Uusitalo and Verho (2010) have only a relatively small number of observations, while Card et al. (2007a) have many more observations to estimate the effects of severance pay (see also table 11.4). Card et al. compare the search behavior of people who were laid off just before and just after the 36-month cutoff for severance pay eligibility. They find that the lump sum severance pay has a significant effect on the duration of joblessness. The job-finding rate during the first 20 weeks of unemployment (the eligibility period for regular UBs in Austria) is 8–12 percent lower for those who are just barely eligible for severance pay than for those who are just barely ineligible. A substantial share of the behavioral response to longer UBs is attributable to a liquidity effect rather than to moral hazard. All in all, the importance of liquidity constraints is still not well established.

11.5 Interactions with Other Institutions

UBs affect labor force participation, employment, and unemployment through a variety of channels that involve interactions with other institutions, such as collective bargaining institutions (see chapter 3) and active labor market policies (see chapter 12). Because payroll taxes have to be levied to finance the benefits, UBs can be better understood by considering the effects on the labor market equilibrium of taxes on labor (see chapter 13).

UBs and employment protection are supposed to have a similar function: to protect workers against uninsurable labor market risk. There are two key differences between the two institutions:

1. EPL protects only those who already have a job, acting as a deterrent to layoffs, while UBs protect the working-age population at large (although some work experience is generally required to receive UBs).

2. EPL does not impose any tax burden on workers, while UBs are financed by
a payroll tax levied on those who have jobs.

These key differences can be somewhat reduced by appropriate adjustments in
the design of UBs or EPL. For instance, UBs can be experience-rated, as in the
United States and, limited to STW, in Italy and Germany (see chapter 5). In this
case higher payroll taxes should be paid by those employers who are responsible
for the redundancies.

However, even an experience-rated UB system imposes some fiscal externality
on other employers and workers. To prevent adverse selection involving only high-
turnover employers, UB systems require mandatory payment by all employers.
Thus, some sharing of the costs of redundancies occurs. Another reason why EPL
and UBs cannot be perfect substitutes is that EPL in practice requires that some
tax always be imposed on the employers responsible for dismissals. To elicit effort
from their workers, employers should establish stronger sanctions for disciplinary
than for economic dismissals. In the language of jurisprudence, they should treat
subjective just cause differently from objective just cause dismissals, but this different treatment cannot be generally enforced without envisaging some role for labor
judges. Hence EPL, unlike UBs, always involves some deadweight costs in terms of
payment to third parties, like lawyers.

Thus, some differences between UBs and EPL are unavoidable, and these differences are perceived by unemployed individuals. As documented in chapter 10,
EPL reduces labor turnover, making it more difficult to exit unemployment. UBs
are instead more mobility and hiring friendly and, unlike EPL, provide income
support during an unemployment spell. Thus, unemployed individuals are always
likely to rank UBs over EPL. Employees would instead prefer EPL to UBs, especially
if they have a high discount rate. Political economic models of labor market institutions (e.g., Wright 1986) predict that configurations with strict EPL arise when
the median voter is an insider (i.e., a person with a regular contract). Because of
this imperfect substitutability between UBs and EPL, we are unlikely to observe
countries with only one or the other institution. An additional political economic
reason for having both institutions is that because of the moral hazard problems,
neither EPL nor UBs can provide full insurance against job loss. Thus, in countries
where UB predominates, there will always be political pressure to increase EPL,
and vice versa. Yet it is also likely that the pressure for one institution will be lower
in the countries that have more of the other institution.

The term flexicurity is increasingly being used to denote countries, like Denmark, with low EPL and generous UBs. The location of different countries along
this trade-off may well reflect the relative political strength of insiders (who support EPL) and outsiders (who support UBs). An example of how changes in the
balance of power between these two groups can change the institutional mix along
this dimension is provided by Spain, one of the few countries that reduced EPL
for regular contracts. Significantly, the reform was enacted in 1994, just after
unemployed workers and workers with temporary contracts had become more
numerous than employees with regular contracts. Figure 11.5 provides a cross-

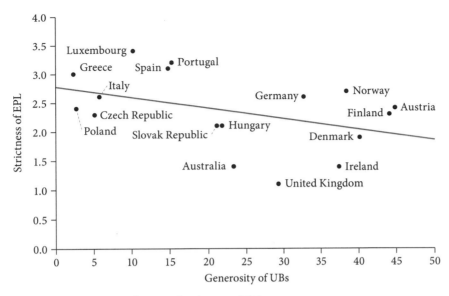

FIGURE 11.5 Generosity of UBs and strictness of EPL
Note: See tables 10.1 and 11.3 for definitions of the indexes used.

country overview. Clearly the relationship between the generosity of UBs and the strictness of employment protection is negative.

There is also an overlap between UBs and ALMPs. A key problem associated with the provision of UBs relates to disincentives to job search because of imperfect monitoring of the job-search efforts of recipients of UBs. The policies characterized in chapter 12 partly reduce these informational asymmetries. Finally, there is an interaction between UBs and taxes. Taxes on labor are levied to finance various social programs, including UBs.

11.6 Why Do UBs Exist?

The theory and empirical evidence reviewed in this chapter suggest that UBs raise a worker's reservation wage and increase unemployment duration. UBs also need to be financed by payroll taxes, which, as will be discussed in chapter 13, are distortional in that they reduce the size of the labor market. The obvious question is why UI is publicly provided. The answer is that UBs provide insurance against an otherwise uninsurable unemployment risk. No private company in the world supplies insurance against the risk of becoming or remaining unemployed, because moral hazard and adverse selection stand in the way of such potential contractual arrangements. Moral hazard arises because workers do not try as hard to avoid unemployment and find new jobs if they are covered against the negative consequences of the event by purchasing insurance at a given market price. Adverse selection arises in the presence of a heterogeneous pool of unemployed individuals, one in which some workers have (unobservable) characteristics that make them more likely to experience job loss. Under these conditions, workers who know that their unemployment risk is particularly high can make the scheme unprofitable for private insurance providers and force them to raise prices, making the insurance scheme unattractive to workers with average risk.

Public provision of UBs therefore remedies the inequitable or unfair labor market treatment of workers who, lacking insurance, become or remain unemployed despite their best efforts. Public provision of UBs solves the adverse selection problem, because participation in the insurance system is compulsory for everybody. However, it does not solve the moral hazard problem, because workers have no less incentive to decrease their job search intensity when covered by public rather than private insurance. Unemployed individuals will not be actively searching for other jobs if their utility is not much different when they work and when they do not work. The evidence reviewed in this chapter suggests that disincentives to job search associated with UB provision can indeed be substantial. Moreover, protection from unfair developments unavoidably decreases the labor market's speed of adjustment by increasing the duration of unemployment. More broadly, labor market institutions that protect workers against unfair market developments unavoidably reduce the intensity of competition, because they trade off lower productive efficiency for ex ante distributional equity. This trade-off is desirable, from an ex ante point of view, in the presence of the informational asymmetries that prevent private insurers from doing the job, but ex post it unavoidably decreases productive efficiency.

The design of UBs described at the beginning of this chapter can be rationalized in terms of optimal insurance arguments. When search effort is unverifiable, and hence the principal (the state) must give to the agent (the unemployed individual) an incentive to make this effort, optimal UI models (Hopenhayn and Nicolini 1997; Pavoni 2007, 2009) prescribe earnings-related UBs offering replacement rates that decrease over time. Another feature of the benefit system—the flat and open-ended benefit provided for longer unemployment durations—is consistent with the prescriptions of economic theory. Because human capital depreciates during the unemployment spell, for longer unemployment durations, eliciting search effort may become too costly relative to offering support to nonemployed individuals (Pavoni and Violante 2007). Finally, the welfare-to-work schemes that combine passive income transfers with ALMPs (characterized in chapter 12) all involve a sequence of actions and sanctions at different durations of unemployment.

Another trade-off related to the provision of UBs that has been more recently highlighted by the literature has to do with the *quality of jobs* and the effects of UBs on structural change. Acemoglu and Pischke (1999), Acemoglu et al. (2000), and Marimon and Zilibotti (1999)—who considered bilateral job search models with heterogeneous workers and jobs—showed that a positive level of UBs is required to maximize output, because otherwise jobseekers, notably poorer jobseekers, would be discouraged from applying for high-productivity jobs that are more difficult to get, and firms would not create these types of jobs. In these models unemployment generated by UBs has an efficiency-enhancing function, in that it allows economies to generate better matches and hence higher-productivity jobs. There is some evidence (Boeri and Macis 2010) that historically the introduction of UBs has indeed been associated with an increase in job reallocation and structural change. The experience of countries transitioning from central planning is also consistent with UBs increasing job reallocation and structural change (Boeri and Terrell 2002). At the same time, when UBs are too generous, efficiency-enhancing job reallocation may be reduced, because unemployment duration increases and stagnant unemployment pools are created. And, as discussed before, empirical studies often find no relationship between the generosity of UBs and the quality of post-unemployment jobs.

11.7 Suggestions for Further Reading

Although some surveys are a bit dated, they can still be highly instructive. We recommend in particular the surveys by Atkinson and Micklewright (1991) from the *Journal of Economic Literature*, Devine and Kiefer (1991), the survey of results from duration analysis offered by Kiefer (1988), and the more recent surveys by Meyer (1995) and Krueger and Meyer (2002) (which, however, cover mainly the U.S. experience). Tatsiramos and van Ours (2013) provide a recent overview of the potential labor market effects of UI design.

11.8 Review Questions and Exercises

1. Why do replacement rates offer an incomplete measure of the generosity of UBs?

2. Do UBs redistribute in favor of low-skilled workers?

3. What effects should we expect UBs to have on first-time jobseekers when benefits are conditional on previous work experience?

4. How does the introduction of a UB system affect labor force participation?

5. What type of relation do we expect to observe between generosity of UBs and structural change?

6. Why is UI not provided by private insurance companies?

7. Why is there a socially optimal replacement rate?

8. What are the main differences between a static and a dynamic reservation wage?

9. What happens to the static reservation wage when UI benefits are increased? Explain the main mechanism.

10. What happens to the dynamic reservation wage when UI benefits are increased? Explain the main mechanism.

11. A worker is looking for a job. His marginal revenue from the job search is $MR = 50 - 1.5w$, where w is the wage offer at hand, whereas his marginal cost of job search (in the presence of UBs) is $MC = 5 + w$.

    (a) Provide an interpretation for these MR and MC curves: why is MR a negative function of the wage at hand? What does the intercept of MC represent? And its slope?

(b) What is the worker's reservation wage?

(c) Suppose UBs are cut, so that the marginal cost of search increases to $MC = 20 + w$. What is the new reservation wage? Will the worker accept a job offer at 15 euros?

12. Mike's utility function for consumption C and leisure l is

$$U(c, l) = cl.$$

There are 168 hours in the week, and he earns 15 euros per hour.

(a) Write down Mike's budget constraint and graph it.

(b) What is Mike's optimal amount of consumption and leisure?

(c) What happens to employment and consumption if Mike receives 320 euros of UBs each week?

(d) What value of UBs would make Mike indifferent between working and not working?

13. (Advanced) In a job search model the flow value of employment can be written as

$$\rho V_e(w) = w + q(V_u - V_e(w)),$$

where ρ is the discount factor, w is the wage, q is the job separation rate, and V_e and V_u are the value of employment and unemployment, respectively. The flow value of unemployment is

$$\rho V_u = z + \lambda \int_x^\infty [V_e(w) - V_u] dH(w),$$

where z is the flow value of leisure, λ is the job offer arrival rate, $H(w)$ is the wage distribution, and x is the reservation wage.

(a) Explain the intuition behind these value functions.

(b) Derive the reservation wage equation.

(c) Derive the average duration of unemployment.

(d) Show that the reservation wage increases with the job offer arrival rate.

(e) Discuss why in theory the relationship between the job offer arrival rate and the duration of unemployment is ambiguous.

11.9 Technical Annex: Search Theory and Duration Models

11.9.1 Search Theory

As discussed in the chapter, changes in the generosity of UBs are bound to affect search intensity, wage bargaining, and labor force participation. In this annex—based on Tatsiramos and van Ours (2012)—we formally characterize these effects.

UBs aim to protect workers against uninsurable labor market risk. The generosity of UBs is determined by all the different features of this institution, for example, eligibility conditions, duration of benefits, and amount of transfers. Nevertheless, in this simplified job search model we initially treat UBs as a one-dimensional institution where only the benefit level b matters and benefits last indefinitely.

The basic search model is central to examining the effect of UBs on the exit rate from unemployment to a job. We start by considering the partial equilibrium model under the assumption that all unemployed workers receive the same amount of UBs, which are paid for over the entire duration of unemployment. Workers have their (dynamic) reservation wage as the only instrument of search to influence their unemployment duration. In a stationary environment, the flow value of having a job is equal to

$$\rho V_e = w + \delta(V_u - V_e), \tag{11.7}$$

where ρ is the discount rate, V_e is the asset value of having a job, w is the wage rate (which is constant over the duration of employment), δ is the exogenous job separation rate, and V_u is the asset value of being unemployed. The employment value function is equal to the current wage w plus the future value of becoming unemployed, which is actually a loss, since $(V_u - V_e)$ is negative.

Similarly, the flow value of being unemployed is equal to

$$\rho V_u = b + \mu \int_{w^r}^{\infty} [V_e - V_u] dH(w), \tag{11.8}$$

where b represents the benefit level, μ denotes the exogenous arrival of job offers, and $H(w)$ is the wage offer distribution.[9] Again, the value function is equal to the current utility (which is the unemployment compensation b) plus the future value of finding a job (which occurs at rate μ).

Unemployed workers can influence the exit rate from unemployment to work by choosing the reservation wage (i.e., the minimum wage that they require for accepting a job offer). From (11.7) the gain from being employed can be written as

$$V_e - V_u = \frac{w - \rho V u}{\rho + \delta}, \tag{11.9}$$

which implies that a jobseeker accepts a job offer if $V_e > V_u$ or if $w > \rho V_u$. In a stationary environment, δ, μ, and w are constant. In such an environment, the reservation wage w^r is equal to the flow value of being unemployed: $w^r = \rho V_u$.

---

9. So the wage offer w, which is connected to a job offer, is a random variable with the distribution function

$$H(w) = \int_0^w h(w) dw.$$

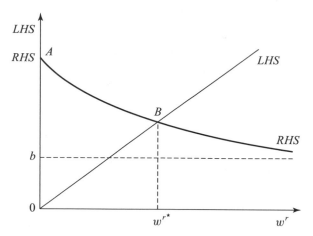

FIGURE 11.6 Left-hand side (*LHS*) and right-hand side (*RHS*) of (11.11)

Substituting (11.9) and $w^r = \rho V_u$ into (11.8), the reservation wage is implicitly defined by

$$w^r = b + \frac{\mu}{\rho + \delta} \int_{w^r}^{\infty} [w - w^r] dH(w).$$ (11.10)

Using integration by parts, this can be rewritten as

$$w^r = b + \frac{\mu}{\rho + \delta} \int_{w^r}^{\infty} [1 - H(w)] \, dw.$$ (11.11)

There is a unique solution of w^r, as is shown graphically in figure 11.6.[10] Using the implicit function theorem, from (11.11), we can derive the following comparative statics:

		w^r	D
1	$b \uparrow$	$\uparrow$	$\uparrow$
2	$\mu \uparrow$	$\uparrow$	Ambiguous
3	$\rho \uparrow$	$\downarrow$	$\downarrow$
4	$\delta \uparrow$	$\downarrow$	$\downarrow$

If UBs (1) or the job offer arrival rate (2) goes up, the reservation wage goes up. If the discount rate (3) or the job separation rate (4) goes up, the reservation wage goes down. In a stationary labor market, the job-finding rate is defined as $\lambda = \mu[1 - H(w^r)]$, which is the product of the rate at which unemployed workers receive job offers and the probability that a given offer is acceptable. Variables that

10. Note that for $w^r = 0$, the left side of (11.11) is equal to 0, while the right side is equal to $b + \frac{\mu}{\rho+\delta} E(w) > 0$ (point A in figure 11.6). Furthermore, $\frac{\partial LHS}{\partial w^r} = 1$, so the left side is upward sloping in w^r, while $\frac{\partial RHS}{\partial w^r} = -\frac{\mu}{\rho+\delta}(1 - H(w^r)) < 0$, so the right side is downward sloping. *LHS* and *RHS* cross at point B of figure 11.6.

lead to an increase in the reservation wage lower the job-finding rate λ and increase the average duration of unemployment $D = \frac{1}{\mu[1-H(x)]} = \frac{1}{\lambda}$.

From this we can derive the comparative statics for the duration of unemployment D, as indicated in the preceding table. The effect of the rate of incoming job offers is ambiguous, because on the one hand it increases the reservation wage and therefore indirectly has a positive effect on the duration, but on the other hand it also increases the exit from unemployment, thereby reducing the unemployment duration. For most wage distributions, the second effect dominates.

Introducing Search Intensity

Allowing for search effort as an additional choice for the unemployed jobseeker does not alter the main effect of benefit receipt. An increase in benefit level b not only increases the reservation wage w^r but also leads to lower search effort, which further reduces the exit rate. Denoting the intensity of job search by s, the job offer arrival rate is $\mu = \alpha\mu(s)$, with $\mu' > 0$ and $\mu'' < 0$. The cost of search as a function of search effort is denoted by $c(s)$ $(c' > 0, c'' > 0)$, which means that the instantaneous utility of an unemployed individual becomes $b - c(s)$. Furthermore, α is an indicator of the state of the labor market, which also affects the arrival rate of job offers. Unemployed workers can influence the exit rate from unemployment to work by choosing not only the reservation wage but also how much effort to exert on searching for a job. Using (11.10), the optimal value of search effort satisfies the condition $\partial w^r / \partial e = 0$, or

$$c'(s) = \frac{\alpha\mu'(s)}{\rho + \delta} \int_{w^r}^{\infty} [w - w^r] \, d\Pi(w). \tag{11.12}$$

Thus, the optimal search effort is the one that equates the marginal cost of effort with the marginal benefit.

Nonstationary Search Model

We now consider the nonstationary case, in which the benefit level differs over the unemployment spell and benefit duration is limited (see Mortensen 1977; van den Berg 1990a). When the UI system defines a declining profile of benefit payments or a termination of them, the main theoretical prediction is an increasing job-finding rate over the spell of insured unemployment. When the instantaneous income while unemployed declines over time, we get that $b(t') \leq b(t)$ for all $t' \geq t$, which results in a reduction of the value of unemployment, with $V_u(t') \leq V_u(t)$. The decline in the value of unemployment over time and close to benefit exhaustion leads to a drop in the reservation wage, with $w^r(t') \leq w^r(t)$, or alternatively, a higher search intensity $s(t') \geq s(t)$, both of which result in a higher exit rate.

Entitlement Effects

In most UI systems, benefit entitlement depends on previous employment experience, which is in contrast with the assumption of the basic model that all unemployed individuals receive benefits. Typically, new entrants in the labor market and long-term unemployed workers are not entitled to receive UBs. Finding a job for these types of unemployed persons means also becoming entitled to UBs in case they lose their jobs in the future. The behavioral effect of this case has similarities with the nonstationary case described above, where individuals close to benefit exhaustion experience a lower value of unemployment compared to those at the beginning of unemployment. In general, we can consider two different types of jobseekers. The first group consists of those who are entitled or are at the beginning of their unemployment spell, who receive benefits b with value of unemployment V_u. The second group consists of those who are close to benefit expiration or are not entitled to benefits, with instantaneous income denoted by $b_n < b$ and the value of unemployment by V_{un}. The flow value of being employed for a nonentitled unemployed worker is equal to

$$\rho V_e = w + \delta(V_u - V_e),$$
(11.13)

which suggests that nonentitled unemployed workers become entitled for the full unemployment compensation once they find a job and again become unemployed in the future with probability δ. Similarly, the flow value of being unemployed for a nonentitled unemployed individual is

$$\rho V_{un} = b_n + \mu \int_{w_n^r}^{\infty} [V_e(w) - V_{un}] dH(w),$$
(11.14)

where b_n represents the flow of income other than UBs, with $b_n < b$. For the entitled workers, their reservation wage satisfies $w^r = \rho V u$. The reservation wage of the second group, w_n^r, satisfies $V_e(w_n^r) = V_{un}$. Using these relations and (11.13), we can express the value of unemployment for the nonentitled workers as a function of the two reservation wages in the following way:

$$\rho V_{un} = \frac{\rho w_n^r + \delta w^r}{\rho + \delta}.$$
(11.15)

Using (11.13), (11.14), and (11.15), we can express the reservation wage of the nonentitled unemployed workers as a function of the reservation wage of the entitled ones:

$$\rho w_n^r = (\rho + \delta)b_n - \delta w^r + \mu \int_{w_n^r}^{\infty} [w - w_n^r] dH(w).$$
(11.16)

This characterization shows that there is a negative relationship between the two reservation wages. An increase in the benefit level b of the entitled workers (which leads to an increase in their reservation wage w^r) is associated with a decline in the reservation wage of the nonentitled ones. This occurs because the immediate gain from the increase in the benefit level for the nonentitled workers is zero or very small for those close to benefit exhaustion, while the value of becoming qualified for benefits in the future increases. This *entitlement effect* increases the incentive to accept jobs for UI recipients close to exhausting their benefits and for those who are not entitled to UBs.

Changes in PBD and Benefit Levels

The change in the behavior of jobseekers over the spell of unemployment and the entitlement effect imply that individuals with different lengths of benefit entitlement behave differently. For a given length of unemployment and for a given level of benefits, an increase in PBD will lead to an increase in the reservation wage, and consequently to a rise in the average duration of unemployment. An increase in PBD entails only a small immediate disincentive effect (at the beginning of the unemployment spell). The largest effect of an increase in benefit duration is expected for unemployment durations close to the benefit expiration period before the change of the system. This is because the reservation wage at that time will be significantly higher under the new system with longer benefit duration compared to the system without a benefit extension, in which the reservation wage is at its lowest level.

An increase in the benefit level will also affect unemployed workers differently, depending on their elapsed unemployment duration. Contrary to an extension of the benefit duration, an increase in the replacement rate has its largest effect at the start of the unemployment spell. For a recent unemployed worker, an increase in the benefit level will lower the exit rate from unemployment as a result of a higher value of unemployment. The jobseeker will demand a higher wage before accepting a job offer. For an unemployed worker close to benefit exhaustion, a higher benefit level will lead to a higher exit rate due to the entitlement effect.

Theoretically, the overall effect of an increase in the generosity of benefits on the average duration of unemployment depends on the balance of two opposing effects. First, a higher level of benefits and a longer benefit duration will lower the exit rate from unemployment. Second, for the ineligible and for those close to benefit exhaustion, more generous benefits will create an incentive to find a job faster because of the entitlement effect. However, since the entitlement effect is second-order, it is likely that the disincentive effect will dominate, so that an increase in benefit generosity will lead to longer unemployment durations.

Two-Sided Job Search and Matching Model

In contrast to the one-sided search model, in the matching model frictions are modeled in a reduced form by using a constant returns-to-scale matching function $M = M(U, V)$ (see chapter 12), where M is the flow of hirings, U denotes the number of unemployed workers and V the number of vacancies. The probability of filling a vacancy is $m(\theta) = M(U, V)/V$, which is a decreasing function of labor market tightness $\theta = V/U$. The probability of a jobseeker finding a job is $\theta m(\theta) = M(U, V)/U$, which is an increasing function of labor market tightness. Firms post vacancies, which are filled at the rate $m(\theta)$. The expected flow of profits from a filled job is

$$\rho \Pi_e = y - w + \delta(\Pi_v - \Pi_e),\qquad(11.17)$$

where y is the output, w is the cost of labor, δ is the exogenous separation rate, and Π_v is the profit from a vacant job. The expected flow of profits from a vacant job is

$$\rho \Pi_v = -\kappa + m(\theta)(\Pi_e - \Pi_v),\qquad(11.18)$$

where κ is the cost of posting a vacancy. With the assumption of free entry, $\Pi_v = 0$, and in equilibrium the average cost of a vacant job must be equal to the expected profit from a filled job. Solving (11.17) and (11.18) for Π_e and equating, we get

$$\frac{\kappa}{m(\theta)} = \frac{y - w}{\rho + \delta}, \tag{11.19}$$

which implies a negative relationship between labor market tightness and the wage. The behavior of workers is very similar to the basic search model with the value of unemployment defined as

$$\rho V_u = b + \theta m(\theta)(V_e - V_u). \tag{11.20}$$

Wages are endogenously determined through wage bargaining, which is the mechanism that shares the rents created by frictions between workers and firms. For both firms and workers, the rents are the difference between what they could obtain through forming a match and the best outside opportunity. The sum of the rents creates the surplus to be shared, which is $S = V_e - V_u + \Pi_e - \Pi_v$. If β represents the bargaining power of the worker and $(1 - \beta)$ is the bargaining power of the employer, the resulting negotiated wage is

$$w = \rho V_u + \beta(y - \rho V_u), \tag{11.21}$$

which can be written as

$$w = b + \Gamma(\theta)(y - b), \tag{11.22}$$

with $\Gamma(\theta) = \frac{\beta[\rho + \delta + \theta m(\theta)]}{\rho + \delta + \beta\theta m(\theta)}$ representing the overall bargaining weight of the workers, which not only depends on the "direct" bargaining weight β but also increases with labor market tightness θ. It is also dependent on the discount rate ρ and job separation rate δ.

The increase in UBs b increases the value of unemployment for the jobseeker, which leads to an increase in the wage in the bargaining process. Since a higher wage lowers firms' expected profits—the right-hand side of (11.19)—to restore equilibrium, firms lower the average cost of vacancies by reducing the number of vacancies, which lowers θ. To deduce the effect of an increase in UBs on unemployment, we consider the equilibrium in steady state, in which the flows into unemployment equal the flows out of unemployment:

$$\delta L = \theta m(\theta)U, \tag{11.23}$$

where U denotes the number of unemployed workers, and L denotes the number of employed. The stationary value of the unemployment rate is then given by

$$u = \frac{\delta}{\delta + \theta m(\theta)}, \tag{11.24}$$

which generates a relationship between unemployment and vacancies—the Beveridge curve. It also shows that an increase in benefits and the corresponding drop in labor market tightness θ leads to an increase in the unemployment rate.

11.9.2 Duration Models

The job-finding rate λ from the search and matching model has a clear empirical equivalent. In a stationary labor market the job-finding rate is constant, and the average duration of unemployment is $D = 1/\lambda$. Therefore, data on unemployment durations of individuals can be used to derive the job-finding rate.

Hazard rate models are econometric models of lengths of time spent in a given state before transitioning to another state. If T is the duration in a state, the density function is $f(t) = dF(t)/dt$, the probability that the duration or spell length is less than t is $F(t) = \Pr[T \le t] = \int_0^t f(s)ds$, and the probability that duration equals or exceeds t (called the survivor function) is $S(t) = \Pr[T > t] = 1 - F(t)$.

The hazard function is the instantaneous probability of leaving a state conditional on survival to time t, defined as

$$\lambda(t) = \lim_{\Delta t \to 0} \frac{\Pr[t \le T < t + \Delta t | T \ge t]}{\Delta t} = \frac{f(t)}{S(t)}. \tag{11.25}$$

Integrating $\lambda(t)$ and using $S(0) = 1$, we can show that

$$S(t) = \exp\left(-\int_0^t \lambda(u)du\right) \tag{11.26}$$

and

$$f(t) = \lambda(t) \exp\left(-\int_0^t \lambda(u)du\right). \tag{11.27}$$

For descriptive purposes nonparametric methods are useful. If a sample of complete durations is available, the obvious estimator of the survivor function is one minus the sample cumulative distribution function. Then $\widehat{S}(t)$ equals the number of spells in the sample of duration greater than t, divided by the sample size N. Let $t_1 < t_2 < \ldots < t_j < \ldots < t_k$ denote the observed discrete failure times of the spells in a sample of size N, $N \ge k$. Define the following:

- d_j: the number of spells that end at time t_j,
- m_j: the number of spells right censored in $[t_j, t_{j+1})$, and
- r_j: the number of spells at risk at time t_j.

The estimator for the hazard function is the number of spells ending at time t_j divided by the number at risk of failure, or $\widehat{\lambda}_j = \frac{d_j}{r_j}$. The Kaplan-Meier estimator is the sample analogue of the survivor function

$$\widehat{S}(t) = \prod_{j|t_j \le t} (1 - \widehat{\lambda}_j) = \prod_{j|t_j \le t} \frac{r_j - d_j}{r_j}. \tag{11.28}$$

This is a decreasing step function with a jump at each discrete failure time. The following table gives an example of how hazard rates and survival functions can be calculated (see Cameron and Trivedi 2005):

j	r_j	d_j	m_j	$\widehat{\lambda}_j = d_j/r_j$	$\widehat{S}(t_j)$
1	80	6	4	6/80	$(1 - 6/80)$
2	70	5	3	5/70	$(1 - 6/80) \times (1 - 5/70)$
3	62	2	1	2/62	$\widehat{S}(t_2) \times (1 - 2/62)$

Notes: At time t_j, r_j is the number of observations at risk, d_j is the number of failures, m_j is the number of missing spells (censored), $\widehat{\lambda}_j$ is the estimated hazard rate, and $\widehat{S}(t_j)$ is the estimated survivor function.

If micro data on durations are available, the hazard rate can be specified as a function of observed personal characteristics x. In a proportional hazard model, the conditional hazard rate $\lambda(t|x)$ can be written as

$$\lambda(t|x) = \lambda_0(t)\phi(x), \tag{11.29}$$

where $\lambda_0(t)$ is called the baseline hazard, a function of t alone. Furthermore, $\phi(x) = \exp(x'\beta)$ is a function of x alone and is the scale factor. There are various ways to specify the baseline hazard:

- Exponential distribution: $\lambda_0(t) = \lambda_0$.
- Weibull distribution: $\lambda_0(t) = \alpha t^{\alpha-1}$, with $\alpha > 0$. If $\alpha = 1$, we get the exponential; if $\alpha > 1$, the hazard is monotonically increasing; if $\alpha < 1$, the hazard is monotonically decreasing.
- Step function of k segments: $\lambda_0(t, \alpha) = e^{\alpha_j}$, $c_{j-1} \leq t < c_j$, $j = 1, \ldots, k$, with $c_0 = 0$, $c_k = \infty$, and the parameters $\alpha_1, \ldots \alpha_k$ are to be estimated.

It is also possible that the researcher does not observe all relevant characteristics. Then the hazard rate can be specified as a function of observed characteristics x and unobserved characteristics v. In a mixed proportional hazard model, the conditional hazard rate can be written as

$$\lambda(t|x, v) = \lambda_0(t)\phi(x)\exp(v). \tag{11.30}$$

In this case the density function is specified as

$$f(t|x, v) = \lambda(t|x, v) \exp\left(-\int_0^t \lambda(u|x, v)du\right), \tag{11.31}$$

and the unobserved characteristics can be removed by integrating them out:

$$f(t|x) = \int_v f(t|x, v)dG(v), \tag{11.32}$$

where $G(v)$ is the distribution function of unobserved heterogeneity.

CHAPTER TWELVE **Active Labor Market Policies**

Active labor market policies have a long-standing tradition in many countries. At the beginning of the twentieth century employment offices were built up. During the depression of the interwar years government programs were established to put the unemployed to work. Later, labor market retraining was organized to stimulate occupational and regional mobility and thus facilitate structural adjustments. More recently, there has been experimentation with activation schemes that put pressure on UB recipients to avoid their getting trapped in a long-term dependency on public transfers.

ALMPs currently implemented in OECD countries aim mainly at improving the functioning of the labor market by enhancing labor market mobility and adjustment, facilitating the redeployment of workers and their investment in human capital. They are also intended to overcome market failures arising from generous UB and welfare benefit schemes by alleviating the moral hazard problem of UI. All this contributes to maintaining the size of the effective labor force and keeping up competition for available jobs (Calmfors 1995).

There are four main types of ALMPs: (1) training, (2) subsidized employment, (3) public employment services, and (4) activation. *Labor market training* concerns training for unemployed adults, those at risk of losing their jobs, and employed adults. *Subsidized employment* consists of targeted measures to promote or provide employment for the unemployed and other priority groups. It also concerns wage subsidies paid to private-sector firms to encourage the recruitment of targeted workers or continued employment of those whose jobs are at risk, and support of unemployed persons starting enterprises, as well as direct job creation in public or nonprofit organizations for the benefit of the unemployed. *Public employment services* concern placement, counseling, and vocational guidance, job search courses, and administration of UBs. *Activation* measures provide incentives for the unemployed to increase job finding either directly through benefit sanctions or through mandatory participation in training or subsidized employment. Key examples of activation programs are requirements that unemployed individuals attend intensive interviews with employment counselors, apply for job vacancies as directed by employment counselors, independently search for job vacancies and apply for jobs, accept offers of suitable work, participate in the formulation of an individual action plan, and attend training or job creation programs. If unemployed workers are unwilling to participate in the activation programs, they may lose their benefits permanently or temporarily (in the case of benefit sanctions). Some activation programs are *workfare* in the sense that they do not deliver further services except for keeping the unemployed busy. The main motivation for workfare schemes is that they enable a distinction between involuntarily and voluntarily unemployed persons. In other words, they allow the administration to enforce a *work test* assessing the actual willingness to work of the individual. Most OECD countries' activation strategies in principle aim not to use workfare: all programs are intended to function as employment services (OECD 2005b).

ALMPs may reduce mismatch in the labor market; promote more active search behavior on the part of jobseekers; and function as screening, because they substitute for regular work experience to help reduce employer uncertainty about the employability of job applicants. Placements in labor market programs may provide a work test as an alternative to eligibility for UBs since some of those who are not genuinely interested in work will prefer to lose registration rather than participate in a program. An adverse side effect of ALMPs is that workers are locked into training and job creation programs: because of their participation, they reduce their search intensity.

12.1 Measures and Cross-Country Comparisons

ALMPs are often but not always expensive. Depending on the amount of money, there may be few workers in expensive programs or many workers in cheap ones. Therefore, to indicate the importance of ALMPs at a country level, two measures are used. First, the number of workers participating in ALMPs as a share of the labor force; second, the amount of money spent on ALMPs as a percentage of GDP.

There are large cross-country differences in the share of the labor force participating in ALMPs, ranging from a low of 0.2 percent in the United Kingdom to a high of 12.8 percent in Spain in 2010. As shown in table 12.1, expenditures on ALMPs measured as a percentage of GDP differ greatly across countries.

Whereas Mexico only spends 0.01 percent of GDP on labor market training, Finland spends 0.53 percent. While Korea spends 0.01 percent of GDP on public employment services and countries like Italy, Luxembourg, and the United States devote little more to public employment services, Denmark and the Netherlands spend more than 0.40 percent of GDP on such services. With respect to expenditures on subsidized jobs, the differences between countries are also quite large. Italy, Mexico, New Zealand, the United States, and the United Kingdom spend 0.01 percent or less of GDP on subsidized jobs, while Belgium and Hungary spend more than 0.30 percent of GDP on this ALMP.

Finally, table 12.1 provides an overview of sanction rates (expressed as a percentage of the stock of UB claimants) for some OECD countries. The sanctions refer to behavior during benefit periods.[1] The sanction rates range from very low in Belgium, Japan, Sweden, and New Zealand to quite large in the Netherlands

---

1. Other sanctions may concern a lack of effort to prevent job loss (voluntary unemployment). In terms of the flow of initial benefit claims, these sanctions range from 3.4 percent in Finland to 13.5 percent in the United States. See Grubb (2000) for details on the system of benefit sanctions in various countries.

TABLE 12.1 ALMPs: Participation, public expenditures, and sanction rates

Country	Labor force involved (%)	ALMP Public expenditures (percentage of GDP)					Sanction rates (%)
		Total	Training	PES	Job creation	Other	
Australia	1.7	0.32	0.03	0.17	0.03	0.09	3.30
Austria	3.9	0.84	0.52	0.18	0.04	0.10	—
Belgium	11.9	1.47	0.16	0.22	0.36	0.73	0.80
Canada	1.3	0.31	0.13	0.14	0.02	0.02	6.10
Czech Republic	1.1	0.32	0.04	0.11	0.04	0.13	—
Denmark	6.5	1.91	0.42	0.51	0.00	0.98	2.10
Finland	4.0	1.05	0.53	0.18	0.09	0.25	10.20
France	5.8	1.13	0.38	0.30	0.22	0.23	—
Germany	3.6	0.95	0.31	0.38	0.05	0.21	1.10
Greece	1.8	0.23	0.02	—	0.00	0.21	—
Hungary	4.0	0.62	0.05	0.09	0.39	0.09	—
Ireland	4.9	0.97	0.46	0.18	0.26	0.07	—
Italy	5.1	0.46	0.18	0.11	0.01	0.16	—
Japan	—	0.27	0.07	0.05	0.05	0.10	0.02
Korea	—	0.41	0.07	0.01	0.28	0.05	—
Luxembourg	8.0	0.55	0.04	0.05	0.13	0.33	—
Mexico	—	0.02	0.01	0.00	0.00	0.01	—
Netherlands	4.5	1.22	0.13	0.43	0.17	0.49	36.00
New Zealand	2.1	0.34	0.14	0.12	0.01	0.07	0.40
Norway	2.4	0.50	0.22	—	0.04	0.24	7.30
Poland	4.0	0.69	0.04	0.09	0.04	0.52	—
Portugal	3.6	0.72	0.40	0.14	0.05	0.13	—
Slovak Republic	3.8	0.33	0.01	0.10	0.01	0.21	—
Spain	12.8	0.90	0.20	0.17	0.10	0.43	—
Sweden	3.1	1.14	0.09	0.34	0.00	0.71	0.60
Switzerland	1.5	0.44	0.22	0.13	0.00	0.09	38.50
United Kingdom	0.2	—	—	—	—	0.00	5.50
United States	—	0.13	0.04	0.04	0.01	0.04	35.40

Sources: OECD Online Statistics, 2012, for data on ALMP participants and expenditure; Boone and van Ours (2009), Grubb (2000) for data on sanction rates.

Notes: Active labor market expenditures are for 2010 (2009 for the United Kingdom); sanctions and benefit refusals for behavior during benefit periods are as a percentage of the average stock of benefit claimants, 1997–1998. The numbers refer to sanctions for labor market behavior conditions (not to administrative infractions). — = not available; PES = public employment service.

and Switzerland. The Swedish system is sometimes considered to be one that puts pressure on the unemployed—including possible denial of benefits—both to look for work and to accept suitable job offers. Nevertheless, Björklund and Holmlund (1991) report that yearly benefit denials amount to no more than approximately 1–2 percent of all those who receive unemployment compensation during a year, and this rate has recently been falling. Thus, whereas the Swedish system is known for its ALMP, in terms of benefit sanctions it is the least strict of all the OECD countries represented in table 12.1. In principle, there are two reasons observed sanction rates in a country are low. First, it may be that sanctions are seldom imposed because the system is lax and not credible. Second, a low sanction rate can be

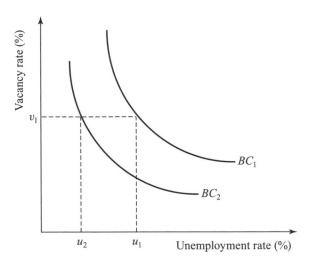

FIGURE 12.1 The Beveridge curve

due to the (equilibrium) reaction by workers to comply with the search guidelines: as sanctions are a deterrent to opportunistic behavior, optimal sanctions should never be applied, in line with the well-known Becker theory of optimal deterrence (Becker 1968). In the case of Sweden, there are indications that the first reason is the cause. Since the sanction is a 100 percent reduction in the UB, monitors are very reluctant to impose this sanction (see Björklund and Holmlund 1991 for details).

12.2 Theory

Figure 12.1 illustrates how ALMPs might affect the functioning of a labor market using the well-known Beveridge curve (see box 12.1), the empirical relationship between unemployment rates and vacancy rates (unfilled vacancies as a percentage of the labor force). Curve BC_1 in figure 12.1 slopes downward, because in a boom there are many vacancies and few unemployed, while in a slump there are many unemployed and few vacancies. As an economy experiences cyclical fluctuations, the unemployment-vacancy combination moves up and down the curve BC_1. At a particular moment it may be that the labor market has an unemployment rate of u_1 and a vacancy rate of v_1. The exact location of the Beveridge curve depends on how efficient the labor market is. ALMPs may improve the efficiency of the labor market, causing an inward shift of the Beveridge curve, for example from BC_1 to BC_2. If that is the case, conditional on the vacancy rate v_1, the unemployment rate will go down from u_1 to u_2.

BOX 12.1   *The Beveridge Curve and the Matching Function*

In many labor markets there appears to be an inverse relationship between unemployment rates and vacancy rates. The graphical representation of this relationship is named the Beveridge curve after William Beveridge (1879–1963), a British economist who was the first to note this empirical regularity (in 1944).

He explained this relationship as due to mismatch between vacancies and the unemployed, ongoing reallocation of workers across industries, cyclical effects, and measurement errors. Later, theoretical foundations for the Beveridge curve were provided in which the labor market is characterized by frictions delaying and making costly the matching of jobseekers and vacancies. Through this matching process vacancies are filled and unemployed workers find jobs. The process may be described by an *aggregate matching function* (Pissarides 1979; Blanchard and Diamond 1994):

$$m = A(U)^{1-\alpha} V^{\alpha}, \tag{12.1}$$

where m is the number of matches per time period, U (V) is the number of unemployed workers (vacancies) at the beginning of that time period, A represents the efficiency of the matching process, and α is usually assumed to be equal to 0.5. The statistical foundations of the matching function are discussed in technical annex 12.9.1. Clearly $m = 0$ if either the stock of unemployed or the stock of vacancies is zero. Moreover, unemployment outflows increase with U and V, although at a decreasing rate. In a dynamic labor market individuals change positions frequently. Not only do unemployed workers find jobs, but also many employed workers lose their jobs, because firms reduce their workforce temporarily or permanently. The reallocation of labor across different firms causes a regular flow of workers into and out of unemployment. Often the flow of workers from employment to unemployment is assumed to be a constant fraction of total employment:

$$F_{in}^{u} = \delta L, \tag{12.2}$$

where F_{in}^{u} is the inflow into unemployment, δ is the job separation rate, and L is the number of employed workers. In a steady state labor market there are constant stocks of unemployed workers and vacancies; the inflow into unemployment F_{in}^{u} equals the outflow from unemployment m, and therefore

$$\delta L = AU^{1-\alpha} V^{\alpha}, \tag{12.3}$$

or

$$\frac{\delta}{A} = \left(\frac{U}{L}\right)^{1-\alpha} \left(\frac{V}{L}\right)^{\alpha} \approx u^{1-\alpha} v^{\alpha}, \tag{12.4}$$

where u is the unemployment rate and v is the vacancy rate. If δ and A are constant, there is a stable hyperbolic relationship between the unemployment rate and the vacancy rate: the Beveridge curve, as depicted in figure 12.1. If the matching process becomes more efficient, for example, through ALMPs, the parameter A increases and the Beveridge curve shifts toward the origin.

Boone and van Ours (2009) present a theoretical search-matching model in which they distinguish three types of ALMPs: training of unemployed workers, subsidized employment, and public employment services. They model training as a subsidy to training costs of unemployed workers. The idea is that placement workers help unemployed workers find the most suitable training for them so that they do not waste time and effort enrolling in less effective courses. Furthermore, the government sometimes creates courses that are directly relevant to targeted groups of the unemployed. This is less costly for the unemployed than doing bits and pieces from different courses, one of which is targeted at them. The effect of employment services is modeled as a subsidy to search costs of workers. Here the placement workers help filter all vacancy information so that only the vacancies most relevant for an unemployed worker are considered. This reduces the search cost for the unemployed. Finally, subsidized employment is modeled as a subsidy to the value of the match to low-productivity jobs. In the model of Boone and van Ours there are two channels through which ALMPs can potentially reduce unemployment. First, the job-finding rate may be increased. Second, through training the unemployed can get better jobs (with higher wages and lower job destruction rates). If ALMPs cause more unemployed workers to end up in high-skilled jobs, this reduces unemployment by decreasing the flow from employment to unemployment. It turns out that the effects of ALMPs on the job-finding rate are theoretically ambiguous. However, the mechanism that associates the quality of the job with the flow from employment to unemployment can discriminate among the different ALMPs. Boone and van Ours (2009) show that training may do very well in reducing unemployment, while subsidized jobs and public employment services may not be as effective in reducing unemployment. They also show that there may be an interaction effect between UBs and training: training is more effective if UBs are more generous, so that the two policies are self-reinforcing in favoring the take-up of higher quality jobs.[2]

Boone and van Ours (2006) present a theoretical framework to analyze the impact of benefit sanctions, an activation measure to increase job-finding rates of recipients of UBs. They present a search-matching model in which benefit sanctions affect the intensity with which unemployed workers search for a job. Benefit sanctions may affect unemployment duration through two channels: the first operates ex post and the second ex ante. Benefit sanctions will increase the search intensity of the sanctioned because of the reduction in the value of being unemployed. This mechanism is the *ex post effect:* an actual benefit reduction stimulates a worker's search efforts. Furthermore, those not sanctioned may also increase search intensity because of stricter enforcement of job search requirements. This second effect is the *ex ante effect:* the risk of being sanctioned also influences the search behavior of unemployed workers who have not been sanctioned. The two effects are formally derived in technical annex 12.9.2.

12.3 Empirical Evidence

Figure 12.2 provides empirical examples of the Beveridge curves for Germany, Norway, Sweden, and the United Kingdom.[3] In each of these countries the rela-

2. See Bassanini (2006) for similar results.
3. Many OECD countries do not have long series of vacancy data, which makes it difficult to generate Beveridge curves for more than a few countries.

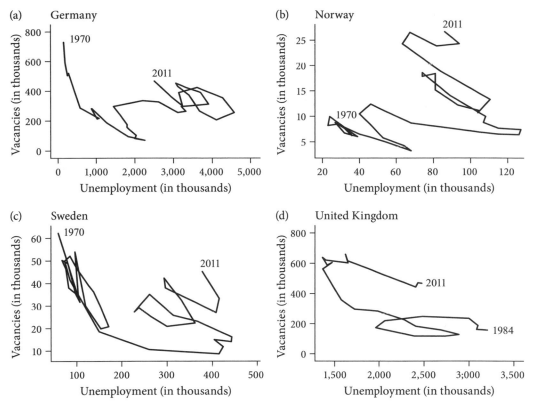

FIGURE 12.2 The Beveridge curve in four countries: (a) Germany; (b) Norway; (c) Sweden; (d) the United Kingdom.

Source: OECD Labor Force Statistics.

tionship between unemployment and vacancies has a hyperbolic curvature. There are also fluctuations and shifts outward of the curve.

A large empirical literature estimates the relationship between, on the one hand, unemployment and unfilled vacancies, and, on the other hand, outflows from unemployment. This relationship underpins the Beveridge curve, that is, the aggregate matching function (see Petrongolo and Pissarides 2001). This literature confirms that unemployment outflows are increasing in both the stock of vacancies and the stock of unemployment, and both affect exits from unemployment at a decreasing rate. However, the relationship is found to be unstable over time, as if the technological parameter A described in box 12.1 were shifting in and out the matching function (and the Beveridge curve) over time. Boeri and Burda (1996) looked into determinants of this shifter of the matching function and found that it was indeed associated with the scale of ALMPs.

However, it is difficult to draw conclusions on the effectiveness of ALMPs on the basis of shifts in the Beveridge curve, which is, after all, an equilibrium condition, potentially capturing both changes in vacancy formation and job search, labor demand and labor supply. Moreover, not only are there direct effects of ALMPs, but there are also indirect effects that can be quite important (Calmfors 1994). First, there are *displacement effects,* because jobs created by one program can replace other jobs. Second, there are *deadweight effects,* because labor market programs subsidize hiring that would have occurred anyway in the absence of the program. Third, there are *substitution effects,* because jobs created for a certain category of workers replace jobs for other categories as wage relativities change. Finally, there are *fiscal substitution effects* (taxes required to finance the programs) on the behavior of everyone in society. Thus, even if ALMPs were found to increase outflows from unemployment to jobs, this would not necessarily imply an improvement in labor market conditions.

An effective public employment service can not only increase the job-finding rate but also the quality of matches. The role played by the public employment service in increasing the quality of job matches can be assessed by comparing wage premiums (or penalties) from finding jobs through formal channels versus through personal contacts. This may explain why research in this field points to a wide dispersion of results: some countries display a wage premium for jobs obtained via formal channels, while other countries display a penalty. Indeed, reforms improving the effectiveness of formal job intermediation are found to increase the premium of formal versus personal job-finding channels (Pellizzari 2010).

12.3.1 Experimental Studies

ALMPs are an ongoing area of experimentation. Quite naturally then, a large empirical literature has developed that exploits an experimental setup to address the effectiveness of ALMPs. The problem with these experiments is their external validity, that is, whether their conclusions are sufficiently general or hold only in the specific institutional context where the experiment was carried out. However, the results are very interesting in that they highlight a number of issues that may arise in the implementation of ALMPs and are useful in understanding what works and what does not.

Gorter and Kalb (1996) analyze the effects of intensive counseling and monitoring. By way of experiment, in seven employment offices in the Netherlands some unemployed workers were exposed to more intensive counseling and monitoring than others who got the usual treatment. The unemployed themselves were unaware of being part of the experiment. The allocation to more intensive counseling and monitoring was done randomly and at the start of the unemployment spell; the only way out of the experiment was through finding a job. Both the unemployed in the treatment group and in the control group had monthly meetings with staff of the employment office. The control group had traditional meetings in which progress in finding a job was discussed and occasionally the information provided by the unemployed worker was checked. The treatment group had longer meetings, because the applications were more thoroughly discussed and more advice was given on potentially suitable vacant jobs and direction of search. Furthermore, the employment office staff spent more time checking information given by the unemployed. People who did not make sufficient applications or listed false applications to disguise their lack of search effort had a larger probability of being detected and penalized accordingly. Gorter and Kalb find that the treatment group had a higher application rate and a higher job-finding rate with a somewhat smaller matching probability—for the unemployed who previously had a permanent job, the application rate increased by 20 percent, while the job-finding rate increased by 15 percent. Thus, more intense counseling and monitoring stimulated unemployed workers to make more applications for jobs. Because of this, the job-finding rate increased, which shows that the additional applications were not fake applications.

Dolton and O'Neill (1996) present an analysis of the British Restart program, which consisted of a series of compulsory interviews every six months for unemployed workers, starting after they had been registered as unemployed for six months. During this mandatory interview the counselor assessed the recent unemployment history of the worker, offered advice on search behavior and training courses, and sometimes initiated direct contact with employers. Unemployed workers were randomly assigned to the treatment group or the control group, whose members were eligible for benefits but did not have to attend the first interview. Those who were assigned to the treatment group were faced with the possibility of having their benefits reduced if they did not attend the Restart interview or if they were considered to be making insufficient effort to find a job. Dolton and O'Neill find that the Restart interviews significantly decreased unemployment durations. Some individuals left the unemployment registers without having found a job; this was common among women and other groups "who are most likely not to be genuinely available for work." This type of outflow from unemployment was particularly high around the timing of the first Restart interview, which indicates a threat effect. However, measured over 18 months, exits to a job were also significantly different for the treatment and the control groups. In a follow-up article Dolton and O'Neill (2002) investigate the long-run effects of the Restart program and find that the Restart interviews reduced the male unemployment rate five years later by 6 percentage points compared with a control group for whom participation in the first interview took place six months later. Klepinger et al. (2002), who study the effects of alternative work search requirements in Maryland, find that imposing additional search requirements speeds up the job-finding process (see box 12.2 for details).

ALMPs in the United States

BOX 12.2

Daniel Klepinger, Terry Johnson, and Jutta Joesch present the results of an experimental evaluation of alternative work-search requirements imposed on UB recipients in Maryland. Assignment to control and treatment groups was random, based on Social Security numbers. The control group of unemployed workers had the standard obligation to contact two employers per week and report those contacts to remain eligible for UB payments. The Maryland experiment distinguished four treatment groups, who were informed about their duties within one week after registing for a benefit claim. The first group had to make four employer contacts per week, the second group was informed that they had to search actively without specifying the number of contacts they had to make, and the third group had to attend a four-day job-search workshop lasting 16 hours early in the unemployment spell. The fourth group was informed that their claimed employer contacts would be verified. As discussed in the main text, there are two effects of increased work search requirements. First, the treatment effect: the unemployed may make more job contacts, which increases the job-finding rate. Second, the threat effect: the additional requirements raise the nonmonetary costs of remaining unemployed, which leads to more intense job search or a reduction in reservation wages (or both). Comparing the four groups allows a distinction between the two effects. The results for various outcome measures in the first year after the start of the unemployment spell are as follows:

| | | Treatment group effect | | | |
Outcome measure	Control group	Additional contacts	No reporting of contacts	Workshop	Verify contacts
Total UI benefits paid ($)	2,085	−116*	34	−75*	−113*
Weeks of benefits	11.9	−0.7*	0.4*	−0.6*	−0.9*
Exhausted benefits (%)	28.3	−2.5*	1.5*	−1.1	−2.8*
Percentage worked	80.0	1.1	0.8	−0.8	1.3
Earnings ($)	8,407	54	347*	−163	124

Note: * means significantly different from the control group at the 5 percent level.

The nonmonetary costs of imposing additional search requirements are important for the duration of benefit claims. Increasing the required weekly number of employer contacts from two to four and indicating that employer contacts would be verified reduced the duration of unemployment benefit spells by almost a week, which is a substantial effect, since the average unemployment benefit duration was about 12 weeks. Eliminating a specific number of required contacts increased UB duration. Finally, the obligation to attend a job search workshop also reduced UB duration. This was at least partly because many unemployed workers left unemployment shortly before their search workshop was planned. Effects on the quality of post-unemployment jobs in terms of employment and earnings were small or absent.

Source: Klepinger et al. (2002).

A large literature has developed recently on *profiling,* that is, involvement in employment and training services of claimants with long *predicted* unemployment spells or high predicted probabilities of UB exhaustion at relatively early stages of their unemployment spells. Profiling seems to be rather effective for specific categories of workers, such as women re-entering the labor force, while it is less so for others. Box 12.3 summarizes the main results of an experiment carried out in Kentucky on profiling and re-employment services.

Dan Black, Jeffrey Smith, Marsh Berger, and Brett Noel present an analysis of a nat-ural experiment on profiling UI claimants to provide mandatory re-employment services in Kentucky. Unemployed workers were ranked in 20 categories according to a profiling score based on the expected unemployment duration. The expected duration was estimated on the basis not only of individual characteristics but also of variables capturing local labor market conditions. Local budgets available for re-employment services were allocated to the unemployed according to profil-ing scores, starting with the highest score, that is, the longest expected duration. In case there was insufficient funding for all the unemployed and the marginal group could not be covered completely either, there was a random allocation of re-employment services to the unemployed in the marginal group. The figure below provides the timeline of the treatment.

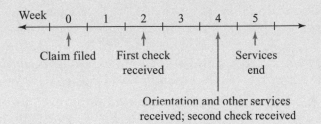

The first UB payment is received in week two of the spell. After this first check but before the second—that is, in week three or four—treated individuals receive a letter stating the following:

> You have been identified as a dislocated worker and selected under the UI Claimant Profiling Program to receive job search assistance services. You are obligated under the law to participate. Failure to report or participate in re-employment services without justifiable cause may result in denial of your unemployment insurance benefits.

Within ten working days following notification of the program, claimants selected for treatment report to a local office for an orientation, where they learn about the program and complete a questionnaire. Using this information, Employment Ser-vices staff assesses the claimants and then refers them to specific services, such as assisted job search, employment counseling, job-search workshops, and retrain-ing programs. Claimants need to contact the UI office in week three or four to verify their continuing eligibility and then to receive the second check. Thus, the deterrent effect exerted by the letters, and the mandatory re-employment services they imply, should be observed between weeks two and four. By comparing the treated with the nontreated, the authors find that the re-employment services in-duced workers to leave unemployment more quickly; those who left unemploy-ment quickly did not earn lower wages, which suggests that there is "no long-term harm from the treatment provided by the program." The main action caused by the mandatory re-employment services was at the beginning of the unemployment spell. The unemployed workers who were notified of their obligations to attend the re-employment service program left unemployment quickly to avoid having to enter the program. In other words, the threat effect was driving the results. Apparently, many unemployed workers consider the re-employment service programs sanctions that they prefer to avoid. The authors also evaluated profiling as an allocation mechanism, by assessing whether it targeted the treatment to those for whom it has the largest impact. Their conclusions are not very encouraging in this respect, as they state that "the evidence calls into question the wisdom of using expected UI spell duration as means of allocating treatment."

Source: Black et al. (2003).

Van den Berg and van der Klaauw (2006) analyze the outcome of a small-scale experiment on counseling and monitoring in the Netherlands. They distinguish between two types of job search: formal and informal. *Formal* job search is conducted through personnel advertisements and public employment offices. *Informal* job search refers to direct contacts with employers and search through friends, relatives, or employed workers. They argue that counseling and monitoring only affects formal job search. Monitoring leads to a substitution of effort from informal to formal search, which reduces the effectiveness of monitoring. At the time of the experiment in the Netherlands, at the start of the unemployment spell unemployed workers were classified into one of four types on the basis of objective characteristics and subjective evaluation. Types 2, 3, and 4 are offered assistance to find a job, while type 1 individuals are expected to have sufficient skills to find a job without assistance. The experiment was limited to type 1 unemployed, who were randomly assigned to a treatment group or a control group. The control group had to report on search activities every week. In addition to this requirement the treatment group had regular meetings with counselors, during which initially quality of application letters and résumés were examined and a plan was made, while during follow-up meetings plans from previous meetings were evaluated and planning for the next period was done. Unemployed workers who did not comply could be punished with a benefit sanction (a reduction of UBs by 10 percent for two months). In their baseline estimate van den Berg and van der Klaauw find no significant treatment effect; that is, counseling and monitoring do not help the unemployed find a job more quickly. However, they also find that counseling and monitoring affect the type of search: unemployed workers who are subject to counseling and monitoring shift their search from informal to formal channels. Van den Berg and van der Klaauw conclude that focusing monitoring on the unemployed with less favorable characteristics may make more sense, because these individuals have less scope for substituting informal for formal search channels. Finally, Graversen and van Ours (2008) show that mandatory programs help Danish unemployed workers find a job more quickly (see box 12.4 for details).

BOX 12.4

Brian Graversen and Jan van Ours analyze data from a Danish experiment that randomly assigned unemployed workers to control and treatment groups on the basis of their birth dates. The treatment group was confronted with mandatory activities, whereas the control group was not. The unemployed in the treatment group were informed by letter about their duties within one or two weeks after becoming unemployed. The letter gave a short description of the activities contained in the program. After five or six weeks of unemployment individuals had to participate in a job-search program that lasted two weeks. After the program individuals had to attend meetings once a week or once every second week. The purpose of the meetings was to assist individuals in their job search and to monitor job-search efforts. Individuals could also receive job offers mediated by the public employment service. Before individuals were unemployed for four months, they had to receive an offer to participate in an activation program with a duration of at least three months. Longer classroom training courses (with a duration of more than three months) could not be offered at this stage. Individuals who did not find a job after six or seven months had to participate in a longer meeting with a caseworker, and a new job plan was made. The job plan contained a description of the activities to improve the chances of finding a job. The services offered to the control group during the early stage of the unemployment period were much less intensive than those offered to the treatment group. Unemployed workers in the control group could voluntarily participate in some of these activities, but this did not happen frequently. Individuals in the control group typically would have to participate in an activation program after one year of unemployment. Graversen and van Ours find that even before the start of the job-search program the job-finding rate in the treatment group was higher than in the control group. The figure below presents the survival functions separately for the two groups.

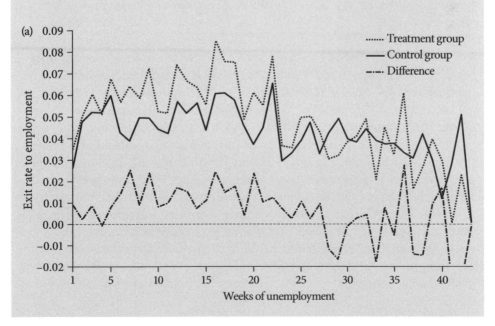

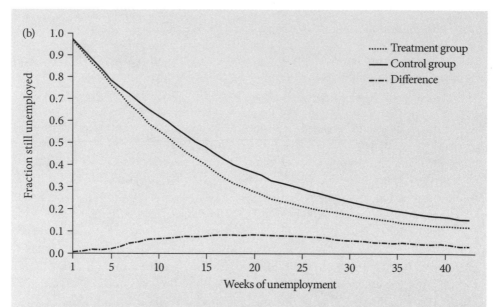

As shown, the treatment group left unemployment more quickly than did the control group. After three months 47 percent of the control group and 54 percent of the treatment group had left unemployment. After six months 28 percent of the control group was still unemployed, while only 21 percent of the treatment group was still unemployed. The difference between both survival functions increased up to 13 weeks of unemployment, stayed constant until 26 weeks, and declined after that. The figure also shows that the median unemployment duration for the control group was about 14 weeks, while for the treatment group it was 11.5 weeks. Clearly there is a substantial treatment effect.

Source: Graversen and van Ours (2008).

12.3.2 Nonexperimental Studies

Nonexperimental studies are based on cross-country comparisons or micro-oriented evaluation studies. Based on a review of experimental and nonexperimental studies, Card et al. (2010) conclude that "non-experimental evaluations are not significantly biased relative to the benchmark of an experimental design."

The most recent evaluation studies are not very optimistic about the benefits of many of these programs. Heckman et al. (1999) provide a detailed overview of microeconometric evaluation studies. They conclude that ALMPs have, at best, a modest impact on participants' labor market prospects. Furthermore, there is considerable heterogeneity in the impact of these programs, so that for some groups of workers the programs are more effective than for other groups. Card et al. (2010), analyzing 199 program estimates drawn from 97 studies carried out between 1995 and 2007, find that longer term evaluations are more favorable than short-term ones. As suggested by table 12.2, many programs exhibit insignificant or even negative impacts over one year and positive impacts over two to three years.

TABLE 12.2 Summary of estimated impacts of ALMPs

Impact estimate	Sample size	Percentage of estimates that are:		
		Significantly positive	Insignificant	Significantly negative
Short term	183	39.3	32.8	27.9
Medium term	108	50.0	39.8	10.2
Long term	50	54.0	40.0	6.0

Source: Card et al. (2010).

Note: Short term = 12 months; medium term = 24 months; long term = 36+ months.

Finally, when programs are implemented on a large scale, displacement and general equilibrium effects may be sizable. Thus, if they are not incorporated into a macro framework, micro treatment effect evaluations will provide poor guidance to public policy. Calmfors et al. (2001) conclude that the evidence on the effectiveness of Swedish ALMPs is rather disappointing. Labor market retraining, for example, has no or negative employment effects. Martin and Grubb (2001) draw similar conclusions in their overview of what works and what does not among ALMPs in OECD countries. They conclude that subsidies to employment and direct job creation have not been effective in helping the unemployed get permanent jobs.

If one can draw a general conclusion from the empirical studies based on micro data, it is that the effects of ALMPs on job-finding rates are rather small.[4] An important drawback of many ALMPs is that they encourage workers to reduce their search efforts rather than increase them, inducing the so-called *locking-in effect* (van Ours 2004). Other effects are important too. What is effective for an individual unemployed worker may not be effective in terms of the aggregate level of unemployment. One reason for this may be crowding out. If a training program brings an unemployed worker back to work more quickly at the expense of another unemployed worker finding a job more slowly, the training program is not very efficient. Another reason for the differences between individual and aggregate effects is that a training program may make workers more attractive for firms, which stimulates job creation. It may also be that a training program induces a better match between a worker and a job. In that case job tenure will increase, causing a reduction of unemployment through a reduced inflow into unemployment.

Activation measures seem to be more effective than training programs or employment subsidies. From recent micro studies on the effect of benefit sanctions in the Dutch labor market, we know that a reduction of UBs may have a substantial

4. Kluve and Schmidt (2002) and Kluve (2010) present overviews of many evaluation studies concerning ALMPs in Europe. They conclude that providing job-search assistance and counseling and monitoring, accompanied by appropriate sanctions for noncompliance, are especially effective, and these methods are often quite cost-effective, because they are rather inexpensive.

effect on the outflow from unemployment to jobs. Abbring et al. (2005) study the effect of financial incentives by comparing the unemployment durations of individuals who faced a benefit reduction with those of similar individuals who had not been penalized. In the Netherlands people who receive UBs have their benefits reduced if they do not follow the rules related to the benefits. According to the UB law, an unemployed worker has three obligations that must be met to be entitled to UBs. First, the worker has to prevent unnecessary job loss. Second, the worker has to take actions to prevent staying unemployed (search for a job and accept appropriate job offers, register as a job searcher at the public employment office, participate in education and training, etc.). Third, the worker has to keep the administrative organization informed about everything that is relevant to the payment of the UB. Related to these obligations are four categories of infringements for which workers can have benefit sanctions imposed: (1) blameworthy unemployment after dismissal, (2) lack of effort to find a job (e.g., search intensity too low, declining job offers), (3) administrative infringements (reporting too late), and (4) other infringements (e.g., fraud, inaccurate information). The sanction is temporary or permanent (full or partial) reduction of the benefit level. In practice, the temporary partial reduction of the benefits ranged from 5 percent for 4 weeks to 25–30 percent for 13 weeks. Abbring et al. (2005) analyze how benefit sanctions affect the transition out of unemployment and find that re-employment rates are significantly and substantially raised by imposition of a sanction of from 58 to 67 percent.

Van den Berg et al. (2004) perform a similar analysis on the effects of sanctions on the behavior of Dutch recipients of unemployment assistance in the city of Rotterdam. A benefit sanction raises the transition rate from welfare to work substantially: the job-finding rate more than doubles. A straightforward comparison between individuals who got a benefit sanction imposed and those who did not is incorrect. If this is done, the selectivity of the imposition of a sanction (workers with low motivation who have a low job-finding rate anyway are more likely to get penalized) is not taken into account. Then the estimated sanction effect is seriously underestimated. Although the benefit sanction itself is temporary, the effects turn out to be long-lasting. Even after the sanction period expires, the transition rate from welfare to work is higher than before the sanction was imposed.

Similar effects of benefit sanctions are found for the Swiss labor market. From an analysis of Swiss data on benefit sanctions, Lalive et al. (2005) conclude that imposing a benefit sanction reduces unemployment duration by roughly three weeks. They also find evidence of the existence of an ex ante effect. Arni et al. (2013) evaluate the effects of sanctions on post-unemployment outcomes. They find that warnings of a PBD do not affect subsequent job stability, whereas they reduce post-unemployment earnings.

12.4 Policy Issues

The 1994 OECD *Jobs Study* recommended that governments strengthen the emphasis on ALMPs and reinforce their effectiveness. In the reassessment of the jobs strategy, OECD (2006b) concludes "that well-designed programs can have a positive impact ... but that many existing programs have failed to do so" (OECD 2006b, p. 72). Nevertheless, the same OECD report concludes that "enough successful programs have been documented to confirm that an appropriate mix of properly designed ALMPs can reduce unemployment by improving the efficiency of the job-matching process and by enhancing the work experience and skills of those who take part in them" (OECD 2006b, p. 74). This section discusses the main policy issues concerning employment services and activation policies.

12.4.1 Do We Need Public Employment Services?

Employment services are usually provided by government agencies, although there are also private employment services. Public services are provided to unemployed workers to assist them in finding jobs. Services range from assistance in locating relevant vacancies and help in job finding to training programs that update the skills of the unemployed worker. To benefit from market mechanisms, some countries set up quasi-market arrangements for the provision of public employment services and other ALMPs. The OECD (2005b) argues that to implement a quasi-market, public employment services have to separate the public authority and multiple employment service providers. The public authority is responsible for the determination of individual eligibility for benefits and services, the assignment of the unemployed to specific service providers, and measurement of the outcome of the service provision. The local employment service providers can choose their own strategies aimed at bringing their unemployed clients back to work. The main idea is that through the survival of the fittest, successful strategies will persist, even when it is difficult to identify why these strategies are successful. In public employment services the issue of profiling unemployed workers is important. For an optimal allocation of resources, those unemployed workers with longer expected durations of benefit receipt should receive more or different employment services. There is room for improvement in the functioning of public employment services with regard to profiling of unemployed workers. The results depend sensitively on the quality of caseworkers. For instance, Lechner and Smith (2007) show that Swiss caseworkers do not do better in their profiling than does random assignment, while Swedish caseworkers contribute considerably to the success of ALMPs.

12.4.2 Do We Need Activation Policies?

Activation policies put requirements and obligations on UB recipients, such as the obligations to attend intensive interviews with employment counselors, search actively for a new job, and accept job offers. Activation programs differ from public employment services because participation is obligatory for unemployed workers who want to remain entitled to UBs. Therefore, activation policies make it less attractive for unemployed workers to collect benefits. This may affect both the inflow of benefit recipients (some unemployed workers will not apply for benefits) and the outflow of benefit recipients (either because the unemployed find jobs or because they drop their benefit claims). Workfare programs provide unemployed workers with temporary jobs in exchange for the payment of UBs, but they do not provide additional services. A workfare program may act as a screening device but does not encourage the unemployed worker to search more intensively. Benefit sanctions imply temporary or permanent reductions of UBs to increase the difference between benefits and post-unemployment wages. This will stimulate job-search activities. Instead of sticks (e.g., benefit sanctions), carrots (e.g., wage subsidies or ECI offered to unemployed individuals taking up relatively low-paid jobs) may be used to make it more attractive for workers to search for a job. Both activation and ECI widen the gap between wages and the reservation wage. The former increase the net wage, while the latter reduce the reservation wage.

Overall, the evidence in favor of activation programs is rather strong. One may question the role of these policies during recessions, as the moral hazard problems related to UB receipt are likely to be less serious when there is a shortage of jobs.

12.5 Interactions with Other Institutions

The above discussion suggests that ALMPs are part of a comprehensive strategy to help transitions from unemployment or inactivity to work and to smooth transitions from job to job. This role creates a strong connection between ALMPs, payroll tax schemes, and in-work benefits (see chapter 13).

ALMPs have long been defined in opposition to "passive" income support policies for the unemployed. However, as discussed in this chapter and in chapter 11, a key problem associated with the provision of UBs relates to disincentives to job search because of imperfect monitoring of the search efforts of UB recipients. ALMPs partly reduce these informational asymmetries. In particular, the offer of slots in some ALMP (subsidized jobs, training schemes, or public works) can be used as a device to enforce work tests, eliciting whether the UB recipient is actually willing to work and is actively seeking employment. Benefit sanctions can also be used as a deterrent to discourage opportunistic behavior by UB recipients (Pavoni and Violante 2007).

To the extent that ALMPs reduce moral hazard associated with the provision of UBs, they help reduce the efficiency costs of UI, improving the trade-off between insurance and unemployment duration that was discussed in chapter 11. Hence, ceteris paribus, one would expect to observe a positive cross-sectional correlation between the generosity of UBs and the investment made by individual countries in policies and infrastructures (e.g., a public employment service) that encourage UB recipients to go back to work.

Figure 12.3 displays expenditure on ALMPs as a fraction of GDP versus the summary measure of UB generosity (adjusted by the fraction of unemployed workers receiving the benefits). The two institutions seem to be positively correlated across countries, consistent with the preceding theoretical insights.

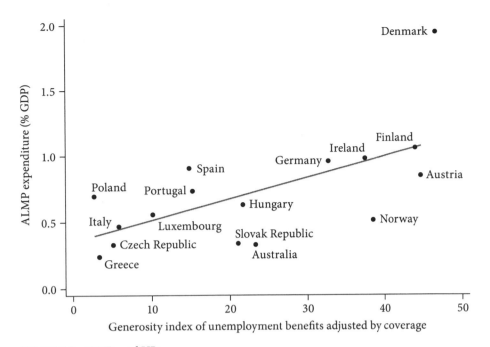

FIGURE 12.3 ALMPs and UBs

Sources: OECD for the indicators and ECHP for the coverage.

Notes: The vertical axis displays expenditure on ALMPs as a fraction of the GDP; the horizontal axis displays the OECD summary measure of UB generosity (discussed in chapter 11) multiplied by the fraction of unemployed workers receiving the benefits. See tables 12.1 and 11.3.

12.6 Why Do ALMPs Exist?

ALMPs exist because UBs provide disincentives for unemployed workers to find jobs. These disincentives may lead to a number of traps (OECD 2005b). The *unemployment trap* arises because benefits paid to unemployed workers and their families are high relative to net income from work. This may discourage job search and put upward pressure on wages (see also chapter 11 on UBs). The *inactivity trap* is similar to the unemployment trap but concerns individuals of working age who are not receiving UBs. Often, income-related benefits will be lost upon taking paid work, reducing the net gains from work. The *poverty trap* is also called the *low-wage trap*, because it discourages those already in low-paid work from increasing working hours or moving into higher paid employment. An increase in gross earnings fails to translate into an increase in net income because of the withdrawal of income-tested benefits. Countries with a relatively generous UB system also spend much on ALMPs. The latter induces those who are voluntarily unemployed to find a job more quickly than they otherwise would have. However, even without the existence of UBs, ALMPs can improve the efficiency of the labor market. Unemployed workers who stay unemployed too long may lose some or all of their skills. Involuntarily unemployed workers who want to invest in themselves to acquire the skills necessary to find a job will not always find it easy to finance this investment. Capital market imperfections provide a justification for public training of unemployed adults and for start-up loans. In all these cases, governments may step in and provide financial support.

12.7 Suggestions for Further Reading

Calmfors (1994) presents a theoretical framework to understand how ALMPs operate. Heckman et al. (1999) present a detailed discussion of the measurement of the effectiveness of ALMPs. Kluve and Schmidt (2002) provide a nice overview of many studies exploring the effectiveness of ALMPs. Various years of the OECD *Employment Outlook* contain overviews and discussions of ALMP topics. Finally, Card et al. (2010) carry out a meta-analysis (contrasting and combining results from studies carried out between 1995 and 2007) of ALMPs.

12.8 Review Questions and Exercises

1. Why might one criticize subsidized jobs as a policy instrument to bring the unemployed back to work?

2. Why is training possibly more effective in reducing unemployment than are subsidized jobs or public employment services?

3. Through what mechanisms do benefit sanctions affect unemployment?

4. How do ALMPs affect the Beveridge curve?

5. In what way does the lump-of-labor fallacy affect the discussion concerning the effectiveness of ALMPs?

6. How do intensive interviews with employment counselors affect the behavior of unemployed workers?

7. What does profiling mean, and what is known about its effectiveness in reducing unemployment duration?

8. What is the relationship between the unemployment trap and upward pressure on wage levels?

9. Why would training be more effective in countries where UBs are high?

10. The main elements of a system of benefit sanctions are the monitoring intensity and the size of the penalty. Explain the different ways in which these two components affect the behavior of unemployed workers. Use the concepts of ex ante and ex post effects in your explanation.

11. Consider a matching function specified as $M = AU^{\alpha}V^{1-\alpha}$, in which M is the number of matches per time period, U is the stock of unemployed workers, V is the stock of vacancies, and A represents the efficiency of the matching process. The job separation rate is δ, and there is a constant labor force normalized to one for convenience.

    (a) Show that the Beveridge curve shifts outward if δ increases.

    (b) Show that if the government invests in increasing the match efficiency the Beveridge curve shifts inward.

12. (Advanced) Assume the following system of equations in a situation in which unemployed workers may be confronted by a benefit sanction:

$$\rho V_u = \max_{0 \leq s \leq 1} \left[b - \gamma(s) + \mu s(V_e - V_u) + \phi(1 - s)(V_s - V_u) \right], \qquad (12.5)$$

$$\rho V_s = \max_{0 \leq s \leq 1} \left[(1 - p_s)b - \gamma(s) + \mu s(V_e - V_s) \right], \qquad (12.6)$$

where ρ is the discount rate, V_u is the value of being unemployed, b is the level of benefits, s is the intensity of search, $\gamma(s) = \frac{1}{2}s^2$ represents the search cost function, μs is the job-finding rate, V_e is the value of being employed, V_s is the value of being unemployed after receiving a benefit sanction, $\phi(1 - s)$ is the monitoring intensity, p_s is the penalty, s_u is the search intensity before a benefit sanction is imposed, and s_s is the search intensity after a benefit sanction is imposed. Jobs are assumed to last forever.

(a) Interpret the two equations.

(b) How large is the ex ante effect of a benefit sanction?

(c) How large is the ex post effect of a benefit sanction?

(d) Under which conditions is $s_u > s_s$?

(e) Provide an intuition for these results.

13. (Advanced) Use the same system of equations as in the previous question. Show under which conditions:

(a) s_u increases with p_s.

(b) s_s increases with p_s.

(c) s_u increases with ϕ.

(d) s_s increases with ϕ.

12.9 Technical Annex: ALMP

12.9.1 The Statistical Foundations of the Matching Function

Consider an uncoordinated application process by workers to a given set of vacancies. Lack of coordination implies that even when the number of applicants is equal to the number of vacancies—as in a standard random placement of balls into urns (Petrongolo and Pissarides 2001)—some vacancies may receive more than one application and others may receive none. If a vacancy attracts more than one application, it is matched randomly to one of those. Each vacancy then receives an applicant with probability $(1/V)$, and conversely, the probability that the vacancy does receive that applicant is $(1 - 1/V)$. The probability that a vacancy does not receive *any* applications is then $(1 - 1/V)^U$, and the probability that it receives at least one is $1 - (1 - 1/V)^U$. Total matches occurring at any round of applications will be then $V[1 - (1 - 1/V)^U]$. For large V and U, a good approximation of $(1 - 1/V)^U$ is the exponential $e^{-U/V}$. Thus, total hirings M_1 are given by

$$M_1 = M(V, U) = V[1 - (1 - 1/V)^U] \simeq V(1 - e^{-U/V}). \qquad (12.7)$$

It is easy to check that this function has the desirable properties of the matching function discussed in box 12.1, that is:

1. $m(0, V) = 0$ and $m(U, 0) = 0$;
2. $\frac{\partial M}{\partial U} > 0$, $\frac{\partial M}{\partial V} > 0$; and
3. $m(\lambda U, \lambda V) = \lambda M$.

By fixing M_1, and allowing V and U to vary, one obtains a Beveridge curve.

Consider now that only a fraction, say γ, of the vacancies is advertised to jobseekers, who consequently only apply to a subset of positions. It follows that the matching function would be

$$M_2 \simeq \gamma V [1 - e^{-\gamma U/V}]. \tag{12.8}$$

Now a larger number of vacancies (and unemployed workers) will be needed to originate a given level of hirings with respect to M_1. In other words, the Beveridge curve shifts out.

ALMPs, such as a public employment service, make the labor market more transparent, increasing γ. Active policies may also increase search intensity among the unemployed, in which case they increase the number of referrals per any given stock of unemployed. In both cases, ALMPs increase the number of matches per any given V/U (or market tightness) ratio, inducing an inward shift of the Beveridge curve.

12.9.2 Activating Unemployed Workers

This technical annex shows how a system of benefit sanctions intended to activate unemployed workers can affect job-finding rates by influencing the job-search behavior of unemployed jobseekers (see, e.g., Boone and van Ours 2009; Boone et al. 2007). Unemployed workers are assumed to receive UBs b, where generally $b < w$, and w is the wage rate. Jobseekers pay a search cost $\gamma(s)$, which is increasing in search intensity s. In a model without benefit sanctions, the flow value of being unemployed equals the difference between UBs and the cost of search, plus the expected benefits from finding a job:

$$\rho V_u = \max_{0 \leq s \leq 1} \left[b - \gamma(s) + \mu s \left(V_e - V_u \right) \right], \tag{12.9}$$

where μs is the job-finding rate.

Activation measures are intended to overcome market failures arising from generous UBs and welfare benefit schemes. Activation can be introduced through UB sanctions, p_s while the monitoring rate is equal to ϕ. Because monitoring is imperfect, the probability of being sanctioned, conditional on being monitored, is $(1 - s)$. Then, assuming that each unemployed individual can receive only one sanction, we have that

$$\rho V_u = \max_{0 \le s \le 1} \left[b - \gamma(s) + \mu s (V_e - V_u) + \phi(1-s)(V_s - V_u) \right], \qquad (12.10)$$

$$\rho V_s = \max_{0 \le s \le 1} \left[(1 - p_s)b - \gamma(s) + \mu s (V_e - V_s) \right], \qquad (12.11)$$

where V_u and V_s are the values of unemployment for a nonsanctioned and a sanctioned worker, respectively. Thus, sanctions reduce the value of unemployment and increase search intensity. Now, optimal search intensity (denoted by an asterisk) requires that

$$\gamma'(s_u^*) = \mu \left(V_e - V_u \right) - \phi(V_s - V_u) \qquad (12.12)$$

$$\gamma'(s_s^*) = \mu \left(V_e - V_s \right). \qquad (12.13)$$

As γ is increasing in s and $V_s < V_u$, (12.12) tells us that a positive monitoring rate increases search effect of those unemployed workers who have not been sanctioned. This is the ex ante effect. Sanctions also increase search efforts of the sanctioned unemployed, because they increase the difference $(V_e - V_u)$. This is the ex post effect.

In words, the ex ante effect refers to the optimal search intensity of workers, which is higher than it would be if workers did not face the possibility of being sanctioned. The ex post effect refers to the effect on the search of having lower benefits once a sanction is imposed. For some systems of benefit sanctions, the ex ante effect turns out to be more important than the ex post effect, while for other systems the reverse is true. The comparison between the two depends on the difference between the job arrival rate for workers and the intensity of monitoring. With a low monitoring intensity, the possibility of suffering a sanction is small, and the job search will not be affected very much. The main effect is after the sanction is imposed. In this case the ex post effect dominates. With a high level of monitoring, the unemployed workers will try to reduce the sanction rate by increasing their search intensity. Then the ex ante effect dominates. It is even possible that the ex post effect is very small, which in micro research could lead to the erroneous conclusion that sanctions do not have an effect. They do, but the main effect is in the threat of a penalty, not in its imposition.

CHAPTER THIRTEEN **Payroll Taxes**

Historically, taxes emerged from seigneurial arrangements by which the king could obtain extraordinary revenues to meet unusual temporary conditions, such as wars. From these extraordinary revenues medieval taxation developed, which ultimately became the fiscal basis for government expenditures (Ames and Rapp 1977). Since then, the history of taxation is one of levies introduced to cope with extraordinary events, but the taxes survived well after these circumstances were no longer in place. For the most part the famous 1783 Benjamin Franklin quote is still uncontroversial: "In this world nothing can be said to be certain, except death and taxes."

Payroll taxes are levies on the wage bill. They consist of income taxes and social security contributions. Income taxes are also levied on nonlabor income, but earnings are the dominant source of income for households. The tax base of social security contributions is the wage bill. Payroll taxes drive a *wedge* between the cost of labor to the firm and the net wage of the worker and therefore reduce the size of the labor market. Workers will supply fewer hours of work, if any, than they would have with lower taxes, and employers create fewer jobs than they would have with lower taxes. However, payroll taxes do not necessarily reduce the perceived income of the worker. Social security contributions may also be considered as a form of deferred consumption. For instance, in the case of contributions to the public pension programs characterized in chapter 6, individuals give up income today in exchange for a higher future income. Social security contributions also provide insurance against income fluctuations (e.g., UBs).

The incidence of taxation is relevant in assessing the impact of payroll taxes on labor market behavior; the effects of taxes on behavior do not necessarily coincide with the side of the market (demand or supply) where the tax burden is put. It may be that taxes imposed on employers actually mostly affect workers' behavior, as the tax burden is shifted onto them in terms of lower wages.

Payroll taxes are the last institution discussed in this book, as the effects of taxes on the behavior of workers and firms are related to the use made of the tax proceeds. Many labor market institutions presented in this book (e.g., subsidized short-time work, retirement plans, education, UBs, ALMPs) need to be funded by payroll taxes. Moreover, tax deductions are used in combination with UBs, minimum wages, and other transfers to reduce disincentives to work. Therefore, this chapter also discusses social transfers to households and tax credits to workers and firms, and how payroll taxes and social transfers together influence work incentives.

13.1 Measures and Cross-Country Comparisons

Employers are required to withhold payroll taxes from their employees' pay. These taxes are usually levied as a percentage of the gross wage called the *tax rate*. The *average tax rate* is the total tax paid divided by the total amount the tax is levied on; the *marginal tax rate* is the percentage tax paid on the next amount of money earned. In a *progressive tax system* the average tax rate increases with income; that is, the marginal tax rate is higher than the average tax rate. The *marginal effective tax rate* may differ from a marginal tax rate, because the taxpayer may be in an income range in which that person is subject to a phaseout of some exclusion, deduction, or social transfer, so that an increase in earnings is de facto taxed with the removal of the transfer. Eligibility for several social programs is indeed conditional on passing an income and asset test (*means testing*). As previously noted, payroll taxes consist of two components: taxes and social security contributions. There is a further distinction between social security contributions paid by employees and those paid by employers, but this distinction is irrelevant in the medium-run from an economic point of view, as the tax burden is partly (or fully) shifted onto the other party. Tax systems are complex, and to summarize them by one particular number is impossible. Therefore, tax levels are often calculated for various types of situations.

Table 13.1 presents a cross-country overview of taxes and social security contributions for a single worker earning the average wage.[1] Countries differ greatly in overall tax burden, as well as its composition. The average payroll tax ranges from a low of 15.9 percent in New Zealand to a high of 59.8 percent in Germany. In most countries social security contributions are relatively large; in Australia, Denmark, Iceland, and New Zealand income taxes dominate social security contributions. The relative importance of private pension arrangements plays an important role in cross-country differences in social security contributions. The penultimate column of table 13.1 presents the marginal tax wedge, which also differs considerably from country to country. The lowest marginal tax rate is in Mexico (18.7 percent), the highest in Belgium (66.3 percent). In almost every country the marginal tax rates are substantially higher than the average tax rates. However, in countries like Germany and Poland the differences are small, indicating that the taxes are close to being proportional. Value-added taxes (VATs) are sometimes included in the calculation of the overall tax burden.[2] Table 13.1 shows that there are also big

---

1. The average wage is equal to the average annual gross wage earnings of adult, full-time manual and nonmanual workers of the private sector (mining and quarrying; manufacturing; electricity, gas, and water supply; construction; wholesale and retail trade; repair of motor vehicles, motorcycles, and personal and household goods; hotels and restaurants; transport, storage, and communications; financial intermediation; and real estate, renting, and business activities).

2. Nickell and Layard (1999), for example, advocate that the total tax wedge should also include consumption taxes (VATs), because it is the difference between product and consumption wages that matters for labor market behavior.

TABLE 13.1 Payroll taxes and VAT rates, 2011

Country	Average tax wedge (%)				Marginal tax wedge (%)	VAT (%)
	Income tax	Employee SSC	Employer SSC	Total		
Australia	22.3	0.0	6.0	26.7	35.4	10
Austria	15.3	18.1	29.1	48.4	60.6	20
Belgium	28.2	14.0	30.0	55.5	66.3	21
Canada	15.5	7.3	11.7	30.8	40.8	5
Czech Republic	12.0	11.0	34.0	42.5	48.6	20
Denmark	28.0	10.7	0.0	38.7	42.3	25
Estonia	16.8	2.8	34.4	40.1	42.9	20
Finland	22.7	7.2	22.5	42.7	57.2	23
France	14.3	13.7	42.3	49.4	51.3	20
Germany	19.0	20.9	19.7	59.8	60.4	19
Hungary	17.5	17.5	28.5	49.4	63.5	27
Iceland	27.8	0.5	8.7	34.0	43.5	26
Ireland	14.9	4.0	10.8	26.8	56.7	23
Italy	21.3	9.5	32.1	47.6	54.1	21
Japan	7.6	13.4	14.2	30.8	35.8	5
Korea	4.3	8.1	10.1	20.3	28.8	10
Luxembourg	15.0	13.1	12.3	36.0	54.9	15
Mexico	4.9	1.4	11.8	16.2	18.7	16
Netherlands	16.0	15.4	10.2	37.8	47.0	19
New Zealand	15.9	0.0	0.0	15.9	30.0	15
Norway	21.5	7.9	13.1	37.5	51.2	25
Poland	6.8	17.8	14.8	34.3	36.1	23
Portugal	13.5	11.0	23.8	39.0	50.7	23
Slovak Republic	9.5	13.4	26.2	38.9	44.4	20
Slovenia	11.3	22.1	16.1	42.6	51.0	20
Spain	15.6	6.4	29.9	39.9	48.1	18
Sweden	17.8	7.0	31.4	42.8	47.9	25
Switzerland	10.0	6.2	6.2	21.0	27.7	8
Turkey	12.4	15.0	16.5	37.7	42.2	18
United Kingdom	15.6	9.5	11.0	32.5	40.2	20
United States	17.2	5.7	9.5	29.5	41.8	—

Source: OECD tax database, 2012.

Notes: Both average and marginal tax rates concern single persons without dependents who earn 100 percent of the average wage. The total average tax wedge is the combined central and subcentral government income tax plus employee and employer social security contribution taxes as a percentage of labor costs, defined as gross wage earnings plus employer social security contributions. The tax wedge includes cash transfers. Note that in Australia, Canada, and New Zealand, VAT is known as GST (goods and service tax); the United States does not have VAT but does have sales taxes. The total tax wedge is calculated as the income tax plus employee and employer social security contribution taxes, as a percentage of labor costs (defined as gross wage earnings plus employer social security contributions):

$$\text{Total tax wedge} = 100 \times \frac{\text{Income tax} + \text{Employee SSC} + \text{Employer SSC}}{100 + \text{Employer SSC}}.$$

SSC = social security contributions; — = not available.

differences for VATs, ranging from a low of 5 percent in Canada and Japan to a high of 25 percent or more in Denmark, Hungary, Iceland, Norway, and Sweden.

Table 13.2 presents information about the way in which the tax-benefit system affects the net income position of workers in various types of households. The numbers represent net income as a percentage of the average wage for an average worker.[3] By taking the difference between 100 and the numbers reported in the first column, one can see that the tax wedge ranges from a minimum of 16 percent in New Zealand to a maximum of 56 percent in Belgium. Because of specific benefits or tax concessions to lone parents or households with children and one earner, these families' tax wedges are lower than those of working singles: in the case of New Zealand, for these households net income is even larger than gross income (net income greater than 100, implying a negative tax wedge, second column). In contrast, households with children and two earners (third column) often benefit from small tax concessions if compared to single individuals without children, even though these concessions are lower than those for single earner households.

For a two-earner couple with two children, net income in case of nonemployment in the initial phase ranges from a low of 52 percent in Belgium to a high of 86 percent in Switzerland. For a single earner moving from inactivity to 67 percent of the average wage (H1 column in table 13.2), the marginal tax rate in the Slovak Republic is more than 100 percent, while in Austria, the Czech Republic, Sweden, and Switzerland the marginal effective tax rate is about 100 percent. In these countries, for nonemployed persons there are no incentives to search for a job if the expected wage is two-thirds of the average wage. This contrasts sharply with Italy, where the marginal effective tax rate is below zero, due to a lack of universal UBs or social assistance. In the presence of income thresholds defined at the household level, there are relevant interactions in effective tax rates between members of the same family. Table 13.2 shows the marginal effective tax rate in the case where one spouse earns 67 percent of the average wage and the partner is moving from inactivity to 33 percent of the average wage (column H2). The highest marginal effective tax rate presented is 89 percent (in Denmark), while the lowest is 7 percent (Korea). Except for Italy and the United States, the marginal effective tax rates in the first situation are higher in every country than in the second situation. These characteristics of the tax-benefit system induce a polarization in both work-rich and work-poor families. If neither of the partners is working, the disincentives for one of them to accept a job are quite substantial, but if one of the partners is already working, the disincentives for the other partner also to find a job are much smaller.

Finally, table 13.2 (column H3) shows that the marginal effective tax rate for one earner moving from 67 percent to 100 percent of the average wage ranges from a low of 11 percent in Korea to a high of 89 percent in the Slovak Republic. It is clear that in many countries, in households where one person is already working, it is financially more advantageous for the nonworking partner to enter employment

3. The calculations include earnings, social assistance, family benefits, housing benefits, income tax, own social security contributions, and in-work benefits.

TABLE 13.2 Total net income and marginal effective tax rates
of first and second earners

Country	Net income (%)			Marginal effective tax rates (%)		
	T1	T2	T3	H1	H2	H3
Australia	73	85	76	69	63	66
Austria	52	63	60	99	21	41
Belgium	44	60	52	71	44	51
Canada	69	81	73	54	53	65
Czech Republic	57	78	65	99	31	37
Denmark	62	73	66	94	89	61
Estonia	60	69	64	—	—	—
Finland	57	62	62	94	50	77
France	51	58	55	89	36	43
Germany	50	66	58	76	54	54
Greece	—	—	—	16	16	17
Hungary	51	67	62	38	18	37
Iceland	66	79	69	89	45	45
Ireland	73	93	81	88	34	42
Italy	52	61	57	−8	38	52
Japan	69	77	74	86	53	52
Korea	80	82	82	75	7	11
Luxembourg	64	87	77	84	62	62
Mexico	84	84	85	—	—	—
Netherlands	62	69	69	88	42	41
New Zealand	84	101	87	77	56	62
Norway	63	69	66	87	27	36
Poland	66	72	69	87	65	68
Portugal	61	71	64	55	51	52
Slovak Republic	61	75	67	125	83	89
Slovenia	57	77	66	—	—	—
Spain	60	66	63	62	16	19
Sweden	57	63	61	100	34	47
Switzerland	79	92	86	99	14	22
Turkey	62	64	62	—	—	—
United Kingdom	67	74	72	72	67	77
United States	70	82	75	46	52	52

Sources: OECD (2005b); OECD online statistics, 2012.

Notes: Family types (2011): T1 = single person earning the average wage; T2 = one-earner (100 percent average wage) married couple with two children; T3 = two-earner (100 and 67 percent average wage) married couple with two children. The tax wedge and tax rates include social security contribution and are net of cash benefits. Types of changes (2005): H1 = one earner moving from inactivity to 67 percent of average wage; H2 = first earner at 67 percent of average wage, second earner moving from inactivity to 33 percent of average wage; H3 = one earner moving from 67 percent to 100 percent of average wage.

than for the partner who is already working to work more. The only exceptions are Denmark, Japan, and the Netherlands.

13.2 Theory

Economic theory suggests that the *structure* of taxation is often more important than the *level* of taxation in affecting labor market outcomes. We first illustrate how the structure affects individual labor supply incentives for consumption and leisure in a competitive labor market. Next we consider the interaction of taxes with other institutions in an imperfect labor market.

13.2.1 A Perfect Labor Market

The interaction of taxes, social security contributions, transfers, and withdrawals described in tables 13.1 and 13.2 implies that the budget constraint of an individual is nonlinear; that is, it is composed of different segments of a line (unlike those considered for simplicity in other parts of this book). Taxes are thus likely to deeply affect not only the choice along the extensive margin but also the decision as to how many hours of work are to be supplied. As taxes and social security contributions are needed to fund many of the institutions discussed in this book, it is also important to take into account the potential additional effects of these policies along the intensive margin.

Figure 13.1a describes a typical income tax system in which individual incomes are not taxed below a certain level (the so-called no-tax area, which is also supposed to cover the costs related to the generation of income), say y^0; it is taxed at rate τ_0 above that level and below y_1 and at tax rate $\tau_1 > \tau_0$ for $y > y_1$. These features of the tax system generate the convex and multisegment budget constraint hitting the vertical axis at point F. This budget constraint can be analytically described as

$$C = \begin{cases} wh & \text{if } h \leq h_0 \\ wh_0 + w(1 - \tau_0)(h - h_0) & \text{if } h_0 < h \leq h_1 \\ wh_0 + w(1 - \tau_0)(h_1 - h_0) + w(1 - \tau_1)(h - h_1) & \text{if } h > h_1, \end{cases}$$

where $h_0 = \frac{y_0}{w}, h_1 = \frac{y_1 - y_0}{w(1 - \tau_0)} - h_0$.

Without the tax, the budget constraint will be given, to the left of h_0, by the dashed line hitting the vertical axis at C_{notax} (figure 13.1b). With a strictly proportional tax system (at rate τ_0) the budget constraint would instead be given by the dashed line segment hitting the vertical axis at C_{prop}. For any given preferences of the individual, the presence and the structure of taxes are therefore bound to affect the choice as to the hours of work. In this example, the individual would have chosen point A without the tax, B with the progressive tax system, and C with the proportional tax system. Thus, both the presence and the structure of taxes matter for labor supply decisions. Notice that a purely proportional tax system may induce an individual with stronger preferences for leisure to work less than in the progressive tax system (as shown in figure 13.1b), because a proportional tax system does

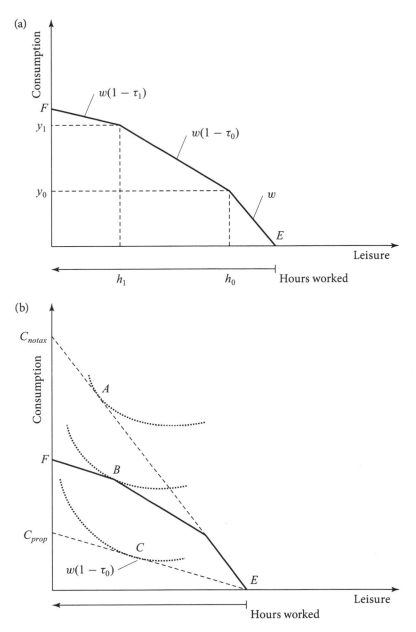

FIGURE 13.1 (a) A progressive tax system; (b) leisure-labor choices in different tax regimes

not have a no-tax area. In general, however, a progressive tax system is bound to affect the intensive more than the extensive margin, as the tax can be significantly reduced by working fewer hours.

The reduction in hours of work is induced by the presence of relatively flat segments of the budget constraint, making any additional hour of work pay little, if any, additional consumption. Figure 13.2 displays a case where a segment of the budget constraint is completely flat. This happens in the presence of a minimum

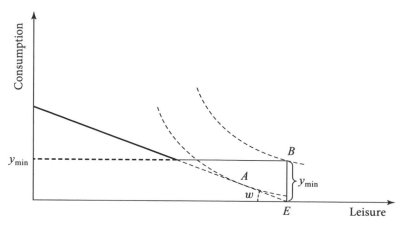

FIGURE 13.2 Minimum guaranteed income

guaranteed income (MGI) scheme, that is, a social assistance scheme topping up income to guarantee to individuals at least a given subsistence level income, say, y_{min}. Due to the presence of the MGI, consumption cannot fall below y_{min}; hence an individual who, without the scheme, would work less than required to attain this subsistence level, would choose not to work at all, moving from A to B. It is because of these disincentives to work that MGI schemes are typically integrated with earning disregards or ECI (e.g., those discussed in section 13.4), which make the budget constraint negatively sloped also to the left of the zero hours of work locus.

Overall, when taxes affect labor supply along the extensive margin, they will always reduce participation, inducing individuals not to work irrespective of the structure of taxation, because only the substitution effect matters. When instead taxes affect the number of hours supplied, their effect will depend in general on the structure of taxation and on the relative sizes of the substitution and income effects. If the substitution effect is larger than the income effect (which is usually considered to be the case), a progressive tax system will reduce labor supply more than a proportional tax system would. The opposite happens when the income effect dominates.

In addition to affecting labor supply, payroll taxes may also affect labor demand, or they may increase labor costs. Who pays the burden of payroll taxes depends on labor supply and labor demand elasticities (see box 13.1).

BOX 13.1   *Labor Supply and the Evaluation of Payroll Taxes*

In a pure tax model workers do not benefit from taxes, but in reality payroll taxes (e.g., social security contributions) may be used to finance programs that are beneficial to workers. If that is the case, a tax increase buys the workers some benefits. In a static model payroll taxes affect labor supply (L^s) and labor demand (L^d) in the following way:

$$L^d = L^d(w(1 + t_f)) \tag{13.1}$$

$$L^s = L^s(w(1 - \rho_w t_e) + \rho_e w t_f), \tag{13.2}$$

where w is the pretax wage, t_f is that part of payroll taxes paid by the employer, t_e that part paid by the worker, ρ_w is the discounting of employee taxes by employees, and ρ_e the valuation of employer taxes by employees relative to cash income. Two extremes can be distinguished. First, in a pure tax model, $\rho_w = 1$ and $\rho_e = 0$; the worker does not benefit at all from taxes. Second, in a *full valuation* model, $\rho_w = 0$ and $\rho_e = 1$; all taxes are experienced as benefits for the worker and are an equivalent to cash income. By imposing the equilibrium condition $L^d = L^s$ and using the implicit function rule, a small increase in payroll taxes paid by the employer from $t_f = 0$ has the following effect on labor supply:

$$\frac{dw/w}{dt_f} = -\frac{\varepsilon - \eta \rho_e}{\varepsilon - \eta(1 - \rho_w t_e)}, \tag{13.3}$$

where ε is the inverse elasticity of labor supply, and η is the inverse of labor demand elasticity. There are three situations in which a change in payroll taxes is fully shifted to wages ($\frac{dw/w}{dt_f} = -1$):

1. $\varepsilon = \infty$; inelastic labor supply, that is, a vertical labor supply curve;
2. $\eta = 0$; perfectly elastic labor demand, that is, a horizontal labor demand curve; and
3. $\rho_w = 0$ and $\rho_e = 1$; the full valuation model; all taxes are considered benefits.

In all three cases tax changes are fully compensated through a wage change, so a change in taxes should not have an effect on employment (L): $\frac{dL/L}{dt_f} = 0$.

The sharing of taxes between employers and workers is graphically characterized in figure 13.3. Initially, labor market equilibrium is at the wage/employment combination (L_0, w_0). After the introduction of a tax, employment declines to L_1, the wage costs for the firm are equal to w_d, and the net wages for the worker are equal to w_s. The total tax wedge is equal to $w_d - w_s$, of which the employer pays $w_d - w_0$ and the worker pays $w_0 - w_s$. The steeper the supply curve is, the higher will be the share of the tax paid by the worker; the steeper the demand curve is, the higher will be the share of the tax paid by the firm. As is spelled out in more detail in technical annex 13.9.1, the burden is shifted to the side of the labor market that is less elastic. If labor supply does not respond much to changes in wages (as in the case of prime-aged men), employees pay a high proportion of the payroll tax. Insofar as taxes increase the wage cost to employers and reduce the net wages of workers, taxes will reduce employment. The after-tax equilibrium will be inefficient, because employment is not at the level that maximizes total gains from the trade of labor services and introduces a deadweight loss, the triangle ABC.

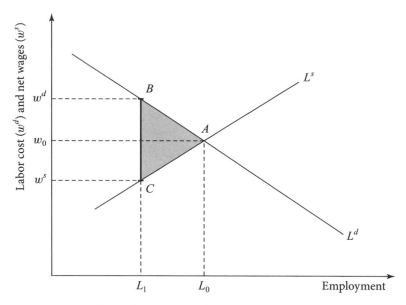

FIGURE 13.3 Payroll taxes in competitive labor markets

13.2.2 An Imperfect Labor Market

The impact of taxes on employment and wages can be better investigated in an imperfect labor market, involving some unemployment at the equilibrium. In a perfect labor market, taxes involve only adjustments in labor force participation and reductions in employment, but no unemployment.

Consider, in particular, a labor market with frictions, like the environment described in chapters 11 and 12, where workers are matched to unfilled vacancies and then bargain with employers as to how to split the rents created by these frictions.[4] In this context, the effect of taxes depends on the relationship between UBs and wages. Suppose initially that UBs are indexed to (net) wages, that is, to the purchasing power of workers, w_s. As shown in technical annex 13.9.2, a higher *proportional* payroll tax in this context implies an equivalent reduction in the reservation wage of the jobseekers, w^r (the lowest wage at which they are willing to accept a job offer), and of the actual wage w_s. As both wage offers and wage aspirations shift down by the same amount, labor supply is unaffected. Graphically, the labor supply curve is vertical; tax rates are entirely absorbed by a decline in take-home pay with no effects on labor costs. Thus, there is no effect on employment and unemployment.

Changes in the structure of taxation instead affect unemployment. A revenue-neutral increase in the progressiveness of taxation increases employment and reduces unemployment, because it makes the labor-leisure trade-off more favorable to work. The increase in labor supply reduces wages, and this in turn increases la-

---

4. A problem with this framework is that it does not consider changes in participation. However, the effects of taxes on labor force participation in imperfect labor markets operate in the same direction as in the competitive market, and the reader can refer to that case.

bor demand and the equilibrium employment level. The intuition is that, when unemployment benefits are indexed to wages, a proportional tax affects only the total rent to be split between workers and employers, while progressive taxes affect the sharing rule itself, making it less favorable to workers.

The analysis can be enriched by allowing for adjustment of hours and not just of head counts (Cahuc and Zylberberg 2004). Progressive taxes, in this case, increase employment at the extensive margin (where taxes are lower) and reduce hours worked by those initially working longer hours and earning more.

When UBs are not indexed to net wages (i.e., are defined as a fraction of the gross, before tax, wage), taxes affect unemployment even when they are proportional. This is because the change in the outside option would then affect the sharing rule and no longer only the surplus. Put another way, when UBs are indexed to gross (as opposed to net) wages, labor supply is positively sloped, and hence employers face higher labor costs when taxes are levied.

Overall, the employment and wage effects of a tax depend on the slope of the wage-setting function. If this function is relatively flat, a tax hike will lead to a large reduction in employment. If the function is relatively steep, as in the case of labor supply of prime-aged men, tax hikes are absorbed by wages, and employment does not change much. These two situations are depicted in figure 13.4. We simulate the effect of an increase in social security contributions of employers, increasing labor cost per any given wage paid to the worker: the increase in taxes causes the demand curve to shift from L_0^d to L_1^d. Figure 13.4a shows a large decrease in employment (from L_0 to L_1) and a small decrease in wages. Figure 13.4b shows a small decrease in employment and a large decrease in net wages (from w_0 to w_1).

The above results also hold when bargaining over wages does not take place at the individual level but is organized by unions. If wages are determined through bargaining between firms and unions, unemployment disciplines union wage demands. Taxes affect the wage platform of unions (the union wage curve; see chapter 3), because unions and firms perceive that the tax paid depends on the equilibrium wage level. Because firms and unions take taxes into account, progressive taxation implies lower unemployment, while regressive taxation implies higher unemployment. When taxes are proportional and UBs are indexed to net wages, labor demand and the wage equation shift down by the same amount when taxes are levied, so that taxes are absorbed in wages without affecting employment, just as in the case of individual wage setting.

Pissarides (1998) also considers the effects of taxes in an efficiency wage model. In this context the role of unemployment is to discipline workers and prevent shirking on the job. Given unemployment income, taxes do not influence the wage offer. Furthermore, as in the competitive model, it is the amount of taxation that matters, not the structure of taxation. The intuition is that the effects of the structure of taxation come from the bargaining rule, and in the efficiency wage environment there is no bargaining—the employer unilaterally sets wages.

Therefore, whether changes in the structure of taxation—that is, more or less progressive taxes—affect employment depends on the nature of the labor market. If wages are determined in a competitive market or in an efficiency wage model setting, the structure of taxation is irrelevant. The only thing that matters is the

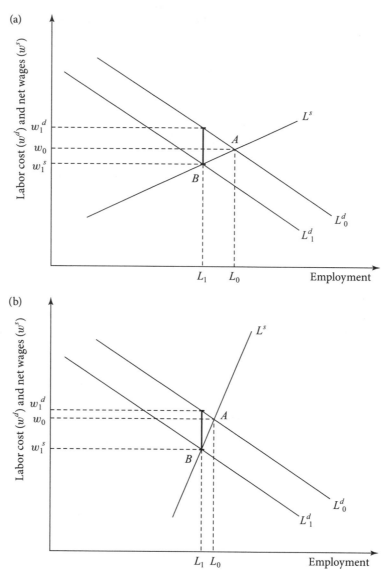

FIGURE 13.4 Increase in employers' social security contributions: (a) with relatively elastic labor supply (flat wage-setting function); (b) with relatively rigid labor supply (steep wage-setting function)

level of taxes. However, in markets with frictions and bargaining (either individual or collective) over the rents created by these frictions, the structure of taxation is very important.

13.3 Empirical Evidence

As discussed in section 13.2, the response of labor supply to changes in wages and taxes is critical when evaluating the efficiency costs of payroll taxes. A large empirical literature has studied labor supply and behavioral responses to taxes and transfers (for an overview, see Blundell and MaCurdy 1999; Keane 2011). The labor supply of men is found not to be much affected by changes in tax rates, but that of women is usually found to increase significantly if net wages increase.

Eissa (1995) uses the U.S. Tax Reform Act of 1986 as a natural experiment to identify the labor supply responsiveness of married women to changes in the tax rate. The tax reform reduced the top marginal tax rate by 44 percent (from 50 percent to 28 percent), but changed the marginal tax rate less drastically for those further down the income distribution. Eissa analyzes the response of married women at or above the 99th percentile of the distribution, using as a control group women from the 75th percentile of the distribution. The tax effect is identified as the difference between the change in the labor supply of women with large tax rate reductions and that of women with small rate reductions. Eissa finds evidence that the labor supply of high-income married women increased because of the tax reform, implying an elasticity with respect to the after-tax wage of approximately 0.8. At least half of this elasticity is due to a labor supply response along the extensive margin, that is, labor force participation.

Several studies find relatively strong effects of tax reductions on participation of single parents (Eissa and Liebman 1996). Payroll taxes will only lower employment if taxes cannot be passed on to workers in the form of lower wages. If there is full compensation, employers are not confronted with higher labor costs, and higher taxes will not lead to lower employment. The question is whether taxes are fully incident on those who are formally liable to pay them.

Gruber (1997) exploits a change in the financing of social insurance in Chile to assess the incidence of payroll taxation. The reduced costs of payroll taxation to firms appear to have been fully passed on to workers in the form of higher wages, with little effect on employment levels.

In his overview of the labor market impact of taxes, Disney (2000) concludes that the labor supply of a regular full-time worker is probably inelastic to tax changes. He identifies four groups of workers whose behavior may be affected by high tax rates: those with high-income work, those with low-income work who are eligible for in-work benefits, those nearing retirement, and those considering entering the labor force. At the upper end of the wage distribution, high marginal tax rates may reduce labor supply and work effort.[5] At the low end of the income distribution, means-tested benefits discourage workers from participating in the labor market. For this reason, most OECD countries have introduced in-work benefits (discussed in section 13.4).

At the high end of the age distribution of the labor force, high tax rates have induced workers to retire early (see also chapter 6 on retirement schemes). For younger prospective workers, entry to work may be discouraged by high effective marginal tax rates. This problem too has been tackled by in-work benefits. Several

5. However, according to Disney, the effects are not sufficient to generate Laffer curve–type effects, that is, conditions in which reductions in taxes may increase fiscal revenues. The so-called Laffer curve displays a bell-shaped relationship between tax rates and tax revenues. Although Arthur Laffer does not claim to have invented this concept, it was popularized with policymakers following an afternoon meeting of the economist with Dick Cheney, the 46th vice president of the United States, in which the former reportedly sketched the curve on a napkin to illustrate his argument.

studies have tried to infer from labor supply elasticities the optimal structure of payroll taxation that would minimize distortions. The key contributions to this *optimal taxation* literature pioneered by Mirrlees (1971) are those from Saez et al. (2009), Brewer et al. (2010), and Atkinson et al. (2011).

13.4 Policy Issues

The structure of the tax-benefit system often does not generate strong incentives for low-income unemployed workers to find jobs. Policies aimed at "making work pay" introduce financial incentives to employment. The specific design features of these schemes are also very important. Here we explain the relationship between MGI and ECI, and the alternative between tax credits and wage subsidies as well as the targeting to families' individual incomes.

13.4.1 How to Make Work Pay?

In a means-tested welfare system individuals without income receive a welfare benefit, an MGI, that is reduced one-for-one when the individual starts making money. This is because the MGI tops up income to raise it to the level of a given poverty threshold. In this system individuals are only tempted to enter the labor market if they can earn at least the amount of the welfare benefit. This gives rise to flat segments of budget constraints, such as that displayed in figure 13.2.

To reduce the disincentive effects of an MGI,[6] *earning disregards* are often allowed. In other words, benefits are withdrawn only as a percentage of the increase in earned income to preserve financial incentives to work. In practice, fractions of workers' compensation are not counted when establishing the amount of the top-up transfer. MGIs with earning disregards operate like a "negative" income tax (see figure 13.5), that is, a transfer declining gradually as the income of the individual increases. In figure 13.5, A is the "guarantee" level, the benefit paid to an individual (or family) with no income, and the slope of the segment AB gives the rate at which the benefit is reduced as income increases.

In-work benefits, unlike the negative income tax, are paid only to individuals working. They aim at reducing poverty among those working. The design of an in-work benefit is presented in figure 13.6a. Individuals receive benefits only if they work. The size of the benefits provided depends on the gross income of the worker. Over the gross income range OA the benefits initially increase to the maximum at D. This is the *phase-in* region. Then there is a flat region AB with constant in-work benefits. Finally, over the gross income range BC the in-work benefits are slowly reduced—the *phase-out* region, which operates like a negative income tax. Figure 13.6b provides another representation of an in-work benefit, in relation to the overall budget constraint of the individual.

Financial incentives to work are increased by in-work benefits. Card and Hyslop (2005) show that even for long-term welfare recipients, earnings subsidies have a

---

6. MGI experiments in the United States in the late 1960s showed that labor supply responses of men along both margins of labor supply were small. For women, especially single female heads of household and young workers, the behavioral response was higher and concentrated along the extensive margin. Participation elasticities were between 0.5 and 1.

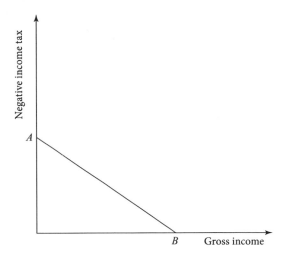

FIGURE 13.5 Design of the negative income tax

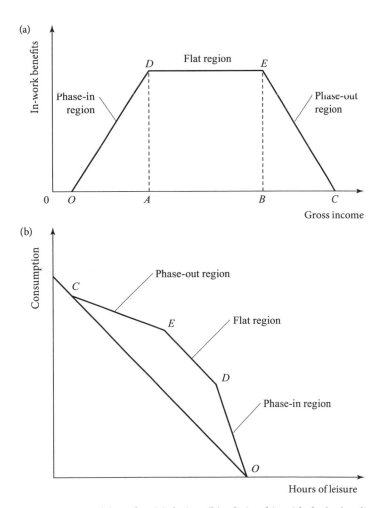

FIGURE 13.6 In-work benefits: (a) design; (b) relationship with the budget line

positive effect on employment rates. However, temporary wage subsidies do not have a permanent effect (see box 13.2).

In-Work Benefits in Action

In Canada in the early 1990s a system of time-limited earnings subsidies for long-term welfare recipients was introduced. This system, the Self-Sufficiency Project (SSP), was intended to help welfare recipients make a permanent break from program dependency. The subsidy scheme applied only to individuals who accepted full-time jobs and could last for up to three years, and once workers were offered the scheme, they had to begin to work within a year. The SSP was evaluated using a randomized design. Half of the long-term welfare recipients were offered the SSP, while the other half remained in the regular welfare system. Data were collected for six years to measure both the short- and the long-term effects of the subsidy scheme. Card and Hyslop (2005) find that SSP had a large effect in the short run. The percentages of individuals who were on income assistance by years since random assignment were as follows:

Months since program start	Control group	Program group	Effect of program
6	90.8	83.1	7.7
12	83.7	72.4	11.3
24	73.0	63.3	9.7
36	65.4	58.8	6.6
48	56.7	53.5	3.2
60	50.6	48.4	2.2
69	45.0	45.0	0.0

After the first six months of the program a difference of 7.7 percentage points existed between the treatment group and the control group. After one year the difference had increased to 11.3 percent. However, over time the effect faded away. After three years the difference between the two groups had fallen to 6.6 percent and after five years to 2.2 percent. After 69 months all subsidy payments ended, and the welfare participation rates of the two groups were equal. Once the financial incentives for some individuals to find a full-time job were gone, these individuals no longer behaved differently from those who did not get this financial stimulus. Card and Hyslop conclude that the SSP experiment offers little support for the idea that temporary wage subsidies can have a permanent effect on the labor market position of welfare benefit recipients.

Source: Card and Hyslop (2005).

Many countries have introduced some sort of in-work benefits with payments in the form of lump sums. Blundell (2001) offers a nice comparison of in-work benefits in Canada, the United Kingdom, and the United States.

The earliest scheme was the Earned Income Tax Credit (EITC) introduced in 1975 in the United States. The generosity of the modest program was increased in

1986, 1990, and 1993. The EITC is provided through the tax system rather than the welfare system. Eligibility for the EITC is awarded to all low-income families with children, irrespective of marital status.

Countries differ greatly in terms of benefit levels, withdrawal rates, time limits, hours limits, and targeting of programs. The entitlement criteria vary across countries. Whereas in Australia, Belgium, and Ireland entitlement is restricted to long-term unemployed individuals, in Canada, the Netherlands, and New Zealand all benefit recipients who find a job are entitled to an employment-conditional benefit. Except for Canada, hours-of-work requirements accompany the bonus payments: full-time employment in Australia and Ireland, and part-time work in all other countries. Benefit levels vary widely across programs, with the United Kingdom's Working Family Tax Credit (WFTC, up to 30–35 percent of average earnings for low-income families with children) and the Irish Family Income Supplement (paying 32.5 percent of the average wage to working families with children) being the most generous. The U.S. system is less generous, with maximum payments of 13 percent of average earnings to families with two children. However, benefits are withdrawn faster in the United Kingdom (at the rate of 55 percent) than in the United States (rate of 20 percent).

In-work benefits, just like MGI schemes, may reduce work incentives in the phase-out region. In-work benefits are introduced to encourage individuals without labor income to find a job by relating the provision of benefits to being employed. However, on the one hand, in-work benefits push individuals to find a job, while on the other hand, they generally reduce incentives to work longer hours (or earn higher wages). This is because the in-work benefit has to be taxed away at some point further up the income distribution and thus imposes labor supply disincentives along the intensive margin for workers in the phase-out region. Therefore, in-work benefits stimulate labor supply at the extensive margin, but they reduce incentives at the intensive margin. Furthermore, in-work benefits programs do not provide income support to individuals with no earnings, whereas MGI schemes provide the largest transfers to the lowest-income earners, who are presumably the most in need of support. Relative to MGI programs, incentives to enter the labor force are enhanced with in-work benefits. This comes at the cost of the neediest people with no earnings, who receive no support.

Saez (2002) shows that when the behavioral response of individuals is along the intensive margin of labor supply, the MGI program is the optimal welfare program, with a large guaranteed income level that is taxed away at high rates. If the behavioral response is concentrated along the extensive margin of labor supply, then the optimal program is an in-work benefit with smaller guaranteed income levels and transfers that increase with earnings at low income levels.

It should be stressed that the two schemes are not mutually exclusive, and they can work well in combination if there are enough resources to fund both of them. Depending on budgetary allocations to antipoverty schemes, one could also have an MGI and an in-work benefit established just above the poverty line of the MGI scheme.

13.4.2 How to Pay and Target Beneficiaries

Tax Credits versus Wage Subsidies

Hiring decisions of firms may be influenced by payments to employers. These payments may be given as a direct transfer to the employer (wage subsidy) or as a tax credit. Wage subsidies may be provided as an incentive for firms to expand their employment (marginal wage subsidies). Tax credits are sometimes provided to firms to hire specific categories of workers. The trade-off between tax credits and wage subsidies is influenced by the costs of the payments. Tax credits do not increase public expenditures and are administered through the tax system, so there is no need for a separate administration, as is often the case for wage subsidies.[7] The reduction in labor costs for specific types of workers may induce employers to hire more of these workers.

In the United States the Targeted Jobs Tax Credit program began in 1979, targeting disadvantaged youth, the handicapped, and welfare recipients and providing employers with a tax credit lasting one year. The program was discontinued in 1995. There is evidence that this type of tax credits may have had stigmatizing effects on potential participants. Burtless (1985) found that if tax credits were offered for disadvantaged welfare recipients, the probability that these workers were hired was in fact lower than if these tax credits were not offered. Wage subsidies are sometimes targeted to low-wage employees and provided as employment subsidies to employers or as reductions to employers' social security contributions. Since the wage level is often the only qualifying condition, there could be an incentive for workers with high hourly wages to work part-time. An example of such a wage subsidy is the Dutch SPAK (Specifieke Afdrachtskorting), which was introduced in 1996 as a reduction of employers' contributions on low wages and was phased out in 2003 over four years for cost-saving reasons. Evaluations suggested that the wage subsidy increased employment of low-skilled workers by 1–5 percent.

Similar programs in France and Belgium also had significant employment effects (see Boeri 2005 for details). Tax credits and transfers to firms can generate large deadweight losses if they subsidize existing jobs that would have existed in any event. To reduce the size of deadweight losses, governments may only subsidize new job creation. But some of the job creation would have occurred anyway. Hence deadweight losses may still be large at least in relative terms. A better method to avoid deadweight costs is to target those jobs that would disappear without the subsidy, identified as those where the subsidy is less likely to be transferred to wages. But this theoretical solution cannot be easily implemented.

Targeting Individuals versus Households

The other key issue relates to the targeting of taxes and benefits to the individual or to the household. A tax and benefit system based on individual incomes raises distributional concerns regarding the family income of those receiving the tax credit. For instance, it may reward part-time spouses of wealthy individuals. However, it

---

7. Note that tax credits are not likely to be effective where tax noncompliance is high.

is more effective in raising female labor supply, as it generally raises work pay for married women. Income-tested tax credits based on family income are better targeted to needy people, but they may discourage the second family member to work, if the additional income would move the household to partial or total withdrawal of the credit.

For administrative convenience, the target of the tax credit is generally the tax unit of use in each country. For instance, in France it is the family and in Italy the individual. However, the United Kingdom adopts individual tax returns and assessment of family income in determining eligibility for the WFTC. Thus, the choice as to the level at which the income assessment determining eligibility should be made depends on the relative importance in government strategies of poverty relief versus increasing rewards from labor force participation. Poverty relief targets the family. Increasing rewards from participation targets the individual. If eligibility is targeted on family income, the benefits go to families who need support the most, but there may be adverse effects on participation decisions of secondary earners in couples. If it is targeted on individual incomes, this disincentive problem does not occur, but part of the benefits will go to high-income families.

13.5 Interactions with Other Institutions

Payroll taxes interact with most, if not all, labor market institutions and other forms of taxation. Indeed, they interact with all institutions funded by public revenues, such as education, retirement programs, and UBs. By the same token, payroll taxes interact with other forms of taxation (e.g., VAT taxes and taxes on capital income). To support job creation, it is often recommended that taxes be shifted from labor to consumption by reducing payroll taxes and increasing VAT rates, but the macroeconomic evidence in this respect is rather weak (Lee and Gordon 2005).

In addition to these *accounting* effects, payroll taxes alter incentives, thus modifying the effects of other institutions. To give an example, payroll tax credits, like ECI, are often used in conjunction with minimum wages (see chapter 2) to prevent displacement of workers. At the same time, the minimum wage prevents the tax credit from being entirely transferred to the employer.

Unions (see chapter 3) are also important, because union bargaining affects the relationship among taxes, the structure of taxation, and the incidence of payroll taxation.

Early retirement programs (see chapter 6) are affected by payroll taxes, since high tax rates may induce workers to retire early, particularly at the high end of the income distribution. To the extent that payroll taxes are earmarked for paying retirement plans or UBs (see chapter 11), they will be less distortional when perceived by workers as a form of deferred consumption or insurance. Under these circumstances workers may be more keen to accept reductions in their current net wage, because they know that these reductions will improve their living standards later in life. This reduces the labor supply response to the level of social security contributions (see box 13.1).

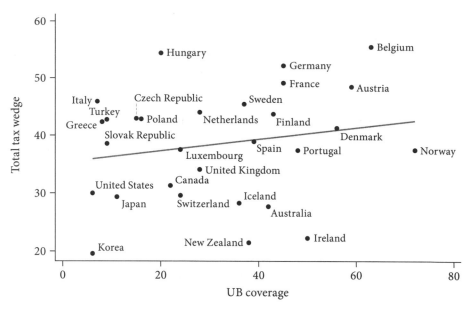

FIGURE 13.7 Taxes and UBs
Source: OECD (2007).

Notes: The vertical axis displays the total tax wedge measure discussed in this chapter; the horizontal axis displays the OECD summary measure of UB generosity discussed in chapter 11. The solid line is the fit to data.

Across countries a positive correlation exists between the total tax wedge on labor and the coverage of UBs (see figure 13.7). This correlation can be attributed to accounting (higher contributions are required to pay more generous UBs), but could also possibly capture the less distortionary effect of contributions when perceived as an insurance by many workers.

Finally, there is an important interaction between payroll taxes and ALMPs (see chapter 12) to the extent that incentives affect the behavior of unemployed workers in their search for jobs and wage subsidies offer an alternative to ECI (see section 13.4.2).

13.6 Why Do Payroll Taxes Exist?

Payroll taxes exist to fund government expenditures. The social security contribution to the tax wedge is directly related to the functioning of labor markets, for example, because it provides insurance to workers in case of unemployment. The payroll tax structure is important to ensure that workers have sufficient incentives to put effort into their jobs or search for new jobs once they become unemployed.

Although contributions to public pension programs are considered to be part of the tax wedge, it is not a priori clear whether these contributions are a tax, savings, or an insurance premium. Disney (2004) shows that the distribution over tax or savings of contributions to public pension programs is especially important for women. A higher tax component reduces employment rates of women, while a higher retirement savings component has the opposite effect. Employment rates of men are largely insensitive to tax rates.

Payroll taxes are, however, unavoidably distortionary. They reduce employment along both the extensive and the intensive margins. Tax rates are indeed a significant factor in explaining differences in the amount of market work undertaken by the working-age population in different countries. However, tax differentials explain only a minority of the market differentials, the majority being explained by other relevant labor market institutions (Nickell 2006).

13.7 Suggestions for Further Reading

Pissarides (1998) presents an analysis of the way taxes affect the functioning of the labor market under different assumptions concerning wage formation. Blundell and MaCurdy (1999) provide an overview of the empirical literature on labor supply and behavioral responses to taxes and transfers. Chapter 3 of OECD (2005b) gives a detailed overview of the characteristics of in-work benefits systems in various countries. Boeri (2005) discusses the components of an activating social security system in which in-work benefits and tax credits or transfers to firms are important. Keane (2011) provides a survey on the effects of taxes on labor supply.

13.8 Review Questions and Exercises

1. How does a change in marginal taxes—with constant average taxes—affect labor demand and supply?

2. How do in-work benefits affect incentives of unemployed workers?

3. What happens during the phase-in and phase-out regions of in-work benefits?

4. How do supply and demand elasticities affect the distribution of the wedge between workers and firms?

5. How does the structure of payroll taxes affect the functioning of the labor market?

6. Why does the impact of taxes depend on the nature of the labor market?

7. What are the main purposes of MGI schemes and in-work benefits, and what are the essential differences between the two systems?

8. What is the trade-off between wage subsidies and tax credits?

9. Should contributions to public pension programs be considered part of the tax wedge?

10. The utility function of an individual is $U(c, l) = \sqrt{cl}$. The price of the consumption good is p, the wage rate is w, and nonlabor income is m. The individual has T hours to work (h) or consume leisure (l).

    (a) Write down the utility maximization problem. Given $p = 1$, $w = 5$, $m = 20$, and $T = 16$, what is the optimal labor supply? What is the optimal level of consumption?

(b) Assume that m increases to $m = 30$. What is the new labor supply and consumption?

(c) An ECI program is introduced that provides a \$1 tax credit for every hour of work. The effective wage rate is now $w = 5 + 1 = 6$. Calculate optimal labor supply and consumption under this program. Explain the result.

11. Suppose that, in the market for blue-collar workers, labor supply is equal to $w = 20 + 8L$, while labor demand is given by $w = 80 - 12L$.

(a) Characterize the labor market equilibrium (wage w, employment L, and unemployment U) without taxes.

(b) How do these equilibrium levels change with the introduction of a payroll tax on take-home pay of 50 percent, to be paid by the employers?

(c) Assume now that supply becomes more rigid. Is the effect of an employer-paid payroll tax stronger or weaker on wages? And what about employment?

(d) What happens if supply is unchanged, but demand becomes more rigid?

12. Suppose the supply curve of fast-food employees is given by $w = 10 + 5L$, while the demand curve is given by $w = 50 - 3L$.

(a) Compute the equilibrium levels of wage w, employment L, and unemployment U.

(b) How do these levels change with the introduction of a payroll tax of 25 percent, to be paid by employers?

(c) How do these levels change if the same payroll tax is instead paid by employees, on wages?

13. (Advanced) Consider the general equilibrium model of the labor market of technical annex 13.9.2. Evaluate the effects of the following institutional interactions:

(a) A *flexicurity reform* type 1, reducing employment protection while increasing the generosity of UBs.

(b) A *flexicurity reform* type 2, reducing employment protection while increasing ECI.

(c) A *flexicurity reform* type 3, reducing employment protection while increasing hiring subsidies.

(d) A revenue-neutral increase in the progressiveness of taxation combined with an increase in ECI.

13.9 Technical Annex: Payroll Taxes

13.9.1 Taxes, Benefits, and the Structure of Taxation

The purpose of this annex is to show that in a competitive market when the UBs are fully indexed to wages, the structure of taxes does not affect the equilibrium wage and employment levels. We proceed in three steps. First, we characterize how the tax burden is shared between employers and workers. Next, we consider the role played by the indexation to taxes of nonemployment income on the elasticity of labor supply. Finally, we look at the progressiveness of taxes.

Tax Incidence

As shown in box 13.1, the way in which the tax burden is shared between employers and employees depends on the relative elasticity of labor supply and demand. Take the simple static model used throughout this book (notably in the technical annexes to chapters 1–3) and consider a simple proportional tax on nominal wages w, imposed on workers, so that w is the gross labor cost, and $w^s = w(1 - t)$ is the net take-home pay. At the competitive equilibrium, there is no unemployment, hence $L^s = L^d$. Then we have

$$L^s = [w(1 - t)]^{\frac{-1}{\eta}} \equiv L^d. \tag{13.4}$$

It follows that the equilibrium wage will be

$$w = A^{\frac{\varepsilon}{\varepsilon + \eta}} (1 - t)^{\frac{-\eta}{\varepsilon + \eta}}, \tag{13.5}$$

and the net take-home pay of workers is

$$w^s = w(1 - t) = [A(1 - t)]^{\frac{\varepsilon}{\varepsilon + \eta}}, \tag{13.6}$$

while the equilibrium level of employment is

$$L = [A(1 - t)]^{\frac{1}{\varepsilon + \eta}}. \tag{13.7}$$

As also shown in box 13.1, the incidence of taxation will fall on employers and employees depending on the relative elasticity of labor supply and demand. In particular, a small increase of t from $t = 0$ implies

$$\frac{\partial \ln(w)}{\partial t} = \frac{\eta}{\varepsilon + \eta} \tag{13.8}$$

$$\frac{\partial \ln(w^s)}{\partial t} = -\frac{\varepsilon}{\varepsilon + \eta}. \tag{13.9}$$

It follows that under an infinitely elastic labor demand (when $\eta = 0$), taxes are entirely shifted onto workers ($\frac{\partial \ln(w^s)}{\partial t} = -1$); but when the labor supply is infinitely elastic ($\varepsilon = 0$), it is the other way around ($\frac{\partial \ln(w)}{\partial t} = 1$ and $\frac{\partial \ln(w^s)}{\partial t} = 0$). Finally, when the labor supply is rigid ($\varepsilon = \infty$), the tax burden falls entirely on workers ($\frac{\partial \ln(w)}{\partial t} = 0$ and $\frac{\partial \ln(w^s)}{\partial t} = -1$). In this case we also have that $\frac{\partial \ln(L)}{\partial t} = 0$; that is, there is no change in employment.

Summarizing, we have two cases in which the tax burden falls entirely on workers and taxes have no effect on employment:

Case	ε	η	w	w^s	L
1	$\varepsilon = \infty$	$0 \leq \eta < 1$	A	$A(1-t)$	1
2	$0 \leq \varepsilon < \infty$	$\eta = 0$	A	$A(1-t)$	$[A(1-t)]^{\frac{1}{\varepsilon}}$

Supply Elasticity and the Indexation of Benefits

The elasticity of labor supply depends on whether nonemployment income (including any transfer to persons not working) is indexed to wages or to prices. Assume that time off work is rewarded as a nonemployment benefit b. As we are in a perfectly competitive market, there is no unemployment. In an imperfect labor market, b would be the UB. Normalize to unity both the total endowment of time (l_0) and the potential labor supply. Actual labor supply depends on the preferences of the worker, which are assumed to be represented by a Cobb-Douglas–type utility function

$$U(c, l) = c^\alpha (1-h)^{1-\alpha}, \qquad (13.10)$$

where U represents utility; c represents consumption; $h = l_0 - l = 1 - l$ is working time, that is, labor supply; and α is a positive parameter with $0 < \alpha < 1$. The budget constraint of this individual can be specified as $c = hw(1-t) + (1-h)b$, with $b < w(1-t)$. Thus, the utility derived from leisure and labor supply becomes

$$U = [hw(1-t) + (1-h)b]^\alpha (1-h)^{1-\alpha}. \qquad (13.11)$$

In a competitive labor market the worker maximizes utility by choosing hours, which delivers the following first-order condition:

$$\alpha[hw(1-t) + (1-h)b]^{\alpha-1}[w(1-t) - b](1-h)^{1-\alpha}$$
$$- [hw(1-t) + (1-h)b]^\alpha (1-\alpha)(1-h)^{-\alpha} = 0, \qquad (13.12)$$

from which, after some rewriting, we find the labor supply equation:

$$h = \frac{\alpha w - b}{w - b} = \frac{\alpha w(1-t) - b}{w(1-t) - b}. \qquad (13.13)$$

Let us now consider the role played by the way in which nonemployment income reacts to changes in taxes. Consider first the case where benefits are indexed to prices; that is, real nonemployment income is constant at b. In this case, as shown by (13.13), the labor supply curve is always upward sloping $\left(\frac{\partial h}{\partial w(1-t)} = \frac{b(1-\alpha)}{[w(1-t)-b]^2}\right)$, hence taxes reduce labor supply. Suppose now that nonemployment income is instead indexed to wages, so that the ratio of benefits to wages (or the replacement rate) is constant at $b/w(1-t) = b^w$. Dividing the numerator and the denominator of (13.13) by w, we obtain

$$h = \frac{\alpha - b^w}{1 - b^w}. \qquad (13.14)$$

If the replacement rate is constant, labor supply does not depend on the wage; that is, there is a vertical labor supply curve, just like the case where $\varepsilon = \infty$ characterized above. All changes in the tax rate are absorbed by the (net) wage, leaving employment unaffected. This is an extreme case, and it is related to the Cobb-Douglas specification of the utility function. With a more general specification, the labor supply curve will be upward sloping when UBs are indexed to wages, but the slope will be steeper than in the case where benefits are indexed to prices.

The Progressiveness of Taxation

A general structure for payroll taxes T is the linear tax,

$$T = tw + a, \tag{13.15}$$

where w is the wage that the worker receives, t is the marginal tax rate on wages, and a is the per worker lump-sum tax or employment subsidy. The average tax rate $\frac{T}{w}$ is equal to $t + \frac{a}{w}$; the marginal tax rate $\frac{\partial T}{\partial w}$ is equal to t. Both a and t are tax instruments where t is assumed to be positive or equal to zero, and a can be zero, positive, or negative. This linear tax subsumes various tax systems. Taxes are proportional if every worker pays the same tax rate irrespective of the level of the wage, in other words, if the average tax rate equals the marginal tax rate, which holds if $a = 0$. Taxes are progressive if the marginal tax rate is higher than the average tax rate, which holds if $a < 0$. Finally, the tax system is regressive if the marginal tax rate is lower than the average tax rate, which holds if $a > 0$.

Consider then a labor market in which nonemployment income is indexed to (net) wages. We know from the above that in this case labor supply is rigid, employment is unaffected by taxes, and wages are determined by labor demand. Now, profits are maximized when the marginal value equals the marginal wage costs, that is, the costs to the firm of an additional worker, including payroll taxes:

$$AL^{-\eta} = (1+t)w + a, \tag{13.16}$$

from which we obtain the optimal choice as to the number of workers:

$$L^* = \left[\frac{A}{(1+t)w + a} \right]^{\frac{1}{\eta}}. \tag{13.17}$$

From this equation it follows that a tax hike—irrespective of whether it occurs through t or a—reduces labor demand. Provided that T is the same, the structure of taxation is immaterial. In a competitive market firms are price-takers. Hence labor demand is affected only by the total tax level and not by the structure of the taxes.

13.9.2 General Equilibrium Effects of Taxes

Consider a two-sided job search model like the framework developed by Mortensen and Pissarides (1999) and proposed in technical annex 11.9. There is a constant returns-to-scale matching function, hence θ, the vacancy to unemployment ratio or market tightness, is a sufficient statistic. Let $m(\theta)$ denote the vacancy filling rate, where $m' < 0$. Allow for a linear labor tax $T = tw + a$, where a parametrizes tax progressiveness, nominally imposed on workers so that the take-home pay is $w(1 - t) - a$. We also extend the model by considering skill differences and endogenizing job destruction to better characterize the effects of redistributions carried out by means of the tax system.

Suppose that there is a continuum of labor markets indexed by $s \in (0, 1]$ where s stands for years of schooling. Workers supply labor inelastically and cannot change their skill level; they are either unemployed (with income b) or employed at wage $w(s)$. Firms either produce with one worker, or search for one with an open vacancy. They can enter freely and search in any labor market at zero cost, but they must pay a periodic recruitment cost of $s\kappa$ per unit period. For production to occur, a worker must be matched with a job. When matched, a firm and a worker generate periodic productivity sy, where $y \in (0, 1]$ is a match-specific component. All newly formed matches (i.e., filled jobs) begin at the highest possible value of y ($y = 1$). Immediately thereafter, match productivity can change at Poisson frequency λ, in which case it is a random draw with a fixed, known cumulative distribution $F(y)$.

We can now write the equilibrium valuations of states for an arbitrary skill level as follows:

flow value of unemployment:

$$\rho V_u = b + \theta m(\theta)[V_e(1) - V_u] \tag{13.18}$$

flow value of a vacancy:

$$\rho V = -s\kappa + m(\theta)[\Pi_e(1) - \Pi_v] \tag{13.19}$$

flow value of employment:

$$\rho V_e(y) = w(y)(1 - t) - a$$
$$+ \lambda \int_R^1 (V_e(z) - V_e(y))dF(z) + \lambda F(R)(V_u - V_e(y)) \tag{13.20}$$

flow value of a job:

$$\rho \Pi_e(y) = sy - w(y)$$
$$+ \lambda \int_R^1 (\Pi_e(z) - \Pi_e(y))dF(z) + \lambda F(R)(\Pi_v - \Pi_e(y)). \tag{13.21}$$

The lower bound of the definite integral, R, is the cutoff or threshold value of match productivity, determined endogenously in the model. If idiosyncratic productivity y falls below R, the match is no longer profitable, and the job/worker pair is destroyed. Hence the product $\lambda F(R)$ captures the probability that the job is hit by a productivity shock, making it no longer profitable (i.e., it is the probability of job loss).

Partial Equilibrium Effects

Gross wages are determined as a (Nash) bargaining process solving

$$w(y) = \arg \max(V_e(y) - V_u)^\beta (\Pi_e(y) - \Pi_v)^{1-\beta}, \tag{13.22}$$

yielding the first-order condition:

$$(1 - \beta)[V_e(y) - V_u] = \beta(\Pi_e(y) - \Pi_v)(1 - t). \tag{13.23}$$

Imposing the free entry condition $\Pi_v = 0$ and rewriting the two asset value conditions results in

$$\Pi_e(y) = \frac{y - w(y) + \lambda \int_R^1 \Pi_e(z) dF(z)}{r + \lambda} \tag{13.24}$$

$$V_e(y) = \frac{(w(y)(1 - t) - a) + \lambda \int_R^1 V_e(z) dF(z) + \lambda F(R) V_u}{r + \lambda}, \tag{13.25}$$

with the adequate substitutions

$$w(y) = \frac{(1 - \beta)(r V_u + a)}{1 - t} + \beta y. \tag{13.26}$$

To get a closed-form expression for $r V_u$, we can use the free entry condition

$$\Pi_e(1) = \frac{s\kappa}{m(\theta)} \tag{13.27}$$

to obtain

$$\rho V_u = b + \frac{\beta(s\kappa)\theta}{1 - \beta}. \tag{13.28}$$

Substituting, we finally obtain

$$w(y) = \beta y + \frac{\beta s\kappa\theta + (1 - \beta)(b + a)}{1 - t}. \tag{13.29}$$

As indicated by the above, the marginal tax rate t unambiguously increases labor costs of the firm as part of the tax is rebated by wage bargaining onto the employers. The effect becomes greater with increasing bargaining power of workers and market tightness. The parameter a instead affects labor costs proportionally to the bargaining strength of employers. This is because a increases the reservation wage of workers, forcing employers to pay at least $b + a$ to their workers. Notice that when benefits are fully indexed to wages and hence $da = -db$, an increase in the progressiveness of taxes will have no effects on the equilibrium wage. However, a change in a compensated by variations in t (e.g., a reduction of a "financed" by an increase in t) so that

$$dt = -\frac{da}{w} \tag{13.30}$$

will increase labor costs. Symmetrically, increases in the progressiveness of taxation allowing for reductions in the marginal tax rate t will reduce the gross wage.

General Equilibrium Effects

To characterize the general equilibrium (of the labor market) effects of labor taxes, we have to derive the equilibrium job creation and destruction conditions of this model and consider whether taxes affect the range of skill levels for which a labor market is properly working (there are vacancies and jobseekers). The *job creation condition* can be derived using (13.23) together with the asset value condition for a job evaluated at the entry productivity level (see Boeri 2011 for the full derivation) to obtain

$$(\rho + \lambda)\frac{s\kappa}{m(\theta)} = (1 - \beta)(y - R). \tag{13.31}$$

Hence taxes do not directly affect the equilibrium job creation condition. However, they affect job creation indirectly, by increasing the reservation productivity threshold, R. To see this, we have to derive the *job destruction condition* of this model. The latter (see once more Boeri 2011 for the full derivation) reads

$$sR(1 - \beta) + s\lambda \int_R^1 (z - R)dF(z) = \frac{\beta s\kappa\theta + (1 - \beta)(b + a)}{1 - t}. \tag{13.32}$$

The two equilibrium conditions endogenously determine the equilibrium market tightness θ^* and reservation productivity R^* levels. Plugging these in the steady state unemployment condition, we obtain the equilibrium unemployment level:

$$u^* = \frac{\lambda F(R^*)}{\lambda F(R^*) + \theta^* m(\theta^*)}. \tag{13.33}$$

Implicit differentiation of the job destruction condition shows that R^* is increasing in both a and t. By the job creation condition, an increase in R (remember that the vacancy filling rate is declining with θ) implies a decline in the equilibrium job-finding rate. Thus, unemployment unambiguously increases when taxes are higher. However, when UBs are fully indexed to the net wage, then an increase in a has no effects on the equilibrium job destruction and unemployment conditions. Intuitively, in this case there is no change in the reservation wage of the worker. In this context, a revenue-neutral increase in the progressiveness of taxation (an increase in a allowing for a reduction of t) involves a reduction in the equilibrium unemployment level. When UBs are not fully indexed, for reasonable values of the parameters, a revenue-neutral increase in the progressiveness of taxes will still reduce unemployment. However, it will also increase the range of skill levels for which a labor market is not operating. This can be seen by taking the limit of the job destruction condition when R approaches unity, that is, there is no skill-productivity level sy for which a job is viable or, equivalently, by taking the limit of the job creation condition when θ approaches zero and there are no vacancies available for individuals with that skill (Boeri and Burda 2009). This generates a critical skill level $\hat{s}$, below which a labor market is not operating, and the latter is increasing with a.

Possible Extensions

Payroll taxes are collected to finance a number of labor market policies. Hence, the effects of taxes can be better evaluated by considering taxes in conjunction with other labor market institutions affecting the job creation and destruction margins.

The above framework can be readily extended to evaluate the general equilibrium effects of the following institutions:

- UBs $b = b^w \bar{w}$, where $\bar{w}$ is the average wage, and b^w is the replacement rate;
- ECI (α is paid to the employee at a flat rate to increase job-finding rates of low-skilled workers);
- hiring subsidies h, or a more efficient public employment service, reducing the recruitment costs c of employers; and
- a firing tax F, like the employment protection (pure) tax discussed in chapter 10.

As shown by Boeri (2011), we have the following qualitative results:

	Effect of an increase in			
Variable affected by increase	b^w	F	α	h
R^*	$+$	$-$	$-$	$+$
θ	$-$	$-$	$+$	$+$
u^*	$+$	?	$-$	?
Probability of job loss	$+$	$-$	$-$	$+$
Job-finding rate	$-$	$-$	$+$	$+$
Average wage	$+$	?	$-$	?

The economics behind these results is as follows.

- An **increase in the replacement income** b^w offered by UBs. Insofar as gross job destruction increases, unemployment unambiguously increases, bringing down the equilibrium level of market tightness, θ^*. The new equilibrium features a higher probability of job loss, a lower job-finding rate $\theta^* m(\theta^*)$, and a higher unemployment and average wage.
- An **increase in firing taxes** F has the opposite effect of maintaining jobs with a lower match productivity. This reduces the gross job destruction rate. Firing taxes also positively affect wages, as in partial equilibrium. The effect on wages is partly offset by the reduction in market tightness induced by the larger firing tax and by the wage hike, which reduces the number of vacancies

available at equilibrium. As both job-finding and job-loss rates decline, the effect on equilibrium unemployment is ambiguous. The new equilibrium features lower job-loss and job-finding probabilities, while there is ambiguity as to the effects on unemployment and average wage.

- An **increase in ECI** α makes the labor market tighter. The reduction in entry wages, hence the increase in θ^*, is larger the stronger the bargaining position of employers and the larger recruitment subsidies become. As continuing jobs are subsidized, the productivity threshold, R^*, also declines, increasing the duration of jobs. The new equilibrium involves a higher job-finding rate and a lower job-loss probability, as well as a lower unemployment and average wage. The latter declines because wages are lower at any productivity realization and there are more low-productivity jobs.

- Finally, an **increase in the activation scheme** h, reducing recruitment costs, has similar effects on the job creation margin as the other ALMP tool. As the costs of filling a vacancy are lower, the vacancy to unemployment ratio increases. However, lower turnover costs allow for jobs to be destroyed at a higher productivity threshold. The new equilibrium features higher job-finding and job-loss rates, while the effects on unemployment and the average wage are ambiguous.

Another extension to the framework involves endogenizing taxes by considering a government budget constraint like

$$(t\bar{w} + a)(1 - u) = b^w \bar{w} u + \alpha(1 - u). \tag{13.34}$$

However, introducing a government budget constraint may generate multiple equilibriums. In particular, we may have a *bad equilibrium* with high unemployment, large outlays for UBs, and high taxes and a *good equilibrium* with low unemployment, modest UB expenditures, and low taxes. The intuition is that endogenous taxes mitigate the positive externality caused by unemployment on job finding via the matching function by also generating a negative *fiscal externality* of unemployment.

References

Abbring, J. H., G. J. van den Berg, and J. C. van Ours (2005). The effect of unemployment insurance sanctions on the transition rate from unemployment to employment. *Economic Journal 115*, 602–30.

Abowd, J., F. Kramarz, T. Lemieux, and D. Margolis (1999). Minimum wage and youth employment in France and the United States. In *Youth employment and the labor market*, ed. D. Blanchflower and R. Freeman. Chicago: University of Chicago Press.

Acemoglu, D. (1997). Training and innovation in an imperfect labor market. *Review of Economic Studies 64*, 445–64.

——— (2001). Good jobs versus bad jobs: Theory and some evidence. *Journal of Labor Economics 19*, 1–22.

Acemoglu, D., and D. Autor (2011). Skills, tasks and technologies: Implications for employment and earnings. In *Handbook of labor economics 4B*, ed. D. Card and O. Ashenfelter. Amsterdam: Elsevier.

Acemoglu, D., and J. Pischke (1998). Why do firms train? Theory and evidence. *Quarterly Journal of Economics 113*, 79–119.

——— (1999). Beyond Becker: Training in imperfect labor markets. *Economic Journal 109*, F112–F142.

Acemoglu, D., P. Aghion, and G. Violante (2000). Deunionization, technical change, and inequality. *Carnegie-Rochester Conference Series on Public Policy 44 (1)*, 229–64.

Adams, S. J. (2004). Age discrimination legislation and the employment of older workers. *Labour Economics 11*, 219–41.

Addison, J., and M. Blackburn (1999). Minimum wages and poverty. *Industrial and Labor Relations Review 52 (3)*, 393–409.

——— (2000). The effects of unemployment insurance on post-unemployment earnings. *Labour Economics 7*, 21–53.

Addison, J., and J.-L. Grosso (1996). Job security provisions and employment: Revised estimates. *Industrial Relations 35 (4)*, 585–603.

Agell, J. (1999). On the benefits for rigid labour markets: Norms, market failures and social insurance. *Economic Journal 109*, 143–64.

——— (2000). On the determinants of labor market institutions: Rent-sharing vs. social insurance. Working Paper 16, Uppsala.

——— (2001). On the determinants of labor market institutions: Rent-sharing vs. social insurance. *Research Papers in Economics 1001:12*, Stockholm University, Department of Economics.

Agell, J., and K. E. Lommerud (1992). Union egalitarianism as income insurance. *Economica 59*, 295–310.

Ahmed, A., L. Andersson, and M. Hammarstedt (2011). Are homosexuals discriminated against in the hiring process? IFAU Discussion Paper 2011: 21.

Aigner, D. J., and G. G. Cain (1977). Statistical theories of discrimination in labor markets. *Industrial and Labor Relations Review 30*, 175–87.

Akerlof, G. A. (1980). A theory of social customs, of which unemployment may be one consequence. *Quarterly Journal of Economics 94 (4)*, 749–75.

Alderman, H., L. Haddad, and J. Hoddinott (1994). Intrahousehold resource allocation: An overview. Policy Research Working Paper Series 1255, World Bank, Washington, DC.

Alesina, A., and R. Perotti (1997). The welfare state and competitiveness. *American Economic Review 87*, 921–39.

Algan, Y., and P. Cahuc (2005). Theory roots of low European employment: Family culture? In *NBER macroeconomics annual*, ed. C. Pissarides and J. Frankel. Cambridge, MA: MIT Press.

——— (2009). Civic virtue and labor market institutions. *American Economic Journal: Macroeconomics 1*, 111–45.

Alogoskoufis, G., C. R. Bean, G. Bertola, D. Cohen, J. J. Dolado, and G. Saint-Paul (1995). Unemployment: Choices for Europe. CEPR Report. London: Centre for Economic Policy Research.

Altonji, J., and R. Blank (1999). Race and gender in the labor market. In *Handbook of labor economics*, ed. O. Ashenfelter and D. Card. Amsterdam: Elsevier.

Ames, E., and R. T. Rapp (1977). The birth and death of taxes: A hypothesis. *Journal of Economic History 37*, 161–78.

Andersen, T. M., and M. Svarer (2010). State dependent unemployment benefits. *Journal of Risk and Insurance 78*, 325–44.

Andrews, M. J., T. Schank, and R. Simmons (2005). Does worksharing work? Some empirical evidence from the IAB-establishment panel. *Scottish Journal of Political Economy 52*, 141–76.

Angrist, J. D. (1990). Lifetime earnings and the Vietnam era draft lottery: Evidence from social security administrative records. *American Economic Review 80*, 313–36.

——— (1991). Instrumental variables estimation of average treatment effects in econometrics and epidemiology. Technical Working Paper 0115. Cambridge, MA: National Bureau of Economic Research.

Angrist, J. D., and A. B. Krueger (1991). Does compulsory school attendance affect schooling and earnings? *Quarterly Journal of Economics 106 (4)*, 979–1014.

——— (1999). Empirical strategies in labor economics. In *Handbook of labor economics*, ed. O. Ashenfelter and D. Card. Amsterdam: Elsevier.

Antecol, H., D. Cobb-Clark, and S. Trejo (2003). Immigration policy and the skills of immigrants to Australia, Canada and the United States. *Journal of Human Resources 38 (1)*, 192–218.

Antón, J., and R. Muñoz de Bustillo (2011). The impact of the minimum wage on Spanish youth: Evidence from a natural experiment. Munich Personal RePEc Archive Paper 33488.

Arni, P., R. Lalive, and J. van Ours (2013). How effective are unemployment benefit sanctions? Looking beyond unemployment exit. *Journal of Applied Econometrics*, doi: 10.1002/jae.2289.

Arrow, K. (1973). The theory of discrimination. In *Discrimination in labor markets*, ed. O. Ashenfelter and A. Rees. Princeton: Princeton University Press.

Ashenfelter, O. C., and J. N. Brown (1986). Testing the efficiency of employment contracts. *Journal of Political Economy 94 (3)*, 541–87.

Ashenfelter, O. C., and D. Card (2002). Did the elimination of mandatory retirement affect faculty retirement flows? *American Economic Review 92*, 957–80.

Ashenfelter, O. C., and G. E. Johnson (1969). Bargaining theory, trade unions, and industrial strike activity. *American Economic Review 74*, 35–49.

Ashenfelter, O. C., and C. Rouse (1998). Income, schooling, and ability: Evidence from a new sample of identical twins. *Quarterly Journal of Economics 113*, 253–84.

Ashenfelter, O. C., H. Farber, and M. R. Ransom (2010). Labor market monopsony. *Journal of Labor Economics 28*, 203–10.

Atkinson, A., and J. Micklewright (1991). Unemployment compensation and labor market transitions: A critical review. *Journal of Economic Literature 29*, 1679–1727.

Atkinson, A., T. Piketty, and E. Saez (2011). Top incomes in the long run of history. *Journal of Economic Literature 49 (1)*, 3–71.

Aubert, P. (2003). Productivity, wage and demand for elder workers: An examination of French matched employer-employee data. Paris: Institut National de la Statistique et d'Études Economiques.

Autor, D. (2001). Why do temporary help firms provide free general skills training? *Quarterly Journal of Economics 116 (4)*, 1409–48.

Autor, D., J. Donohue, and S. Schwab (2006). The costs of wrongful discharge laws. *Review of Economics and Statistics 88 (2)*, 211–31.

Avolio, B. J., D. A. Waldman, and M. A. McDaniel (1990). Age and work performance in non-managerial jobs: The effects of experience and occupational type. *Academy of Management Journal 33 (2)*, 407–22.

Bacache-Beauvallet, M., and E. Lehmann (2008). Minimum wage or negative income tax: Why skilled workers may favor wage rigidities. *Spanish Economic Review 10 (1)*, 63–81.

Baker, M., and K. Milligan (2010). Evidence from maternity leave expansions of the impact of maternal care on early child development. *Journal of Human Resources 45 (1)*, 1–32.

Banks, J., and S. Smith (2006). Retirement in the UK. *Oxford Review of Economic Policy (Spring)*, 40–56.

Barth, M. C., W. McNaught, and P. Rizzi (1993). Corporations and the aging workforce. In *Building the competitive workforce: Investing in human capital for corporate success,* ed. P. H. Mirvis. New York: John Wiley and Sons.

Bassanini, A. (2006). Training, wages and employment security: An empirical analysis on European data. *Applied Economics Letters, 13 (8)*, 523–27.

Bauer, T. K., R. Flake, and M. G. Sinning (2011). Labor market effects of immigration: Evidence from neighborhood data. IZA Discussion Paper 5707. Bonn: Institute for the Study of Labor.

Baum, C. L. (2003). Does early maternal employment harm child development? An analysis of the potential benefits of leave taking. *Journal of Labor Economics 21*, 409–48.

Bean, C. (1994). European unemployment: A survey. *Journal of Economic Literature 32 (2)*, 573–619.

Becker, G. (1968). Crime and punishment: An economic approach. *Journal of Political Economy 76 (2)*, 169–217.

——— (1971). *The economics of discrimination* (2nd ed.). Chicago: University of Chicago Press.

Becker, G. S. (1964). *Human capital: A theoretical and empirical analysis, with special reference to education.* New York: Columbia University Press.

Behaghel, L., B. Crépon, and B. Sédillot (2004). Contribution Delalande et transitions sur le marché du travail. *Economie et Statistique 372*, 61–88.

——— (2008). The perverse effects of partial employment protection reform: The case of French older workers. *Journal of Public Economics 92*, 696–721.

Bell, L. A. (1997). The impact of minimum wages in Mexico and Columbia. *Journal of Labor Economics 15*, S102–S135.

Belot, M., and J. C. van Ours (2001). Unemployment and labor market institutions: An empirical analysis. *Journal of the Japanese and International Economies 15*, 403–18.

——— (2004). Does the recent success of some OECD countries in lowering their unemployment rates lie in the clever design of their labor market reforms? *Oxford Economic Papers 56*, 621–42.

Belzil, C. (2001). Unemployment insurance and subsequent job duration: Job matching versus unobserved heterogeneity. *Journal of Applied Econometrics 16*, 619–36.

Ben-Porath, Y. (1967). The production of human capital and the life cycle of earnings. *Journal of Political Economy 75 (4)*, 352–65.

Bentolila, S., and G. Bertola (1990). Firing costs and labour demand: How bad is eurosclerosis? *Review of Economic Studies 57*, 381–402.

Bentolila, S., and J. Dolado (1994). Labor flexibility and wages: Lessons from Spain. *Economic Policy 18*, 55–99.

Bentolila, S., J. Dolado, P. Cahuc, and L. Barbanchon (2012). Two-tier labor markets in the Great Recession: France versus Spain. *Economic Journal 122*, F155–F187.

Bertola, G. (1990). Job security, employment, and wages. *European Economic Review 34 (4)*, 851–79.

Bertola, G., and T. Boeri (2002). EMU labour markets two years on: Microeconomic tensions and institutional evolutions. In *EMU and economic policy in Europe*, ed. M. Buti and A. Sapir. Cheltenham, UK, and Northampton, MA: Edward Elgar.

Bertola, G., and R. Rogerson (1997). Institutions and labour reallocation. *European Economic Review 41*, 1147–71.

Bertola, G., T. Boeri, and S. Cazes (2000). Employment protection in industrialized countries: The case for new indicators. *International Labor Review 139 (1)*, 57–72.

Bertola, G., J. F. Jimeno, R. Marimon, and C. Pissarides (1999). EU welfare systems and labor markets: Diverse in the past, integrated in the future? In *Welfare and employment in Europe,* ed. G. Bertola, T. Boeri, and G. Nicoletti. Cambridge, MA: MIT Press.

Bertrand, M. (2010). New perspectives on gender. In *Handbook of labor economics 4B,* ed. D. Card and O. Ashenfelter. Amsterdam: Elsevier.

Bertrand, M., and S. Mullainathan (2004). Are Emily and Greg more employable than Lakisha and Jamal? A field experiment on labor market discrimination. *American Economic Review 94,* 991–1013.

Biddle, J., and D. S. Hamermesh (1994). Beauty and the labor market. *American Economic Review 84,* 174–94.

Bils, M., and P. Klenow (2000). Does schooling cause growth? *American Economic Review 90,* 1160–83.

Binmore, K., A. Rubinstein, and A. Wolinsky (1986). The Nash solution in economic modelling. *Rand Journal of Economics 17 (2),* 176–88.

Björklund, A., and B. Holmlund (1991). The economics of unemployment insurance: The case of Sweden. *Labour market policy and unemployment insurance,* ed. A. Bjorklund, R. Haveman, R. Hollister, and B. Holmlund. Oxford: Clarendon Press.

Black, D. A. (1995). Discrimination in an equilibrium search model. *Journal of Labor Economics 13,* 309–34.

Black, D. A., J. Smith, M. C. Berger, and B. L. Noel (2003). Is the threat of training more effective than training itself? Evidence from random assignments in the UI system. *American Economic Review 93,* 1313–27.

Blanchard, O. J. (2004). The economic future of Europe. *Journal of Economic Perspectives 18,* 3–26.

——— (2006). European unemployment: The evolution of facts and ideas. *Economic Policy 22,* 5–59.

Blanchard, O. J., and P. A. Diamond (1994). Ranking, unemployment duration, and wages. *Review of Economic Studies 61 (3),* 417–34.

Blanchard, O. J., and L. H. Katz (1992). Regional evolutions. Brookings Papers on Economic Activity. Washington, DC: Brookings Institution.

Blanchard, O. J., and J. Tirole (2003). Redesigning the employment protection system. *De Economist 152,* 1–20.

Blanchard, O. J., and J. Wolfers (2000). The role of shocks and institutions in the rise of European unemployment: The aggregate evidence. *Economic Journal 110,* 1–33.

Blanchflower, D. (2007). A cross-country study of union membership. *British Journal of Industrial Relations 45 (1),* 1–28.

Blau, D. (2000). Child care subsidy programs. Working Paper 7806. Cambridge, MA: National Bureau of Economic Research.

——— (2001). *The child care problem: An economic analysis.* New York: Russell Sage Foundation.

Blau, D. M., and P. K. Robins (1986). Job search, wage offers, and unemployment insurance. *Journal of Public Economics 29,* 173–97.

Blau, F., M. A. Ferber, and A. E. Winkler (2010). *The economics of women, men and work* (6th ed.). Boston: Pearson.

Blau, F. D., and R. G. Ehrenberg (1997). *Gender and family issues in the workplace.* New York: Russell Sage Foundation.

Blau, F. D., and A. Grossberg (1992). Maternal labor supply and children's cognitive development. *The Review of Economics and Statistics 74 (3),* 474–81.

Blau, F. D., and L. M. Kahn (1996). The gender earnings gap: Some international evidence. Working Paper 4224. Cambridge, MA: National Bureau of Economic Research.

Blinder, A. S. (1973). Wage discimination: Reduced form and structural estimates. *Journal of Human Resources 8,* 436–55.

Blundell, R. (2001). Welfare reform for low income workers. *Oxford Economic Papers 53,* 189–214.

Blundell, R., and M. Dias (2000). Evaluation methods for non-experimental data. *Fiscal Studies 21,* 427–68.

Blundell, R., and T. MaCurdy (1999). Labor supply: A review of alternative approaches. *Handbook of labor economics,* ed. O. Ashenfelter and D. Card. Amsterdam: Elsevier.

Blundell, R., A. Bozio, and G. Laroque (2011). Extensive and intensive margins of labour supply: Working hours in the US, UK and France. IZA Discussion Paper 6051. Bonn: Institute for the Study of Labor.

Böckerman, P., and R. Uusitalo (2006). Erosion of the Ghent system and union membership decline: Lessons from Finland. *British Journal of Industrial Relations 44 (2)*, 283–303.

Bodvarsson, Ö. B., H. F. van den Berg, and J. J. Lewer (2008). Measuring immigration's effect on labor demand: A reexamination of the Mariel Boatlift. *Labour Economics 15*, 560–74.

Boeri, T. (1996). Is job turnover countercyclical? *Journal of Labor Economics 14 (4)*, 603–25.

——— (1999). Enforcement of employment security regulations, on-the-job search and unemployment duration. *European Economic Review 43*, 65–89.

——— (2005). An activating social security system. *De Economist 153 (4)*, 375–97.

——— (2010). Immigration to the land of redistribution. *Economica 77*, 651–87.

——— (2011). Institutional reform and dualism. In *Handbook of labor economics 4B*, ed. D. Card and O. Ashenfelter. Elsevier.

——— (2012). Setting the minimum wage. *Labour Economics 19*, 281–90.

Boeri, T., and H. Bruecker (2005). Why are Europeans so tough on migrants? *Economic Policy 44*, 629–704.

——— (2011). Short-time work benefits revisited: Some lessons from the Great Recession. *Economic Policy 26 (68)*, 697–765.

Boeri, T., and A. Brugiavini (2008). Pension reform and women's retirement plans. *Journal of Population Ageing 1*, 7–30.

Boeri, T., and M. C. Burda (1996). Active labour market policies, job matching and the Czech miracle. *European Economic Review 40*, 805–17.

——— (2009). Preferences for collective versus individualized wage setting. *Economic Journal 119*, 1440–63.

Boeri, T., and P. Garibaldi (2006). Two tier reforms of employment protection: A honeymoon effect? *Economic Journal 17*, 357–85.

Boeri, T., and J. Jimeno (2005). The effects of employment protection: Learning from variable enforcement. *European Economic Review 49*, 2057–77.

Boeri, T., and M. Macis (2010). Do unemployment benefits promote or hinder structural change? *Journal of Development Economics 93 (1)*, 109–25.

Boeri, T., and K. Terrell (2002). Institutional determinants of labor reallocation in transition. *Journal of Economic Perspectives 16 (1)*, 51–76.

Boeri, T., G. Hanson, and B. McGormick, eds. (2002). *Immigration policy and the welfare system*. Oxford: Oxford University Press.

Boeri, T., D. Del Boca, and C. Pissarides (2005). *Women at work: An economic perspective*. Oxford: Oxford University Press.

Boeri, T., M. Burda, and F. Kramarz, eds. (2008). *Working hours and job sharing in the EU and USA: Are Europeans lazy? Or Americans crazy?* Oxford: Oxford University Press.

Boeri, T., P. Garibaldi, and M. Ribeiro (2011). The lighthouse effect and beyond. *Review of Income and Wealth 57*, 54–78.

Boeri, T., J. I. Conde-Ruiz, and V. Galasso (2012). The political economy of flexicurity. *Journal of the European Economic Association 10*, 684–715.

Boeri, T., P. Garibaldi, and E. Moen (2013). The economics of severance pay. IZA Discussion Paper 7455. Bonn: Institute for the Study of Labor.

Boldrin, M., J. J. Dolado, J. F. Jimeno, and F. Peracchi (1999). The future of pension systems in Europe: A reappraisal. *Economic Policy 29*, 289–323.

Boockmann, B., T. Zwick, A. Ammermüller, and M. Maier (2012). Do hiring subsidies reduce unemployment among older workers? Evidence from natural experiments. *Journal of the European Economic Association 10*, 735–64.

Boone, J., and J. C. van Ours (2006). Modelling financial incentives to get unemployed back to work. *Journal of Institutional and Theoretical Economics 162 (2)*, 227–52.

——— (2009). Bringing unemployed back to work: effective active labor market policies. *De Economist 157 (04-87)*, 293–313.

——— (2012). Why is there a spike in the job finding rate at benefit exhaustion? *De Economist 160*, 413–38.

Boone, J., P. Fredriksson, B. Holmlund, and J. C. van Ours (2007). Optimal unemployment insurance with monitoring and sanctions. *Economic Journal 117*, 399–421.

Booth, A. (1995). *The economics of the trade union*. Cambridge: Cambridge University Press.

Booth, A., and J. C. van Ours (2008). Job satisfaction and family happiness: The part-time work puzzle. *Economic Journal 118*, F77–F99.

Booth, A., and J. C. van Ours (2009). Hours of work and gender identity: Does part-time work make the family happier? *Economica 76*, 176–96.

——— (2013). Part-time jobs: What women want? *Journal of Population Economics 26*, 263–83.

Booth, A. L., and L. Bryan (2005). Testing some predictions of human capital theory: New training evidence from Britain. *Review of Economics and Statistics 87*, 391–94.

Booth, A. L., and A. Leigh (2010). Do employers discriminate by gender? A field experiment in female-dominated occupations. *Economics Letters 107*, 236–38.

Booth, A. L., and M. Ravallion (1993). Employment and length of the working week in a unionized economy in which hours of work influence productivity. *Economic Record, Economic Society of Australia 69 (207)*, 428–36.

Borghans, L., B.H.H. Golsteyn, J. J. Heckman, and J. E. Humphries (2009). Identification problems in personality psychology. NBER Working Paper 16917. Cambridge, MA. National Bureau of Economic Research.

Borjas, G. J. (1999). The economic analysis of immigration. In *Handbook of labor economics*, ed. O. Ashenfelter and D. Card. Amsterdam: Elsevier.

——— (2001). Does immigration grease the wheels of the labor market? *Brookings Papers on Economic Activity 1*, 69–133.

——— (2003). The labor demand curve is downward-sloping: Reexamining the impact of immigration on the labor market. *Quarterly Journal of Economics 18 (November)*, 1335–74.

——— (2009). *Labor economics (5th ed.)* Cambridge: McGraw-Hill.

Börsch-Supan, A., and H. K. Jürges (2006). Early retirement, social security and well-being in Germany. NBER Working Paper 12303. Cambridge, MA: National Bureau of Economic Research.

Bratberg, E., T. H. Holmås, and Ø. Thøgerson (2004). Assessing the effects of an early retirement program. *Journal of Population Economics 17*, 387–408.

Brewer, M., E. Saez, and A. Shephard (2010). Means-testing and tax rates on earnings. In *Dimensions of tax design, the Mirrlees review,* ed. Institute for Fiscal Studies. Oxford: Oxford University Press.

Brown, C. (1999). Minimum wages, employment, and the distribution of income. In *Handbook of labor economics*, ed. O. Ashenfelter and D. Card. Amsterdam: Elsevier.

Browning, M., F. Bourguignon, P. Chiappori, and V. Lechene (1994). Income and outcomes: A structural model of intrahousehold allocation. *Journal of Political Economy 102*, 1067–96.

Brugiavini, A., M. C. Burda, L. Calmfors, D. Checchi, R. Naylor, and J. Visser (2001). The future of collective bargaining in Europe. In *The role of unions in the twenty-first century,* ed. T. Boeri, A. Brugiavini, and L. Calmfors. Oxford: Oxford University Press.

Brunello, G., P. Garibaldi, and E. Wasmer (2007). *Education and training in Europe.* Oxford: Oxford University Press.

Brusentsev, V., and W. Vroman (2012). *Stabilizing employment: The role of short-time compensation.* Kalamazoo, MI: Upjohn Institute Press.

Buddelmeyer, H., G. Mourre, and M. Ward (2005). Part-time work in EU countries: Labour market mobility, entry and exit. IZA Discussion Paper 1550. Bonn: Institute for the Study of Labor.

Burda, M. (1995). Migration and the option value of waiting. *Economic and Social Review 27*, 1–19.

Burda, M., and J. Hunt (2001). From reunification to economic integration: Productivity and the labor market in Eastern Germany. *Brooking Papers on Economic Activity 2*, 1–92.

Burda, M. C., and P. Weil (2008). Blue laws. *Working hours and job sharing in the EU and USA: Are Europeans lazy? Or Americans crazy?,* ed. T. Boeri, M. Burda, and F. Kramara. Oxford: Oxford University Press.

Burda, M., D. Hamermesh, and P. Weil (2008). *Understanding transatlantic differences in working hours.* Oxford: Oxford University Press.

Burdett, K., and R. Wright (1989). Unemployment insurance and short-time compensation: The effects on layoffs, hours per worker and wages. *Journal of Political Economy 97*, 1479–96.

Burgess, P. L., and J. L. Kingston (1976). The impact of unemployment insurance benefits on reemployment success. *Industrial and Labor Relations Review 30*, 25–31.

Burtless, G. (1985). Are targeted wage subsidies harmful? Evidence from a wage voucher experiment. *Industrial and Labor Relations Review 39,* 105–14.

Cahuc, P., and S. Carcillo (2011). Is short-time work a good method to keep unemployment down? CEPR Discussion Paper 8214. London: Centre for Economic Policy Research.

Cahuc, P., and J. Michel (1996). Minimum wage, unemployment and growth. *European Economic Review 40,* 1463–82.

Cahuc, P., and A. Zylberberg (2004). *Labor economics.* Cambridge, MA: MIT Press.

Caliendo, M., K. Tatsiramos, and A. Uhlendorff (2013). Benefit duration, unemployment duration and job match quality: A regression discontinuity approach. *Journal of Applied Econometrics 28 (4),* 604–27.

Calmfors, L. (1994). Active labor market policy and unemployment—A framework for the analysis of crucial design features. *OECD Economic Studies 22 (1),* 7–47.

——— (1995). What can we expect from active labor market policy? *Konjunkturpolitik 43,* 11–30.

——— (2001). The Future of Collective Bargaining in Europe. In *The role of unions in the twenty-first century,* ed. T. Boeri, A. Brugiavini, and L. Calmfors. Oxford: Oxford University Press.

Calmfors, L., and J. Driffil (1988). Bargaining structure, corporatism, and macroeconomic performance. *Economic Policy 6,* 12–61.

Calmfors, L., and M. Hoel (1989). Work sharing, employment and shiftwork. *Oxford Economic Papers 41,* 758–73.

Calmfors, L., A. Forslund, and M. Hemström (2001). Does active labor market policy work? Lessons from the Swedish experiences. *Swedish Economic Policy Review 85,* 61–124.

Cameron, A. C., and P. K. Trivedi (2005). *Microeconometrics: Methods and Applications.* Cambridge: Cambridge University Press.

Card, D. (1990). The impact of the Mariel Boatlift on the Miami labor market. *Industrial Labor Relations Review 43,* 245–57.

——— (1992). The effects of unions on the distribution of wages: Redistribution or relabelling. NBER Working Paper 4195. Cambridge, MA: National Bureau of Economic Research.

——— (1995). Using geographic variation in college proximity to estimate the return to schooling. In *Aspects of labour market behaviour: Essays in honour of John Vanderkamp,* ed. L. N. Christofides, E. K. Grant, and R. Swidinsky. Toronto: University of Toronto Press.

——— (1999). The causal effect of education on earnings. In *Handbook of labor economics,* ed. O. Ashenfelter and D. Card. Amsterdam: Elsevier.

——— (2001). The effects of unions on wage inequality in the U.S. labor market. *Industrial and Labor Relations Review 54,* 296–315.

——— (2005). Is the new immigration really so bad? *Economic Journal 115,* 300–24.

——— (2012). Comment: The elusive search for negative wage impacts from immigration. *Journal of the European Economic Association 10,* 211–15.

Card, D., and D. R. Hyslop (2005). Estimating the effects of a time-limited earnings subsidy for welfare-leavers. *Econometrica 73,* 1723–70.

Card, D., and A. Krueger (1994). Minimum wage and employment: A case study of the fast food industry in New Jersey and Pennsylvania. *American Economic Review 84,* 772–93.

——— (1995a). *Myth and measurement: The new economics of the minimum wage.* Princeton, NJ: Princeton University Press.

——— (1995b). Time-series minimum-wage studies: A meta-analysis. *American Economic Review, AEA Papers and Proceedings 85,* 238–43.

——— (2000). Minimum wages: A case study of the fast food industry in New Jersey and Pennsylvania: Reply. *American Economic Review 90,* 1397–1420.

Card, D., and P. Levine (2000). Extended benefits and the duration of UI spells: Evidence from the New Jersey Extended Benefit Program. *Journal of Public Economics 78,* 107–38.

Card, D., R. Chetty, and A. Weber (2007a). Cash-on-hand and competing models of intertemporal behavior: New evidence from the labor market. *Quarterly Journal of Economics 122,* 1511–60.

——— (2007b). The spike at benefit exhaustion: Leaving the unemployment system or starting a new job? *American Economic Review 97,* 113–18.

Card, D., J. Kluve, and A. Weber (2010). Active labor market policy evaluations: A meta-analysis. *Economic Journal 120,* 452–77.

Card, D., C. Dustmann, and I. Preston (2012). Immigration, wages, and compositional amenities. *Journal of the European Economic Association 10,* 78–119.

Carling, K., P. Edin, A. Harkman, and B. Holmlund (1996). Unemployment duration, unemployment benefits, and labor market programs in Sweden. *Journal of Public Economics 59,* 313–34.

Carling, K., B. Holmlund, and A. Vejsiu (2001). Do benefit cuts boost job findings? Swedish evidence from the 1990s. *Economic Journal 111,* 766–90.

Carlsson, M., and D. Rooth (2007). Evidence of ethnic discrimination in the Swedish labor market using experimental data. *Labour Economics 14,* 716–29.

Carrington, W., and P. de Lima (1996). The impact of the 1970s repatriates from Africa on the Portuguese labor market. *Industrial and Labor Relations Review 49 (January),* 330–47.

Centeno, M. (2004). The match quality gains from unemployment insurance. *Journal of Human Resources 34,* 839–63.

Centeno, M., and A. Novo (2007). *Unemployment insurance generosity and post-unemployment wages: Quantile treatment effects.* Lisbon: Bank of Portugal.

Chan, S., and A. H. Stevens (1999). Employment and retirement following a late-career job loss. *American Economic Review 89,* 211–16.

——— (2001). Job loss and employment patterns of older workers. *Journal of Labor Economics 19,* 484–521.

Chetty, R. (2008). Moral hazard vs. liquidity and optimal unemployment insurance. *Journal of Political Economy 116,* 173–234.

Chiappori, P.-A., and F. Bourguignon (1992). Collective models of household behavior: An introduction. *European Economic Review 36,* 355–65.

Clark, X., T. J. Hatton, and J. G. Williamson (2007). Explaining U.S. immigration, 1971–1998. *Review of Economics and Statistics 89,* 359–73.

Classen, K. (1977). The effect of unemployment insurance on the duration of unemployment and subsequent earnings. *Industrial and Labor Relations Review 30,* 438–44.

Contensou, F., and R. Vranceanu (2000). *Working time: Theory and policy implications.* Cheltenham, UK: Edward Elgar.

Corneo, G. (1997). The theory of the open shop trade union reconsidered. *Labour Economics 4,* 71–84.

Crépon, B., and F. Kramarz (2002). Employed 40 hours or not employed 39: Lessons from the 1982 mandatory reduction of the workweek. *Journal of Political Economy 110,* 1355–89.

Crépon, B., N. Deniau, and S. Pérez-Duarte (2003). Wages, productivity, and worker characteristics: A French perspective. Working paper, CREST-INSEE. Paris: Institut National de la Statistique et d'Études Economiques.

Crépon, B., M. Leclair, and S. Roux (2005). The shorter working week, productivity and employment: New estimates based on business data. *Economie et Statistique, Institut National de la Statistique et des Études Economiques 376,* 55–89.

Damm, A. P. (2009). Ethnic enclaves and immigrant labor market outcomes: Quasi-experimental evidence. *Journal of Labor Economics 27,* 281–314.

D'Amuri, F., G.I.P. Ottaviano, and G. Peri (2010). The labor market impact of immigration in western Germany in the 1990s. *European Economic Review 54,* 550–70.

Daniel, K., and J. S. Heywood (2007). The determinants of hiring older workers. *Labour Economics 14,* 35–51.

Daniels, R. (2002). *Coming to America: A history of immigration and ethnicity in American life* (2nd ed.). New York: Harper Perennial.

De Henau, J., D. Meulders, and S. Padraigin O'Dorchai (2007). Making time for working parents: Comparing public childcare provision. ULB Institutional Repository 2013/7708, Université Libre de Bruxelles, Brussels.

De Silva, D. G., R. P. McComb, Y. Moh, A. R. Schiller, and A. J. Vargas (2010). The effect of migration on wages: Evidence from a natural experiment. *American Economic Review: Papers and Proceedings 100,* 321–26.

Del Boca, D., and C. Wetzels, eds. (2008). *Social policies, labour markets and motherhood.* Cambridge: Cambridge University Press.

Devine, T., and N. Kiefer (1991). *Empirical labor economics: The search approach*. Oxford: Oxford University Press.

Di Nardo, J., N. Fortin, and T. Lemieux (1996). Labor market institutions and the distribution of wages: A semi-parametric approach. *Econometrica 64*, 1001–44.

Di Tella, R., and R. MacCulloch (2005). The consequences of labor market flexibility: Panel evidence based on survey data. *European Economic Review 49*, 1225–59.

Disney, R. (2000). The impact of tax and welfare policies on employment and unemployment in OECD countries. IMF Working Paper 164. Washington, DC: International Monetary Fund.

——— (2004). Are contributions to public pension programs a tax on employment? *Economic Policy 19 (39)*, 267–311.

Docquier, F., and H. Rapoport (2012). Quantifying the impact of highly skilled emigration on developing countries. In *Brain Drain and Brain Gain*, ed. T. Boeri, H. Brücker, F. Docquier, and H. Rapoport. Oxford: Oxford University Press.

Dolado, J., F. Kramarz, S. Machin, A. Manning, D. Margolis, and C. Teulings (1996). The economic impact of minimum wages in Europe. *Economic Policy 23*, 317–72.

Dolton, P., and C. R. Bondibene (2011). The international experience of minimum wages in an economic downturn. *Economic Policy 65*, 99–142.

Dolton, P., and D. O'Neill (1996). Unemployment duration and the restart effect: Some experimental evidence. *Economic Journal 106*, 387–400.

——— (2002). The long-run effects of unemployment monitoring and work-search programs: Experimental evidence from the United Kingdom. *Journal of Labor Economics 20*, 381–403.

Dorn, D., and A. Sousa-Poza (2005). Early retirement: Free choice or forced decision? CESifo Working Paper 1542. Munich: Center for Economic Studies, Ifo Institute.

Dostie, B. (2006). Wages, productivity and aging. *De Economist 159 (2)*, 139–58.

Doucouliagos, H., and T. D. Stanley (2009). Publication selection bias in minimum-wage research? A meta-regression analysis. *British Journal of Industrial Relations 47*, 406–28.

Draca, M., S. Machin, and J. van Reenen (2011). Minimum wages and firm profitability. *American Economic Journal: Applied Economics 3*, 129–51.

Dunlop, D. M. (1944). The karaits of East Asia. *Bulletin of the School of Oriental and African Studies 11 (2)*, 276–89.

Dustmann, C., and A. Glitz (2005). Immigration, jobs and wages: Theory, evidence and opinion. CREAM-CEPR technical report. London: Centre for Economic Policy Research.

Dustmann, C., and U. Schönberg (2011). Expansion in maternity leave coverage and children's long-term outcomes. *American Economic Journal: Applied Economics 4*, 190–224.

Dustmann, C., T. Frattini, and I. P. Preston (2013). The effect of immigration along the distribution of wages. *Review of Economic Studies 80*, 145–73.

Duval, R. (2003). The retirement effects of old-age pension and early retirement schemes in OECD countries. Working Paper 370. Paris: OECD Economics Department.

Dygalo, N. N., and J. M. Abowd (2005). Estimating experience-productivity profiles from earnings over employment spells. Working paper. London, University of Western Ontario.

Edin, P., P. Fredriksson, and O. Åslund (2003). Ethnic enclaves and the economics success of immigrants—Evidence from a natural experiment. *Quarterly Journal of Economics 118*, 329–57.

Ehrenberg, R., and R. L. Oaxaca (1976). Unemployment insurance, duration of unemployment, and subsequent wage gain. *American Economic Review 66*, 754–66.

Ehrenberg, R. G., and R. S. Smith (2006). *Modern labor economics* (9th ed.). New York: Addison Wesley.

Eissa, N. O. (1995). Taxation and labor supply of married women: The tax reform act of 1986 as a natural experiment. NBER Working Paper W5023. Cambridge, MA: National Bureau of Economic Research.

Eissa, N. O., and J. Liebman (1996). Labor supply responses to the Earned Income Tax Credit. *Quarterly Journal of Economics 111*, 605–37.

Elmeskov, J., J. P. Martin, and S. Scarpetta (1998). Key lessons for labor market reforms: Evidence from OECD countries' experience. *Swedish Economic Policy Review 5 (2)*, 205–52.

Emerson, M. (1998). Regulation or de-regulation of the labour market: Policy regimes for the recruitment and dismissal of employees in industralised countries. *European Economic Review 32*, 775–817.

Estevão, M., and F. Sá (2008). The 35-hour workweek in France: Straightjacket or welfare improvement? *Economic Policy 23*, 417–63.

Eurostat (2010). Eurostat labor force survey.

———— (2013). Percentage of part-time employment of adults by sex, age groups, number of children and age of youngest child. European Union.

Falch, T. (2010). The elasticity of labor supply at the establishment level. *Journal of Labor Economics 28*, 237–66.

Fallick, B. C. (1991). Unemployment insurance and the rate of re-employment of displaced workers. *Review of Economics and Statistics 2*, 228–35.

Farber, H. S. (1993). The incidence and costs of job loss: 1982–1991. Brookings Papers on Economic Activity: Microeconomics. Washington, DC: Brookings Institution.

Fernandez, R. (2004). Mothers and sons: Preference formation and female labor force dynamics. *Quarterly Journal of Economics 119*, 1249–99.

Flanagan, R. (1999). Macroeconomic performance and collective bargaining: An international perspective. *Journal of Economic Literature 37 (3)*, 1150–75.

Flinn, C. (2007). Minimum wage effects on labor market outcomes under search, matching and endogenous contact rates. *Econometrica 74*, 1013–62.

Fogli, A. (2011). Nature or nurture? Learning and the geography of female labor force participation. *Econometrica 79*, 1103–38.

Fortin, B., and G. Lacroix (1997). A test of the unitary and collective models of household labour supply. *Economic Journal 107*, 933–55.

Frazis, H., and M. A. Loewenstein (2005). Reexamining the returns to training: Functional form, magnitude, and interpretation. *Journal of Human Resources 40*, 453–76.

Freeman, R., and R. Schettkat (2005). Marketization of household production and the EU-US gap in work. *Economic Policy 20*, 6–50.

Freeman, R. B. (1999). Demand for education. In *Handbook of labor economics*, ed. O. Ashenfelter and D. Card. Amsterdam: North-Holland.

———— (2005). What do unions do? *Journal of Labor Research 26*, 641–68.

Freeman, R. B., and J. L. Medoff (1984). *What do unions do? The 2004 M-Brane Stringtwister edition*. New York: Basic Books.

Friedberg, R. M., and J. Hunt (1995). The impact of immigrants on host countries' wages, employment, and growth. *Journal of Economic Perspectives 9*, 23–44.

Fryer, R. G. (2010). Racial inequality in the 21st century: The declining significance of discrimination. In *Handbook of labor economics 4B*, ed. D. Card and O. Ashenfelter. Amsterdam: Elsevier.

Fryer, R. G., and G. C. Loury (2005). Affirmative action and its mythology. *Journal of Economic Perspectives 19*, 147–62.

Galasso, V. (2006). *The political future of social security in aging societies*. Cambridge, MA: MIT Press.

García Pérez, J. I., and V. Osuna (2012). The effects of introducing a single open-ended contract in the Spanish labor market. Working paper, Universidad Pablo de Olavide, Sevilla.

Garibaldi, P., and P. Mauro (2002). Anatomy of employment growth. *Economic Policy 17 (34)*, 67–114.

Garibaldi, P., and G. Violante (2005). The employment effects of severance payments with wage rigidities. *Economic Journal 115*, 799–832.

Garibaldi, P., J. Konings, and C. Pissarides (1997). Gross job reallocation and labor market policy. In *Unemployment policy: Government options for the labour market*, ed. D. J. Snower and G. de la Dehesa. Cambridge: Cambridge University Press.

Garibaldi, P., A. Borgarello, and L. Pacelli (2003). Employment protection legislation and the size of firms: A close look at the Italian case. *Giornale degli Economisti e Annali di Economia 63 (1)*, 33–68.

Garibaldi, P., J. O. Oliveira-Martins, and J. C. van Ours (2008). *Ageing, health, and productivity: The economics of increased life expectancy*. Oxford: Oxford University Press.

Gertler, M., and A. Trigari (2009). Unemployment fluctuations with staggered Nash bargaining contract. *Journal of Political Economy 117*, 38–86.

Gibson, J., and D. McKenzie (2011). The microeconomic determinants of emigration and return migration of the best and brightest: Evidence from the Pacific. *Journal of Development Economics 95*, 18–29.

Gielen, A., and J. C. van Ours (2006). Age-specific cyclical effects in job reallocation and labor mobility. *Labour Economics 13*, 493–504.

Gindling, T. H., and K. Terrell (2004). Minimum wages and the wages of formal and informal sector workers in Costa Rica. Working Paper 04-102. Ann Arbor, MI: University of Michigan.

Godard, J. (2011). What has happened to strikes? *British Journal of Industrial Relations 49*, 282–305.

Goldin, C. (1988). Marriage bars: Discrimination against married women workers, 1920's to 1950's. NBER Working Paper 2747. Cambridge, MA: National Bureau of Economic Research.

Goldin, C., and C. Rouse (2000). Orchestrating impartiality: The impact of "blind" auditions on female musicians. *American Economic Review 90*, 715–41.

González, L., and F. Ortega (2011). How do very open economies adjust to large immigration flows? Evidence from Spanish regions. *Labour Economics 18*, 57–70.

Goos, M., B. M. Fraumeni, A. Manning, and A. Salomons (2009). Job polarization in Europe. *American Economic Review 99*, 58–63.

Gornick, J. C., and M. K. Meyers (2003). Support for working families: Work and care policies across welfare states. *CESifo DICE Report 4*, 13–18.

Gorter, C., and G. Kalb (1996). Estimating the effect of counselling and monitoring the unemployed using a job search model. *Journal of Human Resources 31*, 590–610.

Gramlich, E. (1976). Impact of minimum wages on other wages, employment and family incomes. *Brooking Papers on Economic Activity 2*, 409–51.

Graversen, B. K., and J. C. van Ours (2008). How to help unemployed find jobs quickly: Experimental evidence from a mandatory activation program. *Journal of Public Economics 92*, 2020–35.

Gregg, P. (2000). The use of wage floors as policy tools. *OECD Economic Studies 31*, 133–46.

Gregg, P., and A. Manning (1997). Skill-biased change, unemployment and inequality. *European Economic Review 41*, 1173–1200.

Gregg, P., and J. Waldfogel (2005). Symposium on parental leave, early maternal employment and child outcomes. *Economic Journal 115*, F1–F6.

Grout, P. (1984). Investment and wages in the absence of binding contracts: A Nash bargaining approach. *Econometrica 52*, 449–60.

Grubb, D. (2000). Eligibility criteria for unemployment benefits. In *OECD Employment Outlook*. Paris: Organisation for Economic Co-operation and Development.

Grubb, D., and W. Wells (1997). Employment regulations and patterns of work in EC countries. *OECD Economic Studies 21*: 7–58.

Gruber, J. (1997). The incidence of payroll taxation: Evidence from Chile. *Journal of Labor Economics 15 (3)*, S72–S101.

Gruber, J., and D. A. Wise (1997). Social security programs and retirement around the world. NBER Working Paper 6134. Cambridge, MA: National Bureau of Economic Research.

——— (1999). Social security programs and retirement around the world. *Research in Labor Economics 18*, 1–40.

——— (2010). *Social security programs and retirement around the world: The relationship to youth employment*. Cambridge, MA: National Bureau of Economic Research.

Hairault, J., F. Langot, and T. Sopraseuth (2010). Distance to retirement and older workers' employment: The case for delaying the retirement age. *Journal of European Economic Association 8*, 1034–76.

Hall, R. E. (1995). Lost jobs. *Brookings Papers on Economic Activity 1*.

Hall, R. E., and E. Lazear (1984). The excess sensitivity of layoffs and quits to demand. *Journal of Labor Economics 2*, 233–57.

Ham, J., and S. Rea (1987). Unemployment insurance and male unemployment duration in Canada. *Journal of Labor Economics 5*, 325–53.

Hamermesh, D. S. (2011). *Beauty pays: Why attractive people are more successful*. Princeton, NJ: Princeton University Press.

Hanel, B. (2010). Financial incentives to postpone retirement and further effects on employment—

Evidence from a natural experiment. *Labour Economics 17*, 474–86.

Hanushek, E., and L. Woessmann (2011). How much do educational outcomes matter in OECD countries? *Economic Policy 26*, 427–91.

Hanushek, E. A., S. Machin, and L. Woessmann, eds. (2011). *Handbook of the Economics of Education* (vols. 3 and 4). Amsterdam: Elsevier.

Hatton, T. J. (2004). Seeking asylum in Europe. *Economic Policy 19*, 5–32.

Hatton, T. J., and M. Tani (2005). Immigration and inter-regional mobility in the UK, 1982–2000. *Economic Journal 115*, F342–F358.

Hatton, T., and J. Williamson (1998). *The age of mass migration: Causes and economic impact.* New York: Oxford University Press.

Heckman, J. J. (1998). Detecting discrimination. *Journal of Economic Perspectives 12*, 101–16.

Heckman, J. J., R. J. Lalonde, and J. A. Smith (1999). The economics and econometrics of active labor market programs. In *Handbook of labor economics,* ed. O. Ashenfelter and D. Card. Amsterdam: Elsevier.

Hellerstein, J. K., D. Neumark, and K. R. Troske (1999). Wages, productivity and worker characteristics: Evidence from plant-level production function and wage equations. *Journal of Labor Economics 17*, 409–46.

Hicks, J. R. (1932). *The theory of wages.* London: Macmillan.

Hijzen, A., and D. Venn (2011). The role of short-time work schemes during the 2008–09 recession. OECD Social, Employment and Migration Working Paper 115. Paris: OECD.

Hirsch, B. T. (2008). Sluggish institutions in a dynamic world: Can unions and industrial competition coexist? *Journal of Economic Perspectives 22*, 153–76.

Hirsch, B. T., and D. A. Macpherson (2003). Union membership and coverage database from the current population survey: Note. *Industrial and Labor Relations Review 56*, 349–54.

Hirsch, B. T., T. Schank, and C. Schnabel (2010). Differences in labor supply to monopsonistic firms and the gender pay gap: An empirical analysis using linked employer-employee data from Germany. *Journal of Labor Economics 28*, 291–330.

Hirschman, A. O. (1970). *Exit, voice, and loyalty: Responses to decline in firms, organizations, and states.* Cambridge, MA: Harvard University Press.

Hoelen, A. (1977). Effects of unemployment insurance entitlement on duration and job search outcome. *Industrial and Labor Relations Review 30*, 45–50.

Hoffman, S., and S. Averett (2010). *Women and the economy.* Boston: Addison-Wesley.

Holden, S., and O. Raaum (1991). Wage moderation and union structure. *Oxford Economic Papers 43*, 409–23.

Holmlund, B. (1998). Unemployment insurance in theory and practice. *Scandinavian Journal of Economics 100 (1)*, 113–41.

Holzer, H. (1986). Reservation wages and their labor market effects for black and white male youth. *Journal of Human Resources 21*, 157–77.

Holzer, H., and D. Neumark (2000). Assessing affirmative action. *Journal of Economic Literature 38*, 483–568.

Holzmann, R., and E. Palmer (2006). Pension reform: Issues and prospects for non-financial defined contribution (NDC) schemes. Washington, DC: World Bank.

——— (2012). *Nonfinancial defined contribution pension schemes in a changing pension world.* Washington, DC: World Bank.

Hopenhayn, H. A., and J. P. Nicolini (1997). Optimal unemployment insurance. *Journal of Political Economy 105*, 412–38.

Hosios, A. J. (1990). On the efficiency of matching and related models of search and unemployment. *Review of Economic Studies 57*, 279–98.

Hoxby, C. M. (2000). Does competition among public schools benefit students and taxpayers? *American Economic Review 90*, 1209–38.

Hunt, J. (1992). The impact of the 1962 repatriates from Algeria on the French labor market. *Industrial and Labor Relations Review 45*, 556–72.

——— (1995). The effect of unemployment compensation on unemployment duration in Germany. *Journal of Labor Economics 13*, 88–120.

——— (1999). Has work-sharing worked in Germany? *Quarterly Journal of Economics 114*, 117–48.

——— (2006). Staunching emigration from East Germany: Age and the determinants of migration. *Journal of the European Economic Association 4*, 1014–37.

Hutchens, R. (1986). Delayed payment contracts and a firm's propensity to hire older workers. *Journal of Labor Economics 4*, 439–57.

Hyslop, D., and S. Stillman (2007). Youth minimum wage reform and the labour market in New Zealand. *Labour Economics 14*, 201–30.

Ichino, A., and R. T. Riphahn (2005). The effect of employment protection on worker effort: Absenteeism during and after probation. *Journal of the European Economic Association 3*, 120–43.

Ilmakunnas, P., and M. Maliranta (2005). Technology, labor characteristics and wage-productivity gaps. *Oxford Bulletin of Economics and Statistics 67*, 623–45.

Isacsson, G. (1999). Estimates of the return to schooling in Sweden from a large sample of twins. *Labour Economics 6*, 471–89.

ISSPC (2005). International Social Survey Programme, 2005 module, Work Orientations III, no. 4350.

Jackman, R., R. Layard, and S. Nickell (1996). Combating unemployment: Is flexibility enough? CEP Discussion Paper 0293. London: Centre for Economic Performance.

James-Burdumy, S. M. (2005). The effect of maternal labor force participation on child development. *Journal of Labor Economics 23*, 177–211.

Jaumotte, F. (2003). Female labor force participation: Past trends and main determinants in OECD countries. OECD Economics Department Working Paper 376, Paris: Organisation for Economic Co-operation and Development.

Johnson, P. (1993). Ageing and European economic demography. In *Labour markets in an ageing Europe,* ed. P. Johnson and K. F. Zimmermann. Cambridge: Cambridge University Press.

Jones, P. (1997). The impact of the minimum wage legislation in developing countries where coverage is incomplete. WP/98-2. Oxford: Institute of Economics and Statistics.

Jones, S., and C. J. McKenna (1994). A dynamic model of union membership and employment. *Economica 61*, 179–89.

Kahn, L. M. (1998). Collective bargaining and the interindustry wage structure: International evidence. *Economica 65*, 507–34.

——— (2000). Wage inequality, collective bargaining, and relative employment from 1985 to 1994: Evidence from fifteen OECD coun-

tries. *Review of Economics and Statistics 82 (4),* 564–79.

Kaitz, H. (1970). *Experience of the past: The national minimum, in youth unemployment and minimum wages.* Bulletin 1657, 30–54, Washington, DC: U.S. Department of Labor, Bureau of Labor Statistics.

Kapteyn, A., A. Kalwij, and A. Zaidi (2004). The myth of work-sharing. *Labour Economics 11*, 293–313.

Katz, L. F., and B. D. Meyer (1990). Unemployment insurance, recall expectations, and unemployment outcomes. *Quarterly Journal of Economics 105*, 973–1002.

Kaufman, B., and J. Hotchkiss (2006). *The economics of the labor market.* Mason, OH: Thomson South-Western.

Kawaguki, D., L. Jungmin, and D. S. Hamermesh (2012). A gift of time. IZA Discussion Paper 6700. Bonn: Institute for the Study of Labor.

Keane, M. P. (2011). Labor supply and taxes: A survey. *Journal of Economic Literature 49*, 961–1075.

Kennan, J. (1986). The economics of strikes. In *Handbook of labor economics 2,* ed. O. C. Ashenfelter and R. Layard. Amsterdam: Elsevier.

——— (1995). The elusive effects of minimum wages. *Journal of Economic Literature 33*, 1950–65.

Kerr, S. P., and W. R. Kerr (2011). Economic impacts of immigration: A survey. *Finnish Economic Papers 24*, 1–32.

Kiefer, N. (1988). Economic duration data and hazard functions. *Journal of Economic Literature 26*, 646–79.

Kiley, M. T. (2003). How should unemployment benefits respond to the business cycle? *Topics in Economic Analysis and Policy 3*, 1–30.

Klepinger, D. H., T. R. Johnson, and J. M. Joesch (2002). Effects of unemployment insurance work-search requirements: The Maryland experiment. *Industrial and Labor Relations Review 56*, 3–22.

Kluve, J. (2010). The effectiveness of European active labor market programs. *Labour Economics 17*, 904–18.

Kluve, J., and C. M. Schmidt (2002). Can training and employment subsidies combat European unemployment? *Economic Policy 35*, 411–48.

Kramarz, F., P. Cahuc, B. Crépon, T. Schank, O. Nordstrom Skans, and G. van Lomwel (2008). Work sharing. In *Working hours and job sharing in the EU and USA,* ed. T. Boeri, M. C. Burda, and F. Kramarz. Oxford: Oxford University Press.

Kroft, K., and M. J. Notowidigdo (2010). Should unemployment insurance vary with the local unemployment rate? Theory and evidence. NBER Working Paper 17173. Cambridge, MA: National Bureau of Economic Research.

Krueger, A. (1993). How computers have changed the wage structure: Evidence from microdata, 1984–89. *Quarterly Journal of Economics 108,* 33–61.

Krueger, A., and B. Meyer (2002). Labor supply effects of social insurance. In *Handbook of public economics,* ed. A. Auerbach and M. Feldstein. Amsterdam: Elsevier.

Kugler, A., and G. Pica (2008). Effects of employment protection on worker and job flows: Evidence from the 1990 Italian reform. *Labour Economics 15,* 78–95.

Kugler, A., and G. Saint-Paul (2000). Hiring and firing costs, adverse selection and long-term unemployment. Working Paper 447. Barcelona: Universitat Pompeu Fabra.

Laing, D. (2011). *Labor Economics.* New York: Norton.

Lalive, R. (2008). How do extended benefits affect unemployment duration? A regression discontinuity approach. *Journal of Econometrics 142,* 785–806.

Lalive, R., and J. Zweimüller (2009). How does parental leave affect fertility and return to work? Evidence from two natural experiments. *Quarterly Journal of Economics 124,* 1363–1402.

Lalive, R., J. C. van Ours, and J. Zweimüller (2005). The effect of benefit sanctions on the duration of unemployment. *Journal of the European Economic Association 3,* 1386–1417.

——— (2006). How changes in financial incentives affect the duration of unemployment. *Review of Economic Studies 73,* 1009–38.

Lalive, R., A. Schlosser, A. Steinhauer, and J. Zweimüller (2011). Parental leave and mothers' careers: The relative importance of job protection and cash benefits. IZA Discussion Paper 5792. Bonn: Institute for the Study of Labor.

Landais, C., P. Michaillat, and E. Saez (2010). Optimal unemployment insurance over the business cycle. NBER Working Paper 16526.

Cambridge, MA: National Bureau of Economic Research.

Lang, K., and J.-Y. K. Lehmann (2012). Racial discrimination in the labor market: Theory and empirics. *Journal of Economic Literature 50,* 959–1006.

Layard, R., S. Nickell, and R. Jackman (1991). *Unemployment.* New York: Oxford University Press.

Lazear, E. (1979). Why is there mandatory retirement? *Journal of Political Economy 87,* 1261–84.

——— (1990). Job security provisions and unemployment. *Quarterly Journal of Economics 105 (3),* 699–726.

Leamer, E., and J. Levinsohn (1995). International trade theory: The evidence. In *Handbook of International Economics,* ed. G. Crossman and K. Rogoff. Amsterdam: Elsevier.

Lechner, M., and J. Smith (2007). What is the value added by caseworkers? *Labour Economics 14,* 135–48.

Lee, Y., and R. Gordon (2005). Tax structure and economic growth. *Journal of Public Economics 89,* 1027–43.

Legros, F. (2006). NDCs: A Comparison of the French and the German Point System. In *Pension reform: Issues and prospects for nonfinancial defined contribution (NDC) schemes,* ed. R. Holzmann and E. Palmer. Washington, DC: World Bank.

Lemos, S. (2004). Minimum wage policy and employment effects: Evidence from Brazil. *Economia 5,* 219–66.

Lester, R. 1947. Marginalism, minimum wages, and labor markets. *American Economic Review 37,* 135–48.

Leuven, E. (2005). The economics of private sector training: A survey of the literature. *Journal of Economic Surveys 19,* 91–111.

Lewis, E. (2005). Immigration, skill mix, and the choice of technique. Working Paper 05-8. Philadelphia: Federal Reserve Bank of Philadelphia.

Lindbeck, A., and D. J. Snower (1988). Cooperation, harassment, and involuntary unemployment: An insider-outsider approach. *American Economic Review 78,* 167–88.

Lippman, S. A., and J. J. McCall (1979). *Studies in the economics of search.* Amsterdam: North-Holland.

Ljungqvist, L., and T. J. Sargent (2003). European unemployment and turbulence revisited in a matching model. CEPR Discussion Paper 4183. London: Centre for Economic Policy Research.

Lochner, L. (2004). Education, work, and crime: A human capital approach. NBER Working Paper 10478. Cambridge, MA: National Bureau of Economic Research.

Loewenstein, M. A., and J. R. Spletzer (1998). Dividing the costs and returns to general training. *Journal of Labor Economics 16,* 142–71.

——— (1999). General and specific training: Evidence and implications. *Journal of Human Resources 34,* 710–33.

Lundberg, S. J., R. A. Pollak, and T. J. Wales (1997). Do husbands and wives pool their resources? Evidence from the U.K. child benefit. *Journal of Human Resources 32,* 463–80.

Lynch, L. (1983). Job search and youth unemployment. *Oxford Economic Papers 35,* 271–82.

Malcomson, J. M. (1999). Individual employment contracts. In *Handbook of labor economics,* ed. O. Ashenfelter and D. Card. Amsterdam: Elsevier.

Manacorda, M., A. Manning, and J. Wadsworth (2012). The impact of immigration on the structure of wages: Theory and evidence from Britain. *Journal of the European Economic Association 10,* 120–51.

Manning, A. (2003). *Monopsony in motion.* Princeton, NJ: Princeton University Press.

——— (2004). Monopsony and the efficiency of labour market interventions. *Labour Economics 11,* 145–63.

——— (2011). Imperfect competition in the labor market. In *Handbook of labor economics,* ed. O. Ashenfelter and D. Card. Amsterdam: Elsevier.

Manning, A., and B. Petrongolo (2005). The part-time pay penalty. CEP Discussion Paper 679. London: Centre for Performance.

Marimon, R., and F. Zilibotti (1999). Unemployment vs. mismatch of talents: Reconsidering unemployment benefits. *Economic Journal 109,* 266–91.

——— (2000). Employment and distributional effects of restricting working time. *European Economic Review 44,* 1291–1326.

Martin, J. P., and D. Grubb (2001). What works and for whom: A review of OECD countries' experience with active labor market policies.

Working Paper 2001 14. Paris: Organisation for Economic Co-operation and Development.

Mayhew, H. (1851). *London labour and the London poor: The condition and earnings of those that will work, cannot work, and will not work.* London: Charles Griffen and Company.

McConnell, C. R., S. L. Brue, and D. Macpherson (2008). *Contemporary labor economics.* Boston: McGraw-Hill Irwin.

McCormick, B.E.A. (2002). Managing migration in the European welfare state. In *Immigration policy and the welfare state,* ed. T. Boeri, G. Hanson, and B.E.A. McCormick. Oxford University Press.

MaCurdy, T. E., and J. Pencavel (1986). Testing between competing models of wage and employment determination in unionized markets. *Journal of Political Economy 94,* S3–S9.

McDonald, I. M., and R. M. Solow (1981). Wage bargaining and employment. *American Economic Review 71,* 896–908.

McIntosh, M. F. (2008). Measuring the labor market impacts of Hurricane Katrina migration: Evidence from Houston, Texas. *American Economic Review, Papers and Proceedings 98,* 54–57.

Metcalf, D. (2004). The impact of the national minimum wage on the pay distribution, employment and training. *Economic Journal 114,* C84–C86.

Meyer, B. D. (1990). Unemployment insurance and unemployment spells. *Econometrica 58,* 757–82.

——— (1995). Lessons from the U.S. unemployment experiments. *Journal of Economic Literature 33,* 91–131.

Miles, T. (2000). Common law exceptions to employment at will and US labor markets. *Journal of Law, Economics and Organization 16,* 74–101.

Mincer, J. (1974). Unemployment effects of minimum wages. *Journal of Political Economy 84,* 87–104.

Mirrlees, J. A. (1971). An exploration in the theory of optimum income taxation. *Review of Economic Studies 38,* 175–208.

Mitman, K., and S. Rabinovich (2011). Procyclical unemployment benefits? Optimal policy in an equilibrium business cycle model. PIER Working Paper 11-01. Philadelphia: Penn Institute for Economic Research.

Moffitt, R., and W. Nicholson (1982). The effect of unemployment insurance on unemployment: The case of federal supplemental benefits. *Review of Economics and Statistics 64*, 1–11.

Montizaan, R., F. Cörvers, and A. De Grip (2010). The effects of pension rights and retirement age on training participation: Evidence from a natural experiment. *Labour Economics 17 (1)*, 240–47.

Mortensen, D. (1977). Unemployment insurance and job search decisions. *Industrial and Labor Relations Review 30*, 505–517.

Mortensen, D., and C. Pissarides (1999). *New developments in models of search in the labor market*. Amsterdam: Elsevier.

Mueller, G., and E. Plug (2006). Estimating the effect of personality on male and female earnings. *Industrial and Labor Relations Review 60*, 3–22.

Myers, R. J. (1964). What can we learn from European experience? In *Unemployment and the American economy*, ed. A. M. Ross. New York: John Wiley and Sons.

Nash, J. (1950). The bargaining problem. *Econometrica 18*, 155–62.

——— (1953). Two-person cooperative games. *Econometrica 21*, 128–40.

Naylor, R., and M. Cripps (1993). An economic theory of the open shop. *European Economic Review 37*, 1599–1620.

Naz, G. (2004). The impact of cash-benefit reform on parents' labor force participation. *Journal of Population Economics 17*, 369–83.

Neumark, D. (2012). Detecting discrimination in audit and correspondence studies. *Journal of Human Resources 47*, 1128–57.

Neumark, D., and W. Stock (1999). Age discrimination law and labor market efficiency. *Journal of Political Economy 107*, 1081–1125.

Neumark, D., and W. Wascher (2000). Minimum wages: A case study of the fast food industry in New Jersey and Pennsylvania—Comment. *American Economic Review 90*, 1362–96.

——— (2007). Minimum wages and employment. IZA Discussion Paper 2570. Bonn: Institute for the Study of Labor.

Neumark, D., M. Schweitzer, and W. Wascher (2004). Minimum wage effects throughout the wage distribution. *Journal of Human Resources 39*, 425–50.

Nickell, S. (1979). The effects of unemployment and related benefits on the duration of unemployment. *Economic Journal 89*, 34–49.

——— (1997). Unemployment and labor market rigidities: Europe versus North America. *Journal of Economic Perspectives 11 (3)*, 55–74.

——— (2006). Work and taxes. In *Tax policy and labor market performance*, ed. J. Agell and P. B. Sørensen. Cambridge, MA: MIT Press.

Nickell, S., and M. Andrews (1983). Unions, real wages and employment in Britain, 1951–79. *Oxford Economic Papers 35 (1)*, 183–206.

Nickell, S., and R. Layard (1999). Labor market institutions and economic performance. In *Handbook of labor economics*, ed. O. Ashenfelter and D. Card. Amsterdam: Elsevier.

Nickell, S., L. Nunziata, and W. Ochel (2005). Unemployment in the OECD since the 1960s: What do we know? *Economic Journal 115*, 1–27.

Oaxaca, R. (1973). Male-female wage differentials in urban labor markets. *International Economic Review 14 (3)*, 693–709.

OECD (Organisation for Economic Co-operation and Development) (1994). *Jobs study*. Paris: OECD.

——— (1998). *Employment outlook*. Paris: OECD.

——— (1999). *Employment outlook*. Paris: OECD.

——— (2001). *Employment outlook*. Paris: OECD.

——— (2002). *Employment outlook*. Paris: OECD.

——— (2003). *Employment outlook*. Paris: OECD.

——— (2004). *Employment outlook*. Paris: OECD.

——— (2005a). *Education at a glance*. Paris: OECD.

——— (2005b). *Employment outlook*. Paris: OECD.

——— (2006a). *Boosting jobs and incomes: Policy lessons from reassessing the OECD jobs strategy*. Paris: OECD.

——— (2006b). *Employment outlook*. Paris: OECD.

——— (2006c). *Live longer, work longer*. Paris: OECD.

——— (2007). *Employment outlook*. Paris: OECD.

——— (2008). *Employment outlook*. Paris: OECD.

——— (2009). *Labor market performance of immigrant children*. Paris: OECD.

——— (2010). *Employment outlook*. Paris: OECD.

——— (2011a). *International migration outlook*. Paris: OECD.

——— (2011b). *Employment outlook*. Paris: OECD.

——— (2012a). *OECD Factbook 2011–2012: Economic, environmental and social statistics*. Paris: OECD.

——— (2012b). OECD family database. Paris: OECD.

——— (2013). *Employment outlook*. Paris: OECD.

Ohanian, L., A. Raffo, and R. Rogerson (2006). Long-term changes in labor supply and taxes: Evidence from OECD countries 1956–2004. NBER Working Paper 12786. Cambridge, MA: National Bureau of Economic Research.

Okkerse, L. (2008). How to measure labor market effects of immigration: A review. *Journal of Economic Surveys 22*, 1–30.

Olsson, M. (2009). Employment protection and sickness absence. *Labour Economics 16*, 208–14.

Oreopoulos, P. (2006). Estimating average and local average treatment effects of education when compulsory schooling laws really matter. *American Economic Review 96*, 152–75.

Osborne, M., and A. Rubinstein (1990). *Bargaining and markets*. San Diego: Academic Press.

Ottaviano, G.I.P., and G. Peri (2012). Rethinking the effect of immigration on wages. *Journal of the European Economic Association 10*, 152–97.

Pacheco, G. (2011). Estimating employment impacts with binding minimum wage constraints. *Economic Record 87*, 587–602.

Pavoni, N. (2007). On optimal unemployment compensation. *Journal of Monetary Economics 54*, 1612–30.

——— (2009). Optimal unemployment insurance, with human capital depreciation, and duration dependence. *International Economic Review 50*, 323–62.

Pavoni, N., and G. Violante (2007). Optimal welfare-to-work programs. *Review of Economic Studies 74 (1)*, 283–318.

Pedersen, P., and N. Westergård Nielsen (1993). Unemployment: A review of the evidence from panel data. *OECD Economic Studies 20*, 65–114.

Pellizzari, M. (2010). Do friends and relatives really help in getting a good job? *Industrial and Labor Relations Review 63*, 494–510.

Pencavel, J. (2003). The surprising retreat of union Britain. NBER Working Paper 9564. Cambridge, MA: National Bureau of Economic Research.

Pereira, S. C. (2003). The impact of minimum wages on youth employment in Portugal. *European Economic Review 47*, 229–44.

Persson, T., and G. Tabellini (2000). *Political economics: Explaining economic policy*. Cambridge, MA: MIT Press.

Pestieau, P. (2003). Ageing, retirement and pension reforms. *World Economy 26*, 1447–57.

Petrongolo, B., and C. Pissarides (2001). Looking into the black box: A survey of the matching function. *Journal of Economic Literature 39 (2)*, 390–431.

Picchio, M., and J. C. van Ours (2011). Market imperfections and firm-sponsored training. *Labour Economics 18*, 712–22.

——— (2013). Retaining through training; Even for older workers. *Economics of Education Review 32*, 29–48.

Piketty, T. (1998). L'impact des incitations financières au travail sur les comportements individuels: Une estimation pour le cas français. *Economie et Prévision 132–133*, 1–36.

Pissarides, C. (1979). Job matchings with state employment agencies and random search. *Economic Journal 89*, 818–33.

——— (1998). The impact of employment tax cuts on unemployment and wages: The role of unemployment benefits and tax structure. *European Economic Review 42*, 155–83.

Portegijs, W., M. Cloïn, S. Keuzenkamp, A. Merens, and E. Steenvoorden (2008). *Verdeelde tijd; waarom vrouwen in deeltijd werken [Divided time; Why women work part-time]*. The Hague: Sociaal en Cultureel Planbureau.

Portugal, P., and A. R. Cardoso (2001). Disentangling the minimum wage puzzle: An analysis of job accession and separation from a longitudinal matched employer-employee data set. CEPR Discussion Paper 2844. London: Centre for Economic Policy Research.

Postel-Vinay, F., and A. Clark (2006). Job security and job protection. IZA Discussion Paper 1489. Bonn: Institute for the Study of Labor.

Prescott, E. C. (2004). Why do Americans work so much more than Europeans? *Federal Reserve Bank of Minneapolis Quarterly Review 28*, 2–13.

Rangazas, P. (2002). The quantity and quality of schooling and U.S. labor productivity growth (1870–2000). *Review of Economic Dynamics 5*, 932–64.

Ransom, M. R., and D. P. Sims (2010). Estimating the firm's labor supply curve in a "new monopsony" framework: Schoolteachers in Missouri. *Journal of Labor Economics 28*, 331–55.

Rebitzer, J. B., and L. J. Taylor (1995). The consequences of minimum wage laws: Some new theoretical ideas. *Journal of Public Economics 56 (2)*, 245–55.

Reid, F. J. (1985). Reductions in work time: An assessment of employment sharing to reduce unemployment. In *Work and pay: The Canadian labour market,* ed W. C. Riddell. Toronto: University of Toronto Press.

Remery, C., K. Henkens, J. Schippers, and P. Ekamper (2003). Managing an aging workforce and a tight labor market: Views held by Dutch employers. *Population Research and Policy Review 22*, 21–44.

Riach, P. A., and J. Rich (2002). Field experiments of discrimination in the market place. *Economic Journal 112*, F480–F518.

Robinson, C. (1989). The joint determination of union status and union wage effects: Some tests of alternative models. *Journal of Political Economy 97*, 639–67.

Robinson, J. V. (1933). *Economics of Imperfect Competition.* London: Macmillan.

Rodrik, D. (1998). Why do more open economies have bigger governments? *Journal of Political Economy 106*, 997–1032.

Røed, K., and T. Zhang (2003). Does unemployment compensation affect unemployment duration? *Economic Journal 113*, 190–206.

Rogerson, R. (2009). Market work, home work, and taxes: A cross-country analysis. *Review of International Economics 17*, 588–601.

Rønsen, M., and M. Sundström (2002). Family policy and after-birth employment among new mothers—A comparison of Finland, Norway and Sweden. *European Journal of Population 18*, 121–52.

Rothstein, J. (2007). Does competition among public schools benefit students and taxpayers? A comment on Hoxby (2000). *American Economic Review 97*, 2026–37.

——— (2011). Unemployment insurance and job search in the Great Recession. *Brookings Papers on Economic Activity 43*, 143–213.

Roy, A. D. (1951). Some thoughts on the distribution of earnings. *Oxford Economic Papers 3*, 314–17.

Ruffle, B. J., and Z. Shtudiner (2010). Are good-looking people more employable? Working Paper 1006. Beer-Sheva, Israel: Ben-Gurion University of the Negev.

Ruhm, C. J. (1998). The economic consequences of parental leave mandates: Lessons from Europe. *Quarterly Journal of Economics 1*, 285–317.

Saez, E. (2002). Optimal income transfer programs: Intensive versus extensive labor supply responses. *Quarterly Journal of Economics 117*, 1039–73.

Saez, E., J. Slemrod, and S. H. Giertz (2009). The elasticity of taxable income with respect to marginal tax rates: A critical review. NBER Working Paper 15012. Cambridge, MA: National Bureau of Economic Research.

——— (1993). On the political economy of labor market flexibility. CEPR Discussion Paper 803. London: Centre for Economic Policy Research.

——— (1997). *Dual labor market: A macroeconomic perspective.* Cambridge, MA: MIT Press.

——— (2000). *The political economy of labor market institutions.* Oxford: Oxford University Press.

Scarpetta, S. (1996). Assessing the role of labor-market policies and institutional factors on unemployment: A cross-country study. *OECD Economic Studies 26*, 43–98.

Schivardi, F., and R. Torrini (2008). Identifying the effects of firing restrictions through size-contingent differences in regulation. *Labour Economics 15*, 482–511.

Schmieder, J. F., T. von Wachter, and S. Bender (2012a). The effects of extended unemployment insurance over the business cycle: Evidence from regression discontinuity estimates over 20 years. *Quarterly Journal of Economics 127*, 701–52.

——— (2012b). The long-term effects of UI extensions of employment. *American Economic Review: Papers and Proceedings 102*, 514–19.

Schnalzenberger, M., and R. Winter-Ebmer (2009). Layoff tax and employment of the elderly. *Labour Economics 16*, 618–24.

Shannon, M. (2011). The employment effect of lower minimum wage rates for young workers: Canadian evidence. *Industrial Relations 50*, 629–55.

Shapiro, C., and J. Stiglitz (1984). Equilibrium unemployment as a worker discipline device. *American Economic Review 74*, 433–44.

Smith, A. 1776. *An Inquiry into the Nature and Causes of the Wealth of Nations [The Wealth of Nations]*. Reprinted in 1998 by Oxford: Oxford University Press.

Smith, J. P., and B. Edmonston (1997). *The new Americans: Demographic and fiscal effects of immigration*. Washington, DC: National Academy Press.

Snower, D., and G. de la Dehesa (eds.) (1996). *Unemployment policy*. Cambridge: Centre for Economic Policy Research and Cambridge University Press.

Sobel, R. S. (1999). Theory and evidence on the political economy of the minimum wage. *Journal of Political Economy 107*, 761–85.

Sociaal en Cultureel Planbureau (1998). *Sociaal and Cultureel Rapport, 1998*. The Hague: Staatsuitgeverij.

Soskice, D., and T. Iversen (2000). The non-neutrality of monetary policy with large price or wage setters. *Quarterly Journal of Economics 115*, 265–84.

Spence, M. (1973). Job market signaling. *Quarterly Journal of Economics 87*, 355–74.

Staiger, D. O., J. Spetz, and C. S. Phibbs (2010). Is there monopsony in the labor market? Evidence from a natural experiment. *Journal of Labor Economics 28*, 211–36.

Stewart, M. (2004). The employment effects of the national minimum wage. *Economic Journal 114*, 110–16.

Stigler, G. (1946). The economics of minimum wage legislation. *American Economic Review 36*: 535–43.

Stock, J. H., and D. A. Wise (1990). Pensions: The option value of work and retirement. *Econometrica 58*, 1151–80.

Swinkels, J. M. (1999). Education signalling with preemptive offers. *Review of Economic Studies 66*, 949–70.

Tanaka, S. (2005). Parental leave and child health across OECD countries. *Economic Journal 115*, F7–F28.

Tatsiramos, K. (2009). Unemployment insurance in Europe: Unemployment duration and subsequent employment stability. *Journal of the European Economic Association 7*, 1225–60.

Tatsiramos, K., and J. C. van Ours (2012). Labor market effects of unemployment insurance design. Discussion paper. Tilburg, Netherlands: CentER, Tilburg University.

——— (2013). Labor market effects of unemployment insurance design. *Journal of Economic Surveys 27*, forthcoming.

Topel, R. H. (1986). Local labor markets. *Journal of Political Economy 54*, 111–43.

US Office of Immigration Statistics (2011). *2011 Yearbook of immigration statistics*. Available at www.dhs.gov/yearbook-immigration-statistics-2011-1.

Uusitalo, R., and J. Verho (2010). The effect of unemployment benefits on re-employment rates: Evidence from the Finnish unemployment insurance reform. *Labour Economics 17*, 643–54.

Van Audendrode, M. A. (1994). Short-time compensation: Job security, and employment contracts: Evidence from selected OECD countries. *Journal of Political Economy 102*, 76–102.

Van den Berg, G. J. (1990a). Nonstationarity in job search theory. *Review of Economic Studies 57*, 255–77.

——— (1990b). Search behavior, transitions to nonparticipation and the duration of unemployment. *Economic Journal 100*, 842–65.

Van den Berg, G. J., B. van der Klaauw, and J. C. van Ours (2004). Punitive sanctions and the transition rate from welfare to work. *Journal of Labor Economics 22*, 211–41.

Van den Berg, G. J., and B. van der Klaauw (2006). Counseling and monitoring of unemployed workers: Theory and evidence from a controlled social experiment. *International Economic Review 47*, 895–936.

Van der Wiel, K. (2010). Better protected, better paid: Evidence on how employment protection affects wages. *Labour Economics 17*, 16–26.

Van Lomwel, A.G.C., and J. C. van Ours (2005). On the employment effects of part-time labor. *De Economist 153*, 451–60.

Van Ours, J. C. (2004). The locking-in effect of subsidized jobs. *Journal of Comparative Economics 32 (1)*, 37–52.

Van Ours, J. C., and M. Vodopivec (2006). How shortening the potential duration of unemployment benefits affects the duration of unemployment: Evidence from a natural experiment. *Journal of Labor Economics 24*, 351–78.

Van Ours, J. C., and M. Vodopivec (2008). Does reducing unemployment insurance generosity reduce job match quality? *Journal of Public Economics 3 (4)*, 684–95.

Venn, D. (2009). Legislation, collective bargaining and enforcement: Updating the OECD employment protection indicators. OECD Social, Employment and Migration Working Papers 89. Paris: Organisation for Economic Co-operation and Development.

Visser, J. (2011). Data base on institutional characteristics of trade unions, wage setting, state intervention and social pacts, 1960–2010, version 3.0. Amsterdam: Amsterdam Institute for Advance Labor Studies (AIAS), University of Amsterdam.

Von Below, D., and P. S. Thoursie (2010). Last in, first out? Estimating the effect of seniority rules in Sweden. *Labour Economics 17*, 987–97.

Von Wachter, T. (2002). The end of mandatory retirement in the US: Effects on retirement and implicit contracts. Center for Labor Economics Working Paper 49. Berkeley: University of California, Berkeley.

Wacziarg, R., and K. Welch (2003). Trade liberalization and growth: New evidence. NBER Working Paper 10152. Cambridge, MA: National Bureau of Economic Research.

Walker, A. (1998). Adjusting to an aging workforce in Europe—Policy and practice. In *Aging of the Workforce workshop*, Brussels, March 23–24.

Warr, P. (1998). Aging, competence and learning at work. In *Aging of the Workforce workshop*, Brussels, March 23–24.

Wasmer, E. (2006). The economics of Prozac: Do employees really gain from strong employment protection? IZA DP 2460. Bonn: Institute for the Study of Labor.

Weiss, A. M., and A. M. Ching-to (1993). A signaling theory of unemployment. *European Economic Review 37*, 135–57.

Welch, F. (1976). Minimum wage legislation in the United States. In *Evaluating the labor market effects of social programs*, ed. O. Ashenfelter and J. Blum. Princeton, NJ: Princeton University Press.

Whitehouse, R. E. (2011). Decomposing notional defined-contribution pensions. OECD Social, Employment and Migration Working Paper 109. Paris: Organisation for Economic Co-operation and Development.

Williamson, O. E. (1975). *Markets and hierarchies, analysis and antitrust implications: A study in the economics of internal organization.* New York: Free Press.

Winter-Ebmer, R. (1998). Potential unemployment benefit duration and spell length: Lessons from a quasi-experiment in Austria. *Oxford Bulletin of Economics and Statistics 60*, 33–45.

World Bank (2011). Database.

Wright, R. (1986). The redistributive roles of unemployment insurance and the dynamics of voting. *Journal of Public Economics 31*, 377–99.

Zavodny, M. (2000). The effect of the minimum wage on employment and hours. *Labour Economics 7*, 729–50.

Zimmermann, K. F. (2005). *European migration— What do we know?* Oxford: Oxford University Press.

Johnson, T., 359
Jones, P., 45
Jones, S., 82
Jürges, H. K., 157

Kahn, L. M., 80
Kaitz, H., 36, 58
Kalb, G., 358, 359
Kapteyn, A., 141
Katz, L. F., 260, 322
Kaufman, B., xiv
Kawaguki, D., 141
Keane, M. P., 387, 395
Kennan, J., 58, 77
Kerr, S. P., 259
Kerr, W. R., 259
Kiefer, N., 341
Kiley, M. T., 335
Kingston, J. L., 334
Klenow, P., 209
Klepinger, D. H., 359
Kluve, J., 365, 370
Kramarz, F., 76, 141, 142, 301
Kroft, K., 335
Krueger, A., 45, 46, 47, 48, 51, 52, 58, 224, 228, 326, 341
Krugman, P., 4
Kugler, A., 292, 296

Lacroix, G., 201
Laing, D., xiv, 247
Lalive, R., 185, 196, 323, 326, 329, 330, 332, 333, 366
Landais, C., 335, 336
Lang, K., 118
Layard, R., xv, 2, 68, 322, 376
Lazear, E., 134, 170, 171, 284, 285, 292
Leamer, E., 256
Lechner, M., 367
Lee, Y., 393
Legros, F., 157
Lehmann, E., 57
Lehmann, J.-Y. K., 118
Leigh, A., 113
Lemos, S., 45
Leuven, E., 216
Levine, P., 324
Levinsohn, J., 256
Lewis, E., 260

Liebman, J., 387
Lindbeck, A., 220
Lippman, S. A., 318
Ljungqvist, L., 22
Lochner, L., 232
Loewenstein, M. A., 221, 230
Lommerud, K. E., 76
Loury, G. C., 116
Lundberg, S. J., 201
Lynch, L., 319

MacCulloch, R., 81, 292
Machin, S., 49
Macis, M., 340
Macpherson, D. A., 83
MaCurdy, T. E., 73, 387, 395
Malcomson, J. M., 221
Maliranta, M., 170
Malthus, T., 187
Manacorda, M., 259
Manning, A., xv, 43, 58, 87, 103, 135, 146, 151, 292
Marimon, R., 135, 340
Martin, J. P., 365
Mauro, P., 146, 151
Mayhew, H., 136
McCall, J. J., 318
McConnell, C. R., xiv
McCormick, B. E. A., 256, 260, 268
McDonald, I. M., 73
McIntosh, M. F., 273
McKenna, C. J., 82
McKenzie, D., 273
Medoff, J. L., 82
Metcalf, D., 58
Meyer, B. D., 46, 322, 323, 341
Meyers, M. K., 179
Michel, J., 44
Micklewright, J., 322, 341
Miles, T., 297
Milligan, K., 194, 195
Mincer, J., 44, 224, 242
Mirrlees, J. A., 388
Mitman, K., 336
Moffitt, R., 323
Montizaan, R., 235, 236
Mortensen, D., 324, 345, 399
Mueller, G., 98
Mullainathan, S., 113

Muñoz de Bustillo, R., 54
Myers, R. J., 4

Nash, J., 30, 61, 71, 89, 90, 319, 320, 401
Naylor, R., 76
Naz, G., 192, 193
Neumark, D., 48, 50, 51, 58, 112, 116, 167
Nicholson, W., 323
Nickell, S., 2, 68, 71, 292, 322, 376, 395
Nicolini, J.-P., 340
Noel, B., 361
Notowidigdo, M. J., 335
Novo, A., 327, 334

Oaxaca, R. L., 110, 334
Ohanian, L., 150
Okkerse, L., 259
Olsson, M., 295, 296
O'Neill, D., 359
Oreopoulos, P., 228, 229, 230
Ortega, F., 260
Osborne, M., 71
Osuna, V., 301
Ottaviano, G. I. P., 259

Pacheco, G., 54
Palmer, E., 157
Pavoni, N., 340, 368
Pedersen, P., 322
Pellizzari, M., 358
Pencavel, J., 73, 83
Pereira, S. C., 53
Peri, G., 259
Perotti, R., 84
Persson, T., xv
Pestieau, P., 155, 172
Petrongolo, B., 146, 151, 357, 371
Pica, G., 296
Picchio, M., 230, 231
Piketty, T., 192
Pischke, J., 44, 217, 221, 230, 231, 234, 340
Pissarides, C., 355, 357, 371, 385, 395, 399
Plug, E., 98
Portegijs, W., 105

Subject Index

Page numbers followed by letters *b, f,* and *n* refer to boxes, figures, and notes, respectively.

Deunionization, 64

Difference-in-differences: effect of migration on wages and employment of natives, 261–262; employment protection legislation and, 292–293; estimators, 46; family policies and, 193; reduction in work hours and, 142; in within-countries studies, 292

Discrimination: audit studies on, 112; coefficient of market discrimination, 99; correspondence studies on, 112–114, 113t; employer-specific coefficient of discrimination, 99; prejudice, 95, 98; statistical discrimination, 102, 103–104, 105f; taste-based, 98, 102

Displaced workers, return to new jobs, 166

Displacement effects, 358

Dual labor markets, minimum wages in, 44, 44f, 57

Dual-track reform strategy, 279

Duration analysis, 341

Early childhood education and care, 179

Early retirement programs, 155–178; employment and, 162–168; mandatory retirement age and, 170–171; measures and cross-country comparisons in, 156–160; optimal retirement age and, 177–178; productivity and, 169–170; reasons for existence of, 174–175; reasons for phasing out, 171–172; theory on, 160–162

Earned Income Tax Credit (EITC), 390–391

Education, 209–243; government subsidies for in-company, 234; market failures concerning, 210–211; measures and cross-country comparisons, 211–214; on-the-job, 231; productivity and, 210–211, 214–216, 243; reasons for government-provided, 237. *See also* Schooling; Training

Efficiency wages: employment protection and, 286–287b; unemployment benefits and, 320–321b

Efficient bargaining: unions and, 73n, 74f, 75, 89

Employer concession curve, 78f

Employment gap, 107–109, 108t, 109f

Employment protection legislation (EPL), 17–18, 21, 234, 275–306; administrative procedures and, 275; advance notice period and, 275; behavior of workers and, 295; contract undoing, 284–285b; cross-country analyses of, 291–292; defined, 275; difference-in-differences approach and, 292–293; economic and disciplinary dismissals, 275–276, 285–286; efficiency wages and, 286–287b; endogeneity

of, 297; individual and collective dismissals, 275–276; legal minima, 275; measures and cross-country comparisons in, 276–284; neutrality and, 284–287; permanent and temporary contracts, 276, 301n; procedural costs and, 276; reasons for existence of, 302–303; reforms in, 22; removing risk neutrality in, 287; retirement programs and, 161, 167, 172; rigid wages and, 287–289; severance payments and, 275; tax component, 275; taxes and, 275, 289–290; transfer component and, 275; trial costs and, 275; two-tier regimes in, 290–291; unions and, 84

End-of-benefit spikes, 322–324b

Entitlement effect, unemployment benefits and, 321

Equal pay legislation, 115

European Trade Unions Confederation (ETUC), 63

Excess coverage of trade unions, 64, 65t, 67

Exit routes from work, 163–164

Family allowances, 16

Family day care, 203

Family income, fertility and, 188

Family policies, 179–207; child care facilities in, 205–206; empirical evidence in, 189–192; measures and cross-country comparisons in, 180–182; parental leave in, 185–187; reasons for existence of, 203; trade-off between fertility and employment, 200

Fertility: factors affecting, 187–189; total, 189, 190f; trade-off between employment and, 200

Firm-specific training, 216–217

Fiscal substitution effects, 358

Free-rider problem of unions, 67

Gender wage gap, 98, 100, 100f, 101, 102–103

General training, 216–217

Globalization, labor demand and, 32–33

Great Recession, 1–5

Guaranteed minimum income scheme, 254

Hicks paradox, 77, 78f

Holdup problem, 211, 220–221

Honeymoon effect, 290–291, 291f, 301n

Hours of work. *See* Working hours regulation

Household. *See* Family policies

Human capital, 209–211. *See also* Education

Identical twins, returns to schooling and, 226–227

Immigration policies. *See* Migration policies

Immigration surplus, 252

Imperfect labor market, definition, 7–8

In-company training: government subsidies for, 234; provision of, 211

Innate ability, 215–216

In-work benefits, 388–391

Isocost curve, 116, 116*f*, 132

Isolabor curve, 132–133

Job polarization, 224

Job search, 317; formal, 362; informal, 362; theory of, 317–319; unemployment benefits and, 317–319, 342–345

Kaitz index, 36*n*

Labor demand: effect of payroll taxes on, 13, 382–383; part-time work and, 128–131; wedge between labor supply and, 30–32

Labor market institutions, 8, 15, 22–27; economic performance and, 1; functions performed by, 21; interactions in, 15–17, 18; quantities and, 17–18; reasons for existence of, 19–22; reforms of, 22–27

Labor market status: employed individual, 5; inactive individual, 6; unemployed individual, 6

Labor supply: aggregate, 12–13; effective, 17; effect of payroll taxes on, 380–382; part-time work and, 128–131; reservation wages and, 8–12; wedge between labor demand and, 19–20

Labor taxes. *See* Payroll taxes

Laffer curve, 387*n*

Late-career job loss, economic consequences of, 166

Layoff taxes, 294–295*b*

Length of stay, migration policies and, 245

Lighthouse effects, 46

Liquidity constraint, 336–337

Locking-in effect, 365

Lump of labor fallacy, 136–137

Lump-sum taxes and transfers, 20

Mandatory retirement age, 155; elimination of, 168*b*; reasons for increasing, 170–171

Mandatory schooling age, 17, 232

Marginal effective tax rate, 376

Marginal hiring cost of monopsonist, 103

Marginal tax rate, 376

Mariel boat-lift, 261–263

Marketization hypothesis, 198

Matching function, 347, 354–355

Maternity leave. *See* Parental leave

Means testing: unemployment benefits and, 307–308; welfare benefits in, 376

Migrant integration policy, 250*t*

Migration policies, 245–273; admission procedures and, 245; asylum seekers and, 245–246; brain-drain effect of, 269; citizenship and, 245; competitive labor market and, 251–252; cross-country comparisons in, 247–249; economy with wage rigidities and, 252–253; effects on income distribution of skill-biased, 255–256; effects on wages and employment of natives, 251, 256–261; factors driving decisions and, 253–255; fiscal effects in, 263–264; labor market performance of migrants in, 264–265; length of stay and, 245; net gains from, and option value of waiting, 272–273; points system in, 245, 268–269; quotas and, 245; reasons for existence of, 270; restrictions and, 17; wage rigidities and unemployment benefits in, 252–253; welfare and, 267–268

Minimum wages, 17, 21, 35–62; based on natural experiments, 46–50; based on workers' histories, 50–51; collective bargaining and, 43; in competitive labor market, 39–40; cross-country comparisons in, 36–39; defined, 35; in dual labor markets, 44*f*; effects of hikes in, on United States fast-food industry, 47–48*b*; implementing, 15; national government-legislated, 36; in noncompetitive labor market, 40–45; positive effects of minimum wages on welfare, 44–45; ratio of, to average wage, 36–39; reasons for existence of, 57–58; in reducing earnings inequality and poverty, 57–58; studies of, based on firm-level data, 45–46; unions and, 52–56, 86. *See also* Wages

Monopoly: bilateral, 43; pure, 40

Monopsony power, 40; degree of, 43; training and, 221; working hours and, 148

Moral hazard: family policies and, 203; labor market institutions and, 21; unemployment benefits and, 339, 368

Nash-bargaining rule, 89–91; unions and, 89; wage effects and, 319–320

Natives: skill composition of, 255; wages and employment of, 251–252, 256–261

Negative income tax (NIT), 388–390

Net replacement rate, 308–312

Target efficiency, 57

Taste-based discrimination, 98, 102

Tax credits, 375, 388

Taxes: average rates of, 376; employment protection legislation and, 275, 289–290; on labor, 15, 22; negative income, 388–390; progressive systems, 376, 380–382; unemployment benefits and, 314, 317; value-added, 376–378. *See also* Payroll taxes

Tax incidence, 397–398

Tax rates, 376; average, 376; marginal, 376

Temporary workers, 277–284, 278*t*, 293*b*

Trade unions. *See* Unions

Training, 216–217; firm-specific, 210, 216; in-company, government subsidies for, 234; as investment, 210; market failures concerning, 210; on-the-job, 210, 216; paying for general, 243; provision of, 211; self-financed, 230. *See also* Education; Schooling

Transfer component, employment protection legislation and, 275

Trial costs, employment protection legislation and, 275

Twins, return to schooling and, 226–227

Two-sided job search, 347–348

Two-tier: reforms, 26–27; regime of employment protection, 290–291

Underemployment, 131; involuntary part-time work, 131

Unemployment: bargaining coordination, union density, and, 81–82; effect of unemployment benefits on duration of, 322–333; effects of, on generosity of unemployment benefits, 322, 333; of older workers, 166; as trap, 369

Unemployment assistance, 307–308

Unemployment benefits, 21, 307–350; active labor market policies and, 351, 352, 359, 367, 369, 372; competitive labor markets and, 314–317; defined, 307; duration of, 322–333; effects of unemployment on generosity of, 320–321*b*, 322, 333; eligibility, 307; employment protection legislation and, 298; entitlement effect and, 321; imperfect labor market and, 317; inactivity trap, 369; institutions and, 375; interaction effect of training and, 356; job search effect and, 317–319; labor market participation and, 354–355*b*; measures and cross-country comparisons, 308–313; migration policies and, 246, 252–253, 321; nonexperimental studies on, 364–366; payroll taxes and, 339, 393–394, 396–399; poverty trap,

369; reasons for, 339–341; reservation wages, 315–316*b*, 316, 318–319*b*; retirement and, 155; shortening duration of, 328–329*b*; taxation effect, 314; in two-sided job search model and, 347–348; unemployment trap, 369; wage bargaining and, 317, 319–320; wage effects of, 320

Unemployment insurance fund, 64–67, 307

Union density: bargaining coordination, unemployment, and, 81–82; influence, 86–87; presence, 86–87

Union resistance curve, 77–78

Unions, 21; collective bargaining and, 63–93; decline in membership, 66; effect of, on efficiency, 82–84; effects of, on wages, 79–81; excess coverage of, 64, 67; free-rider problem in, 67; migration policies and, 269; monopoly union, 89–90; power of, in wage bargaining, 18; reasons for existence of, 86–87; regulation of working hours and, 123; strength and efficiency of, 89–91; wage compression and, 234; wage gaps and, 79, 80*b*

Unitary model of household behavior, 201

Vacancies: for high-productivity jobs, 45; matching of workers and, 7, 43, 319, 347, 354–355; part-time workers and, 145; posting, 319; public employment services in locating, 367; unemployment and, 319, 347, 348, 351, 357

Value-added taxes (VATs), 376–378

Wage bargaining: power of unions in, 18; unemployment benefits and, 320

Wage deferrals, 305–306

Wage effects of unemployment benefits, 317, 319–320

Wage insurance, 56

Wage rigidities, migration policy and, 252–253

Wages: defined, 5; effects of unions on, 70–71; ratio of average to minimum, 36; relationship between productivity and, 167; reservation, 7; union-induced compression of, 234. *See also* Minimum wages; Reservation wages

Wage share, 68

Wage subsidies, 392; for older workers, 172; versus tax credits, 392

Wedge between labor supply and demand, 30–32

Weekly working hours, regulating, 135–136

Welfare: migration and, 267, 270; positive effects of minimum wage on, 44–45

Welfare-to-work schemes, 340

Women: balance of work and family life for, 197–200; child care and, 182–185; early retirement programs for, 162–164; employment rates and fertility, 187–189, 192, 197–200; employment rates of, 162, 189; hours of work for, in Norway, 193–194*b*; maternity leave for, 185; parental leave for, 185–187, 194; trade-off between fertility and employment of, 200; with young children, 192–193*b*

Workers: activating unemployed, 372–373; displaced, 166; employed, 5; inactive, 6; incumbent, 83; older, 166, 171; restrictions on cross-border flows of, 245; unemployed, 5–6; unemployment among low-productivity, 356

Workfare programs, 368

Working day, optimal length of, 123

Working Family Tax Credit (WFTC), 391

Working hours: annual, 139; decline in, per week, 139; mandatory reduction of, in France, 141–142; reduction of standard, 152–154; regulation of, 8, 123–154; weekly, 124–125

Working hours regulation, 123–154, 179; collective bargaining and, 123; measures and cross-country comparisons in, 124–128; part-time, 128–132, 143–147; reasons for, 147–148; reduction of standard, 152–154; theory of, 128–139; unions and, 123; working hours and, 139–141. *See also* Working hours

Working poor, 51